THE
GREAT WAR

RANDOM HOUSE

New York

THE
GREAT WAR

PERSPECTIVES ON THE

FIRST WORLD WAR

EDITED BY

ROBERT COWLEY

946.4
Cow

The essays in this work were originally published in *Military History Quarterly*.

Permission acknowledgments are located on p. 491.

Maps created by MapQuest.com, Inc.

LIBRARY OF CONGRESS CATALOGING-IN-PUBLICATION DATA

The Great War: perspectives on the First World
War/edited by Robert Cowley.

p.   cm.

Includes index.

ISBN 0-375-50909-7

1. World War, 1914–1918—Historiography.   2. World War, 1914–1918—
Campaigns—Western Front.   3. War and society.   4. Europe—History, military—
20th century.   5. Military art and science—Europe—History—20th century.

I. Cowley, Robert.

D522.42.G74 2003   940.4—dc21

2002036993

Random House website address:
www.atrandom.com

Printed in the United States of America on acid-free paper

2 4 6 8 9 7 5 3

FIRST EDITION

Book design by Barbara M. Bachman

"The time will come when the single unprotected rifleman will be ground between the millstones of machinery. . . . It is a question no longer of launching men in mass, but machines."

ERNST JÜNGER, *Copse 125*

CONTENTS

———

v. THE FIRST AIR WAR

vi. TIPPING POINTS

vii. AFTERMATH

LIST OF MAPS

———

INTRODUCTION

—

"Life will never be the same." Repeated mantra-like these days, it's a sentence that threatens to become a cliché. How accurate will it prove to be? Or to what extent self-fulfilling? For the moment, the international disruptions set in motion with the crumbling of two towers have not turned (at least not yet) into the trauma of a world coming apart, as happened nine decades ago. The trauma was the First World War—or the Great War, as people then called it. As the eminent military historian Michael Howard writes, "This somber spondee, like a tolling bell, seems a far more appropriate description of that huge tragedy." That war, that unnecessary but perhaps inevitable war, is the subject of this book.

Comparing cataclysms should not, of course, be treated as a game. But you can make a good argument that the Great War was the true turning point of the century just past. It brought down dynasties and empires—including the Ottoman, one of the roots of our present difficulties. It changed the United States from a provincial nation into a world power. It made World War II inevitable and the Cold War as well. It created the modern world—and that greatest of growth industries, violent death. Even at the time, people seemed aware of the war's potential for permanent upheaval. In the summer of 1915 the Abbé Breuil—in years to come one of the discoverers of the Lascaux caves—wrote to his friend, the Jesuit philosopher Teilhard de Chardin, then a frontline chaplain in trenches north of Ypres. "We are all, Boche and Allies, floating downstream towards a cataract hidden from us by a bend," Breuil wrote, "but whose roar we can hear. What will come next, we don't know. Civilization is in the melting-pot again; but what the mold will be we do not know. . . ."

Winston Churchill, whose political career was nearly engulfed by the cataract, called his history/memoir of the Great War *The World Crisis*. But writing in the 1920s, he had no way of recognizing that the story had just begun. Pick a major upheaval in the next decades and the chances are that it is rooted in the Great War. Increasingly, historians have come to regard the two world wars (in Howard's words) "as a single Thirty Years' War interrupted by a long truce." There is even a reasonable argument for extending the date of the end of the crisis from 1945 to 1989, when the Berlin Wall came down.

Churchill avoided the term "First World War," though it was already in vogue. The first "First World War" was actually the Seven Years' War of the mid-eighteenth century, its major actions ranging from Europe to the Indian Ocean and North America. But in 1921, Colonel Charles à Court Repington, the former military correspondent of the London *Times*, published his war diaries under the title *The First World War*. If the phrase had a cynical ring, he meant it. According to Samuel Hynes in *A War Imagined*, a Major Johnstone, a Harvard professor whom the U.S. government sent to Europe to plan an official history of the war, visited Repington in September 1918. Among other matters, they talked about what to call the war. Later, Repington noted in his diary:

> We discussed the right name of the war. I said that we called it now *The* War, but that this could not last. The Napoleonic War was *The Great War*. To call it *The German War* was too much flattery for the Boche. I suggested *The World War* as a shade better title, and finally we mutually agreed to call it *The First World War* in order to prevent the millennium folk from forgetting that the history of the world was the history of war.

Whether appropriate or not, the title took hold and has long since supplanted the more accurate designation, Great War. If it was not the *first* world war, it was history's first "total war." As the editors (Jay Winter, Geoffrey Parker, and Mary R. Habeck) of *The Great War and the Twentieth Century* remark in their introduction, here was "something the world had never seen before: armed conflict on a world stage between industrialized powers. . . . Total war entailed the brutalization of millions and thereby raised radically the tolerance of violence in some of the societies caught up in armed conflict."

The brutalization that trench warfare, with its mass killings, visited on the men who fought in the Great War would scar not just them but the entire century. It is no accident that many of those responsible for the Holocaust were veterans of the trenches. We live in an age of fierce boundaries, political, military, ideological, and now, religious: Has any affected our lives more conclusively than the fiercest of all, the Western Front? The excavations that stretched 470 miles from the North Sea to the Swiss border gave us a modern metaphor for relentless slaughter, for stalemate without hope. Here was a barrier on which shattered traditions of humanism and refinement nurtured over centuries—not just a physical presence but one of the genuine dividing lines of history.

The importance of the Great War cannot be overstated. At the same time, some corrective generalizations are worth recognizing. The war, as the Australian military historians Robin Prior and Trevor Wilson remind us, was shorter and less bloody than the Second World War, costing one fifth the number of lives. The areas of utter devastation were limited to the relatively narrow band that ran across Belgium and France; the fought-over landscapes of Russia and Austria-Hungary were even less battered. (There was an unreality to the war: Men on leave could in a matter of hours hop back to London or Paris, which the war had left physically unchanged—and then return to die.) Because the stalemate on the Western Front lasted so long, armies had no chance after 1914 to rampage over the land of the enemy, burning and destroying towns and cities. Wars of maneuver always leave havoc in their wake, much of it deliberate. (There can be no better example than Sherman's March in the Civil War.)

But it is the human havoc of the Great War that has always concerned us more. The popular image is of the trenches that sheltered a lost generation waiting to be mown down by machine guns, crushed by massed artillery, and sucked into the mud. To that mix we add the notion of lions—the common soldiers—led by donkeys—the generals. "[O]nce radical views of the generals' and the staff's incompetence," the military historian Brian Bond writes, "have . . . become the received wisdom to the extent that to many people it now seems bizarre to insist that there were many able generals and highly efficient staff officers." The disappointing results of the war have been distilled into the adjective "senseless." This negative emphasis has been particularly felt in Great Britain beginning with the pacifism of the early 1930s and resurfacing with the antinuclear, anti-Vietnam, antiestablishment attitudes of the 1960s. If the Second World War had been a "good" war, the First had nothing to recommend it. That became the theme of countless popular histories, novels, plays, and television documentaries. To quote that historian of culture, Modris Eksteins, the "real" historical Great War has been "swallowed by imagination in the guise of memory."

Too often, it has been pointed out, there now seem to be two Great Wars—the one of literature and popular culture and the other of history. Fortunately, serious historians have begun to reclaim the Great War, with often fascinating results. The war that they have begun to portray is not the war we have too long imagined. Some of their work will be found in this volume. To think only in terms of the undeniable misery and massive losses of the war is to distort its meaning, or to miss it altogether. I wouldn't describe this collection as revisionist history but rather as history without tears. There has been altogether too much emotion and not enough measured reflection devoted to a subject incompletely understood—and, for all the millions of words expended on it, still too narrowly explored.

PART ONE

———

PROLOGUE

EUROPE 1914
Sir Michael Howard

I HOLD WAR TO BE INEVITABLE, AND THE SOONER THE BETTER."
The frequently quoted words of General Helmuth von
Moltke, the Chief of the German General Staff, were part of a
memorandum to the Reich chancellor written at the end of
1911. "Everyone," Moltke added, "is preparing for the great
war, which they all expect." He was merely putting on paper a
fatalistic anticipation that had become increasingly widespread. A series of intensifying international crises seemed to
justify an ever-heightening military preparedness—which, in
its turn, only ratcheted up Continental tensions. It was clear
that soon enough scores would be settled not at the conference table but on the battlefield.

More than just expecting war, most Europeans wanted it.
They snapped up novels about war in the near future, which
had developed into something of a literary subgenre. (Only
the 1898 *Is War Now Impossible?* by the Russian industrialist
Ivan S. Bloch envisaged a long war leading to major up-
heavals, in which "the spade will be as indispensable to the
soldier as his rifle.") The heroic paintings of Detaille and Lady
Butler, full of bright uniforms, grim-nostrilled chargers, eager
marksmen, and clean deaths, were the most familiar images
of combat; few, probably, had glimpsed the American Civil
War photographs of Alexander Gardiner, with their bursting
corpses. "In the popular mind, as in the military mind,"
Michael Howard notes in the essay that opens this book,
"wars were seen not as terrible evils to be deterred but as necessary struggles to be fought and won."

Howard, one of the preeminent military historians of our time, reexamines the fateful decisions taken in the midsummer days of 1914, as well as the near-universal mood that sustained them, decisions that would finally bring on the great Continental civil war. What, he asks, did Europeans—governments, armies, and ordinary citizens—think would happen to them if they did *not* go to war? "Why did war, with all its terrible uncertainties, appear to be preferable to remaining at peace?" Every potential belligerent, except perhaps Russia, could summon convincing rationales for an immediate score-setting. The risks of continued peace seemed greater than those of a quick and decisive war. Politicians like to deal in sure things. Going to war seemed to be one. Meanwhile, military leaders on both sides maintained publicly that the best chance for victory lay in taking an immediate offensive: To yield the initiative, as the French had done in the Franco-Prussian War, was to court defeat. (New documents discovered in the former East German military archives indicate that even before 1914, many German senior war planners had private qualms about whether they could indeed achieve a quick win.) "The lessons of history," Howard concludes, "seemed to reinforce the strategic imperatives of 1914." But how dangerous such "lessons" can be, he points out—and how often they can lead us to opt for short-term gains that may have unforeseen long-term consequences.

———

SIR MICHAEL HOWARD is the former Regius Professor of Modern History at Oxford University and the Robert A. Lovett Professor of Military and Naval History at Yale University. This article was included in Howard's collection, *The Lessons of History*, published by Yale University Press.

I N A PLACE OF HONOR IN THE OXFORD EXAMINATION SCHOOLS, THERE HANGS a portrait of Kaiser Wilhelm II of Germany, wearing the robes of the honorary doctorate of civil law bestowed on him by the University of Oxford in November 1907. Seven years after the kaiser received his degree, out of a total of seven Oxford honorands in June 1914, five were German. The duke of Saxe-Coburg-Gotha, Professor Ludwig Mitteis of the University of Leipzig, and the composer Richard Strauss all received their degrees at the encaenia on June 25. Special sessions of convocation were held to bestow honorary doctorates on the king of Württemberg and the German ambassador, Prince Karl Lichnowsky. At a banquet in the latter's honor, the professor of German reminded his audience that the kaiser's great-grandfather, King Frederick William III of Prussia, had also received an honorary doctorate of civil law exactly one hundred years before. He welcomed the presence of so many German students in Oxford (fifty-eight German Rhodes Scholars had matriculated over the previous ten years) and expressed the hope that thereby the two nations would be "drawn nearer to one another," quoting the belief of Cecil Rhodes "that the whole of humanity would be best served if the Teutonic peoples were brought nearer together and would join hands for the purpose of spreading their civilization to distant regions."

Three days after this encaenia, Archduke Franz Ferdinand of Austria was assassinated at Sarajevo. When the university reconvened three months later in October 1914, many of the young Germans and Englishmen who had rubbed shoulders at those celebrations had enlisted in their respective armies and were now doing their best to kill one another. The Examination Schools had been turned into a hospital. The number of undergraduates in residence had dwindled by over half, from 3,097 to 1,387. (By 1918 it would be down to 369.) During the vacation over a thousand of them had been recommended for commissions by a committee established under the vice-chancellor, and they were already serving with the army. As yet, only twelve had been killed; the slaughter of the First Battle of Ypres was still a few weeks away.

Several colleges had been taken over to house troops. Organized games had virtually ceased, while the Officers' Training Corps, to which all able-bodied undergraduates now belonged, trained for five mornings and two afternoons a week. As if this were not enough, the Chichele Professor of Military History,

Spenser Wilkinson, advertised a course of lectures "for those who are preparing themselves to fight England's battles." The course was to begin with a description of "the nature and properties of the weapons in use—the bullet, the shell, the bayonet, the sword and the lance."

In one way it can therefore be said that the war came out of a clear sky. But these events do not indicate a profoundly pacific community taken totally by surprise and adjusting only with difficulty to astonishing and terrible new conditions. Everyone seems to have known exactly what to do, and to have done it with great efficiency. Arrangements to take over the Examination Schools and colleges had been made by the War Office two years earlier. The OTC was already flourishing: One undergraduate in three belonged to it, and five hundred were in summer camp at Aldershot when the news of the assassination came through. And insofar as such iconographic evidence can be legitimately adduced, group photographs of Oxford colleges and clubs show how the lolling dandies of the turn of the century, with their canes, blazers, and dogs, had given way soon after the Boer War to a new generation of muscular young men—fit, serious, short-haired, level-eyed—whose civilian clothes already seemed to sit uneasily upon them. This generation may not have expected war to break out in the summer of 1914 but was psychologically and physically ready for it when it came. The challenge was expected, and the response full of zest.

In this respect Oxford was a microcosm, not only of Britain but of Europe as a whole. Europe was taken by surprise by the occasion for the war—so many comparable crises had been successfully surmounted during the past five years—but not by the fact of it. All over the Continent long-matured plans were put into action. With a really remarkable absence of confusion, millions of men reported for duty, were converted or, rather, reconverted to soldiers, and were loaded into the trains that took them to the greatest battlefields in the history of mankind. It cannot be said that during the summer weeks of 1914, while the crisis was ripening toward its bloody solution, the peoples of Europe in general were exercising any pressure on their governments to go to war, but neither did they try to restrain them. When war did come, it was accepted almost without question—in some quarters indeed with wild demonstrations of relief.

The historian is faced with two distinct questions: Why did war come? And when it did, why was it so prolonged and destructive? In the background there is a further, unanswerable question: If the political and military leaders of Europe had been able to foresee that prolongation and that destruction, would the war have occurred at all? Everyone, naturally, went to war in the expectation of victory, but might they have felt that at such a cost even victory was not worthwhile? This is the kind of hypothetical question that laymen put and historians cannot answer. But we can ask another and less impossible question: What did the governments of Europe think would happen to them if they did *not* go to war? Why did war, with all its terrible uncertainties, appear to be preferable to remaining at peace?

Clausewitz described war as being compounded of a paradoxical trinity: the government for which it was an instrument of policy; the military for whom it was the exercise of a skill; and the people as a whole, the extent of whose involvement determined the intensity with which the war would be waged. This distinction is of course an oversimplification. In all major states of Europe, military and political leaders shared a common attitude and cultural background, which shaped their perceptions and guided their judgments. The same emotions that inspired peoples were likely also to affect their political and military leaders, and those emotions could be shaped by propaganda, by education, and by the socialization process to which so much of the male population of Continental Europe had been subject through four decades of at least two years' compulsory military service at an impressionable age. (It must be noted that the British, who were not subjected to the same treatment, reacted no differently from their Continental neighbors to the onset and continuation of the war.) Still, the triad of government, military, and public opinion provides a useful framework for analysis.

First, the governments. Although none of them could foresee the full extent of the ordeal that lay before them, no responsible statesman, even in Germany, believed that they were in for "a fresh, jolly little war." It was perhaps only when they had made their irrevocable decisions that the real magnitude of the risks came fully home to them. But that is a very common human experience. The German chancellor, Theobald von Bethmann-Hollweg, in particular saw the political dangers with gloomy clarity: A world war, he warned the Bavarian minister, "would topple many a throne."

There had indeed been a certain amount of wild writing and speaking over the past ten years, especially in Germany, about the value of war as a panacea for social ills; and the remarkable way in which social and political differences did disappear the moment war was declared has tempted some historians to assume that this effect was foreseen and therefore intended: that the opportunity was deliberately seized by the Asquith cabinet, for example, to distract attention from the intractable Irish problem to Continental adventures, or that the German imperial government saw it as a chance to settle the hash of the Social Democrats for good. One can only say that minute scrutiny of the material by several generations of historians has failed to produce any serious evidence to support this view.

Rather, the opposite was the case: Governments were far from certain how their populations would react to the coming of war, and how they would stand up to its rigors. A whole generation of English publicists had been stressing the social consequences of even a temporary blockade of the British Isles: soaring insurance rates, unemployment, bread riots, revolution. The French army, for ten years the butt of left-wing agitation, hardly anticipated an enthusiastic response from conscripts recalled to the colors, and the French security services stood by to arrest left-wing leaders at the slightest sign of trouble. It was only with the greatest reluctance that the German army forced military service on the supposedly unreliable population of the industrial regions. The Russian government had within the past ten years seen one war end in revolution, and for at least some of its members this seemed good reason to keep out of another.

It was one thing to enhance the prestige of the government and undermine support for its domestic enemies by conducting a strong forward policy, whether in Morocco or in the Balkans. It was another to subject the fragile consensus and dubious loyalties of societies so torn by class and national conflict, as were the states of Europe in 1914, to the terrible strain of a great war. Governments did so only on the assumption, spoken or unspoken, that the war, however terrible, would at least be comparatively short—no longer, probably, than six months, the length of the last great war in Europe in 1870. How could it be otherwise? A prolonged war of attrition, as Count Alfred von Schlieffen had pointed out in a famous article in 1909, could not be conducted when it required the expenditure of milliards to sustain armies numbered in millions. The only person in any position of responsibility who appears to have thought differently was Horatio Herbert, Lord Kitchener, a British imperial soldier who had served outside Europe throughout his career and who had never, as far as we know, seriously studied the question at all.

But whether the war proved to be short or long, it was for all governments a leap into a terrible dark, and the penalties for defeat were likely to be far greater than the traditional ones of financial indemnities and territorial loss. So we inevitably come back to these questions: What appeared to be the alternatives? And in the event of victory, what appeared to be the probable gains? Why, in the last resort, did the governments of Europe prefer the terrifying uncertainties of war to the prospect of no war?

Let us begin where the war itself effectively began, in Vienna. Was not the prospect that lay before the statesmen of Vienna, even if this crisis were successfully "managed," one of continuous frustration abroad and disintegration at home? Of a Serbia, doubled in size after the Balkan Wars, ever more boldly backing the claims of the Bosnian irredentists, while other South Slavs agitated with ever greater confidence for an autonomy that the empire would never permit them to exercise? What serious prospect was there of the empire hanging together once the old emperor had gone? A final settling of accounts with Serbia while Germany held the Russians in check must have seemed the only chance of saving the monarchy, whatever Berlin might say; and with a blank check from Berlin, Vienna could surely face the future with a greater confidence than had been felt there for very many years. No wonder Count Leopold von Berchtold and his colleagues took their time drafting their ultimatum: They must have found the process highly enjoyable. A successful war would put the monarchy back in business again, and keep it there for many years to come.

What about the government in Berlin? Was this the moment it had been waiting for ever since the huge expansion of the army resulting from the famous Council of War in December 1912? The controversy about this has consumed many tons of paper and gallons of ink. But if one asks again what the imperial German government had to lose by peace and gain by war, the answers seem very clear. One of the things it had to lose by peace was its Austrian ally, which would become an increasingly useless burden as it grew ever less capable of solving its internal problems or protecting its own (and German) interests in the Balkans against the encroachments of Russia and Russia's protégés.

Another thing Germany stood to lose was her capacity to hold her own against a dual alliance in which French capital was building up a Russian army whose future size and mobility appeared far beyond the capability of any German force to contain. It would not be too anachronistic to suggest that the shadow of Russia's future status as a superpower was already rendering out of date all calculations based on the traditional concept of a European balance. If war was to come at all—and few people in the imperial government doubted that it would—then it was self-evidently better to have it now, while there was still a fair chance of victory. By 1917, when the Russians had completed the great program of rearmament and railway building that they had begun, with French funding, in 1912, it might be too late.

And, for Germany, there was a lot to be gained by war. The domination of the Balkans and perhaps the Middle East; the final reduction of France to a position from which she could never again, even with allies, pose a military threat to German power; the establishment of a position on the Continent that would enable Germany to compete on equal terms with England and attain the grandiose if ill-defined status of a world power—all this, in July 1914, must have appeared perfectly feasible. In September, when the program of her war aims was drafted, it looked as if it had almost been achieved. Even in a less bellicose and more self-confident society than Wilhelmine Germany, the opportunity might have seemed too good to miss.

In Vienna and Berlin then, there seemed much to be lost by peace and gained by war. In St. Petersburg, the ambitions for Balkan expansion and the "recovery" of Constantinople, which had been checked in 1878 and 1885, were far from dead, but they can hardly be considered a major element in Russian political calculations in July 1914. More serious were the costs of remaining at peace: abandoning Serbia and all the gains of the past five years; facing the wrath of the Pan-Slavs in the Duma and their French allies; and watching the Central Powers establish and consolidate an unchallengeable dominance in southeast Europe. Even so, these costs were hardly irredeemable. Russia had been humiliated before in the Balkans and had been able to restore her authority. She had no vital interests there that, once lost, could never be recovered. Above all, she had nothing to lose in terms of military power by waiting, and a great deal to gain. Of all the major European powers, Russia's entry into the war can be categorized as the least calculated, the most unwise, and ultimately, of course, the most disastrous.

As for Paris and London, a successful war would certainly remove—as it ultimately did—a major threat to their security. But the advantages to be gained by war did not enter into their calculations, whereas the perils of remaining at peace evidently did. The French government took little comfort from the long-term advantages to be gained from the growth of Russian military power and paid little heed to the consequent advisability of postponing the issue until 1917. It was more conscious of its immediate weakness in the face of the growing German army. In 1914, after the increase of the past two years, German peacetime strength had reached 800,000 men, its wartime strength 3.8 million.

Thanks to their new and controversial Three-Year Law, the French could match this with 700,000 men in peace, 3.5 million in war. But with a population of only 60 percent of the Germans', that was almost literally their final throw. Completion of the Russian reforms was three years away. In the long run Russian strength might redress the balance, but in the long run a large number of Frenchmen could be dead and their nation reduced to the status of Italy or Spain. So the French government saw no reason to urge caution on St. Petersburg, and even less reason to refrain from supporting its ally when Germany declared war on her on August 1.

To the British government, composed largely (although by no means entirely) of men to whom the whole idea of war was antipathetic and who were responsible to a parliamentary party deeply suspicious of militarism and of Continental involvement, there appeared nothing to be gained by war. Indeed, perhaps more than any of its Continental equivalents, the British government was conscious of the possible costs, but was equally conscious of the cost of remaining at peace. She had no demands to make on any of the belligerents, no territorial aspirations, no expectation of economic gain. So far as the British government was concerned, Norman Angell's famous book *The Great Illusion* was preaching to the converted. But if the Dual Alliance defeated Germany unaided, the two victors would regard Britain with hostility and contempt. All the perils of imperial rivalry that were temporarily dispersed by the Entente with France in 1904 and the British accords with Russia of 1907 would reappear. If, on the other hand, Germany won and established a Continental hegemony, Britain would face a threat to her security unknown since the days of Napoleon.

Leaving aside any consideration of honor, sentiment, or respect for treaties—and let us remember that that generation of Englishmen did *not* leave them aside but regarded them as quite central—every consideration of *realpolitik* dictated that Britain, having done her best to avert the war, should enter it on the side of France and Russia once it began.

WHEN THE STATESMEN OF EUROPE DECLARED WAR IN 1914, THEY ALL SHARED ONE assumption: that they had a better-than-even chance of winning it. In making this assumption they relied on their military advisers, so it is now time to look at our second element in the triad: the soldiers.

The first thing to note about the soldiers—certainly those of western Europe—is that they were professionals, and most of them professionals of a very high order. Those of them who were wellborn or socially ambitious certainly shared the feudal value system so excoriated by Professor Arno Mayer in his book *The Persistence of the Old Regime.* Those who were not probably had more than their fair share of the prevalent philosophy of social Darwinism and regarded war not as an unpleasant necessity but as a test of manhood and of national fitness for survival. In all armies, then as now, there were incompetents who through good luck or good connections reached unsuitably high rank; but a study of the military literature of the period strongly indicates that the military professionals—especially those responsible for the armament, training, organization, and deployment of armies—were no fools, worked hard, and took their jobs very seriously. And they, too, shared certain assumptions.

The first was that war was inevitable. The now much-quoted statement made by General Helmuth von Moltke (namesake of his famous uncle) at the so-called Council of War in December 1912, "I hold war to be inevitable, and the sooner the better," can be paralleled with comparable expressions by responsible figures in every army in Europe. They may have differed over the second part of the sentence—whether it was better to get it over with quickly or wait for a more favorable moment—but from 1911 onward it is hard to find any military leader suggesting that war could or should be avoided any longer.

The change of mood in the summer of that year, provoked by the 1911 Agadir crisis over conflicting French and German interests in Morocco, was very marked. In France a new political leadership appointed a new group of military chiefs who belatedly and desperately started to prepare their ramshackle army for the test of war. The Dual Alliance was reactivated, Russian mobilization schedules were speeded up, and the Great Program of Russian military mobilization was set afoot. In Germany, the agitation began that contributed so powerfully to the German army's massive increase in military strength. In Britain, the government gave its blessing to the army's plans for sending the British Expeditionary Force to France, and Winston Churchill was sent to the Admiralty to bring the navy into line.

The extent to which war was generally regarded as inevitable or desirable by the public as a whole is still difficult to gauge—although if the "distant drummer" penetrated into the summer idylls of A. E. Housman's poetry, it is reasonable to suppose that less remote figures found the sound pretty deafening. Certainly the evidence is overwhelming that the question in military minds was not "whether" but "when." They saw their job as being not to deter war but to fight it.

The second assumption, which they shared with the statesmen they served, was that the war would be short. It required exceptional perspicacity to visualize anything else. Ivan Bloch, in his work *La Guerre Future*, published in 1898, had forecast with amazing accuracy that the power of modern weapons would produce deadlock on the battlefield and that the resulting attrition would destroy the fabric of the belligerent societies. Bloch's thesis was widely known and much discussed in military periodicals. But since he was saying in effect that the military was now faced with a problem it could not solve, it was unlikely that many soldiers would agree with him.

In 1904–1905 Russia and Japan had fought a war with all the weapons whose lethal effects were so gruesomely described by Bloch, and Japan had won a clear-cut victory that established her in the ranks of the major powers. The effect on Russia had been much as Bloch described, but revolution and defeat always stalked hand in hand. The war had indeed lasted well over a year, but it had been fought by both belligerents at the end of long and difficult supply lines. In Europe, where lines of communication were plentiful and short, and armies at hair-trigger readiness, the pattern of the German wars of unification seemed much more relevant: rapid mobilization and deployment of all available forces; a few gigantic battles—battles, indeed, that might be prolonged for days if not weeks as the protagonists probed for a flank or a weak point in the enemy defenses; and a decision within a matter of months. Because that decision would be reached so quickly, it was important that all forces be committed to action. There was no point in bringing up reserves after the battle had been lost. It was even more pointless—if indeed it occurred to anyone—to prepare an industrial base to sustain a war of matériel that might last for years. The idea that any national economy could endure such an ordeal seemed absurd.

This shared assumption—that the war would inevitably be short—led to another: that the best chances for victory lay in immediately taking the offensive. With the wisdom of hindsight, it is easy for subsequent generations to condemn the suicidal unreality of this idea; but in the circumstances of the time, it appeared reasonable enough. An offensive held the best hope of disrupting or preempting the opponent's mobilization and bringing him to battle under conditions favorable to the side taking the initiative. As in a wrestling match, which has to be settled in a matter of minutes, to yield to the initiative was to court defeat. The French had remained on the defensive in 1870 and been defeated. The Russians had remained on the defensive in 1904–1905 and been defeated. Those who had studied the American Civil War—including all of the students of the British Army Staff College at Camberley—concluded that the only hope of a Confederate victory had lain in a successful offensive; and that once Lee passed over to the defensive after the Battle of Gettysburg, his defeat had been only a matter of time. The lessons of history seemed to reinforce the strategic imperatives of 1914.

And let us not forget what those strategic imperatives were. The Germans had to destroy the French power of resistance before the full force of Russian strength could be developed. The Russians had to attack sufficiently early, and in sufficient strength, to take the weight off the French. The Austrians had to attack the Russians in order to take the weight off the Germans. For the French alone a defensive strategy was in theory feasible, but the precedent of 1870 made it understandably unpopular, and the national mood made it inconceivable. The doctrine of the offensive was certainly carried to quite unreasonable lengths in the pre-1914 French army, but that in itself does not mean that a posture of defense would have been any more effective in checking the German advance in 1914 than it was in 1940.

Finally, we must remember that the stalemate on the Western Front did not develop for six months, and that on the Eastern Front it never developed at all. The open warfare of maneuver for which the armies of Europe had prepared was precisely what, in the autumn of 1914, they got. It resulted in a succession of spectacular German victories in eastern Europe, and given bolder and more flexible leadership it might very well have done the same in the west. The terrible losses suffered by the French in Alsace in August and by the British and Germans in Flanders in November came in encounter battles, not in set-piece assaults against prepared defensive positions; and they were losses that, to the military leadership at least, came as no great surprise.

For this was the final assumption shared by soldiers throughout Europe: that in any future war, armies would have to endure very heavy losses indeed. The German army, for one, had never forgotten the price it paid for its victories in 1870, when the French had been armed with breech-loading rifles that, in comparison with the weapons now available, were primitive. Since then the effects of every new weapon had been studied with meticulous care, and no professional soldier was under any illusions about the damage that would be caused—not simply by machine guns (which were in fact seen as ideal weapons of a mobile offensive) but by magazine-loading rifles and by quick-firing artillery hurling shrapnel at infantry in the open and high explosives against trenches. Their effects had been studied through controlled experiment and also in action, in the South African and Russo-Japanese Wars. The conclusion generally drawn was that in the future, infantry would be able to advance only in open formations, making use of all available cover, under the protection of concentrated artillery fire.

But whatever precautions they took, sooner or later troops would have to charge with the bayonet across open ground, and they must then be prepared to take very heavy losses. This had happened in Manchuria, where the Japanese were generally seen as owing their success not simply to their professional skills but to their contempt for death. European social Darwinians gravely propounded the terrible paradox that a nation's fitness to survive depended on the readiness of its individual members to die. Avoidance of casualties was seen as no part of the general's trade, and willingness to accept them was regarded as a necessity for commander and commanded alike. Into the literature of prewar Europe crept a term that was to become the terrible leitmotiv of the coming conflict: "sacrifice"—more particularly, "the supreme sacrifice."

That may have been all very well for professional soldiers, whose job it is, after all, to die for their country if they cannot arrange matters any less wastefully. But the people who were going to die in the next war would not be just the professional soldiers. They would be the people: men recalled to the colors from civilian life or, in the case of England, volunteering to "do their bit." Would these young men, enervated by urban living, softened by socialist propaganda, show the same Bushido spirit as the Japanese? This question was constantly propounded in military and right-wing literature during the ten years before the war. Kipling, for one, surveying the civilians of Edwardian England in the aftermath of the Boer War, very much doubted it, and the writer taunted his fellow countrymen in a series of scornful philippics:

Fenced by your careful fathers, ringed by your leaden seas,
Long did ye wake in quiet and long lie down at ease;
Till ye said of Strife, "What is it?" of the Sword,
  "It is far from our ken";
Till ye made a sport of your shrunken hosts and a toy
  of your armed men.

In Germany Heinrich Class and Friedrich von Bernhardi, in France Charles Maurras and Charles Péguy, all expressed the same doubts about the capacity of their people to rise to the level of the forthcoming test. But the astonishing thing was that when the time came, they did so rise. Why?

This brings us belatedly to the third element in the triad, the people. Without the support, or at least the acquiescence, of the peoples of Europe, there would have been no war. This is the most interesting and most complex area for historians to investigate. We know a lot—almost to excess—about the mood of the intellectuals and the elites in 1914, but what about the rest? There are now some excellent studies of local and popular reactions in Britain, largely based on the superb sources at the Imperial War Museum. Jean-Jacques Becker had done pathbreaking work for France in his study *1914: Comment les Français sont entrés dans la guerre* (Paris, 1977), but elsewhere there remains much research to be done or, where done, brought together. My own ignorance forces me to treat this vast subject briefly and impressionistically, and I hope that others will be able to correct some of my misconceptions and fill some of the yawning gaps.

What does appear self-evident is that the doubts many European leaders felt about the morale of their peoples proved in 1914 to be ill-founded. Those who welcomed war with enthusiasm may have been a minority concentrated in the big cities, but those who opposed it were probably a smaller minority still. The vast majority were willing to do what their governments expected of them. Nationalistically oriented public education; military service that, however unwelcome and tedious, bred a sense of cohesion and national identity; continuing habits of social deference—all of this helps explain, at a deeper level than does the strident propaganda of the popular press, why the populations of Europe responded so readily to the call when it came. For the "city-bred populations" so mistrusted by right-wing politicians, the war came as an escape from humdrum or intolerable lives into a world of adventure and comradeship. Among the peasants of France, as Becker has shown us, there was little enthusiasm, but rather glum acceptance of yet another unavoidable hardship in lives that were and always had been unavoidably hard; but the hardship fell as much on those who were left behind as on those who went away. The same can no doubt be said of the peasants of central and eastern Europe.

Probably only a tiny minority considered the idea of war in itself repellent. Few military historians, and no popular historians, had yet depicted the realities of the battlefield in their true horror, and only a few alarmist prophets could begin to conceive what the realities of future battlefields would be like. Their nations, so the peoples of Europe had learned at school, had achieved their present greatness through successful wars—the centenaries of the Battles of Trafalgar and Leipzig had recently been celebrated with great enthusiasm in Great Britain and Germany—and there was no reason to think that they would not one day have to fight again. Military leaders were everywhere respected and popular; military music was an intrinsic part of popular culture. In the popular mind, as in the military mind, wars were seen not as terrible evils to be deterred but as necessary struggles to be fought and won.

I have touched on the social Darwinism of the period: the view, widespread among intellectuals and publicists as well as among soldiers, that struggle was a natural process of development in both the social and natural orders of the world, and war a necessary procedure for ensuring survival of the fittest, among nations as among species. It is hard to know how seriously to take this. Its manifestations catch the eye of a contemporary historian if only because they are, to our generation, so very shocking. But how widespread were such views, and to what extent were proponents like F. N. Maude, Sidney Low, and Benjamin Kidd regarded as cranks?

The same applies to the much-touted influence of Nietzsche and Bergson among intellectuals—the creed of liberation from old social norms, of heroic egotism, of action as a value transcending all others. How widespread was their influence? Did it make the idea of war more generally acceptable than it otherwise would have been? Intellectuals tend to overrate the importance of other intellectuals, or at best attribute to them an influence that becomes important only among later generations. Webern and Schoenberg may have been composing in prewar Vienna, but the tunes that rang in the ears of the 1914 generation were those of Franz Lehár and Richard Strauss.

And if there was a "war movement," there was also, far more evident and purposeful, a peace movement, derived from older liberal-rationalist roots. It was stronger in some countries than in others; then as now, it flourished more successfully in Protestant than in Catholic cultures, at its strongest in Scandinavia, the Netherlands, and Britain (not to mention the United States), weakest in Italy and Spain. It was indeed the apparent strength and influence of the peace movement, especially at the time of the Hague Conferences, that provoked so much of the polemical writings of the social Darwinians and caused so much concern to nationalistic politicians.

In imperial Germany the peace movement had an uphill struggle; but if Heinrich Class and the Pan-German League were thundering out the dogmas of the war movement, the far larger and more important Social Democratic party rejected them. So did the overwhelmingly dominant Liberal-Labour coalition in England and the left wing led by Jean Jaurès that triumphed at the polls in France in the spring of 1914. Social Darwinism may have been not so much the prevailing zeitgeist as a sharp minority reaction against a much stronger and deeply rooted liberal, rational, and progressive creed whose growing influence seemed to some to be undermining the continuing capacity of nations to defend themselves.

But the events of 1914 showed these right-wing fears to be misplaced. Everywhere the leaders of the peace movement found themselves isolated: small and increasingly unpopular minorities of idealists, intellectuals, and religious zealots. Events made it clear that whatever their influence among intellectuals and elites, both the peace and the war movements were marginal to the attitudes of the peoples of Europe. Those people did *not* reject war. Nor did they regard it as the highest good, the fulfillment of human destiny. They accepted it as a fact of life. They trusted their rulers and marched when they were told. Many did so with real enthusiasm; perhaps the more highly educated they were, the greater the enthusiasm they felt. None knew what they were marching toward, and any romantic notions they had about war shredded to pieces the moment they came under artillery fire. But they adjusted to the ordeal with astonishing speed and stoicism. It was indeed because they adjusted so well that the ordeal lasted as long as it did.

PART TWO

———

DEADLOCK

UNEXPECTED ENCOUNTER AT BERTRIX

Bruce I. Gudmundsson

—

POLITICIANS AND GENERALS MAY HAVE HAD THEIR strategic goals long fixed, but once populations were mobilized, war declared, and armies unleashed, an operational haze everywhere descended. Nobody seemed to know what the other side was doing, something that still comes as a surprise. It shouldn't. Intelligence was haphazard, depending mainly on cavalry scouts and a handful of reconnaissance aircraft. Telephones were relatively rare and many towns had to depend on the single hand-cranked device in the railway stationmaster's office; radios were bulky, hard to set up, and notoriously unreliable.

Hundreds of thousands of men, whole armies, barged across the landscape, undetected. (That was one problem a continuous trench line would take care of.) Even after the Germans had destroyed the Belgian forts surrounding the Meuse River city of Liège in mid-August and, after occupying Brussels, had begun to wheel southward, the French high command failed to grasp what was happening: the beginning of the Schlieffen Plan, that scythelike swing through Belgium that would soon reach the borders of France. Both sides maneuvered to seize the initiative. General Joseph Joffre, the French Commander in Chief, had a scheme of his own, known as Plan XVII. The idea was to squeeze the fortress city of Metz with pincers from the south and the north and then thrust up along the Rhine, cutting off the German armies at their base. In the process, Joffre's armies would do the politically popular thing: liberate Lorraine and Alsace, the two provinces lost in the Franco-Prussian War. The southern offensive through Lorraine commenced in the third week of August. Faulty intelligence as much as anything doomed it. Waves of attackers melted away before unexpected German prepared positions at Morhange and Sarrebourg. The Germans chased two French armies back across the border and nearly took the great city-prize of northeastern France, Nancy.

Even with two of his armies reeling in disorderly retreat, Joffre elected to go ahead with the second part of Plan XVII, the offensive (again with two armies) in the Ardennes forest. "The enemy will be attacked wherever encountered," France's portly military impresario declared. The Ardennes hardly seemed a promising place to attack. (In the Second World War, the same forest would be the scene of two other epic encounters, Sedan in 1940 and the Battle of the Bulge in 1944.) "A great forest of small trees," its hills and ravines are covered with a tangle of pine and crisscrossed with narrow roads, which made troop movement and supply difficult. Joffre had forbidden scouting: He wanted his attack to be a complete surprise. In cases, his regiments had only rough tourist maps of the area or maps torn from railroad timetables to guide them. He confidently believed that he held a huge numerical advantage, that his offensive would meet with only a thin screen of cavalry, and that he would soon break into open country. Instead, he collided head-on with two German armies, waiting to join the Schlieffen wheel into France. As Sewell Tyng wrote of the Ardennes in his overlooked classic of military history, *The Campaign of the Marne 1914*:

> It was in fact not one battle, nor even two, but a series of engagements, fought simultaneously by army corps, divisions, brigades, and even battalions, for the

most part independently of any central control and independently of the conduct of adjacent units. The character of the terrain rendered liaison between forces fighting almost side by side difficult, if not impossible.

The Germans used their cavalry not just to warn of the enemy approach but to guide infantry to positions it had scouted. They dug trenches in the forest and waited. On the night of August 21, a heavy rain fell, which had turned into a thick, humid summer fog by the following morning. French units literally stumbled on the German trenches. Then the fog lifted, revealing French artillery positions, which were promptly wiped out. By late morning, the French were fighting a desperate defensive action. As troops, badly cut up in piecemeal bayonet charges, panicked, gaps appeared in the line. Regiments suffered losses of up to 70 percent. A brigade of one of the crack units of the French army, the 3d Colonial Division, was trapped at Rossignol. "Hopelessly outnumbered and completely surrounded," Tyng writes, "the Colonials fought with the valour of desperation, and, at last, as darkness fell, with all hope gone, buried their regimental colours in the shell-swept ground, as the final grey assaulting wave swept over the flaming ruins of the little Belgian village." The division itself was destroyed.

In the article that follows, Bruce I. Gudmundsson describes the fighting that took place around another village, Bertrix. It is the Ardennes offensive in microcosm; what happened there was repeated all down the line. German preparation played a big part, he writes, but their superior tactical command and control made the real difference.

That was true—to a point. To quote Gudmundsson: "By sunset, the German victory was complete in all its elements except one. The German leadership . . . had no idea what they had accomplished."

Time and again, that would be the story of the Great War.

BRUCE I. GUDMUNDSSON is the author of several books touching on World War I. These include *Storm Troop Tactics; On Infantry; On Artillery;* and *On Armor.* A former Marine, he advises the armed forces on matters of tactics, policy, and structure. He divides his time between Oxford, England, and Quantico, Virginia.

F OR BOTH THE FRENCH AND THE GERMANS, WORLD WAR I BEGAN AS A monstrous exercise in military administration. Outfitting the hundreds of thousands of reservists called back to the colors and forming them into units was a monumental task. Loading those units into trains and sending those trains to the right place at the right time was an even greater achievement. Both tasks placed a premium on systematic preparation and what American efficiency experts of the time were beginning to call "scientific management." For the first few days, at least, World War I was a conflict in which the timetable took precedence over everything else, the staff officer held sway over the field commander, and the supply sergeant lorded over the squad leader. When, however, the giant armies formed by this process encountered each other on the battlefield, scientific management would fade into the background as the art of command took pride of place. Once the bullets started flying, there would be little demand for the staff officer's exquisitely synchronized railroad timetable or the supply sergeant's painfully correct ledger. The spirit of improvisation would reign supreme. The thoroughly tested plan would give way to the quick decision, the carefully weighed alternatives to the educated guess.

A thorough lesson in the difference between preparation and execution was taught, at a very high price, on August 22, 1914. On that day, some three weeks after the start of World War I, fourteen French infantry divisions marching north through the Ardennes encountered an equal number of their German counterparts marching south and east. The remarkable thing was not that these two armies met—both sides were spoiling for a fight—but that they were so perfectly matched. The number of major formations—seven army corps, each containing two infantry divisions of identical size—on each side was exactly equal, while the number of infantry battalions (174 French to 165 German) and fieldpieces (852 French to 864 German) was nearly so. The weapons employed were likewise remarkably similar, with the Germans having a slightly better rifle and the French a somewhat more powerful field gun. Even such factors as the years of peacetime training of the private soldiers involved (two years), their average age (mid-twenties), and the number of days they had been marching in the hot August sun (three) were identical.

Notwithstanding this remarkable symmetry of the forces involved, the outcome of the Battle of the Ardennes was anything but symmetric. The evening of August 22 found fourteen French infantry divisions retreating from the woods they had entered earlier that day. In most cases, the casualties suffered by the French divisions were horrific. In an engagement named for the village of Virton, the 8th Infantry Division, which had started the day with some 16,000 men, lost some 5,500 to death, capture, or incapacitating wounds. Near the neighboring village of Ethe, the 7th Infantry Division attacked over open fields with trumpets playing, drums beating, and flags flying. By the end of the day, the division had suffered so badly that a contemporary observer described it has having been "stomped" (*écrasse*). (In one French infantry regiment at Ethe, five men were killed, one after the other, while carrying the regimental standard.) At Neufchâteau, the 5th Colonial Infantry Brigade, which entered the Ardennes with 6,600 men, left with 3,400.

German losses were not inconsiderable—at Neufchâteau, some German infantry regiments seem to have suffered as terribly as the French colonial troops they were fighting. At Maissin, where the 25th Infantry Division faced two French divisions, a single German regiment took 1,000 casualties—a loss of a full third of its effectives. As a rule, however, the German losses were significantly less than those of the French. At Virton, the German 9th Infantry Division lost some 1,500 men—about 27 percent of the 5,500 men its French counterpart left on the battlefield. The VIII Reserve Corps, which made a forced march of forty-five kilometers in order to rescue the 25th Infantry Division at Maissin, seems to have lost more of its reservists—many of whom were overweight and out-of-shape—to heatstroke and sore feet rather than to French shells or bullets.

Looking at the encounter as a whole, it is hard to find a simple explanation for the one-sided outcome of the Battle of the Ardennes. Neither the French nor the Germans had any particular advantage of ground or battlefield geometry. Both were marching along narrow forest roads in territory that, being Belgian, was equally unfamiliar. Each force had well-secured flanks and free access to its lines of communication. The one tangible advantage enjoyed by the victors was their superior number of heavy field howitzers—powerful artillery pieces that shot 40-kg shells. The Germans had eighty of these, the French only twelve. A closer look at the engagements indicates that few of these monstrous products of armorer's art got involved in the combats. Those few that did fire on August 22 often arrived so late on the battlefield that the only available targets were French columns already in retreat. In the absence of a wholesale explanation for the lopsided outcome of the Battle of Ardennes, those who would understand the events of August 22, 1914, have to look at the seven division-sized engagements that made up the larger struggle. The best documented of these—and thus, perhaps, a sort of Rosetta stone for making sense of the rest—is the encounter that took place around the three-way road intersection near the village of Bertrix.

Sometime around noon on August 22, the main body of the French 33d Infantry Division—six battalions of infantry and all thirty-six of the division's 75mm field guns—began to enter the Forêt de Luchy, a large wood north of Bertrix. The bulk of the infantry—four battalions—was at the head of the column. The remaining two battalions traveled with the long column of horse-drawn field guns, caissons, and wagons that brought up the rear. This formation was a vulnerable one, designed for efficient marching and ease of command rather than combat. Both the division commander and his immediate superior, the commander of the French XVII Army Corps, saw no problem in this. Both thought that the Germans were far away.

The general in command of the French main body, Général de Brigade Fraisse, had better information than either of his superiors, both of whom were located several miles to the west. About an hour before the forward elements of his column entered the Forêt de Luchy, he had received word that Ochamps, the village 1,400 meters north of the woods, was controlled by German troops and that German cavalry had been seen throughout the area. Fraisse therefore sent an order to the officer in command of the artillery telling him to keep his guns out of the woods until he had finished a reconnaissance of Hill 471, a point four kilometers northwest of Bertrix, four kilometers southwest of Ochamps, and just clear of the western edge of the Forêt de Luchy. This hill, General Fraisse hoped, would provide his guns with a position from which they could effectively protect the forward movement of the rest of the division, particularly if there was to be a fight for Ochamps.

The soundness of this plan was never tested. By the time Fraisse's orders reached the lieutenant colonel in charge of the guns, it was too late to carry them out. In accordance with previous orders from Fraisse, the artillery commander had already limbered up his guns and placed them on the highway to Ochamps. Obeying General Fraisse would have required the artillerymen to turn their six horse teams 180 degrees on the narrow forest road, return to the open area south of the forest, and then proceed to Hill 471. The real impediment to obedience, however, was the fighting already in progress at the northern edge of the woods. At one-thirty—twenty minutes after General Fraisse had written the order telling the artillery to stay out of the woods—two companies of the lead battalion of the French 33d Infantry Division debouched from the northern edge of the Forêt de Luchy and marched into open ground.

It is quite possible that the officer in charge of the French artillery column was aware of the risks of sending his thirty-six field guns—the whole of the division artillery of the 33d Infantry Division—into the Forêt de Luchy. His immediate superior, the commander of the divisional artillery, a colonel by the name of Henri Jules Paloque, had recently published a book on artillery tactics. In that book, *Artillerie dans la Bataille* (*Artillery in Battle*), Paloque explicitly warned against sending columns of guns into the woods when enemy infantry was near. The officer in charge of the guns, however, had not been charged with acting in accordance with what he knew to be right. His task was to obey his explicit orders—and, as the order telling him to keep the guns out of the woods failed to reach him in time, his explicit orders were to take his guns to Ochamps.

The great majority of the French infantrymen were still in the woods when the firing started. Shrapnel shells were exploding above the forest, sending balls and shell fragments into the trees and men scrambling for cover. To French observers at the edge of the woods, the origin of this cannonade was clear; the muzzle flashes of German field guns could be seen just east of the church tower of Ochamps. The source of the rifle fire that accompanied the artillery fire was also readily apparent; the riflemen were firing from the ridge that hid Ochamps from its would-be liberators.

Unknown to the French infantrymen, who had been so sure of their safety that they had entered the open ground in march formation with officers mounted, Ochamps was occupied by a large force of Germans. The field guns, whose fire took the leading French battalion by surprise, belonged to a single German battery. This battery, however, was not alone. There were, in addition, two more batteries of field guns, three battalions of infantry, and a squadron of cavalry. This detachment—one fourth of the combat units of the 21st Infantry Division—had been posted in Ochamps to maintain contact with a neighboring division.

The effect of a battery's worth of German field gun fire on the exposed French infantry was devastating. When the second and third German batteries joined in, the impact was even greater. The lead elements of the forward battalion were annihilated—so affected by casualties and the psychological shock of the sudden bombardment that they were no longer able to participate in battle. This unexpected disaster, however, did nothing to hinder the offensive spirit of the following French battalions—units full of young soldiers who, as yet ignorant of the horrors of war, were eager to fight their first battle.

The remnants of the first French battalion and the as yet unbloodied second battalion formed their skirmish lines and began to move forward. On the right, they made little progress. The fire of the German infantry—which seems to have consisted of little more than a few pickets—could be suppressed without much trouble. The French even succeeded in driving some of these pickets back to the other side of the ridge. The German batteries, however, were some

1,400 meters away—well beyond the reach of the French rifles. To make matters worse, the fields over which the Frenchmen were attempting to attack were crisscrossed by a number of barbed-wire fences. These had not been laid by the defenders of Ochamps—the systematic use of barbed wire in war was still a few months away—but were nonetheless a big help to them, slowing down the French advance until the Germans could organize a proper counterattack.

For the French, things went a little better on their left. There, a slight indentation of the ground protected them from the German artillery fire. Advancing through this dead ground for more than a kilometer, the French battalion on the left soon reached the southwestern outskirts of Ochamps. There, the unit ran into the main body of the German 87th Infantry Regiment moving south through the streets of Ochamps. Aided by the six machine guns of their regimental machine-gun company, the three battalions of the 87th were able to stop the French advance. Nevertheless, as two more French battalions poured out of the woods to join their comrades south of Ochamps, the German regimental commander felt sufficiently hard-pressed to call for help.

The commander of the German artillery battalion responded, not by shifting his fire but by ordering two of his three batteries to limber up. This done, the two German batteries galloped down the back of the hill that they had been hiding behind and through the streets of Ochamps. Reaching the forward edge of the 87th Infantry Regiment, the gunners unlimbered their field pieces, turned them around, and, despite heavy French small arms fire, fired point-blank into the French skirmish lines. This, for the French, decided the issue. They stopped their attack and began to melt back into the forest.

While four French infantry battalions were being decimated in the open terrain south of Ochamps, the three artillery battalions following them were still in the forest, stretched out along the Ochamps road. No more than four kilometers away, and in some cases less than a thousand meters away, the bulk of the German 21st Infantry Division—nine battalions of infantry, nine batteries of field artillery, and four batteries of heavy field howitzers—was also marching through the Forêt de Luchy. This force was using the second major road that ran through the woods, the road from Recogne that intersected the Ochamps road at the southern entrance to the forest. Between two and three o'clock, just as the advance guard of this German force arrived within sight of that intersection, the last few guns of the last French battery could be seen moving north into the woods.

The lead German company promptly deployed into two separate skirmish lines, one on each side of the road. In the excitement of the moment, some Germans fired off a few rifle shots. (The men of the 21st Infantry Division, having previously fought nothing more than a running skirmish, were still rather

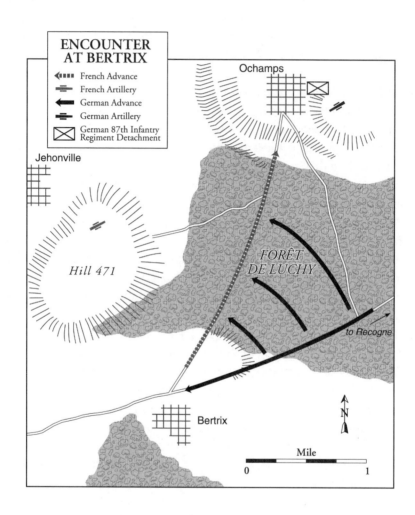

ENCOUNTER AT BERTRIX

French Advance
French Artillery
German Advance
German Artillery
German 87th Infantry Regiment Detachment

Ochamps

Jehonville

Hill 471

FORÊT DE LUCHY

to Recogne

Bertrix

N

Mile

0   1

green.) The reply was swift. The infantry battalion that formed the rear guard of the French column peppered the forest with rifle and machine-gun fire, driving the Germans to ground. The rest of the German vanguard—three more companies—soon arrived on the scene. The French, however, maintained control of the situation, and it looked like the German vanguard might have to pull back.

Marching to the sound of the guns, the German division commander, General-Leutnant von Oven, left his post at the head of the main body of his column and began to ride forward. On the road, he ran into a messenger from the vanguard. From the content of the message—scribbled, no doubt, by an officer more concerned with his immediate situation than with the task of accurately reporting what he saw—it seemed that a large French force was attacking through the woods. Von Oven responded immediately. He ordered the German infantry in his immediate vicinity—the remaining two battalions of the forwardmost German infantry regiment—to attack at once.

This rapid counterattack through the southernmost quarter of the Forêt de Luchy managed to stop the attack of the French infantry battalion. However, despite the employment of a second German infantry regiment, further progress was prevented by the combinations of rifle fire and the fire of the French corps artillery located four or five kilometers to the northeast on heights near the village of Jehonville. The 75mm shells fired by this overstrength regiment combined with the small arms fire of the French infantry, to inhibit the forwardmost German artillery battery from leaving the comparative safety of the forest road.

General-Major von Scherbening, the senior artilleryman of the 21st Infantry Division, Major Petzel, commander of the forwardmost German artillery battalion, and Major Petzel's three battery commanders were at the southern exit of the woods when Petzel received General von Oven's order to move his battalion forward in support of the attack of the German vanguard. General Scherbening, seeing the move into the open as suicidal, countermanded the order and sent an orderly to General von Oven to request infantry support for the deployment of the battery. When this request was refused—all three of the German infantry regiments that had been along the road were already engaged—Scherbening gave the order to move forward.

As the sole French machine-gun company south of the woods attempted to move into a position from which it could enfilade the German skirmish lines, Major Petzel's battalion left the woods at a gallop and took up positions on both sides of the Recogne road. The French answered this bold move with heavy fire from rifles and field guns. Although the Germans lost some men and horses, all eighteen of the German guns were able to make it to their assigned places, unlimber, and fire. Both the French infantry and artillery, it seems, were firing too high. The latter's efforts also suffered from a high percentage of "dud" shells. One of Petzel's batteries directed its attention on the guns of the French corps artillery more than five kilometers away. The other two fired over open sights in support of the infantry. Their main target was a handful of French guns from the column on the road to Ochamps that had turned around and taken up positions just west of the point where that road entered the Forêt de Luchy.

The result of the counterbattery fire against the distant guns of the French corps artillery was uncertain. Whether they were silenced by the fire of one German battery is unlikely. That they were distracted by another task is undocumented. The outcome of the counterbattery fire against the closer French guns, however, was immediately apparent. Subjected to almost (400-meter range) point-blank fire from twelve German fieldpieces, the three or four French guns just west of the Ochamps road were quickly silenced. The French drivers who bravely rode out of the shelter of the woods to recover the now crewless 75s received similar treatment.

The almost instantaneous destruction of this French battery decided the engagement. Deprived the material support and moral comfort of their own artillery fire, the French riflemen hiding in the tall gorse that covered the open ground between Bertrix and the forest lost heart. At the same moment, the German infantrymen trying to advance against an unseen enemy took courage from the fact that only their guns were firing effectively. The Germans, who by now numbered six infantry battalions, advanced. The French infantry retreated south, to Bertrix.

While battles raged to the north and south, General Fraisse, still stuck on the forest road to Ochamps, had come to a decision. On the advice of the lieutenant colonel in charge of the artillery (who had just returned from his reconnaissance of Hill 471), Fraisse ordered one of the artillery battalions—twelve 75mm field guns—to go into action north of the woods, to support the hard-pressed infantry. This order, however, was immediately countermanded by the recently arrived Général de Division de Villeméjane, commanding general of the 33d Infantry Division. Furious that his artillery should have been allowed in the woods in the first place, de Villeméjane commanded the entire artillery column—all thirty-six guns—to return to the open area near Bertrix. Thus, the first order of business for the thirty or so French gun sections in the woods was to get their 15m-long limbered guns to "about-face" on a road that was rarely more than ten meters wide.

The advantage was now clearly with the Germans. In the north, the bulk of General Fraisse's infantry was stuck at the edge of the woods, unwilling to retreat but unable to move forward. In the south, a French battery had been annihilated and the French infantry driven off. In the center, along the forest road between Bertrix and Ochamps, the three French artillery battalions (minus the tail-end battery lost in the south) were in a state of self-imposed confusion.

The Germans, however, did not seem to have recognized the fact that they had gained the upper hand. Rather, the major concern of General von Oven at this time was to protect his own artillery—ten batteries of which were strung out along the Recogne–Bertrix road. Reports from the vanguard fighting to the southwest had caused von Oven to believe that French infantry was moving through the woods toward his position. Similar tales told by the "walking wounded" and drivers of the vanguard's field kitchens as they moved toward the rear of the column spread tales of disaster among troops moving forward along the road. The final contributor to this atmosphere of disarray was the explosion of a handful of stray French artillery shells. Fired, it seems, by French guns defending themselves against the German vanguard, these 75mm shells fell on the piece of road occupied by the 80th Fusilier Regiment, killing the one officer and turning the confusion into panic.

Too weak to defend, General von Oven decided to attack. Hoping, perhaps, to meet the Frenchmen he presumed were attacking on even terms, he ordered his one remaining infantry regiment to counterattack through the woods. This simple maneuver—three thousand German infantrymen turned half-right and moved forward, converting the march column into an instant skirmish line—never made contact with the supposed French attack. Instead, the six companies on the right of the German line that ran into the French positions south of Ochamps joined with the German occupants of that village in fierce forest fighting. The other six companies found themselves slammed against a line of limbered French field guns stretched out along a narrow forest road.

In the hand-to-hand combat that followed, the French gunners fought no less bravely than their comrades of the infantry. Some made use of their carbines. Others found the Germans so close that they had to resort to their fists. A few managed to bring their guns into action—one gun accounting for a number of German riflemen when it fired point-blank into the ammunition limber of its neighbor. In such an uneven contest, however, the artillerymen were bound to lose. Within minutes, the rearwardmost of the three French artillery battalions—the unit which had already lost a battery at the southern entrance of the Forêt de Luchy—was no longer capable of effective resistance.

The two surviving French artillery battalions were now caught in a cruel dilemma. To stay where they were meant annihilation by the German infantry moving through the forest. (The further north the Germans were, the further they had to move through the woods and, consequently, the later they were to hit the Bertrix–Ochamps road. That they would arrive eventually, however, was obvious to all who cared to ponder the situation.) To move south or east brought the same result. To move north would put them under the fire of the German field pieces at Ochamps. The only way out, it seemed, lay to the west.

Sometime before the crisis in the woods, when the lieutenant colonel in direct command of the three French artillery battalions was still looking for a firing position from which he could support the four infantry battalions attacking Ochamps, a French artillery officer had discovered a primitive road running from the Bertrix–Ochamps road to the western edge of the Forêt de Luchy. Reporting this fact to the division commander, he got permission to lead the two surviving artillery battalions down that road and out of the forest.

The safety offered by this maneuver was, however, more apparent than real. About a thousand meters west of the western edge of the forest the retreating Frenchmen of the second battalion of the divisional artillery of the 33d Division found themselves on top of a low hill—the same Hill 471 where General Fraisse had wanted to place all of his guns. To men who had just escaped with their lives, the hill did not seem that significant. The increase in elevation, however, was just enough to expose the moving column to the fire of the German batteries that had been hastily set up just south of the Forêt de Luchy.

In the short time (less than an hour) that passed between the German seizure of the southern exit of the Forêt de Luchy and the attempted escape of the French artillery, the bulk of the German artillery assembled just east of the intersection of the Bertrix–Ochamps and the Recogne–Bertrix roads. North of the road to Recogne, four batteries of field artillery hid behind a low hill that protected them toward the north. South of the road, four more batteries of field artillery and four batteries of heavy field howitzers sheltered in a shallow draw.

As the first French teams pulled their guns into the open, the shells from the German "grand battery" started to fall. Although the accuracy of the first few volleys must have left something to be desired, enough shells hit the ridge to wreck havoc among the limbered guns, stopping seven out of twelve gun teams of the lead French artillery battalion from joining in the mad gallop to safety. The second French battalion, seeing what had happened to the first, wisely avoided what later generations of soldiers would call the "skyline." In moving through the dead ground north of the hill, however, many of the second battalion's guns got caught in a mixture of bog and barbed wire. Of the thirty-six French field guns that entered the Forêt de Luchy earlier that day, only nine remained in French hands at the end of the day.

As the German infantry in the woods pushed west of the Bertrix–Ochamps road, collecting prisoners and driving groups of stragglers before them, the remaining five battalions of the French 33d Infantry Division arrived on the scene. This understrength brigade had spent most of the day in the small forests to the west of Bertrix, serving as corps reserve. Rather than providing material aid to their comrades, however, the *poilus* of these five French infantry battalions found themselves spending the early evening of August 22 battling seven and a half German infantry battalions, six batteries of field guns, two batteries of light field howitzers, and four batteries of heavy field howitzers. For the Germans, the battle provided them with an opportunity for a "textbook" attack, with the field guns firing from the firing line, the light field howitzers a few hundred meters behind them, and the heavy field howitzers a thousand meters behind the light field howitzers. For the French, it was the last disaster of a disastrous day.

Hindered by confused orders and required to push through the remnants of the artillery regiment destroyed earlier that afternoon, the French infantry arrived on the battlefield in pieces. In pieces it faced the overwhelming fire of more than half of a German division. And in pieces it fell back to the south and west. By sunset, the German victory was complete in all its elements except one. The German leadership—the division commander and the brigade commanders—had no idea what they had accomplished. The general in charge of the Ochamps detachment was happy to have beaten off what he thought was an attack by two French infantry brigades. General von Scherbening, the commander of the artillery brigade, had no way of knowing the destruction his guns and howitzers had visited upon the two French artillery battalions on Hill 471. General von Oven, the division commander, had yet to receive the reports of his far-flung units. From his command post on the road to Recogne, all he could see were the long lines of wounded walking back to the regimental aid stations.

The French, of course, realized what had happened. Roll call the next morning would establish that thousands of men were dead, missing, or captured. The 20th Infantry Regiment, which had attacked Ochamps from the woods, was missing 1,300 men—close to half of its effectives. Its partner, the 11th Infantry Regiment, lost more than twice as many—2,700 out of 3,300. The 7th Infantry Regiment, whose three battalions had been in the corps reserve, lost more than 700. Worse still, from the point of view of soldiers who could accept casualties more easily than dishonor, twenty-seven guns and the colors of at least one regiment had been left in the hands of the enemy.

The only German who immediately understood the enormity of what happened was a young lieutenant of the 6th Uhlan Regiment, the divisional cavalry unit of the 21st Infantry Division. During a patrol made late in the afternoon of the twenty-second, he rode through the wreckage of the French batteries on Hill 471. Then, mounting the heights, he saw the survivors of a defeated division retreating to the west. His only regret was that the rest of his regiment was too far away to pounce upon the vulnerable columns.

An examination of the other battles that took place on August 22 indicates that bold, skilled, and decisive leadership by German commanders was not the exception but the rule. Just northwest of Bertrix, near Maissin, for example, the 25th Infantry Division was on the point of being overwhelmed by superior French forces when it was rescued by the arrival of the advance elements of the VIII Reserve Corps. This formation, which had begun the day in the second echelon of the Fourth Army, forty-five kilometers of winding, undulating roads east of the battlefield, had received no orders to take part in the battle. Rather, as its columns were reaching their designated march objectives, the corps commander, General von und zu Egolffstein, received a message describing the plight of the two widely separated brigades of the 25th Infantry Division. Acting without hesitation and entirely on his own authority, Egolffstein ordered his two divisions to continue their march for fifteen to twenty additional kilometers. While neither of these divisions did much fighting that day, their unexpected appearance on the flank of the locally triumphant French division, and their use of long-range artillery fire to protect their hard-pressed comrades, turned certain defeat into an unqualified victory.

Similar things happened in the other engagements of the larger Battle of the Ardennes. German leaders at all levels, from the young men in charge of companies and batteries up to the silver-haired commanders of divisions and army corps, were able to outcommand, and thus outfight, their French counterparts. One element of this was a willingness of German leaders to act on their own authority, to do what was necessary in the absence—and sometimes even in direct contravention—of explicit orders. The other element, a necessary complement to this extraordinary degree of initiative, was the ability of German leaders to consider the impact of their actions on the larger situation. To borrow a phrase sometimes seen on bumper stickers, the German leaders had learned how to "think globally and act locally." This, then, is the secret of the Battle of the Ardennes. In a fair fight—one in which courage, and numbers, and quality of weapons are equal—success came to the side that had the best approach to the art of command.

THE MASSACRE
OF THE INNOCENTS
Robert Cowley

—

NEVER BEFORE IN WAR HAD THERE BEEN LOSSES LIKE THE losses of 1914. French deaths alone may have totaled 300,000 for those first five months, or about one quarter of the Frenchmen killed in the entire war. By September 6, after just a month of fighting, the German armies in Belgium and France had taken some 265,000 casualties. The totals for the first six weeks of war on the Eastern Front were equally as astronomical, equally as appalling: a combined 750,000 for the Germans, Austrians, and Russians.

Even after the setbacks and tactical retreats known collectively as the Battle of the Marne, the German generals still felt that a swift victory was possible. Now began the phase of the war in the West which would be called, as an afterthought, "the Race to the Sea"—although everyone thought a decision would be reached long before the sea was. The real race during those six weeks would be the race to outflank and envelop, first by one side and then by the other. The Germans and French fought a series of desperate, and now forgotten, battles in the open plains of Picardy and the Artois. (How many historians nine decades later even mention the First Battle of Arras, a stand-up affair in the open that had more to do with the nineteenth century than with the twentieth and that saw part of an overextended French army nearly encircled by its German opposite?) For a few weeks more, cavalry mattered. Meanwhile, as the Western Front began to stabilize in the wake of the racers, the opposing troops connected foxholes and dug trenches. They did so less out of a fatalistic acceptance of a possible long war and the need to stay put than as a means of conserving manpower, so profligately spent earlier. It's worth noting that the French encountered the first barbed wire, erected by the Germans near Reims, on September 13.

By mid-October the fighting had returned to Belgium. Now it really was a race to the sea. The new German chief of staff, General Erich von Falkenhayn, thrust his forces toward the ports of Boulogne, Dunkirk, and Calais. To take them would give him a base of operations against England. It would also have opened the door to the Channel, giving the German navy an opportunity to range southward, effectively breaking the newly established blockade of Germany.

First the Belgians barred his way by flooding the plain of the tiny river Yser. The fighting shifted to the walled town of Ypres, once the trading center of the medieval cloth industry. For the better part of a month, Falkenhayn threw his hundreds of thousands at an ever-shrinking Allied perimeter—what would become the Ypres salient. He recognized that victory had to be won now or never. He was forced to use recently called-up reserve divisions, men who were badly trained, inadequately equipped, and lacked good officers. The popular image was that these divisions were mainly composed of young men of university age, who went to their deaths with voices raised in patriotic song. That was how the myth started. But Germany would soon be in need of a myth.

All the combatants had them, some based on fact, some not. The British had their Angel of Mons, the French, the Taxis of the Marne, and the Germans, the so-called Massacre of the Innocents. The latter story was all about loss and the attempt to rationalize failure. Innocents they may have been. But how many were really students? Did the singing attacks really happen? And how, and for what ends, did those in charge of public relations (and later, the Nazi Party) appropriate the cover-up of a disaster?

Ypres did turn out to be a disaster for the Germans. They lost from 80,000 to 100,000 men: Nobody will ever know the exact figure—but then that is the case with most of the statistics of 1914. Once the battle ended, a trench line, however sketchy in places, extended from the North Sea to the Swiss border. There would be no more flanking movements, no more envelopments. On November 18, a week after his offensive had shut down, Falkenhayn visited the German chancellor, Theobald von Bethmann-Hollweg. He announced that the war could no longer be won and suggested that Germany initiate peace overtures. Bethmann-Hollweg turned him down, in effect pronouncing the death sentence for a generation.

———

ROBERT COWLEY is the founding editor of *MHQ: The Quarterly Journal of Military History.* He has edited two earlier *MHQ* anthologies, *No End Save Victory*, about World War II, and *With My Face to the Enemy*, about the Civil War, as well as the *What If?* series. He lives in Connecticut.

AT YPRES IN 1914, GERMANY BOTCHED ITS LAST CHANCE TO WIN THE upper hand on the Western Front—and its last chance, perhaps, to win the Great War. From the middle of October to the middle of November, practically without letup, parts of two German armies, the Fourth and the Sixth, battered the British and French divisions clinging to a narrowing salient. Their immediate objective was Ypres, once the center of the medieval cloth trade in northern Europe; but beyond lay the last real strategic prizes of the fall, the Channel ports of Dunkirk, Calais, and Boulogne, where the British buildup was centered.

Villages, even crossroad features, with hitherto forgettable names like Bixschoote, Zonnebeke, Kortekeer Caberet, and Langemarck, gained sudden notoriety. Time and again the Germans threatened to break through, only to lose momentum or to run up against a determined improvised defense at the last moment. The "last": The repetition applies in every sense but one. Though nobody imagined it at the time, this would not be the last Ypres but the "First."

The losses, hideous for all concerned, were worst for the Germans. They had nothing to show for them. There would be no more turning of flanks, no more opportunity to maneuver, no occupation of the Channel ports. The war in the West had hardened into a trench stalemate. How could Germany's military and political leaders rationalize the disaster at home? How could they put the best heroic gloss—a favorable spin, as we might say—on the shambles of their hopes? Out of this public relations dilemma, apparently, grew one of the enduring legends of the Great War: the massacre of the singing innocents at Ypres.

Few caught the essence of the story better, if with less regard for the truth, than Adolf Hitler, then a private in the 16th Bavarian Reserve Regiment. In *Mein Kampf,* he describes his baptism by fire—or, as he put it, the "iron salute" he received near Gheluvelt on October 29:

> With feverish eyes each one of us was drawn forward faster and faster over turnip fields and hedges till suddenly the fight began, the fight of man against man. But from the distance the sounds of a song met our ears, coming nearer and nearer, passing from company to company, and then, while Death busily plunged his hand into our rows, the song reached also

us, and now we passed it on: "Deutschland, Deutschland über alles, über alles in der Welt!"

By the time Hitler wrote those lines in 1924, while incarcerated for his part in the failed Munich putsch, the invention of myth and not the establishment of fact was uppermost in his mind. In this instance, Hitler was busy pushing what would become one of the most persistent semifictions of the interwar period and a cornerstone of the Nazi experience, a vision of manly young patriots sacrificing their lives for the greater good of the fatherland. This was the story of *Der Kindermord bei Ypern*—the so-called Massacre of the Innocents at Ypres. The "innocents" were the student volunteers in the German reserve corps, who were slaughtered in droves but who went to their deaths singing. In German Bibles, the word "*Kindermord*" was also applied to the children Herod killed after the visit of the Magi, and it had, in both cases, the connotation of "holy innocents."

The story even has its own special locus, the village of Langemarck on the north face of the Salient, and date, November 10, 1914—in both location and day some distance from Hitler. According to the next day's official army bulletin, which appeared on the front pages of many German newspapers, "West of Langemarck youthful regiments stormed the first lines of the enemy trenches and took them, singing 'Deutschland, Deutschland über alles.' " They took approximately two thousand prisoners, the dispatch concluded, French Regulars all. The carefully crafted story, notably repeated in accounts published during the Third Reich, is basically this: The student volunteers, called the children's corps "by mocking veterans," advance silently in the fog, "a wide sea of white air," as one memoirist puts it. There is no preliminary artillery barrage that might tip off the enemy. The volunteers are discovered anyway, and fire from a source they cannot see chops down their close-packed rows. They continue to throw themselves "into this hell with childlike trust." But nothing avails. They lie in the open, unable to advance or retreat. "In this hour, they have become men."

Then the miracle happens. A voice rises in song, then another and another takes up "the holy words." The young soldiers rise up as one and storm forward: They sing as they run. Some are helmetless, their heads wrapped in bloody bandages. With their "burning eyes" they are like "unreal figures from an old saga." In some versions, the volunteers sweep over the enemy trenches; in others, the song dies as they die, and silent gray heaps litter the damp fields in front of Langemarck.

There are all manner of things wrong with the story, beginning with that official dispatch. The singing volunteers took no Allied trenches at Langemarck on November 10. The one incident that comes close to matching the words of the dispatch took place a day earlier. It is recorded in the daily diary of the 206th Reserve Infantry Regiment, published as part of the history of the regiment in 1931. Regimental histories can be the meat and potatoes of military history, but seventeen years had passed since the event, time enough for the author, one Werner Maywald, to buy into, and insert, some of the more improbable details of the story—including the singing of the most patriotic German song, a tune that is not easy to carry under normal circumstances. (Imagine American troops under fire trying to mouth the words of "The Star-Spangled Banner.")

At six in the morning on the ninth, the diary reports, soldiers with unloaded rifles and fixed bayonets leave their lines "almost noiselessly." But French troops detect their advance and begin to fire. At that moment the singing starts. It "reaches heaven like a cry for help: first one man, then a small group, then more and more, until the entire advance sings, 'Deutschland, Deutschland über alles!' Even the wounded sing. The words are on the last breaths of the dying." The attack sweeps over the French lines, taking fourteen officers and 1,154 men prisoner, mostly older soldiers from territorial regiments—the equivalent of our National Guard—but not Regulars, whose capture by green German troops would have added luster to the exploit.

Unfortunately for the myth, the November 9 incident did not occur at Langemarck but three miles away at a village called Bixschoote. *Beck-skota:* that rough, turnip-eating name does not lend itself to myth in the same way that the vaguely Teutonic vibrations of Langemarck do. As one former student volunteer put it in 1933, the first year of Hitler's reign, "the name sounds like a heroic legend." That the actual village had, both in 1914 and in its postwar resurrection, a drably brickbound and distinctly unheroic look seemed beside the point.

But the single dispatch is only the beginning of the confusion that the mythmakers wrought. When we look at contemporary accounts and regimental histories, we come up against an inconvenient fact. There seem to have been not just one Langemarck but several, both in this sector and in others miles away. They occurred on various dates, as early as October 21 and as late as November 16. During that three-week period, singing attacks were reported everywhere from the Yser to the Langemarck sector to Neuve Chapelle, twenty-five miles to the south.

In his diary entry of October 27, for example, a junior staff officer named Rudolf Binding (who was several miles away from Langemarck, at the German-occupied village of Passchendaele) laments that against experienced defenders "these young fellows we have, only just trained, are too helpless,

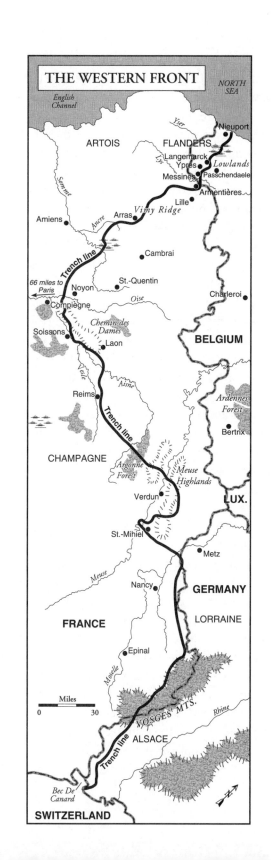

particularly when the officers have been killed." Binding, later to become a prominent man of letters, goes on to note that a battalion of light infantry, or *Jäger*, "almost all Marburg students . . . have suffered terribly from enemy shell-fire." And then: "In the next division, just such young souls, the intellectual flower of Germany, went singing into an attack on Langemarck, just as vain and just as costly." Binding gives no date, but since the Germans temporarily suspended their attacks in the Langemarck sector on October 24, the episode he refers to must have taken place earlier. But then, for all their curious similarity, accounts don't always agree on chronology. This includes Hitler's—if, indeed, he actually did hear singing. He was even farther from Langemarck than Binding.

Allied eyewitness reports only add to the confusion. The closest to Langemarck that a singing attack comes is in the village of Koekuit—no more than a narrowing of the road, actually, about a mile to the north. A battalion of the Gloucester Regiment reported it on the 21st, and the attack did force the British to retreat toward Langemarck. There are military historians who point to that episode. On the same day, at Zonnebeke, five miles away, one of the "old contemptibles" (as the British Regulars called themselves) remembered how German volunteers spilled down the ridge from Passchendaele "singing and waving their rifles in the air." It was, you might say, 1917 in reverse. "As fast as we shot them down, others took their place. Even when their own artillery barrage caught them by mistake, they kept on advancing. They were incredibly, ridiculously brave."

The next day, October 22, at a place called Kortekeer Caberet (named after a crossroads estaminet), about a mile west of Langemarck, *Einjährige*, "volunteers," of the 46th Reserve Division attacked other units of the perilously overstretched Gloucestershires. According to the regimental war narratives, "it was a particularly fine feat of arms. . . . These lads . . . advanced with the utmost determination, singing patriotic songs, and though suffering appalling casualties, actually succeeded in driving back their seasoned opponents." (The British would in turn drive the *Einjährige* back to their starting point.)

At least one British description—of an action in the same area on October 23—seems to buy into the script for the legend, though it also raises questions. This time the attacking volunteers wear not the regulation spiked *Pickelhauben* but what appear to be student caps. (Did the British confuse them with *Feldmützen*, or "field caps"? It is not unlikely.) The defenders hear the distant sound of voices raised in song; the volunteers surge forward, arm-in-arm. (If that is true, how did they hold their rifles?) In the event, batteries firing over open sights, as well as the famously disciplined rifles of the British Regulars, blow them away.

Word of the singing attacks got back to London. Sir Henry Wilson, the British deputy chief of staff, crowed in the October 24 entry of his diary about yet another killing extravaganza some miles from Langemarck: "The I Corps really took tea with the Germans. . . . These Germans attacked five times in close formations singing 'Die Wacht am Rhein' and the place became a shambles. They must have had 6,000 or 7,000 casualties"—surely a vast overestimation.

Perhaps the final recorded instances of the singing attacks in Ypres occurred on two days very late in the battle, November 14 and 16. Both were against the French (the badly mauled British were by then being pulled out of the Salient), and both happened near Bixschoote; they are noted in the journal of the commander of the French 26th Infantry Regiment, Lieutenant Colonel Henri Colin. November 14 began with hailstorms and German assaults; the fighting continued, practically without letup, until dark. Reports began to filter back to Colin in his command post of close, desperate struggles over farm buildings, bits of tattered woodland, and shallow impromptu trenches that were already filling with water. A noncom ran up, out of breath, and blurted out that his company had been almost annihilated. He told Colin that his company commander had been killed, but not before dispatching a German officer with his revolver. Later, Colin's surviving company commanders would describe an even wilder sight in this "day of terrible distress." With fanatic élan, masses of fresh young German troops had thrown themselves at the thin French line, "singing and shouting insults at us. They were finally driven off, leaving a great number of corpses on the ground."

But how are we to take the odd, ghastly episode that Colin records two days later? There may be more to it than met the eye. The first snow had just fallen, and the weather, as much as the rapidly diminishing ardor of the combatants, was about to shut down serious fighting for the next few months.

16 November—Day of Belgian fog . . .

The Germans renewed their epic attacks in which, to make up for their inexperience, the young recruits advanced shoulder to shoulder in a column four men abreast, and singing "Deutschland über alles." It was crazy . . . the human cost meant nothing to them.

Could men have been sent into battle that way? It is a bit improbable. The four-abreast column suggests another scenario. As the tactical historian Bruce I. Gudmundsson points out, this was the marching order German troops adopted when passing through towns or going up to the front. Had the volunteers, singing to keep up their spirits, become lost in the impenetrable murk and blundered into the waiting guns of the French—who must have heard their invisible coming from a long way off? If so, it would be hard to find a better example of the "fog" of war.

The singing attacks happened. Though in a signal twist of the story, recent German historians deny that they did, there is plenty of evidence for them. But their reality is far less exalted and ennobling than the legend would have it.

Begin with the matter of place. Apparently, none of the singing attacks came closer than a mile from Langemarck—and in Western Front terms that might as well have been five or fifty. The Germans did not take the village until the following April, when the French abandoned it during the opening hours of the first poison gas attack. But, in fact, Langemarck did become a convenient generic description for the battles that raged along the whole northern sector of the Salient that fall, the area where most of the reserve divisions, to which the volunteers belonged, were thrown in. On that score—but on that score alone—it would be wrong to fault the legend too harshly.

Why would men sing going into an attack? Except as the stuff of Nazi-era PR, mystical miracles played no part. Among poorly trained soldiers—as most of the volunteers were—singing must have helped to sustain morale and cohesion in the face of unexpected and disconcertingly heavy casualties, including the loss of most of their officers. Singing performed the function of the defunct battlefield drum, allowing units to keep in touch amid the confusion of noise, autumn fogs, unexpected ditches and hedgerows, contradictory orders, and unseen enemies. Singing familiar soldier songs may also have lessened the danger of friendly fire. Still, that the volunteers sang all that much seems unlikely. It is just that when they did, everyone noticed.

But the myth does not square with the most important fact of all. The majority of men in the reserve regiments were not even students. Recent research indicates that only 18 percent were, and that included teachers, hardly the youths of later legend. "The number of actual volunteers serving in the [reserve] regiments was considerable," George L. Mosse writes, "but most of those who fell in battle were older conscripts or men who had been in the reserves, fathers of families, men settled in their trade or profession." The volunteers, on the other hand, were mostly young men who had mobbed the recruiting depots in August: They had either been exempted from military service while they finished their studies or had escaped being called up because the peacetime army could only handle about half of those legally obligated to spend two years on active duty.

The volunteers went into action two months later not just under- but improperly trained. Their instructors had been mainly older noncommissioned officers (NCOs) who taught the close-order tactics favored at the turn of the century, in which men charged in waves, shoulder-to-shoulder, or in squares that would have done justice to a Napoleonic battlefield. Regular officers, especially lieutenants, were in short supply, and the few the reservists did have often led them into battle without maps. It was hardly surprising that they occasionally blundered into enemy lines. As a rule, the better the reserve regiments were trained—which is to say, the smaller the proportion of raw volunteers—the less likely they were to move forward in vulnerable tight-packed skirmish lines, or to rely on song under stress.

One thing is incontrovertible about those attacks. A massacre had taken place, a massacre of innocents in the military sense, and one that deprived Germany of the human potential that a nation wastes at its peril. The violent depletion of the six reserve divisions that fought from Gheluvelt to the Yser was particularly cruel. They lost an average of 6,800 men per division, or about half the infantrymen in each. In the month of fighting around Ypres, some 6,000 were killed in the reserve regiments alone. Their premature commitment to battle was, according to the military historian Dennis E. Showalter, "one of the great mistakes of the World War."

A disturbing command pattern was taking shape: The willingness of Western Front general staffs to continue an offensive long after the prospect of a reasonable return on the investment of lives and matériel had ceased. At Ypres, Germany had suffered its fourth major defeat since September, and one that, coming on the heels of the Marne and the battles for Nancy and the Yser, not only ratified stalemate but ended Germany's chances for a quick victory in the west.

Ypres was the only one of the four that assumed mythic proportions. With casualties somewhere above 100,000, of whom as many as 30,000 were dead, perhaps it had to. The famous army bulletin of November 11—prophetic date—about the youthful regiments at Langemarck must be seen, Mosse writes, "against the background of the rapidly declining enthusiasm of the troops themselves. The myth was necessary, and though it could not influence the soldiers in the trenches, it had an impact on the home front and especially . . . after the war was lost."

The bulletin no doubt originated as an attempted cover-up, but it succeeded beyond the wildest expectations of its designers. *Der Kindermord bei Ypern* would become the Kosovo of the Third Reich, and like the great and terminal defeat of the Serbs by the Turks in 1389, this debacle would be transformed into a holy memory, a moral victory. Would it be churlish to suggest, moreover, that the myth served another purpose? Langemarck was the sector where, the following April, the Germans first released poison gas on the Western Front—and finally took the village. (By this time singing attacks were already a curiosity of the past.) But as far as the home front was concerned, the guilt of a possible war crime would be forever overshadowed, and nullified, by the transfiguring image of a sacrifice raised in song.

In the years that followed, notes the German historian Bernd Hüppauf, the November 11 press release would be glorified in "novels, poetry, dramas and stage performances, (pseudo-) philosophical reflections, public celebrations and monuments, in institutions such as the army, schools and universities, youth organizations and, finally, an NS [National Socialist] program of advanced studies." On the first anniversary of the bulletin, a time when the affliction of stasis had long since begun to spread to the home front, newspapers all over Germany published editorial reflections on the "Day of Langemarck," with the inevitable conclusion that November 10 be made a national day of remembrance. After the war, student and veteran organizations would regularly repeat the suggestions, although the Weimar Republic never acted on it. Not even literature was immune. The hero of Thomas Mann's 1924 *The Magic Mountain* stumbles across a gunswept Flanders turnip field, his voice raised in a song of love and loneliness—a far more likely choice than "Deutschland über alles."

The Nazis in particular seized on the story and exploited it. Langemarck, writes Hüppauf, served as a lure "for the educated youth longing for *metaphysical shelter* and *meaning* in history." Once Hitler and the Nazis came to power, Langemarck was chosen as the day on which the party inducted students, and after 1938, every member of the Hitler Youth paid a compulsory fee, known as the *Langemarck-Pfennig.* As a party publicist put it, "National Socialism and Langemarck are one and the same."

THERE IS A PLACE THAT COMES CLOSE TO BEING A MONUMENT TO THE STUDENT myth—in fact it was specifically created with that in mind. It is the huge but eerily compact German military cemetery just north of Langemarck—in military mortuary parlance, a concentration cemetery. The phrase, in light of subsequent history, is not without irony. What remains of almost 45,000 men lies beneath its placid lawns, including those who were killed at the First Ypres.

The designers of the Langemarck cemetery (which was consecrated in a July 1932 ceremony already heavy with Nazi oratory) tried hard to make the place seem user-friendly, a bit of Germany transplanted. Oaks rise to a modest height, muffling the lawns in shadow: Germans consider the oak, with its symbolic strength, to be their tree. "Nature itself," writes Mosse, "was to serve as a living memorial: The German wood was a fitting setting for the cult of the fallen. Nature's rejuvenating powers would reshape the memory of the war, removing the curse of defeat in the process."

But unnatural things intrude: The reason for this place can't be denied. You feel it in the presence of a pair of blockhouses squatting side by side in the newer, northern section of the cemetery, which is more related to the later years of the war than to that first autumn. Their concrete was probably mixed with high-grade sand imported from the Rhine—another bit of Germany transplanted—but the heavy weight of permanence has caused them to sink so deep into the alien Belgian clay that today only the top foot or so of their entrances show above ground.

You feel that reason, too, in a discreet low-walled rectangle, its inner surface covered with hemlock shrubs. You pace it out to be roughly seventy by forty feet, a surprisingly small receptacle for the bones of 24,834 men, including no doubt some of the singers in the mists, a calcareous jumble of premature terminations dumped there in the 1930s. Nine men per square foot: eternity at rush hour.

You pause for a moment inside the bunkerlike red-stone gatehouse. Behind fretwork screens of iron lily-bursts is a chapel memorializing the students slain here in 1914 and known to be buried in the Langemarck cemetery. The official register notes that there are 6,313 names on the oakwood panels of that somber room. The question is, how many of those were actually students? Given the percentage of the reserve regiments that Mosse cites—eighteen, with teachers—there is no way they could all be. Based on that, just over 1,000 would be more like it: bad enough for the future meritocracy of Germany, a fatal undertow, you might say, in the national gene pool. But if you extend that 6,000-plus figure to include most of the reservists killed at the First Ypres, you probably have a pretty fair estimate of their toll.

The Nazis may be gone, but the myth they promoted lives after them.

THE CHRISTMAS TRUCE
Stanley Weintraub

——

ANY NUMBER OF EPISODES IN THE GREAT WAR SPEAK TO the barbarity of which humankind is capable; only a handful recognize a fundamental decency, and none more so than the Christmas Truce of 1914. The final battles of the year were over. Men exhausted from the nonstop combats of the past five months hunkered down in the shallow line that ran, with hardly a break, from the North Sea to the Swiss border. If the war represented the true beginning of the phenomenon we think of as the modern era, the men in the new trenches were not quite ready to relinquish the values—or the observances—they had grown up with. To fight this sort of war, F. Scott Fitzgerald wrote, "You had to have a whole-souled sentimental equipment going back further than you could remember." For a last moment in the war, that "sentimental equipment" still counted for something. Stanley Weintraub's account of the interval when one of the worst of wars took a holiday may, at the remove of nine decades, sound like fiction. But the Christmas Truce was the sort of event that fiction can only imitate.

The Truce—which was actually many small truces— was largely (though not entirely) concentrated in the twenty or so miles held by the British and their opponents from Saxony, Bavaria, and Westphalia. That was the area south of the Ypres salient itself, which was for the moment entirely garrisoned by the French. (Most veterans of the Great War would agree that the spontaneous time-out from killing would never have happened had the fierce Prussians been in that part of the line: "very vicious indeed" was the way one British officer characterized them.) It was the Germans who made the first overtures on Christmas Eve; but the British, still mainly Regulars, were more than willing to join in. As that always original cultural historian Modris Ecksteins writes:

> Some saw the fraternization as a matter of time-honored courtesies. On a holy day one saluted one's opponent and paid one's respects. During the Peninsular War at the beginning of the preceding century the French and British armies had become so friendly one Christmas that staff officers chanced upon one large group sitting around the same fires, sharing rations and playing cards. The French apparently came to refer to the British as "*nos amis les ennemies.*"

Our friends the enemy. That was less true of the Frenchmen of 1914. They apparently had their reservations, and the meetings in no-man's-land were more scattered, most often taking the form of agreements to bury the dead.

The sort of fraternization that marked the Christmas Truce rarely occurred later on. High commands on both sides discouraged it. British officers who allowed a local truce at Christmas the following year were threatened with court-martial; in December 1916, patrolling British troops gathered in shell holes close to the German lines to sing carols. Nobody shot at them.

The handshakes in no-man's-land would have to wait for the Armistice of 1918.

––––––

STANLEY WEINTRAUB is the author of a book about the Christmas Truce, *Silent Night.* He has also written numerous histories and biographies, including *The London Yankees; A Stillness Heard Round the World: The End of the Great War; Long Day's Journey into War;* and *MacArthur's War.* He is Evan Pugh Professor Emeritus of Arts and Humanities at Pennsylvania State University.

CONFRONTING EACH OTHER ACROSS THE MUDDY, HALF-FROZEN TRENCHES OF Flanders as Christmas 1914 approached were the armies of Queen Victoria's grandsons George and Wilhelm. No-man's-land between the troops was littered with the dead, and hopes for a short, decisive war had died with them. Yet the deadlock of the trenches and the imminence of Christmas gave rise to one of the few humane episodes of the war. It has become almost mythic, but it happened.

Ironically, the initiatives came from the invaders. Most Germans, even leading intellectuals like Thomas Mann, viewed the war as a response to the alleged encirclement of Germany by the hostile forces of cultures less rich and technologies less advanced. To be called "Hun barbarians" when they avowedly represented the higher civilization, and one under threat at that, seemed absurd, a feeling shared by educated young officers at the front.

While the war itself might be justifiable, a Christmas tarnished by war seemed outrageous. Captain Rudolf Binding, a hussar officer, wrote to his father from Flanders on December 20, 1914, that if he were in authority, he would issue a proclamation banning the celebration of Christmas. "Enemy, Death, and a Christmas tree—they cannot exist so close together."

Binding was not appeased by what he labeled as a "Christmas gift stunt organized by . . . snobbish busybodies in a glare of publicity [that] creates such an unsavory impression here that it fairly makes one sick." The *Liebesgabe*, or love gift, had been promoted by German newspapers on behalf of commercial enterprises that packaged them out of profitable patriotism. Binding disparaged them as "packages of bad cigars, indifferent chocolate, and woollies of problematical usefulness." This did not make a Christmas.

The British took their cue from the propaganda success of Victoria's brass box of chocolates for the Boer War troops in 1899, a prized gift even embossed on the lid with her royal profile. Now shipped across the Channel in the name of George V's daughter, Princess Mary, her youthful profile on the lid, were gift boxes of cigarettes, pipe tobacco—in those days everyone smoked—and a greeting card reproduced in facsimile from the king's handwriting, "May God protect you and bring you home safe."

Following the British lead, the German army prepared a wooden box of cigars and cigarettes, emblazoned on the lid—thus implicitly emphasizing the cultural divide—with a flaming sword.

In some sectors of Flanders, firing began to slacken spontaneously on the afternoon leading up to Christmas Eve; in others it was war as usual—at least to begin with. "About half-past four on Christmas Eve," a Private Mullard of the London Rifle Brigade wrote to his parents on the Isle of Wight, "we heard a band in the German trenches, but our artillery spoilt the effect by dropping a couple of shells right in the centre of them. You can guess what became of the band, for we have not heard it since." Yet when darkness fell about an hour later, they "were surprised to see trees stuck on the top of the [German] trenches, lit up with candles, and all the men sitting on top of the trenches. So, of course, we got out of ours and passed a few remarks, inviting each other to come over and have a drink and a smoke, but we did not like to trust each other at first."

To Allied troops, the German impulse not to forgo the rituals of Christmas came as a surprise after the propaganda about German bestiality. They did not expect the supposedly barbaric and pagan Germans to risk their lives in behalf of each prized *Tannenbaum*. Yet when unanticipated gunfire felled the first trees in the trenches, Fritz and his friends stubbornly climbed the parapets to set them upright.

The Christmas tree was a revered German tradition.

At Fromelles, south of the border between France and Belgium, the 2d Battalion of the Scots Guards was opposite the Saxon 15th, 37th, and 158th Regiments. A German who spoke good English shouted across the lines, "Merry Christmas, Scottie Guardie. We not fire tomorrow; have holiday, game of football." An eighteen-year-old second lieutenant, Alan Swinton, commander of a company only a hundred yards off, soon realized that the pauses in enemy fire were lengthening, with his own men happily reciprocating. The Scots listened to the enemy singing into the night, and warily watched their fires and their lighted candles, which by their positions seemed to be on the branches of Christmas trees.

What broke through the suspicion at most places on the line was the singing, stolid and often religious on the German side, informal and often irreverent on the British. An infantryman in the London Rifles trenches reported that the Saxons opposite "sang and played to us several of their own tunes and some of ours, such as 'Home Sweet Home,' 'Tipperary,' etc. while we did the same for them. The regiment on our left all got out of their trenches, and every time a flare went up they simply stood there, cheered, and waved their hats, and not a shot was fired. . . . The singing and playing continued all night." (His description of the incident appeared in *The Times*, which relaxed its customary bellicosity to print such accounts, as did dozens of local newspapers.)

Almost everywhere opposite the British in Flanders, Germans placed lighted candles atop their parapets, and where they could obtain small trees, put them up, too. A lieutenant in the London Rifles said "the Boches' trenches" looked "like the Thames on Henley Regatta night." The numbers of exposed and unarmed men on both sides grew. Where Saxon troops went out to meet the London Rifles, Private Mullard reported, the enemy officers approached "on the rays of a searchlight playing from the German lines, and it made a fine picture to see the six officers meet between the lines. . . . All the boys on both sides gave a tremendous cheer. . . . Then it was the troops' turn, and we swarmed out of our trenches."

To the north of Ploegsteert Wood, the Seaforth Highlanders were fraternizing. The Germans sang Christmas songs; the Highlanders responded impudently with "Who Were You with Last Night?" as well as "Tipperary," both "very badly," a Seaforth officer wrote home. First "horrified at discovering some of our men had actually gone out," he soon excused it as an effort to see what the enemy trenches were like. Halfway between the lines, he reported, they exchanged cigarettes for cigars "and they arranged (the private soldiers of one army and the private soldiers of the other) a 48 hours' armistice. It was all most irregular, but the Peninsular and other wars will furnish many such examples." Eventually, that first night, their officers intervened, and "both sides were induced to return to their respective trenches." Yet not only did "the enemy" sing all night, "during my watch they played 'Home, Sweet Home,' and 'God Save the King,' at 2:30 A.M.!"

Near Armentières, the Queen's Westminster Rifles assumed at first that the lights were a ruse and fired at them. When there was no return volley, it puzzled them more. "The first unusual thing happened," Rifleman Percy H. Jones wrote a few days later in his diary, "when we noticed about three large fires behind enemy lines. This is a place where it is generally madness to strike a match." Then lights began appearing on trench parapets, and Jones heard what he thought were "weird tunes on their peculiarly pitched bugles or horns," as well as singing.

Troops suspected the enemy soldiers were priming themselves up for a big attack. . . . In fact we were about to loose off a few rounds at the biggest light when the following words were heard (probably through a megaphone): "Englishmen, Englishmen. Don't shoot. You don't shoot, we don't shoot."

How it all happened I don't know, but shortly after this our boys had lights out, and the enemy troops were busy singing each other songs, punctuated with terrific salvos of applause.

The scene from my sentry post was hardly creditable. Straight ahead were three large lights, with figures perfectly visible round them. The German trenches, which bent sharply and turned to the rear of our advanced positions[,] were illuminated with hundreds of little lights. Far away to the left, where our lines bent, a few lights showed our A Co[mpan]y trenches, where the men were thundering out "My Little Grey Home in the West." . . . The music then quietened down and some time was spent yelling facetious remarks across the trenches. After this, some dare devils in E Co[mpan]y actually went out, met and shook hands with some of the Germans and exchanged cake and biscuits. As the night went on things gradually grew quieter.

Such early contacts were tentative and timid, and in the darkness, troops returned to their own lines.

Early Christmas morning at Houplines, near Armentières, Private Frank Richards and some chums in the Royal Welch Fusiliers "stuck up a board" on which they had printed "A MERRY CHRISTMAS," then waited to see what would happen. When the placard was not shot at, two men jumped onto the parapet of their trench with their hands above their heads to show that they had no weapons. Two Germans opposite did the same, and began walking toward them. As they met and shook hands, the trenches emptied and men on both sides ran toward each other. "Buffalo Bill," Richards's company commander, rushed into the forward trench to stop them, but his men were already gone. His nickname had come from his habit of cocking his revolver and threatening to blow a man's "ruddy brains out" for some trifling thing—and what he saw was no trifle. Yet he had to accept what had happened, "so company officers climbed out, too," Richards wrote. "Their officers were also now out. . . . We mucked in all day with one another." One English-speaking Saxon confessed that he was fed up with the war, and Richards and his friends agreed.

Discovering in the morning that his men had left their trenches to meet Saxons in no-man's-land, Lieutenant Swinton sought advice from higher authority on how to handle the situation. At battalion headquarters he found his superior officer, Captain George Paynter, being admonished by the brigade commander. "George," he warned, "you are *not* to fraternize with the Huns!" Waiting until Paynter was alone, Swinton reported what the captain obviously knew. Paynter replied, as if he had heard no order from above, "Come on, Alan, show me the Huns." Hurrying forward, they met their Saxon counterparts and arranged for a day's truce.

The enemy was almost too friendly, and asked to visit the British trenches; but Paynter did not want them to see how badly off the Guards were. Casualties and sickness had left their companies woefully understrength. Forbidding his own troops to visit closer than the halfway point between the trenches, an order soon ignored, he directed some of his men to move back and forth in their own breastworks, to give an impression of greater numbers. Meanwhile, they also used the opportunity to repair dugouts and reinforce their barbed wire. "I honestly believe," said another Guards officer of enemy friendliness, "that if we had called on the Saxons for fatigue parties to help with *our* barbed wire, they would have come over and done so." (Opposite the 8th Division, Lieutenant Colonel J. H. Boreston and Captain Cyril E. O. Bax reported that both sides "lent each other implements for reinforcing each other's wire entanglements.")

From the German side, Private Heinrich Knetschke—if we are to trust the humor magazine *Der Brummer, "The Grumbler"*—sent a letter prefaced by a poem to his "Beloved Anna" from somewhere in Flanders. It recorded the mood if not the fact:

The weather is cold in France.
Maybe therefore each soldier
That is on his post is longing
For the room where his girl
Is just now lighting a Christmas tree.

"All rights preserved!" Knetschke joked, hoping, he added, that his verses might stir a tear as Anna thought of him. Many poems were just then being written by his company, he explained. "A postal van of love has arrived and in the same were lots of different packages with rhymed verses, which all of us are answering now." He was also sending his poem, he confessed, to two other ladies whose names and addresses he had found in his *Liebesgabe,* which contained a *gereimte Tabakspfeife*—a pipe with a patriotic motto around the bowl— and a belt decorated with "very beautiful needlepoint and the exhortation, A CALL IS SOUNDING LIKE A ROLL OF THUNDER!"

"Beloved Anna!" he went on, "I well believe that you are astonished that I am attempting poetry. However, war causes changes that in ordinary times one thinks would be impossible." Their situation, he added, which was bad when he last wrote, was now excellent. His platoon had been ordered to an outpost that turned out to be "a very beautiful pavilion," which must have belonged at one time to a marquis for it included a marquee. "And a hundred meters on is a little château; however, we did not move in because behind it is an outpost of the French."

Once in their new quarters, his lieutenant had remarked, "Knetschke, we must secure a Christmas tree!" Knetschke knew exactly where to find one. Reconnoitering the château, he had observed a beautiful evergreen growing near the back entrance. Slipping back, in a daring foray into enemy territory, he cut down the tree and had begun "a strategic retreat" with it when he heard loud voices. Just then, a few "Marseillaise"-singing drunks, precariously carrying bottles of red wine, emerged from the château. "They swayed like rocking horses," Knetschke wrote. He rushed back, not forgetting the tree, and reported the discovery of *Rottwein* to his lieutenant, "who gathered up six men and with me in the lead marched to the château. Well, Anna, you might be joyously expecting that a decisive battle followed. But it's not the case. We reached the rear entrance and entered the ground floor, and couldn't risk a wrong move as we heard the 'Marseillaise' still coming from the cellar, which showed us the way to go. As we stood quietly in the dark vault, a French officer luckily opened the cellar."

Avoiding detection, Knetschke confided, was impossible, but the officer already "had such a load on" that he could not tell friend from foe, and he ordered the Germans (in French) to "move out the champagne." They had come exactly for this purpose, the *Oberleutnant* answered, "and we entered the wine cellar. . . . Their insensibility was obvious. Half of the French outpost was inside, and they were as drunk as loons. After this, you will surely believe me that we thanked our maker that we hadn't come any later because the Frogs would have guzzled up everything all by themselves."

The enemy officer "extended his French paw to our Oberleutnant. . . . A poilu wanted to embrace me. I rejected such fraternization but only, Beloved Anna, because he was belching so powerfully, But then we agreed to a truce for the rest of Christmas on the condition that the parleyvoozes would help us to carry fifty bottles into our pavilion." Back in their own quarters, having left the French to slip fuzzily into unconsciousness, the Germans put candles on their *Tannenbaum* and, inspired by champagne, sang "Stille Nacht" in "voices like oxen." Knetschke's tale recognized that when the irregular line separating forces had been frozen in place, the opposing trenches often had cut through farms and estates; it also acknowledged that despite the Franco-German hatred ever since 1870, some impromptu truces that Christmas involved even the unforgiving French.

Decades later, the novelist Henry Williamson wondered what might have been had a glum soldier in the Bavarian ranks across the line from him stepped forward. "Three weeks after my eighteenth birthday, I was talking to Germans with beards and khaki-covered *Pickelhauben,* and smoking new-china gift-pipes glazed with the Crown Prince's portrait in colour, in a turnip field amidst dead cows, English and German corpses frozen stiff. The new world, for me, was germinated from that fraternization. Adolf Hitler was one of those 'opposite numbers' in long field-grey coats." Later, in the pacifist futility of the 1930s, Williamson would fantasize hopefully about Hitler's experience of 1914–18: If the führer had been one of those involved in the rapprochement across the lines, his memory of *Brüderschaft*, "brotherhood," might contribute to staving off a new war. Yet Corporal Hitler had in fact rejected that opportunity in 1914. Williamson's recollection—it was during the writer's fascist phase—was only a convenient quarter-truth.

To escape Austrian conscription in 1913, Hitler had slipped into Bavaria, volunteering the next year from Munich on the day the Germans invaded France and Belgium. After eight weeks of training, he was a lance corporal and field messenger in Flanders with the 16th Bavarian Reserve Infantry Regiment. But he was out of the line on December 25, and when there was discussion in the ranks about crossing into no-man's-land to share Christmas with the British, he contended, "Such a thing should not happen during wartime." Besides, although he was a baptized Catholic, Hitler rejected every vestige of religious observance. He was only opposite Williamson, opposed to everything the truce promised. As Williamson's alter ego, Phillip Maddison, in the novel *A Fox under My Cloak* (1955) is pedaling back toward a shattered château, from which he had liberated an ancient bicycle, a Tommy shouts that "everyone" is out of the trenches and in no-man's-land—"talking to the Alleymans," he explains. "There's bloody hundreds of'm, Jock!" Maddison cycles toward "what at first sight looked like a crowd on a football field during the interval of a match." What he sees seems like a dream, as is the reality of standing up safely in daylight. "Leaning the bicycle against the British barricade, he . . . found himself face to face with living Germans, men in grey uniforms and leather knee-boots. . . ." Moving on, Maddison is surprised when he sees a football kicked into the air and several soldiers running after it. A soccer match has been proposed, to be played in a field behind the German lines.

Whether a game of "footer" actually occurred inside the German lines is unproven, but the references to football along the front are many. Unit histories include reports of matches, some played within earshot, often within artillery range, of the enemy. One lieutenant in a Highland regiment reported talking during the truce with a footballer from Leipzig who arranged with him to have a two-hour "interval" for a match the next day—Boxing Day, the traditional English day for giving Christmas gifts to servants. "This, however, was prevented by our superiors at HQ." Another soldier, Private William Tapp of the 1st Royal Warwickshires, wrote on Christmas Day from just above St. Yvas, "We are trying to arrange a football match with them for tomorrow, Boxing

Day," but artillery fire prevented it. There were other plans to play, right up until New Year's, especially after the clearance of corpses from no-man's-land furnished areas for competition at least as wide as a conventional soccer field.

Certainly something resembling football occurred between the lines on Christmas itself. A London Rifles officer whose letter about the truce was published in *The Times* described how "on Christmas Day a football match was played between them and us in front of the trench." Rifles sergeant Bob Lovell recalled the preliminaries—that his company commander had sent a sack of tea across the line and received a letter of thanks from his counterpart, after which, later on Christmas morning, a German juggler who had appeared in London music halls "cleared a space" between the lines and gave an exhibition. One of the Saxon officers emerged with a camera—all personal cameras on both sides violated regulations—and took a photograph of a dozen men from both sides, posed with mistletoe from gift packages thrust jauntily into caps and helmets exchanged with the enemy for the picture.

The Times also published a letter from a major in the Medical Corps who claimed that in his sector his regiment "actually had a football match with the Saxons, who beat them 3–2!!!" The account is verified in the war history of the 133d Regiment of the 9th Division, Royal Saxon Infantry, which spoke of the "droll scene" of "Tommy und Fritz" first chasing down wild hares between the lines, then kicking about a football furnished by a Scot. "This developed into a regulation football match with caps casually laid out as goals. The frozen ground was no great matter. Then we organized each side into teams, lining up in motley rows, with the football in the center. One of us took a photograph. Das Spiel endete 3:2 für Fritz."

Sergeant Major F. Naden of the 6th Cheshires, then east of Wulverghem, above the river Douve in Belgium, wrote home, "The Scotsmen . . . started the bagpipes, and we had a rare old jollification, which included football, in which the Germans took part." Private J. Higgins of the same regiment failed to mention football in his letter home, but said the Cheshires invited the enemy, only sixty yards away, for Christmas dinner. "Today we were shaking hands with some of the Germans, and they have given some of our chaps four barrels of beer."

Decades later, Private Ernie Williams, a former territorial in the 6th Cheshires, recalled,

> The ball appeared from somewhere, I don't know where, but it came from their side—it wasn't from our side that the ball came. They made up some goals and one fellow went in for a goal and then it was just a general kickabout. I should think there were about a couple of hundred taking

part. I had a go at the ball. I was pretty good then, at 19. Everybody seemed to be enjoying themselves. There was no sort of ill-will between us. . . . There was no referee, and no score, no tally at all. It was simply a mell—nothing like the soccer you see on television. The boots we wore were a menace—those great big boots we had on—and in those days the balls were made of leather and they soon got very soggy. . . .

Few details of reported games or the conditions of play survive. Lieutenant Charles Brewer of the 2d Bedfordshires wrote home only that "higher up in the line—you would scarcely believe it—they are playing a football match." And a history of the Lancashire Fusiliers records that its A Company played a Christmas game against the enemy just north of Le Touquet, using an old ration tin for a ball, and lost, three to two. Curiously, both recorded scores are the same, but the circumstances and locations are very different. Lance Corporal George Ashurst, who was somewhere on the line with the 2d Lancashires, mentions only that "some of our boys tied up a sandbag and used it as a football"—obviously not the same incident.

No-man's-land in the sectors where the truce was holding had taken on the atmosphere of a panoramic, anecdotal, Victorian scene as painted by W. P. Frith—a Derby Day or a Ramsgate Sands. As on every square inch of Frith's crowded canvases, people gathered and stories unfolded. In the former cabbage and turnip patches, cow pastures and orchards, fattened rabbits were skewered on makeshift spits and a pig caught by the 6th Cheshires was roasted and shared with the Boche. Both sides brought up loads of wood and straw to improve their dugouts, tasks laborious and even impossible under fire. An Englishman in the 3d Rifles had his hair cut by a Saxon who had been his barber in High Holborn, and Captain Josef Sewald of the 17th Bavarians watched several of his soldiers, heads cranked up, being shaved by the enemy. The cartoonist Bruce Bairnsfather, a second lieutenant with the 1st Royal Warwickshires, recalled "one of my machine gunners, who was a bit of an amateur hairdresser in civil life, cutting the unnaturally long hair of a docile Saxon, who was patiently kneeling on the ground whilst the automatic clippers crept up the back of his neck."

Few units were eager to return to a war of attrition that seemed endless. Some had agreed to stretch the cease-fire into a further dawn; others held out for New Year's Day. Headquarters on both sides responded with threats of punitive action; local commanders, realizing that their troops had to be weaned gradually from humane impulses, argued that the continued lull furnished time to drain flooded trenches, repair barbed-wire defenses, and move forward ammunition and supplies. Reluctantly, often perfunctorily, battalions on the line recommenced hostilities. In the 1st Royal Warwickshires, Private Tapp noted, an officer warned the Germans opposite at eight-forty on December 26 to get back into their trenches, as British artillery would begin shelling at nine o'clock. A German shouted back, "We will get into your trenches as we shall be safer."

"This will stop the football match," Tapp mourned. "Shells are exchanged for a few hours but we all stand up at intervals, no fear of being shot with a bullet."

In most instances, the return to hostilities was preceded by a signal to the other side. On the banks of the Lys, Captain Charles Stockwell of the 2d Royal Welch Fusiliers fired three shots in the air at eight-thirty, posted a sign reading "Merry Christmas" above a forward trench, and climbed atop his parapet. The Germans opposite responded with a "Thank you" sheet, and their company's captain stood up on his own parapet. The two officers bowed, saluted, then climbed down into their trenches, from which the German officer fired two shots in the air. The war was resumed. A Saxon unit threw a piece of dirty cardboard across to the British side apologizing for being forced to fight, and announcing, in English, "We shot in the air." "But of course," Captain F. D. Harris of the 1st North Staffordshires wrote to his family, "war is war, and I expect we shall be at it properly again in a short time."

Little enthusiasm for hostile action was displayed in sectors where the truce had held. "During the whole of Boxing Day," Frank Richards recalled, the 2d Royal Welch Fusiliers "never fired a shot, and they the same; each side seemed to be waiting for the other to set the ball a-rolling." In the XIX Saxon Corps, there was almost a mutiny in one of its regiments when it received orders to begin shooting again. When on leave in Leipzig, Vize-Feldwebel Lange told Australian expatriate Ethel Cooper about it. Although she could not mail letters to her sister back home because Australia was at war with Germany, she carefully hid the unsent correspondence in date sequence until peace came. According to Miss Cooper,

> The difficulty began on the 26th, when the order to fire was given, for the men struck. Herr Lange says that . . . he had never heard such language as the officers indulged in, while they stormed up and down, and got, as the only result, the answer, "We can't—they are good fellows, and we can't." Finally, the officers turned on the men with, "Fire, or we do— and not at the enemy!" Not a shot had come from the other side, but at last they fired, and an answering fire came back, but not a man fell. "We spent that day and the next," said Herr Lange, "wasting ammunition in trying to shoot the stars down from the sky."

What had made the truce work was the shared feeling that the war would be decided at another place and time, and in another way—by some massive assault or by negotiations after a wearing down of the desire of governments to keep on fighting. As long as the troops in the trenches saw themselves as a sideshow that only put them at risk, they preferred to make life at least marginally bearable. Yet as units relieved each other on both sides of the line, the links briefly forged now eroded. Fewer companies in the forward trenches knew their counterparts by reputation or by name, and the events of Christmas seemed strange and even surreal to newcomers full of rear-area slogans and enmities.

It was the newcomers, however, on command from generals miles behind the lines, who restarted the war. With the new year approaching, battalions suspected of being unreliable were pulled back and replaced, some of the shifts only normal rotation of troops. As snow gave way to rain, turning the fields of Flanders once more into mud and slime, the weather prolonged a semblance of the cease-fire. Yet it had to end. As Bruce Bairnsfather put it, "It was too much to expect that a table would be suddenly wheeled out into No Man's Land, accompanied by English and German Ministers with fountain pens and documents, ready to sign PEACE." He found that the higher the official echelon, the more annoyed the superior was about what had happened, right up to divisional headquarters.

The holiday having passed, "and the respective soldiers having been sorted out, and put back in their proper slots in the ground, the war went on again. Bullets whizzed around that one-time meeting place, and sundry participants in that social gathering were laid out stiff on parapets, awaiting burial. . . ." In the sector where British-officered (but Indian) Garhwals had greeted Westphalians on Christmas Eve, the 2d Worcesters now were on the front, firing away with "Archibald," an improvised trench mortar made from a large iron drainpipe. It looped into the enemy lines Tickler's jam tins, once bartered for sausages but now stuffed with explosives and nails. It was symbolic of the return to a shooting war that, depending upon which troops were in the trenches, rekindled irregularly as the poor fighting weather in January improved and friendly relations deteriorated. Easter and other holidays came and went, with nothing more than sporadic and abortive war stoppages to aid burial parties. On both sides, there would be more dead than yards gained throughout 1915.

THE GERMAN ARMY HAD AN EVEN MORE INTENSE TRADITION OF DISCIPLINE, AND its high command was just as concerned as the other side about a spontaneous stoppage of the war. Expressions of popular will, soldier or civilian, could topple the governments, endanger the state. Yet some soldiers' letters home trickled through the censorship. Those that appeared in newspaper accounts were mostly watered down to describe spotty truces to bury the dead. In Leipzig, the *Reclams UNIVERSUM* published three pictures from London papers showing artists' renderings of warm fraternization, and followed them with German soldiers' accounts that "proved" the enemy depictions were falsehoods. Throughout Germany, authorities kept photographs of the real thing taken by their own troops out of the illustrated weeklies.

The fading of the 1914 truce had closed off the last practical opportunity for a short war. Soldiers in the trenches might not want to fight on, but their governments did. The Chinese novelist Lu Xun once observed wryly, "Whoever was in power wishes for a restoration. Whoever is now in power is in favor of the status quo." A peace in place was impossible for the western Allies. The British and Belgians and French could not concede the lost national territory; the Germans, having overrun it, could not return it without the collapse of their regime. It made no difference what the men doing the dying felt, as long as they also felt under military discipline.

Paradoxically, discipline would lead inevitably to its opposite as the war reheated. In a play by Hubert Griffith, *Tunnel Trench*, a Tommy tells a captured German long after, "When you woz comin' through Belgium you woz swine— not as bad as they said you woz, but you woz bad. . . . But 'ave you 'ated us when we woz fightin' equal, all these years in trench warfare? 'Ave we 'ated you? Not when you palled up with us Christmas 1914." But, the soldier believes, once the Germans were driven from their positions, as assuredly they would be, it was "Gawd's 'oly bible truth" that "as I'm alive, we'll lose our 'eads as well. . . . We'll chuck bombs down yer dugouts an' laugh. . . . We'll baynet yer wounded. . . . We'll get ter killin' you fer the love of killin'. . . . Gawd knows why it is, but so it will be. 'Tain't, and won't be, our fault, but so it will be."

However much the Christmas Truce of 1914 evidenced the unquenchable desire of men to live in amity with one another, it was doomed from the start. A celebration of the human spirit rather than an abortive mutiny, it was at odds with a fact of war explained by Graham Greene about a very different kind of conflict in a different place and time. "An enemy," Greene wrote in his novel, *The Human Factor* (1978), "had to remain a caricature if he was to be kept at a safe distance: an enemy should never come alive. The generals were right—no Christmas cheer ought to be exchanged between the trenches." War required demonizing the enemy—not recognizing his human face.

A BAD AFTERNOON
AT AUBERS RIDGE
Lionel Sotheby

—

THE BRITISH ARMY HAS KNOWN BETTER DAYS THAN MAY 9, 1915, the date of the Battle of Aubers Ridge. It was one of those Great War actions that have become Western Front epitomes; 11,619 casualties traded for no gain. Its purpose was to divert German reserves from a much bigger French attack that same day at Vimy Ridge, fifteen miles to the south. The British attack failed to accomplish even that.

In a memorable exchange, a corps commander reprimanded one of his brigadiers: "This is most unsatisfactory," he said. "Where are the Sherwood Foresters? Where are the East Lancashires on the right?" "They are lying out in No-Man's Land, sir," the brigadier answered, "and most of them will never stand again."

There must be few more dreary places in which to end a life. The country of French Flanders is so flat, and the water table so high, that trenches could not be dug down but parapets had to be built up instead. (Aubers Ridge itself is a groundswell barely noticeable unless you are looking for it.) The first attack began at five-thirty in the morning, after a bombardment that failed to destroy the German barbed wire and did little damage either to the enemy parapets or the defenders sheltered behind them. Few British or Indian troops managed to get across no-man's-land. The machine gun reigned.

A final attack went forward late in the afternoon, with similarly dismal results. A participant in that forlorn hope, skirled into action by bagpipers, was Lionel Sotheby, a twenty-year-old subaltern in the Black Watch. A graduate of Eton who was more at home in London clubs than the Scottish Highlands—family connections had got him into the regiment—Sotheby had served in the sector since March. In the letter that follows, written to his mother three days after the battle, he describes playing dead under the German parapet after most of his platoon had melted away. (Sotheby speaks of "thousands of German dead"; in reality, the total enemy casualties were just 1,551.)

————

LIONEL SOTHEBY's letter, slightly cut but otherwise unchanged, comes from *Lionel Sotheby's Great War,* edited by Donald C. Richter and published by Ohio University Press. Sotheby's diaries and letters are part of the remarkable Peter H. Liddle collection of British war documents at the University of Leeds.

My dear Mother,

Perhaps you have heard about it by now. The awful losses on Sunday which was to have been the great advance. The old fault, wire not cut.

The Black Watch including myself charged the German trenches 400 yards away. The whole 15 officers were killed except 4. Of these 4, 3 were wounded & I survived. I tell you it was a miracle and I felt quite changed as I lay out 15 yards from the German trenches for 4 hours before crawling back.

The attack in the morning failed. Our shelling was bad as it failed to cut the wire, though thousands of German dead lay behind the trenches so the aeroplanes report. We were rushed up to the front trenches through a hellish fire of shrapnel and heavy gun fire. Many were killed and wounded. The enemy had got wind of the attack, got up huge reinforcements and guns. The high explosive shrapnel shells were fearful, sweeping the ground for yards. All the communication ramparts were swept continually. However we reached the first line ramparts to discover the attack had failed. I think the failure of cutting the wire was due to bombarding too wide a front and not doing it thoroughly. Well, the Germans shelled us very hard in the ramparts then, and many were killed. The day was cloudless, but the smoke from bursting shells made quite a fog over everything. Wounded men crept over the parapet and were hauled in.

This went on all day until 12 noon, when we were told we would attack again. We charged at 4 P.M. . . . The German trenches were 350 to 400 yards away, and had been bombarded again before the attack. We ran 50 yards and then perforce had to walk the remainder. Many of the men actually stopping and firing at the Germans [who were] look[ing] over and firing from their parapets. In places the machine guns wiped men out very rapidly. . . . I was on the extreme right with my platoon and we had no one attacking on our left, thus we got cross-fire.

By the time I reached the German wire. I had only 4 or 5 men left with me and we found the wire uncut!

150–200 yards on our left there was a gap and A Company was getting through all massed together, they were mown down, quite a number however getting into the German rampart. Being only 15 yards from the Germans who were fighting [firing] over their parapet at us, it was impossible to get to that gap, so we sought cover. There were a few shell holes close to the wire and into them we got, firing at the Germans above. We did some good as it prevented them getting a cross-fire into our men getting over on the left a good distance away. We accounted for several. One big German in a helmet stood waist high above the parapet firing and raving at us. I think we got him.

A signaller of ours was right under the lee of the German parapet and bravely kept signalling back various messages, he was 200 yards to the left. As a result our artillery observers directed gun fire on the left and right flanks, and where some of our men got through the wire, in order to protect them a bit, as a result we got a bit of the shelling being a long way to the right. My cap fell off before I got into the small shell hole and was lying 3 yards away outside. We all wore our caps with the Balaclava helmets on top. My cap has about 7 holes from shrapnel and pieces of shell! Lucky it wasn't my head! An explosion from one of the shells stunned me for about 10 minutes. The Germans were well down now and were sniping from loop holes near the base of the parapet. They sniped at anything that moved, wounded and all. Thus we few that were left dug ourselves as low as possible. I was wedged in between 2 dead men. [Lance Corporal] Swan on my left and someone else on my right. Swan was shot through the forehead. These two dead men protected me somewhat from shrapnel of our own guns.

In the charge and while in the hole at first, I had two shots through my haversack and one through the strap of my equipment ½ inch off the flesh. Another shot hit my entrenching tool and smashed it in half. The metal end hit me in the back very hard, making me think I was wounded at first in the back. Never shall I forget that awful experience. For 4 hours (4 P.M. to 8 P.M.) I lay there cramped up and never moved once. I am still stiff and very sore on the right side of the head where a lump of dry earth gave me an awful bang, when a shell burst.

I was afraid a shell would land on me, as our artillery bombarded the Germans continuously over us and we only 15 yards from them. It was awful. I was also afraid they would chuck bombs at us lying there, they did later at the wounded, petrol bombs. But I had crawled back by then. I waited there till 8 P.M. and then being a bit dark I attempted to crawl back. It was rotten and how the snipers missed me is wonderful. The ground was perfectly flat the whole 400 yards. It took me 30 minutes to crawl back, and then on getting over our parapet, I had to rest a bit. Finding the Battalion had left to go to Hinges, 4 miles away by straight line, but 6 by road, I returned getting back by about 12 P.M. I was in a beastly mess! The rotten part was being unsupported. No supports were sent us, and it was beastly thinking any minute they would come but never came. They were ordered not to. Those who penetrated into the rampart on our left held on for about ten minutes and then were stripped of their equipment by the Germans, shot and thrown over the parapet. These were only a few too exhausted. Several men came back and told us that. It was truly wonderful. Here one Battalion had in part succeeded when a whole—[censored] had failed in the morning. The Colonel has been praised by all the other Colonels and Generals for what the Battalion did. Not a man hung back, all charged as far as possible. A finer set of men than these, and mostly Reservists, could not be found anywhere.

On returning I find myself in charge of a Company of 25 men instead of 200. This is temporary as Officers will soon stream out. We lost over 500 men. I feel a changed person at present and unable to laugh or smile at anything, feeling almost in a dream. Next time the Germans will get it. Given a chance with wire down and at close quarters, they will be slaughtered, and I feel quite mad at it, and long for a decent smash at them. I shall get the chance yet with any luck, and I shall never forget May the 9th, 1915, a Sunday, and a marvelously clear day. You can't tell how I want to get at them and not hung up by barbed wire and the G—15 yards away. I cannot write any more as I feel tired, so please excuse an absence of letters for a week. . . .

I trust you will write other relations for me. I will do so by degrees. Must end now, feeling very tired.

> Your affectionate son
> Lionel Sotheby

———

POSTSCRIPT: Sotheby was killed four and a half months later on September 25, 1915, at the Battle of Loos, one of 1,131 Etonians who died in the war. His death occurred not far from the spot where he had once mimicked the real thing. Sotheby's body was never found.

ARTOIS 1915
Douglas Porch

—

I F THE DESPERATE COMBATS OF 1914 HAD BEEN LARGELY improvised encounters between ever-marching opponents—moving targets, as it were—the year 1915 saw the murky dawn of a new phenomenon: the drawn-out set-piece battle. It was characterized by preliminary bombardments that often lasted for days, "with the object," wrote Ferdinand Foch, the commander of the French Army Group North, "of destroying the enemy's morale, disorganizing his defensive measures and breaking up his obstacles and strong points." This would be followed by a methodical sweep across no-man's-land and over the pulverized enemy trenches. The primary objectives would be limited but the ultimate one was a breakout into open country and a return to a 1914-like war of movement and maneuver.

Douglas Porch, an eminent authority on modern French military history, describes two of the first, and most sanguinary, of those set-piece battles, the attacks on the German-held heights north of the city of Arras, in the Artois region. The offensive began on May 9, 1915, was shut down in the middle of June, and then started up again at the end of September. (The French command arm-twisted the British into making simultaneous attacks, first at Aubers Ridge and then at Loos.) By the time the French called off the Artois attacks on October 18, they had managed to penetrate just three miles. The Artois, as Porch points out, became a showcase of error and excess. The long bombardment that was designed to soften up opposition, merely announced the fact that an attack was coming. Moreover, it didn't include enough high-explosive shells to cut the German barbed wire. The limited objectives weren't limited enough. Breakthrough inevitably broke down. French and German alike, Porch writes, "were locked in a siege war of such ferocity that no attack had a chance of advancing more than a few yards." And worst of all, commanders did not seem to sense when to stop. At what point did the cost no longer justify the results?

Practically all the ground won in an extended battle was won in the first three hours. In trench warfare, Murphy's Law prevailed: Communications broke down. Staffs too far removed from the front lines ordered men to respond to situations that no longer existed. Unexpected successes caught them off guard and were not exploited. Reserves failed to arrive when they were most needed—which, as Porch notes, could have delivered the French their principal objective, Vimy Ridge, on the first morning. It would not fall for another two years.

But the blindness of command was not just the monopoly of the French. Max Heinz, a German who served at Vimy (and lived to write about his experience), could not contain his anger:

> In those days even the simplest infantryman had the feeling that his life was being played with—I can find no other word for this insensate squandering of human lives—in a manner which cannot be sharply enough criticized. Or should we give another name to this kind of leadership which flings company after company into the front line during the most severe bombardment—hunting them to their death without sense or reason? . . . There were many regiments practically annihilated through artillery fire without having seen a single enemy soldier.

Still, the French had the most to lose. The Artois fighting may have been a learning experience, but it was one that cost them 150,000 casualties. "The sacrificial élan of the first year was gone," Porch writes, "not to return in this war—or in the next."

———

DOUGLAS PORCH's many books include *The French Secret Services: From the Dreyfus Affair to the Gulf War; The French Foreign Legion: A Complete History of the Legendary Fighting Force;* and *Wars of Empire.* He is Professor of National Security Affairs at the Naval Postgraduate School in Monterey, California.

I N OCTOBER 1914, AS THE SERIES OF FLANKING MOVEMENTS KNOWN COLLECTIVELY as the "Race to the Sea" exhausted themselves near the town of Arras in the Artois, German and French troops faced off across a narrow no-man's-land that ran roughly along the Arras–Béthune road. Rifle pits were dug, which were then joined to become trenches, and the line hardened into one of the most violently contended stretches of the Western Front.

Travelers along that road today are left in no doubt that these few miles of sleepy French *route nationale* were once the scene of immense slaughter: Walled cemeteries rise like bleached islands out of rain-swept fields of wheat, and deserted country roads wander past craters whose depth and dimensions defy any plow to reclaim them.

About five miles out of Arras, the road dips and winds through the village of Souchez, before it climbs the lower slopes of Notre-Dame-de-Lorette, a long, narrow promontory that rises some 500 feet out of the rolling countryside like the prow of some immense ship. Even before the Great War, this butte with its commanding view and its then-modest church was a place of local pilgrimage. Today, the fact that Notre-Dame-de-Lorette and the villages nestled in its shadow were once a vast charnel house is obvious—the flat summit, crowned by an outsize and rather hideous church and a freestanding observation tower, is awash in a regimented sea of crosses. Some 20,000 of them occupy twenty-six acres, and the remains of another 22,000 men are jumbled in ossuaries.

With little effort of imagination, one conjures up the time when this peaceful countryside was the scene of such unbelievable slaughter. The historical literature, limited to a few sparse memoirs or the bleak prose of battlefield narrative that records the movement of battalions, regiments, or divisions, offers little help. The Battle of the Marne in 1914 and Verdun in 1916, both of which produced a profusion of accounts, seem to fit the stereotypes of glorious victory or heroic sacrifice better than what amounted to the pointless butchery of the Artois. Those who survived tended to keep silent about their experiences. It was a battle that, in military terms, achieved nothing—and yet produced unintended consequences. If nothing else, it must be counted as the prototypical trench slaughter of the Great War.

The real objectives of the attack—Vimy Ridge, rising just across a valley, and the immense northern European plain that beckoned beyond—were not reached until the end of the war. Nor did the generic name of the Second Battle of the Artois with which the high command officially baptized the offensive capture the public imagination.

Only the ruins of the church that presided over the fields of sacrifice offered a sufficiently dramatic focus. As for Vimy Ridge, it would become a shrine not of the French who died on its slopes but of the Canadians who eventually conquered it in 1917.

In the late spring of 1915, General Joseph Joffre designated the unremarkable villages of Souchez, Ablain-Saint-Nazaire and Carency nestled at the foot of Notre-Dame-de-Lorette, and those empty fields that rise gently past the straggling crossroads of Neuville-Saint-Vaast toward the summit of Vimy Ridge, as the stepping-stones to his planned breakthrough on the Western Front. Why Joffre believed that this offensive would prove to be the magic one is unclear. A limited but powerful attack in the same sector in December 1914 had been repulsed, as had a spring assault on the Saint-Mihiel salient and attacks that pounded German positions in Champagne throughout February and March. In his memoirs, Joffre claims that in March 1915, when General Ferdinand Foch, commander of the northern army group, proposed a second offensive in the Artois, he thought it "premature."

Nevertheless, by mid-April plans were well advanced for an attack set to jump off on May 1; Joffre had become convinced that the arrival of British reinforcements together with the creation of several new French divisions would free the manpower necessary for the operation. Following the battle, he justified his persistence in keeping up the pressure for six more bloody weeks by the need to come to the aid of the Russians; their front was punctured at Gorlice in southern Poland on May 2 and their armies hurled into a massive retreat. A second objective of the offensive was to prevent disruption of Italian mobilization following the decision of that country on April 26, 1915, as the French suggested unkindly, "to rush to the aid of the victors."

The offensive was assigned to General Victor-Louis-Lucien d'Urbal, the commander of the Tenth Army. Tall, with a large head, thick handlebar mustache, and gray hair cropped into a flattop, the fifty-seven-year-old d'Urbal looked every inch the soldier when he assumed his command in early April 1915. D'Urbal's steady leadership during the Race to the Sea won him the command of the Tenth Army. His service record includes a note by Foch, who praised his immediate subordinate in the Artois as "having always shown great character, straight and uncomplicated, sound judgement, a very great authority, a firmness and spirit of decision above reproach, an open-minded and methodical attitude, the spirit of a great leader organized to achieve success. A first class army commander."

Not everyone shared Foch's high opinion of d'Urbal. Joffre, whose imperturbability was legendary, considered him excitable. General Henri-Philippe Pétain, who commanded the XXXIII Corps charged with attacking Vimy Ridge, worried that his orders to create a "breakthrough . . . pushed from beginning to end with the most extreme vigor and finished off by a pursuit undertaken without delay and pressed without letup" were unrealistic given the shortage of artillery and, even more, of munitions. Colonel Marcel Givierge, serving with the codes and ciphers section in Paris, complained of the "singular mentality" of d'Urbal's intelligence chief, who refused to forward intelligence gathered from German radio intercepts to General Headquarters.

All of this, however, is to bring to bear the selective judgment of hindsight. On paper, at least, French hopes appeared bright even though logistical problems caused them to postpone the offensive to May 7. (Last-minute bad weather added another forty-eight hours to the wait, so that the attack ultimately jumped off on May 9.) Both the terrain and manpower appeared to favor the attackers. The German positions clung precariously to a series of ridges that formed the last natural barrier between the French army and the open plains of northern France. French troops were already entrenched on the butte of Notre-Dame-de-Lorette. A successful attack there to dislodge the Germans from their last hold on the easternmost tip and the slopes of that hill would allow them to support the main thrust toward Vimy Ridge, which angled off toward the south from the foot of Notre-Dame-de-Lorette.

Strength also appeared to be in the French favor. In late April the Russians had reported the presence in the east of eight to ten German divisions lifted from the Western Front. Their places in France had been taken by second-class territorial divisions. The attention of the German high command was obviously directed to the east. Joffre had concentrated twenty divisions in the Artois opposite only six enemy divisions, which gave him a numerical edge of around 200,000 men to 60,000 Germans. But when the Germans began to detect the French buildup in April, they shifted another six divisions from Belgium toward the threatened sector.

In addition, diversionary attacks were planned by the British, who had brought their strength in France to eight army corps. And while Pétain complained that the artillery provisions were inadequate, they were the most massive yet seen in the Great War—1,200 guns, with more in reserve. By May 8, the day the French opened their preliminary bombardment, morale was high. They discounted the failure of an early-evening raid to secure a web of trenches known as the *Ouvrages Blancs*, or "White Works," that the Germans had spun through the chalk soil between Neuville and Carency.

At six o'clock on the morning of May 9, the French guns opened a barrage that was, by the standards of the time, of incredible ferocity. The high command calculated that their artillery could place eighteen high-explosive shells on each yard of front, and the barrage appeared to realize that density of fire. At ten o'clock, troops on a twelve-mile front running from Chantecler, a suburb of Arras, north to Aubers Ridge in the British sector rose out of their trenches and moved forward under a brilliant spring sunshine.

The results were almost everywhere disappointing. The British attack, which followed a minimal preparatory barrage of only forty-six minutes, was the first to falter. Within an hour the British command had recognized the futility of sending waves of men against German machine-gun nests left undisturbed by the shrapnel shells that composed 92 percent of their munitions inventory. But by the time they suspended their attack, they had suffered 9,500 casualties.

That same day, the French XXI Corps attacking Notre-Dame-de-Lorette and Ablain-Saint-Nazaire had advanced barely two hundred yards in the teeth of murderous German artillery counterbarrages and machine guns whose fire plunged down upon the attackers from the slopes above. At one place on Notre-Dame-de-Lorette, French and Germans occupied the same trench, separated by sandbags hastily piled up. They dueled with grenades for shell holes or bits of ground known only by map designations such as sap V or point Q. To the west of Vimy, the 77th Infantry Division burrowed into the ground as German artillery fire brought down the trees that lined the Béthune road and left the wounded screaming for help. But the barrage was of such intensity that it prevented both retreat and reinforcements, forcing the troops to burrow into the earth as best they could.

At nine thirty-five, Colonel H. Colin of the 26th Infantry Regiment observed through his trench periscope that the two mines meant to explode beneath the network of German trenches known as the Labyrinth, which sheltered Neuville, had not been pushed forward far enough, and detonated harmlessly in no-man's-land. He also began to doubt the effectiveness of the barrage when he peered over the parapet to observe its effects at the moment of maximum intensity and immediately drew the fire of German snipers whose bullets only moments before had shattered his periscope.

At ten o'clock, when he ordered the four companies in his first wave forward, his fears were realized. No sooner had the troops left their lines than he heard the German machine guns clank to life over the noise of the regimental band, brought into the forward trench to blow the charge and then a stirring rendition of "Les Gars du 26e," "The Boys of the 26th." He watched helplessly as two of his companies were entangled in the undestroyed enemy wire and annihilated. He sent the second wave forward to support the remnants of the other two companies, which had managed to reach the German lines. But concentrated machine-gun fire shot down this attack before the men had jogged more than a few yards. In ten minutes he had lost 700 soldiers. He ordered his third wave to remain where they were. One of his company commanders spent the remainder of the morning firing at German snipers who were methodically finishing off French wounded twitching in no-man's-land. The Tenth Army's battle diary reported laconically on May 10, "The enemy shot our wounded."

May 9, however, was not a day of unrelieved disaster for the French. Other elements of the XX Corps, of which Colin's 26th Infantry Regiment was part, managed to infiltrate Neuville—but, as the official report put it, in an "indescribable disorder," unable to dislodge Germans who fought from the cellars and ruins along the heavily bombarded streets of the rural village.

The center of the French attack between Notre-Dame-de-Lorette and Neuville had been assigned to the XXXIII Corps, commanded by General Pétain. Before 1914, he had been considered one of the French army's maverick officers, because he preached the virtues of firepower against the *offensive à outrance*, "offensive to the limit," school of officers like Foch. The outbreak of war had demonstrated in striking terms Pétain's professional competence. The colonel who in July 1914 had been preparing a quiet retirement had become a corps commander within a year. In 1917, he was to be named French army commander in the wake of the mutinies of that spring.

In many respects, Pétain's assignment was the least difficult, but he prepared it intelligently and methodically. While the 70th Division on the left of his line had to deal with Carency, he cleverly screened off that village from the south and southeast rather than attack it head-on. This allowed the 77th Division in the center of his line to surge forward through German trenches badly disorganized by French artillery fire to reach the Château de Carleul and the cemetery of Souchez, at the foot of Notre-Dame-de-Lorette. Some elements of the 77th even got as far as Givenchy, a village that flanked the Vimy Ridge; here the French were close to a breakthrough.

However, the laurels of the day fell to the French Foreign Legion, which spearheaded the attack of the Moroccan Division on Pétain's right. Though the 2d Régiment de marche depended administratively on the 1st Régiment of the Foreign Legion at Sidi-bel-Abbès in Algeria, it was not made up of grizzled veterans of North Africa. Rather, its ranks were filled by idealistic and often middle-class foreigners who had volunteered to fight for France and democracy in the euphoria of mobilization in 1914. Breaking with the iron tradition of the legion, these recruits had been arranged into nationally homogeneous battalions or companies of Russians, Poles, or Greeks who carried their national flags into battle.

The legion rapidly overran the Ouvrages Blancs, which had defied the French surprise attack the previous evening. Though these trenches were expected to be difficult to take, they were thinly garrisoned and had been badly disorganized by the French artillery barrage. Having seized their initial objective, the legionnaires forged ahead, impulsively, even enthusiastically, toward a shoulder of Vimy Ridge that the French maps designated as Hill 140.

It was here that their real problems began. To their right, the 156th Infantry Regiment had been stopped cold before the crossroads of La Targette. The 156th was later criticized for not maneuvering to seal off La Targette and Neuville. Because they did not, the legionnaires attacking toward Vimy Ridge were subjected to a murderous flanking fire. German artillery began to find their range. Incredibly, however, the legion reached Hill 140 within the space of two hours, companies and battalions mixed together and largely leaderless.

The Swiss poet Blaise Cendrars, who had joined the legion in Paris when war was declared, gazed out over the Flemish plain that beckoned to the north. The scene to the rear was less reassuring. The attack had left a wake of desolation—stragglers, deserters, liaison officers throwing away their cumbersome signaling gear, and piles of dead and groaning wounded who were strewn over the churned earth. More sinister were the groups of Germans who had escaped attention in the haste of the French advance, and who now began to reemerge from their bunkers to pot the legionnaires from the rear. Cendrars's squad crawled back through the blasted bunkers and collapsed trenches to knife and shoot those who resisted. He discovered to his relief that many preferred to surrender rather than fight against the Foreign Legion, which prewar German propaganda had denounced as a collection of cutthroats and gangsters: " 'Die Fremdenlegion!' " Cendrars wrote. "We put the fear of God into them. And, in truth, we were not a pretty sight."

One of the squad, Ganero—an avid hunter who, despite the terror of the attack, had retained the presence of mind to shoot a rabbit scared up by the advancing troops and fix it to his belt—was apparently killed by the blast of an artillery shell. The men threw some soil over his blood-soaked body and left him, the rabbit still attached. Ten years later, Cendrars was amazed to run into Ganero in Paris—very much alive and equipped with an "American leg," which he put on every Sunday to go to the cinema. Ganero forgave his comrades for leaving him for dead, but refused to absolve the stretcher-bearers who had stolen and eaten his rabbit.

The chaos that Cendrars witnessed to his rear was not merely a normal byproduct of battle, but symptomatic of a deeper confusion produced by the unexpected success of the advance. Desperate appeals for reinforcements could not be satisfied, because the high command held their reserves between five

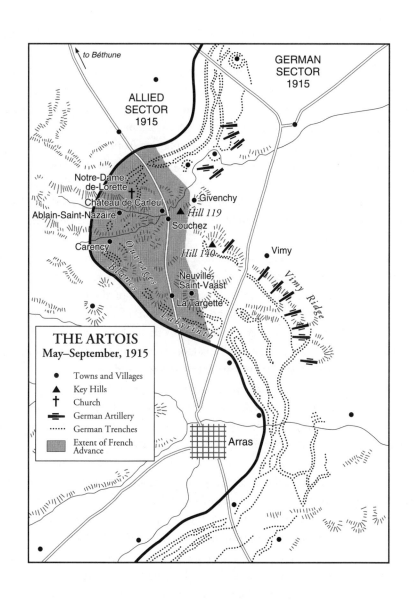

to Béthune

GERMAN
SECTOR
1915

ALLIED
SECTOR
1915

Notre-Dame-
de-Lorette

Château de Carleul

Ablain-Saint-Nazaire

Givenchy

Hill 119

Souchez

Carency

Ouvrages
Blancs

Hill 140

Vimy

Neuville-
Saint-Vaast

Vimy Ridge

La Targette

Labyrinth

THE ARTOIS
May–September, 1915

●   Towns and Villages
▲   Key Hills
†   Church
≡   German Artillery
····   German Trenches
▨   Extent of French
       Advance

Arras

and eight miles behind the original attack lines to protect them from German artillery fire. As almost all the officers, including the regimental commander, had been killed in the attack, no one was able to organize the defense of Hill 140. The brigade commander, Colonel Théodore Pein, whose exploits as a camel corps commander had won him fame in North Africa before the war, came forward, only to be shot down by German snipers.

German shells began to slam into the ridge like runaway freight trains, spewing out shrapnel and clouds of noxious smoke. Less comprehensible to the legionnaires was the fact that their own artillery also began to pummel their positions, and continued to do so, causing great carnage, despite a desperate waving of flags and signaling panels. On the plain in front of them, the legionnaires could see German reinforcements disembarking from city buses requisitioned in occupied Lille, so close that they could read the advertisement boards. Without officers, reinforcements, or machine guns, the legionnaires gave ground in the face of the inevitable German counterstroke that broke over them that afternoon.

The day cost the 2d Régiment de marche its commander, all but one of its battalion commanders, forty-one other officers, and 1,889 legionnaires, or 50 percent of strength, but won for it the compensation of the Croix de guerre. This was the first in a series of decorations that would leave the legion, whose units on the Western Front were amalgated in the autumn of 1915 into the celebrated Régiment de marche de la Légion étrangère (RMLE), the second-most-decorated unit in the French army by the war's end.

Although the advance by Pétain's XXXIII Corps of up to two-and-a-half miles into the German lines, with the capture of 2,000 prisoners as well as a dozen guns and almost fifty machine guns, had left d'Urbal exultant, the success was illusory. By the afternoon of May 9, the German command had already begun to recover its composure—French aircraft reported the arrival of German reinforcements, the first in a steady buildup that within a few days would swing the odds heavily in favor of the defense. And as d'Urbal prepared to reinforce success by urging the XXXIII Corps to advance "with the greatest speed" before the enemy could bring up his reserves, Pétain demurred. In the view of the future commander of the French armies, an advance toward Vimy and the open country beyond was out of the question so long as it had to be funneled between the enemy-held villages along his flanks.

Pétain won the argument in the short run. As the French prepared systematically to reduce Ablain, Carency, Souchez, and Neuville, the deficiencies of their army—and consequently, of Joffre's strategy of breakthrough—were laid bare. Although the French had massed what appeared to be an impressive number of guns for the Artois offensive, most of them were 75s, light straight-trajectory fieldpieces created for mobile warfare, which lacked the ability to strike the enemy in fortifications or behind hills. Nor had they the power to destroy his deep bunkers. Advances were limited to around 3,000 yards, because the 75s could not support a deeper penetration.

The Artois offensive at the height of its intensity was backed by only 355 guns with a caliber greater than 75mm, and many of these were of an antiquated slow-firing design. Shells were also at a premium, a situation complicated by the fact that poor-quality munitions caused barrels to rupture with increasing frequency. So artillery commanders, their casualties mounting, slowed their rate of fire, and saw the number of gun tubes actually diminish even though five artillery divisions were sent to reinforce the front during the course of the battle. Meanwhile, the Germans massed their artillery at a rate that quickly left the French desperately outgunned.

Nor in 1915 were French artillery tactics very sophisticated. While the Germans created false batteries, or fell silent when French spotter planes were above so as not to reveal their positions, the French took little trouble to camouflage or protect their guns. The absence of enfilade fire, as well as what one French commander called "the moral barrier of sector limits," which meant essentially that commanders refused to deviate from rigidly established fire plans, reduced artillery effectiveness still further. French barrage patterns were so predictable that the Tenth Army command complained on May 17 that the Germans merely waited until the French barrage lifted, a sure sign of attack, before opening up on exposed French infantry. The Tenth Army command urged French gunners to "nuance" their barrages, appearing to stop to encourage the German guns to fire prematurely, and then resume their bombardment.

In close fighting, the French were at a disadvantage because of their inferiority in trench mortars and machine guns. Colin complained that his soldiers were sent to attack the Labyrinth with antique grenades armed by pulling a string. By mid-May, Pétain's troops were so short of grenades that he ordered his engineers to manufacture *pétards*, improvised trench bombs, to make up the deficit. While Pétain has received high marks from military historians for refusing to advance until the villages along his path could be occupied, his lack of artillery would make his follow-up attacks costly.

On May 12, the XX Corps on his left inched its way along the plateau of Notre-Dame-de-Lorette and up its northern slopes to seize the church, or what was left of it. At the south foot of the butte, Ablain was declared a French possession, although the Germans still clung to a few shattered houses. Carency fell to Pétain's XXXIII Corps, complete with one thousand prisoners, and Pétain prepared to seize Souchez.

However, this would prove a perilous and mostly frustrated enterprise so long as the Germans clung to Notre-Dame-de-Lorette. Attacks on May 14 and 17 designed to isolate the defenders on the slopes of the butte did little to dent enemy defenses in Souchez, and left d'Urbal seething with impatience at the cautious approach of his subordinate. The tone of his communications became increasingly strained as—replacing the familiar *tu* with which he had addressed his successful corps commander after May 9 with the more formal *vous*—he urged Pétain to seal off Souchez with a screen of troops and push on toward Vimy. While Pétain pretended to obey, he concentrated his artillery on pockets of German resistance that clung to fragments of Ablain and the slopes of Notre-Dame-de-Lorette. But attacks on the cemeteries of Ablain and Souchez on May 22 and May 25–26 yielded minuscule advances.

The reasons for the lack of progress were fairly obvious. By May 20, the Germans had matched and surpassed the French in the weight and quality of artillery, a dominance that they maintained for the remainder of the campaign. Pétain complained that German gunners, guided with unerring accuracy by observers aloft in numerous balloons and aircraft, obliged his troops to keep to their bunkers in the daytime and slowed his attack preparations. Furthermore, attacks inadequately supported by artillery exhausted his infantry, and he asked to postpone a second push until his infantry could recover.

On Pétain's right, the 39th Infantry Division, whose advance before Neuville had for three weeks been measured in inches rather than yards, much less miles, was relieved on May 26 by the 5th Infantry Division under General Charles Mangin. A veteran of numerous colonial expeditions, including the epic march across Africa from the mouth of the Congo River to Fashoda on the upper Nile in 1898 (an event that had brought France and Britain to the verge of war) Mangin was an aggressive commander who did not hesitate to risk his own skin in the front lines—he once dared one of his regimental commanders to join him in raising his head above the trench parapet during intense German sniping. His motto was *"Faire la guerre, c'est attaquer,"* "To make war is to attack." However, at Verdun in 1916 his willingness to pitch his division into costly attacks would win him the nickname of "the Butcher."

On June 1, after sitting for four days under constant German bombardment, the 5th Division jumped off before Neuville. For a week, the 5th did no better than their hapless predecessors in the 39th. The Germans had transformed the village houses into a web of defenses that had to be assaulted piecemeal. The deficiencies of French artillery preparation were such that on the second day Mangin called off all attacks. When he renewed them on the following day, progress was held up by Germans congregated in a single house, which was attacked by the entire 36th Infantry Regiment for a week before it finally fell into French hands. On June 5, despite intense German fire, the 129th

Infantry Regiment broke into the center of the village. When a group of Germans attempted to surrender, a corporal, a cigar dangling from his lips, shot several of them out-of-hand before handing the nine surviving prisoners of war (POWs) to his company commander with the recommendation that he shoot the rest if they proved a nuisance. Two days later the 36th finally cracked the German defenses and captured another portion of the village.

Captain J. La Chaussée led his company of the 39th Infantry Regiment through shallow trenches, over walls, and beneath collapsed roofs and strands of barbed wire to prepare the final assault to clear Neuville, his men cursing as their cumbersome packs snagged on the debris. Hardly had they arrived than General Mangin appeared, dressed in red trousers and a braided kepi. "What I want is a *fuite en avant* ["flight forward"]," he shouted at the battalion commander. La Chaussée watched as one of his sections rushed forward, only to be caught by a flanking fire from the German defenders. "One man who was out in front of his comrades was struck by a bullet at the very moment that he reached a wall, behind which he probably hoped to shelter," La Chaussée remembered. "Disarmed by the shot, as he struck the wall with his fist crying: 'AH!' a second bullet hit him. He squatted down his body trembling. He held out his arms and shouted: 'Mother!' A third shot finished him off." The remainder of the section, which was within a whisker of annihilation, was saved by the arrival of a soldier from an engineering unit, who broke up the troublesome German defenses with a few well-placed grenades.

On June 9, after a concentrated artillery barrage, the last defenders were cleared from the northeast corner of the village. (La Chaussée noted that, contrary to the French practice of packing the front lines, the German forward positions seemed to be occupied only by an elusive handful of grenadiers and snipers, the start of the defense-in-depth concepts that in later months were to frustrate every French offensive innovation.) The Frenchmen pulled together debris of the village to construct individual shelters as the German shells rained down around them—harmlessly, as it turned out, because most were shrapnel, which had little destructive power against well-dug-in troops.

The Germans had left behind three 77mm artillery pieces, fifteen machine guns, many grenades, and over 1,000 corpses. But the French success had been a costly one—the cellars of the village were filled with dead and dying French soldiers whose evacuation had been impossible amid the chaos of destroyed houses. The 5th Infantry Division counted 3,500 casualties at Neuville. Once they were withdrawn to the rear, the survivors of La Chaussée's 39th Infantry Regiment threw themselves into a wild celebration, with soldiers dressed up as clowns. One private entertained Mangin, who attended the festivities, with an original musical composition played out on his machine gun.

The assault upon Neuville allowed the XX Corps to devote its full attentions to the Labyrinth, that maw of trenches, bunkers, and shell holes that had swallowed Colin's 26th Infantry Regiment on the first day of the attack. By June 16, after bitter, close-quarter fighting with mines and grenades, most of the Labyrinth was in French hands.

When d'Urbal resumed his offensive on June 16, he had twenty divisions with more in reserve, supported by 800 light and 355 heavy artillery pieces, each with 800 shells; twelve German divisions faced him. This time, he prepared to exploit the expected breakthrough by keeping his reserves close to the front.

The breakthrough never materialized. For those soldiers preparing the approaches to the northwest of Notre-Dame-de-Lorette for the coming offensive, the reason was obvious: They were locked in a siege war of such ferocity that no attack had a chance of advancing more than a few yards. They spent the daylight hours with forty men crammed into shelters designed for a dozen. Anyone who sought to escape the flea-ridden suffocation of the bunkers for a little fresh air invited a hailstorm of German artillery. As darkness fell, they emerged exhausted from their pestilential holes to shore up positions that had been churned and mangled by daytime bombardments, a labor interrupted by flares that obliged everyone to freeze as the shadows gradually lengthened before blending once again into the blackness of the lunar landscape, or by shelling and the ceaseless chatter of machine guns. They incorporated corpses into trench walls. A shell erupted only a few yards from the position of Corporal Louis Barthas and disinterred a body, upon which a swarm of black flies immediately coagulated. "What a stark contrast such a tempest makes in the midst of the calm serenity of a beautiful summer night," he reflected.

On June 16, Pétain's corps, spearheaded by the Moroccan Division, did make some serious progress toward Hill 119, one of the lower slopes of Vimy Ridge across from Souchez. They held their positions despite enfilading fire from Souchez, which still defied the best efforts of the French to take it. The relative success of the Moroccan Division was spoiled by mutinies in two battalions of the legion. A battalion of Greeks, complaining that they had enlisted to fight Turks, not Germans, had to be forced to attack by Algerian *tirailleurs,* "riflemen," with fixed bayonets. A second battalion composed of "Russians"— they appear to have been mainly Jews of Eastern European descent living in Paris, who had been cast into the legion against their will—refused to fight and agitated to be transferred out of the legion; nine of them, seven Jews and two Armenians, were executed. The mutinous "Russians" protested that they had met much anti-Semitism in the legion and preferred more congenial, and perhaps less dangerous, service in a French line regiment.

During the night of June 22–23, the advanced trenches occupied by the Moroccan Division on the slopes of Hill 119 were abandoned after Pétain concluded that they had become too costly to defend. Elsewhere the Germans, firmly entrenched, threw back the French attacks by concentrating all their artillery on the French infantry, ignoring the largely ineffective French counter-battery fire, and then launching quick counterattacks. The French put down their failure to the lack of artillery and the inexperience of their junior leadership: "Our battalions often only attacked straight ahead, bravely, but without dreaming of maneuvering," the official history concluded, and lamented the fact that ground won at the cost of so much blood was so often forfeited in counterattacks.

Though they tried to put a good face on it, the results of the Artois offensive were disastrous for the French. Since German control of Vimy Ridge was never seriously threatened, the French objective of a strategic breakthrough was never close to being realized. Nor did their attack do anything to halt the precipitous Russian retreat. In his memoirs, Erich von Falkenhayn, the German commander, devotes hardly a paragraph to the Artois offensive in the course of a long chapter on the German breakthrough in the east. The series of attacks in May and June cost the Tenth Army 102,000 casualties. And while the French estimated German losses at around 80,000, Berlin admitted to less than 50,000: "Certainly, there were deplorable losses on the German side," Falkenhayn confessed. "But they were small in proportion to the greater damage inflicted on several occasions upon this more numerous enemy."

D'Urbal's failure in Artois sent his career into a slow decline. He remained commander of the Tenth Army long enough to lead it in the Third Battle of Artois, which took place between September 25 and October 18, 1915, over much of the same ground. Souchez was liberated, as were the last few yards of Notre-Dame-de-Lorette remaining in German hands, but at the cost of another 48,000 casualties. The hill that dominated the battlefield was a French possession once again. But it was no more than a formless heap of shell craters, stinking, rat-infested bunkers, and decomposing corpses. The chapel that had once crowned its summit had been blasted into oblivion. The view from the summit—one of the few bits of high ground the Allies possessed on the Western Front—remained impressive, if more inaccessible than ever. It was one of the scant consolations d'Urbal could take with him after he was relieved of command. For the rest of the war, his main duty was to inspect cavalry depots.

But the Second Battle of the Artois was an important turning point in the war, though one that was not immediately recognized. For some contemporaries like Pétain and a growing number of French parliamentarians, Joffre and Foch had failed to draw the obvious conclusion that they lacked the strength to make the breakthrough, that strategically the effect of their attacks upon German operations elsewhere was minimal, that they should wait until their British allies had built up their strength and their own heavy artillery had come on line.

Instead, Joffre and Foch allowed themselves to be convinced that they had come within an eyelash of victory on May 9, that their failure had been technical rather than systemic: If they had possessed just a little more artillery, if the reserves had been held within striking distance of the lines of attack, if offensive operations had been pursued with audacity, surprise, and method, then their armies would have punctured the front and spilled through the breech into the enemy's rear. "The opportunity for success is fleeting and the opportunity is lost if the reserves do not intervene on the spot," Joffre had concluded when the battle was barely a week old. This theory would be tested in September in Champagne, with equally disastrous results.

The Second Battle of the Artois had at least two important long-term effects on the French army. First, it accentuated the trend in the French command to depend upon firepower and the "controlled battle." This came as the Germans began to emphasize flexible small-unit tactics, which ultimately culminated in the infiltration techniques perfected at Verdun, Riga, and Caporetto before being used with initially devastating success on the Western Front in 1918.

This does not mean, however, that the French command failed to draw the "correct" lesson from their experience. After all, the storm-trooper tactics used by the Germans failed ultimately to deliver victory. But more to the point, those techniques probably would not have worked well in the French army, which lacked a tradition of devolution of command responsibility to lower levels, was less well trained and armed for trench warfare, and less able to define and disseminate a doctrine, especially one based on the trench experience of lieutenants and captains. In the French context, it was far easier for the staff "mandarins" to perfect the organization, coordination, and control of attacks than to turn practice and tradition on its head by relinquishing the control of the fighting to lower-echelon commanders. So while the French recognized that their army lacked the flexibility to allow them to seize fleeting opportunities, the ability of their military culture to deal with them effectively was limited. But in its continued reliance on these murderous offensives, the French command nearly destroyed its own army.

Second, this battle also marked the beginning of a shift from a strategy of *percée,* or "breakthrough," to one of *grignotage*—the realization by the French high command that the breakthrough was not possible until German reserves had been "nibbled" away. The American military historian Leonard V. Smith has argued that this strategic shift reflected a deeper psychological change that came over the French army, as its soldiers became increasingly reluctant to sacrifice themselves for what they saw as the unrealistic goals of their commanders. This change was already apparent as early as the autumn of 1915, when attacks in the Artois and in Champagne were broken off by units on their own initiative, the first step in a series of confrontations between French soldiers and the high command over the conduct of operations, which climaxed in the mutinies of the spring of 1917. French soldiers remained committed to victory, but refused to be sacrificed in "useless violence" that brought that goal no nearer. The sacrificial élan of the first year was gone, not to return in this war— or in the next.

It was this psychological shift that was ultimately responsible for the success of Henri-Philippe Pétain as a commander. The Artois experience confirmed that in Pétain the French possessed a commander with vision, who concluded that his country was engaged in a war of attrition and that it must husband its resources, especially its manpower. But Pétain also recognized that the confidence of French soldiers in the ability of their commanders to deliver victory had been shaken in the Artois, a confidence eroded further by the carnage of Verdun in 1916 and by the utter failure of Nivelle's 1917 "*bataille de rupture*" at the Chemin des Dames, which goaded many of them into mutiny. Pétain realized that French soldiers were not against the war, merely that they opposed the way it was being fought. But for France, that recognition almost came too late.

THE STAKES OF 1915
Robert Cowley

—

N O YEAR COULD BE LIKE THE ONE JUST ENDED, 1914, AND yet the next twelve months would have more than their share of notable events. Poison gas. Gallipoli. The *Lusitania*. The Stalingrad-like surrender of the huge Austrian garrison of Przemyśl, the failed Anglo-French offensives of the Artois, Loos, and Champagne. The crushing of Serbia. The German-led sweep into Russia. What 1914 had torn asunder, 1915 could not put together again.

On the Allied side, the British were resolute, the Russians were reeling, and the French were demoralized. The Central Powers seemed to hold a stronger hand: Was it an illusion? The German people—who had not been told of the defeat on the Marne or the consequent sacking of their Commander in Chief, General Helmuth von Moltke, the chief of staff—still believed in victory. Their leaders were less sure. Even the generals had discarded the vision of a triumphal march down the Champs-Elysées, as the Prussian besiegers of Paris had done in 1871. Meanwhile, the Austrians, incompetently led, had suffered losses in the hundreds of thousands. Long before 1915 was over, they would find themselves completely beholden, and subservient, to the Germans. But already time was running out for the Central Powers. The longer it took them to attain an unassailable advantage, the more perilous their situation became.

All over Europe that year, people in ever greater numbers were beginning to feel the pain of a struggle that seemed not just endless but unwinnable. On her first day of work as a nurse in a military hospital outside London, Vera Brittain (whose own fiancé would shortly be swept away) talked with a convalescing Scottish sergeant. "Jock," as people called him, told her of how, in Flanders, he had frequently stood up to his waist in icy water in midwinter; he had been sent back with frostbitten feet. "We shall beat them," he said, "but they'll break our hearts first."

———

ROBERT COWLEY is the founding editor of *MHQ: The Quarterly Journal of Military History*. He has edited two earlier *MHQ* anthologies, *No End Save Victory*, about World War II, and *With My Face to the Enemy*, about the Civil War, as well as the *What If?* series. He lives in Connecticut.

T HE YEAR OF DEADLOCK. THE YEAR OF IMPROVISATION. *L'ANNEE TERRIBLE.* The Forgotten Year. Each of these descriptions fits 1915 to varying large degrees, depending on your national point of view. For both the Allies and the Central Powers, the only thing that 1915 seemed to decide was that there would be no decision. Following on the nonstop suspense of the first five months of the Great War—one of the truly wild intervals in the history of arms—1915 felt a bit like a dress rehearsal after the big show had folded.

The year would be much more than that, of course. The order and balance of society carefully nurtured in the century since the Congress of Vienna was coming apart—an order that only a quick victory for one side or the other could have saved. But 1915 established that there would be none, and that the disintegration of European society that leaders had so long feared would go on and on. In that respect the year must be considered a continental divide of history.

In the west, the year began with rain that seemed never-ending. "Ghastly night and wicked trenches," a Scottish officer noted on January 2. "The whole place is a river." The French were doggedly pursuing what their generals called *la guerre d'usure,* "the war of wearing down," as day after day they sent men against barbed wire and machine guns, with no result. An angry former lieutenant, Jean Bernier, would later write of "the unpardonable offensives of that first winter" and of "the mud, and the rain, and the veritable jelly of corpses." The British secretary of state for war, Horatio Herbert Kitchener, first Earl Kitchener of Khartoum, complained, "I don't know what is to be done. . . . This isn't war."

On the Eastern Front, in the Battle of Masuria, Germans and Russians fought in a continuous blizzard, sometimes in snow chest-deep. The Germans expelled the invaders from East Prussia, returning their national soil to its inviolate state. Meanwhile, in a sandstorm at the beginning of February, Indian troops stopped Turkish columns at the banks of the Suez Canal.

Isolated events these may have been, but in fact little that happened in 1915 can, or should, be regarded in isolation. British fears for a repetition of the Suez attack helped delay preparations for a Dardanelles landing, so full of early promise, by several weeks. The war in the east always affected the war in the west, and in fact the year's most significant dramas were played out in

Poland and Austria. The Germans believed that once they knocked Russia out of the war, the western Allies would come to the peace table. They almost succeeded. Time and again—Masuria was but one example—they were willing to call on their western reserves to achieve an advantage in the east. As late as April, the German Commander in Chief, Erich von Falkenhayn—who may be the key figure of the year—had built up a reserve of fourteen divisions on the Western Front and was planning to attack the depleted British in south Flanders, splitting them apart from the French and rolling them back against the sea. But the plight of Germany's allies, and the threat of a war without them, forestalled Falkenhayn's grand intention. In Austria-Hungary, disaster beckoned. An offensive against the Russians in the Carpathians turned into a deadly fiasco. The horrors of that winter campaign have seldom been told. "Hundreds freeze to death daily; every wounded soldier who cannot get himself back to the lines is irrevocably sentenced to death," an Austrian colonel reported. Wolves preyed on the dead and the near-dead. Casualties, three quarters of whom were felled by sickness, approached 800,000. Counterattacking, the Russians forced their way through the Carpathian passes and seemed ready to break into the plains beyond. For six months they had been besieging the fortress city of Przemyśl; in March, they took it with its garrison of 120,000. There was talk in Vienna of a separate peace—which would have left Germany's southern flank unprotected.

Falkenhayn rushed his reserves eastward, and ordered the divisions still in France and Belgium to go on the defensive. This decision, wrote the historian C.R.M.F. Cruttwell, was one of the turning points of the war: "If new troops had been sent to France, the effects of a great spring attack, supported by gas, against a British army, tired and short of men, crippled by the acutest crisis of the munitions shortage, would have been disastrous."

A great attack in Galicia would go forward on April 28; in the first two weeks, the Germans covered ninety-five miles. In June they retook Przemyśl. By the end of September, when more than two thirds of all German combat divisions were on the Eastern Front, the armies of the Central Powers had driven the Russians back by as much as 300 miles.

There was little in common between the war of maneuver on the Eastern Front and that of static siege on the Western; Eastern Fronters abhorred the prospect of being sent to the west. In the area where the Germans attacked in Galicia, 3,000 to 4,000 yards separated the opposing armies, and peasants farmed no-man's-land. Cavalry actually played a role. Experiments in the east would become norms in the west. Poison gas was tried out against the Russians in January. Saturation bombardment of the sort Verdun made famous routed the Russians from their shallow Galician dugouts. For the first time, German aircraft made harassing attacks on rear areas. The war of maneuver that Western Front generals dreamed about was the quotidian reality in the east.

The operational and tactical pressures that a two-front war exerted on Germany are easier to overlook than the strategic ones; they go far to explain the unexplainable. It often seems, for example, that after their famous chlorine gas attack in the late afternoon of April 22, the Germans could practically have walked into Ypres. But what few attacks they now carried out on the Western Front were all for a single purpose: to straighten the line, and thus conserve men. The Germans never intended to take Ypres. They regarded poison gas merely as a convenient way of capturing Pilckem Ridge, a position of local dominance, at minimal cost. When their troops dug in that night and consolidated, they had accomplished their main purpose. It was only when they discovered the extent of the bite they had taken from the Salient apple that they followed their initial advantage with more attacks, but ones again designed to straighten the line.

April and May were the key months of 1915, a time, you might say, of interlocking impacts that would forever alter the character of the Great War. Three days after the gas attack at Ypres, untried and unprepared Allied troops went ashore at the Dardanelles, into the teeth of Turkish machine guns. The Gallipoli campaign has been portrayed as the one potential strategic masterstroke of the war, which could have led to the capture of Constantinople and opened a supply route to Russia. It quickly became an extension of the Western Front, trench warfare gone vertical, and for both sides an unsought epic of endurance that ended only when the British slipped away the following January.

On May 7, in the Irish Sea, a German U-boat under orders from Berlin torpedoed the British liner *Lusitania,* with the loss of 1,198 lives, 124 of them American. The German government viewed the episode as a warning to the Great Neutral not to ship war supplies to the Allies; but from that point on, it was headed on a collision course with the United States. Two days later, the Allies on the Western Front attacked in the Artois and south Flanders; by now not just *la guerre d'usure* but relief of the beleaguered Russians was the object. Then, on May 23, Italy entered the war on the Allied side, apparently expecting a quick pickup of Austrian territories. Instead, it got an Alpine stalemate that produced little else besides Mussolini, an annexed Trieste, and *A Farewell to Arms.*

At that point, the British would have been content to lie quiet for the remainder of the year while they waited for Kitchener's volunteer New Armies to arrive. But for the moment they were very much junior partners in the Western Front alliance and had to defer to the French—who, in midsummer, still controlled about five sixths of the front.

What turned out to be their major offensive for the year, Loos, was part of a grandiose scheme by the French Commander in Chief, General Joseph Joffre, to pinch off the bulge that reached its blunt apex at Noyon, seventy threatening miles from Paris. On maps it seemed so simple. Wondrous arrows from the north and from Champagne would converge, forcing a German withdrawal of strategic proportions.

To give Joffre's British counterpart, Sir John French, his due, and it isn't always easy, his first reaction was to resist—and then to call for an attack at Loos "chiefly with artillery." The German line in that sector was, he said, "so strongly held as to be liable to result in the sacrifice of many lives."

But the French were in no mood for British half measures. Now their own home front—those interlocking impacts again—was torn between a majority who demanded immediate expulsion of the Germans and a vocal minority who were ready to pull out of the war. Warsaw fell to the Germans on August 8, and Russia teetered on the edge of military collapse; the government discussed the possible evacuation of Petrograd. (Its former name, Saint Petersburg, had been discarded when war broke out: It sounded too German.) As the Eastern Front disintegrated, the Germans made peace overtures to Czar Nicholas II through Dutch intermediaries: He let it be known that he would hold to the pledge he had made to Britain and France. (Soon after, the czar took charge of his armies and prorogued the Russian parliament, the Duma, an ill-considered move that would, as much as anything, doom his monarchy.) Germany and Austria now attacked and overran Serbia; Bulgaria threw in its lot with the Central Powers. As the historian Holger H. Herwig writes: "Strategically, Serbia's defeat gave the Central Powers control over a huge belt of Mitteleuropa stretching from the North Sea to the Dardanelles, and even beyond to the Tigris River. Pan-German dreams of a Berlin to Baghdad connection had been realized: the first train from Berlin arrived at Constantinople on 17 January 1916. Militarily, Berlin and Vienna had consolidated their interior position." But they never managed to exploit what could have been a strategic opening of Alexandrine proportions.

These were perilous moments for the Entente alliance. Kitchener himself interceded. Like it or not, Sir John French had to proceed with a full-scale offensive at Loos. In doing so, he would doom his own career and would condemn 48,000 men to death or maiming—60,000 if you count the October extension of the Loos campaign. Joffre's attacks in the Artois and Champagne achieved an even more costly lack of success.

What did the Allies get in return for the enormous—some would say inexcusable—casualties of 1915? On the Western Front their losses approached two million. The Russians lost an equal number. The human capital of Europe was being spent at a reckless rate. Of the 19,500 square miles of German-occupied France and Belgium, the Allies recovered just eight square miles. In terms of operations, 1915 was a year of undisputed triumph for Germany; in terms of its ultimate hopes, a catastrophe in the making. For all the square mileage its brilliant tacticians racked up on the Eastern Front, they failed to put Russia out of the war. Every day that Germany missed achieving a resolution was a day it could not afford to lose. There was no greater confession of failure than Falkenhayn's decision, set forth in his so-called Christmas memorandum, to return to the Western Front. His intention was to bleed France white at Verdun—to lure his enemy into a high explosive trap "in which not even a mouse could live!" Stripped to its bare bones, his object could not be more cynical: mass death. As it proved, his "Meuse mill" would grind up Germans as well as Frenchmen.

For the western Allies, 1915 may have been an operational catastrophe but it was an interval full of strategic promise. The British, especially, found the breathing space to build up their citizen army and to put their industry on a war footing. In 1915, the western Allies bought the time—expensive time to be sure—that would bring them victory.

NO-MAN'S-LAND
Malcolm Brown

—

T HE GREAT WAR ADDED INDELIBLE WORDS AND PHRASES
to our language: "the trenches," "over the top," "attrition," "shell shock," "killed in action," "three on a match."
But no term is chiseled so deeply into our imaginations as "no-
man's-land." How had it originated? In my own roamings
through the battlefields of Belgium and France, I had often
wondered about this, especially in the old sectors of the Western Front where you can still see what once was that deadly
interval between trench systems. There is no better place to
feel its pull than on the Somme. There you can walk across the
wide, long, downward-sloping field where, on July 1, 1916,
German fire cut down 684 men of the 1st Newfoundland Battalion. The Newfoundland trenches are still there, carefully
maintained, as are those of the Germans at the foot of the
hill—and in between, where no-man's-land once was, like
some spectral Brancusi sculpture, the pale gray skeleton of
what the Newfoundlanders once called the Danger Tree. Neither I nor the resourceful documents department at the Imperial War Museum, which I consulted, could point to a
satisfying explanation for the first use of no-man's-land.
Spontaneous generation, probably by some anonymous Brits
in the new trenches of 1914–15, was our best guess.

Malcolm Brown, a prominent chronicler of the Great
War, has come up with the answer, which he details in the article that follows, and it is an explanation that should settle
the question once and for all. The indications are that one
man, an influential British officer with a literary bent, Sir

Ernest Swinton, was the originator of the phrase. (At the same time, 1908, and in the same short story, he made an uncanny prediction, along the lines of Ivan Bloch, of what the next war would be like). Not satisfied with that distinction, Swinton also tried to figure out how to get across no-man's-land, a tactical conundrum that occupied many minds in those years. He had the notion of tunneling under no-man's-land, allowing troops to emerge behind German lines and take them from the rear. Another idea not only worked but is still with us. Sent to France as Kitchener's official reporter in the fall of 1914—he was the first person to use no-man's-land in a dispatch—"Swinton became convinced," Brown writes, "that revolutionary means were required to meet the challenge of the new warfare on the Western Front." He was one of those who came up with the concept of the "land iron-clad"—or, as he called it in a flash of inspiration, the "tank."

———

MALCOLM BROWN, a historian attached to the Imperial War Museum in London, has written extensively on the First World War. His books include *Tommy Goes to War; Christmas Truce* (with Shirley Seaton); *Verdun 1916;* and an Imperial War Museum series on the First World War, the Western Front, the Somme, and 1918. In 2002 he became an Honorary Research Fellow of the Centre for First World War Studies at the University of Birmingham.

I
T COULD BE HALF A MILE WIDE, IT COULD BE TWENTY YARDS WIDE. IN PLACES IT
dwindled to nothing as one army's trench line ran straight into its opponent's. The enemy might be a distant stranger or he might be so near you could
hear him talk, cough, laugh, give or respond to orders, scream with pain.

It could be a place where larks sang and flowers grew. One young British
officer, as he advanced across it in the wake of the huge mine explosions that
opened the Battle of Messines in 1917, was astonished to see clumps of grass
and yellow iris. He mused later: "How these plants and grasses escaped destruction I cannot imagine."

But mostly, no-man's-land on the Western Front of World War I was a region of horror and desolation. Its standard terrain was a mix of shell holes and
mud. Its decor consisted of rotting cadavers and smashed weaponry—the inevitable human and technological detritus of a close-fought, industrialized
war. And lining it on both sides were warrens of trenches fronted by vicious entanglements of barbed wire. The wire was where so many attacks failed because for all the efforts of the artillery in the countdown to zero, the necessary
gaps often were not cut. As you clawed at the uncut wire you were the easiest
of targets. Sometimes bodies stayed exposed on it for days. This phenomenon
provided the grim payoff line to one of the most cynical of British soldiers'
songs:

If you want to find the old battalion,
I know where they are, I know where they are. . . . They're
hanging on the old barbed wire.

No-man's-land might be defined as the disputed space between Allied and
German trenches—from the coast at one end to Switzerland 470 miles away at
the other—which became the principal killing field of a notoriously cruel and
inhuman war. Inevitably it drew sharp comment from those who contemplated it, or faced the prospect of going out into it. The writer Edmund Blunden
scorned it as "no man's ditch." The artist Keith Henderson exclaimed: "Of no-
man's-land itself, perhaps, the less said the better. No beast's land—call it that
rather." Before having cause to fear it, Charles Carrington and his comrades
dubbed it "the Racecourse." The poet Charles Hamilton Sorley, stimulated by it,

even finding "a freedom and a spur" in seeking out the enemy in its dangerous spaces, nevertheless saw its hazards and named it "the long graveyard"; he himself died on its edge, shot by a sniper during the Battle of Loos in October 1915. A greenhorn British infantry officer, Lieutenant Colin Hunt, peered through a periscope at the "desolate scene" facing him in 1916 at Ploegsteert ("Plugstreet" to the British) on the Franco-Belgian border and commented in a letter to his wife: "It is indescribably weird to watch the country behind the enemy lines and think of the impossible gulf that separates it from us."

Yet against popular conception—certainly against the vision of most film-makers, who would have the Western Front as one long tornado of frenzied ac-tion—trench life for the most part was a matter of watching and waiting rather than fighting, so that Lieutenant Hunt's "impossible gulf" could often appear to the observer as merely a frieze of dead ground, a still-life, not a rat stirring. It was thus for Second Lieutenant E. J. Ruffell when in 1917 he climbed to an ob-servation point at the top of a broken pit-gantry in the industrial zone where the ill-fated Battle of Loos had been fought two years earlier. He found his first sight of the trench world oddly different from his expectations:

> I shall never forget the disappointment of my first view of the "front"—shell-pocked ground, ruined houses, rusty barbed wire every-where and a maze of trenches, and No Man's Land—not a soul to be seen, and not a sound except a solitary "plop" of a sniper's rifle.

At other times, however, no-man's-land could provide a fair simulation of hell on earth (or "hell let loose," to quote one of the ordinary Tommy's favorite clichés). A British staff officer attached to an Australian division, Captain A. M. McGrigor, saw it from a vantage point called Kemmel Hill during one of the se-ries of actions that finally heaved Field Marshal Haig's 1917 offensive up to that fearsome and infamous destination, the ridge called Passchendaele:

> I had the most extraordinary and wonderful panoramic scene of the whole battle from well to the north of Ypres to beyond Messines. One could see the bursts from all our guns and from many of the Bosche's [sic], and between the two the awful barrages that were being put down in "no man's land." It was a terrible and awe-inspiring sight and made one won-der how human beings could live in that inferno.

Human beings, of course, frequently did *not* live in such infernos. It also claimed countless victims between attacks. Not in the mass, perhaps, but by ones and twos daily—or rather nightly, for no-man's-land during routine trench warfare was preeminently a nocturnal arena. In August 1916 during the Battle of the Somme, Captain D. C. Stephenson described an episode typical of many in a letter to his mother:

> I had a nasty experience yesterday. Another gunner officer and I, with one of my signallers, were reconnoitring a very new trench the Germans have dug. We got a good long way out in No Man's Land and suddenly got severely sniped at. The other officer got back safely, and my signaller and I started to crawl back. All of a sudden he got up for some reason and ran. He hadn't gone two steps before he spun round and fell, just in front of me. I plugged up his wound as well as I could, and then a very gallant infantryman came out, on his own, to help me dress him. This man raised his head for a moment while bandaging, and then fell, shot through head and helmet, on top of me. I shouted to the other fellows to try and scratch a small trench out to us, and I got hold of a telephone wire, tied it on to my poor signaller's legs, and they pulled him in. The poor infantryman who had come out to help was quite dead when I got back to him. I am sorry to say the signaller died on the way to the dressing station.

This was no-man's-land at its most elemental and vicious, the sort of episode that made it one of the enduring concepts of this disturbed and violent century. Indeed, the phrase has been wheeled out again in every war since, right down to the Falklands Conflict, the Gulf War, and the savage struggle over the corpse of Yugoslavia. Clearly, if it didn't already exist, it would have had to be invented.

So how *did* the phrase come into existence? Did it arise spontaneously, a natural product of circumstances? Or did some one person coin it, its appositeness being such that it could not fail to catch on? If so, who was the inventor? Who held the smoking gun?

Many wars, of course, have produced zones of dead ground situated between opposing forces: They are the inevitable consequence of trench warfare, itself a variant of old-style siege warfare. There were trenches in Spain during the Peninsular War, in the Russo-Japanese War, in the Crimea—above all, in the American Civil War. One might think the obvious name for terrain into which no one would dream of stepping if he wished to remain whole in wind and limb would be—no-man's-land. The more so since the phrase itself had been around, constantly acquiring new meanings, for a good many centuries.

In its ancient form of "nanesmanes-lande" it is as old as the Domesday Book, and in the England of the Middle Ages it was applied to all kinds of unowned or unwanted ground—generally waste or barren stretches between defined areas such as provinces or kingdoms. (There is a scatter of small areas bearing the name No Man's Land or Nomansland around England today, some among them significantly sited on ancient regional boundaries.) In the traditional open-field system, it was a useful label for odd scraps of ground here and there, which also attracted the name of "Jack's land," or "anyone's land." Later it was the name of an area outside the north wall of the city of London that was used as a place of execution. In the days of sail it was a section of deck assigned to the storing of blocks, ropes, tackles, and other equipment that might be required on the forecastle. Daniel Defoe used it in 1719 in the sequel to *Robinson Crusoe*, his so-titled *Farther Adventures*, as "a kind of border." Thomas Hughes wrote in 1881 of "a small bit of noman's land in the woods."

All examples so far given hail from Britain. A remarkable American use of the phrase occurs in a poem by the late-nineteenth-century literary figure Thomas Bailey Aldrich, friend of Hawthorne, Longfellow, Lowell, and Whittier, and famous for his influential tenure of the editorial chair of the *Atlantic Monthly*. In his poem "Identity," he wrote:

> *Somewhere—in desolate wind-swept space*
> *In Twilight-land—in No-man's land—*
> *Two hurrying Shapes met face to face,*
> *And bade each other stand.*
> *"And who are you?" cried one a-gape*
> *Shuddering in the gloaming light.*
> *"I know not," said the second Shape,*
> *"I only died last night!"*

For the literary aficionado these lines might seem to resonate with omens of things to come—even read, almost, like a preview of Wilfred Owen's superbly imagined encounter of fallen enemies, "Strange Meeting"—but it has to be admitted that there is no hint that Aldrich's ghosts are in uniform or are casualties of war.

However, first sightings of the phrase in a military context were also beginning to appear, though not at first in the form now generally employed. In a memoir published in 1899 called *The Queen's Service: Being the Experiences of a Private Soldier in the British Infantry at Home and Abroad*, its author, Horace Wyndham, wrote of the unoccupied zone between the British garrison on Gibraltar and the town of La Línea beyond the Spanish frontier: "This is the 'Neutral Ground'—a sort of No Man's Territory."

Almost, but not quite. For the real breakthrough, the use of no-man's-land in its now-classic and most widely understood form, we have to move on another nine years. According to that magisterial source of linguistic wisdom, the *Oxford English Dictionary*, 1908 was the first year in which the phrase was used in relation to the terrain between opposing lines in war.

The context, however, seems an odd one, a short story called *The Point of View*, printed originally in the popular Edinburgh-based *Blackwood's Magazine* and later, in 1909, in a book called *The Green Curve and Other Stories*. The author was Ernest (later Major-General Sir Ernest) Swinton, soldier and historian, who wrote not under his own name but under the alias of "Ole Luk-Oie." (Apparently a Danish phrase meaning "Shut-Eye," this was not the only bizarre pseudonym adopted by Swinton; he had earlier written a treatise on tactical lessons to be learned from the Boer War—cast as a fiction and titled *The Defence of Duffer's Drift*—under the name of "Backsight Forethought.")

The setting of *The Point of View* is a battle in some future conflict, in which the opposing sides are in close, destructive proximity.

> As soon as the light faded altogether from the sky, the yellow flames of different conflagrations glowed more crimson, and the great white eyes of the searchlights shone forth, their wandering beams lighting up now this, now that horror. Here and there in that wilderness of dead bodies—*the dreadful "No-Man's-Land" between the opposing lines* [my italics]—deserted guns showed up singly or in groups, glistening in the full glare of the beam or silhouetted in black against a ray passing behind. These guns were not abandoned—the enemy's fire had stripped them of life as a flame strips a feather. There they remained inert and neutral, anybody's or nobody's property, the jumbled mass of corpses around them showing what a magnetic inducement guns still offer for self-sacrifice, in spite of the fact that for artillery to lose guns is no longer necessarily considered the worse disgrace.

Yet surely this raises the question: Could the trip wire that transformed this hoary old phrase into its present incarnation have been a mere short story, a—by now—long-forgotten military yarn?

Then let me call as witness the late Charles Carrington, the author of a famous early memoir of the Western Front entitled *A Subaltern's War* (written under the pseudonym of Charles Edmonds), and, later, of the equally outstanding *Soldier from the Wars Returning*. In this second book he wrote revealingly about the cultural climate of the years before 1914.

> Among the many books published in Edwardian days forecasting the character of a future war there was one which was much discussed by

professional soldiers and which may be seen to have affected the art of generalship in the First World War. That book was *The Green Curve. . . .*

Carrington went on to name, specifically, *The Point of View* as a subject of serious discussion when he was himself a young soldier. The reason for this was that the story raised a matter of considerable importance in the world of military theory. Since future wars were likely—or so Swinton believed—to be large-scale affairs dominated by artillery and fought by massed armies in strongly defended positions, the role of the commander in the field clearly needed to be rethought. In particular it was vital that he should be clear as to where he should place himself while serious action was in progress. Was it to be on the battlefield itself for the glamour and the glory, or away from the fighting so as to be in a position to take a view overall and make the necessary operational and tactical decisions? Crucial to the story, and doubtless the key to Swinton's own viewpoint, is the quotation with which he headed it, from the writings of Baron Colmar von der Goltz, Prussian soldier and military thinker in the late 1800s: "The more that clear-sightedness and intellectual influence upon the course of a battle is demanded by a general, the more he must keep himself out of serious danger to life and limb." Swinton's solution in his story was that having launched his battle the best thing a commander could do was—go fishing!

This was no joke. In fact, through the writing of *The Point of View,* Swinton was focusing prophetically on an issue that would much concern generals—and their critics—throughout the whole of this century, from Joffre and Haig through Rommel and Eisenhower to Schwarzkopf. His story explains why the last named based himself at Riyadh in the Gulf War as much as it explains why Haig lived for much of the First World War in the Château de Beaurepaire or Montgomery spent numerous crucial nights in the Second War asleep in his caravan. (No-man's-land, it should be added, was strictly incidental to the theme of Swinton's story—an evocative, memorable phrase added, it must be presumed, to give resonance to his austere vision of the shape of conflicts to come.)

The thought therefore emerges that Ole Luk-Oie's stories were far from being merely tales to amuse, yarns for boys of all ages whether in or out of uniform. Rather they were, in the biblical sense, *parables*—serious theses presented by a prescient thinker in a form that would attract his readers' attention far more successfully than if he had written a military textbook.

In the matter of no-man's-land, there seems no doubt that in *The Green Curve*—and in particular in *The Point of View*—we have the actual moment of its arrival on the military scene. A seed was planted, to await its appropriate time to burgeon and flower.

That time came in 1914 on the Western Front, and Swinton was on hand to record the flowering. Indeed, recording was precisely his job in that he had been sent to France by Secretary for War Lord Kitchener as an official reporter.

The French had forbidden the battlefields to all civilian correspondents. They were prepared, however, to accept some suitably qualified officer, and Winston Churchill—then First Lord of the Admiralty and hyperactive member of the British cabinet—nominated Swinton for the role on the basis of his admiration of *The Defence of Duffer's Drift*. Swinton seized his opportunity and produced a stream of vivid and widely syndicated dispatches under the nom de guerre of "Eye-Witness present with General Headquarters." The arrival, before the year was out, of static trench warfare gave Swinton the chance to transfer his evocative buzz phrase from fiction to fact. He seized it in his dispatch of December 21, in which he seems to have been describing the sector in front of the French town of Armentières. This, I believe, is the first published use of our keynote phrase in the war, which would turn it—literally—into a commonplace.

Of the forward area of the already well-developed trench system he wrote:

> Seamed with dug-outs, burrows, trenches, and excavations of every kind, and fitted [*sic*] with craters, it is bounded on the front by a long discontinuous irregular line fringed with barbed wire and broken by saps wriggling still more to the front. This is the Ultima Thule. Beyond, of width varying according to the nature of the fighting and of the ground, is *neutral territory, the no-man's-land between the hostile forces* [my italics]. It is strewn with the dead of both sides, some lying, others caught and propped in the sagging wire, where they may have been for days, still others half buried in craters or destroyed parapets. When darkness falls, with infinite caution, an occasional patrol or solitary sniper may explore this gruesome area, crawling amongst the *débris*—possibly of many fights— over the dead bodies and the inequalities of the ground till some point of vantage is gained whence the enemy's position can be examined or a good shot obtained. On the other side of this zone of the unburied dead bristles a similar fringe of wire and a long succession of low mounds and parapets—the position of the enemy. And woe betide the man who in daylight puts up his head carelessly to take a long glance at it.

Swinton was basically writing for civilians back home who would read his dispatch at the earliest with their breakfast on Boxing Day, December 26. But by this time at the front, here and there, soldiers had already caught the phrase and were beginning—just—to accept it as part of the culture. It is not hard to imagine officers who remembered Swinton's stories calling up the term as they saw his vision of no-man's-land re-created before their eyes. Swinton himself was doubtless using it in conversation as well as print. One way or another it began the process of becoming the obvious, state-of-the-art phrase for a phenomenon of which everybody in frontline trenches was now very much aware.

The famous 1914 Christmas Truce, which began on December 24 and produced a major fraternization on Christmas Day, offers an interesting snapshot of its progress. Thousands of men from both sides met in no-man's-land, but the phrase is markedly absent from the contemporary descriptions, whether in letters, diaries, or newspapers that publicized the story with what now seems amazing frankness and approval. There is much reference to meeting "between the lines" or "in the space between the trenches." Yet the phrase does occur. Writing in his diary on Christmas Day, Lieutenant Colonel Lothian Nicholson, C.O. of the 2d Battalion, East Lancashire Regiment, commented that he had suddenly become aware that afternoon of "a lot of our men hobnobbing with the Hun in No Man's Land." This diary was retyped after the war and could conceivably have been adapted but there is no doubt about the authenticity of the use by a young soldier of the London Rifle Brigade, Private Oswald Tilley. On December 27, he wrote in a letter to his family that two days earlier he had been "out in 'No Mans Land' shaking hands and exchanging cigarettes, chocolate, and tobacco."

By early 1915, the phrase was sufficiently established for the British tabloid press to offer it to its readers as a new state-of-the-art coinage from the war. On January 5 the London-based *Daily Sketch* printed two contrasting pictures, of British and German trenches; the accompanying caption noted that: "The ground between them is known as No Man's Land." The phrase was employed increasingly throughout 1915, and soon it was even finding its way into official military documents. No-man's-land had arrived, for good.

Should any question remain that this is the course of events, there is the modest confirmation of the alleged author himself. In a footnote to his book of war reminiscences, *Eyewitness*, published in 1933, Swinton stated: "To the best of my knowledge this term, which became part of the English language during the war, was first used by myself in a story called *The Point of View*, to describe this neutral zone between two opposing trench-lines."

No-man's-land soon ceased to be merely a matter of phraseology; it became the basis of an aggressive philosophy. It might well be a handy piece of jargon for journalists; it was also a matter of high seriousness for generals, particularly British ones, who first informally, then officially, adopted the view that the German wire should be seen as the Allied front line. British troops were not to accept no-man's-land as such, rather they were to use every opportunity to get out into it and to make it their own. Hence Robert Graves, in *Good-bye to All That,* could write of the entry of his 2d Royal Welch Fusiliers into the line: "As soon as the enemy machine guns had been discouraged, our patrols would go out with bombs to claim possession of No Man's Land."

This notion had its enthusiastic supporters; it also had its bitter denigrators. For the first category there could be no better spokesman than the Irish brigadier general, F. P. Crozier, most thrusting of commanders, whose view was that "training facilities outside the line are good, but the finest training ground of all is no man's land and the German trenches." For the ultimate anti-statement, we need look no further than Wilfred Owen in a letter to his mother dated January 19, 1917. He was writing from the zone that had just been devastated by the four-month Battle of the Somme:

> They want to call No Man's Land "England" because we keep supremacy there.
>
> It is like the eternal place of gnashing of teeth; the Slough of Despond could be contained in one of its crater-holes; the fires of Sodom and Gomorrah could not light a candle to it—to find the way to Babylon the Fallen.
>
> It is pock-marked like a body of foulest disease and its odour is the breath of cancer. . . .
>
> No Man's Land under snow is like the face of the moon chaotic, crater-ridden, uninhabitable, awful, the abode of madness.
>
> To call it "England"!
>
> I would as soon call my House(!) Krupp Villa, or my child Chlorina-Phosgena.

British ambitions, however, did not stop at claiming no-man's-land; beyond it lay the German trenches, which were to be harassed and harried whenever this was deemed appropriate. Hence, the trench raid—the purpose of which was to cause general mayhem, kill as many of the enemy as possible, and bring back prisoners for interrogation. Impromptu and random at first, the raids became increasingly sophisticated and ambitious as the war went on. They were often savage, high-risk affairs, with many casualties.

Nor were the Germans slothful in mounting similar efforts. It was in just such a raid in February 1917 that Lieutenant Colin Hunt, having first been wounded, was snatched across the "impossible gulf," which had so powerfully impressed him five months earlier, to become a prisoner of war until the end of hostilities.

As there were two views on claiming no-man's-land, however, there were also two views on raids. A New Zealander, Sergeant James Williamson MM (Military Medal), denounced them in a postwar memoir:

> Raids every night in the dark, always casualties and perhaps consid-
> ered a great success if they got back with one prisoner. All these raids were
> mostly just to find out what Division was opposite us. As if it mattered, no
> action was taken no matter what Division was opposite us.

It should be pointed out, however, that occasionally raids did have important results; it was a raid on French trenches in April 1917 that gave the Germans the battle plan of the disastrous offensive about to be launched on the
Chemin des Dames.

No-man's-land could have its lighter side. One Canadian private on the
Western Front reported the activities of a resourceful cat that regularly carried
out its independent patrols and knew the mealtimes on both sides. The period
being late 1916, before the United States joined the war, the cat was christened
"Wilson" on account of his scrupulous observance of neutrality! Earlier the
same year Captain H. C. Meysey-Thompson of the Kings Royal Rifle Corps, in-
troducing some officers of the Sherwood Foresters to trench routine in the
"Plugstreet" sector in Belgium, decided one night after dinner on a "little en-
tertainment" for his guests. It took the form of a foray into no-man's-land "to
hang my old breeches on a tree as a signal of defiance of the Hun." A particularly athletic Sherwood Forester shinned up a pollarded willow and "disposed
them most artistically in its topmost branches, where they looked very well."

Such jaunts, however, could sometimes turn out badly, for no-man's-land
was rarely to be trifled with. In the spring of 1915 at Col de Grenay, in the sector soon to become the battlefield of Loos, a huge flowering cherry that had
gained itself the name of "Lone Tree" challenged the imagination of a young
lieutenant of the Seaforth Highlanders. Out on night patrol he climbed it to at-
tach a Union Jack to its upper branches. Caught in the light of a flare as he
made his way down, he was promptly dispatched by enemy machine-gun fire.
His cadaver hung on the tree for several days.

Yet no-man's-land could be benign, being, despite its usually dour reputation, the scene of numerous standoffs and mutually agreed cease-fires—it was
not only at Christmas 1914 that men walked tall between the trenches.
Amazed at a similar, if smaller, effort at Christmas 1915 (by which time fraternization was a strictly prohibited rarity), a young Welsh officer, Wyn Griffith,
commented: "This was the first time I had seen No Man's Land, and it was now
Every Man's Land, or nearly so." At other times there were truces to bring in

the dead, or because trench conditions were so frightful that both sides called a halt to hostilities.

Men could assert important values, flourish even, beyond the wire. "I love being out of trenches and searching for adventure in No Man's Land," Lieutenant Kenneth Macardle of the 17th Manchester Regiment wrote in his diary in May 1916, adding that he was honored in his battalion for his special skills: "I live in HQ in great luxury and sometimes when I am out on a fighting patrol, the Colonel sits up for me." In 1917 on the Salonika front (by which time the phrase had plainly been exported to other theaters), Captain T. M. Sibly of the Gloucestershire Regiment could write in a letter to his family: "No Man's Land provides the one touch of romance in trench warfare." Describing a patrol in January of that year, Sibly commented that "as long as one was not discovered, the expedition was rather like a picnic . . . but of course it was a somewhat exciting picnic."

Nor was no-man's-land always a place of grim desolation. When the fighting moved elsewhere, it could revert to nature with astonishing speed, even acquire its own surreal magic. This is how the war artist William Orpen saw the carnage-ground of the Somme after the lines had moved on, in 1917:

> I had left it mud, nothing but water, shell holes and mud—the most gloomy, dreary abomination of desolation the mind could imagine; and now, in the summer of 1917, no words could express the beauty of it. The dreary, dismal mud was baked white and pure—dazzling white. White daisies, red poppies, and a blue flower, great masses of them stretched for miles and miles. The sky a pale dark blue, and the whole air, up to a height of about forty feet, thick with white butterflies: your clothes were covered with butterflies. . . . Everything shimmered in the heat. Clothes, guns, all that had been left in confusion when the war passed on, had now been baked by the sun into one wonderful combination of colour—white, pale grey, and pale gold.

What did other countries make of this area of dispute between the lines?

For the Germans to begin with it was *Vorfeld*—the space in front, but later they adopted the term *Niemandsland*. Similarly the French seem initially to have used the phrase *la terre neûtre* and then switched to, or extended their vocabulary to include, *le nomansland*. That these are almost certainty straight lifts from the English version tends, surely, to support a British origin. The Russians, by contrast, seem to have kept their own counsel; their dictionaries simply refer to "the space between enemy trenches."

And what of the doughboys when they went into the line in 1918? Ever rich in producing new and resonant phraseology, did they simply pick up the accepted coinage or did Uncle Sam's soldiers invent their own vivid term of reference? No-man's-land, it is good to report, appears to have been safe in their hands, judging by the following remarkable description from the reminiscences of a young brigade commander who was to win a world-famous name in the Second World War and beyond, Douglas MacArthur. Sensing at one point that the Germans were retiring he determined to see for himself and with the help of guides he went out to explore "what had been No Man's Land." He wrote in his *Reminiscences:*

> I will never forget that trip. The dead were so thick in spots we tumbled over them. There must have been at least 2,000 of those sprawled bodies. I identified the insignia of six of the best German divisions. The stench was suffocating. Not a tree was standing. The moans and cries of the wounded sounded everywhere. Sniper bullets sung like the buzzing of a hive of angry bees. . . . I counted almost a hundred disabled guns of various sizes and several times that number of abandoned machine guns.

It is Swinton's vision of exactly ten years before fully realized, and more so. Historically, the no-man's-land of the Western Front may now be with the ages, but the concept is still acquiring ever new shades of meaning, although it will, surely, always carry with it the distinctive aura of the 1914–18 War. It is an analogy that comes to mind in any situation—personal, moral, spiritual, cultural, political, industrial, sporting—where there are dilemmas, uncertainties, standoffs, areas of doubt or prevarication. In this respect it is one of a number of products of that four-year deadlock that have taken up more or less permanent residence in our language. We have such phrases as "entrenched positions," "over the top," "shell shock," "war of attrition," "killed in action," "walking wounded," "keeping your head down."

But I would nominate no-man's-land for pride of place. Older than the others, it will surely outlast them, whether as a territory on a map, or as a territory of the mind. I somehow doubt whether such recently offered bias-free substitutions as "limbo," "wasteland," or "nowheresville" will seriously challenge a phrase with such a long and deep history. Until men and nations cease to confront each other in close encounters of a martial kind, its future is assured.

PART THREE

THE
NAVAL WAR

FISHER'S FACE
Jan Morris

—

I T WAS THE FACE OF THE FIRST SEA LORD THAT PEOPLE always remembered—that ever-changing heavy-lidded countenance, sometimes scowling, sometimes breaking into an unexpected smile, that gave his person such power. As Jan Morris writes here, "the absolute belligerent self-assurance" of the man never ceased to amaze. John Arbuthnot Fisher was, someone once said, "a veritable volcano"—by turns energetic, tenacious, ruthless, and charming. He learned early on how to manipulate both the press and the liberal governments of the first decade of the twentieth century.

"The only thing in the world that England has to fear is Germany," he said, and he created a Grand Fleet whose main purpose was to destroy its German counterpart, the High Seas Fleet, in a latter-day Trafalgar. As First Sea Lord from 1904 until 1910, he was responsible for a revolution in warship design, most notably in the HMS *Dreadnought*, the first all-big-gun battleship, and in the battle cruiser, which sacrificed armor for speed. (His maxim, "speed is armor," would not hold up at Jutland.) Would there have been an arms race with Germany without "Jacky" Fisher? Possibly not.

Jan Morris, that consummate English prose stylist, chronicler of the British Empire, and one of the best travel writers of our time, describes Fisher's astonishing rise—and his fall, equally astonishing. In October 1914, Winston Churchill, First Lord of the Admiralty (the political head of the Royal Navy), would ask him to return to his former position. Fisher was then seventy-three, but as vigorous as ever. Could two such dominating (and domineering) personalities work together? Their relationship, originally close, would fray under the stress of Churchill's obsession: the Dardanelles adventure. When Churchill broached the project early in 1915, Fisher went along with him—if only, he said, to divert his younger partner from his "wilder and more dangerous schemes," notably the invasion of North Sea islands close to the German coast. Fisher was against sideshows of any kind. *"A failure or check in the Dardanelles would be nothing,"* he said, underlining the words. *"A failure in the North Sea would be ruin."* He felt that his Grand Fleet should be used exclusively to blockade Germany. But Churchill would have his way. The result, Gallipoli, would prove to be a naval and military disaster, one that would bring down the last Liberal government and break the man once described as the greatest British admiral since Nelson.

––––––

JAN MORRIS's travel writing has ranged the earth from Oxford, Sydney, Spain, and Hong Kong to Manhattan after the Second World War and Wales (where she lives). She is also the author of a trilogy, *Pax Britannica,* on the rise and fall of the British Empire; an autobiography, *Conundrum;* a novel, *Last Letters from Hav;* a biographical study, *Lincoln: A Foreigner's Quest;* and the book that grew from this article, *Fisher's Face.*

APPEARANCES HAVE ALWAYS COUNTED IN WAR, AND NOT LEAST IN THE hyperbolic epoch of European naval rivalry, spanning the late nineteenth and the early twentieth centuries. In those days the epithet "fierce-faced" was applied to warships of particularly fearsome stance, and half the art of being an admiral was to express in one's person the power, threat, audacity, and confidence of the vessels one commanded.

Nobody did it better than John Arbuthnot Fisher of the Royal Navy, the volcanic naval innovator who died in 1920 as Admiral of the Fleet the First Baron Fisher. "Jacky" Fisher's strange appearance was unforgettable, and he built around it so formidable a presence and reputation that he was like a living eponym of the tremendously named battle cruisers that were his most spectacular inventions—*Invincible, Indefatigable, Inflexible,* or *Indomitable.*

As it happens, all too many of these ships, born out of Fisher's gung-ho energy, were destroyed in action in humiliating circumstances. "There's something wrong with my bloody ships today," said Sir David Beatty as he saw his battle cruisers blowing up around him at the Battle of Jutland in 1916, and in the end there turned out to be something wrong with Fisher, some weakness at the keel, some lack of armor, which made him, too, fail at the ultimate crisis of his life. The time would come when the king of England would say he ought to have been hanged from the yardarm.

FISHER WAS BORN IN 1841, IN WHAT WAS THEN THE BRITISH COLONY OF CEYLON, and twice was First Sea Lord, the professional head of the Royal Navy: from 1904 to 1910, when he was responsible for converting the navy from an antiquated imperial display into a modern fighting force; and for seven months early in the First World War, when he worked in partnership with Winston Churchill, his political chief as First Lord of the Admiralty. Fisher transformed the matériel of the then-supreme Royal Navy, and thus of all other navies, too; but he made innumerable enemies along the way, and was thought by many in the navy to have fatally betrayed the clublike spirit of brotherhood that had been part of the naval tradition since Nelson's day. Personally, he was the most delightful of men (and a lifelong practicing Christian). Professionally, he thrived on intrigue, shamelessly exploited the press, could be horribly vindictive, and would stoop to almost anything that he believed would make the navy more efficient.

Fisher was loved and loathed with equal intensity. But nobody disputed the astonishing force of his presence, which he evidently developed as a work of art around the gift of his striking appearance. He was a man of medium build, medium height, inclining to stoutness, with the Victorian naval officer's conventional trace of swagger to his posture. It was specifically his face that gave his persona such power. In later years this became rather yellow, some say as a result of dysentery, but from boyhood it had always exhibited a curiously Oriental cast. Fisher's enemies called him the Malay, the Mulatto, or the Asiatic, and whispered that his mother was Sinhalese. To me his face has always rather suggested a mild form of Down's syndrome.

Whatever its origins, that face was the foundation of a marvelous stylistic pungency. It was extremely changeable, especially around the mouth, which could smile with a particular sweetness but also could be turned down at the corners in a look of unappeasable contempt—he said himself that he looked sometimes like an angel, sometimes like a devil. He was a merry fellow, for all his dedication, and his face could be very endearing, especially when it collapsed into the helpless laughter he was prone to, or simply flashed in fun. It could also be baffling, because he developed the ability to mask it in a kind of vacuity, his eyes perfectly blank, so that no hint of his responses escaped. In his old age it could be appallingly curdled with scorn and complacency, like one of those malignantly fork-bearded elders of Japanese art.

Most characteristically, though, it expressed absolute belligerent self-assurance—the fierce-face look made human—and this was the face that was generally remembered.

FISHER JOINED THE NAVY WHEN HE WAS THIRTEEN, AND BY THE TIME HE WAS nineteen had seen action (against the Chinese in the Second Opium War) and briefly commanded a ship (the sloop *Coromandel*). From the start he idolized Nelson, and all his life he professed to base his conduct upon Nelsonic precedents and ideals. The mantras in which he habitually expressed himself were all about risk, thrust, the offensive spirit, the Nelson touch: "Think in oceans, sink at sight." "Hit first, hit hard, and hit anywhere." "Any bloody fool can obey orders." It was not mere victory that the Royal Navy must always aim for, but annihilation.

Down the years, as he rose in rank and reputation, he assiduously put these principles into practice. He was captain of the battleship *Inflexible* at the bombardment and occupation of Alexandria in 1882, and he got his name into the newspapers as the dashing deviser of the first armored train, which he equipped with naval guns, crewed with sailors, and sent cruising up and down the railway tracks shelling dissident Egyptians. He was Commander in Chief of the North Atlantic station in 1898, at the time of the Fashoda crisis, which nearly led Britain into war with France—and proposed, if war came, to abduct the imprisoned Captain Dreyfus from Devil's Island and deposit him in France to stir up trouble. He was always eager to explore aggressive new tactics and weapons—the torpedo, the submarine, and later the airplane—and he loved to brag of his absolute ruthlessness: in peacetime, against pettifogging critics and reactionaries; in war, against anybody who dared challenge the Royal Navy.

It was in 1899 that this formidable sailor first became known to the world at large: He went to The Hague as British naval representative at an international peace conference, held at the suggestion of the Russian government in a wan attempt to limit armaments and mitigate the horrors of war. Fisher was in the prime of life then, a rear admiral of fifty-eight shortly to assume command of the most powerful single instrument of war on earth: Britain's Mediterranean Fleet. A photograph of the British delegation to the conference shows him looking splendidly dapper, sitting in his gray top hat and spats in the front row of the group, a stick between his knees and a faintly amused smile on his face, like a performer in *My Fair Lady.*

Socially he was a great success at The Hague. Everyone found him entertaining, especially the women, who were almost invariably enchanted by his charm, his bravura, and his passion for dancing (if he could find no partner, male or female, he would often dance alone, humming or whistling one of the evangelical hymn tunes of Moody and Sankey). At formal sessions of the conference, too, he seems to have behaved with perfect diplomatic propriety. At informal meetings among the delegates, though, he projected his personality very differently, and it was at The Hague that he perfected its professional exploitation.

Fisher despised the purposes of the conference—"Moderation in war is imbecility," he liked to say. His views, as representative of the paramount naval power, certainly affected the attitudes of the other European nations and bolstered his own legend as an inflexible, remorseless, fighting sailor. Behind him stood the vast and somewhat arcane prestige of the Royal Navy, unchallenged since Trafalgar. It was more than simply an armed service; it was a statement of triumphant heritage whose status in world affairs was almost mythical. Attended by a gilded mystique of tradition, captained by aristocrats and lofty originals, burnished to an immaculate degree of spick-and-span, it was at once a discouragement to challenge and an incitement to rivalry. Fisher was its allegorical spokesman. What he told the delegates carried an immeasurable weight, and what he told them was ferocious.

A British journalist, Harold Begbie, described the delegates' reactions to some of Fisher's more bloodthirsty passages. He said they "sat listening with blanched faces, with horror in their eyes." Fisher himself claimed to have made their blood run cold with his forecasts of what would happen if the Royal Navy went to war under his command. It would be merciless, he said. Neutral ships supplying an enemy would be sunk without compunction. Captured submarine crews would be put to death. The mightiest weapons of naval warfare would instantly be hurled at the enemy, no holds barred. It was, Begbie said, the most fearful exposition of the prospects of war that anyone present could remember.

Of course, much of it was rodomontade—Fisher loved exaggeration—but it was calculation, too. "If you rub it in," as he later wrote, "that you . . . intend to be first in and hit your enemy in the belly and kick him when he is down, and boil your prisoners in oil (if you take any!), and torture his women and children, then people will keep clear of you." With his magnificent scowl and his vocabulary of invective, he was the personification of his own warnings. His purpose was to demolish the wistful idea that war would ever again be fought under gentlemanly rules: It would be all or nothing, kill or be killed. *Totus porcus*, "the whole hog," was another of his innumerable mottoes.

NOT LONG AFTER HIS MEDITERRANEAN COMMAND, FISHER WENT TO THE Admiralty in London for his first term of office as First Sea Lord. His personality then was at its most attractive, and pictures show him generally looking genial in his command—the angel more often than the devil. It was nevertheless the start of the most passionately conducted period of his life, in which by fair means and foul he created a new navy, ready to meet the challenge of war after a century of complacent peace.

It was clear now that Germany was the likeliest enemy the Royal Navy might have to face, and soon the two North Sea powers were embarked upon the race for naval strength that did indeed contribute so fatefully to the coming of the Great War. On the German side the kaiser and his navy minister, Admiral Alfred von Tirpitz, hastened the building of a powerful, brand-new fleet, capable at last of challenging British supremacy. On the British side Fisher vehemently set about modernizing the Royal Navy, reequipping it with new weapons, shaking it out of its ornamental self-satisfaction, and concentrating its power not in the distant waters of empire but around the North Sea.

The Germans, no doubt remembering his postures at The Hague, genuinely feared him. It was not simply his patent dedication to the maintenance of British readiness for war. It was his native pugnacity, expressed so vividly in his person, which made people think that he might well precipitate war himself. They had cause for their nervousness. Teamed with a succession of generally compliant political bosses, the First Lords of the Admiralty, Fisher remorselessly forced through his own ideas. He instituted (and named) the destroyer. He sponsored the steam turbine, oil fuel, and the revolutionary water-tube boiler. He built the *Dreadnought*, the all-big-gun battleship, which at a stroke made all other battleships obsolete. He invented a new class of capital ship, presently to be named the battle cruiser. It was perhaps the most beautiful of warships, long, lean, graceful, immensely fast, powerfully gunned, but lightly armored—his greyhounds, Fisher liked to call the cruisers, or his New Testament ships. They were swift enough to choose their own ranges and battlegrounds, and strong enough to sink anything afloat.

He was convinced that the Germans meant war, and he seriously considered the idea of a deterrent strike against them. The launch of the *Dreadnought* in 1906 inevitably obliged the Germans to build ships of similar size and power. This meant that the Kiel Canal, which gave the German navy access to both the Baltic and the North Seas, had to be enlarged to handle them. Fisher rightly guessed that the Germans would not start a war until this work was completed, and he reckoned that the British had until the later months of 1914 to take matters into their own hands.

His hero Nelson had, in a preemptive attack, destroyed the Danish navy at Copenhagen in 1801. Fisher coined the verb "to Copenhagen" to justify similar actions. He argued that the High Seas Fleet, Germany's main battle fleet, should be Copenhagened while the going was good and the Royal Navy was still in sufficient preponderance to do it. He made no secret of this cataclysmic resolve. In Britain it was generally dismissed—"My God, Fisher, you must be mad," said Edward VII when he learned of it—but in Germany people took it more seriously. It was an age of sensational rumors, international plots, and alarmist novels and journalism. Fisher became something of a bogeyman in the German press, and among the officers of the German navy.

Perhaps he did not really mean it, but he was certainly in earnest about his plans for offensive action against Germany once a war had started. He believed that the small, professional British army was no more than a projectile, to be fired at its target by the navy. He was consistently against protracted British military commitments on the European continent, and he thought Britain's strategic emphasis should be on the amphibious warfare for which its naval power qualified it. His first plan for war against Germany was therefore the headlong landing of an army, like a bolt from the blue, upon Germany's northern coast—"the coast of the enemy," he loved to say, "is Britain's frontier."

The Baltic project was a characteristically Fisherian scheme, involving as it did terrific risks, colossal possibilities, a mighty conception, and a cavalier disregard of awkward objections. He believed that the Royal Navy could enter the Baltic and disembark a force—British in his original thinking, Russian later—on the sandy coast of Pomerania, only ninety miles north of Berlin. The German fleet would be immobilized by minefields and submarines, by the threat of the British battle fleet, and perhaps by the blocking of the Kiel Canal.

Between 1904 and 1910 Fisher created the matériel of the Royal Navy that would fight the next war. It was generally assumed, especially in Germany, that if he were in power when the conflict happened, something like the Baltic project would be his violent contribution to the British war effort.

FISHER RETIRED FROM THE NAVY IN 1910, BUT HE WAS CERTAINLY IN FIGHTING mood when, three months after the Great War started—in the summer of 1914, just as he had predicted—he was recalled to the Admiralty as First Sea Lord again. His First Lord of the Admiralty was Winston Churchill, and for seven nerve-racking months they ran the naval war in volatile tandem. They were infatuated with one another. Fisher was a tempestuous seventy-three, Churchill a bumptious forty, but they were men of similar energy, originality, and force of character. Churchill said Fisher was like ozone to him; Fisher thought Churchill a genius. They were like a pair of elemental forces, the one so deceptively cherubic, the other now becoming so fiercely wrinkled as to look almost sinister; but their personalities were too strong for easy partnership. As was said at the time, their association was like "the collision of two powerful but uncongenial chemicals."

They had it in common that they believed above all in taking the offensive, and in taking it suddenly. Fisher considered the very core of the British war machine to be the Royal Navy's main battle fleet, the Grand Fleet, poised in its North Sea harbors to fall upon the German High Seas Fleet if it ever emerged from its bases around the Elbe. He had made the Grand Fleet. Its ships were largely his creations. Its commander, Sir John Jellicoe, was his protégé. He believed the Grand Fleet should be preserved at all costs for the ultimate sea battle, when the whole course of the war might be decided by its actions; but in the meantime he advocated the sort of ancillary action that Nelson fought at the Nile in 1798—audacious, unexpected, overwhelming.

Things were going badly for the navy when he returned to the Admiralty. It had signally failed to do what the public expected of it—namely, achieve some shattering instant victory. Its successes had been limited, its setbacks disillusioning. Within a few months of the war's start, German submarines had sunk four cruisers and a battleship. Two powerful German warships, the *Goeben* and the *Breslau*, had humiliatingly evaded the British in the Mediterranean and made their way to Constantinople. And in November there came the horrifying news that a German squadron under Admiral Graf Maximilian von Spee had defeated a British force off Coronel, in Chile, sinking another two cruisers with no loss to itself. It was at this exact moment that Fisher reassumed office, and he came brilliantly into his own. Every principle he stood for he was now able to translate into action, and all the menace and power of his personality came momentarily true.

Detaching two of his beloved battle cruisers from the Grand Fleet, Fisher had them fitted out at Portsmouth Dockyard so fast that when they put to sea they carried some of the dockyard workmen with them. Three weeks later the squadron they headed was at the Falkland Islands, in the South Atlantic, and the very day after its arrival von Spee's ships appeared over the horizon. Four of them were sunk there and then, without British loss. The fifth was destroyed three months later. Fisher's philosophy of war was dramatically justified: instant action, overwhelming force, merciless onslaught (though he grumbled, nevertheless, that the fifth German ship was not sunk at the same time).

How proud he was! Not only had he created that great battle fleet of the North Sea, waiting superbly in its Scottish haven to beat the High Seas Fleet, but now he had justified the creation of his battle cruisers and restored to the Royal Navy some of its languishing reputation for dash and epic efficiency. But after the Battle of the Falkland Islands all went sour for Fisher, and as the months passed his face lost its all-confident splendor and curdled with disappointment.

Nobody in London knew what to do about the war. The main alliances were firmly established—it was Britain, France, and Russia against Germany and Austria-Hungary—but nobody seemed to be winning. In France and Belgium the armies were stuck in squalid stalemate; in the North Sea the German navy declined to come out and fight; in the east the Russians were floundering; the Balkans were in a state of perilous indecision; the Italians sat on the fence; the Turks, impressed by the audacious arrival of the *Goeben* and the *Breslau*, had joined the German cause and attacked the Russians in the Caucasus.

Herbert Asquith, the British prime minister, was hardly the kind of war leader Fisher preferred, and his celebrated slogan, "Wait and see," was interpreted by the old admiral as waiting to see where or when one was going to be kicked next. Churchill and Fisher were among those who pressed most forcibly for the opening of a fresh front, to relieve the Allied armies so helplessly slogging it out in France and Russia. There were two chief alternatives. One was some variety of the Baltic project, together perhaps with attacks upon the German North Sea coast. At first Fisher and Churchill were so dedicated to this idea that they caused to be built an armada of landing craft and warships designed especially for the Pomeranian invasion (the biggest ships, *Furious*, *Courageous*, and *Glorious*, had enormous guns but very shallow draft, and were nicknamed by the navy *Spurious*, *Outrageous*, and *Uproarious*).

The other alternative, more generally accepted, was the idea of forcing the Turkish Dardanelles, the heavily fortified strait separating the Mediterranean from the Sea of Marmara and Constantinople. Getting to Constantinople, it was argued, would have profound effects on the course of the war: Turkey would be knocked out, relieving pressure on the Russians; the uncommitted Balkan States would be brought into the Allied cause; and the Germans themselves would be threatened on their southeastern flank.

By January 1915, Churchill was enthusiastically favoring the attack on the Dardanelles over the Baltic alternative, and despite misgivings Fisher seemed persuaded, too. The original proposal was that the strait should be forced by the use of naval power alone, and this majestic idea perhaps appealed to his romantic imagination. The British admiral in the eastern Mediterranean thought it could be done, and nothing could be more Nelsonic than the passage through the strait of the Royal Navy's *superbia*, defying all that the Turkish forts could do. Fifteen old battleships were allocated for the task, but Fisher offered to send also the magnificent brand-new *Queen Elizabeth*, the most powerful warship afloat. "By God, I'll go through tomorrow!" he cried, already assuming the glory of it, when it seemed that the ships were indeed going to force their way through to Constantinople, and at one time he really did volunteer to go out and command the operation himself. But the ships never got through, and the Dardanelles were to prove Fisher's downfall.

He was aging fast now. He had pushed through a colossal building program since his return to office, he was living in a perpetual state of emotional excitement, his relationship with Churchill was charged with exhausting nuance—for the first time in his life Fisher was dealing with a man his equal in force of character, but intellectually his superior. When the Dardanelles project began to go wrong, Fisher faltered. The attempt in March to force the narrows by ships alone was a disastrous failure—three of Fisher's beloved battleships were sunk—but Churchill was determined to go ahead, if not with another naval assault, then with a military landing on the Gallipoli Peninsula.

The old admiral, if he really knew his own mind by now, certainly made his feelings unclear to others. Sometimes he seemed enthusiastic still, sometimes despondent, sometimes he claimed to have been against the campaign from the start. Eight times he threatened to resign. He quarreled with Churchill; he made up again. He claimed that the Dardanelles attack was fatally weakening the navy's resources for its real task, the containment of the High Seas Fleet in the North Sea, and he insisted on the withdrawal of the *Queen Elizabeth.*

When German submarines were reported on their way to the Aegean, when yet another British battleship was sunk, and when the Gallipoli landings bogged down in tragic stalemate, Fisher became distraught. He was perhaps having a breakdown. Immediately after one of their reconciliations, Churchill resolved to send yet more ships to the Dardanelles, and Fisher cracked. This time, on May 15, he resigned in earnest. He then simply walked out of his office and disappeared. Couriers scoured London for him, but he was nowhere to be found.

In fact, he had shut himself up in a room at the Charing Cross Hotel, just around the corner from the Admiralty (though he probably spent part of the time meditating in Westminster Abbey, as was his custom). When he was eventually tracked down there, Asquith sent him the curtest of messages: "In the King's name I order you at once to return to your post." He took no notice, and almost at that moment, with nobody at the First Sea Lord's desk, news came that the German High Seas Fleet was about to leave its North Sea bases—it seemed the naval Armageddon for which Fisher had for so long prepared was about to happen. It proved to be a false alarm, but the admiral's absence from duty at this dramatic juncture tarnished his reputation forever. Even some of his besotted friends and admirers thought he had behaved unworthily—un-Nelsonically—and it was for this defection that the king later said he should have been hanged from the yardarm.

Far from being ashamed of himself, however, Fisher now sent Asquith a half-crazed list of conditions under which he would return to duty. Churchill was to be removed, and he himself would assume "complete professional charge of the war at sea, together with the absolute sole disposition of the Fleet and the appointment of all officers of all ranks whatever," and "absolutely untramelled [*sic*] sole command of all the sea forces whatever," plus "sole absolute authority for all new construction and all dockyard work of whatever sort whatsoever, and complete control over the whole of the Civil establishments of the Navy."

Asquith responded predictably to this farrago. After sixty years of service, Fisher's naval career ended with a letter from the prime minister containing a single formal sentence: "I am commanded by the King to accept your tendered resignation of the Office of First Sea Lord of the Admiralty."

Fisher's breakdown had wide repercussions. It led to the collapse of the Asquith Liberal government, which was replaced by a coalition, and to the temporary eclipse of Churchill, who, having guided the affairs of the world's greatest navy for four years, was made chancellor of the Duchy of Lancaster. ("Where is Lancaster?" asked a mocking magazine of this deflation. "And what is a Duchy?") Fisher, in this sad apogee of his life, preferred not to go home to his loyal wife and family in Norfolk, but instead went to Scotland to take comfort from one of his more luxuriant admirers, the duchess of Hamilton. Nelsonian that he was, perhaps he liked her name.

Pathos, but by no means despondency, characterized the rest of his life. Churchill declared the old sailor temporarily mad, and he was probably right, for Fisher soon seemed to recover his spirits and his by now somewhat manic self-assurance. He even got a new job, as chairman of the Board of Inventions and Research, which did important work in the development of sonar. His forebodings about Gallipoli proved justified; his prophecies about submarines and aircraft came true; he spent the rest of his life criticizing government policies, trying to engineer a return to power, and reminding people how right he had been about almost everything. He had many supporters still, and there were periodic campaigns to have him reappointed—some months later even Churchill, in a fit of quixotic generosity, suggested in Parliament that he should be recalled. For the rest of his life, though, he was really no more than a very public gadfly.

NOWADAYS FISHER IS GENERALLY HONORED IN HISTORY AS ONE OF THE GREATEST of all naval visionaries, the man who, by his own re-creation of the Royal Navy, ensured the defeat of Germany in 1918. In a shorter perspective his wartime achievements hardly seemed to live up to his self-publicized personality. For one thing, if he had thrown himself wholeheartedly into the Dardanelles campaign, taking those terrific risks that he had always advocated—"Moderation in war is imbecility"—sacrificing ships and men with the ruthlessness he affected, it might well have succeeded after all. For another thing, although the Royal Navy won the war by its very existence, it never achieved the modern Trafalgar that he had dreamed for it, and Jellicoe, the admiral he had chosen to be the commander of the Grand Fleet, turned out to be no Nelson either: The Battle of Jutland, the one battle-fleet action of the war, was tactically indecisive, and Fisher's darlings, the battle cruisers, proved so vulnerable that three were sunk in a matter of minutes. When, in 1918, the demoralized German High Seas Fleet steamed into Rosyth, Scotland, to surrender, led by a British cruiser, the aged admiral who saw himself as the architect of its defeat was not invited to the ceremony.

Was he downhearted? Never for long. He was depressed, of course, to be confined to the sidelines for the last three years of the war. He was saddened by the loss of his wife, at whose deathbed he (perhaps remorsefully) sat. But he soon recovered his exuberance. At the peace conference, where he appointed himself an unofficial delegate, he danced the nights away with a succession of delighted partners. He bombarded the editor of the London *Times* with splenetic letters, written in his famously explosive handwriting—furiously underlined, littered with exclamation marks—denouncing the errors of authority and constructed around the last of his great slogans: "Sack the lot." His ideas were as boldly vatic as ever. Now he advocated the abolition of conventional navies and a drastic reduction in arms expenditures. Submarines were the thing, and air power, and radio. He became more and more radical in view— socialistic, his enemies said. He admitted no mistakes, he justified his life with irrepressible gusto, and in 1920, at seventy-nine, he died, after a trip to Monte Carlo, in the arms of his duchess in her grand London home in St. James's Square—a last expression, so his detractors sneered, of the Nelson touch.

But pathos, yes—if not to himself, at least to posterity. I suspect Fisher thought to the very end that he should be summoned back to the seats of power, to save the nation from all the varied perils facing it. In his last years he began to appear a lovable but half-senile eccentric. His funeral was a fine enough occasion, admirals of the fleet attending his catafalque as it was drawn slowly through London to Westminster Abbey. The editorial writers were generous in their obituaries. The general public, which had always had a soft spot for "Jacky," was genuinely moved.

Yet no public memorial was erected in his honor, and for decades to come his detractors vilified his memory. He declared himself impervious to criticism—"Never explain, never apologize"—but in the last famous image of him, Jacob Epstein's bust now in the Imperial War Museum in London, the grand euphoria has gone. Fisher's marvelous face is preposterously congealed with pride, its eyes hooded, its cheekbones more Oriental than ever, its mouth twisted in a megalomanic sneer of arrogance. Although the humor is still there, ineradicable behind nearly eighty years' accretion of struggle and achievement, now there is a touch of sadness, too. The fierce-face look is only a mask.

THE FIRST BATTLE OF
THE FALKLANDS
Ronald H. Spector

—

O N NOVEMBER 1, 1914, THE DAY AFTER ADMIRAL FISHER once more became First Sea Lord, the Royal Navy experienced the unthinkable: its first defeat in more than a century. In an early evening action, a German cruiser squadron, commanded by Admiral Count Maximilian von Spee, sank two British cruisers, which went down with all hands. The engagement took place in the rough waters off a nondescript seaport called Coronel on the coast of Chile: No longer just a Continental eruption, the war had genuinely become world war. Coronel was so remote that it took three days for the news to reach London.

There was blame; there was consternation. British, Australian, and Japanese warships had already chased von Spee across the Pacific. Where would he turn next? Would he pounce upon convoys carrying troops westward from the outposts of the Empire? Would he take his ships through the Panama Canal to menace weak French and British naval forces in the Caribbean? Would he head around Cape Horn to the South Atlantic to escort German reservists from South America to South Africa, where they might aid a brewing anti-British revolt by the Boers? Or wreak havoc on the Atlantic sea lanes as he dashed for home? The only thing limiting von Spee—and this the British suspected, albeit dimly—was the precariousness of his coal and ammunition supply.

In the event, Fisher would take a calculated risk that would prove to be one of his finest moments; another subordinate, Vice Admiral Frederick Sturdee, the former Royal Navy chief of staff, would redeem himself for the uncertain directions that may have caused the Coronel disaster. The action, which the naval and military historian Ronald H. Spector describes, would take place on a December afternoon—late spring in the South Atlantic—in one of the most distant and lonely of British colonies, the Falkland Islands. An unlikely place it may have been for a major encounter, but in the century just passed, the islands would be no stranger to war. "Like the second battle of the Falklands almost seventy years later," Spector writes, "the first had begun in muddle and humiliation, been retrieved by prompt and brilliant improvisation, and ended in sweeping military success." It may have been no less than the only decisive naval battle of the Great War.

———

RONALD H. SPECTOR is Professor of History and International Affairs at the Elliott School of International Affairs of George Washington University in Washington, D.C. His most recent books are *After Tet: The Bloodiest Year in Vietnam; Eagle Against the Sun: The American War with Japan;* and *At War at Sea: Sailors and Naval Combat in the Twentieth Century.*

THE GREAT WAR WAS BARELY THREE MONTHS OLD WHEN NEWS OF THE FIRST British naval defeat in more than a hundred years reached London. At seven in the morning on November 4, 1914, as sleepy code clerks and watch officers were preparing to turn over duty to the daytime staff at the Admiralty, a telegram arrived from Valparaíso, Chile. Two British cruisers had been sunk and another damaged in a sea battle with a German cruiser squadron off the rugged southern coast of Chile near the small town of Coronel.

A few hours later, a message from the light cruiser *Glasgow* confirmed the report. Two British armored cruisers, the *Good Hope* and the *Monmouth*, under Rear Admiral Sir Christopher Cradock, had been sunk with all hands by the German squadron of Admiral Count Maximilian von Spee.

Von Spee's squadron—consisting of the armored cruisers *Scharnhorst* and *Gneisenau* and the light cruisers *Dresden*, *Nürnberg*, and *Leipzig*—had been a major headache for the British since the first days of World War I. Sightings and rumors of sightings of his ships, and fears as to what they might do, had caused panic throughout the Far East and the South Pacific. Merchant shipping was thrown into confusion or halted. Troop convoys from Australia and New Zealand were delayed or rerouted. More than twenty British and French cruisers, the entire Royal Australian and New Zealand navies, and a substantial portion of the Japanese navy (which had entered the war on the Allied side in mid-August) were occupied in searching for von Spee.

Eluding all these forces, von Spee made his way eastward across the Pacific, after first detaching his fastest light cruiser, the *Emden*, on a commerce-raiding cruise to the Indian Ocean. The *Emden* sank seventeen merchant ships in two months and became a kind of sea legend before finally being sunk by the Australian cruiser *Sydney* near the Cocos, or Keeling, Islands.

On the far side of the Pacific, off the coast of South America, Cradock's squadron at last found von Spee. At first glance the two small fleets seemed fairly evenly matched. Cradock had two armored cruisers, a light cruiser, and an armed merchant liner, the *Otranto*. Von Spee had two armored cruisers and two light cruisers. (A third German light cruiser, the *Nürnberg*, was not present until late in the battle.)

In fact, however, the Germans had a decided advantage. Cradock's two armored cruisers, the *Good Hope* (his flagship) and the *Monmouth*, were older and slower than von Spee's big ships. The *Scharnhorst's* and *Gneisenau's* modern 8.2-inch and 5.9-inch guns fired a total of 2,200 pounds of shell each, compared to about 1,200 pounds for the *Good Hope* and 600 pounds for the *Monmouth.* Cradock's light cruiser, the *Glasgow,* was far more heavily armed than her German counterparts, but she was outnumbered two to one by them.

Altogether the German ships could fire a total broadside of 4,750 pounds, whereas the British ships could fire only a scant 2,100 pounds. And the modern German guns could fire faster. More important, the German armored cruisers were the crack gunnery ships of the German navy, while Cradock's cruisers were manned by inexperienced reservists hastily mobilized at the beginning of the war. The *Monmouth,* noted one of the *Glasgow's* officers, "had been practically condemned as unfit for further service, but was hauled off the dockyard wall, commissioned with a scratch crew of coast guardsmen and boys, and . . . is only kept going by superhuman efforts."

There was one other ship in Cradock's command, which was supposed to even the odds. This was the old battleship *Canopus,* built around the turn of the century and armed with a main battery of four 12-inch guns. But these guns were of an old type and could actually be outranged by those of the *Scharnhorst* and *Gneisenau,* while the *Canopus's* armor was little better than the *Good Hope's.* Like the crew of the latter ship, the *Canopus* crew were mainly reservists who had never even had the opportunity to fire her heavy guns in practice.

The *Canopus's* only good point was that her aged reciprocating engines could still propel her along at close to her maximum designed speed of sixteen knots. But the battleship's chief engineer suffered a nervous collapse upon arrival in the South Atlantic, perhaps brought on by age and the strain of wartime operations. After closeting himself in his cabin, he emerged to declare that the ship's engines were suffering from faulty condensers and could make no more than twelve knots! Upon receiving this report Cradock, unaware of the engineer's condition, left the *Canopus* behind at Port Stanley in the Falkland Islands, to follow his squadron through the Strait of Magellan once repairs had been made.

In fact, the deranged chief engineer was fabricating his reports. There was nothing wrong with the battleship's engines, and she could easily keep up with Cradock's slowest cruiser. But by the time the falsehood was discovered, it was too late.

At four-thirty in the afternoon on November 1, as Cradock's squadron steamed north up the coast of Chile in search of the Germans, the *Glasgow* sighted smoke to the northeast. The weather was intermittently clear and squally, and heavy seas broke across the ships' bows as the British and German men-of-war maneuvered for position. The Germans to the east would have the late-afternoon sun in their eyes. This was a serious disadvantage in the days before radar, when the visual observations and calculations of the gunlayers and fire controllers counted for everything, particularly in the precision gunnery at which the *Scharnhorst* and *Gneisenau* were expert. Using his superior speed, von Spee kept out of range until the British ships were silhouetted against the setting sun, then closed in for the kill.

The German shooting was excellent from the start; within a few minutes both of the big British cruisers had been hit repeatedly and were on fire. The poorly armed and unprotected *Otranto* quickly pulled out of the line and retreated into the night while the *Glasgow* attempted to engage the two German light cruisers.

Aboard the *Glasgow*, Lieutenant Lloyd Hirst could see a shot from the *Scharnhorst*'s third salvo send up "a heavy burst of flame in the forepart of *Good Hope* and after this the curious effect of a continuous sheet of flame along the sides of *Good Hope* and *Monmouth* on which flame the heavy seas appeared to have no effect."

Events on the *Glasgow* must have been like those on the other ships: Gunlayers were frequently blinded by heavy spray, and fire-control officers reported that they could see no splashes in the gathering darkness. After a short time the British gunners were reduced to aiming at the gun flashes of the German ships.

Both the *Good Hope* and the *Monmouth* were burning fiercely by now. At seven-fifty a giant explosion rocked the *Good Hope* and flames roared 200 feet into the air. Recalled Hirst:

> She lay between the lines [of German and British ships], a low, black hull gutted of her upper works and only lighted by a dull red glare which shortly disappeared. Although no one on board *Glasgow* actually saw her founder, she could not have survived the shock more than a few minutes.

The *Monmouth*, still able to navigate, attempted to withdraw but was engaged by the light cruiser *Nürnberg* just then entering the battle, and went down with her flag still flying. The speedy *Glasgow*, which had miraculously escaped serious injury, fled south to warn the *Canopus* and report the disaster to the world.

In England, the initial shock and incredulity at the news of Cradock's defeat soon turned to anger and frustration at what was widely perceived as blundering in the Admiralty. Who, it was demanded, was responsible for placing an inferior British squadron in the path of a superior German force? "Cradock's death and the loss of the ships and the gallant lives in them can be laid at the door of the incompetency of the Admiralty," wrote Rear Admiral David Beatty, who commanded the British Grand Fleet's battle-cruiser force. "They have as much idea of strategy as a board school boy."

The First Lord of the Admiralty was the irrepressible Winston Churchill. Only thirty-nine years old, Churchill was the embodiment of energy and boldness, but his understanding of naval operations and of how best to utilize the Admiralty and its staff to direct a worldwide war was limited. The Admiralty itself was not an effective organization in the first weeks of the war. The First Sea Lord, Prince Louis of Battenberg (father of the future viceroy of India and First Sea Lord Louis Mountbatten), the professional head of the navy, had just been driven from office by a campaign of slander and rumor about his supposed "German sympathies." The chief of staff, Vice Admiral Frederick Charles Doveton Sturdee, though a fine seaman and a student of naval tactics, was a poor manager who could not delegate responsibility and did not understand how to make a staff system work. Members of the Admiralty staff were afraid to stand up to their bosses and were seldom consulted by them.

Under this regime the Admiralty had misread von Spee's movements and intentions, and repeatedly sent confused and misleading instructions to Cradock. They also refused his request for reinforcements while conveying the impression that they expected him to fight no matter what the odds.

In fact, Churchill assumed that Cradock would always stay within supporting distance of the *Canopus*. "Admiralty orders were clear," declared the beleaguered First Lord. "The *Canopus* battleship was sent to him for his protection. . . . Keeping together with the *Glasgow* he had a good chance of finding and holding them until reinforcements arrived."

Critics were quick to respond that the *Canopus* was of doubtful value as an insurance policy even if she could have kept up with the cruisers. "Had the *Canopus* joined Cradock's flag it would merely have swelled the casualty lists," said one of the battleship's own officers after the battle, "and instead of being in the happy position of writing you, I, together with the whole ship's company, would have died that night."

"A good many moves are necessary in consequence of this contretemps," wrote Churchill to the secretary of state for war, Horatio Herbert Lord Kitchener. And the energetic young First Lord wasted no time in making them. In a sense the most important move occurred a few days before Coronel when Prince Louis, worn out by the slander campaign (which continued unabated even after his nephew, Prince Maurice, was killed in action in France), asked permission to resign. To replace him Churchill urged the appointment of Admiral Sir John Arbuthnot Fisher.

Fisher, retired since 1910, was probably the best-known and ablest officer in the Royal Navy. As First Sea Lord from 1904 to 1910, he introduced the dreadnought battleship and reformed and modernized almost every department of the navy. However, his sweeping reforms and ruthless, driving administrative style made him many enemies, including King George V, who opposed his recall to the Admiralty. In addition, by 1914 Fisher was seventy-three years old, and many wondered whether he was up to the demanding job. Yet Churchill threatened to "leave the Admiralty and go to the war and fight" if Fisher was not appointed. When the king protested that for a man of Fisher's age the strain would prove fatal, Churchill replied, "Sir, I cannot imagine a more glorious death."

With the backing of Prime Minister Herbert Henry Asquith, Churchill prevailed, and Fisher arrived at the Admiralty breathing fire and ready to punish malingerers and incompetents. "Did twenty-two hours' work yesterday but two hours' sleep not enough so I shall slow down," wrote Fisher to a friend soon after his return. A glance at the charts convinced Fisher that Cradock's squadron was ill-suited to deal with von Spee, and he immediately dispatched reinforcements to the South Atlantic and signaled Cradock to this effect. But as Churchill later wrote, "We were already talking to the void."

Only hours after receiving word of Cradock's defeat—flashed halfway around the world by the newly perfected transatlantic wireless—Churchill and Fisher, shaken but determined, were planning countermeasures. In a bold gamble, Fisher suggested to Churchill that three of the Grand Fleet's new battle cruisers be secretly dispatched from their war bases in northern Scotland to the South Atlantic.

The battle cruiser was a new type of supercruiser that had been introduced under Fisher's guidance at the same time as the dreadnought. It was as large and as heavily armed as a battleship, but was only lightly armored and could steam as fast as any cruiser. The British Grand Fleet had only a few more battleships and battle cruisers than the German High Seas Fleet a few hundred miles across the North Sea, and the British had just lost a brand-new battleship, the *Audacious*, to a mine the week before. The absence of three more capital ships would make the odds even thinner. Nevertheless Fisher and Churchill did not hesitate. The battle cruisers *Invincible* and *Inflexible* were ordered to the South Atlantic, while the even more modern *Princess Royal* was sent to protect British possessions in the West Indies.

The *Invincible* and *Inflexible* were the most powerful elements of a new South Atlantic force that was intended to hunt down von Spee and annihilate him. In addition to the two battle cruisers, it included the armored cruisers *Cornwall* and *Kent*, sisters to the ill-fated *Monmouth*, and the slightly larger

Carnarvon, plus the light cruiser *Bristol,* as well as the *Canopus* and the one Royal Navy survivor of Coronel, the *Glasgow.*

To command this armada, Churchill and Fisher selected Sturdee, who had performed less than brilliantly as chief of staff at the Admiralty during the preceding weeks. Fisher, who cordially detested Sturdee from the days when they had been on opposite sides in various Royal Navy feuds, made no secret of his determination to be rid of him. Sturdee just as firmly refused to leave—and he had the backing of the king, who had strongly pushed him as a candidate for First Sea Lord on Battenberg's departure.

However, Sturdee could not well refuse an independent command at sea, certainly not one likely to provide an early chance of action. So it was that the man whom many junior officers blamed in part for the foul-ups leading to Coronel was now given the chance to redeem himself for what Fisher called his "criminal ineptitude."

Three thousand miles away, in windswept, fogbound Stanley Harbor in the Falkland Islands, Captain Heathcoat Grant of the *Canopus* now found himself the principal defender of this most desolate and remote of British colonies. Ever since news of the defeat at Coronel had reached the islands, the inhabitants, a thousand-odd British and Scotch farmers and shepherds, had been in a state of gloom and apprehension. The gray, treeless town of Port Stanley, with its English cathedral, government house, and scattered cottages ringing the inner harbor, had been Cradock's last base before his departure for the Pacific. Many recalled a final church service conducted by the *Good Hope*'s chaplain, whose wife had just given birth to a girl. The chaplain and all his shipmates who had been present that day had gone down with the *Good Hope.*

The return of the *Canopus,* which had left port to meet the *Glasgow* after the battle, greatly cheered the Falklanders, for it seemed clear to all that after the defeat at Coronel the Falklands would be von Spee's next target. The Admiralty instructed Captain Grant:

> Moor the ship so that your guns command the entrance [to Stanley Harbor]. Extemporize mines outside the entrance. Be prepared for bombardment from outside the harbor; send down your topmasts. Stimulate the governor to organize all local forces and make determined defense. Arrange observation stations on shore. . . . No objection to your grounding ship to obtain a good berth.

Grant had already gone far toward carrying out these instructions. And the governor, Sir William Allerdyce, a tall, spare career civil servant of the old school, required no stimulation. The *Canopus's* Marine detachment under Captain R. M. Avery became the nucleus of an infantry reserve of about 200 Marines and local volunteer militia. The *Canopus* herself was grounded in the soft mud and camouflaged in a position where her big guns commanded the entrance to the harbor. The ship's light 12-pounders were sent ashore to act as coast-defense batteries. Telephones linked these batteries and the *Canopus* with observation points on high ground all around the harbor. Directed by spotters in these observation posts, the *Canopus's* gun crews daily practiced firing the ship's 12-inch guns at targets in the outer harbor and far out at sea.

This experiment with indirect fire control—what contemporary seamen called "blind" shooting—was to stand the British in good stead: Von Spee's squadron was indeed headed for the Falklands.

ON THE WEST COAST OF SOUTH AMERICA, VON SPEE RECEIVED A HERO'S WELCOME from the large German community in Valparaíso and was awarded 300 Iron Crosses to be presented to his officers and men. Yet the admiral was well aware that the victory had not improved his strategic situation. He was still thousands of miles from the safety of his German home port—and probably aware that more than thirty Allied warships were now hunting him.

Returning to the South Atlantic via Cape Horn, von Spee determined to raid the Falklands, destroy the wireless station and coal stockpiles, and capture the governor in retaliation for the British capture of the governor of German Samoa. Only a minority of von Spee's officers favored this course of action. The rest believed it held little advantage and considerable risks; far better, they argued, to raid the crowded trade routes off the River Plate on the east-central coast of South America, then break for home. But von Spee would not be dissuaded. The squadron would attack the Falklands.

WHILE VON SPEE'S FORCE WAS CLOSING IN ON THE FALKLANDS, STURDEE'S armada was steaming south along the east coast of South America, also bound for Port Stanley. Captain John Luce of the *Glasgow,* who had joined Sturdee's command, had repeatedly warned his admiral that von Spee would probably raid the Falklands and that time was of the essence. Sturdee believed von Spee to be still at large in the Pacific and expected to search for him for several weeks after reaching the Falklands. In the end, however, Captain Luce finally succeeded in persuading Sturdee to make for the Falklands at top speed and to keep his position secret by observing radio silence.

Sturdee had not taken such measures on his voyage out from England to his rendezvous with the *Carnarvon, Cornwall,* and *Kent* at the Abrolhos, a lonely island group off Brazil. As a result, German agents and wireless operators had picked up ample information about the presence of the *Invincible* and *Inflexible* in the Atlantic. Incredibly, none of this vital intelligence had gotten through to von Spee, who steamed on toward the Falklands expecting to meet nothing more formidable than a couple of British cruisers.

In Port Stanley, lookouts on watch in Captain Grant's observation towers early on the morning of December 7 excitedly reported the smoke of many ships on the horizon. While the *Canopus* crew rushed to their action stations and Captain Avery's Marines and militia took position near the twelve-pounders ashore, the lookouts continued to report. A total of eight ships were now in sight, all of them men-of-war. On the bridge of the *Canopus,* Captain Grant and one of his officers exchanged a brief, bleak glance: eight to one! Then came better news: The ships were British—two of the eight were battle cruisers, and one of the others appeared to be the *Glasgow.* Sturdee had beaten the Germans to Port Stanley.

The British admiral, still convinced he would be hunting von Spee for many days, gave his crew shore leave and ordered his ships to begin coaling immediately. Governor Allerdyce had ordered the island's pubs closed—perhaps as a "war measure," or perhaps because the *Good Hope'*s crew had busted up a few bars on their last visit. Still, Sturdee's men were happy to get ashore after their long voyage south. Midshipman E. A. Woodland of the *Invincible* climbed one of the hills surrounding the harbor and was invited to tea in a watchtower.

"The volunteers," Woodland observed, "are mostly shepherds. They are all mounted on small ponies with sheepskins on their saddles and look rather like Boers. The ponies are small but very strong."

The next morning, December 8, dawned clear and bright, rare weather for the Falklands. It was late spring in the South Atlantic. The *Glasgow* and the armored cruiser *Carnarvon* had completed their coaling and the two battle cruisers had begun taking on coal soon after midnight. The *Kent, Cornwall,* and *Bristol* still awaited their turn to fuel from the available colliers. At seven-thirty an island volunteer in one of the lookout towers spotted two columns of smoke on the southwestern horizon. It was the *Gneisenau* and the *Nürnberg,* to whom von Spee had assigned the task of raiding Port Stanley, covered by the remainder of his squadron.

The *Gneisenau* and the *Nürnberg* had sighted Port Stanley much earlier but were unable to see more than smudges of smoke from the harbor. Around nine o'clock, with the two German ships less than ten miles from Port Stanley, a lookout high up in the *Gneisenau*'s foretop reported that there were warships in the harbor. As the range closed, Lieutenant Hans Busch in the fire-control station thought he could make out the tripod masts of battleships or battle cruisers. Captain Maerker of the *Gneisenau* signaled the news to von Spee and continued to close in on the harbor.

Admiral Sturdee was just completing his morning shave when he received the news that von Spee's ships were in sight. From a tactical point of view, the Germans could not have come at a worse time. Only two of Sturdee's ships—the *Kent* and the armed liner *Macedonia*—were ready to get under way, and the *Macedonia* was of little use in a stand-up fight. The battle cruisers, the *Carnarvon,* and the *Glasgow,* whose engines had been shut down for minor repairs, would need at least an hour to get under way, and the other ships somewhat longer. In the meantime the German ships could close in on the harbor and rake the anchored ships at leisure.

"I had a distinct fellow feeling with 'the young man at Cape Horn who wished that he'd never been born,' " wrote the *Inflexible*'s gunnery officer, Commander Rudolph Verner, in a letter, "and judging by the cheeriness of everyone else he must have been in other people's minds as well as my own."

Unruffled, Sturdee ordered all ships to raise steam for full speed and the *Canopus* to open fire as soon as the Germans were in range. He then went down to breakfast. If, as chief of staff at the Admiralty, Sturdee could not be hurried, now he could not be panicked either, and his calm confidence was contagious.

That the British escaped disaster, however, was due far more to the much-despised reservists on board the *Canopus* than to Sturdee's sangfroid. For at nine-twenty in the morning, as the German ships were about to open fire on the Falklands' wireless station, the *Canopus*'s forward 12-inch turret fired its first shots in anger.

The *Canopus*'s gun crews were no longer the raw recruits of a few weeks before. They had trained rigorously for this moment. All of the sea area within range was divided into target squares, and observers in the shore towers were trained to spot the fall of a shot and report by telephone. The *Canopus*'s gunnery had achieved a precision that fire controllers in World War II and Korea might have envied. This very day, in fact, she had been scheduled to demonstrate her prowess to Admiral Sturdee, and the eager crew of one of her 12-inch turrets had crept out the night before to load with practice shells.

Even fired at maximum elevation, the *Canopus*'s first two shells fell a little short of the *Gneisenau* at 11,500 yards (six and one-half miles). The next two shells—the practice ones—were also short, but instead of bursting on impact as live shells would have, they ricocheted across the water and scored a hit on the *Gneisenau*'s afterfunnel. Shaken but undeterred, Captain Maerker was continuing his course toward the wireless station when he received a message from von Spee: "Do not accept action. Concentrate on course east by north and proceed at full speed."

"The difference between a successful leader and an unsuccessful one," Admiral Arleigh Burke, a brilliant naval commander of World War II, once observed, "is about ten seconds." In the ten seconds von Spee had taken to issue that order, he had lost the battle. A correct decision would have been to attack Port Stanley with his entire squadron while the British were unready and trapped inside.

Yet von Spee also suffered from another common disadvantage of commanders—incomplete information. He knew, from Maerker's reports and the fact of the 12-inch-shell hit, that there were some sort of capital ships at Port Stanley, but he had little reason to think they were battle cruisers. Since his cruisers could outrun any ordinary capital ships, such as the *Canopus* or the Japanese ships hunting him in the Pacific, the prudent course seemed to be immediate retirement. The *Gneisenau* and *Nürnberg* caught up with von Spee's other ships by ten-thirty and now were headed southeast at over twenty knots.

At last the British squadron began to leave harbor: first the *Kent*, which had been waiting beyond the entrance for some time; then the *Glasgow*; then the *Carnarvon, Cornwall, Invincible*, and *Inflexible*; and finally the *Bristol* and the *Macedonia*. The last two ships headed south to deal with von Spee's colliers, which had just been spotted thirty miles from Port Stanley near a creek called Point Pleasant. The other ships headed southeast in pursuit of the German squadron.

"When we got clear we saw the enemy hull down and belching thick, black smoke from every funnel," recalled Lieutenant Commander James Giffard of the *Inflexible*. The *Glasgow*'s paymaster wrote:

> No more glorious moment do I remember in the war than when the flagship hoisted the signal for general chase. The sun was shining gloriously from a cloudless sky, a light cold breeze from the northwest scarcely ruffled the sea . . . astern the grey-green low-lying islands of our base and between us and them a straggly line of cruisers' white bow waves showing their haste and the clouds of smoke the urgency of their errand.

At eleven-thirty Sturdee reduced speed to allow his armored cruisers to catch up to the battle cruisers, and all hands were piped to lunch. On the *Invincible*, sailors wolfed down sandwiches of tongue, peanut butter, and jam before returning to their action stations. Around one in the afternoon they cheered as the *Invincible* and *Inflexible* opened fire with their forward 12-inch guns at the

German ships more than 15,500 yards (nine miles) away. In the battle cruisers' engine spaces, oil was sprayed onto the coal in the furnaces to gain maximum power as the *Inflexible* and *Invincible* worked up to twenty-six knots. Von Spee's big ships could not do much better than twenty knots; thus after about twenty minutes, heavy shells began falling near his rearmost ship, the *Leipzig*.

Realizing that the only hope for his speedier light cruisers now was to delay the British pursuers long enough to allow them to flee, von Spee signaled the *Dresden, Leipzig,* and *Nürnberg* to "leave the line and try to escape." At the same time, he swung his two big ships around to the east to engage the *Invincible* and *Inflexible*. At that moment the armored cruisers *Cornwall* and *Kent*, well coached by Sturdee on what action to take in this contingency, immediately turned away, together with the *Glasgow*, in pursuit of the fleeing German light cruisers.

The *Scharnhorst* and the *Gneisenau* now opened fire at the British battle cruisers at a range of almost 14,000 yards (eight miles). "The range was so long you could hear the shells before they got to us," recalled Lieutenant Commander Giffard of the *Inflexible*. "First a shrill whine which got deeper and then 'pop pop pop' as they burst in the water." The German shelling was accurate from the beginning, and some hits were scored, but the battle cruisers' armor protected them against any serious injury.

The British fire, on the other hand, was ragged—a foretaste of the problems British capital ships would have with long-range gunnery at the Dogger Bank and Jutland. In addition, the prevailing wind continued to blow thick clouds of brown smoke back at the British ships, making spotting all but impossible. After about twenty minutes, Sturdee turned sharply away to the south. "During the lull, the upper deck was covered with men hunting for splinters as mementos," recalled Lieutenant Commander Giffard.

When the British battle cruisers came within range again, von Spee turned sharply across the bows of the British ships in an attempt to "cross the T." At this closer range the German fire was again very accurate. One 8.2-inch shell from the *Scharnhorst* hit a 4-inch gun on the *Invincible*, "cut it in two, passed downward through the conning tower, the upper and main deck and the admiral's stateroom and lay there unexploded." Most of the German hits broke up against the stout armor of the battle cruisers, while the heavy British 12-inch shells tore through the lightly protected German cruisers, smashing men and machinery to bits and starting fires raging in all parts of the ships.

"Death was very busy aboard and it was merely a question of whom he would take first," recalled Commander Hans Pochhammer, executive officer of the *Gneisenau*.

A shell fell in the galley deck, shattering the men's galley. . . . The tin walls of the galley had been hurled in all directions, the huge cooking vessels had been smashed, the men—reserves and stretcher-bearers—killed and mutilated, hurled by the air pressure and crushed, their clothing split at the seams or bodily torn off. . . . Another shell, which penetrated the aft dressing station and released the wounded there from their suffering, killed the senior staff surgeon and the squadron chaplain.

At around four o'clock the *Scharnhorst*, with her flag still flying, listed heavily to port and disappeared beneath the waves. The *Gneisenau* managed to keep up the fight for two more hours. Then, a little before six, with all ammunition expended and power lost in all boilers, her captain gave orders to scuttle the ship. "Through gaping holes in the deck and sides, men were clambering out of the ship, black from the bunkers and stove holes, all calm and orderly as if for roll call," recalled Pochhammer.

Officers were standing in the battered boats handing out wooden fittings and buoys. . . . Then the captain, who had preserved his wonted calm to the last, ordered three cheers for HM the emperor and our good gallant *Gneisenau* and proceeded to sink the ship. Our crew, who had really given their utmost in endurance and courage, complied with enthusiasm and the strains of "Deutschland Über Alles" echoed throughout the ship followed by the hymn of the black, white and red flag which was flying riddled with shot at the main masthead.

Lieutenant Hans Busch, the *Gneisenau*'s gunnery officer, found himself in the water shortly after the ship capsized.

Men clinging to objects around me were singing the song of the flag and other patriotic songs. One man gave three cheers for the sunken ships and the cheers were repeatedly taken up by others. . . . The temperature of the water was only thirty-nine degrees and during half an hour's immersion many of my companions perished.

The *Scharnhorst* went down with all hands, including von Spee, but about two hundred men were rescued from the *Gneisenau*. Commander Pochhammer, the senior surviving officer, was housed in the admiral's vacant cabin aboard the *Inflexible*. That evening, wrapped in an old traveling rug, he was entertained at dinner by the officers of the *Inflexible*.

While the *Scharnhorst* and *Gneisenau* had been exchanging final salvos with the British battle cruisers, the *Kent, Glasgow,* and *Cornwall* were still in pursuit of the *Leipzig, Nürnberg,* and *Dresden.* The *Glasgow* was faster than any of the three German ships, but the two British armored cruisers were slower than any of their opponents. For this reason Captain Luce of the *Glasgow* made the controversial decision, still debated in British naval circles, to fight a delaying action with the *Leipzig* until the slower *Cornwall* caught up. This he did very skillfully, and by five o'clock the *Cornwall* had closed up and was pouring her full broadside of nine 6-inch guns into the *Leipzig.* The delay, however, let the faster *Dresden,* aided by deteriorating weather conditions, make good her escape.

Like the *Scharnhorst* and *Gneisenau,* the *Leipzig* did not surrender but exhausted all of her ammunition in an unequal gun battle with the *Cornwall* and *Glasgow.* At eight-thirty Captain Luce observed through the mist and rain the *Leipzig* heeling over to port and sinking by the bow with her flag still flying and her captain still aboard. Only twenty survivors were picked up by the *Cornwall.*

Meanwhile, the armored cruiser *Kent* was left to pursue the faster *Nürnberg.* In the *Kent's* engine room, firemen and stokers coaxed and battered the ship's old reciprocating engines into action. All available wood—such as accommodation ladders, hen coops, and wooden lockers—was broken up and passed down into the stokeholds to be used in the furnaces. The ship's engines were designed for 22,000 horsepower, but they developed 27,000 that day, and the old ship's speed rose to almost twenty-five knots. Nevertheless, the *Nürnberg* might have escaped into the thickening mist and rain had not two of her boilers suddenly burst.

Her speed dropping to under sixteen knots, the *Nürnberg* turned to face her enemy. "Her salvos went off very quickly and she was hitting us all over," wrote Lieutenant James Marshall, one of the *Kent's* officers. But the *Nürnberg's* small, 4.1-inch shells did little damage against the *Kent's* armor, while the *Kent's* 6-inch lyddite shells did enormous damage to the *Nürnberg.* Around seven-thirty the *Nürnberg* heeled to starboard and slowly sank. "She was a horrible sight," observed Lieutenant Marshall, "with large holes in her sides through which flames were pouring."

The *Kent's* boats had all been badly damaged by shell fragments and splinters, but Captain J. D. Allan ordered the least damaged patched up and lowered to look for survivors. James Marshall in the *Kent's* badly leaking cutter managed to rescue nine men before having to return to the ship. Altogether, twelve men were picked up, but only seven survived. Among those who perished was von Spee's son, Otto.

Historians often refer to the Falklands as "the only decisive naval battle of World War I." Admiral Sturdee's complete destruction of the German overseas squadron (the *Dresden* was sunk three months later) gave the Allies an immense moral and psychological boost—and helped Sturdee's career as well. (He was promoted and made commander of the Fourth Battle Squadron.) The strategic consequences were equally important. As Churchill observed,

> The strain was everywhere relaxed. All our enterprises, whether of war or commerce, proceeded without the slightest hindrance. Within twenty-four hours orders were sent to a score of British ships to return to home waters. For the first time we saw ourselves possessed of immense surpluses of ships of certain classes, of trained men, and of naval supplies of all kinds.

Like the second battle of the Falklands almost seventy years later, the first had begun in muddle and humiliation, been retrieved by prompt and brilliant improvisation, and ended in sweeping military success. Yet if Sturdee's victory was decisive, it was only in contrast to the frustrating and indeterminate actions of other World War I campaigns: the stalemate on the Western Front, the bungling of Gallipoli, the lost opportunities at Jutland. Like the Falklands/ Malvinas War of the 1980s, which left the Argentines defeated but the Falkland Islands' fate still in question, the First Battle of the Falklands failed to resolve the basic strategic issues of World War I. Britain's sea power was, for all Churchill's phrases, only marginally strengthened, Germany's even more marginally weakened, the land campaigns virtually unaffected.

Yet the battle lives on in the imagination, perhaps less because of its historical than its symbolic importance. It was, in the words of Admiral Sturdee's son, "the last battle to be fought out in the old style, against a worthy foe whose force displayed splendid courage, determination, and efficiency, between ships by gunfire alone, unaided by aircraft, in waters entirely free from minefields and submarines."

Like so many of their friends and relatives who were at that moment fighting in Flanders and France, most of the men who fought at Coronel and the Falklands were destined never to return. The *Good Hope, Monmouth, Scharnhorst, Gneisenau, Nürnberg,* and *Leipzig* were sunk with no survivors or only a tiny handful. The *Inflexible* was damaged four months later in the attack on the Dardanelles and lost over thirty men, including her gunnery officer, Commander Verner. The *Invincible* was sunk at the Battle of Jutland in May 1916, and only five of her more than 1,000-man crew survived.

Like the millions who died on the Western Front, the German and British sailors represented the end of an era, the end of a time in which war was viewed as the ultimate sport and one's opponent the ultimate sportsman. ("Tell my people I played the game" were reportedly Commander Verner's dying words at the Dardanelles.)

The courage and determination that led British and German sailors to spurn surrender and fight to the last continues to excite admiration. But in retrospect the more unusual aspect of these battles is that surrender was still an option. By the conclusion of World War I, the British sailors who had chivalrously entertained von Spee's surviving officers in their wardrooms were denouncing the Germans as war criminals for their conduct of the V-boat campaign. By World War II, survivors of sunken ships were frequently machine-gunned in the water. The idea of war at sea as somehow a clean and honorable activity died with Cradock and von Spee's sailors at Coronel and the Falklands.

THE WRECK OF THE
MAGDEBURG
David Kahn

———

REAT BRITAIN OFFICIALLY WENT TO WAR WITH THE
Central Powers at midnight on August 4, 1914. Even
before the sun was up the next morning, the cable ship *Telco-
nia* was fishing up with grappling irons and cutting German
transatlantic cables. Soon Germany's only contact with the
outside world would be through a powerful wireless station located near Berlin. This meant that anyone could pluck messages from the air. That was the easy part; breaking the
German codes was a problem far more formidable. From the
outbreak of the war, cryptographers had been at work in
quarters at the Admiralty Old Building in London, called simply: Room 40, OB. So far, they had been unable to read the pil-
fered messages. They badly needed a bit of luck. Soon enough
the Great War version of Bletchley Park would be handed one.

The running aground of the German light cruiser *Magdeburg* in the Gulf of Finland seemed a decidedly minor event,
coming on a day (August 26) when the Battle of Tannenberg
began in East Prussia and British Regulars managed to hold
off a superior German force, and slip away, at Le Cateau in
northern France. After the order came to abandon ship, the
Magdeburg's secret documents were carefully removed—all
except one codebook, which a Russian boarding party discovered. David Kahn, the world's foremost authority on the history of codes and codebreaking, relates the story of that

codebook, which the Russians would present to the British. It gave the cryptographers of Room 40 the opening they needed. They could now read German naval messages—and eventually this first key would help to unlock other cryptographic doors. (The Germans had compromised British naval codes, but in a less dramatic fashion.) Still, as Kahn points out, the British could never quite trust their luck. Time and again, good intelligence would be misused or disregarded, especially in the biggest naval battle of all, Jutland. But there was one exception, the intercepted Zimmermann telegram, and it would play a major role in bringing the war to an end.

———

DAVID KAHN is the author of *The Codebreakers* and *Seizing the Enigma: The Race to Break the German U-Boat Codes, 1939–1943.*

O N THE AFTERNOON OF AUGUST 24, 1914, THE GERMAN WARSHIP *MAGDEBURG* steamed out of the East Prussian harbor of Memel toward the most fateful accident in the history of cryptography.

A four-stacker, the *Magdeburg* was what the Germans called a small cruiser, different from the larger light cruisers. She was new (three years old), well armed (twelve fast-firing, 4-inch guns), fast (27.6 knots)—and unlucky. Her acceptance test had not gone well. Her commissioning had been delayed several months. She had never participated, as was intended, in the autumn 1912 naval maneuvers. Some equipment was still not in order when she was declared "ready for war" and when the ancient city of Magdeburg, for which she was named, sponsored her in two days of festivities. One of her turbines gave trouble. And unlike her sister ships, which got assignments suitable for cruisers, the *Magdeburg* merely fired test torpedoes.

The *Magdeburg* was part of Germany's Baltic fleet. When war with Russia, France, and England broke out in August 1914, she dropped her test assignment and undertook more typical cruiser tasks. These were directed against the Russians, whose empire included Finland, Estonia, Latvia, and Lithuania—the countries bordering the eastern Baltic. In her first operation, the *Magdeburg* and another small cruiser, the *Augsburg*, arrived off Liepaja, Latvia's naval port, to lay mines. They gained an unexpected success: The Russians, thinking the appearance of the two ships portended a major fleet operation, blew up their own ammunition and coal dumps and scuttled ships in the harbor entrances. In the two ships' second and third operations, they shot up some lighthouses and a signal station and laid a minefield not far from the mouth of the eastern arm of the Baltic Sea, the Gulf of Finland, at whose farther end lay the Russian capital, St. Petersburg.

A few days later, on August 23, the commander of a new flotilla ordered his vessels, which included the two cruisers, to assemble for an operation. The *Magdeburg*, in Danzig, then a German port, went first to Memel, at the extreme east of Prussia, for some gunnery exercises to reassure the population, nervous because the Russian border was not far from the city limits. The next afternoon the warship set out for the rendezvous. She joined the *Augsburg*, three torpedo boats, a submarine, and three other warships early on the twenty-fifth off Hoburgen lighthouse on the southern tip of the Swedish island of Gotland.

There, the officers were told of the plan: The ships were to slip by night behind a Russian minefield believed to protect the entrance of the Gulf of Finland, and attack whatever Russian ships they found.

At eight-thirty in the morning that same day, the flotilla set out, moving to the northeast at the fairly high speed of twenty knots. The sailors aboard the *Magdeburg,* who suspected the presence of enemy armored cruisers, thought the assignment would prove to be just a suicide mission.

By five o'clock, in a calm sea, the air misty, the navigational plots of the *Magdeburg* and the *Augsburg* differed by a mile. But this raised no concern, since the *Magdeburg* was to follow the flagship *Augsburg* by half a mile: If the *Augsburg* struck a mine, the *Magdeburg* had time to avoid hitting any herself.

Soon, however, fog—common in those waters in summer—rolled in. By nine o'clock it was so thick that even with binoculars an officer on the bridge of the *Magdeburg* could not see the lookout on the stern. At eleven the *Augsburg,* intending to run along the supposed Russian minefield before swinging east to enter the Gulf of Finland, turned onto a course south-southeast one-half point east (151 degrees, 32 minutes, 30 seconds) and ordered the *Magdeburg* to do the same. She did so, maintaining the same 230 engine revolutions per minute, or about fifteen knots, that had kept her at the proper distance from the *Augsburg* during the afternoon. But she was a mile farther south than her plot showed her to be.

Her captain, Lieutenant Commander Richard Habenicht, had soundings taken. These showed the depth decreasing: 190 feet, 141 feet, and, at twelve-thirty, now August 26, 112 feet. At the same time the radio shack reported that a message from the *Augsburg* was coming in; four minutes later it was decoded and on the bridge. It ordered that her course be altered to east-northeast one-half point east (73 degrees, 7 minutes, 30 seconds). The helmsman turned the rudder twenty degrees, and at twelve thirty-seven, just as he reported that the new course was being steered, still at fifteen knots, the luckless vessel hit something. She bumped five or six times and, shuddering, stopped. The cruiser had run aground. As a consequence of her earlier navigational error, she had struck shallows 400 yards off the northwestern tip of Odensholm, a low, narrow island two and one-half miles long at the entrance to the Gulf of Finland.

At once, Habenicht sought to get his ship off. He reversed engines. The ship stayed stuck. He rocked her with various engine speeds. He assembled the entire 337-man crew on the quarterdeck to push the *Magdeburg*'s stern down and her bow up and then went full speed astern. He had the crew carry munitions aft. The ship didn't budge. Soundings showed that at the bow, where the *Magdeburg* normally drew sixteen and one-half feet, the water to starboard was only nine feet deep; at the stern, with normal draft just under twenty feet, the depth was thirteen feet. The vessel needed to rise seven feet.

Habenicht jettisoned the anchors and their chains. He had the drinking and washing water pumped out. Ash ejectors flung coal into the sea. All but sixty boxes of munitions were dumped over the side. All movable steel parts— the mine-laying rails, bulkhead doors, doors on the forward turrets, steel cables, coaling equipment—were pushed overboard. Habenicht then ran the engines forward and backward at various speeds. The *Magdeburg* moved not an inch.

The Germans' efforts were spurred by the likelihood that the officials on Odensholm, which was Russian territory with a lighthouse and a signal station, had alerted superiors at the major Russian port of Tallinn, only fifty miles away. Habenicht worried that the cruiser's secret documents might fall into Russian hands. In addition to the charts of German minefields and the ship's war diary, these included the main Imperial German Navy code and the key used to encipher its code words and thus to provide another layer of secrecy.

Lieutenant Walther Bender, who as first radio officer was in charge of destroying these documents, brought one of the codebooks and its cipher key from the steering room to the stokehold and burned it. Sailors did the same for other secret documents. But two codebooks—one on the bridge and one in the radio shack—as well as a cipher key were retained for possible use in communicating with rescuers and higher commands. A fourth lay hidden and apparently forgotten in a locker in Habenicht's cabin.

As dawn approached, the seabed and the stones on which the ship was lying became visible. At eight-thirty, with the fog lifting, the fast and powerful torpedo boat *V-26* appeared, attached a line, and tried to pull the *Magdeburg* off. She failed. Habenicht decided he might as well do some damage and fired about 120 shots at the lighthouse, chipping it, and at the signal station, setting it ablaze. By then the radio shack was picking up many signals from Russian ships; apparently they were on their way. Since all attempts to free the *Magdeburg* had failed, Habenicht regretfully concluded he had to blow her up rather than let her fall into enemy hands.

Charges were set fore and aft. The crew was to get off the ship and onto the *V-26*, which was to come alongside. But suddenly a shout rang through the ship: "The fuses are lit!" Habenicht had not ordered this; it had been done by mistake. The vessel would blow up in only four and a half minutes.

In the midst of the tumult that ensued, Bender directed the second radio officer, Lieutenant Olff, to have the codebook and cipher key from the radio shack taken off the ship and onto the *V-26*. On Olff's instructions, Radioman Second Class Neuhaus grabbed the codebook and Radioman Third Class

Kiehnert the cipher-key papers. The bridge's codebook was in the hands of Radioman Second Class Szillat. The first officer, unable to find Habenicht as the seconds ticked away, ordered the crew to the afterdeck, where the *V-26* was to pick them up. He called for three cheers for the kaiser, had the two ships' boats lowered, and commanded, "All hands abandon ship!"

Upon hearing this, Szillat flung the codebook he was carrying over the side, toward the stern. It splashed into what he said was a "dark" place about fifteen feet from the ship and immediately sank. Then he leaped overboard. Kiehnert, too, jumped into the water, holding the radio shack's cipher key. He was struck by men following him, and when he came to the surface, he noticed that he had lost the key.

At ten minutes past nine the forward charge detonated. It split the vessel in half, tore open the forepart from near the bow to the second smokestack, and hurled huge pieces of steel into the air. They rained down upon scores of men who were trying to swim to the *V-26*. Neuhaus, carrying the radio shack's code, had been seen in the water before the explosion but was missing for a while later; no one knew what had happened to the codebook.

The *V-26* picked up many of the swimming men, including Szillat and Kiehnert. Fear of being destroyed in the explosion of the *Magdeburg*'s aftercharge—which never fired—kept the torpedo boat from coming near enough to rescue the men still aboard. Meanwhile Russian ships, closing, began to fire at the speedy vessel. One shell swept eight men overboard; another smashed into her starboard side, destroying the officers' wardroom and killing all who were in it, mainly wounded men from the *Magdeburg*. But the *V-26* got away.

Habenicht, who had appeared briefly on the bridge when he heard the cheers for the kaiser and then vanished again into the bowels of his cruiser, did not abandon ship but awaited his fate on it, together with a few others. Bender and a few dozen sailors, among them Neuhaus, swam to Odensholm, where they were taken prisoner. One of the Russian ships, the torpedo boat *Lejtenant Burakov*, sent a boat with armed men, led by her first officer, Lieutenant Galibin, to the *Magdeburg*. The crew members still on board offered no resistance and were taken prisoner. Habenicht, whom Galibin thought "a true gentleman," offered the Russian his dagger, which Galibin chivalrously declined. The Germans were rowed from both the ship and the island to one of the Russian cruisers and later sent to a prisoner-of-war camp in Siberia.

Galibin lowered the black-white-and-red German naval war flag and raised the white czarist flag with its light blue cross of diagonals. Then, revolver in hand, he searched the wreck of the *Magdeburg*. He found a locker in Habenicht's cabin and broke it open. Hidden deep within it was the German codebook, forgotten in the excitement of the catastrophe. Galibin removed it, together with other documents, and had it transferred to the *Lejtenant Burakov*. The Allies thus came into possession of the key cryptographic secret of the Imperial German Navy—the one that gave them access to many others.

Knowing that possession of the German code and its key would be enormously helpful to Britain's Royal Navy, the Russians loyally notified their allies of the find and said they would give them the documents if the British would send a small warship to escort the officers accompanying the documents to Britain. The Russians courteously set aside for the British the original code, which bore serial number 151, making a copy of it for themselves.

The task of bringing Codebook 151 to England was assigned to two naval captains, Kedrov and Smirnow, and to another naval officer, Count Constantine Benckendorff. A cosmopolitan, mustachioed combat veteran of the Russo-Japanese War, Benckendorff was the son of the ambassador to Great Britain and had served a year as a cipher clerk in the London Embassy. He was on watch on the battleship *Poltava* in the Tallinn roadstead, pacing the quarterdeck and listening to the sailors' choir chanting the Russian Orthodox mass on a Sunday morning in September, when a yeoman handed him an order to report to the flag captain. On the flagship, he was "amazed and delighted" to be told he would be going to London.

He was given the precious codebook in St. Petersburg. It was in a satchel with a large piece of lead sewn in to make it sink in case he had to throw it overboard. He took the satchel to Archangel, where he boarded a Russian volunteer fleet steamer. The vessel was to meet the British escort, the aging cruiser HMS *Theseus*, at Aleksandrovsk (now Polyarny), a port near Murmansk, whence it had arrived early in September from Scapa Flow, the deep, circular, islands-sheltered bay in the Orkneys just north of Scotland.

Owing to the time needed for copying the codebook and to bureaucratic delays and misunderstandings, the *Theseus* and the steamer did not sail until September 30. After an uneventful crossing over the top of Norway, punctuated only by a few vague V-boat alarms, the *Theseus* arrived in Scapa Flow on October 10; the Russian steamer, with Benckendorff aboard, went on alone to Hull, arriving there a couple of days later.

After a slow night-train ride, Benckendorff reached the Russian Embassy at dawn. He greeted his parents, then routed out the naval attaché, and the two went, early on the morning of October 13, to the Admiralty. There, in a moment heavy with history, they handed Winston Churchill, the First Lord of the Admiralty, a gift more precious than a dozen jewel-encrusted Fabergé eggs: the big, fat, blue-bound *Signalbuch der Kaiserlichen Marine*.

It went at once to the fledgling group of codebreakers set up at the outbreak of war by the director of naval education, Sir Alfred Ewing, an engineer who had long been interested in ciphers. A short, thickset Scot, given to wearing mauve shirts with white wing collars, he was a good friend of the director of naval intelligence, who had asked him to see what he could do with the encoded German radio messages being intercepted by British stations. Ewing had gathered some instructors in German from the Royal Naval Colleges, sat them around a desk in his cramped office, and, with them, examined the intercepts. But though they classified the messages into different kinds based on their appearance and addressees, they had not been able to read any of them.

Now, two months later, the German naval codebook landed on their desk. It contained hundreds of pages of columns of five-digit groups and three-letter groups standing opposite the German words they were to replace. For example, *63940* or *ÖAX* were the secret substitutes for *Oktober.* The encoder looked up each word of his message in the codebook as in a dictionary and replaced it with the five-digit code number or—more usually—the three-letter code word next to it. The succession of these code numbers or code words formed the secret message, or cryptogram. But British attempts to decipher the intercepts by this simple method still did not work. Some code words could not be found in the codebook, and those that could produced gibberish.

Gradually the British discovered that the *letters* of the code words had also been disguised. Other letters replaced them, so that the codebook's *ÖAX* might become the transmitted *JVM.* By early November the British had worked out the letter substitutes and were able to read many German naval messages.

Among the first were some that dealt with a possible ambush. The German naval commander, encouraged by the success of a bombardment and minelaying off the British port of Yarmouth, which some Britons feared presaged an invasion, decided to repeat the action with two ports in northern England, Scarborough and Hartlepool. He hoped to lure some British battle cruisers into the arms of his full High Seas Fleet, destroy them, and thus regain at least near-parity with British naval forces. On December 14, 1914, his scoutingforce commander, Vice Admiral Franz von Hipper, wirelessed a request for extensive aerial reconnaissance to the north, northwest, and west on the next two days. He added that German forces would sail from their roundish harbor in the estuary of the Jade River at Wilhelmshaven at three-thirty in the morning.

The British intercepted and deciphered the message. It went to retired admiral Sir Arthur Wilson, a former First Sea Lord (equivalent to a U.S. chief of naval operations) who had returned as Churchill's adviser on intelligence and other matters. At seven o'clock on the fourteenth, he brought it to Churchill, who summoned the First Sea Lord and the chief of staff. What did it mean? It specified no objective, but Wilson said that it probably indicated a movement of the German battle cruisers against English coasts and that the High Seas Fleet as a whole seemed not to be involved. The others agreed with his conclusions, though they acknowledged that hypotheses were needed to bridge the gaps in the evidence.

Within hours the Admiralty ordered units of the British fleet to proceed at once to a "point where they can intercept the enemy on his return." But thinking the German battleships were staying in port, the Admiralty refused to let more than a single squadron of British battleships sail from their home base of Scapa Flow. The commander of the British Grand Fleet, Admiral Sir John Jellicoe, chose the perfect intercept point: on an almost direct line between Scarborough and the German island fortress of Heligoland off Wilhelmshaven.

The Germans sailed at three in the morning on December 15, the British soon thereafter. By the morning of the sixteenth, the Germans were bombarding Hartlepool and Scarborough. Churchill, notified in his bath at eight-thirty, hopped out, put his clothes on over a damp body, and hurried downstairs to the War Room. The admirals assembled there were confident of their dispositions, but they knew that weather in the wintry North Sea could shut down visibility, and thus the possibility of contact, within minutes. What they did not know was that, despite their assumptions, the whole High Seas Fleet had sailed. If it met with the reduced force of British ships, it could destroy the British squadrons and regain the equivalence in forces that could change the course of the naval war.

Indeed, in the predawn blackness of December 16, one of the German destroyers ran into the British advance screen. The contact created the very situation that the Germans had sought since the start of the war. But the German commander did not recognize it. Believing himself to be confronted by the whole of Britain's Grand Fleet, and mindful of the kaiser's fears about losing the navy, he turned for home. He thus lost the greatest opportunity the German navy was ever to have.

Meanwhile, Hipper's forces were likewise racing for home after the bombardment. British intelligence had placed their ships so precisely in Hipper's path that at ten-thirty the light cruiser *Southampton* spotted them. But fog and rain were reducing visibility, and before either the *Southampton* or the heavier British forces could attack, Hipper's ships escaped behind the veils of mist, reaching home safely.

The British were angry and disappointed. Not only had the navy failed to defend Britain's coast, it had failed to sink any Germans. Their anger was compounded by frustration. Churchill later said that he had

> to bear in silence the censures of our countrymen. We could never
> admit for fear of compromising our secret information where our

squadrons were, or how near the German raiding cruisers had been to their destruction. One comfort we had, the indications upon which we had acted had been confirmed by events.

Similar indications came the next month. Wilson strode into Churchill's office around noon on January 23, 1915, and said, "First Lord, those fellows are coming out again."

"When?"

"Tonight. We have just time to get Beatty there," he said, referring to Vice Admiral Sir David Beatty, commander of the battle cruisers. Wilson explained that the codebreakers had read a message sent at ten twenty-five that morning to Hipper, ordering a reconnaissance of the Dogger Bank, a sandy shallows in the North Sea about sixty miles east of Britain.

Britain elected to use the same tactics as before, and units under Beatty sailed to block the German homeward trip. This time they were luckier. Contact was made at seven-thirty on the morning of January 24 at a point on the Dogger Bank. When Hipper saw the numerous English forces, he followed directives, collected his ships, and ran. The British, in their faster, superdreadnought-class battleships, gave chase. By nine o'clock, the *Lion,* carrying Beatty, opened fire at 20,000 yards (eleven miles). The action soon became general between the four British and four German capital ships. The *Blücher* was sunk and the *Seydlitz* and *Derfflinger* heavily damaged. Confusion in the British squadron after a shell crippled the flagship permitted the German ships to escape. Nevertheless, the Germans staggered into port, flames leaping above their funnels, their decks encumbered with wreckage and crowded with the wounded and the dead. The German ships did not stir out of port again for more than a year.

The codebreakers had by this time expanded slightly and taken up the quarters in the Admiralty Old Building that soon gave them their unofficial name: Room 40, OB. The Battle of the Dogger Bank earned them the confidence of the Admiralty, and shortly afterward the terrifying Lord John "Jacky" Fisher, the builder of the dreadnought fleet who had just returned as First Sea Lord, gave Ewing carte blanche to get whatever he needed for the betterment of his work. Ewing augmented his staff, added to his intercept and radio direction-finding stations, and improved their equipment.

But some of Room 40's effectiveness was lost due to excessively tight control by the director of the operations division, Captain Thomas Jackson. Boorish and self-opinionated, Jackson distrusted civilians' ability to deal with naval affairs and was unpleasant to them. He hardly visited Room 40 at all, and on one of those occasions came only to complain that he had cut his hand on one of the red boxes in which the intercepts were circulated. Another time, when a change of cipher key temporarily interrupted the flow of solutions, he called to express his relief that he would not be further bothered by such nonsense. This attitude was to have grave effects.

In the late spring of 1916, the new commander of the German High Seas Fleet, Vice Admiral Reinhard Scheer, was chafing at his inactivity. He decided to try to repeat, with a variation, some of the tactics that sought to bring parity between his fleet and his enemy's. He would attempt to entice the British Grand Fleet to where his submarines could attack it and his High Seas Fleet fall upon a section of it without risking a general engagement.

His orders, however, lay at the mercy of British radio intelligence. Cryptanalysis was part of this; another was radio direction-finding. In this, radio stations take bearings on the emissions of a transmitter from two or more points; a control center plots these bearings on a map, and the transmitter is located where they cross. Successive plottings can determine the movement of a transmitter—its direction and speed.

It seems to have been such intelligence that led the Admiralty to inform its forces at five o'clock, May 30, 1916, that the High Seas Fleet was apparently about to put out to sea. At this news, virtually the entire Grand Fleet, that mighty armored pride of England, built up steam and sallied forth majestically from Scapa Flow, Invergordon, and Rosyth. It sought a major fleet action that would give England the undisputed control of the seas on which her strategy in the war so heavily depended.

There then occurred one of those trifling errors on which history so often turns. On sailing, Scheer had transferred the call sign *DK* of his flagship *Friedrich der Grosse* to the naval center at Wilhelmshaven in an attempt to conceal his departure. Room 40 was aware of this procedure, but it was the insufferable operations director, Captain Jackson, who came in on May 31 to ask where call sign *DK* was. He was not the sort of person to whom one offered unsolicited advice, so he was merely told, "In the Jade River." Jackson passed along this message, and the Admiralty thereupon radioed Jellicoe that directional wireless placed the enemy flagship in the harbor at eleven-ten. Three hours later, with Jellicoe believing that the Germans were still in port, the two fleets made contact in the middle of the North Sea.

This rather shook Jellicoe's faith in Admiralty intelligence. It was further jolted when he plotted the position of the German cruiser *Regensburg* as given by the Admiralty report and found that it appeared to be in almost the very same spot as he himself then was! At the time no one knew that the *Regensburg* navigator had made an error of ten miles in his reckoning and that blame for the absurd result lay with the German officer, not with the cryptanalysts of Room 40 reading the German report of the ship's position.

After the brief flurries of action, damaging but inconclusive and unsatisfactory to both sides, that constituted the Battle of Jutland, Scheer at nine-fourteen ordered: "Our own main body is to proceed in. Maintain course SSE 1/4 E; speed 16 knots." At nine forty-six he altered it slightly to south-southeast three-quarter point east. Both messages were decoded with almost unbelievable alacrity by Room 40, and by ten forty-one a summary of them had been received aboard the flagship.

But Jellicoe had had enough of Admiralty intelligence. Furthermore, the summary had omitted Scheer's call at six minutes past nine for air reconnaissance off the Horn Reefs, which would have confirmed his intentions to head for home, and thus there was nothing to contradict a battle report from the *Southampton* that suggested a different enemy course. Jellicoe therefore rejected the Admiralty information, which this time was right. As a result, he steered one way, Scheer fled another, and Britain's hope of a decisive naval victory evaporated in a welter of errors, missed chances, and distrust.

But if Room 40, through no fault of its own, did not enable Britain to win a major naval battle, it did play a critical role in helping her to win the war.

In 1917, Germany on one side and Britain and France on the other were gasping in exhaustion from a war that both had thought would be over—as the kaiser said—"before the leaves fall" in 1914. Germany thought she saw a way to win: Unrestricted submarine warfare would starve the Allies into submission. She recognized that this would probably bring the United States into the conflict against her. But her new foreign minister, Arthur Zimmermann, thought of a way to neutralize this danger. He would distract America by getting Mexico to wage war on her. And he would persuade Mexico to do this with an offer she could not refuse: Upon victory, Mexico would get back the territories she had lost in the Mexican-American War of 1846.

He put his proposal into code and cabled it on January 15 via Sweden to the Western Hemisphere. But the cable touched British soil. The British intercepted the message, and Room 40 deciphered it. The director of naval intelligence, Captain Reginald Hall, whom the American ambassador called a genius ("all other secret service men are amateurs by comparison"), saw that he had a propaganda weapon of the first water. With permission, he gave it to the Americans. President Woodrow Wilson, stunned by the German proposal, gave it to the Associated Press. The story made headlines in papers all over the nation on March 1. The isolationist Midwest, previously unconcerned with the distant poppings of a war in Europe, jerked awake at the thought of a German-officered Mexican army advancing up toward Chicago.

Five weeks later President Wilson—who had been reelected just months earlier on the slogan "He kept us out of war"—went up to Capitol Hill to ask

Congress to "make the world safe for democracy" by declaring war on Germany. Congress complied. And soon the fresh strength of the young nation was pouring into the factories and trenches of the Allies. The Germans were driven back and back until they had no choice but to surrender. The codebreakers, who had gotten their start with a codebook recovered from a stricken German warship at the beginning of the war, had played a major role in bringing that war to an end.

POSTSCRIPT: FOR THE TWENTY-FIFTH ANNIVERSARY OF THE MAGDEBURG'S stranding, the old battleship *Schleswig-Holstein* was sent to Poland to commemorate the cruiser's dead, who were buried in a Danzig cemetery. The ceremonies lasted a day, but the battleship remained moored at the port as tension between Poland and Nazi Germany mounted. At four forty-eight in the morning on September 1, 1939, her 11-inch guns roared, shattering and setting ablaze some Polish installations on the Westerplatte, a sandy tongue of land. The shots were the first of World War II.

JUTLAND

John Keegan

NE HISTORIAN OF THE IMPERIAL GERMAN NAVY SUBTITLED his chapter on the battle of Jutland "Missed Opportunity or Fortunate Escape?" Indeed, most discussions of the largest battleship encounter in history concentrate on what it achieved—or did not. How, they ask (as does John Keegan in the following article), could a battle so indecisive be a turning point? The question is inescapable. But there is one, less frequently asked, that may be fully as pertinent, because it speaks volumes about the military capacities of Great Britain and Germany. What would have been the result if one side *had* decisively defeated the other? Winston Churchill, in his monumental history/memoir of the Great War, *The World Crisis,* speculates on what was at stake on May 31, 1916, and saw a great disparity between the sides.

Had that decisive advantage gone to the British and the Commander in Chief of the Grand Fleet, John R. Jellicoe, Churchill points out, "The psychological effect upon the German nation . . . might conceivably have been profound." Also, a British victory might have meant that their naval vessels could have entered the Baltic with impunity, bringing aid to the Russians. Whether that would have prevented the Russian Revolution is a speculative question—but one that cannot be overlooked. Still, the destruction of the High Seas Fleet would not have been immediately fatal; Germany was, after all, mainly a land power. For Great Britain, however, defeat might have changed the course of the war, sooner than later:

The trade and food-supply of the British islands would have been paralyzed. Our armies on the Continent would have been cut from their base by superior naval force. All the transportation of the Allies would have been jeopardized and hampered. The United States could not have intervened in the war. Starvation and invasion would have descended upon the British people. Ruin utter and final would have overwhelmed the Allied cause.

No wonder so much was riding on the person of "Silent Jack" Jellicoe. Fisher once complained that he had "all the Nelsonic virtues save one": Jellicoe was "totally lacking in the great gift of insubordination." His handling of his battleships at Jutland was inspired—he twice "crossed the German *T*"—but also overcautious. To quote Churchill again: "His responsibilities were on a different scale from all others. It might fall to him as to no other man—Sovereign, Statesman, Admiral or General—to issue orders which in the space of *two or three hours* might nakedly decide who won the war. . . . Jellicoe was the only man on either side who could lose the war in an afternoon."

All this should be kept in mind as we read Keegan's account, which was originally excerpted from his book, *The Price of Admiralty.* There can be few more vivid, or harrowing, descriptions of Jutland than this one.

———

JOHN KEEGAN, who was for many years senior lecturer at the Royal Military Academy, Sandhurst, has taught at Princeton University and Vassar College, and is defense correspondent for *The Daily Telegraph* in London. He is the author of sixteen books, including *The Face of Battle; The Price of Admiralty; The Second World War; A History of Warfare;* and the bestselling *The First World War.*

ADMIRAL REINHARD SCHEER, THE COMMANDER OF GERMANY'S HIGH SEAS Fleet during World War I, proved a sailor of Nelsonian stamp. Reserved in expression and unassuming in manner, Scheer achieved high command only because fatal illness removed his predecessor. Once established in office, however, he showed a marked capacity for dismissing difficulty, concentrating on the strengths rather than the weaknesses of the German navy. A torpedo specialist, he believed that his surface and submarine forces had the capacity to inflict unacceptable damage on the British Grand Fleet if it could be maneuvered into unfavorable circumstances. Throughout the spring of 1916, he worked on refining plans for an extended operation that would run his opponents' battleships and battle cruisers onto a series of submarine-laid minefields, and allow his capital ships to pick off casualties and detached units at small cost to himself.

In 1916 the High Seas Fleet counted sixteen dreadnoughts (revolutionary new turbine-driven battleships that were more heavily armed and armored than any ship then afloat) and five battle cruisers to the Grand Fleet's twenty-eight dreadnoughts and nine battle cruisers; it also had six pre-dreadnoughts (the heaviest battleships carrying mixed-caliber batteries before development of the dreadnought). The balance of force, given what was then being built, could not improve in Scheer's favor. He therefore concluded that the time to act was now or never; and in the early morning of May 31, 1916, he ordered his squadrons to sea in the hope of returning to port with losses fewer than those he inflicted.

Altogether twenty-two battleships, five battle cruisers, eleven cruisers, and sixty-one torpedo boats of the High Seas Fleet put to sea. The modern capital ships were organized into two battleship squadrons of eight dreadnoughts each, as well as the First Scouting Group of five battle cruisers. Scheer commanded the battleships; Vice Admiral Franz Hipper was in command of the battle cruisers. Hipper's ships began to leave their North Sea ports at one o'clock in the morning; Scheer followed at two-thirty. The best speed of the dreadnought squadrons, determined by their slowest ships, the *Posen, Rheinland, Nassau,* and *Westfalen,* was twenty knots; but it was further reduced to eighteen knots by six pre-dreadnoughts that Scheer had included to bulk out numbers. The First Scouting Group had a maximum speed of twenty-six knots and was committed to the role of finding and "fixing" the location of the enemy's fleet until the heavier ships came up.

Scheer's plan did not envisage a decisive action. Realistically he recognized that his inferiority in numbers of ships and in weight of broadside (400,000 to 200,000 pounds, reflecting the lighter calibers of his ships' main armament) ruled out a German Trafalgar. He hoped nevertheless to come off the better by entangling the Grand Fleet with a U-boat line he had deployed off the British bases and by inflicting losses on ships and squadrons temporarily separated from the main body. The High Seas Fleet was to steer due north, toward the outer mouth of the Baltic, the Skagerrak, by which the Germans were to name the ensuing battle. News of its sortie was trusted to draw the Grand Fleet southward to a rendezvous.

However, the news came to the Grand Fleet much sooner than Scheer had expected. Through the capture of three cipher books, the Admiralty had acquired the key to the whole German maritime and overseas cipher system—a priceless advantage that enabled the Admiralty to detect Scheer's intention to "come out" as early as May 16, when his U-boats departed for their patrol lines. It was confirmed on May 30, and Admiral Sir John Jellicoe, commanding the Grand Fleet, was immediately warned. As he had on hand plans for a "sweep" of his own, the third undertaken that year, he rapidly translated his scheme for a probe into orders for a major action. Two hours before Hipper left Jade Bay, the Grand Fleet, including its Battle Cruiser Fleet, was already at sea, heading for an encounter off the west coast of Danish Jutland.

The battle that followed is conventionally divided by naval historians into five phases: the battle-cruiser action, encompassing two of the phases—a "run to the south" and a "run to the north"; the first and second encounters of the battleships; and a night action, involving many clashes between light forces, in which the High Seas Fleet made its escape to the Elbe River and Jade Bay.

The Battle Cruiser Fleet, commanded by Vice Admiral Sir David Beatty, comprised his six fastest ships—the *Lion, Tiger, Princess Royal, Queen Mary, Indefatigable,* and *New Zealand*—and was accompanied by the fast battleships of the Fifth Battle Squadron, the *Barham, Valiant, Warspite,* and *Malaya.* These were the most formidable ships on either side, heavily armored, mounting 15-inch guns, and capable of twenty-five knots—as close to the kaiser's cherished ideal of a "fast capital ship" as was then possible. They were superior to any other battleship and barely slower than the fastest battle cruisers, which were safe against them only by taking flight.

The Battle Cruiser Fleet passed undetected through Scheer's U-boat patrol line (as Jellicoe's battleships later would), thus robbing the High Seas Fleet's sortie of much of its point—and gravely compromising its security. But the Admiralty staff had perversely misinterpreted the cipher intelligence, and so assured Jellicoe that the enemy was still in port nine hours after it had put to sea.

In consequence, Beatty's and Hipper's battle cruisers managed to arrive within fifty miles of each other, some ninety miles west of the mouth of the Skagerrak, at two o'clock in the afternoon, without either having knowledge of the other's proximity. Chance drew them together: Light forces on each side detected a neutral merchant ship lying between their axes of advance and blowing off steam. Diverting to investigate the unknown vessel, they found each other. Fire was exchanged, signals were sent (HMS *Galatea:* "Enemy in sight. Two cruisers probably hostile in sight bearing ESE course unknown"), and the battle cruisers were ordered by their commanders to change course and steer for each other.

By the sort of mischance that would have been excusable at Trafalgar, when flags were the only medium of intercommunication, but not at Jutland, where radio provided a means of duplication, Beatty's fast battleships missed his hoist directing them toward the Germans and persisted in a prearranged turn northward to rendezvous with Jellicoe. The result was that Beatty led his lightly armored battle cruisers to challenge Hipper's ships unsupported. And when action was joined, at three forty-five in the afternoon, it did not go the British way.

Hipper, on sighting Beatty's ships, ordered a turn to draw them down onto Scheer's battleships following forty miles in his rear. The British, silhouetted by the sun in the western sky, showed up crisply in the German range finders. "Suddenly my periscope revealed some big ships," recorded Georg von Hase, gunnery officer of *Derfflinger.* "Black monsters; six tall, broad-beamed giants steaming in two columns." A few minutes later Hipper signaled "Open fire" and the German battle cruisers began observing and correcting their fall of shot. Beatty, whose range takers had overestimated the distance separating the two lines, was busy getting a radio message off to Jellicoe and did not yet respond. Some five minutes after the Germans had begun to engage, Beatty's flag captain ordered the "open fire" on his own responsibility and also began to observe effects.

Because British range-finding was inferior to German (due to the better quality of German optics), the Battle Cruiser Fleet, which outranged the First Scouting Group, had allowed itself to run within the fire zone of the enemy's guns. Hipper's 11- and 12-inch armaments were therefore straddling and scoring hits on Beatty's 12- and 13½-inch-gun ships when more prudent ship-handling would have denied them the opportunity. Bad signaling also misdirected British gunners so that one of the five ships in Hipper's line (*Derfflinger*) was spared altogether from attack by Beatty's ships for nearly ten minutes. The consequences were not long delayed. Gunnery control officers on both sides were trying to hit hulls and particularly turrets that, even if heavily armored, were the access points to magazines, detonation of which was the quickest way to put an enemy out of action.

Such a direct hit on a lightly armored and unprotected sector of the ship normally killed or wounded everyone who was in the vicinity. On armor, however, shells exerted erratic effects. In Q turret of HMS *Tiger,* which was hit on its armored roof at three fifty-five by an 11-inch shell from the *Moltke,* two men were killed outright and a midshipman was mortally wounded. Four other sailors were wounded, but three of them were able to help bring the turret back into action. "The dead were placed to one side," according to one report, "the wounded given first aid, and necessary substitutes were brought up from below to replace casualties."

A quick survey of the damage revealed that the more fragile machinery and instruments had been disabled but that the guns and loading gear still were in working condition; as the directors of strategic bombing were to discover during World War II, it is almost impossible to destroy high-grade steel machinery with explosive, however accurately it is delivered.

But there was one thing that put the German guns at an advantage: All the British capital ships had a fundamental design defect—an insufficiency of "antiflash" devices between the turrets and the magazines. The Germans had learned a lesson from the battle cruiser *Seydlitz*'s near-fatal internal fire after a direct hit on a turret the year before at the Battle of Dogger Bank. The fire had traveled down the turret trunk—the tube for bringing shells up from the magazine. Consequently, the High Seas Fleet's ships had been modified to avert the passage of flash down their turret trunks. The British ships had not. A subsequent investigation revealed that the British crews, in their determination to achieve the highest possible rates of fire in gunnery competitions, had removed anti-flash devices from the trunks without realizing that cordite flash in the turret labyrinth posed the gravest danger to dreadnoughts. A third of the British battle cruisers would be destroyed as a result.

This nearly happened to Beatty's flagship, the *Lion.* Her Q turret was hit by a 12-inch shell from the *Lützow* at four o'clock, killing everyone in the gunhouse. But one of the gun numbers, as he died, involuntarily sent the loading cage of the right gun down into the working chamber. A fire, apparently spreading down the turret's electrical cables, ignited the cordite in the cage and the working chamber; and fire passed thither down the turret trunk toward the magazines. The turret officer, Major F.J.W. Harvey, managed with his dying breath (he had lost both his legs) to order that the magazine doors be closed and the magazine flooded. In giving this order, for which he was posthumously awarded the Victoria Cross, he saved the ship.

The fire that the shell started below the turret was fatal to all the crew in the workspaces above the magazine. As was stated in a later report:

> [It] passed down the main trunk into the shell room and handling room and up the escape trunk into the switchboard compartment. In this latter compartment were stationed, beside the switchboard men and certain of the electrical repair party, the after medical party under the charge of a surgeon. All these men, together with the magazine and shell-room crew, were killed by the cordite fire. . . . [Their] bodies and clothes were not burnt and, in cases where the hands had been raised involuntarily, palms forward, to protect the eyes, the backs of the hands and that part of the face screened by the hands were not even discolored. Death to these men must have been instantaneous.

Beatty's flag captain pulled the ship out of the line to take her from the danger zone. The Germans believed her finished.

Shortly afterward, the *Indefatigable,* which had been exchanging salvos with the *Von der Tann,* also suffered hits. The *Lion*'s were to prove survivable; the *Indefatigable*'s were not. One salvo penetrated her thinly armored deck. Another, hitting near her fore turret, set off a fatal internal explosion, and at two minutes past four she turned over and sank.

In terms of battle cruisers, numbers were now equal. "I gazed at this in amazement," remembered Beatty's flag captain. "There were only five battle cruisers in our line. . . . I glanced quickly toward the enemy. How many of them were afloat? Still five." Beatty now ordered his light forces into action in the 15,000-yard space separating the two battle lines. Light cruisers and destroyers, engaged by the German battle cruisers' secondary armament, tried to launch torpedoes against the enemy's heavy units; Hipper's light forces swung into action against them. And then, while light cruisers and destroyers fired their 6- and 4-inch guns against each other, the four battleships of the Fifth Battle Squadron, redirected at last onto their proper targets, began to fire their shells, tossing columns of water larger than any that had yet been seen around the German battle line. Suddenly the odds among the heavy ships were again in Beatty's favor: nine against five, with greater range and weight of shell on his side.

But German gunnery achieved one more success: A full 12-inch salvo hit the *Queen Mary,* consort of the *Tiger* and *Lion.* She did not survive. About twenty-six minutes after four, after several earlier hits, she was struck on one of her forward turrets. A cordite fire entered the forward magazine, and the resulting explosion blew off the forepart of the ship. Shortly afterward a hit on X turret blew up the after magazine, and the remains of the ship capsized. Gunner's Mate E. Francis, a survivor of the X turret crew, described the sequence:

> Then came the big explosion [the detonation of the forward magazine], which shook us a bit, and on looking at the pressure gauge I saw the [hydraulic] pressure had failed. [Hydraulic power trained the turret, elevated the guns, and worked the ammunition lifts and loading rammers.] Immediately after that came . . . the big smash and I was dangling in the air on a bowline, which saved me from being thrown onto the floor of the turret. . . . Numbers two and three of the left gun slipped down under the gun, and the gun appeared to me to have fallen through its trunnions and smashed up these two numbers. Everything in the ship went as quiet as a church, the floor of the turret was bulged up and the guns were absolutely useless. . . . I put my head up through the hole in the roof of the turret and I nearly fell back through again. The after four-inch battery was smashed right out of all recognition and then I noticed the ship had an awful list to port. [X turret, behind the bridge, gave no view of the missing foreparts of the ship.] I dropped back inside the turret and told Lieutenant Eward [the turret officer] the state of affairs. He said, "Francis, we can do no more than give them a chance; clear the turret." "Clear the turret," I called out, and out they all went.

Francis and Midshipman Lloyd-Owen of X turret were to be among the *Queen Mary*'s twenty survivors, of a crew of fifty-eight officers and 1,228 men. The *Indefatigable* sank with the loss of all but two of her crew of a thousand. These catastrophes, with the later loss of the *Invincible*, were to be the great tragedies of Jutland, because of their unexpectedness. The vulnerability of the *Invincible* and *Queen Mary* to long-range, armor-piercing fire was the most unsettling outcome of all the events of the Jutland encounter. It was the *Queen Mary*'s loss that prompted Beatty's notorious remark, "There seems to be something wrong with our bloody ships today."

Meanwhile, however, under the cumulative effect of Beatty's much heavier gunnery, Hipper's line was now running ever deeper into danger. Well-aimed salvos were falling about his ships every twenty seconds; some were scoring hits, and the British officers on the bridges of the battle cruisers and battleships who could see enough to judge the course of the action were now certain that the destruction of the First Scouting Group was at hand.

Then, at four-thirty, Beatty received a signal from one of his advance light cruisers that she had "sighted enemy battle fleet bearing approximately SE, course of enemy N." The implication was clear: If Beatty continued making his "run to the south," he would arrive under the guns of Scheer's battleships, against which his Battle Cruiser Fleet, even with the support of the Fifth Battle Squadron, could not hope to stand without devastating consequences. At four-forty, therefore, he signaled a turnaway, toward Jellicoe's approaching squadrons, and the "run to the north" began.

Commodore W. E. Goodenough, commanding the British light cruisers that had sighted Scheer's ships—it was the dense clouds of black smoke from their coal burning engines, working at full revolutions, that had drawn his attention toward the eastern horizon—held on far into the danger zone while he established their number and bearing. When he at last turned away, he was followed by torrents of shells, any one of which could have obliterated him or a consort. Forty large shells fell within seventy-five yards of the cruiser *Southampton* as she made her escape at twenty-five knots toward Jellicoe, zigzagging between the shell fountains to confuse the German range takers.

Beatty's battle cruisers had meanwhile put enough distance behind them to be out of danger. But the fast battleships of the Fifth Battle Squadron, once again misled by a signal, had not. They were five minutes late in turning away, and in the interval the *Barham* and *Malaya* were hit by German fire, the *Malaya* heavily. One of her secondary batteries was knocked out and she was holed beneath the waterline. But the fast battleships' advantage in gunpower told in reply. Several German battleships and battle cruisers were struck by salvos from the retreating British ships, the *Seydlitz* so hard that she risked sinking.

But the *Seydlitz* herself scored hits, notably on the battleship *Warspite*. At about five-thirty the *Warspite* was hit several times. In the next few minutes a shell burst in the starboard secondary battery. Commander Walwyn reported that "a sheet of flame came down through the slits of sliding shutters . . . [and he] heard a lot of groaning." When he went forward, he found that the burst had started a fire in the ready-use cordite among the guns of the starboard secondary battery. The fire had "frightfully burnt" two gun crews and was also blazing around the conning tower, through the slot of which "signalmen and messengers peering out . . . looked like thrushes in a nest, gaping and shouting, 'Put the fire out.' We eventually got a steam main connected and got water."

The fire had also taken hold below, in the navigating officer's cabin, burning a store of four hundred life jackets nearby.

> The stench of burning rubber being perfectly awful . . . smoldering wooden uprights of doors kept on breaking out again . . . decks were all warped and resin under corticine [deck covering] crackling like burning holly. . . . [E]verything in the fore superstructure was wrecked and it

looked like a burned-out factory all blackened and beams twisted every-where. . . . [A] twelve-inch had come through the after funnel, through the beef-screen [meat-storage area] and smashed the second cutter to matchwood. On its way through the beef-screen it had carried a whole sheep with it, which was wedged into the gratings. At first I thought it was a casualty.

That a sheep's carcass could be mistaken, even briefly, for a human casu-alty testifies to the appalling nature of wounds that high-explosive projectiles frequently inflicted in the confined spaces of armored ships.

But the "run to the north," though a withdrawal, had scored hits on Ger-man ships and reunited Beatty with Jellicoe. It was therefore as much a British success as the "run to the south" had been a British setback. Still, both had been preliminary engagements. Shortly after six o'clock the battle fleets them-selves at last drew within range of each other. Their covering screens of cruis-ers and light cruisers had already been in action and the Germans had fallen under the guns of Beatty's battle cruisers with disastrous results: Three cruis-ers—the Wiesbaden, Pillau, and Frankfurt—had suffered crippling damage. But so too had a British destroyer, the Shark, overwhelmed by heavier fire, and a cruiser, the Chester, in which the boy hero of Jutland, Jack Cornwell, had been killed. (The sixteen-year-old Boy First Class, though wounded, remained at his post and received the Victoria Cross posthumously.) And there were to be more losses before the dreadnoughts began their artillery duel. Two British armored cruisers, supporting Jellicoe's battleships, came under fire from Scheer as they steamed ahead of the Grand Fleet; the Warrior was rapidly wrecked and the De-fence blown up, both hit by shells against which their thin sides offered no pro-tection, at ranges too long for their 8-inch guns to straddle.

And there was to be another catastrophe before Jellicoe's and Scheer's bat-tleships saw each other. Three battle cruisers, the Indomitable, Inflexible, and In-vincible, oldest and weakest of their type, were accompanying the Grand Fleet. At one minute past six, the Lion, which had returned to the fight, had come within sight of Jellicoe, who signaled to Beatty, "Where is the enemy's battle fleet?" The answer was ambiguous, but it persuaded the commander that he must now anticipate imminent action and deploy from column into line—the formation best suited for the concentration of maximum gunpower on the enemy. As his six columns began their fifteen-minute deployment, the Invinci-ble, steaming ahead of the main formation, out of sight of Jellicoe but in sight of Beatty, also came within view of the Germans.

It was an unlucky rendezvous. Cloud and mist, which until now had con-cealed its presence, suddenly parted to reveal the isolated squadron of three battle cruisers to the leading German battleships, which opened fire instantly. The *Invincible*, the leading ship, was the focus of the attack and was hit repeatedly. At six thirty-three, a shell penetrated the roof of Q turret amidships and blew her into halves. Among the six survivors of her thousand men was the composer Richard Wagner's godson, who had been observing the fall of shot from the highest point in the ship.

Fortunately, the surviving battle cruisers were not to bear the brunt of the ensuing action, while the battleships, which were, had external armor sufficiently thick to keep out the projectiles that had damaged the *Invincible* and Beatty's ships so fatally. Moreover, Jellicoe's battleships were to join action with Scheer's on highly advantageous terms.

Ambiguous and intermittent though the signaling of his advance forces had been, Jellicoe was the more fully alerted of the two commanders to the approach of his opponent. Hipper had been able to warn Scheer of the imminence of fleet action with no clearer signal than "Something lurks in that soup. We would do well not to thrust into it too deeply." Scheer, who had thitherto believed he had the British Battle Cruiser Fleet in a trap, now had to grapple with the anxiety that it might be supported by the rest of the Grand Fleet, yet without clear indication of its location. Jellicoe, on the other hand, not only knew Scheer's positions and heading but also could calculate that his own heading put him between Scheer and his line of retreat to the northern German ports, and therefore that he could "Trafalgar" the enemy if daylight and the accuracy of his gunnery availed.

The Grand Fleet's twenty-eight battleships, deploying from columns to line as they passed the wreck of the *Invincible* (many British sailors thought she was a German ship and cheered as they saw her), now enjoyed the advantage of the light—an advantage that earlier in the day had been the enemy's—and could see their targets clearly on the western skyline. To Scheer's range takers, Jellicoe's ships were "indicated on the horizon ahead of us [only] by the firing of heavy-caliber guns. The entire arc stretching from North to East was a sea of fire. The muzzle flashes were clearly seen through the mist and smoke on the horizon, though there was still no sign of the ships themselves."

The opening range was about 12,000 yards, well within the reach of the guns on the leading British ships, which, by classic tactics, had "crossed the *T*" of the German line and were pouring fire at its head. British observers were convinced they were scoring a succession of hits and sinking ships. Several German battleships—and battle cruisers, leading the fleet—were hit in this exchange; twenty-two shells struck altogether. The Germans inflicted thirty-three in return, all on British battle cruisers, cruisers, and fast battleships of the Fifth Battle Squadron; Jellicoe's line of dreadnoughts was not touched. As it steamed imperturbably onward, steadily closing the range and interposing itself more deeply between the High Seas Fleet and home, Scheer's nerve cracked. After only ten minutes' engagement, he ordered a simultaneous turnaway to take his fleet out of danger.

The German ships disappeared instantly and mysteriously from the British range takers' field of vision as the smoke and gathering dusk of a misty evening enclosed them. They might have turned south. Jellicoe correctly guessed that Scheer had chosen the quickest way out of danger and turned due west, toward the English coast. He ordered an alteration of course southward, to better his chances of cutting off the enemy's retreat, and held onward. So, too, for some ten minutes (from six forty-five to six fifty-five) did Scheer, until, hoping to escape across the rear of the Grand Fleet, he signaled a reversal of course and began to steer due east. His intention was to reach the coast of Jutland and then work his way home behind the minefields fringing it in German territorial waters.

His order, however, was timed too early. Overestimating the speed of Jellicoe's advance, he suddenly found himself at about ten past seven under fire once more from the British battleships, his *T* crossed again, his weakest ships—the battle cruisers—in the van, and last light silhouetting his line while it hid the British ships from his guns. This "second encounter" of the battle fleets went far worse than the first for the Germans. They scored only two hits on Jellicoe's line (both on the *Colossus*) while the British scored twenty-seven in return, on the already heavily stricken battle cruisers.

Less than ten minutes of this treatment persuaded Scheer to break off action. At seven-eighteen, he signaled another simultaneous reversal of course to his battle line, having meanwhile ordered the battle cruisers to "charge" the enemy and his light cruisers and torpedo boats to lay smoke and mount a torpedo attack. Hipper's "death ride"—an allusion to the last charge of Prussia's armored horsemen in 1870—put all but one of his ships out of action. The torpedo attack was more profitable. Jellicoe deployed his own light cruisers and destroyers against it as the Germans approached and caused most to launch at extreme range, or not to launch at all. Nevertheless twenty-one torpedoes traveled the distance, forcing Jellicoe to order a general turnaway and individual ship captains to maneuver sharply. No hits were scored, but by the time Jellicoe resumed his pursuit, Scheer had put himself at extreme range of the Grand Fleet—some ten to eleven miles—and was heading south for home with the British abreast of him to the east and slightly to his rear.

Light was failing fast as the last phase of the battle—later to become known as "the night action"—opened. The sun set at eight twenty-four. At eight-thirty Scheer ordered his squadron of six pre-dreadnoughts to go to the aid of his battle cruisers, which, lying to his east, were still under fire from Beatty's ships; his, in turn, were running ahead of Jellicoe's line of advance. While the pre-dreadnoughts exchanged fire with Beatty's fleet, Hipper's battle cruisers were able to make good their escape; eventually, as Beatty's range takers lost definition on the darkening horizon, so did the pre-dreadnoughts, which were able to disengage unscathed.

While the darkness grew thicker, the battle fleets converged on southerly courses in complete ignorance of each other's whereabouts. In the six miles of sea that separated them, there were to ensue nine encounters between German and British light forces, and between British light forces and the German battle fleet. In the first, none of the four torpedoes fired struck a target. In the second, the British destroyer *Castor* was hit a number of times and in the confusion failed to report the German position to Jellicoe for half an hour. In the third, the British cruiser *Southampton* sank the German cruiser *Frauenlob* by torpedo. In the fourth and largest engagement, the destroyer *Tipperary* was sunk with heavy casualties, and the *Elbing*, the ship that had opened the battle hours earlier, was fatally crippled; it sank four hours later. In the fifth, British destroyers attacked the German dreadnoughts at ranges that closed to a thousand yards and damaged one by ramming. In the sixth, a British destroyer put a torpedo into the German pre-dreadnought *Pommern*, found its magazine, and blew it up. In the seventh, a British armored cruiser, the *Black Prince*, was set on fire by salvos from a German dreadnought and also blew up. The eighth and ninth were destroyer actions, in which one German torpedo boat was lost.

While these brief and chaotic encounters—the last timed at three-thirty in the morning on June 1—were taking place, the High Seas Fleet, holding to its southerly course and making several knots less than the Grand Fleet, had passed behind the British and gotten safely to the coast of Jutland and its minefields. It was in sore straits. One of its battle cruisers, the *Lützow*, had sunk; of the four remaining, only one, the *Moltke*, was still capable of fighting.

The *Lützow*'s captain described her end, which came early on the morning of June 1:

> After it became clear that it was not possible to save the ship, because she had 8,300 tons of water in her and was on the point of heeling over, I decided to send off the crew. . . . She was so down by the bows that the water came up to the control tower and the stern was right out. On my orders the ship was sunk by a torpedo fired by G-38 [a German torpedo boat]. She heeled over and after two minutes swiftly sank with her flag flying.

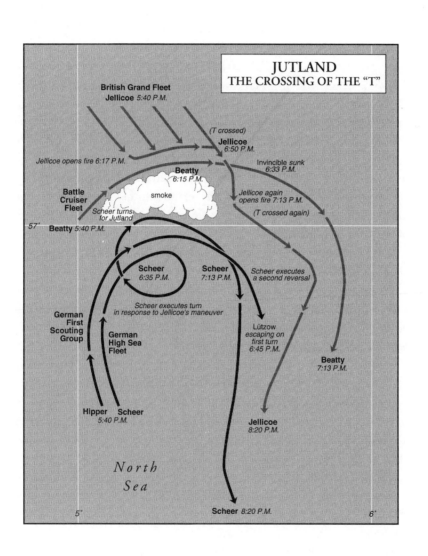

JUTLAND
THE CROSSING OF THE "T"

British Grand Fleet
Jellicoe *5:40 P.M.*

(T crossed)
Jellicoe
6:50 P.M.

Jellicoe opens fire 6:17 P.M.

Invincible *sunk*
6:33 P.M.

Beatty
6:15 P.M.

smoke

**Battle
Cruiser
Fleet**

*Jellicoe again
opens fire 7:13 P.M.*

*Scheer turns
for Jutland*

(T crossed again)

57°   **Beatty** *5:40 P.M.*

Scheer
6:35 P.M.

Scheer
7:13 P.M.

*Scheer executes
a second reversal*

*Scheer executes turn
in response to Jellicoe's maneuver*

**German
First
Scouting
Group**

**German
High Sea
Fleet**

*Lützow
escaping on
first turn
6:45 P.M.*

Beatty
7:13 P.M.

Hipper   Scheer
5:40 P.M.

Jellicoe
8:20 P.M.

*North
Sea*

Scheer *8:20 P.M.*

5°   *6°*

The only other German capital ship not to return from Jutland was the pre-dreadnought *Pommern*, which had been blown up during the night action by a torpedo fired from the destroyer *Onslaught*. The German pre-dreadnoughts were not elaborately subdivided and had no underwater protection. The explosion broke *Pommern* in half. There were no survivors from her crew of 844.

That terrible toll is largely explained by the near impossibility of finding survivors on the surface of the sea during the hours of darkness. That some initially did survive her wreck is suggested by the aftermath of the *Queen Mary* and *Invincible* disasters, in which twenty-six were picked up; even from the *Indefatigable*, two crewmen survived and landed in German hands. The *Pommern's* broken hull remained afloat for at least twenty minutes after the torpedo strike. The surmise is that the ship was destroyed by a succession of explosions, beginning in the magazines of the secondary armament and spreading to where the 11-inch charges and shells were stored. Men in the tops and on the bridge must have been thrown into the sea, and others in the upper decks would probably have been able to make an escape. All were subsequently lost, however, to the darkness and the cold.

Those most imperiled by internal explosion—indeed without hope of escape at all—were the ammunition and engine-room crews. Ammunition handlers, if at the flash point, suffered instantaneous extinction. Stokers and mechanics might undergo a protracted and awful agony. That must certainly have been the fate of the engine-room crews on the *Pommern*, as well as on the *Indefatigable* and *Queen Mary*, trapped in air pockets belowdecks, plunged into darkness, engulfed by rising water, perhaps also menaced by escaping superheated steam and machinery running out of control.

The details of the last minutes of those engine-room spaces are mercifully hidden from us. Some impression of what the victims underwent is conveyed by the experience of the engine-room crew of the *Warrior*, the British armored cruiser attacked by *Derfflinger* and other German battle cruisers at about six o'clock in the evening. The *Warrior*, which was quite inappropriately attempting to support the British battle-cruiser line, suffered hits by fifteen heavy shells, one of which struck at the water line, causing flooding in the whole engine-room space.

The damage trapped the survivors among the engine-room crew in the working spaces. There were initially eight of them. The engineer officer in charge attempted to lead the others out of the engine room, but he was defeated. He "found by the glimmer of the sole remaining oil lamp that the water was coming over the floor plates, and the crank pits were full up and the cranks were swishing round in the middle of it." The *Warrior* was not a turbine ship but a reciprocating-engine one—massive pistons worked in cylinders that were as tall as the engine-room ceiling, perfectly safely while the ship was proceeding normally, but at great risk to the engine-room crew as soon as anything went awry. According to a later report, the engineer officer first

> tried to ease the engines and shut off steam, fearing further accidents, but by this time the water was breast high over the floor plates, and he decided the only thing to do was to clear out. But by this time the ladders were inaccessible as the floor plates were dislodged, and there was every chance of being drawn into the racing cranks. They climbed up over pipes and condensers, holding hands to prevent the swirling water carrying them away. Unfortunately their chain was twice broken, with the result that several men were jammed somehow and drowned. The remainder climbed from one vantage point to another as the water rose until they reached the upper gratings, but by this time it was quite dark, and having no purchase anywhere they could not dislodge the gratings overhead, and apparently found themselves doomed to certain death.
>
> Not only were they expecting to be drowned, but escaping steam almost suffocated them, and they kept splashing oily water over their faces to keep themselves from being peeled. Some men had wrapped scarves round their heads to protect themselves, and all kept as much of their heads as they could in the water. The surprising thing was that the engines went on working till the water was halfway up the cylinders and only stopped then because the boilers were shut off. . . .
>
> [T]his agony of terror went on for nearly two and a half hours in pitch darkness and apparent hopelessness. . . . A stoker petty officer . . . absolutely refused to recognize the horror of the situation and kept talking and cheering them all up. . . . [T]hey kept hold of each other to save their lives as long as possible, but one by one they kept dropping off and getting lost and drowned in the water, till at last there were only three of them left. (The engineer officer himself would have been lost, having slipped from his hold and finding himself being drawn into the machinery, but the petty officer held on to him and kept him up until he recovered somewhat.) They thought at one time that the ship had been abandoned . . . then they felt a noticeably cold stream of water coming in . . . and from this they apparently had the idea that the ship must be under way, and therefore in tow of someone, which encouraged them. At last they heard some order being "piped" round the ship and they all shouted together and this led to their rescue.

There was to be no rescue for the engine-room crew of the battleship *Pommern*, any more than there had been for those of the battle cruisers *Queen Mary* and *Indefatigable*. The crews of the turbine-driven battle cruisers were spared the horror of crushing and dismemberment by cranks and pistons as the shattered hulls of their ships carried them down into the deeps. The older *Pommern*, a juggernaut of the sea, must have mangled many of her stokers and mechanics as she made her last plunge. And in all three ships the escape of propulsive steam would have flayed men alive before drowning deprived them of life.

By six-thirty on the morning of June 1, most of the ships in the High Seas Fleet had reached the safety of the Jade estuary; the last casualty was the battleship *Ostfriesland*, which at five-thirty struck a mine laid by HMS *Abdiel* but managed nevertheless to limp home. The *Seydlitz*, which twice grounded on the approach to the Jade, had to be hauled ignominiously into harbor stern first. The Battle Cruiser and Grand fleets, with their accompanying shoals of destroyers and cruisers, had returned to Scapa Flow and Rosyth by June 2. At nine forty-five that evening Jellicoe reported to the Admiralty that his warships were ready to steam out again on four hours' notice.

That signal writes the strategic verdict on Jutland. Britain's navy remained fit for renewed action, however soon it should come. Germany's did not. The kaiser preferred to ignore this fact. He exulted that "the magic of Trafalgar has been broken," distributed Iron Crosses wholesale to the crews of the High Seas Fleet when he visited it on June 5, and kissed many of the captains. He promoted Scheer to full admiral and invested him with the Pour le Mérite, Germany's highest military honor. Scheer himself, however, was much less convinced of his "victory." Shortly after the battle, reflecting on its conduct to fellow admirals, he conceded that "I came to the thing as the virgin did when she had a baby," and in his official report on Jutland to the kaiser on July 4, he warned that "even the most successful outcome of the fleet action," which he implicitly conceded Jutland had not yielded, "will not force England to make peace."

"The High Seas Fleet," Scheer said in his report to the kaiser, "will be ready by the middle of August for further strikes against the enemy." However, contemplating and acting are two different things.

True to Scheer's word, the High Seas Fleet did put to sea, on August 19, and steamed north to bring the English east coast town of Sunderland under bombardment. Scheer's approach was covered, however, by ten of the zeppelins he had not been able to take to Jutland, and when one reported that the Grand Fleet was bearing down on him from the Scottish anchorages, he reversed course and raced for home. The Admiralty cryptographers had detected his sortie, and were to do so again when he next put to sea, in October, with the same humiliating outcome. That was to be the High Seas Fleet's last open challenge to the Royal Navy. In April 1918, when it slipped out of port once more, its mission was mere commerce raiding against the Scandinavian convoys. An engine-room accident in one of the battle cruisers, causing the battleships also to reduce speed, then obliged Scheer to call off the operation and return to port.

For more than half the war, therefore—from June 1, 1916, until November 11, 1918, twenty-nine months in all—the High Seas Fleet had been at best "a fleet in being," and for its last year scarcely even that. Much explains its inactivity: the growth of the Grand Fleet's strength relative to its own (Britain launched nine capital ships between 1916 and 1918, Germany only three), the addition of the Americans to the British dreadnought fleet after April 1917, and the kaiser's increasingly neurotic opposition to taking any naval risk whatsoever. But the central factor in the reduction of the High Seas Fleet to an inoperative force was the action of Jutland itself. Germany had built a navy for battle. But in the only battle fought by its united strength, the navy had undergone an experience it did not choose to repeat.

Germany could publicly celebrate Jutland because the raw "exchange ratio" was in its favor. The High Seas Fleet had inflicted far greater damage than it had suffered. Three British battle cruisers, the *Indefatigable, Invincible*, and *Queen Mary*, were sunk, as were three armored cruisers, the *Black Prince, Defence*, and *Warrior*, and eight destroyers. And five British capital ships had suffered hits by 11-inch shells or heavier, notably the *Lion, Tiger*, and *Warspite*. The High Seas Fleet, by contrast, had lost only one battle cruiser, the *Lützow*; the other ship casualties were either pre-dreadnoughts like the *Pommern* or secondary units like the four light cruisers and five torpedo boats.

Three to one, in rude terms, did make Jutland look more like a German than a British victory. But calculated in refined rather than crude terms, the "exchange ratio" was very much more in Britain's than Germany's favor. Three of her fast battleships—*Warspite, Barham*, and *Malaya*—had suffered damage requiring dockyard attention. But the battleship fleet itself was almost unscathed; and despite losses, the Battle Cruiser Fleet on June 1 still outnumbered the German First Scouting Group, which moreover was crippled by damage. The German dreadnought battleships had also suffered grievously. *König, Markgraff*, and *Grosser Kurfürst* all needed major refits when they returned to port, and the German battle line could not have met the British at four weeks' notice, let alone four hours', except at risk of outright defeat. The balance of forces had not been significantly altered by relative losses. The Grand Fleet still outnumbered Scheer's, twenty-eight dreadnoughts to sixteen.

The human cost, however, had fallen far more heavily on the British. True, her long tradition of "following the sea" and her large seafaring population made her losses easier to replace than the German. But the truth was that over 6,600 British officers and sailors had gone down with their ships or been killed on their decks while the Germans had lost only a few more than 2,000.

The casualties of ironclad warfare, as compared with those of wooden-wall warfare, were gruesome. The solid shot exchanged by the ships at Trafalgar dismembered or decapitated, and tossed showers of wooden splinters between and across decks. But if the missiles did not kill outright, their victims retained a chance of clean and quick recovery, even under the hands of surgeons whose only tools were the probe and the knife. The casualties at Jutland suffered wounds almost unknown to an earlier generation of naval surgeons: metal fragmentation wounds, scouring trauma by shell splinter, and, most painful and hardest of all to treat, flash and burn effects and flaying by live steam. An officer on the destroyer *Tipperary* described coming across a sailor "with a large portion of his thigh removed, probably the result of scouring by a shell splinter. 'What can I do with this, sir?' asked the torpedo gunner who was attempting first aid. . . . I merely covered the wound with a large piece of cotton wool and put a blanket over him. 'Feels a lot better already,' said the wounded man." He was among the majority who drowned when the *Tipperary* foundered two hours later.

Even the wounded who came for care where care was organized—as well as it could be—did not find great comfort. The medical officer of the battle cruiser *Princess Royal* described a surgical center in which wounded men were wounded again by incoming German shells ("the next day about 3 lbs weight of shell fragments . . . were swept up from the deck") and where fumes from explosions elsewhere in the ship, sinking through the internal spaces because heavier than air, forced staff and patients to don respirators.

> Casualties began to arrive, amongst them a gun-layer from the after turret, which had been put out of action by a direct hit. He . . . had a foot nearly blown away. . . . This gun-layer had developed German measles about two days previously, and should by rights have been landed, but owing to the mildness of his complaint, and because he was an important rating, he had been isolated on board and permitted to come to sea. Later on I amputated his leg. . . . I proceeded to operate on a . . . marine who had been brought down bleeding seriously from a punctured wound of the face. . . . We had hardly started operating before rapid firing developed, and the tray with all my instruments was deposited on the deck . . . [but we] proceeded to operate on the gun-layer. The light was most trying [gunfire had forced the doctors to depend on barely adequate oil lamps], the securing of arteries during the operation being particularly

difficult. . . . The dressing of large numbers of burns, some very extensive ones, now fully occupied the time of the whole staff. . . . Most of the wounded, who numbered exactly 100, were seriously burned.

Aboard the cruiser *Southampton*, which was a smaller ship, the doctors were forced to work under even more makeshift conditions. The operating room, according to one of her lieutenants,

> was the stokers' bathroom . . . about eight feet high, twelve feet broad, and twelve feet long. The centre of the room was occupied by a light portable operating table. A row of wash basins ran down one side and the steel walls streamed with sweat. . . . Stepping carefully between rows of shapes who were lying in lines down each side of the passage-way, I put my head inside the narrow doorway. Bare-armed the fleet surgeon and a young doctor were working with desperate but methodical haste. They were just taking a man's leg off above the knee. . . .
>
> I went aft again and down to the ward-room. The mess presented an extraordinary appearance. As it was the largest room in the ship we placed in it all the seriously wounded. [The *Southampton* had suffered forty killed and forty to fifty wounded.] The long table was covered with men, all lying very still and silently white. As I came in (the doctor) signalled to the sick-berth steward to remove one man over who[m] he had been bending. Four stokers, still grimy from the stokehold, lifted the body and carried it out. Two men were on top of the sideboard, others were in armchairs. A hole in the side admitted water to the ward-room, which splashed about as the ship gently rolled. In the ankle-deep flood, blood-stained bandages and countless pieces of the small debris of war floated to and fro. . . . [T]he most dreadful cases were the burns—but this subject cannot be written about.

Both fleets, as they made their way back to harbor from their inconclusive North Sea encounter, were encumbered belowdecks with "dreadful cases" that "cannot be written about." The first—it was to be also the last—great clash of dreadnoughts had inflicted appalling human damage on their crews. But the toll of casualties is not to be compared with the bloodlettings of the Western Front. Exactly one calendar month after Jutland, the British Expeditionary Force was to attack the German trench line on the Somme and suffer 20,000 killed in a single day of action. There had been such massacres before, and others would follow before the exhaustion of the combatant armies would bring the agony of trench warfare to an end. Set against the five million deaths in action suffered during the First World War by the British, French, and German armies alone, Jutland is small beer. As a proportion of crews present, some 110,000 in all, the total of fatal casualties, approaching 9,000, is high, but it must be set against the consideration that the event was unique. Earlier actions had not been costly in lives, and there were to be no major fleet actions after May 31, 1916.

Jutland ranks among the costliest naval battles ever fought. Not until the great Japanese-American clashes of the Second World War in the Pacific would action at sea bring death to so many sailors. And there is another dimension to the engagement: It called into question all the presumptions on which the great ironclad fleets—the dreadnoughts being their ultimate embodiment—had been built.

As Ernle Chatfield, Vice Admiral Beatty's staff commander in the Battle Cruiser Fleet, put it in retrospect:

> What would happen [in Nelson's time] when two ships met and engaged was, as far as material was concerned, known within definite limits from handed-down experience and from a hundred sea-fights. [Nelson] knew exactly the risks he ran and accurately allowed for them. He had clear knowledge, from long-considered fighting experiences, how long his ships could endure the temporary gunnery disadvantage necessary in order to gain the dominant tactical position he aimed at for a great victory.... We had to buy that experience, for our weapons were untried. The risks could not be measured without that experience.... Dreadnoughts had never engaged, modern massed destroyer attack had never taken place.

The passing of the wooden walls and the coming of the iron, steam-driven warship had wrenched naval strategy from its foundations. For about two centuries, admirals had manipulated a naval system in which the fighting qualities of their ships and the rare "clash transaction" of battle—Clausewitz's term—had been but two among the factors by which the balance of sea power was struck. There were many others, including the possession of overseas bases at strategic points, the availability of trained seamen, the distribution of ports that were adaptable to naval operations, the interoperability of land with sea forces, and, besides all these, the will and capacity of a government to maximize its material advantages for military purpose in great waters.

The British had proved supremely successful at the adjustment of means to ends in the pursuit of national power through the maintenance of a wooden-wall navy. But the supersession of wood by iron and sail by steam in the middle of the nineteenth century had consigned the Royal Navy to the working-out of an invisible crisis that, though it would take decades to emerge in its plenitude, threatened to undermine all the assumptions on which wooden-wall supremacy had been established. Ironclad navies, vulnerable to defeat "in an afternoon," as Winston Churchill percipiently put it, were fragile instruments of national supremacy. They were expressions of the strength not of a whole national system—social, financial, and industrial—but of no more than a single one of its technological aspects.

Germany's naval technology was proved by Jutland to be superior to Britain's. Her ships were stronger, her guns more accurate, her ordnance more destructive. German shells had usually penetrated British armor when they struck; the reverse had not been the case. Because the German navy took second place in national life to the German army, on which the bulk of the state's wealth was spent, Germany's admirals could not transform technological into strategic advantage over their British counterparts. But because Britain's admirals were themselves the servants of a naval technology supported by a financial and industrial power that since the 1870s had been in relative and irreversible decline, their strategic posture was also defective. In the years from 1914 to 1916, the Grand Fleet, and its battle-cruiser appendix, was perhaps the largest embodiment of naval strength the world had ever seen—in weight of firepower, it unquestionably was. But it was a pyramid of naval power trembling on its apex, at risk of being toppled by any new technological development that threatened its integrity.

PART FOUR

A WORLD
AT ARMS

GALLIPOLI: THE OTHER SIDE OF THE HILL

Tim Travers

—

G ALLIPOLI HAS BEEN PORTRAYED AS THE ONE POTENTIAL strategic masterstroke of the war; it soon became just another unsought epic of endurance. Few campaigns better define the essence of military misfortune; none better sums up the frustrations of 1915. The voluminous literature on Gallipoli, predominately Anglo- or ANZAC-centric, tends to dwell on the missed opportunities of the venture. And indeed the episode is one that lends itself splendidly to both the macro- and micro-managing of hindsight. The chroniclers of the Dardanelles inevitably ask why the Allies lost but never why the Turks won. Tim Travers's article, "Gallipoli: The Other Side of the Hill," based on his researches in Ottoman military archives, tells a story that has not been told before: the Turkish version.

The original idea concocted by Churchill and Fisher was to send battleships through the Dardanelles to the Sea of Marmara: Once the Ottoman capital, Constantinople, was under their guns, and had capitulated, the Turkish straits would be open to Allied shipping. A direct route to Russia would be opened. But on March 18, 1915, Turkish mines sank three Allied battleships and shore batteries put three more out of action—just at the point, some writers claim, when the Allies were on the verge of breaking through. They maintain that the shore batteries were running out of ammunition. As

Travers points out, that was not the case, and it would have been folly for the Allied ships to continue.

As for the Gallipoli landings themselves, cobbled together after the naval failure, enthusiastic but inexperienced British, Australian and New Zealand Army Corps (ANZAC), and French troops would come up against some of the best-trained and best-led units in the Ottoman army. "Johnny Turk," Travers writes, may have "often been poorly fed and badly clothed" but he was "still willing to fight to the death." Moreover, the Turks had been working on the defenses of the Gallipoli Peninsula for decades. (As recently as 1913, during the Second Balkan War, they had successfully defended it against a Bulgarian army that had broken through to the Sea of Marmara). The Turks also had a reasonably clear idea of where the Allies would land, and when. Travers reveals here for the first time how a captured British officer, threatened with death, tipped them off.

But even with the odds in their favor, Gallipoli was a near-run thing for the Turks. Travers discloses missed opportunities never before recognized or even suspected. Again and again, gaps would open that the Allies failed to exploit. Reserves would arrive at the very last moment, and the Turkish lines, ready to disintegrate, would hold. As the Australian historian Trevor Wilson has written: "When the Gallipoli operation is scrutinized without the prior assumption that it was entirely feasible, the 'great ifs' do not accumulate; they recede. Only 'little ifs' remain."

———

TIM TRAVERS is a professor of history at the University of Calgary in Canada. In addition to his *Gallipoli 1915*, recently published in the United Kingdom, he is the author of two highly regarded studies of Western Front leadership, *The Killing Ground* and *How the War Was Won*.

IN ENGLISH-LANGUAGE HISTORIES OF THE 1915 GALLIPOLI CAMPAIGN, THE soldiers of the Ottoman Empire are usually portrayed as tough but simple fighters whose unexpectedly stubborn resistance—magnified by the Allies' mistakes and poor generalship—largely explains the invasion's failure. There is more to the story, however. While it is true that the Ottomans, with the assistance of German officers such as General Otto Liman von Sanders, who commanded the Fifth Army on Gallipoli, were a more organized, efficient, and tenacious foe than the Allies expected, the Ottoman defenses were clearly in severe disarray on several occasions.

In 1915 the Ottoman army was still suffering from the effects of the disastrous Balkan Wars of 1912–13, which had cost the empire its European possessions, and the equally unhappy 1914 Caucasus campaign against Russia, which resulted in the Turks' defeat at Sarikamish. Despite a German military mission that worked to improve the Ottoman armed forces, there was still much to be done, especially in regard to the army's officer corps.

The Ottomans' greatest handicap was their lack of qualified and energetic senior officers, together with a shortage of staff officers. The Staff College had only been operational since 1909, and many of its graduates had been killed in the Balkan Wars. The shortage of officers trained in administrative duties often resulted in chaos. A letter from a German staff officer assigned to the Turks, Major Carl Muhlmann, to his parents in May 1915 gives an amusing but alarming picture of the Ottoman officer corps at work: "It is incredible what levels of talent the senior Turkish officers can attain when it comes to disappearing. . . . Divisional and Regimental commanders were nowhere to be seen. . . ."

Qualitatively, senior Ottoman officers were a mixed bag throughout the Gallipoli campaign, and if prisoner-of-war statements are to be believed, many regimental officers were not much better. Some of these prisoners (especially if they were Arabs, Armenians, Kurds, Macedonians, or Greeks) complained of bad treatment by their Ottoman officers. Indeed, a message from the Fifth Army on August 17, 1915, anticipated an Armenian revolt within the army. Desertion from Ottoman units—particularly from the 17th Regiment, 5th Division; 34th Regiment, 12th Division; and 11th Division—generally increased as the winter weather compounded ill-treatment by officers. To exacerbate the difficulties, junior Ottoman officers were also in very short supply.

On the other hand, the enlisted men of the Ottoman army, unless conscripted from an "unreliable" ethnic group, were excellent soldiers (the Ottomans were often referred to as Turks although the empire was a conglomeration of many other ethnic groups). A typical Ottoman soldier would be a young Anatolian Turk, often poorly fed and badly clothed but still willing to fight to the death. Early in the campaign Major Muhlmann had realized the true value of the Ottoman soldier, and he frequently remarked on the high morale of the Ottoman infantryman, even under conditions approaching chaos. Muhlmann wrote admiringly of the Turkish soldiers at dawn on May 4, 1915, nine days after the Allies landed at Gallipoli: "One has to pay the troops the highest tribute for not falling into disarray; for my part, I have once again gained the conviction that all is possible with this raw human material." Again, on May 8, when Muhlmann found the Turkish trenches shallow and full of corpses, he showed the Ottoman soldiers how to dig proper trenches, and "as I left, they began to dig. Really, truly contented and willing soldier material." Although Muhlmann's views are those of only one individual, they are supported by Allied observations of "Johnny Turk" ("*mehmetcik*" to the Ottomans), who was seen as a brave and worthy opponent.

EARLY IN NOVEMBER 1914, NEARLY THREE MONTHS AFTER FIGHTING HAD ERUPTED on the Western Front, Britain, France, and Russia declared war on the Ottoman Empire because of various provocations involving the Dardanelles—the Turkish straits that led from the Aegean Sea to the Sea of Marmara, the Bosporus, and Russian ports on the Black Sea—and the status of the German battle cruisers *Goeben* and *Breslau,* which had found refuge at Istanbul. Then on January 2, 1915, Russian Grand Duke Nicholas appealed to Britain for a demonstration against the Ottomans, who were attacking Russia in the Caucasus. Lord Kitchener, Britain's secretary of state for war, met with First Lord of the Admiralty Winston Churchill to consider the situation. Later that day, Kitchener informed Churchill that troops were not available to help the Russians and that the only place where a demonstration might prevent Ottoman troops from going east to the Caucasus was at the Dardanelles. The next day Lord Fisher, the First Sea Lord, advocated an audacious but impractical joint army-navy attack against the Ottomans.

Stimulated by these ideas, Churchill telegraphed Vice Admiral Sackville Carden, who commanded the Eastern Mediterranean Squadron. Churchill sought Carden's opinion about the possibility of a naval operation against the Dardanelles. Carden replied that the straits could not be rushed but that a methodical naval operation with a large fleet might succeed. Carden worked out a stage-by-stage naval assault, and because of France's interests in the area, the French navy also became involved. Hence the French and British fleets planned to open the Gallipoli campaign with bombardments of the forts guarding the straits. The concept was for the combined Anglo-French fleet to methodically destroy the Dardanelles's forts and batteries and then enter the Sea of Marmara and bombard key Ottoman gunpowder and ammunition factories as well as selected targets in Istanbul.

The attack on the straits' forts commenced on March 18, 1915, and was a disaster. Three battleships were sunk and three others were severely damaged. Almost all the destruction was done by mines—part of a group of just twenty-six laid on the night of March 7–8 parallel to the shore at Eren Keui Bay, which Ottoman observers had noted was used as a turning point by the Allied fleet. The naval attack had been something of a gamble because a series of maneuvers by Allied ships in February and March to sweep the mines from the straits had been thwarted by fire from Ottoman coastal guns. Commander Worsley Gibson, a British naval officer present at the planning conference for the March 18 attack, observed: "A certain amount of hot air talked but very little achieved. Everyone, or nearly so I believe knew really that it would be madness to try and rush them [the straits]. The Narrows are sure to be mined. It has been proved that bombardment silences guns but does little material damage to guns and only silences [them] because the gunners take cover." This was an accurate assessment; during the attack the Ottoman artillerymen suffered light casualties but scored 139 hits on Allied ships. In the end, the attack did little more than alert the Turks to Allied intentions and strengthen their resolve. One badly wounded Ottoman gunner exclaimed as he was carried away: "Let me just see one more ship go down," while another shouted during the heat of the battle, "Comrades, now comes the hour for which our mothers bore us."

Back in London, Churchill pressed for the attack to be renewed, believing that the Ottomans had fired off most of their ammunition, especially their large-caliber shells. Brigadier General C. F. Aspinall-Oglander, the official British historian of the campaign, agreed with that opinion and later wrote that Ottoman "ammunition [was] practically exhausted." The Allied naval attack, however, was not renewed, perhaps fortunately for the Allies. The Turkish official history reveals that the straits' forts had more than enough shells left to continue the battle.

After the failure of the naval attack, the Allies' focus shifted to an army landing on the Gallipoli Peninsula. The object of this landing, often forgotten now, was to secure the Dardanelles so that the fleet could pass safely through and complete its mission. From various intelligence sources, and from simple logic, the Ottomans easily deduced that a landing was imminent. Indeed, on

March 24 the Ottoman military attaché in Athens learned that the Allied fleet would not continue up the straits because of the mines, and by the twenty-eighth Ottoman sources confirmed that an Allied landing would take place. But where would it occur? One possible answer was provided by none other than the British former consul on Gallipoli, Lieutenant C. S. Palmer, who had been captured while on board submarine *E15*, which had been driven ashore on April 17, 1915. Brigadier General Cevad, commander of the straits fortifications, sent a cipher to the Supreme Military Command in Istanbul, headed by Enver Pasha, laying out a statement by the consul. It had been given after the Turkish general had threatened to shoot Palmer as a spy because the lieutenant was also an officer in the British naval reserve but had been serving as a civilian consul before being captured. Palmer's statement included the information that the Allies planned to land a hundred thousand troops on Gallipoli. Perhaps realizing his mistake, he then attempted to divert his captor's attention by claiming there would be another Allied landing on the northwest side of the Gallipoli Peninsula, along the Gulf of Saros, near Bulair. Palmer, said Cevad, gave this information "on the condition that his life be spared. Please do not give the origin of the information, because of his safety. . . . I ask that you accept him as a war prisoner."

Palmer was either deliberately spreading misinformation about a Gulf of Saros-area landing or did not know the real story. His information that the Allies would definitely land and his figure of a hundred thousand Allied troops appeared in several Ottoman documents. In any case, Fifth Army commander Sanders believed that logical military strategy dictated that the Allies would land near Bulair and Besike. In so doing, their widely separated landings could apply the greatest leverage and open up the area between them. Sanders's summary of the situation for Enver Pasha, dated January 26, 1915, had already stressed the probable landing places of Besike or Kum Kale (where the French did land on April 25), then Sedd-el-Bahr and Gaba Tepe (again the general area of landings on April 25), and finally the area around Bulair, where Sanders concentrated two divisions. Thus, Palmer's report may have strengthened the German general's focus on Bulair. In fact, the Allies' false landing along the shore of the Gulf of Saros on April 25, the same day as their main landings on Gallipoli, did keep Sanders guessing until at least the next day. He was slow to recognize the importance of the Helles and ANZAC landings, reportedly saying of the latter, "It's a demonstration, not the true landing," and "The real landings will be at Bulair." Moreover, because of the considerable distance between Bulair and the actual landing beaches, the infantry from the two Turkish divisions in the north would take some time to arrive at either Gaba Tepe or on Cape Helles.

THE ALLIED LANDINGS AT S, V, W, X, AND Y BEACHES NEAR CAPE HELLES; AT Z BEACH at Ari Burnu on the west side of Gallipoli; and near Kum Kale on the Asian side of the Dardanelles met varying degrees of resistance. At S Beach, a detachment of the South Wales Borderers landed with little trouble at seven-thirty in the morning and was comfortably dug in by ten o'clock. At V Beach, farther to the west, however, there was a disaster. The steamer *River Clyde*, which was ferrying troops to the landing spot, beached offshore and was held fast. When troops from the Royal Munster Fusiliers, the Hampshire Regiment, and the Royal Dublin Fusiliers tried to reach the shore from the grounded ship at six-thirty, entrenched Ottomans mowed them down. The sea became red with blood for some fifty yards out from the water's edge, and only about 400 men managed to land and collect themselves behind a low ridge. Without that ridge probably all of the 700 men who tried to land would have been killed or wounded. It was not until dark that the remainder of the troops aboard *River Clyde* managed to reach the shore.

Next to V Beach was W Beach, where the Lancashire Fusiliers also had to fight their way ashore, winning six Victoria Crosses before breakfast, as the overall commander of the Gallipoli expedition, Sir Ian Hamilton, described it. Thereafter, W Beach was known as Lancashire Landing. Farther west was X Beach, where the Royal Fusiliers waded ashore largely unscathed due to the fact that there were only twelve Ottoman defenders at this spot. Around the corner was the last landing beach at Helles, Y Beach. Here the King's Own Scottish Borderers and the Royal Marines found no defenders. The Ottomans had judged the area an unlikely landing spot because of the 200-foot cliff behind the beach. Problems with organization and command, however, led to an evacuation of Y Beach the next morning.

On the west side of the peninsula was Z Beach, later known as ANZAC cove. Here the navy landed three brigades of troops from the 1st Australian Division and two brigades of New Zealand and Australian troops from the ANZACs. Soon after the landing, heavy Ottoman shell fire and counterattacks, as well as unfamiliar ground and heavy scrub growth, caused the ANZAC troops to become separated from each other and led to some loss of morale. Despite the crisis the troops held firm, and strong naval fire the next day preserved the beachhead.

In addition to the British and ANZAC landings on Gallipoli, French troops landed a diversionary force near the village of Kum Kale, on the Asian side of the straits. Good supporting fire from French ships, a certain Gallic élan, and the Ottoman defenders' surprise and disorganization enabled the French to capture their objective. By prearrangement, the French troops later withdrew from the village on April 27 and moved to reinforce the British right wing on Cape Helles.

Although the story of the Allied landings on the twenty-fifth has often been told, the Ottomans' response to them has received less notice. General Sanders had previously rejected Enver Pasha's plan of lining the coast with troops and instead created strong central reserves while small trip-wire units observed the likely landing places. At Sedd-el-Bahr, Major Mahmut Sabri commanded a thousand men of the 3d Battalion, 26th Regiment, plus 200 engineers. Because of concentrated Allied naval shelling Mahmut had already deduced by the twenty-third that the landings would take place in his area. At four-thirty in the morning on April 25, the major's position began to be shelled once more, and wounded soldiers started to trickle into first aid posts, repeating what they had been trained to say: "I have been wounded and cannot continue my duty, I have given my ammunition to my comrades in the section, here is my rifle, who should I hand it over to?" For almost twenty-four hours he and his men defended nearly five miles of coast before reserves started to arrive. Meanwhile, Mahmut reported that the shore at Ertegrul Cove (V Beach) "became full of enemy corpses, like a shoal of fish. At Seddulbahir [sic] pier 5 boat loads of men were completely sunk."

The major's defense had been costly; by evening his command had suffered 50 percent casualties, and the next day he was ordered to fall back to a second line of defense. The retreat was up two stream beds (Kirte and Kanli Dere), but when Mahmut tried to get his soldiers to man the second line of defense, they would not leave the stream beds. Had they been able, this would have been the perfect opportunity for the British to take advantage of the chaos among the Ottoman troops. Still trying to organize themselves after the landing, however, the Allies were unable to react in time, and the Turks managed to reestablish their line.

The First Battle of Krithia—the first concerted Allied attack on Ottoman positions at Cape Helles—took place on the twenty-eighth, the Allies' objective being the high ground of Achi Baba. The Turks' situation was perilous; Ottoman telegrams on April 28 and 29 complained of a serious shortage of officers and ammunition. Mahmut later recounted that a panicky withdrawal had started among his troops but that he refused to retreat to Soganlidere, the next range of hills behind Achi Baba, as ordered. Just when it appeared that he would be overrun, a company of reserves arrived to strengthen his lines. Although weakened, four Ottoman companies halted the entire Allied advance for three or four hours. Finally, after four more desperate hours, the 19th Regiment of the 7th Division arrived and saved the situation from any further collapse. Once again, the Allies had come close to victory on Cape Helles but had been unable to press home their advantage.

This situation was repeated in another form on Helles around May 4 and

5, when a problem developed between the Ottoman Fifth Army (commanded by Sanders and his chief of staff, Kiazim Bey) and Enver Pasha. The initial Ottoman reaction to the landing was simply to try to sweep the Allies back into the sea. The ranking German adviser in Constantinople, the elderly Field Marshal von der Goltz, supported this response. He had already sent an unhelpful and crude message to Enver Pasha on the first, urging that the Allies be pushed off the peninsula in two days if possible because a long war on Gallipoli would spell disaster. Between May 1 and 5 the Ottomans launched a series of night attacks that resulted in serious losses and only minimal gains. In the early morning of the fourth, Major Muhlmann observed one of these assaults: "A horrible confusion! Thick lines of [Ottoman] skirmishers were streaming backwards; on the other side, new skirmisher lines were again assaulting the slope; all with wild shouts of Allah. I searched for officers, and with my few words of Turkish, I drove the men forward."

That same day, in a sharply worded cipher to Enver Pasha, Kiazim Bey angrily pointed out that his forces had been attacking continuously for nine days: "I request that you please stop these ineffective attacks." Sanders's chief of staff stated that his forces had suffered fifteen thousand casualties since April 25 and that their last reserves had been used up. Moreover, the seven Ottoman regiments in the Helles area were all mixed up; therefore, it was now essential to defend rather than attack. Enver Pasha replied by criticizing the management of the Ottoman forces on Cape Helles and by declaring that the political, economic, and logistical situations required that the Allies be pushed off the peninsula. Despite Enver Pasha's notions, the military situation on Helles demanded that the Ottoman troops now go on the defensive. Kiazim Bey's frantic messages and Muhlmann's recollections reveal another potential window of opportunity for the Allies in early May. Although overall Allied commander Sir Ian Hamilton suspected that the Ottomans had problems, he was unable to exploit them. In fact, in the May 6–8 Second Battle of Krithia, the Allies did attempt to break through but failed because of heavy Turkish artillery and machine-gun fire.

On April 25, during the original landing at ANZAC cove, the Allies had faced crises but were also presented with opportunities to achieve a breakthrough. As previously noted, men from 1st Australian Division and the ANZAC Division had been landed too far north. The reason for this mistake has never been fully established but was probably due to navigation errors by naval officers as the leading landing barges tried to locate landmarks in complete darkness. In any case, the result was initial confusion as the covering force landed, which was compounded when the barges landed troops in the wrong order and in the wrong locations. After landing, battalions moved inland, clambering up steep slopes, and soon became separated into small groups in thick scrub, hidden valleys, and unfamiliar territory.

The isolated and confused ANZAC squads were vulnerable once the Ottoman defenders recovered and began to counterattack. In some areas, such as at the hill Baby 700, stiff fighting took place. At other places the effect of isolation on small groups of soldiers and shell fire on raw troops began to erode morale, and some Allied soldiers retreated down to the beach in the late afternoon. As a result, some British commanders began to conclude that the landing was a failure and wished to reembark their forces that first night ashore. According to Mustafa Kemal, 19th Division commander, some Allied troops had actually already left in rowboats. But the British navy declared that a general reembarkation was not possible, and so Hamilton issued his well-known order to the ANZAC to "Dig, dig, dig," and the tenacious soldiers were able to hold on. Yet, the Ottoman defenders opposing the landings at ANZAC cove also encountered difficulties.

The Ottomans anticipated that the Allied attack would be at Gaba Tepe and therefore deployed the 27th Regiment, 9th Division, behind this point. Recognizing the strength of Gaba Tepe's defenses, the ANZACs aimed to land north of it. Unfortunately, due to navigational errors, the ANZAC landing took place even farther north than intended, at Ari Burnu. This meant that the closest Ottoman division to the actual location of the ANZAC landing place was not the 9th Division but Kemal's 19th.

Ottoman soldiers manning an observation post spotted the landing early—between two-thirty and three o'clock in the morning on April 25—while Kemal, inland at Bigalikoyu, did not personally learn of it until six-thirty. Without waiting for orders, he pushed forward his 57th Regiment to cover the critical high ground of the Sari Bair Ridge, which faced the ANZAC landing site. He also called up his quick-firing mountain guns, which later that day caused serious problems for attacking ANZAC troops. By about ten o'clock Kemal had enough troops from the 57th to launch a series of counterattacks against the ANZACs from the flanks of the Sari Bair Ridge toward the ANZAC landing site. Kemal also inspired his soldiers, believing that "this was no ordinary attack. Everybody in this attack was eager to succeed or go forward with the determination to die." Kemal told his subordinate commanders: "I don't order you to attack, I order you to die. In the time which passes until we die other troops and commanders can take our place." Despite these brave words, however, there were at least three Ottoman crises that day.

First of all, in one landing area near a jutting peak nicknamed the Sphinx, the Ottoman defenders had been reduced to just eight or ten soldiers, who quickly retreated to the northeast. The area was left wide open to ANZAC attackers. They took advantage of the Ottoman retreat but not in sufficient numbers to achieve decisive results. Farther north, at Fisherman's Hut, the 2d Battalion of the 57th Regiment lost soldiers and communications and also retreated inland toward the heights of Chunuk Bair. On the night of April 25 the commander of the battalion reported that his troops were all gone. Back at headquarters, it was assumed that this battalion had split up into small groups, and that the battalion commander "had lost his head." This area, therefore, also was left open to the ANZACs. Nevertheless, most of the 140 Australian and New Zealand soldiers who had attempted to land near Fisherman's Hut had been shot in their boats or as they landed, and only thirty-two remained in action. These few remaining men simply held on in a defensive position.

A second crisis for the Ottomans had emerged at around eleven-thirty, when a staff officer reported to Kemal that the Allies had also landed at Kum Tepe, between Gaba Tepe and Cape Helles. Because of the potential significance of this landing, Kemal left his 57th Regiment fighting in the Ari Burnu area and began marching south with his two other regiments toward the Kum Tepe area. Kemal later recalled that it was not until one o'clock, an hour and a half later, when he reached the heights of Mal Tepe, that he "heard voices shouting his name." Moving toward the shouts, he discovered the corps commander and his staff. The corps staff had made a mistake, and the report of the Allied landing at Kum Tepe was false. Kemal later reflected, "See how in this [original] verbal report the addition of a sentence 'troops have landed at KUMTEPE' was able to change the whole tactical plan and in a very important way at that!" After being given command of the whole area at Ari Burnu, Kemal turned around and started back toward the ANZAC landing area but was not able to return to the scene of operations until late that day. The period during which he and two of his regiments were absent presented the Allies with yet another opportunity to achieve a breakthrough.

Finally, a third Ottoman crisis developed because two of Kemal's three regiments in the 19th Division—the 72d and 77th—were less-reliable Arab units. Of the 72d, Kemal simply said, "it was not possible to employ [this regiment]." He did attempt to use the 77th on the day of the landings and no doubt regretted doing so. Kemal put it between the 57th Regiment and the neighboring 27th Regiment to the south in order to support those two units. Since the Arab soldiers did not understand Turkish, however, the 77th could barely communicate with their neighbors, and after coming under some naval shelling the regiment retreated and hid in the bushes. As night fell the 77th began firing wildly. According to an Ottoman staff officer, Zeki Bey, "The 27th Regiment coming under this fire, and thinking that the 57th was shooting into it, was all night crying out to the 57th not to fire; and the 57th in the same way was calling out to the 27th." The 77th then simply melted away, dragging back the 27th Regiment and leaving the Kanli Sirt region (Bloody Ridge and Lone Pine) open to the ANZACS. Once more, however, the exhausted, disoriented, and decimated ANZAC troops were unaware of their opportunity and were content to simply hang on.

Although the Allied landings had been successful and the Ottoman defense was in disarray, it proved impossible for the Allies to capture Achi Baba on Cape Helles, despite three battles of Krithia. A stalemate developed similar to that on the Western Front. To break the impasse, several officers, including the ANZAC corps commander, Lieutenant General Sir William Birdwood, suggested a breakout on the ANZACS' left flank. The objective would be Sari Bair Ridge. A landing at and near Suvla Bay, to the north of ANZAC cove, was added as a base to support the breakout plan. The Ottomans were suspicious of a new landing, and General Sanders sent a telegram to Enver Pasha on July 18 remarking that "The necessary orders for the Gulf of Saros have been issued. But at the moment I doubt a landing there because for this the enemy will need heavy equipment such as landing piers and magazines and much more." Instead, Sanders suspected "the area of Gaba Tepe, because he can there use existing facilities, and then simultaneously threaten both groups—while his frontline troops tie us down at Ari Burnu [in the ANZAC area] and Sedd el Bahir [on Cape Helles] by way of an attack." Nevertheless, he wrote, the enemy "is up to something."

However, Ottoman expectations of where the August Allied attacks would take place were contradictory. Despite Sanders's suspicions of Gaba Tepe, he remained very conscious of the Bulair area, predicting, "They will attack in the north." Furthermore, a telegram from the director of operations in Istanbul on August 5 (the day before Allied breakout operations began) to the Fifth Army stressed the Bulair region, complained about the lack of information from the Fifth Army, and strongly conveyed Enver Pasha's inexpedient idea that the enemy should be met on the beaches. Of course, this strategy depended on knowing the exact location of the landing, and again, almost the entire Ottoman staff thought the attack would either be on the Asian side of the peninsula or well to the north. Since Ottoman intelligence reports in July all focused on Bulair (prompted by misinformation supplied by Hamilton's headquarters) and paid lesser attention to the Asian shore, the caution about the shore of the Gulf of Saros is understandable. Once again, however, Ottoman confusion concerning the enemy's intentions provided Allied forces with an opportunity at Suvla.

At least one Ottoman officer did not believe that the Allies would land along the Gulf of Saros shore—Mustafa Kemal, who declared that the most significant area was the Sari Bair hills. Kemal recalled that in July his skeptical corps commander, Essad Pasha, asked from where the enemy would come. Kemal replied, pointing

> in the direction of Ari Burnu and along the whole shore as far as Suvla. "From here," I said. "Very well, supposing he does come from there, how will he advance?" Again, pointing towards Ari Burnu, I moved my hand in a semi-circle towards Koca Cimen Tepe, "he will advance from here," I said. The Corps commander smiled and patted my shoulder. "Don't you worry, he can't do it," he said. Seeing that it was impossible for me to put over my point of view I felt it unnecessary to prolong the argument any further. I confined myself to saying, "God willing, sir, things will turn out as you expect."

The early August ANZAC breakout plan was ingenious but too ambitious given the condition of the Allied troops on the peninsula. On the night of August 6–7, two main columns were to climb up through the narrow defiles on the left flank of ANZAC cove, toward three summits on Sari Bair Ridge: Koca Chemen Tepe, Hill Q, and Chunuk Bair. Meanwhile, a large-scale diversionary attack would be launched at Helles in the south and a smaller-scale one at Lone Pine on the right flank of the ANZAC area. The first was designed to draw Ottoman troops away from the ANZAC area (it did not work), while the Lone Pine assault was intended to draw Ottoman troops away from the ANZACs' left flank area (this did work).

Simultaneously, landings were planned for the Suvla area, just to the north of ANZAC, partly to create a port for the hopefully successful main offensive on the Sari Bair Ridge (ANZAC cove being too small and too exposed), and partly to move inland and secure the high ground of the Tekke Tepe heights directly east of the Suvla landing site. For this operation, the 11th Division was to land on the evening of August 6 and the 10th on August 7. Unfortunately, after these two divisions landed, Lieutenant General Frederick Stopford, the commander of the Suvla operation, brought the offensive to a halt. Thereafter, the small Suvla enclave was gradually widened by further attacks in August, but soon this area too settled into stalemate.

The two main ANZAC columns, meanwhile, found their objectives on the Sari Bair Ridge to be overly ambitious in light of the weakened condition of the men because of dysentery and other diseases and the stifling conditions at night in the narrow, confusing defiles. Troops got lost or were slowed down or halted by tentative commanders and came under heavy Ottoman fire from above. Nevertheless, a small group of Gurkhas captured Hill Q, and the New Zealand Wellington Battalion gained the Chunuk Bair heights. The Gurkhas, however, were shelled off Hill Q by friendly fire on August 9, and Kemal swept the defenders off Chunuk Bair in a mass attack at dawn on August 10. This ended the Allies' innovative and bold August ANZAC offensive, which proved too much of a physical and technical obstacle for the troops involved.

Yet, the little-studied Ottoman response to this offensive requires a more detailed examination. The Australians' Lone Pine diversionary attack at five-thirty in the afternoon on August 6 succeeded at considerable cost. The Ottoman defenders were a battalion of Kemal's 72d Arab Regiment, which had just relieved a battalion of the 57th Regiment. Now recovered from its problems of April 25, the 72d fought well, but the Australians achieved their objective of drawing attention and reserves away from the sector where the left hook—the columns aiming for the Sari Bair peaks of Koca Chemen Tepe, Hill Q, and Chunuk Bair—was under way during the night of August 6–7. By August 9, as previously recounted, the ANZAC forces had a tenuous hold on two of the hills, and at the same time landings were taking place just to the north at Suvla. But once again Sanders remained overattentive to the Bulair area and even warned his two divisions to prepare for an attack there. On the morning of the seventh, some Ottoman units were sent from Bulair to assist the German commander defending Suvla, Major Wilhelm Willmer, and finally at ten o'clock a new group of two Ottoman divisions was formed under Colonel Fezi Bey to move from Bulair and throw back the Allies attacking the Sari Bair Ridge. But the Ottoman response to the breakout attempt—Sanders's slow reaction, his fixation on Bulair, and the general confusion of deciding which was the key front—presented the Allies with chances of success between August 7 and 9.

An alert German staff officer, Colonel Hans Kannengiesser, was largely responsible for quashing one of those opportunities. He was at Chunuk Bair, conducting a reconnaissance early on the morning of August 7, when

> suddenly the enemy actually appeared in front of us at about 500 yards' range. The English [as all Allies were called] approached slowly, in single file, splendidly equipped and with white bands on their left arms, apparently very tired, and were crossing a hillside to our flank. . . . I immediately sent an order to my infantry—this was the twenty man strong artillery-covering platoon—instantly to open fire. I received this answer: "We can only commence to fire when we receive the order of our battalion commander." This was too much for me altogether. I ran to the spot and threw myself among the troops who were lying in a small trench. What I said I cannot recollect, but they began to open fire and almost immediately the English laid down without answering our fire or apparently moving in any other way.

Other reserves, including portions of the 72d Arab Regiment, soon arrived to support Kannengiesser's small force, and this particular chance faded away.

The next day, matters remained confused. Willmer and his small command still contained the Allied thrust at Suvla, due to Stopford's pessimism and inaction, but the Ottoman commanders did not understand the situation at Chunuk Bair and Hill Q. The confusion among 9th Division units can be sensed in a message recorded by Kemal: "An attack has been ordered on Conk Bayiri [Chunuk Bair]. To whom should I give this order? I am looking for the Battalion commanders, but I cannot find them. Everything is in a muddle. The situation is serious. At any rate someone who knows the ground must be appointed. There are no reports and no information. I am confused as to what I should do." A second 9th Division intelligence report states that men from various battalions were all mixed up and that "No officers can be found. . . . I have received no information about what is going on. All the officers are killed or wounded. I do not even know the name of the place where I am. I cannot see anything by observation. I request in the name of the safety of the nation that an officer be appointed who knows the area well."

In fact, on August 8 General Sanders was still trying to divine the Allied offensive's objective but decided to order an attack on the northern flank of the ANZAC front to disorganize the Allied assaults on Hill Q and Chunuk Bair and to make the earliest possible use of reserves arriving from Bulair in the north. Fezi Bey commanded this attack of the 7th and 12th Divisions, which had arrived from the Bulair region after two days of hard marching. Major Willmer, who was present, recalled that Sanders ordered Fezi Bey to attack "during the afternoon of the 8th or at the latest during the evening. . . ." But, to the annoyance of the German general, Fezi Bey argued vehemently that he first needed time to collect the two tired divisions, while the commanders of those divisions simply said, "It is not possible to attack." General Sanders asked the Turkish colonel, "What do you say?" Fezi Bey replied, "I am of the same opinion." Thereupon, he was immediately superseded. Regardless, Sanders then called Kemal to the telephone and asked his opinion of the situation. Kemal remembered that he said "there was no other course remaining but to put all available troops under my command." "Won't that be too many?" the German asked, "It will be too few," Kemal responded.

Early the next morning, Kemal attacked the northern flank of ANZAC cove with Fezi Bey's 19,000 men and occupied Hill 60, although the Allies, principally the 4th Battalion, South Wales Borderers, courageously halted the attack at Damakjelik Bair. Meanwhile, despite continuous attacks, the Ottomans had been unable to recapture the vital position of Chunuk Bair. The Allies had now had three full days to exploit their surprise offensives at ANZAC cove and Suvla. Clearly the Ottoman defense was still in disarray, especially with the dismissal of Fezi Bey, but once again the Allies were unable to capitalize on an opportunity. This time, on the ANZAC front and at Suvla Bay, it was due to exhaustion, formidable terrain, disorganization, poor senior commanders, and increasingly fierce Ottoman resistance. At first light on August 10, Kemal launched waves of bayonet assaults at Chunuk Bair, sweeping away the defenders, while the Allies were forced to evacuate the Hill Q position just below the crest.

Captain Richard Hicks of the 10th Battalion, Hampshire Regiment, who was dug in just below the crest of Hill Q, remembered the moment when the Ottoman attack reached his position and panic erupted among the defenders, with men shouting, "Retire, the Turks are on you!" Hicks managed to mount a brief counterattack, but eventually he and his men were ordered to retreat. He recalled that the narrow gully soon "was full of men running for all they were worth. We rallied the Hampshires. . . . Two officers stood in the nullah [gully] and stopped the rest from flying. Very near a panic but not quite." Such was the effect of the Ottoman attack on exhausted and overexerted men.

Meanwhile, near Suvla Bay, another chance for Allied success was thrown away when Stopford again failed to press his attack forward with any urgency. At dawn on August 9 a squad of East Yorkshire Pioneers reached the summit of the Tekke Tepe hills, the ultimate Suvla objective, but they were too late; a wave of Ottoman infantry met them and overwhelmed the squad. Allegedly, the enraged Ottoman troops began to bayonet some of their prisoners, but the rest were saved by the intervention of an Ottoman imam.

In light of charges that Ottoman soldiers mistreated Allied prisoners of war, it should be noted that prisoner-of-war documents, including those of Allied officers captured at Tekke Tepe, tell a different story. During interrogations, Allied prisoners all stressed their good treatment by the Ottomans, as might be expected in such a setting. Thus Captain Elliott, 6th East Yorkshire Pioneers, one of those captured at dawn on August 9 at Tekke Tepe, said: "There is nothing to complain about in regard to the Turks. They had a chance to kill us, but on the contrary they spared my life. I am especially grateful." In any case, it is possible that Ottoman captors did on occasion treat their prisoners reasonably well on Gallipoli.

The failure of the ANZAC breakout and the Suvla supporting operation spelled the end of the Allied effort on Gallipoli, despite further offensives later in August and September. Ottoman documents confirm the early August offensive's heavy cost to the defenders. These official papers are significant because accurate Ottoman casualty figures are scarce. Between August 6 and 11 Ottoman casualties, excluding missing and prisoners, are listed as 4,373. Despite these losses, the Allies' breakout attempt was defeated. Yet the Ottoman commanders still worried that disaster threatened. Mustafa Kemal, in particular, feared another landing to the north of Suvla Bay, at Ejelmer Bay, otherwise known as Ece Limani. In a message dated August 11 and marked "Very Urgent" he warned the local commander, "Your essential duty is to prevent the Allies' disembarkation at Ece Harbour." A landing there threatened to outflank the Ottoman defenses, and the Allies probably should have considered it more seriously as an invasion site. Indeed, both Kannengiesser and Sanders believed the Allied attacks of August 15 and 16 in this same Kiretech Tepe area created a crisis similar to that of the early August offensives. Nevertheless, these attacks also were turned back, and the campaign settled into another stalemate in which climate and disease played as large a role as bullets and shrapnel.

This stalemate, plus the imminent arrival of German heavy artillery and Serbia's need for help in repelling an invasion by Bulgaria, led to the decision to evacuate. Ironically, the December 1915–January 1916 evacuation was the most successful of all the Allies' Gallipoli operations and resulted in no deaths. But contrary to historical accounts, including that of General Sanders, which describe the evacuation as a surprise to the Turks, the Ottoman commanders were aware of Allied moves to abandon the Gallipoli Peninsula. This was evident in a message that Sanders sent to Kemal on November 29, 1915, written in French, referring to an attack that Kemal was planning for the same day: "The violent attack that you had proposed for today at 3 P.M. does not conform to our aims, and I ask you to cancel the attack. You know very well that the enemy is at the moment still in considerable strength, and we have sustained enough casualties already doing this same kind of thing. . . . The spontaneous and radical change in the situation, of which you have clear signs, now commences, that the enemy wishes to withdraw. Until then, you must obtain the permission of Fifth Army [to attack]. . . ."

Other Ottoman officers confirmed the belief that the Allies were slowly withdrawing. On January 4, 1916, an unnamed artillery commander at Helles wrote Kannengiesser that "in my opinion the enemy is withdrawing slowly but certainly. I deduce that from the daily reports of the batteries and from my own observation. Many [Allied] batteries are now only firing with one or two guns . . . I personally believe that in 8–14 days the enemy will have retired, if not earlier. Unfortunately the infantry cannot be induced to attack."

The general conclusion is that General Otto Liman von Sanders and his Fifth Army, when under severe Allied pressure, did on several occasions offer the Allies genuine chances for breakthroughs—chances the Allies, however, were not able to exploit. It was only too easy for them to reflect upon their own casualties and hardships while imagining that their Ottoman opponents were in better condition. Yet the Ottoman forces suffered frequent crises. Whether during the initial April and early May battles on Gallipoli or again during the renewed Allied offensive of early August, these windows of opportunity might have been exploited by the Allies had they but known of them and had they possessed the necessary forces and leadership to achieve success is a question that will always haunt.

KUT

Robert F. Jones

GALLIPOLI WAS NOT THE ONLY PLACE WHERE "JOHNNY Turk" distinguished himself. The odds against him were always daunting. Just consider the nightmare of logistics. The entire Ottoman Empire, an area of 679,360 square miles, had only 3,580 miles of railroad track in 1914. It wasn't until October 1918, just three weeks before the armistice of Mudros took the empire out of the war, that the rail line between Constantinople and Baghdad was finally completed. The Anatolian fighting front on the border with Russia had no rail service at all, the historian Ulrich Trumpener points out, "requiring transportation by oxcart and foot marches over primitive roads from nearest railheads of 370 miles or more." In 1916, six months were needed to move divisions from Gallipoli to the Caucasus. "If one considers that coal and other fuels were in short supply or located in inaccessible places, it is amazing that the Ottoman war effort did not collapse any sooner than it did."

Still, the Turks were tenacious fighters, and they earned the respect of their allies. January 1916 saw the evacuation of the last British forces at Gallipoli. In the months that followed, Turkey sent divisions to help the beleaguered Austrians in Galicia, joined the Central Powers in the overrunning of Romania, and bolstered the Bulgarian line in Salonika. The seldom-reported fighting in the Caucasus (where nearly half of all Ottoman troops were sent) began with catastrophe, gradually stabilized, and, as Russia disintegrated, turned in favor of the Turks.

But no single feat of Turkish arms quite matched the 148-day siege of a British force at Kut, in Mesopotamia. For the first time but not for the last, oil was the magnet. In the early days of the war, the British sent troops of the Indian Army to protect its oil supplies on the Persian Gulf. They found themselves in the same area where, seventy-five years later, the Gulf War would be fought, but the result would be entirely different. The ease with which the British dealt with the Turks on the Tigris and Euphrates at the end of 1914 certainly influenced their decision to continue probing "the soft underbelly" of the Central Powers, notably in the Dardanelles. But in both cases that softness would prove deceptive. Even as the decision to evacuate Gallipoli was reached in London at the end of 1915, the Turks checked the British near Baghdad, at the great ruined Arch of Ctesiphon, one of the archaeological wonders of the Near East. The British commander, Major General Sir Charles Vere Ferrers Townshend, retreated down the Tigris to a mud-walled town called Kut-el-Amara, there to await relief from the south. But the relief would never arrive. When, a month before Jutland, Kut fell, it would be the largest mass surrender of imperial troops between Yorktown in 1783 and Singapore in 1942. As at Gallipoli, the outcome would have less to do with unavailing British resilience than with the determination of an adversary too often maligned. As Robert F. Jones writes, Kut "underscored the need for thorough preparation before attempting any ground offensive in the area"—an area we now know as Iraq.

———

ROBERT F. JONES, who died in 2002, was the author of eight novels and six works of nonfiction. His articles and essays appeared in many magazines. His final book was *The Hunter in My Heart: A Sportsman's Salmagundi.* Jones lived in Vermont.

W HEN ALLAH MADE HELL," RUNS AN OLD ARAB EPIGRAM, "HE DID NOT FIND it bad enough—so He created Mesopotamia." That antique land now goes by the name of Iraq, and in the wake of the Persian Gulf War, more than half a million of Saddam Hussein's troops would no doubt concur. Superb Allied planning, relentless "preparation" of the Kuwaiti battleground before the final assault, near-total interdiction of Iraqi supply and escape routes, and the most devastating American flanking attack since Stonewall Jackson's at Chancellorsville—all combined to produce an overwhelming victory for United States–led coalition forces. It was a hundred-hour masterpiece of firepower and maneuver, the likes of which had not been seen since Hitler's fifteen-day armored blitzkrieg through the Low Countries and northern France in May 1940.

But it might have gone otherwise, as it did for some 36,000 British and Indian troops who fought, bled, shivered, starved, sweated, scratched, and died in Mesopotamia seventy-five years ago during a disastrous but largely forgotten campaign of World War I—an episode that underscored the need for thorough preparation before attempting any ground offensive in the area. It is known to history as the Siege of Kut-el-Amara.

At Kut, from December 3, 1915, to April 29 the following year, about 10,000 officers, men, and camp followers of Britain's 6th Division of the Indian Army endured a siege that lasted 148 days. A relief force struggling vainly up the flooded Tigris River valley to their rescue took 23,000 casualties in attack after failed attack through rain-sodden sands and pestilential marshes against a tough, well-entrenched Turkish army. When Kut's garrison finally surrendered, much was made of the fact that it had survived longer than the besieged forces at Ladysmith during the Boer War (119 days) and Lucknow during the Indian Mutiny (about 140, in two stages).

Indeed, British pluck was about all that could be salvaged from what amounted to the worst debacle of British arms since the Retreat from Kabul during the First Afghan War, when 16,500 soldiers, women, and servants under General William G. K. Elphinstone ("Elphy Bey" to his troops) left only one escapee, Surgeon William Brydon, to complete a bloody winter's walk down the Khyber Pass to Jalalabad. Kut's dubious distinction was not eclipsed until February 15, 1942, when the equivalent of three British divisions surrendered Singapore (and about a million civilians) to the Japanese who had outflanked them.

At the outbreak of World War I in August 1914, Britain had quickly sent a brigade—the 16th of the Indian Army's 6th Poona Division—to protect its oil supplies in Abadan, now vital since Winston Churchill, as First Lord of the Admiralty, had converted the Royal Navy from coal to oil. The Mesopotamian Expeditionary Force had orders from London to "play a safe game" in the region: Its mission was limited to protecting the oil flow to Abadan, no more. After all, Britain was not yet at war with Turkey. When Britain reluctantly declared war on the Ottoman Empire on November 4, that Indian force moved quickly to secure Fao and Basra in Mesopotamia at the top of the Persian Gulf flanking Abadan on the Shatt-al-Arab.

The Turks responded with an attack down the Euphrates River from An Nasiriya toward Kurna, where the Tigris and Euphrates unite to form the Shatt-al-Arab. The British, with the balance of the 6th Division now in place under the command of General Sir Arthur Barrett, had anticipated such a thrust by taking Kurna on December 9, 1914, against light opposition, and then he blunted an attack at Shaiba in April 1915, just upstream, with a bayonet charge.

The ease with which the Turks had been beaten so far at every point of contact bred overconfidence among British commanders, who began looking beyond Kurna toward Baghdad, some 360 miles up the Tigris from Basra. The Indian Army was overconfident to begin with, having dealt with poorly armed, ill-organized hill tribesmen for the most part. Indeed, Britain's toughest fight in nineteenth-century India had been against its own sepoys during the Great Mutiny of 1857–58.

If the Turks were fighting at the far end of a long supply line, the Mesopotamian Expeditionary Force was worse off. In an essentially roadless land, they lacked much in the way of river transport, as well as adequate artillery, mules, medical supplies, even proper wharves and unloading facilities at Basra. Without these, and especially without a light railroad to move men and armaments upcountry, a successful campaign against Baghdad—where British lines of communication would be stretched as thin as the Turks' were at Shaiba—was doubtful to say the least.

But by now, six months into the Great War, the fighting in Belgium and France was settling down to the form it would retain for most of its four-year duration: brutal, bloody, close-range, high-casualty trench warfare. Strategic thinkers in London, such as Churchill and Horatio Herbert, Lord Kitchener, the secretary of state for war, began to see the Middle East as a theater from which pressure could be applied to "the soft underbelly" of the Central Powers, thus drawing German troops away from both France and beleaguered Russia.

In Mesopotamia, the Expeditionary Force was booted up to corps strength, with a new commander, General Sir John Eccles Nixon, a "thrusting" cavalry officer with the requisite bushy mustache, prominent nose, and overweeningly aggressive ambition. To lead the 6th Division in fulfillment of his plans, he chose Major General Sir Charles Vere Ferrers Townshend, a fifty-four-year-old careerist and serious student of military history whose ambitions were as keen as Nixon's.

Most sources concur with the military historian Byron Farwell that Townshend was "a man with a curious, unlikable personality" who "never seemed to fit in or belong, wherever he went." And he had been many places, never content with any of the regiments in which he served, from the Royal Marine Light Infantry to the Central India Horse to the Egyptian Camel Corps to the Royal Fusiliers. Though he distinguished himself enough in the Sudan to win Kitchener's praise at the Battles of Atbara and Omdurman in 1898 against the Mahdists, his closest friends were not soldiers but actors and actresses in the London theater. Possessed of a cutting tongue, he considered himself a great entertainer and raconteur, dropping French quotations, theatrical gossip, and literary aperçus right and left, which only further alienated his bluffer, anti-intellectual military peers. That he had married a French wife did not help, nor did his inveterate pulling of strings to gain better appointments and higher rank.

Townshend did at times demonstrate flashes of military genius, particularly on the offensive. Oddly enough, however, he first gained fame in the most defensive of military postures, a siege situation. In 1895 he was part of a small force sent to Chitral, a Connecticut-size principality in the Hindu Kush, whose *mehtar,* "ruler," had recently died, precipitating a power struggle. When the British force of Sikhs and Kashmiris was ambushed and Captain C. P. Campbell, the senior line officer, caught a bullet in the knee, Townshend—then still a junior captain at the age of thirty-four—took command. He demonstrated a remarkable talent for sitting tight. In a mud fort only eighty yards square, behind walls eight feet thick, with plenty of bullets but only pea soup and horsemeat to eat, Townshend played his banjo, told theatrical anecdotes, quoted from the French classics, popped away at the enemy with a Martini-Henry rifle, and waited until he and his 542 charges were relieved forty-six days later. Then he returned to England, where he received a Companionship in the Order of the Bath, an audience with the Prince of Wales, a command to dine with Queen Victoria, and a most welcome promotion. He was on his way.

On April 25, 1915—the day that landings began at Gallipoli in what would prove to be Britain's other disastrous thrust at that infamous underbelly—Townshend arrived at Kurna with orders from Nixon to eject the Turks from their positions near the town and advance up the Tigris to 'Amara, ninety miles to the north and the most important town between Kurna and Baghdad.

Local legend had it that Kurna had been the original Garden of Eden. If so, it had declined. Townshend found a mud-hutted hamlet fraught with fleas, flies, and mosquitoes that could suck blood through two layers of khaki drill and a Balaclava helmet; light-fingered *Maadan*, "Marsh Arabs," who stung worse; and such boosterish landmarks as Serpent Alley, Rib Road, Adam's Walk, and Temptation Square, where stood the stump of the putative biblical tree from which the serpent tempted Adam and Eve. But the Tommies weren't taken in. As a bit of doggerel ran:

> *I've tried to solve a riddle,*
> *You wish to know it? Well,*
> *If Kurna's the Garden of Eden,*
> *Then where the dickens is Hell?*

It lay upriver.

Arrayed against Townshend outside Kurna was Turkish general Khalil Bey with six battalions of well-trained Anatolian Turks, 600 Arab riflemen, 1,200 poorly disciplined *Maadan*, at least ten artillery pieces, and two armed river-boats, the *Mosul* and the *Marmariss*. With the Tigris in spring spate, the ground Townshend's force would have to advance across was now a shallow, muddy lake studded with the tops of sand hills, clusters of palms, and a few mud huts. The first objective was a trio of island sandhill redoubts flanking the now invis-ible channel of the Tigris. They lay 3,000 to 4,000 yards away, while some 10,000 yards beyond them reared a crescent of sandy ridges—ideal ground for covering artillery.

For a month Townshend readied his assault: The first wave would comprise 328 *bellums*, "oared dugout canoes," ten men to a boat; an advance guard of thirty-two boats armored with machine-gun shields would precede each bat-talion; behind them would come barges and rafts carrying the division's ar-tillery—18-pounders, howitzers, 4- and 5-inch guns, and a mountain battery. Escorting the troops would be three armed sloops (*Odin, Clio,* and the "flagship" *Espiègle*), three armored tugs (*Shaitan, Sumana,* and *Lewis Pelly*), a paddle steamer (the *Comet*), and four launches. Since the Turks had heavily mined the river and its flooded banks, Townshend offered the local Arab population 400 rupees for each mine brought in.

The preparations were meticulous. Each assault *bellum* would carry one NCO and nine men, assigned so that no single *bellum* carried too many oversize passengers. The boats were equipped with picks, shovels, tow ropes, poles, and paddles, even caulking material to plug bullet holes. In the end, the assembled amphibious force came to be known as "Townshend's Regatta."

On May 31, 1915, the attack began with a murderous artillery barrage from the heavy guns in Kurna, the naval flotilla, and the horse-drawn barges and rafts. The Turkish response was feeble, and the *bellums* that landed their sun-helmeted troops at the first redoubt met no opposition to speak of; the enemy trenches had collapsed under the artillery's "volcano of fire" and were filled with dead and wounded. The story was the same at the second and third redoubts.

A captured Turkish officer who had laid the electrically controlled river minefield led the armored tugs through with their sweeps deployed. Then the big guns opened up on the sandhill crescent at Bahran while the *bellums* moved forward for another assault. Again there came no answering fire. A reconnaissance plane flew over the strongpoint and returned to report "Bahran abandoned." Khalil Bey's force was in full rout northward.

Townshend was quick to follow up his success. At Atbara in the Sudan, he had won Kitchener's praise by taking not one but three lines of trenches in one charge. He saw a similar opportunity for glory here. Leaving part of his force to occupy Bahran and clear the channel more completely, he forged upriver in the *Espiègle* to Ezra's Tomb, twenty miles farther on. With only a hundred troops and some staff officers, and escorted by the rest of his "regatta," he reached the sacred shrine with its blue dome glowing in the sunset, closing to within 8,000 yards of the two fleeing Turkish riverboats and damaging them with his artillery.

At four-twenty the next morning the pursuit continued. The battered *Mosul* was found flying a white flag a short way upriver, and by early afternoon the "regatta" had broken clear of the marshes into open river, its banks lush with date palms. By three-twenty in the afternoon the "regatta" reached Kala Salih, where a few rounds from a 3-pounder routed a detachment of Turkish cavalry; the local sheikh surrendered. On June 3 the chase was on again, this time as far as Abu Sidra, seventy-eight miles from Townshend's jump-off point at Kurna. 'Amara itself lay only twelve miles farther. As the most modern and populous town south of Baghdad, with its own garrison, a customs house, and adequate supplies for the six Turkish battalions that had retreated from Kurna, it wouldn't fail as easily as the others—or would it? Townshend decided to take the gamble.

As the armored tug *Shaitan*, in the lead, neared 'Amara, its gunners spotted hundreds of Turkish troops boarding a steamer at quayside. The *Shaitan* fired one round, and such was their panic that they surrendered. 'Amara, with a population of 20,000, was Townshend's at the price of one cannon shell—if he could hold it. But the Turks had no more fight in them, at least for the moment. Townshend brought the rest of his 15,000 men upriver and consolidated his position. Thorough preparation coupled with audacity in following up his initial success had won him a brilliant, low-cost victory at a time when British forces in France and at Gallipoli could gain no ground at all without the payment of outrageous "butcher's bills."

General Nixon was delighted, as were his superiors in India. The corps commander's next step was to send Major General Sir George Gorringe's 12th Division, strengthened by a brigade from Townshend's 6th and most of his artillery, up the Euphrates against An Nasiriya, the town from which the earlier Turkish attack on Kurna had been mounted. After weeks of fighting through lakes, swamps, and date groves, Gorringe was on the outskirts of An Nasiriya, which fell July 23 after a short, fierce fight that cost the British 500 casualties to the Turks' 1,000. It was a hot campaign in more ways than one: Daytime temperatures in Mesopotamia can reach 130 degrees in the shade.

Townshend spent most of that summer back in Bombay, where he had been shipped shortly after the capture of 'Amara to convalesce from the dysentery that had struck him and 1,100 of his men; along with malaria, it was making greater inroads against the Mesopotamian Expeditionary Force than Turkish bullets had so far. He found Charles Lord Hardinge, India's viceroy, and General Beauchamp Duff, Commander in Chief of the Indian Army, flush with the reflected success of his and Gorringe's victories and contemplating grander successes, possibly even the capture of Baghdad.

"I believe I am to advance from Amarah to Kut el Amarah directly I get back to my division," he confided in a letter to a friend in England.

> The question is, where are we to stop in Mesopotamia? . . . We have certainly not got good enough troops to make certain of taking Baghdad. . . .
>
> We can take no risks of defeat in the East. I imagine a retreat from Baghdad and the consequent instant rising of the Arabs of the whole country behind us, to say nothing of the certain rise, in that case, of the Persians, and probably the Afghans, in consequence. . . .
>
> I consider we ought to hold what we have got and not advance any more as long as we are held up, as we are, in the Dardanelles. All these offensive operations in secondary theatres are dreadful errors in strategy: the Dardanelles, Egypt, Mesopotamia, East Africa—I wonder and wonder at such expeditions being permitted in violation of all the great fundamental principles of war, especially that of Economy of Force. Such violation is always punished in history.

Townshend's prescience was confirmed two days later at a luncheon with Duff, who told him he would be advancing on Kut as soon as Whitehall's approval was granted. Arriving back at Basra on August 21, Townshend reported to Nixon, who informed him that 11,000 Turks and Arabs with thirty-eight fieldpieces under a new general, Yusef Nur-ud-Din (who had replaced the ineffectual Khalil Bey, and whose name, incidentally, was the same as the great Saladin's patron and mentor), were dug in on both sides of the Tigris at a place called Es Sinn, a few miles downstream from Kut. Twelve more battalions were en route downriver from Baghdad by raft to strengthen this force in a few days, another five were in reserve nearby, and Nur-ud-Din had built bridges across the Tigris to enhance the movement of men and artillery to whatever point Townshend chose to hit him.

For his part, Townshend would have some 11,000 men of the 6th Division, a squadron of the 7th Hariana Lancers, twenty-eight guns including heavy howitzers and 4.7-inchers, the armed paddle wheeler *Comet*, the steam launch *Sumana*, two reconnaissance aircraft, and a pair of pack radios—a feeble force to throw against a well-entrenched enemy of better than equal strength. But Nixon and his superiors in India insisted that Kut-el-Amara must be taken to secure the gains already achieved. From Kut, a watercourse called the Shatt-al-Hai ran south-southeast from the Tigris to the Euphrates at An Nasiriya. If the Turks retained Kut, enemy troops could possibly descend the Shatt-al-Hai and take An Nasiriya, then Kurna and Basra, and all thus far would have been for naught. What's more, a British success in Mesopotamia would boost morale at home, where news from the Western Front and the Dardanelles spoke only of deadlock.

On August 23 Nixon ordered Townshend to move on Kut and "disperse and destroy" the enemy there. If all went well, Townshend should be prepared to forge on to Baghdad. By September 16 Townshend's force was concentrated near Es Sinn, still with inadequate river transport but primed to fight. Ten days later he made up for insufficient numbers with a masterful show of maneuver: Feinting a two-pronged attack on Nur-ud-Din's right, Townshend sent his main force across the Tigris via a downstream boat-bridge on a long route march through the night. Skirting two marshes, his battalion fell on the Turks' left flank. They drove the Turks from their position at bayonet point, killing and wounding 4,000 and taking 1,300 prisoners as well as all of Nur-ud-Din's guns. British losses were 1,230.

The bulk of the Turkish force withdrew upstream to Ctesiphon, some forty miles south of Baghdad, to already prepared positions. Meanwhile, Townshend occupied Kut and established his headquarters there. Two months later, with improvised donkey and camel transport to supplement his "regatta," which was hampered by low water in the Mesopotamian dry season, Townshend pursued. He arrived before the ancient Sassanid capital on November 22—only to discover that Nur-ud-Din had been reinforced and now had 12,000 men, with forty-five guns.

Townshend attacked anyway, carrying the first line of Turkish trenches near the third-century ruins of the Arch of Ctesiphon (the prophet Muhammad's barber was also reputed to be buried in the vicinity) before the battle settled down to a four-day "killing match" like those on the Western Front. The Turks lost 6,200 men, the British 4,600. No further gain was possible, and when Townshend was advised that a fresh Turkish force of 30,000 was en route from Baghdad, he decided to withdraw to Kut and wait for reinforcements.

Nur-ud-Din did not press the pursuit vigorously, and after a sharp rearguard action at Umm-at-Tubal, Townshend's exhausted troops—who'd marched eighty miles both night and day with only odd intervals of rest—staggered into Kut on December 3, 1915, and immediately began digging trenches. Sending his cavalry away, Townshend settled down in Kut as he had two decades earlier at Chitral to await relief, meanwhile effectively blocking access to the Shatt-al-Hai and the lower Tigris. By his initial estimate, he had a bit more than two months' worth of food at hand. That should have been more than enough.

Some critics have faulted Townshend for halting and digging in at Kut, where the Turkish army was sure to invest him, rather than pushing on downriver to 'Amara, where the bulk of the British expeditionary force was concentrated. In his postwar memoirs Townshend defended his decision by pointing out that his men had just fought a major battle at Ctesiphon, followed by a double-time fighting retreat of eighty miles to Kut, and were physically spent. 'Amara was another 150 miles downstream, and his force would have been harried by the Turks all the way. What's more, occupation of Kut by British troops would deny the Turks two riverine attack routes—down the Tigris toward 'Amara and Basra, and down the Shatt-al-Hai toward An Nasiriya and the Euphrates. And if Townshend had managed a successful retreat to 'Amara, he or any other commander who in the future wished to move on Baghdad would only have to fight the Battle of Es Sinn all over again.

Kut, with a remaining Arab population of 6,000 (which would also have to be fed), lay in an oxbow of the Tigris, protected by the river against assault on three sides. Townshend's men quickly dug three lines of barbed-wire-barricaded trenches across the fourth (northwestern) side, the first of these trenches anchored on its right flank by a strong, mud-walled fort hard by the Tigris. Across the river from the town lay a village called Yakasum, which the

British renamed Woolpress Village (because it had a wool press), also protected by a short arc of entrenchments: 9,000 yards of seven-tiered barbed wire in all.

Within this perimeter of wire and river were crowded some 20,000 people: four brigades totaling 10,000 men, about 3,500 noncombatant "camp-followers" that were de rigueur in the Indian Army (*bhistis* to tote water, *drabis* and *saises* to feed the horses and mules, sweepers to clean up after them and the fighting men, low-caste bearers to handle the wounded and bury the dead), in addition to the town's potentially hostile citizenry. All hunkered down together in an area that measured little more than two and a half square miles: a maze of narrow, twisting alleys and open drains, mud houses, a small bazaar, a mosque, a brick kiln, a few groves of lime trees and date palms, and a newly established British field hospital.

Townshend had sent the wounded from Ctesiphon downriver with his cavalry at the outset. He had also thrown a bridge of boats across the Tigris from the town, anticipating sorties from Kut to aid the relief force he hoped would soon be forging upriver to his rescue—the bridgehead guarded on the enemy side by a company of tough Punjabis. In the brickyard he positioned most of his artillery—forty-three guns in all, including four 4.7-inchers mounted on barges. To communicate with Basra, he had two radio sets, fastidiously protected, at least initially, by bales of angora wool against the shock of incoming Turkish artillery shells.

The Turks besieging Townshend under his old opponent Nur-ud-Din grew to six divisions by the end, with thirty-two guns, five howitzers, and an enormous brass mortar dating to the eighteenth century that fired a bomb as big and as round as a soccer ball. The Tommies quickly nicknamed this antique weapon "Flatulent Flossie."

An initial Turkish attempt to rush Kut's boat-bridge was repulsed with heavy losses on both sides. Townshend then decided to blow the bridge, cutting his options of sortie or escape. Two British lieutenants and a party of Gurkhas crawled out on the span at night with eight pounds of guncotton apiece, placed their charges, lit the fuses, and fled. The bridge blew spectacularly, and Kut's artillery finished the job when morning came.

Infuriated, the Turks launched attack after attack on Kut's first trench line from dawn to dusk on December 10, and the following day shelled the town in earnest, causing 202 casualties. Day after day throughout the siege, Turkish snipers picked off anyone foolish enough to show himself. Yet the *bhistis*—latter-day Gunga Dins—continued to scamper down to the river's edge to fill their goatskin water bags, never shirking. Tough duty, but the garrison still hoped for early relief. From Basra, Lieutenant General Sir Fenton Aylmer, V.C., radioed

Townshend: "Have assumed command Tigris Line. Have utmost confidence in the defender of Chitral and his gallant troops to keep the flag flying until we can relieve them." Aylmer had been one of the men who had bailed Townshend out of his previous siege, and Kut's commander replied warmly: "Thanks from 6th Division for your inspiring message. Your confidence shall not be misplaced."

But that mutual confidence amounted to mere whistling in the dark. The India government, always tightfisted with men and equipment, and Nixon, always overoptimistic, still had done nothing to rectify Basra's miserable docking facilities. Aylmer's relief force was still short of transport, medical supplies, bridging materials, signaling equipment, even blankets for the troops in the cold Mesopotamian winter nights. His men had never fought together before as a division, yet Nixon—pressed by Townshend for speedy relief—insisted that Aylmer advance at once on Kut.

Townshend sent a message to Nixon:

> The fighting value of my troops was naturally much decreased since Ctesiphon (though discipline maintains), and I am very anxious as to the result if enemy makes determined onslaught with very superior numbers. We are constantly shelled all day and I am very anxious to be relieved in say ten to fifteen days.

Two days later—December 12—Aylmer arrived at 'Amara to concentrate his two newly arrived divisions of green troops at Ali Gharbi for an attack on January 31. Townshend pleaded for greater speed, and just before Christmas his fears that the Turks would take Kut before Aylmer could attack were nearly realized. After two days of intense artillery bombardment, which breached the town's wall in one place, the Turks attacked on December 24, carrying the outlying trenches despite concentrated fire from howitzers, four Maxim machine guns, and 1,000 rifles. The defenders finally drove them out with bayonets and homemade grenades—jam tins crammed with black powder and chopped telephone wire. As German field marshal Colmar von der Goltz, overall commander of the Turkish Sixth Army, looked on, Nur-ud-Din's force took 2,000 casualties while Townshend took 382, bringing his dead and wounded to 1,625 since the siege began. Kut's garrison settled back for Christmas dinner: bully beef, tinned pineapple, and condensed milk for the enlisted men; a five-course feast including asparagus, plum pudding, and whiskey for the officers—all of it gritty, thanks to a yuletide sandstorm.

In early January, far earlier than he had planned, Aylmer moved on the besieging forces downstream near Sheikh Sa'ad—and was stopped, with some 4,000 casualties. (Almost simultaneously, on January 9, 1916, British forces finally withdrew from Gallipoli, ending the ill-fated Dardanelles campaign with 252,000 casualties.) Nur-ud-Din unaccountably withdrew after Sheikh Sa'ad and was replaced by Khalil Pasha (a cousin of the young Turk strongman Enver Pasha).

A second assault at Wadi and a third at Hanna also bogged down—literally, since the rains had come, turning the Tigris valley below Kut into a quagmire. Aylmer's requests for sorties from Kut to relieve some of the frontline pressure against his attacking troops were rejected by Townshend, who was growing increasingly unstable as the siege dragged on. What's more, the Turks had Kut so thoroughly pinned down that it is unlikely many men could have made it very far beyond the walls.

As January neared its end, Townshend issued a communique to his troops:

> The Relief Force under General Aylmer has been unsuccessful in its efforts to dislodge the Turks entrenched on the left bank of the river, some fourteen miles below the position at Es Sinn, where we defeated the Turks in September last, when their strength was greater than it is now. Our relieving force suffered severe loss and had very bad weather to contend with. They are entrenched close to the Turkish position. More reinforcements are on their way up river and I confidently expect to be relieved some day during the first half of the month of February. . . . By standing at Kut, I maintain the territory we have won in the past year at the expense of much blood, commencing with your glorious victory at Shaiba, and thus we maintain the campaign as a glorious one. . . . I have ample food for eighty-four days, and that is not counting the 3,000 animals [horses and mules] which can be eaten. . . . Our duty stands out plain and simple. It is our duty to our Empire, to our beloved King and Country, to stand here and hold up the Turkish advance as we are doing now: and with the help of all, heart and soul with me together, we will make this a defense to be remembered in history as a glorious one. All in England and India are watching us now and are proud of the splendid courage and devotion you have shown. . . . Save your ammunition as if it were gold.

Wise soldiers know that when generals begin spouting rhetoric on that order, the end is near.

Inside the wire, Townshend's trenches filled with cold, yellow water, ankle- and knee-deep in places, footed in mud, into which men hit by Turkish sniper fire disappeared almost without a trace. Trench foot and trench pneumonia were added to the list of medical woes, along with pleurisy, pneumonia, sore throats, frostbite, and gangrene. A plague of green frogs appeared in the trenches, and in their uncomfortable boredom the Tommies quickly organized frog races. But food was also in ever shorter supply, and one night the champion frog of the Norfolk Regiment's 2nd Battalion disappeared from its tin; the Norfolks cast dark, suspicious glances at their Indian trench mates. Lice also came with the rains, vast quantities of them. Troops spent hours picking them out of their blankets, their uniforms, their underwear—one hospital patient claimed a record 420 lice in a single picking session. An infestation of fleas followed the lice, and sand flies bit fiercely whenever the sun shone, leaving boils wherever they burrowed under the skin. When the boils burst, they in turn left pustulant black scars as big as an English penny—"Baghdad Sores," the Tommies called them.

Three times a day the Turks shelled Kut, and now night bombardment was added to the horror. "You try to doze off," an officer wrote in his diary,

> but are intermittently awakened by the sizzling scream of an approaching "obus." You cock up an interested ear to judge whether you are exactly in the line of its flight or not, and if you are, and you have no dugout, you await its fall with still greater interest, only equalled by your relief when it bursts clear or lands with a wump on a neighbouring mud hut. A "whizz bang" on the other hand gives no warning. It comes hissing through the mud wall and there is a tremendous explosion and segments are scattered all over the place, filling the air with poisonous fumes. They are annoying little beasts and are on you before you have a chance to move.

As the siege dragged on, Kut's rations were halved, then halved again. Mesopotamian winters are as cold as its summers are hot, and soon the troops had burned most of the wood in town: windowsills, elaborately carved doors, benches and crates, and superfluous balks from the trenches. Finally, the only fuel left was licorice root, hacked from the bare ground. Tobacco ran short, so men smoked tea leaves and gingerroot, though some swore by the leaves of the lime trees, which they dubbed "Brick Kiln Virginia."

Ration squads ransacked Arab houses for hidden food supplies, digging up floors and smashing walls to find sacks and earthenware jars full of barley, which was ground on hastily improvised millstones and boiled to porridge over fires fueled from the garrison's oil barges. Soon there were no cats or dogs left in Kut—save Major General Sir Charles Melliss's terrier and Townshend's pet dog, Spot (who was gun-shy and yiped at explosions, but survived the siege and was repatriated to England as a favor to its master—indeed rank hath its privileges). Officers popped sparrows and starlings with their shotguns to concoct meat pies; other ranks enjoyed hedgehog fried in axle grease. Horses and mules had already chewed one another's manes and tails down to nubbins, and it was only with the greatest reluctance that the British—always sentimental about animals with big brown eyes and pet names—began eating them. One officer's diary of the siege puts it most poignantly: "April 16, 1916. The day I ate the heart of my beloved Esmeralda."

The Kuttites had quickly learned that a local weed, called *saq* but labeled "spinach" by the Tommies, was nutritious when boiled, but one had to be careful in picking it, because there were poisonous look-alikes. General F. A. Hoghton, one of Townshend's brigade commanders, learned the difference the hard way: On April 11 his batman cooked him up a batch, and he died. Others perished of "starvation dysentery," exacerbated by eating previously discarded tins of now-rancid jam and butter, rotten potato meal, and oats. Among the more fortunate, beriberi was rife. The gunnery officers' sole surviving chicken, a hen named Mrs. Milligan, kept on laying eggs during the most intense of Turkish barrages, and even managed to raise a brood of chicks, which followed her around through the mud, pecking at spent bullets instead of worms.

And the siege wore on. General Nixon was invalided back to India with one of the Middle East's ubiquitous fevers (complicated, no doubt, by London's belated disfavor over his too-ambitious campaign against Baghdad). He was succeeded by General Sir Percy Lake, who in turn sent Gorringe north up the Tigris to relieve Aylmer's failed troops.

In a full-scale attack on March 8, Aylmer had nearly succeeded in relieving Kut—an attempt that ultimately failed, as so many did on all fronts and every side in World War I, due to a too-strict adherence to preconceived plans. The key to the Turkish positions surrounding Kut on the right bank of the Tigris was a heavily fortified node of trenches and bunkers called the Dujaila Redoubt. In a daring night march reminiscent of Townshend's maneuver at Es Sinn the previous September, Aylmer managed to concentrate nearly his entire Tigris Force—some 20,000 men—opposite the redoubt shortly before sunrise. The Turks were clearly unaware of the movement, some being seen standing on the parapets shaking out their blankets and yawning. Indeed, a British intelligence officer, one Major Leachman, had entered the redoubt during the night disguised as an Arab and reported the place nearly deserted, with only about twenty Turks in evidence. A reconnaissance patrol that morning, which also entered the redoubt, confirmed his report.

Though both reports were believed at headquarters, Aylmer's battle plan called for a heavy artillery bombardment before the assault jumped off. No British commander on the scene had the initiative to attack on his own when the position was ripe for the plucking, and when Aylmer's headquarters behind

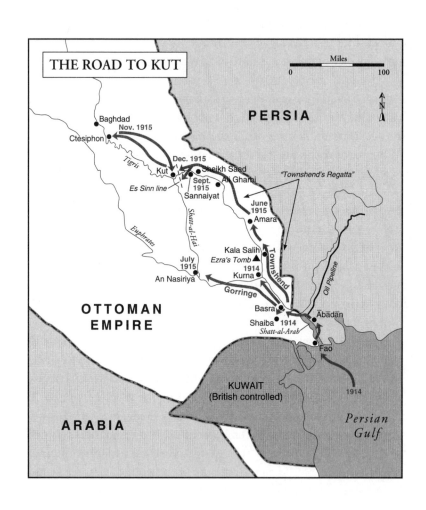

THE ROAD TO KUT

Miles
0   100

PERSIA

Baghdad
Nov. 1915
Ctesiphon

Tigris

Dec. 1915
Kut   Sheikh Saad
             Ali Gharbi
Es Sinn line Sept.
              1915
              Sannaiyat

"Townshend's Regatta"

June
1915
Amara

Shatt-al-Hai

Euphrates

Kala Salih
Ezra's Tomb ▲
              1914
July   Kurna
1915
An Nasiriya

Gorringe

Basra

OTTOMAN
EMPIRE

Shaiba   1914
Shatt-al-Arab

Ābādān

Oil Pipeline

Fao

KUWAIT
(British controlled)

1914

ARABIA

*Persian
Gulf*

the lines was queried by telephone, the orders came back: "Stick to program." Not only that, but when the artillery finally came up almost three hours later, they were allowed to sight in their guns as if they were back home on a firing range.

All chance of surprise ended with that leisurely cannonade. Turkish reinforcements poured into the redoubt, 3,000 of them coursing down the canal from Magasis Fort in coracle-like *moshoofs*, rafts made of skin and towed by motorboats, or on foot across the Dujaila Redoubt; another 3,000 came from the left bank Turkish lines across the river. When the British infantry finally moved on the redoubt at ten o'clock, they were met with withering machine-gun and rifle fire, and cut down in swaths. Toward sunset a few units of the Manchesters and the 59th Rifles managed to occupy two trenches of the redoubt but were thrown back by a crisp counterattack by grenade-hurling Turks.

From the parapets and trenches of Kut, Townshend and his men watched the gunfire flicker out seven miles away as the sun went down. With it went their best chance of rescue. Townshend made no attempt at a sortie to assist Aylmer's assault from the rear, arguing almost fatalistically that "cooperation was of little practical use" at this stage. Yet if a determined attack on the Turkish flank had been mounted from Kut, it might have turned the tide. As it was, Aylmer lost close to 3,500 troops in that bloody day's fighting, and his command as well. Four days later, he air-dropped a letter to Townshend:

My dear Townshend,

The War Office say that my conduct of operations had been unfortunate, and have ordered my suspension. I need not tell you how deeply I grieve that I have not been able to relieve you; but I have every confidence that my successor will be able to do so very soon. I have had a harder task than most people realize. It all looks very easy when you sit in an armchair at the W.O.! The business a few days ago very nearly came off. I cannot tell you how much I admire the splendid way in which you are defending Kut. I heartily pray that you will gain your reward in speedy relief. . . . Goodbye and God bless you all, and may you be more fortunate than myself.

Yours ever,
Fenton Aylmer

But Gorringe fared no better than his predecessor: On April 12 his Tigris Force attacked in the rain at Hanna and carried the first line of Turkish trenches, at a cost of 5,000 casualties. But the Turks retreated to Sannaiyat, along the way destroying dikes that flooded the battleground in front of their previously prepared positions.

On April 22 Gorringe attacked again, his men wading through knee-deep water, with thunder and lightning accompaniment to guns. They gained only 400 yards. At day's end, the Black Watch mustered only forty-eight of its original 842 men; the 6th Jahts, fifty of 825; the 125th Rifles, eighty-eight of 848; and the 1st Seaforth Rifles, 102 of 962. That evening he radioed Townshend: "Much regret that the attack at Sannaiyat position this morning was repulsed. Gorringe, however, will not relax efforts."

But he would have to wait until the end of April—at the earliest—for his badly bled relief force, initially numbering some 30,000 men and 133 guns, to be reinforced to a strength of 23,450. Tigris Force, under two commanders, had lost 23,000 men, killed and wounded, since January, and still stood no nearer than twelve miles from Kut. The intervening ground was now held by the entire Turkish Sixth Army.

And Townshend's garrison was at the end of its endurance. On April 15, British Farman biplanes had tried to drop 5,000 pounds of supplies into Kut by parachute—the first airdrop to a besieged force in military history—but nearly half had drifted into Turkish hands or landed in the Tigris. Subsequent drops fared no better. For weeks Townshend had been contemplating surrender, hoping that by some antique chivalrous turn the Turks—in return for the capture of his artillery and the removal of this strategically placed thorn in Mesopotamia's side—might allow his men to march out of Kut on parole. Indeed, during one fierce artillery duel he had spotted the Sixth Army's commander, Khalil Pasha, within range but ordered his gunners not to fire on him—a nineteenth-century gesture that he hoped might engender a quid pro quo when the white flag ran up.

One last effort remained to be made. At 'Amara, twenty-five miles downriver, the steamer *Julnar* lay at quayside with 270 tons of food for Kut. Naval officers were willing to run the Turkish gauntlet even though they knew the mission was suicidal. The *Julnar*'s sides had been reinforced with steel plates, her deck protected against plunging fire by sandbags filled with lead, but the final decision lay with Sir Percy Lake.

At seven o'clock on April 24, piloted by Lieutenant Commander C. H. Cowley of the Royal Navy, a former skipper of the Euphrates & Tigris Navigation Company (and now regarded by the Turks as a renegade national), the *Julnar* made her run. Officers waiting and watching from Kut's walls could chart her progress up the winding river by the slowly moving flash and boom of Turkish artillery on either bank. They had been advised that she would show a white light to indicate that she was undamaged and could berth, a red light if she was holed and had to run aground.

Neither light appeared. The Turks had strung a hawser diagonally across the Tigris, shunting the steamer into the bank "high and dry at Magasis Ferry" just east of Kut. Swarming aboard, Turkish soldiers killed her officers and most of the crew. Cowley was marched into the desert and summarily shot.

On April 26, Lake radioed Townshend that Lord Kitchener had agreed to Townshend's beginning surrender negotiations with Khalil Pasha. For three days the talks went on, with Khalil smiling politely but referring all decisions to Enver Pasha in Istanbul. Called in to assist in the negotiations were Captains Aubrey Herbert and T. E. Lawrence from the Arab Bureau in Cairo. The intelligence officers tried to bribe Khalil and Enver, first with an offer of a million pounds sterling, then with double that amount, but the Turks and their German partners preferred the propaganda value of an unconditional surrender. (Most of Kut's sick and wounded, however, were finally allowed to be taken downriver to Basra, in exchange for healthy Turkish prisoners, since none of them could have survived the journey to Turkey.) Enver was willing to accept the money and Kut's forty-three guns in exchange only for Townshend's personal parole. "It is obvious," Kut's commander radioed Lake, "that I must go into captivity."

On April 29, Townshend's troops blew up their guns, broke their rifles (only one rifle was retained per company to guard against marauding Arabs), burned their signal books and trenching tools, buried revolvers, hacked saddles and bridles to pieces, smashed binoculars and cameras, and threw their bayonets into the Tigris. The gunners finally killed and ate Mrs. Milligan, who proved as tough on the table as she'd been throughout the siege.

Townshend's final communique to his troops concluded: "I thank you from the bottom of my heart for your devotion and your discipline and bravery, and may we all meet in better times." Moments later Kut's field radio uttered its last message: "Goodbye. Piecemeal." At that final code word, the radio operators fired their rifles into the set until it erupted in flames. They smashed what was left with their rifle butts and hurled the weapons into the Tigris. Then they joined the column of prisoners and marched out into captivity.

It proved a death march, especially for the British and Indian enlisted men. The Turks turned these "other ranks" over to the charge of Arab guards, who whipped, thrashed, bayoneted, or clubbed with rifle butts any stragglers who fell out of the column as it marched northward through the desert. Prisoners were forced to bribe the Arabs with their boots and clothing for minimal food rations. Many of the younger British soldiers were sodomized, and beaten into submission if they objected to the treatment. Captive British officers occasionally witnessed this abuse and its results as they themselves moved north toward Anatolia. As Captain E. O. Mousley wrote in his postwar memoir, *The Secrets of a Kuttite:*

> We tingled with anger and shame at seeing on the other bank a sad little column of troops who had marched up from Kut, driven by a wild crowd of Kurdish horsemen who brandished sticks and what looked like whips. The eyes of our men stared . . . and they held out their hands toward our boat. As they dragged one foot after another, some fell and those with the rearguard came in for blows from cudgels and sticks. I saw one Kurd strike a British soldier who was limping along, he reeled under the blows. . . . Men were dying of cholera and dysentery and often fell out from sheer weakness.

Other observers likened the journey to something out of Dante's *Inferno* or the cruelties of Genghis Kahn and Tamerlane.

The death rate was appalling. Of the 2,592 British officers and men captured at Kut, 1,755 died before war's end. Of the 10,486 Indian sepoys and servants, 3,063 perished in captivity. Townshend himself was treated as Turkey's "honored guest," living in relative luxury in an island villa near Istanbul for the rest of the war. His career, however, was ruined, and to so ambitious a man that may have been as painful as death itself.

Baghdad did not fall to the Tigris Force until March 11, 1917, nearly a year after Kut's surrender, and then only after Britain assembled a force of 166,000 men with adequate supplies, medical support, and transportation.

There are no shortcuts in war.

BRUSILOV'S IMMORTAL DAYS
Jamie H. Cockfield

—

U NTIL THE LAST MONTHS OF 1918, WHEN FERDINAND FOCH orchestrated his great war-ending push along the Western Front, Allied offensives had been mainly notable for what they did not achieve. (The most important Allied victory, the Marne, was less an offensive than a series of coordinated counterattacks along a broad front, like springs suppressed and then released more or less at once.) Midway into the war, however, there was an exception, albeit a largely overlooked one. That was the Russian General Aleksei Brusilov's summer-long dissection of the Austrian army in 1916, which Jamie H. Cockfield recounts here. Along a 200-mile-long front, the four armies Brusilov commanded (and later, a fifth) retook more than 15,000 square miles, and cost the Central Powers 765,000 casualties, including 450,000 prisoners of war. For similar accomplishments, we have to look to the best Soviet commanders of World War II—and, in fact, Brusilov would end his career in the Red Army.

Brusilov was sixty-three in 1916, a former cavalryman, and an aristocrat. He now headed one of the three Russian army groups. C.R.M.F. Cruttwell (whose *A History of the Great War 1914–1918* is still, after seven decades, one of the best) wrote of him that "This general had supreme energy and self-confidence. He knew the ground thoroughly, for he had fought over areas of it in 1915 as an army commander, and had visited the front assiduously since he had been promoted. Unlike so many Russians, he realized the value of minute or-ganization, and saw to it that his orders were actually carried out." Brusilov recognized that the bludgeoning tactics of the Western Front would not work here. He counted on deception and surprise. He would rush his reinforcements not to places where resistance stiffened but to places that showed weakness. To return to Cruttwell's appreciation: Brusilov's "first task is best described in a metaphor much quoted at the time: 'He is like a man tapping on a wall to find out what part of it is solid stone and what is lathe and plaster.' " Time and again that summer, Brusilov would cause the wall to collapse.

For the Russians, eventually battered into revolution, Brusilov was the one real hero whom the Eastern Front produced, a captain of war who has to rank with the best on both sides. Perhaps his broad-front operations might not have worked against the Germans; Brusilov has his detractors. But it is far more likely that the failure of nerve of the other army group commanders prevented him from achieving more than he did. As Brusilov wrote in his memoirs, "In war, it is no new discovery that a lost opportunity never returns." Even so, the Brusilov offensive saw the end of Austria-Hungary as an independent power. "We are now totally and completely under the thumb of the Germans," an Austrian general said. The Brusilov offensive didn't knock Austria out of the war; it merely made certain that Austria no longer had a chance of victory.

———

JAMIE H. COCKFIELD is the author of *With Snow on Their Boots: The Tragic Odyssey of the Russian Expeditionary Force in France during World War I.* He is a professor of Russian history at Mercer University in Georgia.

IN JUNE 1916 RUSSIA LAUNCHED THE MOST MASSIVE AND SUCCESSFUL ALLIED offensive of the Great War. The string of stunning successes is generally called the Brusilov offensive after its mastermind, General Aleksei Brusilov. World War I historian Cyril Falls, however, bestowed a loftier title: "Brusilov's Immortal Days." The operation permanently secured more enemy territory than any other Allied offensive on either front. Although its objectives changed as the months wore on, it achieved every one of them. Moreover, the Russian drive came perilously close to knocking the Austro-Hungarian Empire out of the war and forced the Central Powers to terminate a threatening operation of their own in France and doubly guaranteed the failure of another in Italy. Yet, the cataclysmic revolution that followed the next year in Russia, with the subsequent disintegration of Csar Nicholas II's army, caused the offensive's impact to be largely forgotten.

General Brusilov was undeniably the greatest Russian commander to serve in World War I, with perhaps a nod to Grand Duke Nicholas Nicholaevich. He was an individualist in an officer corps that discouraged individualism, an innovator in an army bereft of innovation. He was also a general both loved and respected by his men in an army whose officer corps was both hated and feared. One wonders how such a man rose to a leadership position in the csar's army.

Brusilov's headquarters lacked the pomp of other generals'. His office was furnished simply and was guarded by only two sentries. Grand Duke Nicholas Mikhailovich Romanov, a pessimist and severe critic by nature, encountered Brusilov in the fall of 1915 and got "an encouraging impression" from both the general and his staff. The grand duke was delighted that Brusilov did not always ask for "cartridges and shells," like other generals, and his total absence of posturing inspired in Nicholas a supreme "confidence in all our forces." Warm and friendly by nature, Brusilov made light, bantering conversation with visitors, telling them jokes and stories. All found him above class snobbery and noticed that he picked men for their ability, not their position in society. His contempt for aristocratic incompetence was a major factor that would lead him to serve both under the Bolshevik banner against the Poles and in the Red Army in the 1920s.

The "Iron General," as he was called, was born in Tiflis, Georgia, in 1853 into a gentry family with a military background. In his youth, he constantly read works on military history and entered the prestigious Corps des Pages in preparation for officer training. His first service was in the Caucasus with the 15th Tver Dragoon Regiment, and his baptism fire came during the Russo-Turkish War of 1877–78. In the years following the war, he served in the Cavalry School for Officers in St. Petersburg, distinguishing himself as one of its best teachers. Following Brusilov's stint as an instructor, his superiors selected him to command two divisions of the elite Guard Cavalry, and in 1909 he was appointed to the command of the XIV Army Corps. In 1912 he was transferred to the important Warsaw Military District, one of the Russian army's far western commands.

Believing war with Germany was inevitable, Brusilov studied Kaiser Wilhelm II's army in depth during these years, becoming a great believer in preparedness. In 1913, he was transferred to the Kiev Military District where he commanded the XII Army Corps. Again he stressed readiness. His preparations in this theater greatly contributed to his successes in the early days of World War I.

During the first five months of the conflict, Brusilov successfully led the Eighth Army of the Southwestern Army Front, advancing through the Carpathian Mountains onto the Hungarian Plain. He received a commendation from Csar Nicholas in 1915, when during the great retreat from Poland, he launched a counterattack that bagged more than 44,000 enemy soldiers, including 720 officers. At one point, he retook the city of Lutsk, and during the winter of 1915, his army continued to attack the enemy. For his actions, the csar awarded him the Cross of St. George, Fourth Class.

In March 1916, Brusilov was made Commander in Chief of the Southwestern Army Front, replacing the timid General Nikolai I. Ivanov. The Russians divided the Eastern Front, as it was known by both the western Allies and the Central Powers, into three sections. The Northern Army Front, under the command of General A. N. Kuropatkin, stretched from the Gulf of Riga to west of Vilna and consisted of the Twelfth, Fifth, and First Russian Armies. The Western Army Front, under General Aleksei Evert, ran from north of Molodechno, west of Vilna, to south of the Pripet Marshes and consisted of the Second, Third, Fourth, and Tenth Armies. Brusilov's Southwestern Army Front was composed of the Eighth Army under General Aleksei M. Kaledin, the Eleventh under General V. V. Sakharov, the Seventh under General D. G. Shcherbachev, and the Ninth under General Platon A. Lechitsky.

The Allies had planned major offensives on all fronts in 1916, hoping that they would bring an end to the war. Unfortunately, the Germans and Austrians struck first. In February, the German attack against Verdun began, and the

French pleaded with their Russian allies to strike in the east. The result was an ill-fated offensive in March at Lake Narocz, where the Russians, greatly out-numbering the Germans, were stopped cold and slaughtered as they advanced through thawing fields of knee-deep mud. Many wounded suffocated after they fell into the mire, and the Russian army sustained 100,000 casualties. Not one German unit was redeployed from Verdun to meet the offensive. What is more, the Commander in Chief of the attack, General Evert, was terribly shaken. If 350,000 Russians and a thousand guns could not defeat 50,000 Germans, he feared that no offensive could succeed. This reasoning would have dire conse-quences come summer.

Ever loyal to their allies, the Russians nonetheless planned another major offensive for 1916. In a meeting at headquarters in April, it was decided that the hammer would fall north of the Pripet Marshes, along the Northern and Western Fronts where most of the German forces in the east were deployed and where the Russians held a 750,000-man numerical advantage. Curiously, no action at all was planned for Brusilov's front. The offensive would take the same form as the failed Lake Narocz operation, with an attack by six corps along a twelve-and-a-half-mile front preceded by a 1,000-piece artillery barrage. The assembly of this force would, of course, alert the Germans, and neither Evert nor Kuropatkin was enthusiastic about it.

At the meeting, Brusilov insisted that he be allowed to attack the Austrians along his front as well, if only as a diversion. He believed that such a strike would draw troops from the Evert-Kuropatkin sectors and guarantee the suc-cess of their offensive. Brusilov suggested to his fellow generals a novel plan of attack. Concentrated assaults had always failed because of a lack of surprise, and such attacks could not be supported by the artillery after the infantry had advanced because the fieldpieces could not be transported across the ground their fire had just torn up. Also, the troops in the salient that the attack created could be cut to pieces by enfilading fire from the sides. Brusilov instead sug-gested attacking on a broad front to keep enemy forces off balance so they would never know where to send reinforcements. Russian reserves would be brought near the front and hidden in dugouts. The broad-front attack would show "what was plaster and what was lathe," Brusilov said, and reserves could be rushed to the sectors where the Austrians gave way.

No one at the meeting was very optimistic about Brusilov's strategy. If massive artillery assaults and overwhelming superiority in numbers could not effect a breakthrough, how could a weaker broad-front attack succeed? Brusilov later remembered that Kuropatkin looked at him with pity when he suggested the strategy. He was told to go ahead, but no one believed Brusilov had any hope of successfully diverting German troops from the main attack.

Linsingen

Baranovichi

Bug

Brest

Pinsk

Pripet Marshes

Pripet

3rd

Kovel

Guard

4th

Vladimir-Volynski

Lutsk

Rovno

1st

Dubno

8th

Brody

UKRAINE

2nd

Süd

Lvov

Zborov

Tarnopol

11th

Dnestr

Gnila Lipa

Zlata Lipa

Strypa

7th

G A L I C I A

7th

Stanislav

9th

AUSTRO-
HUNGARY

Dnestr

CARPATHIAN MOUNTAINS

Pruth

Miles

0   50

Czernovitz

BUKOVINA

BRUSILOV'S GREAT
OFFENSIVE

Austro-Hungarian

German

Russian

Front line — June 4, 1916

Front line — September 20, 1916

Kimpolung

ROMANIA

Undaunted, Brusilov immediately began preparing for his operation, which was scheduled for late June. In the east, the opposing front lines often were so far apart that cattle grazed in no-man's-land and there were sometimes inhabited villages between the two sides. Brusilov relocated his trenches close to the Austrian lines along his whole front, curiously with no interference from the enemy. In some cases, trenches were actually painted on the ground to deceive Austrian air reconnaissance. Dugouts with high ramparts were made all along the front to hide reserve units. To prepare his troops, the general built replicas of the Austrian trenches against which his men made mock attacks. Brusilov, moreover, relied on aerial reconnaissance to spot the Austrian artillery. Also, for the first time in the war, the Russians had massive amounts of heavy artillery and shells with which to open up a barrage all along the South-western Army Front's 200-mile front.

Brusilov's formal plan was for each of his four armies to launch four separate attacks, each along at least an eighteen-and-a-half-mile-wide sector. The sectors where the enemy gave way would receive the reinforcements. Failed attacks would not be supported. When the Austrians rushed to aid the most threatened sections of their line, they would weaken others, making them more likely to collapse under the general assault. As the Austro-Hungarian front fell into deeper trouble, the Germans would be forced to transfer troops to save their ally, thus ensuring Evert's success with the Russians' main thrust.

Brusilov would be playing the sacrificial role. He had only forty infantry and fifteen cavalry divisions to the Austrians' thirty-five and a half infantry and eleven cavalry (a superiority of only 130,000 effectives for a 200-mile front). In artillery, the Russians had only 1,938 pieces of all calibers to the Austrians' 1,846.

The Russian Eighth Army under Kaledin was to attack on the front in Volhynia between Rovno and Lutsk. The Eleventh, under Sakharov, was to advance to Kaledin's south. Its objective was Lvov, seventy miles to the west. The Seventh, under Shcherbachev, would invade eastern Galicia to the west of Tarnopol, and the Ninth, under Lechitsky, would advance into Bukovina south of the Dniester River near the Romanian border. Evert's advance was to begin five days after Brusilov's, and he would have at his disposal almost all available reserves. Brusilov would have to advance with what he had, and a request on May 24 for additional units was flatly refused. Reserves were to be held for the main thrust north of the Pripet Marshes.

Yet, late in May, the Austrians disrupted Allied plans with a major offensive of their own on the Italian front. The Italians retreated, and very quickly a rout was in the making. On the very day that Brusilov requested additional reserves, General Mikhail Alekseev, Csar Nicholas II's chief of staff, wired him of the Italian difficulties and asked how soon he might attack to relieve pressure on their Italian allies, thus giving Brusilov's forces a different assignment from that of the April conference. Brusilov immediately replied that he was ready now, and his armies could advance within a week of receiving orders. He did suggest that since the situation had changed, Evert also should accelerate his attack schedule to pin down the German troops facing his front.

Alekseev asked for a delay from June 1 to June 4 because Evert could not advance until June 14. Brusilov reluctantly agreed. Yet even this deadline was not set in concrete. On June 3, Alekseev wired Brusilov that Evert was not going to be ready on June 14, and he wanted to delay the attack for a few days. Brusilov heatedly refused. His troops were already in advance positions, and the artillery was ready. Moreover, by the time word got to the armies under his command, the artillery preparation would have already begun. Alekseev suggested that the csar decide but noted that at that point Nicholas II was sleeping and could not be disturbed. Only after Brusilov threatened to resign did Alekseev permit the commencement of the Southwestern Army Front's offensive, adding, "Well, God be with you."

On the morning of June 4, all along the front from the Pripet Marshes to the Romanian border, Russian artillery opened fire on the enemy. The light guns concentrated on blowing breaches in the barbed wire, while the larger pieces attempted to obliterate the frontline trenches and silence enemy guns. Then the artillery was to train its fire on any available targets and cover the infantry advance. For the first time on the Eastern Front, Russian airplanes with radios directed artillery barrages. After shelling all day, the artillery stopped at midnight for two and a half hours to assess the damage, and scouts reported that in some cases even the third Austrian line had been demolished. The enemy soldiers who had weathered the shelling in dugouts and bunkers were generally unharmed, but when the Russians advanced, there was nothing for them to do but surrender.

All along the front the Russian steamroller finally lived up to its name. Kaledin struck on June 5, taking Archduke Joseph Ferdinand's Fourth Army by surprise. The entire Austrian front before him collapsed as he advanced toward Lutsk, the headquarters of the Fourth Army. By June 6, he had captured 40,000 prisoners. The number grew rapidly as the attack continued along the line, and within a few days, the Russians had reached the Styr River at Lutsk and bagged 125,000 prisoners all along the front. In some cases, entire Austrian units in the third line were taken prisoner. At Lutsk, huge numbers of reserves were cut down, captured, or fled in panic. In many cases, units composed of Slavs, including Czechs and Croats, surrendered quite willingly to their Russian opponents.

Russian artillery soon bombarded Lutsk, which was afterward taken by Russian cavalry. Fleeing Austrian troops were caught on their own barbed wire and annihilated. Panicked Hapsburg engineers blew up the Styr River bridges too soon, trapping thousands of their own men and much matériel on the eastern banks. The Austrians did not even try to make a stand along the Styr and, in fact, did not begin to re-form until they had retreated thirty miles west of it. Kaledin did not quickly exploit his army's successes, however, because he feared a trap. He was also concerned about exposing his right flank to the forces opposing the inert armies of Evert to his north.

To Kaledin's south, meanwhile, Sakharov's Eleventh Army broke through at Sapanow, taking 15,000 prisoners. On Sakharov's left, Shcherbachev's Seventh Army simultaneously pushed the Austrians across the Strypa River. Lechitsky's Ninth, on the extreme left, initially drove southward before turning northward toward Shcherbachev, rolling up the flank of the Austrian Seventh Army. The Russian Ninth Army's artillery periodically had ceased firing to give the impression that an attack was imminent and then had resumed firing. When the firing finally halted for the actual attack, the Austrians remained in their dugouts, thinking it was another ruse. The attacking Russians trapped and captured thousands of unsuspecting enemy soldiers. The Seventh Army commander, General Karl Freiherr von Pflanzer-Baltin, one of Austria's best generals, happened to be in the hospital and tried to direct the battle by phone. He ordered his army to hold fast, but it was impossible, and by June 9 Lechitsky's troops had advanced twenty miles. All along the front holes had been torn in the Austrian defenses, and the Seventh Army was outflanked and in danger of being trapped. That day, Pflanzer-Baltin ordered a general retreat. Conflicting orders on the direction of the withdrawal added to the already dangerous confusion. Lechitsky's army arrived on the Pruth River, taking an Austrian bridgehead and 1,500 prisoners with just one Russian casualty. Only the part of Sakharov's Eleventh Army that faced General Count Felix von Bothmer's German *Südarmee* failed to make much headway, with just his right wing making substantial advances north of Tarnopol.

Evert, however, failed to attack. As the Russian armies were advancing victoriously on the Southwestern Front, he announced that he would not be able to assume an offensive on the fourteenth due to "bad weather," but would do so on the eighteenth. An attack by General L. P. Lesh's Third Army, the left wing of Evert's front, would help to relieve pressure on Kaledin's salient near Lutsk. Brusilov pleaded to be given command of the Third Army so that he could make the attack, but Evert refused. The Western Army Front commander, who had two-thirds of the Russian army's heavy artillery and a million men, dawdled. He demanded more shells, changed his points of attack, pointlessly shifted men and matériel, and complained chronically about the weather. At one point, he refused to attack because it was Trinity Sunday. Brusilov appealed to Alekseev, who nevertheless accepted Evert's excuses, and the element of surprise was lost. Even when General Ragosa of the Fourth Army at Molodechno, north of the Pripet Marshes, asked permission to attack, Evert forbade him to move.

To try to mollify Brusilov, Alekseev agreed to send him two corps as reinforcements, which Evert was only too willing to provide, since it would give him a better excuse than the weather not to attack. Brusilov, however, knew that the new troops would be virtually worthless to him. Given the slowness of Russian rail transportation and the superior transport abilities of the enemy, the Germans could move reinforcements much faster to the Austrian front than reserves could reach him. What he needed most was an attack on the Western or Northern Fronts to hold the Germans there, leaving the hapless Austrians to fend for themselves. He even requested that Alekseev ask Csar Nicholas to order Evert to attack, but the Russian chief of staff refused. In his memoirs, Brusilov sadly noted that "In war, it is no new discovery that a lost opportunity never returns, and we had to learn this ancient truth by bitter experience." One of Evert's generals later told Brusilov that the Western Front commander's refusal to attack at such a crucial time was based on his jealousy of Brusilov's successes. Evert may have been jealous, but the battering his troops had taken at Lake Narocz was fresh in his mind, and he clearly feared another mauling at the hands of the Germans.

SOUTH OF THE KALEDIN FRONT, THE RUSSIANS NEVERTHELESS ADVANCED everywhere. The greatest success was in the extreme south, where Lechitsky's troops had forced Pflanzer-Baltin's battered Seventh Army—which had no reserves and no artillery (both had been sent to the Italian front for the offensive there)—into headlong flight. The retreat was so chaotic that only a third of Pflanzer-Baltin's army reached the Czeremosz River by mid-June. Only Lechitsky's limited reserves and supply of shells saved the Austrians from total destruction. Yet, by June 17, Czernowitz had fallen to the Russians, and by June 21 all of Bukovina was in Russian hands. By the twenty-third, the Russians had taken Kimpolung in the foothills of the Carpathians, where they had been the year before, and their advance seriously threatened the *Südarmee*'s right flank. The Austrian Commander in Chief, General Conrad von Hötzendorf, began pleading with German Supreme Commander Erich von Falkenhayn for more troops. The German commander, who had little respect for the Austrian army, agreed to help, but only on the condition that Conrad terminate the Italian offensive, transferring what troops he could to the Eastern Front. The Italian offensive had already faltered by the time Brusilov first attacked on June 4, although desultory fighting sputtered on until mid-June. The Russian advance made its failure a certainty and gave Conrad an excellent face-saving reason to terminate formally the failed Italian operation.

Evert's failure to attack in the north allowed Falkenhayn to transfer five reserve divisions south to buttress the flagging Austrian front. The commander mixed eight German and Austrian divisions along the Stokhod River under General Georg von der Marwitz, and he forced the Austrians to remove Archduke Joseph as the commander of the Fourth Army and replace him with the Hungarian General Karl Ritter von Tersztyanski, who had blundered rather badly in the Carpathians the year before. With these new forces, Falkenhayn even counterattacked on the Kovel front on June 16, but by the twentieth, the Russians had stopped his advance after only a few miles.

By late June, Austrian losses had been horrific. Brusilov had taken 350,000 prisoners, 400 guns, and 1,300 machine guns. Moreover, the enemy had suffered heavy casualties, and a 200-mile-long front had been penetrated forty miles in some places. It was becoming clear that this action to divert troops from the main thrust in the north was becoming the main theater of operations. But the cost to the Russians had been high. As shells ran out and as supply trains were delayed, losses mounted. By late June, the Russians themselves had sustained 300,000 casualties, almost the total number that the Germans suffered in the entire ten-month siege of Verdun. Yet the Russians were still advancing and inflicting worse damage on the enemy. Brusilov later wrote, "These were the happiest days of my life, and my joy was shared by the whole of Russia."

On July 2, Evert at long last launched an attack on his front. The Fourth Army's General Ragosa, who had been told to prepare an attack on Vilna, was ordered by Evert at the end of June to strike instead in the direction of Baranovichi and was given only two weeks to make his preparations and transfer troops from the original attack point. He had to advance over marshy ground, and there was no time to make preparations similar to those Brusilov had made in the south. Moreover, his attack was not launched on a broad front, but in the form of an intensive "French-style" bombardment and mass attack on a narrow sector. Shells fell in soft ground and were often ineffectual, and the bombardment lasted for two days, giving the Germans ample time to bring forward whatever reserves they could muster. By July 7, the Germans had stopped the Russian attack, having inflicted 80,000 casualties while sustaining only 16,000 of their own. Kuropatkin's front remained quiet. It was too little too late.

By early July, Shcherbachev's Seventh and Sakharov's Eleventh Armies had made little progress against Bothmer's *Südarmee.* Heavy rains that month created an additional obstacle. Bothmer himself planned a counteroffensive for July, but the rains stopped, and Sakharov attacked on July 15 before his opponent could do so, taking 13,000 prisoners and much of the matériel amassed for the German offensive. Lechitsky joined him, and they menaced Brody and crossed the Styr. Meanwhile in the north, Kaledin's right made progress against the Austrian Fourth Army around Lutsk, reaching for Vladimir-Volynski. At this late stage, general headquarters finally agreed to Brusilov's request and placed General Lesh's Third Army (Evert's left wing) under Brusilov's command. On July 4–5, it crossed the Styr at Czartorysk with elements of Kaledin's forces, pushing the Austrians back on the river. Lesh was able to seize a number of bridgeheads, taking 12,000 prisoners in the process.

Yet the general staff, without consulting Brusilov, also created a new army. Called the Guard Army, it was formed from the Guards Regiments and placed in the line between Lesh and Kaledin in hopes of creating a breakthrough that the cavalry could exploit. Brusilov was not pleased with this intrusion or with the man leading it: Grand Duke Paul Romanov, an uncle of the csar's and a very likable man, but one devoid of much military ability. Nicholas had appointed him, however, and there was little Brusilov could do to replace him.

Brusilov's successes, meanwhile, now posed a dilemma for the high command. Should these victories be exploited, or should the planned main attack in the north be executed? Brusilov argued that only by defeating the Germans could the war be won, but the supreme command determined after some deliberation to continue pushing the Austrians in the south. It was a bad decision. Brusilov's offensive was only to be a diversion, no matter how successful it had been, and it had clearly fulfilled the objective of drawing troops away from the Western and Northern Fronts. Brusilov did not have adequate reserves for an all-out offensive, and he could not, moreover, get them as quickly as the Germans could supply the Austrians. He was also running out of shells, and the same difficulties in supplying him with reserves would plague him on the question of war matériel. If his front were to become the main theater, it would best be helped by an attack on the Northern Front to pin down German troops and prevent their reinforcing the crumbling Austrians.

General Max von Hoffman, one of the sharpest German strategists on the Eastern Front, later suggested that had the Russians attacked the German lines at this point "regardless of the losses," they would have prevented Falkenhayn from sending forces to support the Austrians. Without the help the German commander was able to send, the Russian drive would probably have "developed into the complete defeat of the Austro-Hungarian army."

Even with their ally's help, however, the Austrians continued to fall back. Brusilov resumed his attack into the Styr salient, essentially obliterating the Austrian Fourth Army, which was in complete disarray after only three days of fighting. The marshes had dried by July, and the advancing Russians captured 30,000 more prisoners before they were stopped by fresh German divisions scraped together from various places. Although their own advance had been halted, the Russians had little trouble fighting off strong German counterattacks. Lesh began to attack to the northwest to try to pursue a defeated enemy and roll up the front before Evert. Brusilov had not sanctioned this move, and he repeatedly tried to get Kaledin to attack in the direction of Kovel, ordering him to remain on the defensive on the Styr front. Yet the Eighth Army commander had a "strange temperament," according to Brusilov, always whining about his position, claiming despite his successes that he was in a critical situation and predicting that any day destruction would overtake both himself and his army. His wavering produced uncertainty in men who, in Brusilov's view, never "loved or trusted him," so seldom did he mingle with, speak to, or even thank them. Brusilov ever after believed that Kaledin's shortcomings prevented the Russians from taking Kovel.

In the south, however, July brought fresh successes. While the Styr front was stabilizing, Lechitsky again drove against the Austrian Seventh Army. Even the German reinforcements broke and ran. The flank of the *Südarmee* was turned on the Dniester River, and the Russian Eleventh Army, the weakest on Brusilov's entire front, advanced and finally took Brody. The *Südarmee*, with both flanks threatened after the Austrians were routed, retreated to within thirty miles of Lvov. Sakharov's Eleventh Army had to repel vigorous German and Austrian counterattacks, which they were able to do without losing any ground and despite the fact that all of the Eleventh's reserves had been sent to other fronts. Yet, late in July, Sakharov's troops, along with the Seventh Army, were able to cross the Zlota Lipa, a tributary of the Dniester River. At the same time to the south, Lechitsky took Kalicz on the Dniester.

On July 27, Lesh's Third Army, Kaledin's Eighth, and the newly formed Guard Army went on the offensive. The Guard Army was supposed to make a flanking attack against the salient before Lesh, but its commander, Grand Duke Paul, considered that cowardly and beneath his dignity and launched a frontal assault instead, never informing headquarters of his change of plans. His men had to attack over three causeways under heavy enemy fire from well-positioned artillery on the heights. The slaughter was tremendous, but they finally took the high ground after losing 70 percent of their effectives. Russian cavalry and reinforcements withdrew, however, and the position taken at such a terrible cost had to be abandoned. Meanwhile, on the southern flank of the

Guard Army, the Eighth Army did have some success, advancing and taking 12,000 prisoners. By the first week of August, this advance had begun to stall. Attacks on Kovel continued intermittently every few weeks until November. Despite the Russians' overwhelming superiority, they were unable to take the city.

Farther south, the Eleventh Army's left in conjunction with the Seventh's right drove deeply into the enemy front, inflicting heavy losses, and by August 13 they held a line west of Zborov. The right flank of the Ninth Army attacked on the Korobtsa River, but enemy reinforcements stopped their advance.

By late summer there was strong evidence that Russian successes were taking their toll on the Central Powers. Not only had the Italian offensive ceased for good, but so had the German attacks at Verdun. Thirty infantry divisions and three and a half cavalry divisions had been redeployed from the Western Front. Moreover, the Germans now had to assume responsibility for the entire Eastern Front, with Field Marshal Paul von Hindenburg given command as far as the Dniester River. In theory, he was under Austrian Commander in Chief Conrad's orders in the south, but even the southern sector had a German chief of staff, General Hans von Seekt, and when Hindenburg replaced Falkenhayn as chief of the general staff, a German, Prince Leopold of Bavaria, was given command of the entire Eastern Front.

Yet the Russian losses had also been mounting. Brusilov had suffered 450,000 casualties by mid-August, and his reserves had been reduced, despite the generous shifting of troops from Evert and Kuropatkin, to only 100,000 men for his entire front. At this point in the war, the Russians in all theaters had sustained five and a half million casualties since 1914.

Despite these losses, however, on August 9 Brusilov reopened his offensive in the south with the Ninth and Seventh Armies. The Seventh attacked a sector of the front that visiting Kaiser Wilhelm had called "impregnable." The Russians enveloped it on the northeast and the southwest, and the strong point was abandoned almost without resistance. The Seventh Army broke the enemy line at Stanislav and advanced ten miles, capturing 8,000 men and 33 guns. The Austrians stopped the push only when they were able to retreat into prepared positions. Meanwhile, Lechitsky with his Ninth Army attacked the enemy after a gas shell bombardment of the artillery batteries, which resulted in the soldiers' abandoning their guns. The Russians took 8,000 prisoners that day—3,500 of them Germans. The offensive ended with the occupation of the region between Stanislav and Nadvorna, 22 miles to the south.

Toward the end of August, Romania, impressed by the Russians' stunning victories and lured by the prospect of easy territorial pickings in Transylvania, declared war on the Central Powers. The Romanian army was probably the worst in Eastern Europe, however, and after some initial successes it retreated after running into determined resistance and counterattacks. Soon, the retreat turned into a pathetic rout. Brusilov had never been enthusiastic about Romania as an ally and had feared just such a debacle. Other Russian generals who knew the quality of the Romanian forces also had never wanted the nation as an ally in the first place, for as one Russian commander sarcastically noted, "Asking the Romanian army to fight is like asking a donkey to perform a minuet."

Brusilov attacked, however, to assist his ally to the south. On August 29, he hit the right flank of the *Südarmee* at Brzezany, and the town of Potutory fell after several costly attacks. The city of Niziov on the Dniester capitulated as well, while the Austrians and Germans farther south fell back. Fighting continued in this sector until the end of September, with the Russians making small gains but sustaining terrible losses. Bulgaria attacked Romania from the south, and in effect, the new ally was eliminated from the war. The Russians suddenly had to cover another 200 miles of front, and this additional burden effectively ended Brusilov's offensive.

Brusilov, for all practical purposes, had given up. Without Evert's and Kuropatkin's assistance, he had no hope of total victory. Even with the stupendous Austrian losses, the enemy's numerical strength along Brusilov's front was now greater than his own. He continued to fight, but with less daring and boldness, trying to conserve his troop strength as much as possible. Gone was the mentality apparent in his order a month earlier that "In Russia now, no one has the right to become tired." The offensive would have no more successes. Powerful Csarina Alexandra Feodorovna had a hand in its formal termination. Pleading with the csar to stop the offensive, she wrote him, "Oh, give your order again to Brusilov to stop the useless slaughter," after which Nicholas commanded Brusilov to cease his efforts.

The offensive's handicaps had been greater than merely insufficient reserves. German air superiority—and in some cases, no Russian air support at all—gave the enemy (and especially the Germans) an enormous advantage, particularly in the drive to take Kovel. Moreover, the poor quality of some of Brusilov's generals, especially Grand Duke Paul and Aleksei Kaledin (whom Brusilov later regretted not having removed), was a great hindrance. Even with his multitude of obstacles, he most certainly would have driven the Austrians onto the Hungarian Plain and possibly out of the war had a timely, substantial attack on Evert's front taken place and deprived the Austrians along Brusilov's front of reinforcements.

German deputy chief of staff General Erich Ludendorff made this point clear in his memoirs. He noted that with Brusilov's one blow, the entire Eastern

Front was in danger. The Germans, he added, were fearing an attack on their front at Smorgon or at Riga, where the Russians had great strength and where the Germans had a shortage of reserves. There, the German troops would have been "but a drop of water on a hot stone" had the Russians advanced. At one point, Ludendorff noted that the only reserve unit for the 600-mile front in the north was a single cavalry brigade. All of their forces were in the south halting Brusilov's attack. Had they been held there, the turn of events on the South-western Front would have been markedly different.

Other observers have been quick to mention that Brusilov's successes were against the Austrians, not the Germans, and his method of attack would not have been as successful had it been used against the Northern or Western Fronts, where the Germans were concentrated. Brusilov's armies indeed were less successful against the *Südarmee* than against the Austrians on their flanks, and when the *Südarmee* did retreat, it was largely due to the collapse of the Austrian forces on either flank. Moreover, the Germans would not have allowed the Russians' preoffensive sapping to continue unhindered. Yet, with 750,000 men in reserve behind the Northern and Western Fronts—almost seven times more in reserve than Brusilov had on his front—an offensive executed all along the line would have caused a grave threat to the Germans. It would have most certainly guaranteed Brusilov's success. If the Russians had reached Budapest and Vienna, the Germans would have had no choice but to abandon Poland.

IN THE FALL OF 1916 THE POLITICAL SITUATION IN RUSSIA RAPIDLY DISINTEGRATED, resulting in an increased desertion rate from the army. With the abdication of Csar Nicholas in the revolution of February 1917, the last linchpin of stability departed. The famous General Order Number One, giving soldiers rights they had never had and allowing them to elect soldiers' committees to protect those rights, was issued by the Petrograd Soviet. Mutinies and mass desertions became daily occurrences, as did officer lynchings. Whole units left the trenches and, in Communist leader Vladimir Ilyich Lenin's words, "voted with their feet" and went home. Those who remained usually refused to fight.

Brusilov had less trouble with his troops than most officers, and there were no lynchings in his units during the early radical changes, mainly due to the commander's popularity and his immediate acceptance of the revolution. He readily cooperated with the soldiers' committees, and within days of Nicholas's abdication he removed all csarist emblems from his uniform. He also announced an amnesty to deserters, and later even extended it an extra month. He likewise declared his conversion to republicanism, for which he would never be forgiven by the Russian émigré community. Aleksandr Kerensky, then the minister of justice in the provisional government, toured the Southwestern Front with Brusilov, trying to restore order. The man who would later become the prime minister of the new Russia was so impressed with Brusilov that he replaced General Alekseev with him.

Both Kerensky and Brusilov believed there was a new spirit in the army—a monumental burst of wishful thinking—and with pressure from the Allies, they planned a second Brusilov offensive for the summer of 1917. But desertions reflected the real mood of the army. Between 1914 and February 1917, the rate had averaged 6,800 per month. After the February revolution, it averaged 34,000 a month between March and May, and rose rapidly as the year passed. Yet, billing the planned operation as a "revolutionary offensive," Kerensky ordered some seventy divisions in the south to attack Austria as had been done the year before, with emphasis on a drive to retake Lemberg.

The preparations for the offensive were the best of the war. There was abundant war matériel, and the army even had 120 spotter aircraft flown mainly by French and British airmen. Two hundred thousand soldiers were winnowed from the best units and formed into a fighting force. Unlike the 1916 attack, there was no effort to maintain secrecy, and the Germans transferred four divisions from the Western Front to the east.

Kerensky later noted in his memoirs that the government and officers held their breath when they gave the soldiers the order to advance because they were not certain that they would attack. The second Brusilov offensive began well, however, since the Austrian army was in no better shape than the Russian. While Austrian units—especially the Slavic ones—surrendered without fighting, and other units fled at the slightest Russian advance, the arrival of Germans troops put some backbone into the Austrians. At the first stiffening of the Austrian lines, the Russian advance stopped, and then a retreat began that became a chaotic rout. The Germans often did not even bother taking prisoners.

The situation was further complicated by the "July Days," an uprising in Petrograd that nearly toppled the provisional government. In the face of the upheaval, Kerensky removed Brusilov as Commander in Chief of the army on July 31, replacing him with General Lavr Kornilov. Within a month, Kornilov and other generals executed a coup of their own to overthrow the Soviet and restore order in the army. As these men plotted, they excluded Brusilov, although it is doubtful that he would have participated in the plan if asked. He was in poor health and was recuperating in a village far from both the front and revolutionary politics when the Bolsheviks seized power. Although a legend was born that continues to this day that he fought for the Reds, Brusilov remained on the sidelines during the Russian Civil War. His son, however, did fight with the Communists and was executed when captured by the Whites.

When the general returned to active duty, it was to fight for Russia in the Polish War of 1920–21, after Poland launched an imperialistic campaign against prostrate Russia in a successful attempt to rectify unilaterally the boundaries given it by the Paris Peace Conference. Brusilov reentered military service and issued a ringing call for all officers to join the new government in repelling the foreign invader. After the war, he served the Communist regime as the Inspector General of cavalry. This action gave the émigré community another reason to hate him. He died in 1926, and his second wife, Nadezhda, devoted the rest of her life to preserving his memory and fighting to destroy the belief that he had ever been a Red sympathizer.

There is no denying that Brusilov's offensive had been, by any measure, a great success—the greatest Allied success of the entire war. He had retaken more than 15,000 square miles of territory, an area almost the size of Belgium, and his offensive had cost the Central Powers 765,000 casualties, of which 450,000 were prisoners of war. It sealed the failure of the Austrian attack in Italy and caused the Germans to abandon the siege of Verdun. Indeed, the Brusilov offensive had so panicked the Austrians that at one point they planned a defensive perimeter on an axis based on Vienna and Budapest and made elaborate plans for the evacuation of Emperor Franz Joseph from the capital by motor car.

Austria was never again to be a factor in the Great War beyond holding trenches against an inferior enemy. The Germans essentially had to fight alone. After Franz Joseph died in November 1916, his successor, Karl, began to send peace feelers to the Allies. Undeniably, Brusilov's Immortal Days were a major factor in prompting such overtures and in denying the Central Powers ultimate victory.

SALONIKA
Dennis E. Showalter

O F ALL THE FAR-FLUNG SIDESHOWS OF THE GREAT WAR,
none seemed to carry a heavier freight of unfulfilled
promises than the Salonika operation in northern Greece. In
October 1915, one British and one French division landed,
more or less uninvited, in a country that was still officially
neutral. Their original mission was to open an escape route for
the Serbian army, then under attack on three sides from the
Germans, Austrians, and Bulgarians. It proved impossible.
The Russians demanded that the western Allies maintain a
presence in the Balkans but that presence never helped them.
Nor did the Salonika operation threaten the Turks or draw
German troops from the Western Front. The British, already
dealing with their failing Gallipoli enterprise, wanted to abandon the Salonika bridgehead, once it became obvious that the
Serbs were beyond their help. (The Central Powers eliminated
Serbia from the war but not the Serbs, whose seventy-one-
year-old King Peter led his army out of his landlocked country
to the coast of Albania; many of those men would turn up in
Salonika.) The French insisted not only that the tiny force remain but that it be reinforced. The British policy-makers, the
historian David French writes, "came to believe that France's
commitment to the campaign had little to do with defeating
the Central Powers and more to do with establishing French
predominance in the Balkans after the war. They were correct."

They gave in anyway. But the operation became mainly a
French enterprise. The universal rationalization was that, like

Gallipoli, the Allies once unkenneled from the Salonika front could rip at the underbelly of the Central Powers. And that they did accomplish, although it took them until 1918.

Dennis E. Showalter describes those demoralizing three years of dreary trench stalemate as a mainly Bulgarian force faced an international assortment of French, British, Serbian, Russian, Italian, and eventually, Greek troops along a 300-mile front. The fighting went nowhere. For the Allies, a particularly virulent strain of malaria claimed more casualties than enemy bullets. The port of Salonika, the second city of Greece, became as much a military hospital as staging area. Only in the late summer of 1918 would this fever-ridden backwater become important, when it witnessed one of the rare brilliant campaigns of the Great War. You have to put it on a par with the Brusilov offensive, if not higher: It succeeded. The man responsible was Louis Franchet d'Esperey, a former hero of the Western Front who had been blamed for the German breakthrough on the Aisne that May and sent packing to the Balkans. Like Edmund Allenby, another failed Western Front general turfed out to the eastern Mediterranean (in his case, Palestine) Franchet d'Esperey would redeem himself, and then some. The British disparaged the bullet-headed general as "Desperate Frankie." They could have used some of his energy. The breakthrough that he led, striking northward toward the Danube and the frontier of Austria, would bring about the final collapse of the Central Powers. It was somehow fitting that Serbians under his command would end by occupying Belgrade, where the war began.

———

DENNIS E. SHOWALTER is the past president of the Society for Military History, joint editor of the journal *War in History*, and the author of *The Wars of Frederick the Great* and *Tannenberg: Clash of Empires*. He is a professor of history at Colorado College.

T HE WORLD'S BIGGEST INTERNMENT CAMP" WAS WHAT GERMAN propagandists called the Allied positions around the Greek city of Salonika. A quarter-million British, French, African, Serb, and Greek troops spent so much time entrenching themselves there that Georges Clemenceau dubbed them "the Salonika gardeners." But Salonika was more than another of the Great War's sideshows, more than another dumping ground for generals who failed on the Western Front. Salonika witnessed the rebirth of the Serbian army and the making of the Yugoslav state. It saw some of the war's fiercest mountain fighting and one of history's last decisive cavalry operations. And it was from Salonika that the new Balkan order emerged—an order to this day being determined by blood as well as words.

The Salonika campaign grew out of Germany's decision in the summer of 1915 to remove the Serbian thorn from its southern flank and consolidate a Balkan position threatened by the Allies' attack on the Dardanelles in March and April. Neither Germany nor Austria-Hungary could spare resources for a major operation. They turned to Bulgaria, still smarting from defeat in the Second Balkan War of 1912 and increasingly concerned by a Serbia now directly allied with France and Britain as well as Russia. With the equivalent of twenty divisions, 1,000 guns, and a well-trained officer corps at his disposal, Emperor Ferdinand of Bulgaria was able to strike a hard bargain. Bulgaria would receive all of Macedonia, parts of Serbia, and further territory from Greece and Romania should these states join the Allies. In addition to a generous loan, the Central Powers contributed a dozen divisions, a strong force of heavy artillery, and a proven command team. Field Marshal August von Mackensen and his chief of staff, Hans von Seeckt, specialized in set-piece offensives built around massive, systematic artillery preparation. They had crippled the Russians in Galicia, at Gorlice-Tarnow, in May. Seeckt was also a first-rate logistician, an important attribute for a commander in a region already devastated by war.

By the fall of 1915, a Serbian army eroded by disease and casualties, low on ammunition and medical supplies, faced attack from three sides by Bulgarians, Germans, and Austrians. Mackensen's offensive began on October 7. Veteran German commanders praised Serbian ferocity and resolution. But courage was no substitute for steel. As its troops were driven back on all fronts, Serbia called on its allies. As early as December 1914, the French general Louis

Franchet d'Esperey, who would later lead the Allies in the theater, had urged opening a "second front" in the Balkans. David Lloyd George, then Britain's chancellor of the exchequer, had visions of a combined Greek, Serb, and Romanian offensive against Austria and Turkey. Their respective general staffs observed that such an operation could only be supported through the Greek port of Salonika, acquired from the Ottoman Empire only in 1912. However, the city's harbor facilities fell far short of those required by a modern expeditionary force. The only railway line from Salonika into Serbia was single-tracked and ran through some of the roughest country in southeastern Europe. Diplomats added that the Greek government was aggressively neutral, and correspondingly unlikely to allow even a landing at Salonika, much less turn over its northern provinces to foreign troops.

Serbia's crisis changed minds, if only temporarily. On September 25, France and Britain had agreed to send a division each from the Dardanelles to Salonika—if they could get ashore. Greek premier Eleutherios Venizelos believed Greece could replace Serbia as the Allies' principal Balkan ally if it acted quickly. King Constantine, of German descent, distrusted Venizelos as a rival for power. The resulting fencing match saw Venizelos simultaneously welcoming the landing, protesting the violation of Greek neutrality, and resigning as the first Allied troops disembarked on October 5.

Britain was an unwilling participant. Greek politics baffled soldiers convinced that only the Western Front mattered and that "wogs begin at Calais." The French were more sanguine. The tension between Venizelos and Constantine offered opportunities to enhance French influence in Greece. France had another reason to encourage the operation. Before 1914 the French army had been riven by internal conflicts. General Maurice Sarrail was one of the chief firebrands, an outspoken republican and a freethinking Freemason whose contacts with left-wing politicians facilitated his rise through the senior ranks while alienating him from his colleagues. In July 1915, General Joseph Joffre dismissed Sarrail from command of the Third Army, where his record had been solid until a surprise local German offensive captured enough ground and inflicted enough casualties to legitimate his relief.

Sarrail's political patrons were unwilling to see him relegated to obscurity. Neither Joffre nor Prime Minister René Viviani were comfortable with having a loose cannon of Sarrail's caliber at loose ends in Paris. Sending him to Salonika appeared a no-lose situation. If Sarrail failed, he would be finished. And he just might help win the war. Sarrail might be a political general; he was not an obvious incompetent. The new generalissimo arrived in Salonika on October 12, eager for action but limited in fighting power. Fewer than fifty thousand men were involved in the initial deployment. Sarrail's sole French division, a composite force of metropolitan and African troops, had suffered heavily at the nearby Dardanelles. The British 10th Division, raised in Ireland as part of Kitchener's New Army, had also suffered heavy losses at Gallipoli and was neither trained nor equipped for mountain warfare. Its commander, Sir Bryan Mahon, was under orders from London to remain near Salonika until the Greek political situation was clarified.

Sarrail nevertheless pushed his French elements forward up the Vardar valley in support of a Serbian army whose situation was changing from exposed to desperate. Not until the end of October was Mahon authorized to cross the Serbo-Greek frontier. The Allies, engaging by battalions and batteries, got less than 100 miles from Salonika before Serbia was overrun. What remained of its army made a fighting retreat to Kosovo, the Field of Blackbirds, site of the fourteenth-century defeat by the Ottoman Empire that symbolized Serb identity. With lines of retreat to the south blocked by Bulgarian troops, Serbia's high command turned west, toward the Adriatic coast.

Serbian prime minister Nikola Pasic denounced "the indecision and inactivity of our allies . . . the determining factor in our decision. . . ." The Serbian evacuation involved as many as 300,000 soldiers and civilians. It included 20,000 prisoners of war, mostly Austrians captured in the fall of 1914 and brought along as a gesture of defiance. Some of the men in Serbian uniforms were in their seventies. Others had scarcely reached their teens. King Peter himself, at seventy-one, rode in a specially constructed cart, a concession to his age and frailty. Meat came from slaughtered artillery horses. Bread was made from cornflower seed, when there was any bread at all. A Scottish volunteer nurse who accompanied the retreat recalled dead unburied and wounded abandoned, surgery without anesthesia, men and women moving in silence through rain and mist, sleet and snow, and always the cold, more bitter as the altitude increased. The landscape was oddly bright, she said, with the colors of defeat: blood on a bandage, the brown of exposed flesh, a yellow cap on the head of a dead child.

If the Central Powers were unwilling to waste resources pursuing an enemy apparently doomed, Albanian guerrillas took a heavy toll of their ancestral enemies. Typhus, dysentery, and frostbite ravaged the survivors. After three weeks of nightmare in a Balkan December, those who reached the Adriatic found . . . nothing. Italy, which had joined the Entente in May, initially accepted responsibility for protecting the delivery of food and medical supplies to the small Albanian ports where the refugees had congregated. But when it came to the crunch, Italy's admirals were unwilling to risk their ships. Instead the Allies decided on evacuation. By April 1916, more than 250,000 refugees had been removed, most of them to the Greek island of Corfu. They were so emaciated that nurses could lift and carry grown men. But 150,000 of them would fight again.

Meanwhile the overextended French and British fell back in the face of brutal weather and Bulgarian pressure. The 10th Division alone lost 1,700 men to frostbite and "general debility." Four British and three French divisions arrived in Salonika from Europe as reinforcements by the end of December. They were enough to hold the Greek frontier against a Bulgaria forbidden by its German ally and paymaster to take the military and political risks of driving immediately for Salonika. But what were they to do next? On December 4, British prime minister Herbert Asquith described Salonika in these terms: "From a military point of view [it is] dangerous and likely to lead to a great disaster." The French disagreed, more for diplomatic than military reasons. The Serbian government in exile saw Salonika as its best chance to return to the war and have a stake in the peace settlement. Russia was willing to send troops. So was Italy, suspicious of the French and nurturing its own aspirations for a Balkan sphere of influence.

While the politicians debated, Sarrail created realities on the ground. Within four months he transformed Salonika into a formidable entrenched camp and a base able to support the offensive he planned for the spring of 1916. In the process the original small port town was all but submerged. The principal camp, through which all reinforcements for the theater passed, was located just to the northeast. Its temporary buildings seemed afloat on a sea of mud, with not even trees to break the desolation. The merchants who set up shop outside the sentry lines charged such outrageous prices for such inferior wares that anyone with time and money spent both in a city whose entrepreneurs, whatever their nationality, quickly began catering to the wants of young men far from home. Restaurants, cinemas, theaters, brothels, and souvenir shops proliferated in a matrix of destitution. Salonika was already crowded with refugees from the Balkan Wars of 1912–13, living in churches and shantytowns. The inflation that accompanied the Allied occupation made their lot even worse.

Most of the troops who reached Salonika had little sympathy to spare for anyone but themselves. Instead of riding trains or trucks to the front they marched, with full packs, as far as 200 miles, along roads little better than tracks, through a wasteland of uncultivated fields and depopulated villages to reach a front line roughly paralleling the prewar Greek-Serbian border. Some of the forward positions were in sectors so barren that dynamite was needed to construct shelters. Others ran through low ground where mosquitoes spread a particularly virulent form of malaria. Its mortality rate was not high—one in over 200 for the British contingent. But it left its victims debilitated and vulnerable to further attacks. In October 1917, more than 20 percent of the British contingent was actually hospitalized, and this was after over a year's experience in controlling the disease. Although their sectors were on higher ground, the French suffered as well.

Malaria's impact was compounded by two major local products: high-proof liquor and high-risk sex. Soldiers in Macedonia had little to do with their off-duty time except absorb enough cheap wine or brandy to dull the misery of their surroundings. A common next step involved a transaction with a lady of professional love and doubtful hygiene. Venereal disease rates soared, including some varieties that defied treatment. As alternatives the British, true to a tradition of sublimation by exhaustion, organized fox-hunting meets for the officers, boxing matches and football games for the men. Some of the latter were played within range of Bulgarian artillery, which out of chivalry or bewilderment usually held its fire. Occasionally as well the hounds ran through the barbed wire separating the combatants, but each time they returned or were sent back. For those more culturally inclined there were theater groups and concert parties. *The Balkan News* appeared daily. The French were less readily placated. Not a few regarded even the Western Front as preferable. There they knew why they were fighting and had some contact with home. No one cared about the Bulgarians. "What in the devil have we come here to do?" asked one *cafard*-stricken *poilu*.

That question was answered by Aristide Briand. He had succeeded Viviani as premier and foreign minister in October 1915, and believed that with twenty divisions Sarrail could achieve the kind of success that would convince both Greece and Romania to join the Allies. The Serbian government was willing to provide six of those divisions, reorganized from survivors of the great retreat. The rest would have to come from outside the theater.

The British responded by arguing for the withdrawal of the forces already in place. The nine divisions currently in Salonika, their general staff pointed out, were more than needed to defend the port but too few for an offensive of any consequence. The French insisted on remaining, both to maintain what they regarded as their primacy in the Entente and to relieve the pressure of the German onslaught at Verdun. On April 30, 1916, Sarrail received orders to attack with the forces in hand: five British divisions, four French, and six of Serbs. The offensive was intended first to prevent the transfer of troops of the Central Powers from the Balkans to the west, then to bring Greece and Romania into the war, and finally perhaps to compel Bulgaria to sue for peace.

It was an ambitious program, and Britain remained skeptical. When, however, on July 4, 1916, Romanian premier Ion Bratianu declared his country willing to join the Allies—if they would mount a major offensive from Salonika—London's grumbling subsided. By this time the Allied order of battle was bewilderingly multicultural. The Serbs, reequipped by a France that was the Great War's arsenal of democracy, began landing from Corfu in April. Many were in their thirties or older. Most bore the marks of hunger. But they were survivors, inured to privation and virtually immune to disease. A brigade of Russians arrived in July, with another to follow. Italy sent in August an oversized division of eighteen battalions, good troops experienced in mountain operations.

The army's core remained its French and British contingents. The French eventually reached a strength of nine divisions. One, the 30th, was an active army formation recruited from around Marseilles. The rest were wartime creations, combining active regiments and battalions with units raised from prewar reservists and wartime conscripts. Three of these divisions were "colonial," with cadres and depots provided by regiments raised in France for service outside the country. Otherwise they differed from the rest of the army primarily in their uniforms: khaki as opposed to horizon blue. There were a few Zouave battalions, European residents of Tunisia and Algeria with an admixture of North African Jews. Attached to the colonial divisions, deployed as well for internal security and as labor units, were as many as two dozen battalions of Senegalese. Drawn from sub-Saharan Africa, they were widely regarded and frequently used as shock troops—not least because their allegedly "primitive" nervous systems were supposed to render them less susceptible than Europeans to the horrors of the modern battlefield. Depending on circumstances, their actual performance varied widely, both in Europe and Salonika. France also sent to Salonika three battalions from Madagascar and four from Indochina. Despite the growing shortage of manpower, these units were used only as labor troops. The Vietnamese were regarded as unable to stand the frontline stress of modern war.

The British 10th Division had been reinforced by two Kitchener divisions of volunteers, the 22d and 26th, and by two more organized from regular army battalions brought back from India upon the outbreak of war. Despite their high proportion of experienced "old sweats," the 27th and 28th Divisions never quite found their feet on the Western Front. After suffering badly in the trench conditions of the winter of 1914–15, they were decimated in the Second Battle of Ypres. Sir Douglas Haig seems to have regarded their departure with relative equanimity. The London territorials of the 60th Division would spend some time in Salonika on their way to Palestine. The British had a new commander as well, Sir George Milne, competent and intelligent but not a man to make waves.

Sarrail was so preoccupied with alliance politics and administrative preparations that he was taken by surprise when, on August 17, the Bulgarian army launched an attack of its own. The strategic context was the Austro-German offensive that overran Romania in the last four months of 1916. The Bulgarians were expected to pin the Salonika army in place and thereby convince Romania it had backed the wrong horse. The offensive was also intended to send the Greeks a message by seizing territory as an insurance policy on their continued neutrality. After the war, the Germans had promised, the conquests would be returned—if Greece behaved itself.

The Bulgarians hit the Serbs, deployed on the Allied left, and simultaneously drove for the Aegean Sea through the Rupel Pass, a hundred miles farther east. In the Rupel sector the French lost ground and prisoners, but the Bulgarian attack petered out as it reached the Struma River. To the west the Serbs rallied and held around the town of Ostrovo in four days of hand-to-hand fighting.

Sarrail coped well with surprise. Perhaps he had learned a lesson from his Western Front misfortune. He kept his contingents in order and proved adept at switching local reserves to threatened sectors with the aid of British trucks. On September 12, he launched his counterpunch. Its projected key was an end run by two French divisions and a Russian brigade from the Allied left, aiming at the transport junction and supply base of Monastir. Two Serb divisions would break the Bulgar center: the massive heights of Mount Kajmakcalan, called the "Butter Churn" for its shape. The British, the Italians, and the rest of the French contingent were to go forward around Lake Doiran and across the Struma. Sarrail expected to push forward to the city of Prilep, then to the Vardar River, cutting the Central Powers' lines of communication and perhaps rolling them up from the flank in the manner of Napoleon.

Hindsight suggests Sarrail's plan took little account of terrain and even less of time. Supplying the projected envelopment would become virtually impossible once the fall rains began. That meant a rapid initial advance. Instead the Serbs fought their way to the top of Butter Churn, were driven back by the Bulgarians, then on September 30 recaptured the mountain and held it. To the epic of the Long Retreat was added a victory that became the stuff of legend in the postwar Yugoslavian army. But like so many of its counterparts between 1914 and 1918, the capture of Butter Churn had no consequences. Elsewhere on the Salonika front, the Italians, under tacit instructions from their government, practiced a policy of "live and let live." British divisions along the Struma and in the Vardar valley demonstrated levels of tactical clumsiness not seen since Loos on the Western Front—a logical consequence of a year spent in a quiet sector. But Sarrail's real problems developed on the left. The Bulgarians in that sector were well entrenched; the French were tired and unenthusiastic.

Sarrail bombarded his subordinates with messages insisting that fighting spirit would overcome barbed wire. He relieved one general who had the initiative to see the frontline obstacles for himself—from the rear cockpit of an airplane, a first in the Great War.

On October 21 it began to rain, further slowing an advance that had already lost most of its momentum. With some German help grudgingly given, the Bulgarians held in front of Monastir until November 19, then withdrew. Serbia's government-in-exile considered it a fair exchange for the fifth of their army lost in Sarrail's attacks. Joffre was less sanguine. In December he peremptorily closed down the Salonika front for the winter. For much of this time Greece had been in a virtual state of civil war. Greek troops, unsure who their enemies were, surrendered strategic frontier positions to the Bulgarians without a fight in August. In September, Venizelos established a provisional government on Crete and began raising an "army of national defense." Sarrail, a republican to his fingertips, enthusiastically supported the Venizelists in Salonika. When, in December, fighting broke out in Salonika between Greek royalists and Allied forces, and the Allies imposed a blockade on Greece, Sarrail increasingly treated Venizelos as the legitimate head of state.

JOFFRE'S DISMISSAL IN DECEMBER 1916 BROUGHT SARRAIL EVEN MORE TO THE forefront of French military politics. In January 1917 he was formally designated commander of the Allied Army of the Orient, with all national contingents under his direct authority. His new orders were to fix the enemy in Macedonia while the French and British decided the war on the Western Front. Sarrail saw opportunity beckoning. His radical supporters in parliament were increasingly influential. He had survived his prewar contemporaries in part by virtue of his assignment to Salonika. Now Salonika would bring him at least a marshal's baton.

Sarrail's operational vision had shifted from the previous autumn's Napoleonic model to something more appropriate for the Western Front circa 1915. This time he would attack all along the line, wearing out and breaking through a Bulgarian army that by his calculations had to be on the edge of exhaustion. The plan's lack of subtlety was compounded when Milne decided to shift the British focus from the swampy, malaria-ridden Struma valley to the high ground around Lake Doiran. The Doiran sector commanded several main roads into Serbia and Bulgaria. It was correspondingly heavily defended, but Milne was confident that his men, well supported by heavy artillery, could break through and break out. Instead the 22d and 26th Divisions were stopped on their lines of departure by gas, artillery, and machine guns. Milne paused for almost two weeks, until May 8, then sent his infantry forward onto the same killing grounds with the same results. Total casualties for the 22d and 26th Divisions' share of the offensive came to around 5,000.

Farther west, French, Italian, and Russian attacks achieved a similar common denominator. A Russian brigade was almost annihilated when it broke through the Bulgarian lines and was left unsupported. The Italian division failed to move its reserves forward quickly enough to support initial successes. French battalions, their ranks by now filled with too many recovered wounded, took no more than necessary chances. The Serbian chief of staff, General Peter Bojovic, was unwilling to sacrifice the rest of his country's army in what was turning into a fiasco. On May 21, he asked Sarrail to halt the operation.

Milne took a stiff-upper-lip approach to the defeat, assigning primary responsibility in his sector to bad staff work. More serious, he noted, was the tendency of each ally "to look over his shoulder at the other." Serbia was in the process of purging officers ostensibly seeking to establish a military dictatorship. The central figure of the alleged conspiracy was Colonel Dragutin Dmitrijevic, better known to history under his nom de guerre of Apis. As chief of military intelligence he had been a key figure behind the young Serbian nationalists whose murder of Franz Ferdinand had initiated war in 1914. Whether Apis was in fact conspiring against the monarchy, whether he knew too much for others' comfort, or whether his trial and subsequent execution on June 26 had even murkier motives still submerged in the Belgrade archives, his demise and those of his close associates shook the Serbians so badly that they were unwilling to test loyalties and morale in a protracted offensive.

Events in Greece were no less unbalanced. By the spring of 1917, Constantine had abandoned any pretense of neutrality—a logical, but imprudent, response to the virtual Allied occupation of his country. In March, Briand was forced to resign as French premier, removing one of the king's staunchest international supporters. Greece was under naval blockade, with French ships ready to land troops in Athens to force the king's abdication. Venizelos saw his opportunity and declared himself willing to accept Constantine's son Alexander as king should his father "choose" to renounce the throne. This seemed a reasonable compromise, even to a British government suspicious in general of Balkan revolutionaries. On June 11, the Allies demanded Constantine's abdication. On June 26, Venizelos returned to Athens. Three days later Greece declared war on the Central Powers. Constantine went into Swiss exile, and Alexander assumed the throne, with Venizelos as premier and de facto chief of state.

The adherence of Greece to the Allied camp went far to transform the Salonika campaign into a Third Balkan War. Venizelos ordered full mobilization.

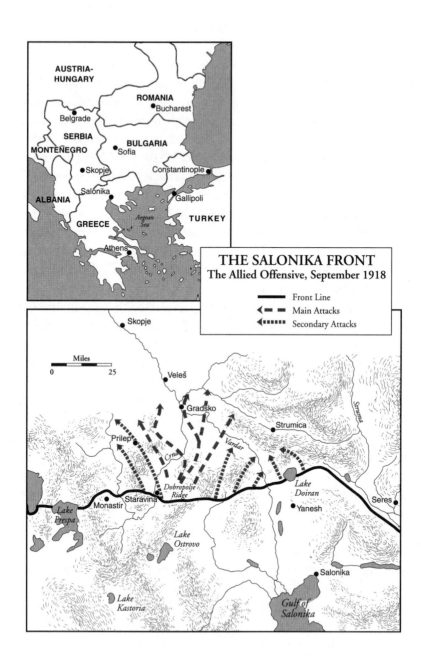

THE SALONIKA FRONT
The Allied Offensive, September 1918

——— Front Line
◄ ▬ ▬ Main Attacks
◄ ▪▪▪▪ Secondary Attacks

AUSTRIA-
HUNGARY

ROMANIA
●Bucharest

●Belgrade

SERBIA

MONTENEGRO

BULGARIA
●Sofia

●Skopje

Salonika

Constantinople●

ALBANIA

Gallipoli

GREECE

Aegean
Sea

TURKEY

Athens

Skopje

Miles
0   25

Veleš

Gradsko

Strumica

Prilep

Crna

Vardar

Strumica

Dobropolje
Ridge

Lake
Doiran

Seres

Staravina

Monastir

Yanesh

Lake
Prespa

Lake
Ostrovo

Salonika

Lake
Kastoria

Gulf of
Salonika

Constantine's authority was respected in the army, but not to a degree that would spark a civil war. Mobilization was implemented with no more than the expected number of cashierings, executions, and minor mutinies. By the summer of 1918, Greece would be able to deliver nine divisions, about a quarter-million men—more than enough to assert postwar claims in Macedonia and Asia Minor.

Greek entry into the war was also more than enough to keep four British divisions—the 22d, 26th, 27th, and 28th—in Salonika, despite the general staff's objections. The question was whether those divisions would be fighting alone. The Russian brigades were suffering from a sense that they were being used as cannon fodder. The csar's abdication in March 1917 and the provisional government's relaxing of disciplinary regulations compounded confusion among all ranks. Disaffection escalated into mutiny; by January 1918, the Russians were disarmed and interned.

The French contingent faced a crisis as well. By the summer of 1917 it was harder than ever for the ordinary *poilu* to see how his presence in Salonika contributed to the war's defining issue: the survival of France. Whatever Sarrail's political popularity, to the men at the front he was a remote figure whose alleged performances in drawing rooms and bedrooms far exceeded his prowess on the battlefield. In June, after the mutinies on the Western Front, the French high command announced more generous and systematic leave policies for that theater: in principle, one week's home leave every four months. Some politicians went further, advocating that any soldier overseas for more than a year and a half should receive a home furlough. Salonika's rumor mills transmuted rhetoric to procedure. In July, most of a division mutinied when informed—accurately—that they had no right to furloughs and that no ships were available to take them home in any case. The issue was resolved without force. It was nevertheless a warning to senior officers to improve conditions in what even optimists called a pesthole.

The quality of life in Salonika significantly diminished on August 18, 1917, when fire broke out in the old quarter. The buildings were tinder-dry; local fire-fighting capacities were soon exhausted. As long as the flames were confined to the poorer districts, Allied response was minimal. Around ten o'clock flames began singeing the well-to-do. By midnight thousands of refugees were being evacuated by truck and ship. Nearly half the city was eventually destroyed—including most of the good-time zones. Some veterans would later suggest that the Allied offensives of 1918 were impelled by boredom as much as strategy. It was worth taking personal risks to get out of Salonika!

The new year brought a new Commander in Chief. Sarrail's position had been shaky ever since the spring. Milne and the Serbian general staff agitated for his replacement. France's new premier, Georges Clemenceau, disliked Sarrail despite their common political sympathies. His feelings were confirmed when, in August, documents from Sarrail's headquarters were found in the office of *Le Bonnet Rouge*, an antimilitarist paper financed in part by German agents. Themselves innocuous, they nevertheless linked Sarrail in Clemenceau's mind with defeatism. Sarrail's connections could no longer protect him. In December 1917 he was recalled.

Sarrail's successor, Marie-Louis Guillaumat, had risen to army command on the Western Front, in the process winning high praise as a master of set-piece battles. His successes in the Verdun sector in the aftermath of the 1917 mutinies had done much to restore French confidence at all levels, from front-line trenches to the *bureaux* of Paris. His service in the colonial army gave him some experience in conducting overseas expeditions. Perhaps best of all Guillaumat was a new broom, an outsider to the gridlocked infighting of Salonika. He improved contact among Allied staffs, in particular establishing cordial personal relations with Milne. He relieved enough officers in the French contingent to encourage the rest. He built bridges to the Balkan contingents, overseeing the Greek army's reequipment to modern standards and cooperating in the Serbs' reinforcement from an unexpected source.

As early as 1916, Serbia had been recruiting ethnic Serbs captured by the Russians from the Austro-Hungarian army. As conditions in the POW camps worsened, Croats and Slovenes also began to volunteer. Weeks of negotiation with the Russian provisional government were followed by months of travel to ports where Allied ships waited—Archangel in the north and Port Arthur at the far end of the Trans-Siberian Railway. But by April 1918, more than 16,000 former prisoners of war were on the ground in the Balkans, in Serbian uniform, just a few days' fighting from home.

Serbia's war aims had developed in the context of restoring and enlarging a centralized, Orthodox Christian state governed from Belgrade. Not until tsarist Russia's collapse removed its traditional protector did Serbia agree to cooperate with Croat and Slovene exiles in establishing Yugoslavia. Even then, Serb acquiescence was as much a matter of expedience as conviction. As for a Muslim role, speaking in the summer of 1917, the leader of the Serbian Popular Radical Party was blunt: "When our army crosses the Drina, we will give the Turks [Muslims] twenty-four hours, or even forty-eight hours, of time to return to their ancestral religion [of Orthodox Christianity]. Those who do not wish to do so are to be cut down." It was not a mind-set boding well for a multicultural state-nation.

Guillaumat tested his improvements in a series of generally successful minor operations in April and May. However, he would not take the armies of Salonika into a major action. In June 1918, he was recalled to France as a possible successor, should one be needed, for Henri-Philippe Pétain as commander of the French armies, or for Ferdinand Foch as Allied generalissimo. He was replaced by General Louis Franchet d'Esperey.

Franchet d'Esperey had begun the war as a corps commander and relieved General Charles Lanrezac at the head of the Fifth Army just before the battle of the Marne. By 1916, he was commanding an army group and was being discussed as a possible successor to Joffre. Franchet d'Esperey's Catholic religion and royalist connections, however, made him suspect in more republican circles. They also made him a convenient scapegoat for the reverses suffered by the French in the German Aisne offensive of May 1918. Franchet d'Esperey's army group bore the brunt of the attacks and suffered the heaviest losses. In a brief interview Clemenceau explained, "I must calm down Parliament. . . . I bear you no ill will." But Franchet d'Esperey had too much influence simply to be dismissed. Instead he was offered command at Salonika.

As early as 1914 the new Balkan generalissimo had suggested a major offensive in that region as an alternative to the stagnating Western Front. Now he saw a chance to make a mark on history that would overshadow his contemporaries. "I expect from you ferocious energy," he informed his welcoming committee on June 17. He found willing listeners. Both the British and the Serbs were convinced Bulgaria would collapse if hit hard in the right place— and the Serbs believed they had found that place. The Moglenitsa Mountains, the prewar frontier between Greece and Serbia, offered some of the worst terrain in the theater. But once they were crossed, the valleys and ridges sloped toward the Vardar, the natural line of advance.

The Serbs, argued their new chief of staff, Zivojin Misic, were ideally suited for a surprise attack and a rapid exploitation across this broken ground. Franchet d'Esperey agreed. He went so far as to place two French divisions under Serb command for the operation, and to strip the depots to provide grenades and light machine guns, those irreplaceable elements of mountain warfare, for the Serb infantry. There remained the task of convincing his superiors. Not until August 3 did the Allies' military representatives in Paris agree to a general offensive from Salonika. It required personal appeals by Guillaumat, who had been a consistent and effective lobbyist for Franchet d'Esperey's plan, to overcome last-minute British and Italian reservations. And like his British counterpart in Palestine, Sir Edward Allenby, Franchet d'Esperey was clearly informed that he could expect neither men nor supplies should anything go wrong.

"Desperate Frankie," as the British dubbed him, set "J-Day" for September

15. Twenty heavy guns had been secretly moved to the summits of mountains overlooking the main Bulgarian positions. Almost 500 more were in position to deliver not the traditional barrage but a one-day hurricane bombardment. In its aftermath the Serbs, French, and Italians would go forward to the Vardar. The British, supported by two Greek divisions, would mount a holding attack around Lake Doiran.

The Central Powers' forces in Macedonia were by now almost entirely Bulgarian. Two corps and one army headquarters, plus some staff officers, were German. So was the commander. General Friedrich von Scholtz had led a corps at Tannenberg and performed well in later assignments in the eastern theater. A former heavy artilleryman, he was undisturbed by the unprecedented weight of the Allied barrage, but did not expect the attack to come where it did. Even with the resulting advantages of tactical surprise, it took two days for the Serbs and French to chew through the Bulgarian positions on the Dobropolje ridge line and around Kozyak Mountain.

THE FRENCH BROUGHT FLAMETHROWERS INTO ACTION FOR THE FIRST TIME IN THE theater. They used Stokes mortars borrowed from the British, 37mm infantry guns, and light mountain howitzers to bring their infantry into grenade range of machine-gun nests whose crews died where they stood. The Serbs depended on cold steel and raw courage. A British observer said of them: "It is possible that if only Western European troops had been available, the attack would at this stage have petered out." Elements of the newly christened "Yugoslav Division" were reported singing as they advanced—a scenario more plausible here than in other Great War accounts of similar behavior. It was the turn of the Bulgars to begin looking over their shoulders. German accounts depict a Bulgarian army unable to apply the concept of defense in depth. Instead its officers purportedly used the obsolete technique of massing their troops in forward positions, and as a result could not sustain resistance. In fact the Bulgarians did initially follow the German principle of immediately counterattacking at every opportunity, but they were unable to push the French and the Serbs out of positions just won. When commanders called for reserves, the units available were composed of middle-aged men, poorly fed, poorly equipped, and increasingly unwilling to advance into the high-tech killing zones created by Allied firepower.

On the Western Front, Allied forces were steadily forcing back a German army bled white and fighting without hope. Austria-Hungary's remaining strength, such as it was, was concentrated in Italy. At Salonika, by September 17, some Bulgarian units were openly refusing orders. Others were falling back spontaneously. Scholtz called for help from Germany and Austria as the Franco-Serbian wedge reached a depth of up to fifteen miles. Then, on September 18, the British and Greeks went forward around Lake Doiran. A division of Venizelist Greeks took ground but was halted by a grass fire. The British were fighting on the scene of earlier defeats, with battalions starved of replacements and so riddled with malaria that some men in the rifle companies could barely walk. Staff work recalled the grimmest days of the Somme in 1916, with orders misdirected and misunderstood, units losing touch, and supporting fire directed on the wrong targets at the wrong times. By September 20, the Doiran sector had stabilized—no gain for much pain.

The Bulgarian general responsible for the repulse urged Scholtz to reinforce victory by mounting a major counterattack against the British and Greeks. Go forward on the Struma and around Doiran, General Nerezov argued. Strike directly for Salonika and leave the French and Serbs hanging in the mountains. This time it was Scholtz who flinched. He could expect no significant reinforcements from outside the theater. The logistic problems of Nerezov's proposed attack impressed him more than its operational prospects. Instead Scholtz and his staff proposed a general withdrawal, luring the Allied spearhead forward and then attacking it from three sides.

Given the often-repeated problems of exploiting victory under the conditions of 1914–18, the plan was sound enough in theory. However, it took too little account of human factors. The Bulgarian troops in the front lines had been on short rations for months. They were outraged by the massive destruction of supplies that accompanied the withdrawal. The regiments in the Doiran sector could not understand why they were retreating from what seemed impregnable positions. Then modern technology took a hand. Air power had to date played limited and conventional roles on the Salonika front: reconnaissance and fire control. But on the morning of September 21, British aircraft reported Bulgarian troops on the move. Quickly, DH9s and Armstrong Whitworths of 47 Squadron turned the roads and trails leading away from Doiran into chaos. Wrecked vehicles and dead animals piled up in the defiles and at the crossroads as planes made strafing runs from as low as fifty feet. Caught in place, with no fighter cover and no antiaircraft, the Bulgarians took to the hills less in panic than despair. The effect, however, was the same: the end of organized, large-scale resistance in the Greek-British sector.

As the Bulgarian left disintegrated, their hard-tried center began crumbling. Serbian advance elements reached the Vardar and crossed the Crna. The French were swinging westward toward Prilep when Franchet d'Esperey turned his cavalry loose. Horsemen had found little to do in the Macedonian mountains. But General François Léon Jouinot-Gambetta commanded two regiments of Chasseurs d' Afrique and a half-dozen squadrons of Moroccan Spahis. He had twenty machine guns and a few 37mm guns on packhorses. He even had four armored cars. Advancing toward Prilep on September 22, the mounted column was overtaken by Franchet d'Esperey himself, using an auto as generals of a later generation would use helicopters. Prilep, he ordered, was to be only the initial objective. After its capture the brigade was to ride for Skopje.

The major city in southern Macedonia, Skopje, was sixty miles from Prilep, through country so wild that a few men with automatic weapons could block a division. But for Jouinot-Gambetta the assignment fitted family tradition. His uncle Léon had escaped from Paris in a balloon during the Franco-Prussian War, and a ride behind enemy lines seemed no more than a walk in the sun. Prilep fell without a fight on September 22. Early on the twenty-fifth, the brigade's advance guards ran into a Bulgarian division. Instead of waiting for infantry to open the road, Jouinot took to the mountains and started his men across the Golenisca Plateau.

Nothing on wheels could cross the broken ground, and the troopers spent more time leading their horses than riding them. But the Chasseurs d' Afrique had learned in Algeria how to make long marches over rough country. The Spahis were near-irregulars, recruited from the hard cases of a hard people. And the horses were North African barbs, hardy and sure-footed. The brigade reached Skopje on the night of September 28, and Jouinot struck at first light.

He did not know that he faced a garrison of six battalions, four batteries, two German machine-gun companies, and an armored train! But the Germans and Bulgarians thought the Allies were still twenty miles away. When the Spahis burst out of the dawn mist shouting Arabic war cries, the Bulgarians decamped in all directions. The Germans were too far from home to make panic an option. Rallying on the armored train, which the French had no means of knocking out, they managed to get out, albeit with heavy losses. But by nine o'clock, Skopje was firmly in Allied hands.

Franchet d'Esperey found the cavalry's feat so incredible that he sent two more aircraft to verify the initial report. Skopje's capture was the final trick in a game that had begun a week earlier, in the Bulgarian capital of Sofia. In theory it was still possible to fight on. Winter was approaching, and the terrain confronting the Allies was still formidable. But Bulgaria had been at war almost constantly since 1912. More than 100,000 of its men had been killed since 1915. Agriculture had fallen to subsistence levels. Urban workers were hungry and dispirited. Politicians feared revolution on the Russian pattern. Deserters were commandeering trains in desperate efforts to get home. One band of mutineers attacked the Army General Headquarters (GHQ)!

On September 23, the first soviets began forming in Bulgarian cities. Two days later the Bulgarian Emperor Ferdinand authorized his Commander in Chief to seek an armistice. The first of two delegations reached Franchet d'Esperey's headquarters on the twenty-sixth. Open revolt broke out in Sofia and was only suppressed with the aid of a German division sent from Russia to reinforce a front that no longer existed. Any negotiating room vanished with the announcement of Skopje's fall. At ten o'clock on the night of September 29, an armistice was concluded. Bulgaria was to demobilize all but token forces for internal security. German and Austrian troops were to evacuate the country or surrender.

"The first of the props had fallen," wrote British diplomat Sir Maurice Hankey. Franchet d'Esperey declared his army able to "cross Hungary and Austria, mass in Bohemia . . . and march directly on Dresden." Instead the British contingent, suffering the ravages of influenza as well as malaria, swung toward Constantinople to support Sir Edmund Allenby's advance from Palestine. The Greeks turned their attention to Asia Minor and Thrace, the projected focal points of a new Magna Graecia. The Serbs fought their way to Nish, then to Belgrade, before collapsing in exhaustion. Franchet d'Esperey's French divisions, eroded by unreplaced casualties, were more eager to survive the fighting than to seek glory on new fields. But the advance from Salonika was the final blow to an Austria-Hungary already at the point of collapse. On October 29, 1918, the Croat Diet in Zagreb declared its allegiance to the new state of "Slovenes, Croats, and Serbs"—Yugoslavia. On November 11, the last Habsburg emperor abdicated. The consequences of the subsequent shifts in governments, boundaries, and populations remain unresolved at the beginning of a new century. But they are in part the harvest of the gardeners of Salonika.

PART FIVE

THE FIRST AIR WAR

THE FOKKER MENACE
Michael Spick

—

THE WORD "ACE" APPARENTLY FIRST APPEARED IN JUNE 1915, when a Paris newspaper dubbed Adolphe Pégoud *l'as de notre aviation,* the ace being the top card in the deck—a term that has now evolved into "top gun." Pégoud then had five "kills"; after reaching ten, he would himself become one. What, beyond the number of confirmed victories, makes an ace? That is the subject of Michael Spick's examination of the brief but spectacular career of Oswald Boelcke, the German aviator known as the father of air combat. A professor's son who disdained things academic, Boelcke preferred sports, the riskier the better. As Spick notes, he "was a great leader, with the power to inspire his men. He was a successful fighter pilot, the ranking ace of the first half of the war. Most important, he was an original tactical analyst and thinker at a time when there was no experience on which to draw."

For the record, the Italians, in their 1911–12 war with Libya, were the first to use the airplane as a military tool, primarily for reconnaissance. By 1914, all the combatants had small air services. French pilots reported the change of direction of General Alexander von Kluck's First Army, which allowed the French to attack his right flank, the battle that initiated the counterattacks of the Marne. About the same time, a German pilot in a Taube dropped some four-pound bombs on a Paris suburb, the first attack from the air of a capital city. In October, a French artilleryman on the Somme pointed up at a German observation plane and said, "There is that wretched bird that haunts us." Aviators and their observers blazed away at enemy planes with revolvers, shotguns, rifles, Verey flare pistols, or slingshots. But human and technological error, not enemy action, caused most of the airplane losses. Often low-flying planes, as yet unmarked, were brought down by friendly fire from the ground.

All that began to change in 1915. The sky became the one remaining domain of maneuver; the airplane took the place of the horse. Once you could dominate the sky, you could prevent the enemy from unlocking the secrets beyond your front line. Pursuit planes that could reach speeds between seventy-five and 100 miles per hour were designed specifically to prey on slower observation craft—which were in turn protected by other fighters; the dogfight developed. "Aeronautical technology," John Keegan has pointed out, ". . . permitted very rapid swings in superiority between one side and the other. 'Lead times' in the development of aircraft, now measured in decades, then lasted months, sometimes only weeks; a slightly more powerful engine . . . or a minor refinement of airframe could confirm a startling advantage."

Oswald Boelcke would benefit from one of those developments, introduced in the summer of 1915. That was an innovation by the Dutch aircraft designer, Anthony Fokker, who built planes for the Germans. Fokker devised a synchronizer gear that allowed a machine gun fixed on the fuselage to fire through the arc of a revolving propeller without hitting the blades. Pilots could now aim their craft at an enemy. The Allies did not introduce fighter planes with synchronized gears until the next winter, which would give German pilots the edge for several months. It was during this time that Boelcke, flying Fokker monoplanes—Eindeckers—began his remarkable string of victories: He preferred, as the World War I aviation authority John H. Morrow, Jr., has written, "to count downed planes rather than fliers." But as Spick reminds us, more than a reliance on technology made Boelcke the foremost ace of his time. He preached the efficacy of actions not by individuals but by groups, the famous Jagdstaffeln, or "hunting swarms."

"As long as one stays calm and deliberate, an air fight in my fast, maneuverable Fokker is scarcely more dangerous than driving an automobile." Boelcke wrote those reassuring words to his parents in November 1915. But increasingly the stress of constant combat would take its toll. There is a photograph, probably taken early in the fall of 1916, that shows a countenance tense and sunken, with the outlines of the skull clearly visible. It is not the face of a twenty-five-year-old but of a prematurely aged man who suffers from a terminal illness, what might be called the malady of the ace. It would soon claim his life.

———

MICHAEL SPICK is a well-known British aviation authority. This article was adapted from his book, *The Ace Factor: Air Combat and the Role of Situational Awareness.*

AT THE OUTBREAK OF WORLD WAR I, MILITARY MEN REGARDED THE airplane as an unreliable toy that might or might not have a certain value for reconnaissance or for artillery observation—provided it didn't frighten the horses. In fact, the new flying machines soon proved they could do a respectable job in both roles. The next step was obvious: To prevent the enemy from carrying out those same functions, airplanes would have to be capable of fighting one another. High above the ruined landscape, away from the mass murder, the mud, and the reek of the battlefield, a new form of warfare had begun.

Arguably the most outstanding fighter pilot and leader of all time was one of the first, the young German Oswald Boelcke. (He was twenty-five when he died.) A reconnaissance pilot at the outbreak of war, he began to fly the new single-seater fighters in 1915; with his compatriot Max Immelmann, he spearheaded what the British called the Fokker Menace, after the plane they flew.

Three basic factors set Boelcke above his fellows. He was a great leader, with the power to inspire his men. He was a successful fighter pilot, the ranking ace of the first half of the war. Most important, he was an original tactical analyst and thinker at a time when there was no experience on which to draw. Nearly three-quarters of a century later, despite all the technical advances, his rules for air fighting are still relevant.

If the case seems overstated, consider that when Boelcke's fighting career started, combat between aircraft was a haphazard affair, with the contestants knowing only what they wanted to do, but having little or no idea how to achieve it. By the time his career ended, less than eighteen months later, he had raised air combat to a science that relied on formations rather than on individuals. He put his own theories into practice, and in the process laid the foundation on which fighter pilots of all other nations built their tactics.

The gulf between the ace and the average fighter pilot is very wide. In fact, there may be almost no average fighter pilots, just victors and victims. A recent analyst, who based many of his findings on First World War aviators, has concluded that only one pilot in every fifteen has a better than even chance of surviving his first decisive combat—but after five such encounters, his probability of surviving increases by a factor of *twenty*. Only about 5 percent of fighter pilots become aces, and this tiny minority tends to run up large scores at the expense of their less gifted opponents.

We know that it happens, but why? What separates people like Oswald Boelcke from the vast majority of fighter pilots? That quality has been identified as *situational awareness* (SA) and is now established as the Ace Factor. SA is the mysterious sixth sense that enables a pilot to keep track of everything happening around him in the middle of a confused dogfight. As Major John R. Boyd, USAF, put it in a 1976 briefing, "He who can handle the quickest rate of change survives." To a degree, SA can be learned, as witness the modern aggressor and Top Gun training programs, but with some pilots it seems innate. It certainly was for Oswald Boelcke, the father of air fighting.

Boelcke made his reputation in the Fokker Eindecker. Equipped with one and later two machine guns firing through the synchronized propeller disk, which was introduced in the summer of 1915, the plane was destined to have a far-reaching effect on air combat and would enable the Luftstreitkrafte—the German Air Service—to attain a measure of superiority for several months. The most used type, the E.III, could manage a top speed of only eighty-seven miles per hour, had a ceiling of 11,500 feet, and took a half hour to reach 10,000 feet. But it was as good as or better than the aircraft that first opposed it. It could dive at a steep angle without shedding its wings, which was not always the case with aircraft in those days. Typical of its opponents was the Vickers FB.5, a two-seater pusher biplane with a maximum speed of only 70 miles per hour and a ceiling of 9,000 feet; it required 19 minutes to struggle up to 6,500 feet.

So far as is known, the first operational flight by a Fokker Eindecker was made on June 24, 1915, with Boelcke at the controls. At this point in the war, there were no fighting squadrons as such, just small units of two or three aircraft whose main task was to protect the artillery spotters. At first, few Fokkers were available, and they tended to stay on their own side of the lines. But as Boelcke said in a letter home in July, "The consequence is that they do nothing but go for joyrides round our lines and never get a shot at the enemy, whereas I have the pleasure of getting a good smack at the fellows over yonder. One must not wait till they come across, but seek them out and hunt them down."

Despite this aggressive attitude, chances were few. Not until August 23 did Boelcke manage a decisive combat in his new single-seater, firing a few shots at a Bristol Scout that later landed behind its own lines. Max Immelmann had opened his score some three weeks earlier by wounding the pilot of a British BE.2c, which was forced to land behind the German lines. After this, the pace increased, and by January 1916 Boelcke and Immelmann had raised their scores to eight each, at which point they were awarded Germany's highest decoration, the Pour le Mérite, or Blue Max.

By the standards of later times, this progress seems painfully slow, but it should be remembered that the young Germans were pioneers in their field and had to find the best methods by trial and error. They had often flown together, and it has been suggested that this was the origin of a fighting pair, working as a team. There seems little evidence that this was the case; it is far more probable that they flew together for mutual support against the Allied formations that were coming into use at this time, rather than trying to operate as a team. Later on, Fokkers usually hunted in pairs, but a pair generally consisted of an experienced pilot showing a novice the ropes, rather than an organized team.

Immelmann, who had started as a noncommissioned officer (NCO) in the Railway Corps, initially gained a reputation for piling up aircraft on landing—actually, in those early days of combat flying, almost everyone did. But his main claim to fame lies in the famous maneuver that bears his name. In essence, the Immelmann turn consists of a fast, diving attack followed by a zoom climb, ruddering over the top, then aileron-turning on the way down to line up for another pass. He seems to have been the first pilot to consistently use the vertical plane for maneuver, rather than the horizontal. This discovery appears to have been instinctive rather than reasoned and required excellent timing and judgment of distance to achieve results. In any case, the Immelmann turn seems to have made a greater impression on the Royal Flying Corps (RFC) on the receiving end than on German Air Service aviators who experimented with it. In time the RFC thought every Fokker they encountered was Immelmann.

Since Boelcke flew more often against the French during this period, he was not as well known to the British. It is interesting that he makes no reference to the Immelmann turn, though he doubtless took note of any innovations likely to bring success.

His own learning process proceeded apace. On October 16, 1915, he was attacked by a French Voisin that approached from the front quarter. "I calmly let him fire away, for the combined speed of two opponents meeting one another reduces the chance of a hit to practically nil—as I have already found by frequent experience. . . ." Closing to between 25 and 50 yards, he pumped 200 shots into the French machine, which fell away vertically and crashed into a woods. (It must have been about this time that a French pilot tried to blast him out of the sky with a blunderbuss.)

On December 29 he joined in a scrap between Immelmann and two British aircraft. As is often the case, the encounter turned into two one-on-one combats, and a whirling, turning dogfight developed, during which over 3,000 feet of altitude was lost. Though Boelcke damaged his opponent, he ran out of ammunition. While he continued to make dummy attacks to confuse the English flier, Immelmann entered the fray, having disposed of his own opponent—but he suffered a jammed gun straightaway. The British plane, though almost forced to the ground, managed to escape across the lines.

Boelcke took the lesson of this combat to heart, and during a similar combat with a two-seater on January 14, 1916, he deliberately conserved his ammunition, firing only when his sights were definitely "on." For several minutes of maneuvering, he did not fire a single shot. At last an opportunity presented itself, and a well-aimed burst put the British machine's engine out of action. With no power, it force-landed between the trench lines. But it had managed to riddle Boelcke's fuel tank (and had even put a bullet hole through his sleeve), so that he also had to force-land.

Boelcke was already emerging as an analytical thinker and theoretician as well as a fighting pilot, and from November 1915 he had begun to send reports on tactics, organization, and equipment directly to headquarters, bypassing the usual channels. This is what set him apart from Max Immelmann, with whom he shared a friendly rivalry. Both men had a technical and mechanical bent, but Boelcke appears to have been much more aware of what was going on in the sky around him and, more important, why.

One of Boelcke's technical reports has been recorded. It concerns the performance of a new Eindecker. The Eindecker had been continually upgraded until it reached the E.IV variant, which had double the engine power of the original E.I and E.II types and carried two machine guns, angled up fifteen degrees from the aircraft axis. Max Immelmann had used the E.IV successfully, but Boelcke was not impressed by it. In his report, he comments that the E.IV was too slow and lost too much speed in the climb, and that the rate of climb fell off rapidly at heights above ten thousand feet. Maneuverability, too, was poor, due to the adverse effects of the torque caused by the large rotary engine, and in his opinion the upward angle of the guns was unsuitable for combat. While Immelmann went on to use the E.IV with no less than three machine guns fitted, trading performance and maneuverability for firepower, Boelcke was pleased to revert to his E.III model, which he considered a more suitable fighting vehicle. It was this total absorption with all aspects of air combat that molded him not only into an ace but into a great combat leader.

A kind of reverse situational awareness among the British fliers stems from this period. The Eindecker—credited with being able to outpace, outclimb, and outmaneuver any RFC aircraft by a good margin—earned a reputation as a superfighter. Allied losses in air combat, negligible until this point, rose dramatically. The future ace James McCudden, flying as an observer in a Morane Parasol, described the Eindecker as "a long dark brown form fairly streaking across the sky," and "when it got above and behind our middle machine it dived onto it for all the world like a huge hawk on a hapless sparrow." Such descriptions did nothing for Allied morale, which reached a low ebb. Even those who repelled an attack—and there were many of them—tended to recount their adventures as epic escapes from mortal danger. Crews lost the will to fight back and were often hacked down as they attempted to escape.

It was not until the beginning of 1916 that the Allies were able to counter the Fokker Menace. They formed their first fighting scout squadrons, which arrived at the front from February 1916 onward and consisted of three main types of aircraft. One was the British Airco DH.2, a single-seat pusher biplane armed with a single Lewis gun. It could reach ninety-three miles per hour at sea level, had a ceiling of 14,000 feet, and could climb to 6,500 feet in just twelve minutes. In absolute performance terms it had only a marginal edge over the E.III, but was far more maneuverable. The second type, the FE.2b, was a two-seater pusher whose performance was roughly comparable to that of the DH.2. The third type, the Nieuport Scout, was a single-seat tractor biplane (meaning its propeller was in front) armed with a single Lewis gun mounted on a top wing and firing over the propeller disk. It had a maximum speed of 107 miles per hour, a ceiling of 17,400 feet, and could reach an altitude of 10,000 feet in nine minutes. The two British pushers held an edge over the Fokker, and the French-built Nieuport completely outclassed it. Encouraged by their new machines, the British in particular started to carry the fight back to the enemy.

Since Boelcke was still engaged mainly with the French in this period, the Nieuport became a principal concern. His seventh victory came on May 21, 1916, and was at the expense of one of the new fighters. He described it in a letter home:

> Two Nieuports were flying at a great height on the far side of their lines, but I did not attack them. . . . Then I saw two Caudrons that had hitherto escaped my notice wandering about below. When I went for one of them and began to shoot, I saw one of the Nieuports diving down on me. . . . I broke away from the Caudrons and bore northward, with the Nieuport behind me in the belief that I had failed to notice him. I kept a sharp eye on him until he was within two hundred meters of me—then I suddenly went into a turn and flew at him. . . . [H]e wrenched his machine round and bolted southward.

But the French pilot made a mistake: He flew straight, giving Boelcke an easy shot from one hundred meters astern. The German infantry saw him crash.

This account contains several interesting points. First is Boelcke's disinclination to attack the Nieuports from a position of disadvantage. Second is Boelcke's admission that he initially overlooked the Caudrons, possibly because he was more concerned with danger from above. Third is that even while shooting at a Caudron—an activity that takes every ounce of concentration—Boelcke was still able to remain aware of the potential threat posed by the two Nieuports and to react as soon as one made a move against him. Fourth, Boelcke was able to present to the French pilot a picture of the situation as it was not. The Frenchman thought he had the advantage of surprise, and appears to have been so disconcerted that he made an elementary error—and paid the supreme price for it. Boelcke was master of the situation at all times, whereas the French pilot only thought he was.

The increasing use of French aircraft in large formations led to the need to counter them in strength. In June, Boelcke formed the first fighting squadron, called a Jagdstaffel (literally, "hunting swarm"), at Sivry on the Verdun front. Although it was not an official formation, it can be regarded as the forerunner of the units that were formed the following August and September. But Boelcke was then overtaken by events, the first of which was the death of Immelmann on June 18.

As is often the case, accounts are conflicting. Immelmann went down in a fight between four Fokkers of the Douai unit and seven FE.2bs of the RFC's Twenty-fifth. German accounts say Immelmann's synchronizing gear failed and he shot his own propeller off. RFC records credit Corporal Waller, the gunner in an FE.2b flown by Lieutenant McCubbin, with shooting him down. Either way, Immelmann was out of the battle, with a final score of fifteen, three behind Boelcke.

The loss was a great blow to the Luftstreitkrafte, coming as it did at a time when command of the air was rapidly passing to the Allies. As a direct result, Boelcke was grounded—the German high command did not want to lose another hero. A few days later he was sent to the east to observe the scene there. Before he left he composed, at the behest of Flugfeldchef Colonel Thomsen, his famous rules for air fighting, the so-called Dicta Boelcke. More than one version of these rules have appeared, and they may later have been embellished a little. The following is the version given by Colonel Thomsen to Professor Johannes Werner for the preparation of the book *Knight of Germany*.

1) Try to secure advantages before attacking. If possible, keep the sun behind you.
2) Always carry through an attack when you have started it.
3) Fire only at close range, and only when your opponent is properly in your sights.
4) Always keep your eye on your opponent, and never let yourself be deceived by ruses.

5) In any form of attack it is essential to assail your opponent from behind.

6) If your opponent dives on you, do not try to evade his onslaught, but fly to meet it.

7) When over enemy lines, never forget your own line of retreat.

8) For the Staffel: Attack on principle in groups of four or six. When the fight breaks up into a series of single combats, take care that several do not go together for one opponent.

Reading between the lines, we can see a determined but cautious pilot, prepared to do everything in his power to load the dice in his favor. The rules themselves are elementary, obviously intended for the novice. The "advantages before attacking," for example, could have been expanded into a minichapter had Boelcke been so inclined, but only the sun is mentioned. In our own time it could have been written "Reduce the enemy's SA!" Rules two and six stress determination, saying in effect, "Do not show that your resolve is weakening," and "The best *defense* is a good *offense*." Rules three and five are concerned with getting results: shooting accurately at close range and with no deflection. The rest are pure situational awareness: Do not be deceived; remember your exit route; and do not leave an opponent unengaged, because he may well use the time to look around and pick his target. The essence of the whole document can be summed up in two words: "win" and "survive."

The First World War was a time of learning, first how to use the new weapon, and then how best to apply it. Tactics played an ever more important role, and the formation leader now counted for more than the individual, leading his flight of Staffel in the careful jockeying and sparring for position before launching an attack. As the numbers of aircraft and the size of the formations increased, so did the confusion factor. Boelcke, for one, recognized that only by learning to minimize confusion could he keep the combat situation under control. The privileged few demonstrated an instinctive understanding of this, while the better leaders tried to instill the basic principles into their followers. But Boelcke alone seems to have formalized those principles into a code for air fighting, which in essence has stood the test of time.

In mid-August, having toured the Balkans and Turkey, Boelcke had reached Kovel, on the Russian front, when he received a telegram recalling him to the west to form one of the new Jagdstaffeln (Jastas for short). By September 2 he was back in action, this time against the British over the Somme battlefield. He immediately brought down a DH.2 flown by Captain Robert Wilson—his nineteenth victory.

It was now Germany's turn to introduce new equipment that would reverse the Allied, and particularly the British, air superiority. This was done with new biplanes, the Fokker and Halberstadt, and most of all with the Albatros D.II Scout. Armed with two Spandau machine guns firing through the propeller disk, the Albatros could top 109 miles per hour and could get up to around 17,000 feet. Its initial climb rate was 3,280 feet in five minutes. Against the Nieuport 17 it was very closely matched, but had the advantage of greater weight of firepower. Boelcke's Jasta 2 was equipped mainly with Albatroses and he would score almost all his final victories in that type of aircraft.

As pilots and aircraft trickled in, Boelcke launched into a thorough training program, aimed primarily at teamwork. As he stressed over and over, it did not matter who scored the victory as long as the Staffel won it. Instilling team spirit into a handpicked bunch of medal-hungry fighter pilots was not easy, and was at times downright exasperating. He was also the first leader to give what today would be called "dissimilar combat training," stressing the weak points of the opponent's machines. This he backed up with practical demonstrations, using captured aircraft and laying down the best methods of dealing with them. For example: Although it was very agile, the Vickers single-seater (really the DH.2) was noted for losing altitude during steep turns. It was best attacked from behind, where the pilot's view was obstructed by the engine, and was also vulnerable to a zoom climb attack from behind and below. The Vickers two-seater (the FE.2b) had a limited rearward firing capability and thus was to be attacked from the rear, preferably from slightly below, but pilots were cautioned to get on its outside in a turning contest. The Nieuport, though fast and agile, generally lost altitude during prolonged turning. But in those days, what aircraft didn't?

Jasta 2 commenced operations on September 16, and Boelcke worked his staff so hard that by the end of the month they had flown a total of 186 sorties, with sixty-nine engagements and twenty-five victories, ten of them scored by the maestro. Now the battlefield had become the classroom, with pre-takeoff instruction and an inquest after each engagement. The instruction took, but even so, four pilots (one third of the complement) were lost during this period. After the first major engagement, on September 17, Manfred von Richthofen, not yet an ace but still an experienced flier, described sighting the enemy: "Of course, Boelcke was the first to see them, for he saw more than most men." To see first, to be aware of all circumstances—whether targets, hazards, or potentialities—this was the key to the ace pilot.

Previously, Boelcke had scored nineteen victories in roughly ten months, most of them against French aircraft. From here on, all his victories were against British opponents, whose aggressive style gave him plenty of opportunity to score, as well as some worrisome moments. "On September 27," he wrote,

> I met seven English machines, near B. I had started on a patrol flight
> with four of my men, and we saw a squadron I first thought was German.
> When we met southwest of B., I saw they were enemy 'planes. We were
> lower and I changed my course. The Englishmen passed us, flew over to
> us . . . then set out for their own front. However . . . we had reached their
> height and cut off their retreat. I gave the signal to attack, and a general
> battle started. I attacked one; got too close; ducked under him and, turn-
> ing, saw an Englishman fall like a plummet.

That same day, Boelcke had an experience that can only be described as weird:

> As there were enough others left I picked out a new one. He tried to
> escape, but I followed him. I fired round after round into him. His stamina
> surprised me. I felt he should have fallen long ago, but he kept going in the
> same circle. Finally, it got too much for me. I knew he was dead long ago,
> and by some freak, or due to elastic controls, he did not change his course.
> I flew quite close to him and saw the pilot lying dead, half out of his seat.

Over the final eight weeks of his life, he added another twenty-one hits to
his tally, the fortieth and last coming on October 26, just two days before his
death. He wrote describing these victories in his always matter-of-fact style.

> About 4:45 seven of our machines, of which I had charge, attacked
> some English biplanes west of P[éronne]. I attacked one and wounded the
> observer, so he was unable to fire at me. At the second attack, the machine
> started to smoke. Both pilot and observer seemed dead. It fell into the sec-
> ond-line English trenches and burned up.

If it seems that his situational awareness deserted him at the last, this was
probably due to fatigue. He had flown intensively over the previous eight weeks,
and his final sortie was his sixth that day. Then came the midair collision with
one of his own men, Erwin Böhme (who would himself account for twenty-
four planes before his own death). Böhme later described what happened that
day:

> We had just begun a game of chess . . . then, about 4:30 P.M., we
> were called to the front because there was an infantry attack going on. We
> soon attacked some English machines we found flying over Flers; they
> were fast single-seaters that defended themselves well.

In the ensuing wild battle of turns, that only let us get a few shots in for brief intervals, we tried to force the English down, by one after another of us barring their way, a maneuver we had often practiced successfully. Boelcke and I had just got one Englishman between us when another opponent, chased by friend Richthofen, cut across us. Quick as lightning, Boelcke and I both dodged him, but for a moment our wings prevented us from seeing anything of one another—and that was the cause of it.

How am I to describe my sensations from the moment when Boelcke suddenly loomed up a few meters away on my right! He put his machine down and I pulled mine up, but we touched as we passed, and we both fell earthward. It was only just the faintest touch, but the terrific speed at which we were going made it into a violent impact. Destiny is generally cruelly stupid in her choices; I only had a bit of my undercarriage ripped, but the extreme tip of his left wing was torn away.

After falling a couple of hundred meters I regained control . . . and was able to observe Boelcke . . . heading for our lines in a gentle glide, but dipping a bit on one side. But when he came into a layer of clouds in the lower regions, his machine dipped more and more, owing to the violent gusts there, and I had to look on while he failed to flatten out to land and crashed near a battery position. . . . He must have been killed outright.

Oswald Boelcke, the man who did so much to make fighter combat a professional activity rather than a sporting pursuit, died at the zenith of his powers. He is the example against whom all fighter pilots, both aces and leaders, must be judged. What sort of man was he that he could achieve so much?

The surviving records depict him as calm and balanced, with few idiosyncrasies except for going early to bed. He was a disciplinarian (both with himself and with others), of a technical turn of mind, and he drank and smoked little. His letters home show that he enjoyed the eminence to which he had risen and the opportunity it afforded of meeting the highest in the land (although he was openly scornful of blatant publicity). A portrait emerges of a man without weakness, with a wry sense of humor as a saving grace. His face was dominated by his eyes, which were very large and pale blue.

Perhaps the closest insights we get are not from Boelcke's own letters home, which were carefully composed so as not to alarm his parents, but from his star pupil, Manfred von Richthofen, who was recruited for Jasta Two in Kovel. Richthofen, who had encountered Boelcke briefly in October 1915, described that first meeting: "I heard a knock on my door early in the morning, and there he stood, a big man wearing the Pour le Mérite."

Boelcke was in fact not a big man. Photographs show him as being on the short side, as was Richthofen. How could Richthofen describe him as big? The answer is that Boelcke's personality made him seem larger. Richthofen also commented:

> It is strange that everyone who came to know Boelcke imagined that he was his one true friend. I have met about forty of these "one true" friends of Boelcke, and each imagined that he indeed was *the* one true friend. . . . It was a strange phenomenon that I have observed only in Boelcke. He never had a personal enemy. He was equally friendly to everyone, no more to one, no less to another.

As Böhme wrote to a friend less than a month before the fatal collision:

> You admire our Boelcke. Who would not? But you admire in him only the successful hero; you can know nothing of his remarkable personality. That is known to only the few who are privileged to share his life. . . . It is most remarkable how [he] inspires every one of his students and carries them along. . . . They will go wherever he leads. . . . He is a born leader.

Boelcke remains an inscrutable character, just slightly too good to be true.

THE WAR LOVER
Robert Wohl

—

OSWALD BOELCKE'S STAR PUPIL WAS MANFRED VON Richthofen, the aristocratic former cavalry officer (Iron Cross, Second Class) and air observer, whose first air combat weapon on the Eastern Front was a rifle. Boelcke had an eye for talent, and it was while touring the Eastern Front in the summer of 1916 that he recruited Richthofen, by then a fighter pilot, for the new Jagdstaffel, or Jasta, that he was forming to fight on the Somme. By the time of Boelcke's death on October 28, Richthofen had already downed six planes. It was in trying to avoid his protégé in a dogfight that Boelcke collided with a wingmate and went down. There is some speculation that he might have survived if he had been wearing a seat belt.

To elevate trench fighters into national heroes was difficult; air aces were ready-made for canonization. Portraits of Boelcke and Richthofen, the historian Peter Fritzsche notes, "appeared on ashtrays, neckties, flags, and other kitschy items." If Boelcke had been the ranking ace of the first half of the war, von Richthofen was that for the second—and, more than that, he became a legend. Robert Wohl, in the article that follows, examines that legend and the man who, perhaps too willingly, allowed himself to be deified. As the leader of Jagdstaffel 11, the "Flying Circus," in its red-painted planes, he seemed to embody the mythical spirit of the Teutonic knight. Home on leave in the late spring of 1917, Richthofen (already famous as the "Red Baron," after the color of his plane) found the time to dictate his memoirs to a ghostwriter. He had just downed twenty-one British planes over the Arras front in a single month. As Wohl observes, hunting is the master metaphor that runs through the autobiography. "Whether hunting men or beasts, the emotions are the same." Richthofen disposed of his adversaries with glee. Listen to his description of his third victory: "He plunged down in flames. One's heart beats faster if the opponent, whose face he has just seen, plunges burning from four thousand meters." Richthofen was a methodical killer—his own brother, Lothar, a lesser ace, described him as a "butcher." That view may be harsh; and yet the fact remains that he killed more than eighty of his adversaries, not to mention the anonymous unfortunates in the "Poor Bloody Infantry" whom he bombed and strafed ("It was special fun to harass the gentlemen below with our machine guns."). When you consider the four planes that Richthofen brought down in a single day, April 29, 1917, it's easy to overlook one unpleasant detail: Six men died. To make as sure as possible that neither plane nor pilot nor observer survived, he deliberately aimed for the fuel tank.

That was not one of the lessons he set down in his *Combat Operations Manual,* on which he put the finishing touches in April 1918, days before his own death. Here are rules that prematurely smack of the triumph of the will: No wonder the Nazis would enshrine his memory. "We need no aerial acrobats; rather, daredevils." "Turning back by pilots whose engines are misfiring or the like is inappropriate." "Through the absolute will of each of us to do battle, the enemy formation will be torn apart." "One should never obstinately stay with an opponent who . . . one has been unable to shoot down, when the battle lasts until it is far on the other side and one is alone and faced by a greater number of opponents."

For reasons unknown, that was a rule that he violated on the last morning of his life.

———

ROBERT WOHL teaches European intellectual and cultural history at the University of California, Los Angeles. He is the author of *The Generation of 1914* and *A Passion for Wings.*

ALMOST NINE DECADES AFTER THE END OF THE GREAT WAR, THE ACES WHO fought and died in the sky continue to fascinate us. This is understandable. Living in the world we do, we look back in wonder at romantic wars in which heroic deeds could be carried out at relatively low human costs. It is difficult to idealize the dehumanized slaughter in the trenches between 1914 and 1918, the confused colonial wars of the twentieth century or, for that matter, even the Second World War—remembered by many as an unambiguously "good" war—in which as many as sixty million people died and civilian casualties were higher, more visible, and often more gruesome than those of combatants.

By contrast, we can repress the more unpleasant aspects of the first air war and thrill vicariously to the exploits of the aces, as we imagine what it would be like to fly a single-seater biplane and blaze away with twin machine guns at a chivalric adversary, the roaring wind in our face, our white scarf waving in the slipstream, and the smell of gasoline and oil in our nostrils. The war in the air, as it was fought between 1915 and 1918, makes for great romance, as Hollywood quickly came to realize in the 1920s and 1930s.

Among the aces of the Great War, Baron Manfred von Richthofen's fame has proved more lasting than that of any other. This was no doubt in part because he downed more enemy aircraft than any other First World War pilot, with a total of eighty victories officially recorded. But the fascination with Richthofen has other sources as well. There are his noble birth, his photogenic features, his piercing blue eyes, his passion for collecting trophies to commemorate his victories, his apparent disdain for death, his bold-faced effrontery in painting his aircraft bright red, the uncompromising standards he set for the fighter pilots in his squadron and later his wing, the controversial circumstances of his death, and the bright, unsullied legend he left behind him. We think we know him from the many photographs that have come down to us. But do we really understand him? What drove Germany's "Red Knight of the Air" (the name came from the color of his aircraft) to do what he did? Love of country? Prussian dedication to duty? Sporting spirit? A Nietzschean urge toward excellence? Simple bloodlust? Or just the sheer excitement and fun of it all?

Manfred von Richthofen was born in May 1892, which placed him solidly in the middle of that cohort of young men who came to be known as "the generation of 1914." His birthplace, Breslau, now lies well to the east of present-day Germany's Polish border and is called Wroclaw, some indication of the massive territorial changes that have occurred in Central Europe during the last hundred years. Where young Manfred differed from most members of his generation (and from most World War I aces) was in the aristocratic title his family had borne since 1741, when Frederick the Great had rewarded the Richthofens for their support in his effort to wrest the province of Silesia from the Habsburg dynasty with the right to designate themselves barons and baronesses. His father, Albrecht, a retired major in the Prussian cavalry, placed him in a prestigious military academy, where he was an indifferent and unhappy student who excelled in athletics, especially gymnastics. Graduated as an officer candidate, he was posted to the 1st Uhlan Regiment, where he was commissioned as a lieutenant in 1912. As a cavalryman, Richthofen was able to indulge his passion for riding. The victim of frequent falls and injuries, he showed the measure of his courage and determination when he won the Emperor's Prize Race, a cross-country event, after having been thrown by his horse and breaking a collarbone. Picking himself up from the ground and remounting, he rode the remaining forty-two miles to victory before seeking medical treatment. The will to win in the face of daunting obstacles would remain throughout his short life one of his outstanding characteristics.

Like other young men of the generation of 1914, Richthofen welcomed the outbreak of war as a test of his mettle and an opportunity to prove himself. His main ambition at the beginning of the war seems to have been to win medals and not to be overtaken by his younger brother, Lothar, who also belonged to a cavalry regiment. Richthofen's war started inauspiciously. Stationed on the Russian border of Poland, he narrowly escaped capture by a troop of Cossacks and was then transferred to the Western Front in August 1914. There he survived an ambush by a force of French dragoons, in which the majority of the men he led were not so lucky. Of the fifteen in his patrol, only four returned. This debacle, however, was quickly forgotten after he participated in General Otto von Below's successful attack against a superior French force at the Belgian town of Virton and experienced the exhilaration of victorious combat.

The next nine months were a period of increasing frustration for Richthofen. Transferred to the German Fifth Army, which had positioned itself opposite the French fortress of Verdun, he saw himself consigned to the role of a communications officer who approached the front lines not heroically, in a cavalry charge, as he had been taught to do, but ignominiously crawling through mud-filled trenches where he stood a chance of being killed by an errant shell. Not even the award of the Iron Cross, Second Class, for his repeated trips to the front lines under heavy fire succeeded in raising his spirits for long. He hungered after even more prestigious decorations and despaired of winning them in a place where his embryonic heroism was confined to taking potshots at the French and tossing an occasional grenade in the direction of the enemy trenches. Here, he complained in a letter to his mother, there was no chance of winning the Iron Cross, First Class, unless he succeeded in entering the fortress of Verdun disguised as a Frenchman and blowing up a gun turret.

Richthofen's boredom only increased when he was appointed ordnance officer of an infantry brigade. Assigned in May 1915 to an administrative position in supply services, Richthofen lost his patience and wrote the commanding general of his division, requesting a transfer to the flying corps. "At first people took offense," Richthofen later wrote, "but finally my request was granted, and so at the end of May 1915 I entered the Air Service. Thus was my greatest wish fulfilled."

Not quite. Richthofen's greatest wish was to distinguish himself, and he still had far to go before fulfilling it. Curiously, the young Uhlan lieutenant did not at first choose to become a pilot. Pilots did not yet have the prestige they would soon acquire—they were, after all, little more than chauffeurs—and to become a pilot Richthofen would have had to commit himself to a three-month training course. Eager to get into combat at the earliest possible moment, he instead opted to become an observer, an objective he achieved in a mere four weeks of instruction.

By the end of June, Richthofen was already flying combat missions on the Russian front. This was the kind of war he had longed for. "Now we are once again in a pure war of movement," he wrote his mother in July 1915. "Almost daily, I fly over the enemy and bring back reports." Richthofen was transferred to Flanders, and on the way back, he stopped by his family's estate at Schweidnitz, south of Breslau. His mother found him looking "splendid." He "was radiant and told of his experiences at the Front, each one more interesting than the other."

In September 1915 Richthofen got his first taste of blood in aerial combat. Flying as Paul Henning von Osterroht's observer in an Aviatik C.I, he shot down a French Farman two-seater on the Champagne front but was not given credit for the victory because the machine went down behind the enemy lines and the kill could not be documented. In October 1915 he was posted to Réthel. On the train going there he met Oswald Boelcke, who had already achieved fame as a flying ace after downing four enemy planes in the new Fokker E single-seater monoplane. Richthofen sought Boelcke out, drank and played cards with him, and asked him for his secret.

Boelcke replied that if Richthofen was really serious about scoring victories, he should become a fighter pilot and learn how to fly a Fokker. Richthofen took Boelcke at his word and persuaded a pilot friend, with whom he had flown in Russia, to teach him. After twenty-five hours of instruction he soloed, and by Christmas 1915 he had passed the three examinations required of German military pilots—more, it seems, through determination and perseverance than through his natural ability for handling an airplane in the air.

Richthofen served briefly at Verdun during the great battle of the spring of 1916, shot down another French plane (for which—again—he was not given credit because once again it came down on the other side of the lines), and was transferred in June with his squadron to the Russian front. There, in the absence of Russian aircraft and strong antiaircraft defenses, he enjoyed himself bombing railroad stations and strafing Russian infantry and cavalry. Yet the glory he sought still evaded him; it could only be found in the kind of aerial combat that had developed on the Western Front.

Richthofen's chance came in August 1916. Forbidden to fly combat missions because of the death of Germany's other great ace, Max Immelmann, in an accident while flying the Fokker E fighter, Boelcke had been sent on a tour of Turkey and Bulgaria, Germany's allies in the Balkans. But British air superiority during the battle of the Somme and anxieties about the morale of German infantrymen, who had begun to complain about the lack of German aircraft above the battleground, overcame the high command's concerns about the possible loss of Boelcke's life. While stopping at the German army's Eastern Front headquarters in Kovel, where his brother Wilhelm was stationed, Boelcke received orders to return to the west with all possible haste to organize and lead a fighter squadron on the Somme front.

Richthofen happened to be at Kovel when Boelcke passed through. Unknown to him, Boelcke recommended Richthofen as a good addition to the squadron his brother was assembling. When "the great man" appeared at Richthofen's door early one morning, he was wearing the Pour le Mérite, Germany's highest military decoration. Asked by Boelcke if he would like to become one of his "pupils," Richthofen leaped at the offer. As he wrote in his autobiography: "I almost hugged him when he asked me if I wanted to go with him to the Somme. Three days later I was on the train traveling across Germany to my new post. My fondest wish was fulfilled, and now began the most beautiful time of my life."

RICHTHOFEN TURNED OUT TO BE AN UNUSUALLY GIFTED STUDENT. ON SEPTEMBER 17, cruising behind Boelcke in a just-introduced twin-gun Albatros D.II, he caught sight of a group of seven British two-seat bombers crossing the German lines in the direction of Cambrai. Richthofen succeeded in getting behind one of the bombers, closed to the point where he was afraid of ramming the enemy machine, and fired a short burst at point-blank range. The British plane began to sway, the observer disappeared from sight, and the British pilot brought his plane down at a nearby German airfield. Richthofen could not contain himself with joy. He landed close to the crippled British aircraft, jumped out of his machine, and ran toward his fallen prey. "Arriving there, I found that my assumption was correct. The engine was shot to pieces, and both occupants were severely wounded. The observer had died instantly, and the pilot died while being transported to the nearest field hospital. Later I placed a stone in memory of my honorably fallen enemies on their beautiful grave."

That night, to celebrate his victory, Richthofen wrote to his jeweler in Berlin and ordered a two-inch-high silver cup engraved with the numeral 1, the type of aircraft he had downed, the number of its occupants, and the date of his victory. He would eventually accumulate sixty such cups before Germany's shortage of silver forced his jeweler to interrupt the production of these trophies, twenty victories before Richthofen himself ran out of luck.

Richthofen was flying with Boelcke on October 28, 1916, when "the great man" collided with Erwin Böhme and plunged to his death while both were attacking a British plane. Though Richthofen was deeply shaken by Boelcke's death and thereafter always kept his photograph in his bedroom, once his leader was gone he set out consciously to take his place as Germany's premier fighter pilot and greatest *Fliegerheld*—"ace." He later expressed annoyance at the fact that whereas in Boelcke's and Immelmann's time it was sufficient to have downed eight enemy planes in order to win the Pour le Mérite, he had been required to accumulate twice as many victories before receiving that honor. Downing enemy aircraft in 1916–17, he insisted, was more demanding than it had been the previous year.

Leaving aside the accuracy of Richthofen's perception about the relative difficulties of winning victories in 1915 and 1916, he clearly had little to complain about when it came to gaining official recognition and public fame. In November 1916 he was decorated with the Saxe-Coburg-Gotha Medal for Bravery and the Order of the House of Hohenzollern with Swords. The following January, after downing his sixteenth plane, Richthofen was awarded the Pour le Mérite and given command of his own fighter group, Jasta 11. It was at this point that he had the ingenious idea of painting his Albatros D.III bright red, yet another way of setting himself (and eventually his pilots, who insisted on following his example) apart from the British planes they relentlessly pursued. Three months later, in recognition of Jasta 11's successes, Richthofen was promoted to *Rittmeister,* or "cavalry captain," a reminder of the arm in which he formerly served, though the mounts he rode now carried him aloft on wings. Reporters came to the front to interview him; his photograph was reproduced in newspapers and on postcards in hundreds of thousands of copies; and fan mail, especially from admiring young women, arrived by the bagful. He was ordered on leave in April 1917 after scoring his fifty-second victory—twelve more than Boelcke. He shot down the last four in a single day. He was given a hero's welcome in Cologne, and invited to breakfast by the kaiser, who presented him with a life-size bronze bust of himself. No honor Germany had to offer seemed beyond his reach.

Richthofen's biographers like to dwell on his famous dogfight with Major Lanoe Hawker on November 23, 1916, which resulted in his eleventh kill. Considered Britain's leading ace, Hawker had nine victories to his credit and was the first airman to receive Britain's highest military decoration, the Victoria Cross. Richthofen's account of their epic struggle emphasizes the masterly manner in which Hawker managed his plane and the sporting nature of their encounter:

> He opens fire with his machine gun. Five shots rip out, and I change my course quickly by a sharp turn to the left. He follows, and the mad circle starts. He is trying to get behind me, and I am trying to get behind him. Round and round we go in circles, like two madmen, playing ring-around-a-rosie almost two miles above the earth.

Richthofen's narrative makes for stirring drama, as he takes us through what seems to be an eternity of twists and turns, zigs and zags, and ever tighter circles. Finally, Richthofen positions himself for the kill. "The gun pours out its stream of lead. Then it jams. Then it reopens fire. That jam almost saved his life. One bullet goes home. He is struck through the back of the head. His plane jumps and crashes down. It strikes the ground just as I swoop over. His machine gun rammed itself into the earth, and now it decorates the entrance over my door. He was a brave man, a sportsman, and a fighter."

But contrary to his legend, the "Red Knight of Germany" did not compile his long list of victories primarily by engaging adversaries of Hawker's caliber in single combat. On the contrary, whenever possible, he pounced on slow two-seater British reconnaissance biplanes, catching them unawares and attacking their blind spot. More typical of his methodical approach to air combat was the report he wrote when requesting acknowledgment of his fifty-seventh victory against a British reconnaissance plane on July 2, 1917:

I attacked the foremost plane [R.E.] of an enemy formation.

After my first shots, the observer collapsed. Shortly thereafter, the pilot was wounded mortally, I believe, by my shots.

The R.E. fell, and I fired into it at a distance of fifty yards. The plane caught fire and dashed to the ground.

By this point in his career, however, Richthofen had begun to think seriously about the construction of his legend. While visiting Air Service Headquarters on his way home to enjoy his triumphant leave in April 1917, Richthofen was persuaded to write his memoirs. The suggestion came from one of Germany's most successful publishers, Ullstein, but the German high command clearly liked the idea because it offered a means of capitalizing on Richthofen's growing celebrity and of stiffening morale at a moment when the German people's willingness to carry on the war effort was beginning to weaken. The first draft of *The Red Combat Flyer* was dictated by Richthofen to a stenographer furnished by the publisher in May and June 1917. It was revised and completed in October during another period of leave, edited and censored by the press office of the Air Service, and published first in the form of magazine articles, then as a small book in late 1917. Though many have dismissed *The Red Combat Flyer* as propaganda, and though the hand of the Air Service censorship office is often visible, it seems to be a faithful enough representation of the way that Richthofen wanted to appear before the German public.

He began his memoir by distancing himself from the profession of arms. This is curious in view of the fact that his father was a retired army officer recalled to active duty; that he was named after a great-uncle who commanded a cavalry corps; and that he himself had spent almost his entire life in the army. While he mentions these military connections, Richthofen prefers to present himself as the product of a family of gentleman farmers whose only concerns had been the cultivation of their lands, riding horses, and hunting game. Hunting, in fact, is the master metaphor that runs throughout the forty-nine chapters of Richthofen's autobiography and unites the carefree prewar youngster with the incomparable flying ace of 1917. How otherwise are we to understand the long account of a hunting expedition on the Silesian wildlife preserve of the prince of Pless that Richthofen dates exactly for us to May 26, 1917?

To be sure, one of Richthofen's aims in narrating this story is to place himself on the same level with "the many crowned heads" and famous generals (including General Paul von Hindenburg) who had earlier traveled this "famous road." But beyond mere name-dropping, Richthofen was also seeking to describe an emotion that hunting inspired in him. When a mighty bison comes into sight two hundred fifty paces away and begins to move in his direction at high speed, he experiences "the same feeling, the same hunting fever that grips me when I sit in an airplane, see an Englishman, and must fly toward him for five or so minutes in order to overtake him." The "giant black monster" disappeared into a gathering of thick spruce before Richthofen could take a shot, and he elected not to pursue the beast because searching for it would have been a difficult task and missing it, once the hunt had been engaged, would have been a disgrace. Before long another bison, equally powerful, appeared and offered a better target. When it was at a distance of about a hundred paces, Richthofen shot, then shot again, and finally brought the animal down when it had come within fifty paces of the platform on which he was standing. Richthofen reports his satisfaction. "Five minutes later the monster was finished . . . all three bullets had lodged just above his heart. Bull's eye."

The message is clear: Enemy airmen and bison can sometimes be difficult to kill. Patience is required. Better to break off combat if the conditions are not right. Another, equally tempting prey can be counted on to appear. Then, if the hunter is skillful, he will have his game. Whether hunting men or beasts, the emotions are the same: excitement at the prospect of the kill and, afterward, satisfaction with a job well done.

Reading *The Red Combat Flyer* is enough to shake anyone's faith in the idea that the air war between 1914 and 1918 was a chivalric contest free of those aspects of technological mass murder that alienated and numbed a generation of men. Richthofen leaves no doubt that his job is killing. He writes with evident relish of bombing and strafing large bodies of soldiers. If he prefers one-to-one combat, it is because success in a single-seater fighter is the road to fame. He has nothing but disdain for aviators who fly for the fun of it and engage in aerobatics. Flying upside down or looping the loop are not necessary to bag your game. Richthofen identifies himself as a sportsman, to be sure, but he is the type of sportsman who likes to load the deck against his quarry. When he hunts bison, he does so from an elevated platform. If you elect to play his game, you can expect to die.

The jaunty tone Richthofen adopted in his memoirs contrasted sharply with his real feelings about the war and his own future at the moment they were published. The best of Germany's pilots and the closest of his friends had been killed, one after another. He himself was shot down and suffered a serious head wound in July 1917. Though he returned to combat flying a month later—it was at this time that Richthofen began flying his trademark red Fokker triplane—he suffered from headaches and depression and was ordered by General von Hoeppner, head of the German Air Service, not to fly in combat unless it was absolutely necessary. Restricted in his flying—between September and November, he shot down only four enemy aircraft—he fretted about being overtaken in his score of victories by his rival Werner Voss and losing his position as Germany's ace of aces. (As it turned out, Richthofen needn't have worried: Voss was shot down in September 1917 after he took on five British SE-5s, his score cut short at forty-eight.)

In January 1918, after observing the peace talks with the Bolsheviks at Brest-Litovsk and hunting bison again, this time in the primeval forest at Bialowicz, where he was invited to stay at the csar's former lodge, Richthofen went home on a brief leave. The young hero had no illusions about the future. His mother found him transformed, almost beyond recognition. He lacked the carefree playfulness that had given him his boyish charm. "He was taciturn, distant, almost unapproachable." There was something hard and painful in his eyes. She was convinced that he had lived too long in the presence of death. Reminded of a dental appointment, he was overheard by his mother to say: "Really, there's no point."

On March 21, 1918, the great German "Peace Offensive" began. Richthofen's tally of victories, which had been halted between late November and mid-March, once more began to mount. In a month, his total would rise from sixty-seven to eighty, including two Sopwith Camels on April 20. The magic figure of one hundred stood within his grasp, and perhaps yet other decorations. Whatever reservations Richthofen had about his future now seemed to evaporate in the exhilaration of combat and the sweet taste of his kills.

On the morning of Sunday, April 21, Richthofen and his squadron waited for the fog to rise at their airfield at Cappy in the valley of the Somme. The *Rittmeister* was in excellent spirits, playing with his dog and joking with his men. "Again and again, the Baron's laughter rang across the airfield," his adjutant Karl Bodenschatz recalled. Then, at ten-thirty, came a report that British aircraft were approaching the German lines. Richthofen and his men sprinted for their Fokker Dr.I triplanes and took off in two flights to intercept the British, eager for combat and sensing the possibility of further victories.

What happened during the next minutes has become the subject of great and unresolved controversy. Everyone agrees that there was a strong wind blowing from east to west, in contrast with the usually westerly wind that worked to the advantage of the German fliers, and that Richthofen broke off from his squadron to pursue a British Camel, flown by Lieutenant Wilfred May, a Canadian novice who had been ordered to stay on the periphery if a fight developed. Tempted by a German triplane that seemed an easy target—thought to be flown by Richthofen's cousin, Wolfram von Richthofen, later notorious for ordering the raid against the Basque town of Guernica—May attacked, only to find himself pursued by Richthofen's bright-red Fokker. Already tasting his eighty-first victory, Richthofen followed May westward along the Somme River valley at low level, thus violating one of the key precepts of his own air combat operations manual: "One should never obstinately stay with an opponent whom, through bad shooting or skillful turning, he has been unable to shoot down when the battle lasts until it is far on the other side [of the lines]."

While in pursuit of May and now well over the British lines, Richthofen was in turn attacked from above by another Canadian, Captain Roy Brown, who succeeded in firing a long burst in the direction of the German triplane before he broke off his pursuit. At the same time, Richthofen was being fired at from the ground by the 53d Australian Field Artillery Battery and the 24th Australian Machine-Gun Company, both of which later claimed credit for bringing the red triplane down. Whatever the source of the fire—and no one will ever know for sure because the bullet was later "souvenired" and then disappeared—Richthofen was hit on the right side by a projectile that then exited through his chest near the left nipple, causing his death within minutes. He evidently had time to rip off his goggles and make a sharp bank to the east before losing control of the plane and plunging into a cattle-beet field nose-first, just off the north side of the Bray–Corbie road.

Brown was given credit for the victory—though he was always careful not to claim it—and his squadron later took as its insignia a red hawk falling to the earth. After the Nazis took power, the official Luftwaffe interpretation of Richthofen's death was that he had fallen "undefeated in his element, in which he so often staked his life for his earthbound comrades." That would seem to imply that Richthofen was brought down by the Australian gun battery. But having weighed the evidence, Richthofen's most recent biographer, Peter Kilduff, concluded cautiously that he could have been killed *either* by ground fire *or* by Brown. Which it was, we will never know.

On the afternoon of April 22, around four o'clock, Richthofen was given a formal military burial by the Australian Flying Corps at the cemetery of Bertangles in the valley of the Somme. A chaplain read from the Church of England service for military funerals, Richthofen's coffin was then lowered into the grave, three volleys were fired, and "Last Post" was played. That night, under cover of darkness, French civilians from the vicinity entered the cemetery and vandalized the grave, tipping over the cross that had been fashioned by the men of the No. 3 Squadron of the Australian Flying Corps and tearing apart the wreaths. They were falsely under the impression that it was Richthofen who had bombed their villages by night.

Richthofen's remains were interred in France until November 1925, when they were retrieved by his youngest brother, Bolko von Richthofen, and returned to Berlin for a state funeral of the sort reserved for heads of state and victorious generals. As the private train bearing Richthofen's coffin made its way across Germany, solemn crowds gathered at every stop, flags were flown at half-mast, and airplanes flew escort. From the Potsdam station, a torchlight procession accompanied the bier to Berlin's Gnadenkirche, where it lay in state for two days, guarded by an escort of highly decorated officers. The next day, on November 19, the official ceremony was held. Richthofen's coffin was placed at the foot of the altar, beneath the cross; upon it lay four of the Spandau machine guns with which the fallen ace had vanquished his foes, and on one end hung an enormous wreath from which projected a broken propeller, symbol of his tragic fate. Upon completion of the ceremony, the coffin was loaded onto a black horse-drawn gun carriage by eight pallbearers, all holders of the Pour le Mérite; from there the procession made its way past immense crowds, gathered to pay their last respects, to Berlin's Invaliden Cemetery for the burial. It was attended by the surviving members of Richthofen's family and a dazzling array of military and civil dignitaries. Field Marshal Paul von Hindenburg, the victor of Tannenberg and recently elected president of the Weimar Republic, tossed the first handful of dirt into his grave.

For the German public, Richthofen was a hero and a patriot, a figure who transcended the political divisions that had already begun to set German against German by the time of his death. Such views extended from the Nationalist Right to the Social Democratic Left. "There is and always will be," the Socialist newspaper *Vorwärts* wrote in April 1918, "something magnificent about the way a Richthofen dared hundreds of times to fight man-to-man for his Fatherland; it is a heroism always to be honored. Such action would be impossible without greatness and firmness of character."

RICHTHOFEN'S MOTHER ALWAYS INSISTED THAT HER SON WAS DRIVEN BY A SENSE of solidarity with the unheralded infantrymen fighting on the ground. "Why do you risk your life like this every day?" she once asked him. "Why do you do it, Manfred?" After pausing to reflect for an instant, he responded: "For the man in the trenches. I want to ease his hard lot in life by keeping the enemy flyers away from him."

On another occasion, when pressed by her to give up flying, Richthofen replied irritably, coming closer to revealing his real feelings: "Would it please you if I were in some safe place and resting on my laurels?" As emerges clearly from this question, what was at stake for the German ace of aces was not so much "the man in the trenches" as the Richthofen honor.

There is also a suggestion in the recollections of Baroness Richthofen, published in 1937, that during his last months of life her son had begun to fear for the social order into which he had been born and which was now showing its fragility. If the professionals faltered in their duty, Richthofen remarked to his mother, what would happen to the country? Germany would soon follow the example of Russia. The implication was that the masses might seize power. It was up to aristocrats like the Richthofens to set an example for ordinary Germans.

Richthofen's posthumous testimony adds yet another dimension to a personality that would soon be lost beneath layers of myth. In "Thoughts from a Shelter," fragments he wrote down shortly before his death, he insisted that the "insolent" person portrayed in *The Red Combat Flyer* did not correspond to the real Richthofen, the one he knew, and he then went on to say:

> From high places, I have been allowed to understand that I myself should give up flying, for one day it will catch up with me. I would be extremely miserable with myself if now, burdened with fame and decorations, I would vegetate as a pensioner of my own dignity in order to save my precious life for the nation, while every poor guy in the trenches does his duty as I do mine.

There seems little doubt that, like other aces, Richthofen felt that the Faustian bargain he had struck with fate required him to risk his life in order to continue to merit the celebrity and recognition he had won and intensely enjoyed. War, for him, was not primarily a means to a patriotic end but more the precondition for his own ascension and the realization of those preeminent qualities that he perceived within himself. Then, too, he enjoyed the hunt and the satisfaction that came with the kill. It amused him to regale his squadron with stories about the Englishmen he had "for breakfast." In every respect a "war lover," he was drawn inexorably to the flame of combat and a "tumult in the clouds."

But Richthofen was more than a seeker after celebrity and a cold-blooded murderer. If his eagle's eye, his coolness under fire, and his methodical approach to the tactics of air fighting explain much of his personal success in downing enemy aircraft, it was his extraordinary self-discipline, his Nietzschean determination to impose himself *and* his men on his adversaries, and the standards he set for himself and his pilots that made him more than a great fighter pilot. During the last year of his life he excelled as a leader and a teacher. In that sense, he was truly Boelcke's heir. After every battle, Richthofen would gather his officers for a conference and discussion of aerial tactics. He was as critical of reckless and overly aggressive pilots as he was of those whom he judged too quick to break off combat. Some measure of his achievement as a mentor is to be found in the fact that of the fifty-nine fighter pilots who received the Pour le Mérite, fourteen were his pupils. These were the qualities that caused him to be chosen leader of a fighter wing at the age of twenty-five. Although not liked personally in the way that Boelcke was, he was respected and admired, and ambitious pilots vied with one another to enter his squadron, knowing that it was the royal road to victories, decorations, and possible fame.

Given his accomplishments as an ace, theorist of air combat, leader, and technical adviser, it is easy to forget how young Richthofen was when he died. Yet the young Uhlan of 1914 had changed almost beyond recognition in less than four years of almost continual combat. By April 1918, as he himself noted in lines never meant for publication, war was no longer fun, no longer a matter of shouts and hurrahs. Nothing remained of "that fresh and joyful war" with which the conflict had begun. Things had become "very serious, very grim." And for all his bravado and his antics with his men, Richthofen admitted that he returned depressed after every aerial combat. "When I put my feet on the ground again at the airfield, I go [directly] to my four walls, I do not want to see anyone or anything." He knew that Germany was on the verge of being vanquished and that, having lost his sense of invulnerability after being shot down in July 1917, he too could—and probably would—die, the victim of an enemy he would never see.

THEIR "GOLDEN GLORY"
Thomas Fleming

—

L OVE UNCONSUMMATED IS ONE OF THE PAINFUL SUBTEXTS of the Great War. In her memoir, *Testament of Youth*, Vera Brittain tells of waiting to be married as soon as her fiancé returns on leave from France—only to receive a phone call telling her not that he has landed in England but that he has just died of wounds. Or a reader may come across Archibald MacLeish's poem, not so familiar as it once was, to his brother Kenneth, lost on a flight over Belgium:

> *. . . The rain gathers, running in thinned*
> *Spurts of water that ravel in the dry sand,*
> *Seeping in the sand under the grass roots, seeping*
> *Between cracked boards to the bones of a clenched hand;*
> *The earth relaxes, loosens; he is sleeping,*
> *He rests, he is quiet, he sleeps in a strange land.*

Kenneth MacLeish would leave behind a grieving young woman and a packet of letters discovered decades later in an attic trunk. And then there was the engagement of Quentin Roosevelt and Flora Payne Whitney, that ultimate American romance, a union-in-the-making of brains and beauty, of political power and wealth.

Some years ago the historian and novelist Thomas Fleming was researching his novel, *Over There*, when he came across the story of Quentin and Flora. Flora's daughter, Flora Miller Biddle, gave him access to another sad cache of love letters. The correspondence of Quentin and Flora begins just after her Newport, Rhode Island, debutante party, where they met late in the summer of 1916, and ends with his death over the Marne two years later. He was the son of a former president, Theodore Roosevelt; she was the granddaughter of one of the richest men in America, Cornelius Vanderbilt. (An uncle, Alfred Gwynne Vanderbilt, had gone down with the liner *Lusitania*, torpedoed by a German submarine in May 1915.) War hardly intrudes on their blossoming relationship, which in the first letters reads like pages ripped from a story by F. Scott Fitzgerald: the attractive young woman with her daring bobbed hair posing for a *Vogue* photographer on the steps of her parents' Newport summer "cottage"; the coming-out party in its ballroom; the dancing until dawn and the sunrise swim, no doubt at the fashionable Bailey's Beach; or the motoring around Ocean Drive in her new Scripps-Booth roadster, as the infatuation between the two takes hold.

All that would change the next April, when America declared war on Germany. A twenty-year-old Quentin would leave Harvard and enlist in the new U.S. Air Service. He would also propose to Flora. In those days you had a better chance of coming through a concentrated artillery barrage in a frontline trench than of surviving either flight training or air combat. Almost 70 percent of all American flight personnel who died in the Great War would be killed in training accidents. Quentin lived to tell that tale to his fiancée, but the odds of making it through the war were not in his favor. In the Air Service especially, the United States paid for its lack of preparation. In two years, its disorganized aircraft industry produced not a single frontline fighter of American design. Planes had to be borrowed from the Allies, and the fighter Quentin and his fellow pilots mostly flew was the already outmoded French Nieuport. As John H. Morrow, Jr., has written, Quentin's instructor, also French, would have "emphasized individual tactics rather than teamwork and formation flying, although 'gang' or 'collective and cooperative' fighting . . . was most efficient and appropriate in 1918." When Quentin reached the front that summer, he would encounter the hunting swarms of Fokker D.7s, the best fighter aircraft of the Great War.

In the early days of July, Quentin wrote Flora that he was leaving a special letter for her in case "I do get it." But he quickly reassured her: "Of course this all sounds foolish. . . . I love you too much not to come back, my darling."

———

THOMAS FLEMING is the author of more than forty books of history and fiction, including, most recently, *Liberty!: The American Revolution; Duel: Alexander Hamilton, Aaron Burr and the Future of America;* and *The New Dealers' War.*

N AUGUST 4, 1916, GERTRUDE VANDERBILT WHITNEY AND HARRY PAYNE Whitney invited some five hundred people to a ball at their cottage on Bellevue Avenue and the Cliffs in Newport, Rhode Island, to celebrate the debut of their older daughter, Flora Payne Whitney. The guest list, crowded with Astors, Biddles, Belmonts, Drexels, Dukes, Harrimans, and similar names, consumed two entire columns in *The New York Times*. For this momentous night in her life, Flora chose Quentin Roosevelt, the fourth son of the former president, as her dinner partner. The young people, who had known each other until then mainly through playful letters, danced until dawn and then shocked Newport summer society by taking a sunrise swim in the ocean. One can be fairly certain that this shock was mild compared to the suddenly visible possibility that Quentin Roosevelt and Flora Payne Whitney might marry.

Born within a few months of each other in 1897, Quentin and Flora were celebrities by accident of birth: They were children of celebrities. Quentin's father, Theodore Roosevelt, had been out of the White House for nearly eight years, but he remained the most famous man in America and probably the world. Flora's maternal grandfather was the eldest son of the richest family in America. At the age of three, the chubby little girl had appeared in newspapers as "Cornelius Vanderbilt's baby sweetheart." Her father and mother combined wealth with energy and talent: Harry Payne Whitney was a world-class sportsman, leader of the polo team that brought back the America's Cup from England in 1909. Horses from his Whitney Stables won races around the world. Gertrude Vanderbilt Whitney was a gifted sculptor and pioneer patron of modern art. Her Whitney Studio on West 8th Street in Manhattan exhibited the controversial moderns—and would eventually become the Whitney Museum of American Art.

In the shadow of these famous forebears, both Quentin and Flora had a tendency to see themselves as ordinary. In neither case was this accurate. Quentin blended his father's gift for language with a maverick imagination that suggested serious artistic talent. He had published surprisingly mature poems and stories in the Groton School magazine. Flora, emulating her father, whom she adored, was a superb horsewoman, a crack shot, and an expert fly fisher—all enthusiasms that Quentin, like his father, a lover of the outdoors, readily shared.

Although they lived only a few miles apart on Long Island, the Roosevelts and the Whitneys were separated by social and political barriers. The Roosevelts were old New York money, content to keep their modest inheritances in government bonds. They tended to disapprove of the lifestyles of the very rich. TR, a progressive Republican and 1912 presidential candidate of the breakaway Progressive Party, saw the great fortunes as a menace to America's stability, grist for the growing anarchist-socialist assault on capitalism. He denounced "the dull purblind folly of the very rich . . . their greed and arrogance."

The Whitneys, on the other hand, were concerned about not only their daughter's future happiness, but also the ultimate destination of her sizable fortune. Harry Payne Whitney's feelings about Quentin were further complicated by his younger sister Dorothy's 1911 marriage to Willard Straight, a Roosevelt admirer who founded *The New Republic*, a weekly that quickly became the bible of the Progressive movement. Harry sometimes referred to Dorothy as his "pink sister."

In several early letters Quentin teased Flora about money. One included a newspaper cartoon in which a bejeweled young woman asks, "Archie, what's the matter with your hand?" Archie holds up his bandaged hand and replies, "Merely a stone bruise, Flora, from holding hands with you last night." With another letter he enclosed a cartoon showing an average citizen struggling with winter, shoveling snow, and cursing a recalcitrant furnace. In the final panel he almost explodes when he opens his newspaper and reads: PALM BEACH SEASON IS AT ITS HEIGHT.

Quentin also used the comics to make fun of the prevailing attitude in his own family that "ladies" should not bob their hair or wear makeup, as Gertrude Vanderbilt Whitney and some of her advanced friends did. He sent Flora a panel picturing a dizzy young woman who asks her father what to do about her shiny nose. He suggests putting some powder on it. She tries to reach into a big flour barrel and falls in headfirst.

But the dominant note of the early letters was wariness on a personal level, with few references to politics or money. Quentin was then extracting himself from a dull relationship with Flora's best friend. Flora herself was very much in the social swim. So both were circumspect; both seemed to sense from the start a powerful attraction that could lead to happiness—or to acute pain.

As Quentin left Newport that August, he wrote a cheerful bread-and-butter letter to Flora's mother that belied any of this conflict. He looked back on three days of "a confused, kaleidoscopic" impression ranging from dances and dinners to Ethel Harriman's imitations to rides with Flora in her Scripps automobile along Ocean Drive—"all accompanied by a pleasant, subdued tinkle, as of ice against the sides of a cocktail shaker."

Beyond Newport, the world was being shaken by other sounds: the thunder of massed artillery at Verdun and on the river Somme. In America, one of the most pervasive sounds was the mounting fury of TR's attack on President Woodrow Wilson, who was running for reelection on the slogan "He kept us out of war."

By 1916, Roosevelt was convinced that America should be in the war, fighting beside France and Great Britain to repel imperial Germany's lunge for world supremacy. He was disgusted by Wilson's neutrality, especially after the Germans sank the Cunard liner *Lusitania* in 1915, drowning over 1,000 noncombatants, including 124 Americans. (One of Flora's uncles, Alfred Gwynne Vanderbilt, was among the dead.) Wilson said Americans were "too proud to fight" and continued to play peacemaker.

The president's policy was absurd, Roosevelt roared in speech after speech, because the United States was virtually disarmed. She could threaten neither side with her displeasure, which made Wilson's pleadings for peace utterly feckless. Instead of speaking softly and carrying a big stick, Wilson spoke loudly and wielded no stick worth mentioning. The 95,000-man American army was a pathetic joke, burdened with antiquated equipment and a sclerotic bureaucracy.

Inspired by Roosevelt, concerned volunteers gathered at army camps, including one in Plattsburgh, New York, in the summer of 1916, to learn soldiering from cadres of Regulars. Roosevelt's four sons, Theodore Jr., Kermit, Archie, and Quentin, were among them. Quentin hated it. He called himself "the family slacker" and made little effort to distinguish himself. One problem he had was a bad back, injured in a fall from a horse during a camping trip in Arizona the previous summer. The strained muscles and tendons made infantry training torture.

Even without this handicap, foot-soldiering had no attraction for Quentin. He was in love with flying. His heroes were the men of the Lafayette Escadrille, the American volunteers who were fighting the Germans in the air over Verdun. From his early teen years, he had been fascinated by engines and displayed a talent for building and repairing them that left the rest of his family baffled and amazed.

In the fall of 1916, to TR's immense frustration, Woodrow Wilson was reelected by the narrowest of margins over the Republican candidate, Charles Evans Hughes. Early in 1917, Wilson issued a call for a negotiated peace, based on the premise that both sides were fighting for the same goals. Roosevelt pronounced this presumption "wickedly false." The Germans seemed to confirm this judgment a few weeks later by attempting to forge a secret alliance with Mexico to attack the United States, as well as announcing that they were about to resume unrestricted submarine warfare, which they had abandoned after Wilson's protests over the *Lusitania*.

Back at Harvard, where he was in his sophomore year, Quentin was struggling against gloom, and the tone of his letters to Flora changed. Life seemed as gray and dismal as the weather and American politics. Part of the reason was his low opinion of his country. He wrote to Flora:

> I just got a very discouraged letter from my Hon. Pa. We are a pretty sordid lot, aren't we, to want to sit looking on while England and France fight our battles and pan gold into our pockets. I wondered, as I sat by my fire, whether there are any dreams in our land any more.

Separation from Flora seemed to have as much to do with his blues. On February 22, he described how he built a fire and got out his papers and books and settled down in his big mohair chair to watch the flames. Usually that cheered him up, but now all he could think about was seeing Flora at the "Maison Whitney." He soon began to miss her "very distinctly."

Trapped in the web of his failed neutralist diplomacy and his stubborn refusal to rearm, an agonized Woodrow Wilson went before Congress on April 2, 1917, and asked for a declaration of war against Germany. The next day, Quentin wrote to Flora from Cambridge. From a headline in the *Boston Evening Transcript* he had clipped the words QUENTIN STRONGLY GUARDED. "As you can see from the enclosed clipping, the police have realized how low I am and have taken measures accordingly," he wrote. In large capitals at the top of the letter, he scrawled "R.S.V.P."

He was beginning to realize how much he loved Flora Payne Whitney— and what the war might mean to the future of that love. As Theodore Roosevelt's son, he had to volunteer, even though at age twenty he was exempt from the conscription act that Congress would soon pass, drafting men between twenty-one and thirty years old. The moment Wilson called for war, TR—who was fifty-eight years old—announced that he wanted to lead a volunteer division to France immediately, to bolster Allied morale. Wilson rejected the idea, and TR defiantly declared that his sons would go in his place.

This collision between love and war plunged Quentin into greater unhappiness. One night in mid-April, during Easter recess, he went to a party at the Whitney house in Old Westbury and got dolorously drunk. The next day he wrote Flora an abject letter.

> I have never before acted as I did last night. . . . I agree to swear off entirely until ____. You fill in the date yourself. . . . I have often thought

the best thing about me was the people I cared for. I am afraid you have meant more to me than anyone else, far more than you imagine.

That episode—and the headlong momentum of the war—swept away the last vestiges of wariness and evasion in Quentin's behavior. He left Harvard, volunteered for the U.S. Air Service, and asked Flora to pledge herself to him. At the end of April, he wrote to her from Washington: "Wild excitement! I have been put in the aviation school at Mineola [on Long Island] instead of the one at Newport News." That meant he would be able to visit Flora constantly while he trained. But he was far more interested in Flora's response to his proposal. He was confident enough to remark, "I haven't yet seen my family. I wonder if they'll approve."

He soon discovered that his parents' approval was the least of his concerns. Quentin's proposal had provoked a crisis for Flora, who was forced to admit for the first time how intimidated she was by Quentin's literary gifts, his quotes from Dostoyevsky, his insider's political observations. She feared she was too ordinary for him. She, too, was troubled by the subtle antagonism between their families, sensing even more disapproval from her own parents.

Quentin responded with an elaboration on the ageless wisdom of the young:

> If two people really love each other nothing else matters. They can be married by [any] ritual, wear paper clothes and buy their supplies from the Bureau of Engraving. . . . I might be a Mormon and you an Abyssinian polyandrist and everything would be all right because you can't get beyond love."

By the end of May, he had the answer he sought. He replied:

> I don't yet see how you can love me. I feel as if it were all a dream from which I shall wake . . . with nothing left to me but the memory of the beauty and wonder of it all. You see I know how very ordinary I am and how wonderful you are.

Meanwhile he was learning to fly in cumbersome Curtiss Jennys, which could barely make sixty miles an hour. Nevertheless, there was a tremendous thrill in conquering the sky. Almost every weekend and every weekday evening when he was not on duty he was with Flora in Old Westbury or at Sagamore Hill, the Roosevelt home in Oyster Bay. They mutually dedicated themselves to persuading their families to accept them as a couple.

In a matter of weeks, Flora had utterly charmed TR and even succeeded in partially defrosting the far more disapproving Edith Roosevelt. A glimpse of Edith's attitude comes from a note Quentin wrote to his mother remarking that he was glad she liked Flora, now that she "had got past the fact that she was one of the Whitneys and powdered her nose."

For her part, Flora was amazed by the Roosevelts' overflowing affection for each other. Teddy and Edith were a stunning contrast to her own mother and father, who led virtually separate social and sexual lives and made little effort to conceal their estrangement. Knowing nothing of either parent's extramarital affairs, Flora resented Gertrude's bitter complaints of loneliness and implications that it was Harry's fault. Unable to understand, Flora blamed Gertrude and told friends that she could not even talk with her mother. It is easy to see why the Roosevelts appealed to her, especially when Teddy told her he was sure she and Quentin would remain "married lovers" all their lives.

An unprepared America was lurching into the war, improvising an army and an air force. With an absolute minimum of thought, the War Department decided Quentin and his group of barely trained fliers would constitute the advance guard of what Secretary of War Newton Baker called "an army of the air." Press releases, Washington's favorite ammunition then as now, volleyed predictions that 20,000 American planes would darken the skies over Germany within a year. Congress approved 625 million dollars to launch this aerial armada.

For Quentin and Flora, this decision meant the most painful word in love's vocabulary, separation. In mid-July 1917, a week before Quentin sailed for France, the young lieutenant brought Flora to dinner at Sagamore Hill and confided to his parents that they were secretly engaged. But they did not perform a similar ritual in Old Westbury. There the secret remained unspoken, while Flora struggled to find the courage to tell her parents.

On July 23, Quentin and Flora motored to a Hudson River pier and walked up and down for hours, waiting for his troopship to sail. Flora struggled for self-control. For two days she had kept a promise to herself not to weep. She had wept enough tears in the previous five days. In a similar agony, Quentin thought she might break down and sent her home. In the Whitney mansion at 871 Fifth Avenue, "the accumulated sea of tears" became a great gulf in her throat. Still she did not weep. She had decided it was unworthy of her love. "Only when there is doubt in the mind do we give way to emotions," she told Quentin's older sister Ethel, who had become a close friend.

In Quentin's pocket when the troopship sailed was a letter from Flora, written on July 19. "All I do from now on will be for you," she wrote. "I will do something—wait and see—so when you do come back I will be more what you want—more of a real person and a better companion and you will care for me as much as I care for you." For the present she was convinced "there is nothing in me that could make you care for me as much as I care for you." If he did not come back, "your influence will have made me what I am."

In France, Quentin and his group, including his Groton and Harvard classmate Hamilton Coolidge, were sent to Issoudun, some 150 miles south of Paris, to set up a flight-training school. It was the worst imaginable site. The clayish soil turned to gumbo when it rained, making it impossible to take off or land. Rain and bone-chilling cold were constants. One night Quentin awoke to find a thunderstorm sending a small river through his tent. He was soon calling the place "a forsaken hole."

Worse, they discovered almost everything they had learned in America about flying was useless. The Curtiss Jenny had almost no resemblance to the plane they would be flying at Issoudun, the French-made Nieuport. This was a second-rate fighter that the French had discarded for the faster, more maneuverable Spad. Among its many defects, the Nieuport had a tendency to shed its wing fabric in a dive. The American Expeditionary Force (AEF) high command had bought a number of them because nothing else was available.

In America, Flora became a constant visitor to Sagamore Hill. Even there she found pain. Every time she went up the road to the big rambling house, she remembered how happy she had been in the spring when Quentin was training at Mineola. At home she struggled to cope with her family. She still hesitated to tell her parents about the engagement. "I never talk about you or mention your name," she wrote him. "I . . . will though."

For Flora, the strain of separation was almost unbearable. "Oh Quentin sometimes it's all I can do to keep from just giving in and breaking down completely," she wrote in November. "It's so hard and there is so little satisfaction. I want you so desperately. The hollow blank feeling that is a living nightmare almost kills me at times. . . . Why does it all have to be? It isn't possible that it can be for any ultimate good that all the best people in the world have to be killed."

Struggling for inner strength, Flora wondered if prayer could help. "I don't pray, I don't know what to pray to," she wrote. Quentin, who described himself as "a throwback to preagnostic days"—he took his religion on faith without analyzing it—recommended his favorite prayer:

> O Lord, protect us all the day long of our troublous life on earth, until the shadows lengthen and the evening comes, and the busy world is hushed, the fever of life is over, and our work is done. Then in Thy mercy grant us a safe lodging and peace at the last, through Jesus Christ our Lord.

Flora's family was not her only problem. She was still a member of New York society. At parties and dinners she met more than a few young men who were eager to woo her. One asked her point-blank if she was engaged to Quentin and, when she declined to say yes or no, told her he thought she was being "perfectly rotten." When she told Quentin about this exchange, he became very upset. He did not want to think of Flora surrounded by amorous young men.

At Issoudun, Quentin and Ham Coolidge had a frank conversation about how to conduct themselves in France. Most of their fellow pilots were already in hot pursuit of everything in skirts. Quentin, reporting this to Flora, wrote that he had told Ham he could never reconcile having Flora one side of the ocean and "chippies over here." Flora replied that she was not worried about him. "I trust you too implicitly," she wrote.

On another crucial point, the lovers began in disagreement. On August 14, 1917, Flora told Quentin that his father wanted to see them married and would do everything in his power to "fix it" with her parents. Quentin hesitated. He was afraid marriage would be "selfishness on my part and might cause you pain in days to come."

He was telling her how dangerous the Air Service was. It was also exhausting. Along with learning to fly the tricky Nieuports, Quentin worked as a supply officer, racing all over France for equipment to build the airfield. His back tormented him, and he was forced to take to his cot one day a week. He lay there thinking of Flora and writing letters to her.

At Sagamore Hill, the Roosevelts were working hard to make Flora feel like a member of the family. They invited her to accompany them on a trip to Canada, where TR would address Parliament. The invitation may have been a hint that TR hoped Quentin would succeed him as the political leader of the next generation. There were indications that he had privately selected him as the son with the ideal combination of talents and personality for the task. Ethel explained the politics behind TR's speech: Canada was trying to decide whether to vote for a draft law similar to America's.

Flora told Quentin she had "the most thrilling time" in Canada. She was "openmouthed" at the enormous crowds, the gigantic receptions. But the experience left her feeling very inadequate. "Please do not go into politics!" she begged Quentin. "My tongue gets paralyzed and my brain gets paresis [meeting so many strangers]. I can only say 'what wonderful air up here' or something equally prosaic." Quentin, unaware of his father's vision of his future, was simply pleased that Flora had participated in a typical Roosevelt adventure.

At Issoudun, Quentin developed a perpetual cold and cough. By mid-November this became pneumonia—a very serious illness in 1917, before doctors had wonder drugs, that killed many a soldier on both sides. The camp doctor sent him to Paris for a three-week leave. He stayed with Theodore Jr.'s wife, Eleanor, who had managed to elude the AEF ban on wives of soldiers and was working for the YWCA. There Quentin soon encountered Ted and Archie, who were both in the 26th Division—Ted as a major, Archie as a second lieutenant. Ted remembered Quentin's poor performance at Plattsburgh and took a dark view of his decision to become a pilot. With Archie's glowering support he arraigned Quentin as a slacker, hiding out in Issoudun while they and their brother Kermit, who had joined the British army in Palestine, were on their way to the front.

Quentin was enormously upset. He appealed to his father and wrote a tense, revealing "apologia" to Archie defending himself and the Air Service. No American pilots had been sent to the front because there were no planes for them to fly. Only the two best pilots had been sent to England for advanced training. He was not one of them. "Father's pull" had gotten him into the Air Service in spite of his bad back and poor eyes, but it had not made him either the best or second-best flier in the army.

This brotherly imbroglio filled Quentin with a fierce determination to get to the front. In a letter rife with anxiety and foreboding, Theodore Roosevelt sympathized with him but urged him to be realistic and to be satisfied with one or two months' service over the lines. In mournful counterpoint was Quentin's growing desire to have Flora come to Europe and marry him. His father's letters repeatedly encouraged him to ask her. TR felt every young man should have his "white hour" with the woman he loved before he went into combat.

Flora wholeheartedly shared Quentin's wish to marry but found herself enmeshed in family and government complications. The War Department prohibited the sisters of soldiers, and all other American civilians under the age of twenty-one, from entering the war zone. Her brother Cornelius was in the Air Service, training in Texas, and she would not be twenty-one until July 29, 1918. Her parents told Flora they might be able to get these regulations waived. But they displayed little enthusiasm for the task. Along with their doubts about Quentin, there were more tangible worries about German submarines and about sending their daughter to Paris when the kaiser's army was poised for a massive assault on the city.

Flora still found it very hard to talk to her family about Quentin. "No one quite understands," she wrote to him. Meanwhile, she was "doing something." She was learning to type and take shorthand, so she could work as a secretary in a government agency. She was also reading serious books, trying to become the better companion she felt Quentin wanted.

Back at Issoudun after his bout with pneumonia, Quentin was made a training-squadron commander. He wrote letter after letter to Flora denouncing the climate and the muddled American war effort, which had yet to produce a single fighter plane. He was haunted by a recurring dream:

> I am coming back to the states wounded, one arm in a sling and my left foot gone. I have not been permitted to telephone from Quarantine to let you know I am coming. The steamer for some reason docks at Hoboken. I am planted there with my luggage and no way to carry it because of my arm. I am stuck in Hoboken. Freud says all dreams have meaning. I should like to have him translate that for me.

In later versions of the dream, he meets a huge military policeman with a red brassard on his arm who orders him onto an outward-bound transport. "Just as I realize . . . with awful despair I shall never come back, I wake up."

Quentin's health continued to be poor: He had constant colds and a racking cough. He wrote to his mother that he had been feeling "all overish" for a long time. Once he had a dizzy spell while performing acrobatics and almost crashed. During another night, the motor of his decrepit Nieuport quit in midair, and he landed in some trees, reducing the plane to kindling wood and badly wrenching his wrist. He was lucky to have escaped with his life. Yet he gave an ultimatum to his commanding officer, demanding to be sent to the front. He extracted a promise that he would get the first available opening. His friend Hamilton Coolidge got a similar pledge.

In New York, Flora wrote to him:

> Quentin I am so worried about you. I am sure you are not a bit well and I wish—oh so much—you could get . . . away somewhere in the south of France. . . . I hardly dare say this but . . . I think with your bad back you ought not to even be in aviation. At the bottom of your heart don't you think there is a good deal of sense in that?

The boom of 4,000 German cannons drowned out her loving voice. On March 21, 1918, Berlin's gray-clad legions launched the *Kaiserschlacht*, "kaiser's battle," a series of violent offensives aimed at knocking the British and French out of the war. In the next two months, they smashed a forty-mile gap in the British front, threatened Channel ports, and sent the French reeling beyond the Marne, putting Paris within artillery range. Swarms of swift new Fokker pursuit planes seized control of the air. Gotha bombers pounded Paris by night. The desperate Allies called on the Americans for help.

The news only made Flora more determined to get to Paris. For a while her parents seemed amenable. Influential friends were enlisted to approach the War Department. But this hope soon shed its fabric like a Nieuport's wing. Flora was told that the answer from the War Department was no. Mournfully, she wrote to Quentin: "It looked so cheerful, the prospects of my coming, it is really . . . mean they should be dashed away so suddenly." Quentin's response was a cable: SO SORRY OUR PLANS IMPOSSIBLE. POOR YOU. LOTS OF TIME YET. MOVING OUT AT LAST WITH HAM. LOVE ROOSEVELT.

He also cabled the news to France. "I can't help feeling a little more resolution on the part of the Whitneys would have done it," TR wrote. He could do nothing himself; his attacks on Wilson had left him with no influence in Washington.

In France, American infantry and airmen went into action to stop a massive German breakthrough at the Aisne River. First Archie, then Theodore, Jr., were badly wounded in the fighting along the river. Ethel's husband, Dr. Richard Derby, had a series of narrow escapes as he worked on the wounded in an aid station just behind the lines. Above the trenches, Quentin and other green American pilots, still flying second-rate Nieuports, dueled German veterans in swift, maneuverable Fokkers and Albatros D.Vs.

Early American air tactics were woefully inept. Imitating the overconfidence of their infantry brethren, whose open-warfare theories ignored the ubiquity of the machine gun, the American airmen sent up three- and four-man patrols, which were constantly outnumbered by the Germans' aggressive Jagdstaffeln, or "hunting flights." The Jastas, as they were usually called, put as many as twelve planes in the air at a time, with the pilots trained to fight as a team.

When Quentin arrived at the 95th Aero Squadron, the commanding officer, succumbing to Quentin's celebrity status, made him a flight commander. Quentin called the other three pilots in the flight together and said, "Any one of you knows more about [this] than I do." He told the most experienced pilot to take command of the flight as soon as they left the ground. "They may be able to make me Flight Commander in name but the best pilot in [this] group will lead it in fact," he said.

On June 25, Quentin wrote to Flora about his first voluntary patrol, "a sort of private Boche hunting party." They did not see any German planes, but "archies"—German antiaircraft shells—burst near enough to "turn me inside out." On the ground he found a big shrapnel hole in his wing.

"Things are getting hotter," he informed her a few days later. On a recent patrol four planes had tangled with six German planes, shooting one down but losing two pilots. Off duty, Quentin spent most of his time resting his back and working on his Nieuport, which had a very balky motor. He frequently fell behind the other members of his flight when they went on patrol. He found high-altitude patrols especially exhausting. "Four miles up is mighty high," he wrote.

He was quartered in a nearby château, overlooking some woods through which he sometimes wandered. The green, shadowy silence, he wrote to Flora, made him think that "however long the war lasts peace will come again. Peace and quiet and just you and I and our island. That's what I almost forget over here. War is only an interlude."

In another letter he was brutally realistic. "If I do get it, Ham is going to take care of my things. I'm leaving a letter for you in my trunk. Of course this all sounds foolish. . . . I love you too much not to come back, my darling."

Then came a letter charged with a new kind of excitement. "I think I got my first Boche," Quentin wrote on July 11. He had become separated from his flight and found himself alone over the lines. In the distance he saw three planes. Thinking they were friendly (an indication of how green he was), Quentin followed them into Germany. Suddenly the leader turned and Quentin saw the black crosses on his wings. A less daring flier would have headed for home. But Quentin "put my sights on the end man and let go. . . . He never even turned. . . . All of a sudden his tail came up and he went down in a *vrille* [tailspin]." The other two Germans pursued him, but Quentin made it safely back to the American lines.

French observers confirmed the kill, and Quentin stormed into Paris to celebrate with his sister-in-law Eleanor and his wounded brothers. Ethel Roosevelt rushed a triumphant note to Flora: "You must be so happy. Those long weary hours at Issoudun are being gloriously repaid." His father told Ethel: "Whatever now befalls Quentin he has had his crowded hour, his day of honor and triumph. . . . How pleased and proud Flora must be."

On July 13, Archie Roosevelt wrote Flora a letter from his hospital bed, telling her "Quentin blew in yesterday." Although he looked well, "one can't help being worried. He is in an American squadron and like everything else in our army we have had to take castoff machines from the allies so they have added dangers."

On the morning of July 14, Quentin took off over the Marne with the other three members of his flight. They were in search of enemy observation planes to prevent them from spying on the American infantry moving into position to block the German army's next offensive, code-named FRIEDENSTURM, "Peace Assault," which was supposed to end the war. Seven red-nosed Fokkers came roaring down on them, with the sun and altitude in their favor.

One of Quentin's flightmates described the ensuing melee:

In a few seconds [they] had completely broken up our formation and the fight developed into a general free-for-all. I tried to keep an eye on all our fellows but we were hopelessly separated and outnumbered nearly two to one. About a half mile away I saw one of our planes with three Boche on him and he seemed to be having a pretty hard time with them so I shook the two I was maneuvering with and tried to get over to him but before I could reach them, our machine turned over on its back and plunged down out of control.

It was Quentin. He was slumped over his instruments with two machine-gun bullets in his brain. The Nieuport smashed to earth behind the German lines, near the village of Chamery. In his pocket Quentin carried two letters from Flora, which helped the Germans identify his body. The later one, written on June 19, was full of her yearning to be with him in Paris. "If you were wounded I could go to you and be of some comfort," she wrote.

Quentin's squadron listed him as missing. In Paris and in America, those who loved him clung to shreds of hope. Eleanor cabled Flora: EVERY REASON TO BELIEVE REPORT QUENTIN ABSOLUTELY UNTRUE. Hamilton Coolidge (who would also be shot down, in October) wrote a letter voicing a similar opinion. But the next day the German Red Cross reported that Quentin had been buried where he fell, with full military honors, which included a guard of one thousand men. (The Germans took a photograph of his body, which is among the Roosevelt papers at Harvard's Houghton Library; the Roosevelt family has barred it from publication.)

"How am I going to break the news to Mrs. Roosevelt?" TR said on July 17 when a reporter on duty at Sagamore Hill told him Quentin was dead. He went into the house and emerged a few minutes later with a statement: "Quentin's mother and I are very glad that he got to the front and had a chance to render some service to his country and show the stuff there was in him before his fate befell him." Then he telephoned Flora.

Consumed with grief, Flora virtually abandoned her own family and became a Roosevelt daughter. In August she went to Maine with TR and Edith to spend a few days with Ethel and her children. She remained with Ethel when the Roosevelts returned to Sagamore Hill, where TR wrote to her:

> Just a line of love, dearest girl, to tell you again how I admire and respect you, because of the way you look upon your engagement to Quentin and because of your fine and gallant bearing in your hour of bitter trial. You made him very very happy and the golden glory of his service and his death is yours also.

In France, the American infantry, fighting under French command, played a crucial role in stopping the German attempt to breach the Marne defenses. A week later, the 1st and 2d Divisions joined in the counteroffensive at Soissons that slammed the German war machine into reverse. Soon Quentin's grave was in Allied territory—and it swiftly became a kind of shrine. Infantrymen hiked miles to see it and decorated it with flowers and mementos. For soldiers fighting to make the world safe for democracy, the death of a former president's son was symbolic proof that Americans practiced what they preached.

However bravely TR tried to face it, Quentin's death was a crushing blow. He told the novelist Edith Wharton that he could not write about it because he would "break down." In a letter to Ethel, he called it "a terrible and irretrievable calamity; nothing atones for it." To Kermit's wife, Belle Willard Roosevelt, he wrote that it was "most [terrible] for poor Flora. . . . I most earnestly hope time will be very merciful to her and in a few years she will keep Quentin only . . . as the lover of her golden dawn, and that she will find happiness with another good and fine man."

For the next six months, Flora worked at Sagamore Hill as TR's secretary. She participated in the Republicans' rout of the Democrats at the polls in the midterm elections of 1918. At Roosevelt's behest, the voters gave the Republicans control of both houses of Congress, in effect repudiating Wilson's plan for a negotiated peace with Germany and for a League of Nations. Instead they endorsed TR's call for unconditional surrender and a more independent foreign policy. Leading Republicans assured TR that he was guaranteed the presidential nomination in 1920 by "acclamation."

Roosevelt told one old friend he was "indifferent on the subject." Since Quentin's death the world seemed to have "shut down on him." Inflammatory rheumatism began ravaging the old Rough Rider's heart. Around four in the morning on January 6, 1919, while the diplomats were gathering at Versailles, Theodore Roosevelt died in his sleep. Flora was among the mourners at Sagamore Hill. Old and new grief mingled as Quentin's favorite prayer was read at the funeral.

For a while, Flora worked in Washington for the Republican National Committee, while living with TR's oldest daughter, Alice Roosevelt Longworth. But without TR's leadership, the Republican Party's vision dwindled to Warren G. Harding. Returning to New York, Flora married former pilot Roderick Tower in April 1920. An old friend from her girlhood days, he had been in Quentin's training squadron at Mineola. After a magnificent society wedding, they moved to Los Angeles, where Tower went into the oil business. They had two children in quick succession and seemed happy.

But Quentin haunted the marriage. With Kermit Roosevelt, Flora created a memorial book, *Quentin Roosevelt: A Sketch with Letters.* Much of it was drawn from Quentin's letters to her from France, with all the personal references excised. In her diary she tearfully commemorated Theodore Roosevelt's birthday—and Quentin's. After four years, the marriage collapsed. Flora returned to Old Westbury and devoted herself to raising her children, Pamela and Whitney.

In 1927, Flora married G. Macculloch Miller, an architect, painter, and writer of witty light verse, with whom she had two more children, Flora and Leverett. By all accounts, Cully Miller was the fine and good man TR had hoped Flora would find. She lived contentedly with him until his death in 1972. During those years, Flora reconciled with her mother and followed in her footsteps, taking a leadership role at the Whitney Museum of American Art. From 1942 to 1961, she supported it virtually single-handedly. She remained a major presence at the museum and in the American art world until her death in 1986, a few days before her eighty-ninth birthday.

Flora saved every letter Quentin had ever written to her. (Many of them are quoted here for the first time.) When World War II began, another Quentin— Ted Jr.'s son, born in 1919—joined the army. While he was training at Fort Devens, Massachusetts, Flora sent him Quentin's prayer and told him she would be saying it for him. (Ted Jr., also served in World War II, earning a Medal of Honor as a brigadier general at Utah Beach on D Day; he died of a heart attack in July 1944.)

In 1968, as the fiftieth anniversary of Quentin's death approached, Flora wrote to Ethel Roosevelt Derby, who replied on the fateful date itself, July 14. Another war was raging beyond another ocean, in a place called Vietnam. "How wonderful it was to hear you have been thinking of Quentin, father and mother, and Sagamore," Ethel wrote. "It has been half a century since we saw Quentin. Fifty long years. . . . How differently many of the young today look at duty, honor and service to our country in this strangely divided world." One can almost hear Ethel sigh as she tried to sum it up: "How incredibly young you both were."

PART SIX

TIPPING
POINTS

"THESE HIDEOUS WEAPONS"

Bruce I. Gudmundsson

T HE IDEA OF PYROTECHNIC PROJECTION GOES BACK AT least as far as the so-called Greek fire, which the Byzantine navy used with such savage effect against Muslim flotillas in 678. The formula for the secret weapon that saved Constantinople has been long-lost but the thick incendiary mix had the properties of napalm, clinging to things organic, such as ship timbers and human flesh. The *Flammenwerfer,* or "flamethrower," which the Germans introduced on the Western Front in 1915 operated on the same principal as Greek fire. While the weapon was hardly a war-winner, it did have a terror-spreading tactical potential. Stationary flamethrowers, as Bruce I. Gudmundsson points out, helped the Germans to take a couple of hundred acres of Verdun woodland that February—a large gain in Western Front terms. They tried out portable backpack versions against the British at Ypres, with similar results, in July. "Jets of flame as if from a line of powerful fire-hoses, spraying fire instead of water, shot across the front trenches of the Rifle Brigade and a thick black cloud formed. . . . The surprise was complete," the British *Official History* noted.

The fire-hose simile was particularly apt. It is one of those ironies of which history seems so fond that one of the men who helped to create "these hideous weapons," Captain Bernhard Reddemann, was in civilian life the fire chief of Leipzig; many of the reservists who joined his special detachment of combat engineers were firemen. The backpack version was ideally suited to trench warfare and, as Gudmundsson tells us, helped German *Stosstrupps*—storm troops or thrust teams—to chalk up notable successes at Verdun and in the Ludendorff offensives of 1918.

Both the French, with considerable success, and the British, with much less, experimented with flame-projection devices. (The principal French portable flamethrower was designed by a manufacturer of cigarette lighters.) But the British apparently never considered employing backpack models where they would have been most useful: against German bunkers. (The U.S. Marines did just that in the Pacific War.) Grisly as it is to think of men consumed by fire in concrete tombs, you also have to think that the flamethrower actually might have saved lives in the costly and demoralizing pillbox-by-pillbox advance at Passchendaele.

Not surprisingly, few accounts exist of what it was like to be on the receiving end of a flamethrower attack. Guy Chapman—whose *A Passionate Prodigality* Gudmundsson quotes here—describes the aftermath of one at Passchendaele. But can there be a narrative more memorable than the concluding paragraph of Hervey Allen's appropriately titled *Toward the Flame,* one of the notable memoirs of the Great War? Allen, better remembered (though mostly forgotten today) as an historical novelist, was a first lieutenant in the American 28th Division, a National Guard unit from Pennsylvania. At Fismette on the Vesle River in August 1918, storm troops swept over Allen and his company:

> Suddenly along the top of the hill there was a puff, a rolling cloud of smoke, and then a great burst of dirty, yellow flame. . . . It was the *Flammenwerfer,* the flame throwers; the men along the crest curled up like leaves to save themselves as the flame and smoke rolled clear over them. There was another flash between the houses. One of the men stood up, turning around outlined against the flame—"Oh! My God!" he cried, "Oh! God!"

BRUCE I. GUDMUNDSSON is the author of several books touching on World War I. These include *Storm Troop Tactics; On Infantry; On Artillery;* and *On Armor.* A former Marine, he advises the armed forces on matters of tactics, policy, and structure. He divides his time between Oxford, England, and Quantico, Virginia.

URING THE FIRST WINTER OF WORLD WAR I, THE ROCKY HILLS AROUND Verdun developed a reputation for being considerably quieter than other sectors. The German and French high commands were occupied elsewhere—primarily to the north, in Flanders and Artois. The local generals had to content themselves with a few small-scale attacks and whatever "strafing" their meager rations of artillery shells allowed.

Frontline troops appreciated this relative lack of activity. In a region where winter brought rain, fog, and an occasional bit of rapidly melting snow, keeping house in a trench not 350 feet from the enemy's was a full-time job. A tacit truce developed between the French who were farthest forward and their German counterparts—a phenomenon the British would later call "live and let live."

On the morning of February 26, 1915, the French who occupied the frontline trenches in the Malancourt Woods northwest of Verdun were doing nothing that would violate the unspoken armistice. Just before ten in the morning, they broke out their mess kits and began work on their standard ration of "monkey" (tinned beef) and biscuit.

On the other side of no-man's-land, a handful of German reservists in baggy gray uniforms were engaged in less innocent pursuits. Conscious of their proximity to their intended victims, the Germans crept silently through shallow ditches dug perpendicular to the main German trench. At the end of each sap (as this sort of ditch had been known since the Middle Ages), less than 100 feet from the Frenchmen, they assembled their weapons, devices that resembled overgrown fire extinguishers.

The picnic ended precisely at ten o'clock. With a deafening crash, a salvo of German howitzer shells struck the first and second French lines. After two hours of steady bombardment, as the clock reached twelve, burning petroleum poured from the German saps into the forward French trench. Blinded by the thick black smoke that covered the battlefield and panicked by the flames around them, the Frenchmen ripped off their burning uniforms, dropped their rifles, and ran.

Hard on the heels of the retreating *poilus* and just behind their own flood of fire and smoke, German riflemen with fixed bayonets rushed into the first trench and, seeing it empty, quickly went on to the second. Hindered more by thick undergrowth than by French resistance, the Germans took that trench, too. Two hours and forty minutes after the first explosions had signaled the start of the attack, 220 acres of the Malancourt Woods were in German hands.

The ease with which the Germans captured the French positions must be credited to one man, a reserve captain named Bernhard Reddemann—in civilian life the Leipzig fire chief. His interest in flame weapons had originally been sparked by a report from the battlefields of the 1904–1905 Russo-Japanese War. During the siege of Port Arthur, Japanese combat engineers had used hand pumps to spray kerosene into Russian trenches. Once the Russians were covered with the flammable liquid, the Japanese would throw bundles of burning rags at them. Although this method does not seem to have been very effective—the amount of kerosene that could be sprayed was limited, and the method of setting it on fire was, to say the least, uncertain—Reddemann saw promise in the idea. Acting almost entirely on his own initiative, he began looking for ways to make a workable flame-throwing weapon.

Reddemann first attempted to remedy the problem of quantity. In 1907, in a mock assault on the fortress of Posen, he used fire engines to simulate dispensing large amounts of burning liquid. Though the only liquid propelled through the hoses was water, Reddemann considered the exercise a success and began to design, build, and test a number of prototype flamethrowers. These, for the most part, seem to have been converted fire-fighting devices.

Soon after the outbreak of war, he teamed up with Richard Fiedler, an engineer from Berlin who had been working on a similar concept. In 1912, after seven years of secret tests on the exercise grounds of the Guard Pioneer Battalion, Fiedler's designs were accepted by the German army. A number were manufactured and issued to the *Belagerungstrain*, "Siege Train"—the organization responsible for reducing any fortresses standing in the way of Germany's field armies.

Fiedler's designs were far more practical than Reddemann's. Rather than gasoline, Fiedler used a mixture of heavier petroleum products that was much less explosive and easier to handle. Instead of Reddemann's hand pumps, Fiedler employed canisters of nitrogen gas to propel the burning liquid. And rather than concentrating on large flamethrowers for fortress warfare, Fiedler designed two basic models—the large one (*Grosserflammenwerfer*, or *Grof*) used at Malancourt and a significantly smaller backpack version (*Kleinerflammenwerfer*, or *Kleif*) that could be carried by one man and operated by two.

What Captain Reddemann lacked as a designer, he made up for as a tactician. In his absence, the flamethrowers of the Siege Train had had little impact.

Though there are unconfirmed reports of German flamethrowers being used as early as October 1914, there is no indication that these potentially fearsome weapons made much of an impression on either the Germans who wielded them or the Frenchmen who were the intended targets. Reddemann's first step in correcting this situation was to remove the flamethrowers from the Siege Train and place them in his "private army"—an independent unit of forty-eight combat engineers known as Flammenwerfer Abteilung Reddemann, "Flamethrower Detachment Reddemann." Many of the reservists who volunteered for this unit had been, like Reddemann, firemen in civilian life.

Thanks largely to the patronage of Crown Prince Wilhelm, son of the kaiser and commander of the German forces around Verdun, Reddemann was able to continue his frontline experiments. One of the most significant was at the village of Hooge, near Ypres in Belgium. On July 19, 1915, in an attack with limited objectives against German positions in the village, British infantry had successfully exploited the detonation of a large mine. But their enjoyment of their newly captured real estate was brief. Eleven days later, on the morning of July 30, taking advantage of the proximity of the British trenches, German flamethrower troops reenacted Malancourt.

Even though French newspapers had published accounts of Malancourt, surprise was complete. The British had no idea what to make of the jets of red flame that lit up the predawn sky. To their credit, however, they did not panic. The combined effects of the flamethrowers, machine guns, trench mortars, and hand-grenade teams pushed them back to their second trench. Nevertheless, they reached it in sufficiently good order to prevent the Germans from installing larger flamethrowers for a second attack. A British officer reported that "the defenders . . . lost few men from actual burns, but the demoralizing element was very great. We were instructed to aim at those who carried the flame-spraying device, who made a good target."

By the end of 1915, Reddemann's private army bore little resemblance to the platoon he had led at the beginning of the year. There were now twelve full companies of flamethrower operators, and the combat engineers in the ranks were joined by volunteers from other arms. The one constant in Reddemann's fast-changing unit was the continued presence of former firemen. Although trained to fight fires rather than start them, firemen had one significant advantage over other would-be flamethrower operators—they had already conquered the very fear of fire that made the weapon so effective.

In addition to the combat troops, Reddemann's unit contained a small research staff, a workshop detachment, a training company, and an experimental company. Ideas for improving existing weapons—whether generated by flamethrower operators returning from an attack or by the engineers on his staff—could be turned into prototypes without delay. Once built, those prototypes would be tested immediately. If the idea worked—and no one was better able to judge than the veteran flamethrower operators—the new design would go into production. Reddemann was able to eliminate the bureaucratic middlemen who do so much to slow down combat development in modern armies.

Because of Reddemann's streamlined organization—what the business world would later call "vertical integration"—some of the initial drawbacks of the flamethrower were eliminated. Early models required one of the operators to light the oil coming out of the flamethrower's tube with a burning rag or torch. This was replaced by a hand-held friction igniter not unlike the ones we use to light charcoal on barbecues—which was, in turn, replaced by an igniter that operated automatically. As soon as the flamethrower operator opened the valve on his hose, the igniter created the sparks that turned the fuel passing it into a cloud of smoke and flame.

The oil mixture the flamethrowers sprayed underwent a parallel development. Fiedler's mixture produced a great cloud of black smoke. While this made a strong impression on the troops being attacked (the psychological effect of the flamethrower was much more powerful than its physical effects), it also made the flamethrower team a convenient target for enemy artillery. The "dirty" oil was thus replaced by a cleaner-burning mixture with smoke that did not attract immediate attention from far away.

The biggest change, however, was the eclipsing of the large-model flamethrower by smaller models. The large flamethrowers could be used only for what Reddemann called "standing attacks"—updated versions of the operation at Malancourt, where trenches were close together. As the war progressed, the distance between the opposing lines tended to increase, and the backpack model, which allowed flamethrower teams to accompany the infantry into the depth of an enemy position, became the only type of flamethrower the Germans used.

This ability to penetrate beyond the enemy's forward trench became increasingly important as the war went on. French and British positions that in the winter of 1914–15 had been little more than a simple ditch tracing the forward line of troops developed into a subsurface city of dugouts connected by an intricate network of communications trenches. The number of machine guns increased by a factor of four or five, and they were often positioned so as to enfilade enemy troops that had managed to advance beyond the forward trench.

To get to these machine guns without falling victim to them, the flamethrower men advanced in small squads of two or three flamethrowers that Reddemann called *Stosstrupps*, "thrust teams." These squads ran from shell hole to shell hole in bounds, moving such a short distance (less than one hundred feet) that enemy riflemen barely had time to aim and fire before the target disappeared again. If shell holes were too far apart, one flamethrower operator would fire a burst of flame. The resulting fireball would provide the few seconds of confusion needed for the team to reach the relative safety of the next shell hole.

In addition to the flamethrower operators, each *Stosstrupp* contained a handful of grenade throwers. Their job was to protect the flamethrowers from short-range counterattacks. They also helped maintain momentum by throwing grenades ahead of the flamethrower operators. Given the fact that trenches were rarely dug in a straight line, the ability of the backpack flamethrowers to shoot fire around corners was also, no doubt, a great help in such work.

The remarkable similarity between Reddemann's *Stosstrupp* tactics and techniques being developed at that time by the first German *Sturmbataillon*, "assault battalion," was no accident. Like Reddemann's unit, this assault battalion was an elite, experimental unit whose chief purpose was to test new weapons and invent new techniques that would help Germany solve the "riddle of the trenches." During the summer of 1915, when both were developing their particular versions of the tactics of deep penetration, Reddemann collaborated closely with Captain Willy Martin Rohr, commander of the first assault battalion. The result of this cooperative effort, which included participation in a small-scale attack, was a single approach to battle based on two different sets of weapons.

In Rohr's system, the role of the large flamethrowers was played by light trench mortars, heavy machine guns, and infantry guns that suppressed key points in the enemy's frontline defenses long enough for the close-combat specialists to get themselves across no-man's-land. Once inside the enemy's trench system, these latter storm troopers, who were also organized into *Stosstrupps*, used hand grenades to fight their way through communications trenches and bundles of grenades to knock out machine-gun nests and other pillars of the enemy's defensive system.

Just as Reddemann's flamethrower-armed *Stosstrupps* were often joined by grenade throwers, Rohr's grenade-wielding *Stosstrupps* were often supported by squads armed with portable flamethrowers. For this purpose, a platoon of six backpack-flamethrower teams from Reddemann's unit was attached to Rohr's assault battalion. As other assault battalions were formed, they too received similar flamethrower platoons.

Adapting Reddemann's tactics to local conditions, the flamethrower companies soon found themselves in action nearly everywhere on the Western Front. The bulk of German flamethrower attacks during the first two years of

World War I, however, took place during the German offensive at Verdun in 1916. In terms of tactics used, the fighting at Verdun was little different from that of the numerous local attacks of 1915. But while these attacks were, in other places, relatively rare events, at Verdun they followed each other in rapid succession. The immediate result of this pace of operations was that Reddemann's men conducted three times as many flamethrower attacks in the first half of 1916 as they had in all of 1915.

At Verdun, attacks supported by Reddemann's flamethrowers were almost always successful. Most German units adopted the habit of moving forward in squads small enough to use minor irregularities in the terrain to shelter them from fire. Many had adopted the technique of using covered routes to push *Stosstrupps* deep into the enemy position. In the absence of truly portable machine guns, however, *Stosstrupps* armed with rifles and grenades couldn't pack the same punch as *Stosstrupps* armed with flamethrowers. The difference that the flamethrowers could make is well illustrated by the German attack on the Caillette Woods on June 1, 1916.

For most of the late winter and spring of 1916, the French position in the Caillette Woods had prevented any significant German advance in the area south of Fort Douaumont. Because the Caillette Woods sat atop the juncture of four major ravines, the French were able to dominate those ravines. Moreover, the location of the Caillette Woods on the relatively steep south slope of Douaumont Ridge made it impossible for the German artillery to knock out the French machine guns. Even the giants of the German artillery park—the 305mm and 420mm heavy mortars—could not place their monstrous projectiles with sufficient accuracy to eliminate the concrete bunkers that sheltered the machine guns.

After three months of fruitless bombardment and a number of failed attacks that had fallen apart at the north edge of the woods, the Germans decided to try a different approach. The artillery would concentrate on isolating the battlefield, heavy flamethrowers would punch a hole in the French forward lines, and *Stosstrupps* with portable flamethrowers would pour through that hole, driving the French machine gunners out of their bunkers. Once the backbone of the defense had been broken, infantry from the 7th Reserve Division would follow a rolling barrage down the steep slope and clear the woods.

Even by the bloody standards of Verdun, the attack would be a difficult one. Just to reach their jumping-off positions the German attackers had to march through an area that, from the point of view of the French artillery, could only be described as a shooting gallery. South of the Caillette Woods, French batteries spread out on a hill sloping gently into the Vaux Ravine could lay their fire along the long axis of the Casemate Ravine, the route that the flamethrower troops would have to take to get within striking distance of the French machine-gun bunkers.

If the German artillery had been able to overpower the French artillery, the aforementioned disadvantages of the terrain would have never become more than a nagging worry in the mind of some German staff officer. However, despite its best efforts, which included the participation of the 305mm and 420 mm heavy mortars, the German artillery failed in the task of neutralizing its French counterpart. The result, for the attacking Germans, was heavy losses and near paralysis.

The flamethrower company moving down the Casemate Ravine found it-self under fire so heavy that five of the ten canisters of compressed nitrogen (for the heavy flamethrowers) were struck by shell fragments. The resulting explosions killed most of the pioneers who had been carrying the canisters. All movement came to a stop as the veterans of countless peacetime fires and wartime flame attacks arrived at a silent consensus that they could take no more. Only the personal intervention of First Lieutenant Theune, the company commander, who returned from a reconnaissance to find the remnants of his command scattered along the ravine, got them moving. Theune ordered his men to stand up, formed them in two columns, and marched them to the line of departure. The German artillery was able to keep the French defenders but-toned up long enough for the remaining five heavy and twelve portable flamethrowers to get forward.

Lacking the resources to attack the Caillette Woods as a whole—not only had he lost half of his large flamethrowers but the infantry company that had been detailed to participate in his attack had been so shot up during its approach march through the Casemate Ravine that it was incapable of combat—Theune concentrated his firepower against the most critical part of the French position. The five large flamethrowers were set up on the eastern edge of the woods, along a 450-meter front that overlooked the concrete machine-gun bunkers that formed the heart of French resistance. Between each of the large flamethrowers, Theune positioned the twelve *Stosstrupps* armed with the back-pack models. The result of this deployment was a solid wall of flame and smoke that engulfed the first French trench.

As had been the case at Malancourt, the shock of receiving such fire was too much for the *poilus* in the front lines. While the smoke still hung heavy in the air, they threw down their rifles, raised their hands, and began walking to-ward German lines in large groups. In the midst of one of the fiercest battles in European history, men who had held their positions against repeated infantry attacks and the monstrous bombardment of the German heavy artillery gave up without firing a shot.

Encouraged by this initial success, Theune's *Stosstrupps*—reinforced by grenade-wielding *Stosstrupps* from Sturmbataillon Rohr—jumped up and plunged deep into the woods, each orienting itself on a particular bunker. For the next few minutes, the fight was entirely out of Theune's hands. Each *Stosstrupp* fought its own battle, using bursts of flame and grenades to clear its path toward its objective and employing the same weapons to drive the French machine gunners out of the little fortresses that had protected them for so long.

With the French machine gunners occupied with their private battles for survival against the *Stosstrupps,* there was little to interfere with the German infantry regiment that swept through the western half of the woods behind a rolling barrage. Before the morning was over, the woods—and 1,911 men of its garrison—were in German hands. The richest booty, however, was the thirty-three French machine guns that had ensured French possession of the Caillette Woods for three months.

The capture of the Caillette Woods did not win the battle of Verdun for the Germans. It can be safely said neither side won that contest. What the flamethrower troops did accomplish, however, was to prove once again the tactical value of their weapon. Two months later, this battlefield prowess was to be recognized by a singular honor. On July 23, 1916, on the occasion of the 150th flamethrower attack, Crown Prince Wilhelm bestowed on Reddemann's Guard Reserve Pioneer Regiment the right to wear a silver "death's head" (as the Germans called the skull and crossbones) as their unit insignia.

During the course of World War I, Reddemann's unit took part in 653 attacks, raids, or defensive actions. In 535 of these, the Germans were able to capture the enemy position, complete the raid, or drive off the enemy attack. In only 118—18 percent of the total—did the German troops accompanied by flamethrower teams fail to accomplish their missions. Just how effective the German flamethrowers were can be seen by contemporary British attempts to denigrate it. One officer reported:

> Its effect may be very easily exaggerated. When you see it for the first time it rather gives you the jumps. It looks like a big gas jet coming towards you, and your natural instinct is to jump back and get out of the way. A man who thinks nothing of a shell or a bullet may not like the prospect of being scorched or roasted by fire. But in my experience the effective range of the flammenwerfer is very limited, and the man who ma-

nipulates it as often as not is shot or bombed by our fellows. . . . The actual cases of burning by devil's fire have been very few.

Nevertheless, given its track record, it is not surprising that the German army decided to make the flamethrower a permanent part of its repertoire. A British officer, Guy Chapman, described a 1917 German counterattack in the autumn mists of Passchendaele:

> The enemy were attacking under cover of flammenwerfer, hose pipes leading to petrol-tanks carried on the backs of men. When the nozzles were lighted, they threw out a roaring, hissing flame twenty to thirty feet long, swelling at the end to a whirling oily rose, six feet in diameter. Under the protection of these hideous weapons, the enemy surrounded the advance pill-box, stormed it and killed the garrison.

The British counterattacked the counterattackers and retook the pillbox. "Then the stream of wounded began," Chapman wrote. "More and more men came in, with black faces, singed hair and eyebrows, and red swollen lips, were bound up and soothed as well as possible, and then sent or carried away."

The flamethrower played a major role in the stunning German victories of early 1918. During that year, Reddemann's troops more than doubled their previous record of 165 flame attacks in a single year—and yet were unable to keep up with the demand for their services. As the tide turned against Germany, the once-offensive weapon turned out to be a handy means of fighting the less-than-fireproof Allied tanks.

The flamethrower even managed to survive Germany's defeat. In the largely urban civil war of 1919, both the left-wing insurgents and the defenders of the new German republic often used it to incinerate their former comrades.

One great mystery is why Germany's enemies failed to develop a parallel affection for such a fearsome weapon. The British made three rather furtive, widely separated attempts to use flamethrowers in combat. In all three cases, the prototypes were large. The "portable" version was about the size of the standard German Grof—the large model that the Germans had all but abandoned by 1916. The other British prototypes were even larger—one had to be carried about on a flatbed railway car. Despite limited tactical success, the British army never followed up on these experiments.

The French were more persistent and, like the Germans, soon settled on light flame weapons. By 1918, a French captain named Schildt—who, like Reddemann, had been a firefighter in peacetime—had trained at least seven companies in the use of portable flamethrowers. Though these weapons, designed and built by a manufacturer of cigarette lighters, were in some respects superior to their German counterparts, the Compagnies Schildt never made the transition from curiosity to tactical staple.

Although it was never fully exploited by either side, the flamethrower was one of the most feared World War I weapons. It is a tribute to its battlefield effectiveness that, along with the submarine, the battleship, heavy artillery, the tank, poison gas, and the zeppelin, the flamethrower appeared on the list of weapons forbidden to the postwar German armed forces by the Treaty of Versailles.

An even greater tribute was paid by the soldiers who, after Hitler's rise to power in 1933, tore up the Treaty of Versailles and began to rebuild the German army. These World War I veterans made sure that backpack flamethrowers of a type similar to those carried by Reddemann's pioneers in 1917 and 1918 were liberally supplied to the combat-engineer battalions of each division, as well as to the elite *Sturmpioniere*, "assault engineers." In the war that soon followed, these weapons proved their worth in Belgium against the great border forts that stood in the way of the panzer divisions, in France against the works of the Maginot line, in Greece against the Metaxis line, and in the Soviet Union against thousands of field fortifications.

On the other side of the world, other descendants of Fiedler's flamethrowers found their way into the hands of U.S. Marines. The island-hopping Pacific campaign against the Japanese was, from the point of view of the Americans on the ground, a monumental exercise in bunker bursting; flamethrowers were distributed not only to combat-engineer battalions but also to every infantry battalion.

Thus, in the space of forty years, the flamethrower had come full circle. A Japanese concept developed during the Russo-Japanese War of 1905 was made a technical reality by a German engineer. A German fireman took that weapon and built a tactical system around it. It took U.S. Marines, however, to use the weapon on a scale that influenced the outcome of battles—battles fought against the very nation whose soldiers had come up with the idea in the first place.

JULY 1, 1916:
THE REASON WHY

Tim Travers

—

HERE IS NO WAY AROUND IT. THE FIRST DAY OF THE SOMME offensive, July 1, 1916, was the greatest disaster in the history of British arms, the worst day (it has been said) since Hastings. Of the 100,000 men who attempted to cross no-man's-land, beginning at seven-thirty that Saturday morning, one out of five would die and more than half would become casualties, as would three out of four officers. Several battalions, 700–800 men strong when they emerged from the cover of the trenches, practically ceased to exist; thirty-two suffered losses of 500 or more each. The total casualties, 57,470, of whom 19,240 were killed, has become a numerical cliché that for many sums up World War I. It gets worse. By the end of the day, the British had taken just under three square miles, although in much of the front they had gained nothing at all. But for most of the attackers, the dream of rolling over the enemy had ended in the first ten minutes.

The list of calamities could go on, as could the arguments about July 1. What had gone wrong? Why, Tim Travers asks, was the British battle plan essentially flawed? And how did an unsatisfactory compromise between the self-righteous and always distant British commander, Sir Douglas Haig, and his more practical subordinate, Sir Henry Rawlinson, ensure failure? (Haig thought that gaining ground was more important than killing Germans; Rawlinson, the exact opposite.) How, too, did a remote and too-rigid command structure contribute to the disaster? Why, in spite of an expenditure of 1,627,824 shells, did the artillery do relatively little damage to the patiently waiting Germans?

The questions multiply. Why were imperfectly trained troops, many of whom had never seen action before or even been in a trench, ordered to walk forward in closely bunched waves that made them such easy targets for German machine gunners? ("The first line appeared to continue without end to right and left. It was quickly followed by a second, then a third and fourth. They came on at a steady, easy pace"—the onlooker was a German officer biding his time with his men in the shell craters opposite—"as if expecting to find nothing alive in our trenches.") Why did each man carry a load of between sixty and seventy pounds? ("Fancy advancing against heavy fire," an Ulster officer remembered, "carrying a heavy roll of barbed wire on your shoulders!") Why did the French, attacking with fewer men on both sides of the Somme River, make big gains at the cost of only 2,000 casualties? And what prevented July 1 from being an even greater disaster—which might well have happened?

Beyond these questions, there is something else worth considering, and it gets to the heart of the vast casualty rolls of World War I. To quote John Keegan: "The simple truth of 1914–18 trench warfare is that the massing of large numbers of soldiers unprotected by anything but cloth uniforms, however they were trained, however equipped, against large masses of other soldiers, protected by earthworks and barbed wire and provided with rapid-fire weapons, was bound to result in very heavy casualties among the attackers. . . . The effect of artillery added to the slaughter."

Days like July 1 could have been better or worse, but given the limitations of the military technology of the time, they could not have been avoided.

TIM TRAVERS is a professor of history at the University of Calgary in Canada. In addition to his *Gallipoli 1915*, recently published in the United Kingdom, he is the author of two highly regarded studies of British Western Front leadership, *The Killing Ground* and *How the War Was Won*.

AT SEVEN O'CLOCK IN THE MORNING ON JULY 1, 1916, A BRITISH AVIATOR named Cecil Lewis was flying a patrol over what was about to become one of the major battlefields of World War I: the Somme. Zero hour for the first great combined Allied offensive was still thirty minutes away, and Lewis described the final countdown. It seemed impossible that a scene so impressive could hold such a potential for disaster.

> Half an hour to go! The whole salient, from Beaumont-Hamel down to the marshes of the Somme, covered to a depth of several hundred yards with the coverlet of white wool—smoking shell bursts! It was the greatest bombardment of the war, the greatest in the history of the world. The clock hands crept on, the thrumming of the shells took on a higher note. It was now a continuous vibration, as if Wotan, in some paroxysm of rage, were using the hollow world as a drum and under his beat the crust of it was shaking. Nothing could live under that rain of splintering steel. . . .
>
> Now the watch in the cockpit, synchronised before leaving the ground, showed a minute to the hour. We were over Thiepval and turned south to watch the mines. As we sailed down above it all, came the final moment. Zero!
>
> At Boiselle, the earth heaved and flashed, a tremendous and magnificent column rose into the sky. There was an ear-splitting roar, drowning out all the guns, flinging the machine sideways in the repercussing air. The earthy column rose higher and higher to almost four thousand feet. . . . A moment later came the second mine. . . . Then the dust cleared and we saw the two white eyes of the craters. The barrage had lifted to the second-line trenches, the infantry were over the top, the attack had begun.

But the first sentence of Cecil Lewis's logbook that day simply stated, "From our point of view an entire failure." And later in the day, he noted, "There must be colossal lack of organisation somewhere."

Unfortunately, Cecil Lewis was right. The first day of the Somme offensive had not gone according to plan. Gradually the magnitude of the disaster became evident. The British alone had suffered 57,470 casualties on July 1,

1916—a figure that the historian Martin Middlebrook computes to exceed the British army's combined losses in the Crimean War, the Boer War, and the Korean War. Of that total, 19,240 men were killed or died of their wounds. Clearly, this was, and has remained, one of the greatest disasters ever suffered by the British army.

Yet to the south, the French army's losses were insignificant in comparison—estimates suggest around 2,000 French casualties for July 1. North of the Somme River, two French divisions reported only about 600 casualties, the same number that some British battalions were suffering. Overall, the British were taking about ten times the casualties of the French. What happened to the British, and why were the French relatively unscathed in the same offensive? Was it the fault of a callous British high command, supplemented by incompetent staff work, as many still suppose? Was it the fault of an unimaginative British plan? Was it because the British army did not understand the new tactics and technology as well as the French? Or was it because the British army did not have the same technical superiority as the French?

The Somme had originally been proposed as a joint Franco-British offensive, and the choice of ground lay with the French. General Sir Douglas Haig, as Commander in Chief of the British Expeditionary Force (BEF), would have preferred the Ypres sector, to the north, and he got his way a year later, at Passchendaele. But the Somme area had better railway access and drier ground; in 1916 the Somme River was also the boundary between the French and British forces. Then, early that year, the German army opened a furious offensive at Verdun, to the southeast, and the French pressed the BEF to launch a joint offensive to relieve the pressure there. The Somme offensive was given the final go-ahead in May. Because of French losses at Verdun, however, the BEF soon became the major partner in the planned offensive.

In the end, the BEF would attack on July 1, 1916, with fourteen infantry divisions, and four more in reserve, while the French, astride the Somme, would attack with five divisions, and another six in reserve. Opposing the British and French attacks north of the Somme would be five German divisions, with another two south of the river. The British planned to attack from Gommecourt in the north to Montauban in the south, and the French would support them with attacks on both sides of the river. The object of the whole offensive was to capture the first lines of German trenches, then take the high ground facing the BEF—the Pozières Ridge—along a ten-mile front, and finally turn north and roll up the German line. The cavalry was then to push through the gaps, capture Bapaume, and also turn north to exploit the panic created in the German back areas. Meanwhile, the French would act as the defensive hinge on the right of the breakthrough, and on the extreme left, as a diversion to the assault, two British divisions would take Gommecourt.

July 1 was a beautiful, misty, and soon to be very hot day. Precisely at seven-thirty in the morning, some 66,000 men in the BEF's first wave left their trenches and started moving steadily across mostly open ground toward the first line of German trenches. An immediate objective was to capture the villages along the German front. In the center of the line, the Germans held the high ground of the Pozières Ridge, with its many valleys and spurs that provided good enfilading fire for the defenders.

Soon after the attack was launched, it became evident to the British that something was terribly wrong. Again and again, reports came back of no ground gained. At Gommecourt, for example, the 46th and 56th Divisions attacked one of the strongest points on the whole line, without much attempt at surprise and without sufficient counterbattery fire to weaken the German artillery. Nevertheless, there was a powerful smoke screen, and in front of the 56th Division, the German wire was well cut, which at least enabled that division to reach its first objectives, and go beyond them. But tremendous German shelling, and counterattacks that bombed the British out of the captured trenches, put the 56th Division back to its own lines by nightfall. Meanwhile, just to the north, the 46th Division had found uncut wire, similar heavy shelling, and enfilading machine-gun fire, which produced serious casualties and not much else. The two divisions had endured over 6,700 casualties for no gain of ground and very little in the way of diversion.

Farther south on the line, the machine-gun defenses of La Boisselle had not been destroyed by the weeklong preliminary artillery bombardment, nor by the final barrage on July 1, and so the German machine gunners, who were on higher ground than the attackers of the 34th Division, simply cut down wave after wave of Tyneside Irish and Scots as they advanced across a mile of open ground. This division suffered the highest casualties of all—6,380—with, again, very little to show for it.

As a final example of futility, opposite Beaumont-Hamel, the first attack of the 29th Division had not succeeded in getting into the first line of German trenches, for many reasons: the failure of counterbattery work; the early firing of the mine at Hawthorn Redoubt, which alerted the defenders; the enfilading fire by machine guns directed at the gaps in the wire through which the infantry had to advance; and the slow pace of the infantry. Consequently, a further attack by the reserves was ordered, mainly involving the 1st Newfoundland Battalion. Without artillery bombardment, and crossing half a mile of downward-sloping open ground, the battalion simply melted away under machine-gun fire. In approximately forty minutes, it suffered 91 percent losses—twenty-six officers and 658 men.

These casualties resulted from the lack of cover; inappropriate infantry tactics; inexperience that meant failure to provide sufficient and well-timed artillery covering barrages for the infantry; uncut-wire, machine-gun, and artillery defenses that had survived the preliminary bombardment; and deep dugouts that sheltered the German infantry and enabled it to survive the artillery fire. Survivors' stories attest to the terrible severity created by these problems. Percy Crozier, getting ready to lead his men in the second wave of the 36th (Ulster) Division assault, wrote later:

> I glance to the right through a gap in the trees. I see the 10th [Royal Irish] Rifles plodding on and then my eyes are riveted to a sight I shall never see again. It is the 32nd division at its best. I see rows upon rows of British soldiers lying dead, dying or wounded, in no man's land. Here and there I see an officer urging on his followers. Occasionally I can see the hands thrown up and then a body flops to the ground. The bursting shells and smoke make visibility poor, but I see enough to convince me Thiepval village [part of the 32nd Division's objectives] is still held [by the German forces]. . . . Again I look southward from a different angle and perceive heaped up masses of British corpses suspended on the German wire in front of the Thiepval stronghold, while live men rush forward in orderly procession to swell the weight of numbers in the spider's webb.

On another part of the line, the future novelist Henry Williamson remembered attacking toward Ovillers.

> I see men arising and walking forward; and I go forward with them, in a glassy delerium wherein some seem to pause, with bowed heads, and sink carefully to their knees, and roll slowly over, and lie still. Others roll and roll, and scream and grip my legs in uttermost fear, and I have to struggle to break away, while the dust and earth on my tunic changes from grey to red.
>
> And I go on with aching feet, up and down across ground like a huge ruined honey comb, and my wave melts away, and the second wave comes up, and also melts away, and then the third wave merges into the ruins of the first and second, and after a while the fourth blunders into the remnants of the others, and we begin to run forward to catch up with the barrage, gasping and sweating, in bunches, anyhow, every bit of the months of drill and rehearsal forgotten, for who could have imagined that the "Big Push" was going to be like this?

About half of all the men involved in the BEF's Somme offensive on July 1 became casualties, as were approximately three out of every four officers. On the German side, where casualty figures were collected only on a ten-day basis, 40,187 casualties were recorded between July 1 and 10, not including the lightly wounded. Probably most of these occurred after July 1. (German records indicate that the German Second Army, defending on both sides of the Somme, also lost 6,960 men from the preliminary barrage between June 21 and 30.) In addition, the BEF divisions took somewhere between 1,983 and about 2,500 unwounded German prisoners on July 1 (these numbers are only estimates, based on various reports). It is possible to estimate that altogether there were some 8,000 German casualties on July 1 from Gommecourt to the junction with the French forces, not counting those caused by the preliminary bombardment. Many of these casualties occurred in the southernmost part of the British line, adjoining the French sector, where three British divisions achieved the best results. Reliable records indicate that the attack by the 7th and 18th Divisions, facing the German 109th Reserve Regiment, produced 2,147 German casualties, while the 6th Bavarian Reserve Regiment, defending against an assault by the 30th Division and the French 39th and 11th Divisions, lost 1,800 men.

Nevertheless, in the BEF sector there was no doubt that the offensive had lost very heavily, so that the overall casualty ratio was around seven to one in favor of the German defenders—and even more skewed in many areas. For example, the 8th Division, attacking toward Ovillers just north of the road to Bapaume, suffered over 5,000 casualties, largely from machine-gun fire, while the German 180th Regiment opposite it lost just 280 killed or wounded. It is probable, in fact, that machine guns did more damage at the Somme than in any other Western Front battle. Henry Williamson recalled the opening moments of the 8th Division advance: "A steam-harsh noise filled the air. He knew what that was: machine gun bullets, each faster than sound, with its hiss and its air crack arriving almost simultaneously, many scores of thousands of bullets in the air together at the same time and coming from all directions."

When German artillery was added to the machine guns, the result was devastating. Brigadier General H. C. Rees, the commander of the 94th Infantry Brigade in the 31st Division, which advanced toward Serre, reported that his brigade

> advanced in line after line, dressed as if on parade, and not a man shirked going through the extremely heavy barrage, or facing the machine gun and rifle fire that finally wiped them out. . . . [Rees] saw the

lines which advanced in such admirable order melting away under the fire. Yet not a man wavered, broke the ranks, or attempted to come back. He has never seen, indeed could never have imagined, such a magnificent display of gallantry, discipline and determination. The reports that he had had from the very few survivors of this marvellous advance bear out what he saw with his own eyes, viz. that hardly a man of ours got to the German front line.

Nor had the BEF divisions captured very much ground, except for an area near Thiepval, another sector just north of Fricourt, and areas to the south, where the villages of Mametz and Montauban had been taken and where the French had captured Curlu and most of their other objectives. The British had captured perhaps a little less than three square miles. What had gone wrong?

THERE WERE ESSENTIALLY FOUR REASONS FOR THE BRITISH FAILURE ON JULY 1, IN contrast to French success: Most important, the artillery, on which so much depended, was technically incapable of fulfilling its role. Partly as a result of artillery shortcomings and inexperience, infantry tactics were poor. The plan of attack was not well thought out. And the BEF high command's structure was inflexible.

Perhaps the greatest difficulty for the BEF at the Somme was that of command. Problems had started at the very beginning of the planning, when Haig entrusted the offensive to Sir Henry Rawlinson, his Fourth Army commander. The two men had very different ideas for the offensive. Rawlinson wanted a limited-objective, "bite and hold" plan, which meant that the BEF would use a lengthy bombardment and a cautious advance under a very heavy artillery barrage to seize a chunk of ground, then consolidate, and finally destroy the inevitable German counterattacks. In other words, killing Germans was more important to Rawlinson than gaining a lot of ground. Yet, according to Rawlinson, Haig's ideas were almost the opposite: "D.H. is for breaking the line and gambling on rushing the 3rd line on the top of a [German] panic." What Haig wanted, therefore, was a quick, hurricane bombardment, then a breakthrough spearheaded by strong patrols, to be eventually followed by the cavalry. In other words, gaining ground was more important to Haig than killing Germans.

Cautious about his career, and conscious of Haig's strong personality and intolerance of opposition, Rawlinson dared not confront Haig too strongly. At the same time, Haig felt that Rawlinson, as the army commander involved, should run the battle, and he believed he had allowed Rawlinson freedom to conduct the offensive as he wanted. There was, in fact, a breakdown in communication—if not a vacuum—between the two men, and there existed no means by which the two could sit down together and thrash out the problems of the attack. As a result, Haig had the erroneous impression that the planning and preparation for the offensive were proceeding smoothly.

The result was a mixed plan, in which Rawlinson was supported with a lengthy barrage and enough artillery, he thought, to take the first line of trenches as a limited objective. But the infantry objectives in the central and northern parts of the attack were actually quite deep; for instance, the 36th (Ulster) Division had to cover 3,000 yards and more—by eight past ten in the morning. (Some of the Ulstermen did reach their deep objectives, but at a fearful cost.) In addition, Haig, obviously thinking of the offensive as a widely based breakthrough, insisted on a series of deeper final objectives. Thus, the plan for July 1, 1916, was a potentially fatal mixture of caution and boldness.

As the chief staff officer of Fourth Army later wrote privately: "I admit at once the objectives were too deep and too broad for the troops and guns available." Even more fundamentally, this was a rigid, detailed plan that attempted too much, dispensed with initiative and surprise, spread out the troops and guns in one long and therefore less effective line, and in the end reflected the orderly hierarchical structure of the BEF at the time. In this respect, Haig, Rawlinson, and Fourth Army staff were apprehensive about the morale of their troops, and sometimes they seemed more worried about their own men than about the enemy. This concern was understandably reinforced by the fact that most of the British troops at the Somme in 1916 were half-trained and inexperienced; only a very small percentage had taken part in the previous offensives of 1915. This, in turn, contributed to the tragedy of the Somme, for Rawlinson told a friend just before the offensive "that the attack must be made in waves with men at fairly close interval in order to give them confidence."

Despite the mixed plan, Rawlinson made three very large and fatal assumptions based on his own "bite and hold" idea. The first was that the artillery would essentially win the battle—perhaps a curious idea, given that Rawlinson was an infantryman. The artillery was assumed to be capable of cutting the German wire during the week's bombardment before zero hour, knocking out German machine guns and artillery, and destroying German trenches and strongpoints. The barrage was also relied on to carry the infantry through at least to the first line of enemy trenches, and perhaps to the more distant infantry objectives as well. The second assumption follows the first: The most important function of the infantry at seven-thirty that morning of July 1 was not so much to fight for and capture its objectives, but to consolidate along the German trenches, already theoretically destroyed by artillery, and then beat off all the counterattacks. The third assumption was that the infantry was not expected to run across no-man's-land, since the artillery would do the job for it; instead, the men would be carrying the extra equipment needed for the all-important task of consolidation, such as coils of wire, iron posts, and shovels. With all this weight, the infantry was supposed to move in orderly fashion across no-man's-land, conforming to the clockworklike lifts of the artillery barrage, which jumped a hundred yards ahead every two minutes. While the plodding pace was not a specific requirement, everything in the plan pointed to a steady, disciplined advance rather than speed.

As an example of this slow pace, Ambrose Ricardo, commanding the County Tyrone Battalion in the Ulster Division, emphasized that his men advance with "no fuss, no shouting, no running; everything orderly, solid and thorough, just like the men themselves. Here and there a boy would wave his hand to me as I shouted 'Good Luck' to them through my megaphone, and all had a happy face. Many were carrying loads. Fancy advancing against heavy fire carrying a heavy roll of barbed wire on your shoulders!"

Rawlinson's three assumptions, and the resulting structure of the offensive, have given rise to much critical abuse of Haig and the BEF's high command over the years for forcing the infantrymen to walk slowly across no-man's-land while carrying seventy pounds or more, thus offering themselves as easy targets to be mowed down by German machine guns. In fact, there was a logic to Rawlinson's assumptions, based on the unfortunate British experience at Neuve-Chapelle and Loos in 1915. Ironically, if the offensive had followed Haig's original cavalry idea for a rapid rush under a hurricane bombardment, casualties would probably have been considerably reduced.

Despite the three assumptions, it is possible to see that the offensive had some potential for success, and that the BEF's attack turned out not to be quite as rigid as historians often portray it. For one thing, the plan to deal with German artillery was far more effective than is generally realized. This was because the BEF and the French had a three-to-one superiority in the air (386 planes versus 129), which enabled pilots and observers to correct the fall of shells on German batteries. Allied gunnery badly defeated the German artillery; German guns were destroyed in large numbers in the valleys north of Mametz and Montauban. The German 12th Division, between Montauban and the Somme, lost most of its guns on June 30 and July 1, while the German defenses opposite the BEF's 30th Division lost most of its garrison artillery and nearly all of its machine guns. Between Montauban and Ovillers, the German 28th Reserve Division also lost most of its artillery, so that on July 1 there were only ten field and thirteen heavy batteries available to stem the attack of three and a half BEF divisions. Hence, at the end of the seven-day preliminary bombardment, General Erich Ludendorff—not yet assigned there—remarked, "The strength of the Allied artillery, well directed by their aeroplanes, has defeated and cut into pieces the German artillery." Seen from ground level, one German soldier in the 109th Reserve Regiment near Mametz wrote, "The English artillery—the English army—the masses of English aeroplanes over our heads always. We are finished, we shall all be wounded or dead." However, these areas of destruction tended to be either in the southern part of the line, where the BEF offensive had its greatest success, or in some areas of the center, but not in the north.

Nor was the BEF's air superiority confined to counterbattery work. There were also contact patrols (to observe the infantry advance and relay this information to infantry headquarters), destruction of enemy observation balloons, and bombing behind the lines to prevent reinforcements from coming up. In the Fricourt area, Lieutenant Basil Liddell Hart said that in the week prior to July 1, "every day one saw as many as 20 or 30 of our bomb-dropping aeroplanes going over the Boche lines." A German prisoner of war later said that two battalions of the German 22d Reserve Division were at the Saint-Quentin railway station on the afternoon of July 1, entraining for the Somme front, when

> English aeroplanes appeared overhead and threw bombs. One bomb fell on a shed which was filled with ammunition, and caused a big explosion. There were 200 waggons of ammunition in the station at the time; sixty of them caught fire and exploded. . . . The train allotted to the transport of troops and all the equipment . . . were destroyed by fire. The men were panic stricken and fled in every direction. One hundred and eighty men were either killed or wounded. It was not till several hours later that it was possible to collect the men of the 71st Regiment. It was then sent back to billets.

If the BEF's artillery in the south and parts of the center generally dominated the German artillery, then the French artillery in the south was absolutely devastating. The French also had complete air mastery, but the difference was that they had a clear overall superiority of heavy batteries as well. (South of the Somme, for example, the French had an astonishing eight-to-one advantage.) Small wonder that the French were successful on their front. Moreover, the French guns north of the river also helped to fire on the front of the BEF's southernmost divisions, the 30th, 18th, and 7th. Hence, one

French heavy mortar fired on Montauban for seven days, reducing it completely to rubble apart from a miraculously undamaged crucifix in the church; one shell alone killed everyone in the German artillery command center. Montauban was also the only place in the British sector where the deep German dugouts were penetrated, and this was due to the French heavies. So it was not surprising that when British troops entered Montauban, they saw many enemy dead. The journalist Phillip Gibbs later wrote: "They looked monstrous, lying there crumpled up, amidst a foul litter of clothes, stick bombs, old boots and bottles. . . . Others might have been old or young. One could not tell because they had no faces and were just masses of raw flesh in uniforms."

Farther south, the French artillery also destroyed nearly all the deep German dugouts opposite the French XX Corps, and a German officer on that front reported that during the preparatory bombardment in the week before July 1, "Our physical and moral resistance naturally diminished. Incredible that we counted as many as 200 explosions a minute. And what a terrible bombardment! At each explosion, the earth shook over a wide area. During the last two days, we just did not receive any food." Basically, the overwhelming artillery strength of the French, in conjunction with their air mastery, made possible the French success of July 1, because of not only successful counterbattery work, but also the almost complete destruction of wire, machine guns, and deep trenches.

But domination in the air and artillery barrages were not the only reasons for the French success and their minimal casualties. It also appears that Erich von Falkenhayn, chief of the German General Staff, had not initially believed that the French would attack there, given their preoccupation with Verdun; instead, he had believed that French preparations were simply aimed at deceiving the Germans as to the point of the attack. In early June, German headquarters had come around to admitting that French support for the offensive was "probable," but as late as June 25 the Germans stated that the French would not be ready to attack south of the Somme "for several days." At least below the Somme, therefore, the French attack was a surprise, which probably accounts for the collapse of the German 121st Infantry Division in that area. Most of the German artillery and nearly six full divisions had been placed north of the Somme, but only three below it. In addition, the two French corps in the extreme south were materially aided by their later start—nine-thirty in the morning—by which time the German defenses were concentrating on the BEF's attack farther north. Most of the German counterattacks on July 1 were launched against the BEF rather than against the southern French corps. Still another advantage for the French was that below the Somme, the ground largely flattened into a plateau, rather than the higher ground and valleys in front of much of the BEF attack. As for the French who attacked north of the Somme, they found that the marshes there produced an early-morning mist that sheltered their advance.

Finally, but by no means least, French offensive tactics were more sensible than those of the BEF. Because of their terrible losses at Verdun, the French were trying to save manpower, so they attacked with the minimum numbers of infantry. Drawing on experience in 1915 and at Verdun, a note from French headquarters on June 20, 1916, called for "a strict economy, in which one asks of the infantry only what it is capable of achieving, and to direct the attack methodically and with close supervision."

The French copied the artillery method employed by the Germans at Verdun—the artillery conquers and the infantry occupies. Hence, General M. E. Fayolle, commander of the Sixth French Army, stated that the French offensive would not be "a rush through enemy lines, or a general offensive leading to exhaustion, but an organized fight, step by step, always with a lot of artillery, precisely prepared and therefore efficient." Nevertheless, after this slow and careful preparation, the execution of the attack would be rapid. The French artillery also seemed to adopt different principles, being far enough forward so that it could fire on the German second line without moving, but concentrating overwhelmingly on counterbattery work. The French had such superiority in heavy artillery that their patrols found much of the German front lines had been evacuated by the time the French advance began.

The attack also seems to have been swifter than that of the BEF. In the area north of the Somme, for instance, the French XX Corps reached its first objectives, northeast of the village of Curlu, in one bound. In addition, French tactics were sensible. When Curlu was found to be heavily defended by machine guns located around the church, in basements, and in the cemetery, the French infantry was simply ordered to halt and wait for another thorough artillery preparation. This took place at six in the evening, when apparently Curlu still had the appearance of a village; after the half-hour hurricane artillery bombardment, an eyewitness reported that the village "was only razed houses, the place full of beams piled up, German bodies scattered among the debris, and shreds of German clothing lying about." On one of these German bodies was found an unposted letter written on June 28: "We are waiting. Let these bandits attack, and they will find out how they are received!" The confidence thus expressed was evidently misplaced, for the French attack took not only Curlu but the next German intermediate line as well. Similarly, south of the Somme, the excellent French I Colonial Corps took both the first and second German positions with a mixture of methodical preparation and élan.

In any reckoning of what went wrong for the British, it is important to understand what went right for the French. The difference resulted from a number of factors. The experience of Verdun had introduced realistic infantry and artillery tactics to the French, of which the speed of the infantry assault and the thorough rebombardment of Curlu were excellent examples. There were orders to use thin lines of attackers, strong enough to resist German counterattacks and overcome isolated points but not expected to take trenches in face-to-face fighting; they relied instead on the methodical artillery preparation and barrage to obtain their objectives. There was a conscious effort to minimize casualties, as well as a considerable element of surprise. To be sure, it also helped that the German defenses were weaker in the French sector, and that German counterattacks that day focused on the British.

But granted that the French had many critical advantages, why did the BEF's air and artillery domination fail to have greater results on July 1? There are many reasons. For example, bad weather between June 26 and 30 prevented proper air observation. The BEF lacked the technical ability to cut the German wire thoroughly, employing shrapnel against wire and trenches instead of using the more effective high-explosive shells. Moreover, it had to contend with poor fuses, many dud shells, and problems with guns, about 25 percent of which were defective. The lack of sufficient heavy-caliber guns and gas shells prevented the kind of penetration of deep German dugouts that the French had achieved, thus enabling the German machine guns to be quickly carried to the surface and brought to bear on the assault. There was also either inefficient or nonexistent counterbattery work in front of some divisions, often due to technical inexperience or simple exhaustion. Further, German artillery had been able to maintain some "silent" batteries, which did not open up until July 1, because observation from the high ground had enabled the Germans to have accurate preregistration. Perhaps most important, British artillerymen had had misunderstandings about the assault barrage at seven-thirty that morning. It not only moved too fast for the infantry, but also lifted off the enemy trenches as soon as the troops went over the top, thus giving German machine gunners about ten minutes in which to come out of the deep dugouts and start firing at the slow-moving British infantry. The German defenders could also see the attackers clearly because of the relatively late hour of the offensive; it did not begin earlier in the misty dawn because the artillery forward-observation officers wanted daylight to check the fall of the shells. (This decision was reinforced by the French, who wanted an even later hour: nine o'clock).

One other aspect is unquantifiable, but it relates to the reluctance of some branches of the British artillery, such as the Royal Horse Artillery, to depart from traditions and to learn new ideas and techniques. In contrast, the French

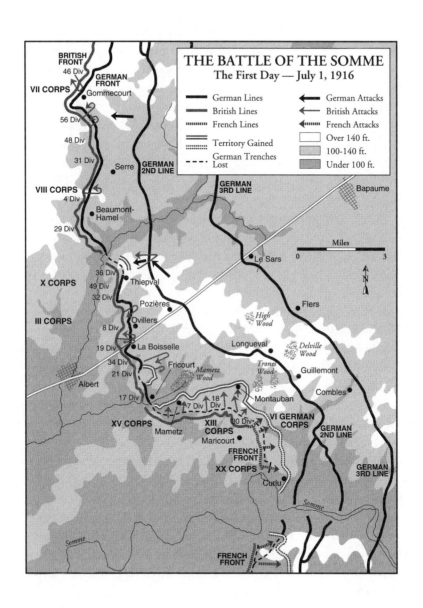

THE BATTLE OF THE SOMME
The First Day — July 1, 1916

▬▬▬ German Lines	◀▬▬ German Attacks
▬▬▬ British Lines	◀▬▬ British Attacks
▪▪▪▪▪ French Lines	◀▪▪▪ French Attacks
≣≣≣ Territory Gained	☐ Over 140 ft.
≣≣≣	▨ 100-140 ft.
▬ ▬ ▬ German Trenches Lost	▨ Under 100 ft.

BRITISH FRONT
46 Div
GERMAN FRONT
VII CORPS
Gommecourt
56 Div
48 Div
31 Div
Serre
GERMAN 2ND LINE
GERMAN 3RD LINE
Bapaume
VIII CORPS
4 Div
Beaumont-Hamel
29 Div
Le Sars
Miles
0   3
N
36 Div
Thiepval
X CORPS
49 Div
32 Div
Pozières
Flers
III CORPS
Ovillers
8 Div
High Wood
19 Div
La Boisselle
Longueval
Delville Wood
34 Div
Fricourt
Mametz Wood
Trones Wood
Guillemont
21 Div
Albert
17 Div
18 Div
Montauban
Combles
7 Div
XV CORPS
XIII CORPS
80 Div
VI GERMAN CORPS
GERMAN 2ND LINE
Mametz
Maricourt
FRENCH FRONT
GERMAN 3RD LINE
XX CORPS
Curlu
Somme
FRENCH FRONT
Somme
Somme

artillery was informal in the extreme, and it had much more experience, including Verdun, to draw upon. An artillery subaltern next to the French XX Corps at Maricourt noted:

> To the British soldier, trained in tidiness, order and discipline of spit and polish, their ways were a revelation and an endless source of amusement. . . . Harness was never cleaned, and was repaired with any material on hand, wire, rope or string. When teams returned to a wagon line all seemed chaos, no horse lines, no gun park. When a wagon and team stopped, their horses were tethered to wagon wheels, trees, fences, anything. They were fed in nose-bags, in tins off the ground, off old sacks. . . . Ammunition was taken up the line in a great variety of military and civilian vehicles. . . . Mediaevalism in equipment was everywhere, but they always got there. For that they held our admiration. . . .
>
> And at the guns, some of which were 1870 mortars, men and every sort of musical comedy uniform wandered about. Uniform—what a misnomer! I cannot remember seeing two French gunners dressed alike. . . . But they were cheery fellows, great workers and always had a smile for us.

One senses that this informality achieved greater efficiency than the more rigid BEF artillery system.

Yet despite all the problems of the BEF artillery, which tended to counteract the overwhelming BEF air domination, and despite the extreme rigidity and detail of the BEF Somme offensive plan—which in the VIII Corps required seventy-six pages from corps headquarters, with a 365-page supplement at the divisional level—there were some attempts at originality in the BEF. At least five divisions quietly advanced their men into no-man's-land before zero hour, to cut down on the distance to be crossed and to escape machine-gun fire for as long as possible. Some divisions also used smoke to protect their attack, especially in the Gommecourt diversion, even though this confused the troops more than it assisted them. Contrary to most historical accounts, some battalions and divisions did run across, such as the 2d Lincolns in the 8th Division, who made short rushes from shell hole to shell hole when 100 yards from the German front trenches; despite heavy losses from machine guns, some men managed to get into the German trenches.

Watching the 50th Brigade attacking toward Fricourt, Lieutenant Liddell Hart also observed an unusual tactic: The German 110th and 111th Reserve Infantry Regiments' fire "was so deadly that our men were forced to crawl. . . . Our Battalion [still] lost about 500 men crossing the 180 yards of No Man's Land." At the extreme southern part of the BEF's line, the XIII Corps had a much shorter distance to cover, and, especially in the 18th Division, there were better fire-and-movement tactics: Covering fire enabled troops to cross the ground more safely. Later in the day, a pilot overhead saw the renewed 34th Division attack on La Boisselle, which he reported was unusually swift:

> Our infantry left the trenches at four o'clock, & rushed across "No Mans Land." They reached the trenches headed by either an officer, or N.C.O. who was about 10 yards in front. They reached the line & could be seen getting through the wire, & hand to hand fighting with the Hun, several fell, & at last the remainder took the line.

There were also five mines to be exploded close to zero hour. In most areas these went up at seven twenty-seven or seven twenty-eight, which helped the men at zero hour. But north of the Ancre River, the commanding officer of the VIII Corps, Lieutenant General Sir Aylmer Hunter-Weston, decreed that the Hawthorn Redoubt mine should go off at seven-twenty, a full ten minutes before zero hour. He had originally wanted the mine to be fired at six o'clock the previous evening, but this was fortunately overruled at headquarters. In the end, the mine went off when it did because the divisional mining company wanted ten minutes to repair possible defects in the fuses, because Hunter-Weston thought that much time was needed to avoid falling debris, and because a special party was sent out to take the crater before the general attack, thus forcing the heavy artillery to lift there ten minutes before zero hour. This early mine explosion gave ample warning of the offensive to the Germans, who immediately deluged every British trench in the area with artillery and machine-gun fire. The special party did not manage to take the crater before the defenders arrived.

Even where the mines were successful, there was bloody fighting for the craters, as one pilot above the Y sap mine, at La Boisselle, reported in his logbook:

> Our infantry were also holding the eastern lip of the large newly formed crater. . . . The fighting around the crater must have been severe as many dozens of bodies could be seen lying about outside crater on the white chalk, & also inside crater. And as shrapnel burst over the crater others could be seen rolling down the steep incline on the inside.

To summarize: The heavy BEF casualties on the first day of the Somme were primarily a result of the three assumptions of Rawlinson, together with the mixed plan, which led to inappropriate infantry tactics. Rawlinson can be blamed, but his assumptions were not random or illogical, and the British high command certainly did not callously send infantrymen to their inevitable deaths. BEF technical shortcomings were evident, especially the lack of heavy artillery and effective ammunition, which prevented the British from dealing effectively with the deep German dugouts and machine guns. Even so, one surprising conclusion presents itself: A still greater disaster with yet higher BEF casualties was actually averted on July 1, because of the strong domination by the air and artillery arms of the BEF. These minimized the German counterbarrage and hindered German reinforcements. Without this advantage, especially in the south, whatever success the BEF enjoyed that day would have evaporated entirely, and the terrible losses would have mounted still higher. Quite apart from this horrific scenario, the careers of Haig and Rawlinson would probably also have suffered an early eclipse.

The tragedy of the first day of the Somme for the BEF has remained an emotional and controversial subject for nearly eighty years. Yet historical opinion may be swinging around to a grudging acceptance of the results of such bloody offensives as the Somme and Passchendaele. Although the whole Somme campaign cost the BEF around 420,000 casualties, and the Allies altogether some 620,000, the German army may have lost approximately 465,000 men. But Germany could less "afford" this total, and it appears, therefore, that the German army's collapse would not have been so complete in 1918 without the heavy casualties already suffered in 1916 and 1917. Thus, the sacrifices of the BEF and the French on July 1, 1916, and for the rest of the Somme campaign do, after all, have meaning.

THE SOMME:
THE LAST 140 DAYS
Robert Cowley

—

EVERYTHING ABOUT THE BATTLE OF THE SOMME STUPEFIES: the pulverized landscape, the profligate expenditure of matériel, the astronomical carnage, and, not least, the infinitesimal gains," this article notes. After four and a half months and more than 400,000 casualties—the remains of some 70,000 of whom have never been found—the British could boast of gaining forty-five villages, eight woods, and a maximum depth of seven miles. The combined casualties of the combatants is just over a million, after the first day. We will never know the exact number. The Somme may well be the bloodiest battle in history.

No one could have imagined the extent of the devastation to come. In hindsight, the "Big Push" should have been shut down after that first day. But offensives on the Western Front inevitably surrendered to the wishful thinking of remote staffs. The need to relieve pressure on the French at Verdun seemed still critical (though in fact, the last and most threatening push to the fortress city on the Meuse had already stalled for good). This was the offensive that had consumed the energies and imagination of Great Britain for two years: To abandon it would have been a demoralizing admission of defeat. Had he believed that his attack had totally failed, Haig was apparently prepared to shift northward, initiating a new offensive in Flanders. But the British Commander in Chief remained convinced that he was on the verge of victory. "Things are going well," he wrote his wife on July 2, "and I hope that, with perseverance and help from Above a considerable success may in time result." A week later, he told her that "In another fortnight with Divine help, I hope some decisive results may be obtained." By the middle of the month, however, he had ceased to invoke divine guidance. He had to admit that there would be no quick breakthrough. Instead, as the military historian and theorist B. H. Liddell Hart wrote, Haig "reverted to the nibbling method" so favored by the generals in the previous year. Even if it took all summer and then some, attrition would grind down the enemy and deplete his reserves.

But the temptation to focus too fixedly on Haig and the British must be resisted. Military historians have mostly portrayed the Somme as a British battle; it wasn't. The French gained more real estate (in their case, gained back) with fewer divisions, and at smaller cost. They advanced as much as five miles in the first ten days of July before they, too, bogged down. Only the French had the opportunity to make an operational triumph out of the Somme. If they had not paused to allow the British to catch up with them—giving the Germans a chance to recuperate—or if they had not lacked the manpower to exploit their early gains, they might have stretched the enemy defenses to their limits. In the end, they too reverted to nibbling.

But the German generals were responsible for fierce, costly nibbling of their own. It would do little to shape the outcome of the battle but much to add to its hecatombs and to hasten the decline of the world's best army. On July 2, Falkenhayn showed up at the headquarters of General Fritz von Below, the commander of the German Second Army. Obviously concerned about his own position (he would be sacked in favor of Hindenburg and Ludendorff before the summer was over), he proclaimed that "the first principle of position warfare must be to yield not one foot of ground; and that if it be lost to retake it by immediate counter-attack, even to the use of the last man." Von Below, in turn worried for his skin because of the enormous success of the French the previous day, backed Falkenhayn: "I forbid the voluntary evacuation of trenches," he said in his Order of the Day. "The will to stand firm must be impressed on every man in the Army. . . . The enemy should have to carve his way over heaps of corpses." The imagery was no more chilling than the result. Increasingly, as the British military historian John Terraine has noted, the Germans would mount a counteroffensive of their own. In the first two weeks of September alone, he has identified no less than seventy-eight counterattacks.

Attrition, the ascendancy of the body count, would become the essence of the Somme—though it was an open question as to who was "attriting" whom. This may explain why the British official historians took such pains to prove that the Germans had lost more men than the Allies at the Somme. During the two months between July 15 and September 15, the British lost more than 82,000 and won less ground than they had done on July 1. The machine gun may have ruled on that dismal first day, but now it was the turn of the artillery, that greatest killer of World War I. (Shell fire accounted for upwards of 70 percent of all casualties.) Artillery would also turn the Somme into a desert. In *The Imperial War Museum Book of the Somme,* Malcolm Brown quotes from the diary of Captain Alfred Bundy of the 2d Middlesex Regiment. The day was October 19, a month before the official end of the battle.

> Mud thin, deep and black, shell holes full of water, corpses all around in every stage of decomposition. . . . One bolt upright, a landmark and guide, another bowed as if trying to touch his toes. Our trenches are little more than joined-up shell holes, mostly with 12 inches of water above 12 inches of mud. A sunken road provides the only access under cover and this is al-

most constantly under shellfire. The casualties on this road are terrible. I had a very narrow escape myself. A 5.9 shell plunged into the mud just in front of me and didn't explode—1,000 to 1 chance. I was smothered with slime and had to scrape it out of my eyes to see. . . . Weather cold and wet. Sat in deep shell holes for shelter completely and utterly miserable.

As Liddell Hart, himself a Somme veteran, put it: "The historic 'cockpit of Europe' became the sump-pit of the British Empire." Or as Americans would say, the cesspool. But the Germans had similar thoughts. The Somme was, one of their officers wrote, "the muddy grave of the German field army."

———

ROBERT COWLEY is the founding editor of *MHQ: The Quarterly Journal of Military History.* He has edited two earlier *MHQ* anthologies, *No End Save Victory,* about World War II, and *With My Face to the Enemy,* about the Civil War, as well as the *What If?* series. He lives in Connecticut.

THE OLD ROMAN ROAD FROM ALBERT TO BAPAUME IS TWELVE MILES LONG and absolutely straight. Even allowing for a token deceleration through the three or four brief villages along the way, with their harsh straggle of brick houses and barns, you can scarcely avoid making the trip in twenty minutes or less. La Boisselle, Pozières, Le Sars: The highway is their main street, and except for an occasional tractor, nothing holds you up.

The beginning of the great plain of northern France is a landscape empty of surprises, until you notice the cemeteries. They seem to sprout up every- where, and in the most unlikely places: not only by the side of the road, but out in the middle of a wheat field or in the shadow of a dark and isolated burst of woodland. A faint groundswell may produce hundreds of headstones, a long gully, thousands, close-packed in orderly rows and boxed behind brick walls, like weathered tent cities turned into marble by mistake. The cemeteries give you a start at first, but you are past them soon enough.

Almost nine decades ago, when the Battle of the Somme was fought here in 1916, it was inconceivable that the land could ever again support anything but cemeteries. A man who was in the battle from beginning to end, and who somehow survived, once described to me the Albert–Bapaume road as it looked by the end of the year: "All you could see was a long line of stumps going straight on to nowhere." Five months of massed artillery fire had turned these rich plains and gentle downlands into a wasteland, "the most terrifying devas- tated area perhaps ever seen on our planet," the poet Edmund Blunden wrote. "I remember coming in sight of it for the first time; gunnery had extinguished every sign of life every step to the horizon and left a specimen of a world with- out a God. . . ."

Everything about the Battle of the Somme stupefies: the pulverized land- scape, the profligate expenditure of matériel, the astronomical carnage, and, not least, the infinitesimal gains. From July until mid-November 1916, the British ground their way up the road from Albert, a few hundred blasted yards at a time. They never did reach Bapaume that year, though troops shivering in the slimy trenches and waterlogged hellholes that passed for the ultimate front line could make out the tallest buildings three miles away, their fractured roofs showing above a last long, tantalizing rise. Nowhere did the British, or their French allies fighting astride the river Somme, drive the German army back more than seven miles on a front twenty-odd miles long; in places they gained nothing at all. They called it a victory anyway, and perhaps it was by Western Front standards. The debate has never been settled to anyone's real satisfaction.

The debate goes on about the losses, too. Nobody knows exactly how many were killed, wounded, reported missing (which mostly meant dead), or taken prisoner in those 140 days that followed July 1: Over the years, informed estimates have varied by the hundreds of thousands. Three million men fought on the Somme at one time or another; perhaps a third of them became casualties. The combined figure generally (but not unanimously) accepted today is just over a million, *after* the first day. If that is not unreasonable, then neither is the estimate of more than 200,000 dead. "I think 7,000 corpses to the square mile is not much of an exaggeration," wrote Charles Carrington, who was there; "ten to the acre shall we say, and your nose told you where they lay thickest."

A different kind of struggle began after July 1, one that would ultimately consume not just the British but everyone involved. The Somme, like a pandemic plague or an earthquake at the upper reaches of the Richter scale, assumed the character less of a battle than of a natural disaster, one of the overriding catastrophes of a catastrophic century. In many respects, after the first day, the worst was yet to come.

ATTRITION NOW REPLACED BREAKTHROUGH AS THE PRINCIPAL OBJECT, THE ANnounced justification for continuing the stalled offensive. The Allied commanders, British and French, turned into sudden converts to *la guerre d'usure*, the "wearing-out battle," the ceaseless step-by-step advance that would gradually exhaust the enemy until his front disintegrated. But this methodical approach only gave the Germans a chance to bring up reinforcements and to dig new defensive lines, particularly in places where gaps, opened on July 1, remained briefly unclosed. That early German weakness was most pronounced as the front approached the Somme and went beyond. (The British never fought on the river for which the battle was named until they extended their line to the south in January 1917.)

The French actually made impressive gains, advancing as much as five miles during the first ten days of July. They reached the high ground overlooking Péronne, the biggest town in the area, and the great bend of the Somme, where the river makes a right angle and heads due south. Troopers of the Chasseurs d' Afrique watered their horses in the river, and Zouaves gathered cherries in the outlying gardens of Péronne. For a brief time the Germans considered abandoning the great bend entirely.

Here the French paused, waiting for the British advance to catch up; it did not do so until the fall. But in the early stages of the battle, the French lacked the manpower sufficient to exploit their gains—or to expand pressure southward, which might truly have stretched the German defense to its limits. In addition, German stubbornness began to tell. The story of Estrées, a village that sits astride another of those plumb-straight Roman roads, is a case in point. The French reached Estrées on July 1, then began methodically to clear it out, house by house. By the fourth they had taken all but a few cellars. But for the next twenty days, a force of some 200 Germans refused to give up, firing their machine guns through vent holes at ground level. Finally, French heavy artillery pounded the tiny area for six hours. When the French stormed what was left of those last cellars of Estrées, they found only fifteen dazed survivors. By this time, as the military historian and theorist Basil Liddell Hart writes, French progress all along the line was "scarcely measurable."

Meanwhile, the British crept up the ridges flanking that other Roman road and spilled over on that plain that seems so high, though it is never more than 500-odd feet above sea level.

The gentle slopes are green to remind you
of South English places

wrote the poet David Jones, who fought with one of the Welsh regiments.

only . . .
grooved and harrowed crisscross whitely and the disturbed,
subsoil heaped up albescent.

Heavy rainstorms coming toward the end of the first week swamped trenches and turned the deranged earth into clinging slime. "Movement was often an agony," reports the British *Official History,* its stiff upper lip quivering ever so slightly. "Men fainted from sheer exhaustion whilst struggling through deep mud; in some localities a team of fourteen horses was required to bring up a single ammunition wagon." On the mistaken assumption that German reserves were limited, and in the fading hope that the British army might still batter its way through the last line of defense, an overoptimistic high command ordered attack after attack. They proved hasty, piecemeal, and mostly ineffective. Troops slogging upward as if in cinematic slow motion were easy targets for machine gunners—it was, unfortunately, a preview of the months to come.

The woods, relics of a forest once vast and unbroken, that lie scattered along the edge of the plain seemed to magnetize the action now. Mametz,

Trones, Delville, High Wood—the British became as obsessed with taking them as the Germans with holding them. In more peaceful times, local men of property had mainly kept them as private hunting preserves; they still do. Two years of neglect had turned these places into formidable obstacles. "To talk of a wood is to talk rot," one British officer said of a leafy objective he had been ordered to secure at all costs. "It was the most dreadful tangle of dense trees and undergrowth imaginable, with deep yawning broken trenches criss-crossing about it; every tree broken off at top or bottom and branches cut away, so that the floor of the wood was almost an impossible tangle of timber, trenches, undergrowth, etc., blown to pieces by British and German heavy guns for a week."

Mametz Wood was probably the most famous: If, on a scale of relative opprobrium, it was not the worst, it was the largest and one of the first to fall. Mametz Wood could also claim as many literary associations as any place on the Western Front. This was partly because persons such as Gerald Brennan and Liddell Hart happened through, and partly because other notable talents such as Jones, Robert Graves, and Siegfried Sassoon had, by chance or by background, found their way into the Welsh regiments that took most of Mametz.

The Welsh went into the wood at dawn on July 10. Let us follow the action of the next twenty-four hours through the eyes and ears of one soldier, Private John Ball, the protagonist of David Jones's *In Parenthesis*—presumably Jones himself. The day begins with a Somme set piece, the men rising "dry mouthed from the chalk" and moving up a shorelike incline, wave after diminishing wave, toward the dark wood ("the high grass soddens through your puttees and dew asperges the freshly dead"). A bewildered half dozen bunch up, "like sheep where the wall is tumbled," at a spot where artillery has blasted a passage, and are picked off by Brandenburghers perched in the trees. The survivors are engulfed by "a denseness of hazelbrush and body high bramble." The struggle for the wood becomes a confusion of bombs winged above thornbushes, of gray figures withdrawing into further thickets, and of the ominous clank of a machine-gun tripod; of coming into a clearing to find newly dead comrades "distinguished only in their variant mutilation"; of stragglers gathering and falling back and trying vainly to dig in ("But it's no good you can't do it with these toy spades"); of the man next to you hit and dying in your arms ("And get back to that digging can't yer—this ain't a bloody wake"); of trees crashing on wounded men and of water parties arriving at last with half their bottles punctured.

Night falls: A barrage mingles with deafening counterbarrage, and platoons grope through the "mazy charnelways" of this nightmare wood, seeking "to distinguish men from walking trees and branchy moving like a Birnam copse." Men panic. In the light of a flare, Ball glimpses the severed head of a friend, grinning "like a Cheshire cat." In the early-morning hours, he too is hit in the legs, but he manages to crawl back to safety: "To groves always men come both to their joy and their undoing."

Green was the color that everyone who had been at Mametz seemed to remember. A Welsh officer named L. W. Griffith, a sometime poet, could never again encounter the smell of cut green timber without "resurrecting the vision" of a tree that "held in its branches a leg, with its torn flesh hanging down over a spray of leaf." Brennan, who came searching for a friend after the capture of the wood, found it extraordinary that "all the dead bodies lay just as they had fallen, as though they were being kept as exhibits for a war museum." Their faces and hands, he said, were "a pale waxy green, the color of rare marble." Robert Graves, too, picked his way through this greening rubble of corpses one chilly July evening, while searching for German overcoats to use as blankets. There was no way to avoid the sight of the dead among the wilting litter of slash. He came across two men who had "succeeded in bayoneting each other simultaneously"—an unforgettable pair whom Brennan had also met— and were sustained in an upright position by the tree trunk against which their bodies had fallen.

Graves collected the overcoats; still feeling superstitious about taking from the dead, he told himself that they were only a loan. But the conventional barriers between living and dead were in fact disappearing. The living cadged food and water and collected souvenirs from the dead, joked about them and slept next to them, and built up their parapets with them when sandbags ran out. The two came to have a kind of ecological interdependence, like that of the Lapp with the reindeer. Once death ceased to be essentially tragic, a whole underlining of life and literature gave way. Heroes died for no reason—if, indeed, there were heroes left. A man who was killed "went west," not to heaven. The veterans of places like Mametz Wood had ventured into that psychological realm that Robert Jay Lifton, in his studies of the Hiroshima survivors, has since described as "death in life," their very boundaries of existence and perception shifting as surely and as permanently as the old frontiers of Europe. These were the men, Edmund Blunden wrote, "who were horrified by schematic death into a new poetry." It is no accident that in many of the memoirs they would one day publish, the experience of the Somme would be central.

But we cannot leave Mametz Wood without mentioning one further item in its catalog of horrors: poison gas. On the night of July 17–18, the Germans fired gas shells filled with lethal diphosgene for the first time on this battlefield, instead of the usual chlorine gas released from stationary cylinders. (The shells, stenciled with identifying green crosses, had been tried out a month earlier at Verdun.) Gas shells until now had been the lacrimatory kind that smelled of strong onions; the standing order was not to bother about gas masks, and that night Graves's company, moving up from Mametz Wood, lost half a dozen men.

At about the same time, Basil Liddell Hart was leading his company of Yorkshiremen through the wood in the opposite direction. "We suddenly heard a lot of shells landing around us, but as they did not explode with a bang, we imagined that they must be duds—until there was a strong smell of gas. . . . Coughing violently, I stayed to warn and divert the platoons that were following." The potentially lethal effects of the diphosgene could take as long as twenty-four hours to manifest themselves, and the next morning Liddell Hart was sent back on a stretcher, "feeling bad, but still unaware how bad." The tall, thin subaltern had been a runner in school, and his strong lungs probably saved his life. His war was over, but the most influential military historian of our time would spend the rest of his life elaborating on the original lessons of the Somme. In eighteen days he had seen enough of generals who bungled and missed chances by what he called the rigidity of their own inertia; his ideas would not be lost on other generations of military leaders. Liddell Hart, then twenty, had come up to the Somme in charge of eight junior officers. Five of them died on the first day of the battle, and the rest, including Liddell Hart, were all casualties by the end of July.

By the middle of the month, the British confronted not only the Germans' second fixed line of defense but the problem of how to avoid a repetition of the July 1 slaughter when they stormed it. This time they tried something new: surprise. In the darkness after midnight on July 14, lines of men, five divisions' worth of the Fourth Army, inched snakelike up the slopes, their faces and figures bathed in an ocher light from gun flashes or in a pale gray from flares arching over no-man's-land. They followed white tapes laid down earlier and assembled as close to the enemy lines as they could get without discovery. Some were as near as a hundred yards or less. Three days of steady shelling had pummeled the defenders and, more important, cut much of their wire. One observer reported that "the German front line system was unrecognizable as such, so severely had it been handled by the artillery."

The Germans were expecting an attack, but not before sunrise at the earliest. At three-twenty, just as the sky was beginning to pale, an intense bombardment erupted. Five minutes later the infantry went forward behind a creeping barrage. (The "creeping barrage" did not really creep; it jumped fifty yards at a bound—though to a distant observer it seemed to move forward at an even pace, hence the name.) The British breached a three-and-a-half-mile gap in the enemy's last completed trench system before the morning was over, and established a secure foothold along the crest of the ridge. Some 22,000 British troops took part, hardly more than the number who had died on July 1.

General Sir Henry Rawlinson, commander of the Fourth Army, saw the possibility of an advance into open country, followed by "a really decisive battle of Bapaume which should go near finishing the war." Indeed, something rare in the experience of the Western Front happened that day. Countryside, untouched by fighting, beckoned. Patrols, and even a careless brigadier, ventured far out into the wheat and barley, growing wild now, and saw nothing but a few horse-drawn guns and limbers disappearing, pell-mell, to the rear. High Wood, a seventy-five-acre copse that managed to dominate the plateau from its slight eminence, lay apparently empty. The surprise storm of Bastille Day, Liddell Hart wrote, had "brought the British to the verge of a strategic decision."

But German reserves arrived quicker than expected. The attack had the bad fortune of colliding with one German division just as 5,000 men of another were coming up to relieve it. A pair of Rolls-Royce armored cars that might have helped to exploit the gains bogged down in the mud before they reached the front. Meanwhile, according to plan, the British infantry in front of High Wood stopped to wait for the cavalry. The ground was so slippery that horses could hardly stand, and the cavalry did not appear until just before seven o'clock. After a day of rain showers, the sky was clearing, and the wide fields were flooded with that haunting amber light of midsummer evenings in northern France, faintly chilly but almost Mediterranean. Two squadrons of the 7th Dragoon Guards and the 20th Deccan Horse advanced—the Indian troopers wore turbans instead of helmets—pennants fluttering, bugles blowing, lances spearing an occasional fugitive hidden in the ripening grain.

It was a scene as memorable as it was meaningless. By nine-thirty, when darkness and German machine guns made further mounted action impracticable, the horsemen drew up in the shelter of a convenient road bank. They had advanced less than a mile, and they were withdrawn under cover of a dense fog in the early hours of the following morning. By that time two battalions of infantry had finally penetrated High Wood, but so had German counterattacks. High Wood—or what was left of it—would not fall for another two months.

Like the sepia-toned photographs of the "Big Push" that appeared week after week in the *Illustrated London News,* there is an unreal quality, monochromatic and at times out of focus, to events during the rest of the summer. The British attacked, the Germans counterattacked: little of territorial value was gained, little was lost. British casualties settled down to a norm of 2,500 per day, and the Germans probably suffered about the same number. That ominous phrase, "at all costs," seemed to creep into the official language of both sides in direct proportion to diminishing results. On July 2 the German supreme commander, Erich von Falkenhayn, made a statement that proved that Allied generals did not have a lock on callousness and bad judgment: "The first principle in position warfare must be to yield not one foot of ground; and if it be lost to retake it by immediate counterattack, even to the use of the last man." The next day, General Fritz von Below, whose Second Army held the Somme front, tried to go his boss one better. "The enemy," he announced, "should have to carve his way over heaps of corpses. . . ." (Before the summer was over, Falkenhayn would be replaced by the famous Hindenburg-Ludendorff partnership—less for his performance on the Somme than for his failure to destroy the French at Verdun.)

Falkenhayn's directive meant that a crack unit such as the Prussian Guards Battalion—called, after its crest, the Cockchafers—was required to hold out in the cellars of Ovillers until surrounded and practically annihilated. "It is said that arms were presented to them when they finally emerged as starving prisoners," the historian C.R.M.F. Cruttwell reports. But this sort of gallant gesture was going out of style. In close fighting, wounded enemies were often systematically dispatched, on the theory that they were still capable of killing. There was an unspoken rule that anyone resisting too long or too zealously—in another favorite official phrase, "to the last"—would not be taken prisoner. If you wanted to be spared, you spared somebody else.

"At all costs": Both high commands made particularly liberal use of the words at Delville Wood, which earned a reputation as the worst battle hell of the Somme. The "Devil's Wood" became an inferno, literally. Smoke and gases formed a canopy impervious to light, and trees continued to burn in spite of heavy rains. Those 154 acres consumed six German divisions. A South African survivor spoke of seeing the earth "strewn every yard with the rags of human bodies"; hundreds of men simply disappeared. Today, only one stump of the original wood remains, wedged between two intertwining trunks of a hornbeam tree.

"At all costs": In July and August, the Australians purchased, for a price of 23,000 men, a mile square of crater fields around the village of Pozières—high even by the going rate. The majority, presumably, were shell-fire casualties. A Lieutenant J. A. Raws of Melbourne wrote home to say that he was still alive but that the strain of the never-ending bombardment had driven two officers in his unit mad. He related how an explosion had buried him; struggling free, he had tried to extricate a man beside him. It was a decomposing corpse. Before the Australians were relieved, Raws himself would be one.

"At all costs": On July 29, the chief of the Imperial General Staff in London, General Sir William ("Wully") Robertson, wrote to warn General Douglas Haig,

British Commander in Chief, that the political "powers that be" were getting restive. "In general, what is bothering them is the probability that we may soon have to face a bill of 2–300,000 casualties with no very great gains additional to the present." But Haig was determined to have his way. He reasoned in his diary a few days later: "Our losses in July's fighting totalled about 120,000 more than they would have been had we not attacked. They cannot be regarded as sufficient to justify any anxiety as to our ability to continue the offensive."

As much as constant offensive wore down the British (and to a lesser extent, the French), constant counteroffensive had the same effect on the Germans—who could afford their losses much less. "By the end of July," writes the military historian John Terraine, "responding to every British or French advance or attempt to advance, the German infantry had made not less than sixty-seven counterattacks, large or small, that I can identify, but in fact a great many more, possibly twice as many." When the battle finally petered out in November, Terraine's count had risen to 330.

IN THE TWO MONTHS FOLLOWING JULY 14, THE BRITISH MANAGED TO PUSH THEIR line forward just 1,000 yards on a five-mile front. "The heavy scale of casualties suffered overall, along with the negligible gains of territory," the historians Robin Prior and Trevor Wilson write, "places this phase on an equal footing with the disastrous opening day of the Somme campaign." The British had had 57,000 casualties on July 1 and gained about three square miles. In the period from July 15 to September 14, they gained two and three-quarter square miles and lost 82,000.

They took most of those casualties in unsupported attacks of battalion size, rarely more than 800 men. Rawlinson did try one multidivision repeat of his July 14 predawn success, but the attacks were so badly coordinated that all hope of surprise was squandered. Inadequate artillery preparation missed defenders dug in on reverse slopes or machine gunners who operated from shell holes. Flares caught the British advancing across no-man's-land, wire held them up, and machine guns brought them down. Gains were negligible. But the Germans, too, were suffering huge losses, not only from their slavish reliance on the counterattack but from the sheer weight of British shell fire—6.25 million shells in this period alone.

That shell fire had an unforeseen effect, and one that completely changed the nature of the fighting. Shell fire killed plentifully; it also made matters more difficult for the attackers. Because the Germans found that it was safer not to depend on rigid trench systems, they took to living in shell holes with waterproof covering. As the tactical historian G. C. Wynne pointed out in the 1930s, "The system of defense from shell holes had the advantage that the enemy's artillery had no recognizable target in the isolated shelters and machine-gun nests. It had to batter a whole area of ground, using an immense quantity of ammunition, instead of a known and easily located trench-line." Too, once the infantry was no longer tied to one place, it "acquired freedom of movement. The foremost line . . . became really a zone or defended area within which the front units moved as the situation demanded." Random shell-hole warfare forced attackers to deal with a new battlefield reality: There had ceased to be, as it were, a there there.

Nothing, apparently not even the introduction of a possibly decisive secret weapon, could alter the inevitability of stalemate. The secret weapon was the tank. Though the idea of a heavily armored vehicle running on caterpillar tracks had been discussed for several years, it took the initiative of Winston Churchill, as First Lord of the Admiralty, to order the earliest working model of a "land battleship." Early in 1915, he illegally allotted some 70,000 pounds of Admiralty funds for the experiment. When he was forced to resign that spring as a result of the Gallipoli fiasco, he convinced his successor, Arthur Balfour, not to scrap his weapon. A single prototype, "Mother," gave a secret performance before a select audience of cabinet ministers and war-office and GHQ representatives in February 1916. David Lloyd George, then minister of munitions, watched the "ungainly monster," trapezoid-shaped and splendidly ponderous, "plough through thick entanglements, wallow through deep mud, and heave its huge bulk over parapets and various trenches. . . . Mr. Balfour's delight was as great as my own, and it was only with difficulty that some of us persuaded him to disembark from H.M. Landship while she crossed the last test, a trench several feet wide."

The boyish enthusiasm of the politicians was catching, and the army ordered a hundred of the "tanks." (The name seems to have originated in the deliberately misleading explanation given to the inquisitive who saw one of the secret machines under wraps and traveling by rail: "It's a tank.") The Mark I tank was big enough to carry a hot and uncomfortable crew of one officer and seven men. Its maximum speed was 3.7 miles per hour and it got a half mile to the gallon. Two heavy wheels connected to the back provided an additional aid to steering. There were two types, the "male" and the "female." The logic of the sexist world prevailed, of course: It was the male that had the cannon.

Much to the consternation of Churchill, who warned about exposing the secret prematurely, Haig determined to use tanks in a third all-out attempt to crack the German line, this time on September 15. It has been observed, in one of those gracefully backhanded conceits the English are so fond of, that a commander makes as great a mistake trying to fight with the weapons of the next war as with those of the last. To an extent this was true of the baptism of the tank, but critics like Churchill and Liddell Hart had a point when they said that Haig appeared more eager to redeem the fading prospects of his offensive than to give the tank a fair trial. Crews were scarcely trained and had only the sketchiest of tactical guidelines to follow; already some of the delicate behemoths were worn out from long hours on the proving grounds.

The habits of attrition were hard to shake. Instead of concentrating the machines in the hope of a single, shattering breakout—the "expanding torrent" principle that Liddell Hart would preach with such effect—Haig allowed them to be parceled out in "packets" scattered along a ten-mile front. In some places the tanks went ahead of the infantry, clearing the way; in others they crawled at a respectful distance behind it, mopping up, accompanied by an officer and six men who moved the wounded from their path. They did not steer very well.

About forty minutes after dawn on the morning of September 15, an eighteen-year-old observation pilot named Cecil Lewis looked down on the smoking front and noticed something curious. Lewis, who in *Sagittarius Rising* (1936) gives us the best account of air combat in the Great War, observed amid the shell bursts "dark lanes, drawn as it might be by a child's stubby finger in dirty snow." Along these lanes, where no shells fell, the tanks were about to advance. He could not know, of course, that line officers were telephoning frantic requests for the artillery to fill the gaps, which were serving no purpose. Of the forty-nine tanks that had set out the previous night, more than half had broken down before they reached their assembly points, or were unable to start at the six-twenty zero hour.

Tanks broke down immediately, split their treads, got stuck in crater fields or hung up astride German trenches, lost direction and fired on their own men, obeyed confused orders to turn back, or cruised around killing aimlessly until hit and disabled (their operative speed turned out to be one-half mile per hour, making them choice targets). A few Germans even panicked at the sight of them and ran or surrendered.

Toward eight-thirty, a reconnaissance plane reported sighting a tank "with large numbers of British troops following it" through the main street of Flers, a village a mile and a half behind the German front line. Correspondents hungering for a bone of good news fleshed out this information with a meaty detail: The troops were cheering. This was the image that caught the imagination at home, and it provided Haig with the public-relations triumph that had eluded him all summer.

For the moment, the cheering men of Flers drowned the rising volume of criticism and persuaded the public that encores were needed. Not for nothing were thousands of families receiving their packets of last effects, which sometimes included shreds of a bloody uniform suitable for burying in the backyard. Possibly the bereaved at home would not have been heartened to know that the "cheering army" behind the tank was a batch of German prisoners being formed up—or that when the tank turned back into the morning mists, it left a breakthrough to be exploited by only two officers and twenty-nine men.

One of the officers, an East Surrey man, strolled alone beyond the village and out into apparently unoccupied country. It was a fine autumn morning, with some clouds, and the uproar of battle was all in back of him now. The road to Bapaume, which he followed, dips down and passes through a brief cut—did he walk that far? He must have looked suspiciously for movement in the high grass, but—shades of July 14—the single sign of life he observed was a team of enemy gunners harnessing up and hauling off a heavy howitzer. He could do nothing to stop them; "unfortunately I had only one precious clip left. Later the vision of Germans advancing in perfect drill-book order sent me back toward the village."

The lengthening casualty lists of the Somme seemed to touch everyone. At the beginning of September, the Liberal prime minister, Herbert Asquith, went to see the battlefield for himself. He inspected the "caterpillars," drank rather too much of Haig's old brandy (Haig thought), and urged the Commander in Chief not to dissipate his surprise in local attacks. One lovely hot day near Fricourt, Asquith met his eldest son, Raymond, who was waiting on horseback at a crossroads. Raymond, though overage for a subaltern at thirty-eight, was yet the model of the New Army volunteer: aloofly handsome, a family man, and a barrister, whose sharp wit and general gifts marked him for greater things. ("Lawyers are a curse to our country," Haig once said.) The prime minister found his son looking "so radiantly strong and confident that I came away from France with an easier mind."

Raymond Asquith was mortally wounded leading the first wave of the September 15 attack. "One might have known that nothing so brilliant and precious could escape," his brother's wife, Lady Cynthia Asquith, wrote in her diary. "Now I feel I have really relinquished all hope and expect no one to survive. . . . all our intellect is being chucked away in the trenches." The prime minister was inconsolable. "Whatever pride I had in the past," he wrote on September 20, "and whatever hope I had for the far future—by much the largest part of both was invested in him. Now all that is gone. It will take me a few days more to get back my bearings." As Asquith's biographer Roy Jenkins notes, it took him much longer than that. He grew uncommunicative, skipped cabinet meetings, and only by an effort of will did he get through a parliamentary speech in mid-October. Meanwhile Lloyd George had initiated his behind-the-scenes campaign against Asquith. The old man was clearly no longer up to a struggle for power, and the events on the Somme did not strengthen his position. In December, after nine years as prime minister, he resigned. Lloyd George formed a new government.

DURING THE NIGHT OF SEPTEMBER 15, SQUALLS SWEPT THE DARKENED battlefield, and Haig's last bid for a breakout subsided into the mud like a derelict tank (how many of them there were now). But the Somme, and the Somme rains, continued. Thiepval and Schwaben Redoubt fell, two objectives of July 1, and the British took over ground still covered by the dead of that day. Intelligence reports had convinced Haig that the enemy was ready to give way, if only suitable pressure could be maintained—and, in fact, not until 1918 would the Germans on the Western Front experience such a dangerous man-power crisis. "In the end," wrote the geographer Douglas W. Johnson, "the water-soaked loam proved the best ally of the Germans."

Though the mud of Ypres in 1917 is more renowned, the mud of the Somme in 1916 had the same rich and heavy body, and the same distinctive bouquet. "The connoisseurs, survivors of both battles," Captain Cyril Falls remarks, "still argue about which was the better year. Ypres the more holding, but the Somme the more slippery is one verdict."

Roads dissolved into deep slime, food and ammunition had to be dragged forward on sledges improvised from sheets of corrugated iron, and horses and mules sank to their bellies and had to be shot. The "dry places" that ration parties used as stepping-stones often proved to be corpses—as Edmund Blunden remembered, "those bemired carcasses . . . have not yet ceased to serve 'the great adventure.' "

James Lockhead Jack, a Scottish colonel commanding a West Yorkshire battalion, noted in his diary entry of October 24 that his men had carried out a relief "in persistent rain, deep mud, shell fire and bullets," following a day of disastrous but otherwise unremarkable attacks in front of a hamlet called Le Transloy. There are few more quietly harrowing accounts of the sullen winding down of the Somme than his, with its record of an exhaustion that was overtaking both sides.

October 25th

The weather has become worse. . . . One patrol . . . captures 16 prisoners, who say they would have surrendered earlier but their sergeant—

evidently a hard-hearted man—would not allow it.

We have lost today 3 officers and 41 other ranks . . . nearly all from shellfire.

October 26th

. . . There are no dugouts in the forward area. . . . officers and men have no cover from the fearful weather except their waterproof sheets rigged up in the trenches to form roofs. . . . The battalion casualties today number 30, chiefly to carrying parties and to support companies. I am quite sick with wondering how to obviate further losses. . . .

October 28th

. . . In the communication trench . . . the knee of a German partially buried by the shell that killed him forms a stile over which we step daily; further on the head of another . . . protrudes from the trench bottom.

The dead of the action of the 23rd lie on the open ground, a daily sickening sight.

Their hardships did not end with their relief on the eighth day: Jack and his men had to march back five miles at night. He was a Regular Army officer who had seen the worst the war could offer, including the slaughter of July 1, and he was not disposed to open emotion. But when he visited with his battalion the next morning, he admitted that "I can scarcely keep sufficiently composed to say a few words to the gaunt, exhausted, patient lads."

BUT THE DUCKBOARDS COULD LEAD TO AN EVEN MORE SURREAL CONCLUSION. ON September 15, Haig's troops had captured Le Sars, a single street of brick astride the Roman road. Beyond the village, the road dips into a broad depression and then starts gradually over the final ridge before Bapaume, now only three miles away. The more that chimera tantalized, the more elusive it seemed to grow: In the next two months, Haig managed to nudge his reluctant line another four or five hundred yards down the forward slope. Charles Carrington— one of those remarkable memoir-writing subalterns—did three tours here in the late autumn. "Life was entirely numbed," he remembered; "you could do nothing. There could be no fighting since the combatants could not get at one another, no improvement of the trenches since any new work would instantly be demolished by a storm of shellfire. . . . We huddled and hid in piles of old brickwork and rafters, or behind hedgerows which had bounded cottage gardens, scrabbing our way deeper into mud-holes, and painfully trying to keep our rifles clean."

This "new valley of humiliation," as Carrington described it, was dominated by a man-made monstrosity, an ancient burial mound that the locals called the Butte de Warlencourt. "What Gallic chieftain slain by Caesar in the land of the Ambiani lay beneath this tumulus we neither knew nor cared," he wrote. When the British had first caught sight of the butte in September, it was still green; but by now all vegetation had been blown away, and it rose out of the mud, a gleaming, pockmarked dome of chalk perhaps sixty feet high. The terror of the machine guns that fired down from the slopes was probably imaginary, but it was an inhibiting terror nevertheless. "That ghastly hill, never free from the smoke of bursting shells, became fabulous," Carrington wrote. "It shone white in the night and seemed to leer at you like an ogre in a fairy tale. It loomed up unexpectedly, peering into trenches where you thought yourself safe: it haunted your dreams." He spent a total of fifteen days and nights under the butte, an experience that left him "a nervous wreck," though he never glimpsed a German soldier. (It is probable that early in October, two future antagonists, Anthony Eden and Adolf Hitler, came within rifle shot of each other here. Hitler was wounded by a shell fragment on October 7.)

How odd, how appropriate that the British advance should spend itself before this death's-head, a place already haunted in its benign aspect. Its capture possessed them, out of all proportion to its real worth: The Germans probably used the butte for observation only. Like men bent on snatching the prize from the top of a glass mountain, the British refused to give up.

Three understrength battalions of the Durham light-infantry regiment made the last serious attempt in a morning downpour on Sunday, November 5. (In London, 150 miles away, Lady Asquith wrote in her diary of the "terrific gale" that raged all day—"by evening it had become mythical and one was told of overturned buses, blown-in shop windows, and so on." The next morning she went out and bought a sou'wester outfit.) You wonder what higher obstinacy refused to intervene, though apparently there was argument. Every so often a personality half emerged from the close-packed but bloodless pages of the *Official History*, in this case the general who commanded the brigade to the right of the Durhams—an Australian, naturally, Brigadier General J. Paton. He wanted a postponement, was overruled, and returned to the front, to be wounded by a sniper.

Nothing seemed to go right. Zero hour had been fixed at nine-fifteen in the morning, but the Durhams reached the line with just fifteen minutes to spare. "The enemy position was exceptionally strong, the trenches from which the attack started were so muddy that several men were drowned in them, and the time for preparation was so short that the attack broke down almost as soon as it had started," reported the historian of the 6th Durhams. In places, they were stopped by their own artillery and machine guns firing short. There was a moment, though, when men of the mired battalions looked up and saw the solitary figure of a British soldier on the summit of the butte. He paused, as if awaiting some sunlit signal of apotheosis, and then passed down out of sight. One battalion of the Durhams clung to the butte all that day. Counterattacks, which they could plainly see forming up, wore them down and threatened to cut them off; reinforcements, if any were available, never arrived. Around midnight they withdrew to their original lines. In a contest between somnambulists, who dreams about winning? According to another historian of the Durhams, "A German in a drunken condition actually walked down the Bapaume road during the attack into the 9th battalion. His sole expressed desire was to sleep."

The monthlong operation, of which the struggle for the butte was a part, was called in the British *Official History* the Battle of the Transloy Ridges. In effect, the British formed themselves at the bottom of a new valley and attempted, without success, to slip and slide upward. Bapaume was the prize; endless small attacks went nowhere. The Germans added a new tactical wrinkle: They withdrew their machine guns beyond the area on which the creeping barrage fell and, unscathed, were able to inflict heavy casualties through long-range fire. In the whole month of October, barely a yard of ground changed hands; failure merely seemed to reinforce failure.

At the beginning of November, Lord Gort, the man who was to command the British army in 1940, came back from an inspection trip to the front. He described to Haig men "living on cold food and standing up to their knees in mud and water." In attacks troops had to "help each other out of the fire trenches as they cannot get out unaided." That same day, November 3, there was even a bit of what the historian Tim Travers describes as an "upper level 'mutiny,' " when Lord Cavan, the corps commander in front of Le Transloy, complained to Rawlinson that all further attacks should be called off: "No one who has not visited the front trenches can really know the state of exhaustion to which the men were reduced. . . . all my General Officers and Staff Officers agree that conditions are the worst they have seen." Cavan even persuaded Rawlinson to take a look for himself. At dawn one morning the two generals actually trudged 150 yards or so beyond the frontline wire. Rawlinson agreed that a general attack was impossible. But Haig overruled him. The attacks—and the casualties—continued.

Haig's reasoning was that constant attacks would wear down the morale of the German army. They were having an even worse effect on his own men.

The Germans may have shared the same unspeakable conditions at the front, but at least they did not have to struggle through several miles of tortured mudscape to reach their uncertain destinations. The crater fields on the German side, which advanced only as the Allies did, petered out after a mile or so, and the countryside beyond was refreshingly green. Roads ran right up to the German communications trenches, and it was easier for supplies to reach the front. Shelter, food, and artillery support were closer at hand. All this gave the Germans a constant edge.

Still, the strain was showing on them. Louis Barthas, a corporal in the French 296th Infantry Regiment, records a strange episode that happened during the Transloy push, one that points to the exhaustion and despair of some German troops. Ordered to attack on the morning of October 23, the French dug attack trenches in no-man's-land, to shorten the distance they would have to cross. In the fog and darkness, one group dug closer to the Germans than they had intended—but the enemy troops were apparently so fatigued that they heard nothing. The next morning, when the fog blew off, the French found themselves just a few steps from the Germans—most of whom simply raised their arms in surrender, shouting, "Comrades! Comrades!" The French took fifty-two prisoners. They also found a dead German officer, his head beaten in, and beside the body, the bloody shovel with which one of his own men had dispatched him.

NORTH OF THE SOMME, THE FRENCH ACTUALLY FOUGHT THEIR WAY ACROSS THE steep valley and gained a foothold on the top of the Transloy Ridges. They reached the linked villages of Sailly-Saillisel, astride the main highway between Bapaume and Péronne, on October 15, and there followed a month of desperate clawing back and forth for possession of smoking rubble heaps. Down the road was Saint-Pierre-Vaast Wood, which was, according to the 1919 Michelin Guide to the Somme, "the most important vestige of the immense Arrouaise Forest that covered the whole of this region in the Middle Ages." The Germans had created a maze of trenches and fortified redoubts in its thickets. In one of those overlooked environmental tragedies of the war, it was reduced to a shattered stump field. The French pushed partway into the wood at the beginning of November, and were pushed out again. The British took over the western fringes in December, and for the next months, grenade fighting from trench to trench was constant and Allied artillery continued to level the wood, which protected Péronne from the north. "The country in front of St.-Pierre-Vaast Wood is a place of horror," wrote a German officer, Rudolf Binding, on January 8, 1917:

I was out there one of the last nights. For days and weeks the earth there has been churned up again and again to its very depths. Dead men and animals, arms and equipment, are tossed about in mud and slime, splashed up on high, pounded down into the earth again, again thrown up and torn to pieces until they are things without form or shape.

Though the French experience on the Somme has been imperfectly recorded (as opposed to Verdun), an impressive number of divisions passed through its meat grinder; no less than thirty served both at Verdun and at the Somme. The fact is that the French gained a good deal more ground than the British, at about half the cost. Their artillery was more effective, and their veteran infantry was the equal of the German. As Liddell Hart explains, "The campaign policy of the French, except when engaged in active operations, was 'live and let live,' and in retrospect there seems little doubt that it was wiser than the British policy of continual 'strafing.' " As a French observer commented about his allies: "They attack in and out of season, break down when they ought to go through; and with a certain spiritual strength, say: 'Oh, well, failed today; it'll be all right tomorrow.' Nevertheless, there are still so many shells wasted and so many men lost. To sum it up, they still lack savoir-faire." The legend of a Somme map in a recent British atlas of World War I is unnecessarily churlish: "Although the French gains appear larger than the British gains on the map, the actual fighting was much harder on the British front." Still, after the first days of July, the French never did come close to a breakthrough. For them, the view of the shattered roofs of Péronne, in the hollow at the great bend of the Somme, remained as teasing as those of Bapaume were for the British.

YOU CAN ALMOST CHART THE PROGRESS OF THE GREAT WAR IN ITS CASUAL exclamations. Sir Edward Grey's remark in August 1914, about the lamps going out all over Europe, had become, by November 1916, the last words of the writer H. H. Munro (Saki): "Put that bloody cigarette out." None would ever be lit again in his lifetime. Lance Sergeant Munro of the Royal Fusiliers, the fashionable author of O. Henry-ish tales who had chosen to bury himself in the ranks, was shot moments later in a crater near Beaumont-Hamel. He was perhaps the most notable literary casualty of the Great War in his own time.

Munro's battalion took part in the last official action of the Somme campaign, an offensive set piece along the Ancre front on November 13–18 that caught the Germans off guard: Given the condition of the terrain and the time of year, further attacks had seemed inconceivable. They obviously had not reckoned on the tenacity of the enemy high command. Though the British managed to advance the line as much as two miles, they still fell short of the objectives of July 1 in this sector. The Battle of the Somme, which had begun in the pleasant sunshine of one morning, ended in the snow and darkness of another, with the indistinct figures of the infantry groping their way forward yet one more time over the white ground.

Do we judge the Somme by this final image? Almost any conclusion about it invites challenge or contradiction. Let us forget the debate over casualties immediately: You can prove anything you want according to what set of statistics you choose. How many skeletons could dance on the head of a pin? Bone counting became an almost religious rite, an Aquinas-like exercise in military theology, conjuring numbers that were both magical and exculpatory. The British *Official History* even found a way of inflating German casualty figures to between 660,000 and 680,000, or considerably more than the combined Allied total. What surer ratification of victory could there be?

If the Allies did not achieve their breakthrough, did stalemate constitute defeat? Which do we weigh more heavily: the slaughter of the first day and the missed opportunities of the 140 following, or the increasing desperation of the defenders? If the process of attrition hardly provided a stirring advertisement for itself, did its dim benefits nevertheless vindicate the principle? Who did win in the end? Or rather, who could least afford what he lost?

On that score, the decision must go to the Allies, narrowly and on points. Their losses, in a strictly military sense, were not irreplaceable; those of the enemy were. The old, highly trained core of the German infantry disappeared on the Somme. The battle was, as a Captain von Hentig wrote, "the muddy grave of the German field army, and of the faith in the infallibility of the German leaders, dug by British industry and its shells." His verdict is echoed again and again. The Germans had lost the most important battle of all, the one they contemptuously referred to as the "material-battle." Hentig added, "The German Supreme Command, which entered the war with enormous superiority, had fallen behind in the application of destructive forces, and was compelled to throw division after division without protection against them into the cauldron of the battle of annihilation." Industry prevailed where men could only endure—that is the lesson of the Somme, as it is of all conventional modern wars.

Attrition did have its risks, for the quality of the British army had also deteriorated since July 1, and in 1916 there was no guarantee of a transfusion of American blood. The Germans would soon remedy that. As the Somme subsided, they came to recognize that victory on the battlefield was no longer possible—but in spite of some unconvincing feelers that winter, so was the peace table. Both sides had simply lost too many men to compromise without fear of the consequences. At the beginning of February 1917, Germany declared a policy of unrestricted submarine warfare. The German Admiralty calculated that their U-boats could starve England into submission before the next harvest. They nearly did—but they also brought America into the war.

The strain of the Somme manifested itself in a second major decision a few days later. Back in September, after the Hindenburg-Ludendorff partnership had taken over the Supreme Command, they had ordered the building of a vast and sophisticated trench system far to the rear of the Somme battlefield; it extended, roughly, from Arras to Soissons. It was thought of only as a precautionary measure then, but by midwinter—the worst in twenty years—the prospect of retirement could no longer be put off. The Germans retreated to their new position, which the British called the Hindenburg Line, leaving a desert in their wake. Towns were destroyed by fire or explosive, wells were fouled with horse manure and dead horses, craters were blown in roads, dugouts were booby-trapped, and apple orchards were cut down. (This last seemed to evoke more indignation than all the deaths on the Somme, the classical-minded recalling the Spartan destruction of the Athenian olive trees 2,300 years before.) Ironically, the Allied infantry and cavalry had become so accustomed to the French stalemate, and were so bewildered by their first taste of open warfare, that they let the enemy slip clean away. You can take the German retreat either as a move of brilliance—by shortening his line, Ludendorff conserved thirteen or fourteen divisions—or as an admission of defeat. It was a little of both. As the British advanced, at last taking possession of the Butte de Warlencourt and the burned-out shell of Bapaume, they noticed a sign erected on a town hall: DON'T BE ANGRY, ONLY WONDER!

Can there be a better epitaph for the Somme?

D DAY 1917
Rod Paschall

—

G ERMANY'S CAMPAIGN OF UNRESTRICTED SUBMARINE warfare against all ships entering designated war zones around Great Britain was inaugurated on February 1, 1917. A blockade in reverse, it was a measure of desperation that nearly worked. The Germans knew that it would almost certainly bring the United States into the war, as in fact it did, and in just two months. That risk would be more than balanced if the submarine campaign could strangle Great Britain before the Americans arrived in numbers great enough to make their presence felt. As the gross tonnage sunk climbed over the million mark, a mood of pessimism seized the British leadership. Food shortages loomed (though the nation would never come as close to outright famine as Germany did). There was talk of shutting down far-flung campaigns like Salonika because of the mounting problem of supply. Would Germany force the Allies to the peace table? No voice of gloom in the government was more influential than that of Admiral John R. Jellicoe, the hero of Jutland who was by now the First Sea Lord. If shipping losses weren't checked, he said, Britain might be knocked out of the war. "There is no good discussing plans for next spring—we cannot go on."

Much of Great Britain's angst settled on the coast of Belgium, which, since 1914, had been mainly held by the Germans. Not only were ports like Ostend and Zeebrugge bases for submarines but they posed a threat to the Channel supply route, should the Germans choose to mass destroyers there. "If the army can't get the Belgian coast ports," Jellicoe told

Haig, "the navy can't hold the channel, and the war is lost." Moreover, should a negotiated peace come to pass, Germany might claim those Belgian ports, and would thus remain, in Jellicoe's words, "a menace to the existence of Great Britain." Possession would trump legitimate ownership.

The need to recapture the Belgian coast became a principal rationale for going ahead with Haig's Ypres offensive. It also gave birth to one of the few genuine inspirations of the war—an invasion of Belgium from the sea. Haig's innovative plan, which Rod Paschall describes here, may have been doomed from the start. But he had glimpsed the future, and in another war his ideas would work.

Meanwhile the submarine menace would largely recede, thanks to the introduction that summer of the convoy system. Jellicoe's lukewarm support of the idea would get him fired before the year was out. And once started, the Flanders offensive would take on a dismal life of its own.

———

ROD PASCHALL is the editor of *MHQ: The Quarterly Journal of Military History*. The former director of the U.S. Army Military History Institute, he is the author of *The Defeat of Imperial Germany*.

O N NEW YEAR'S DAY 1917, THERE SEEMED TO BE LITTLE HOPE FOR EITHER THE Allies or the Central Powers. Despite countless attacks and hundreds of thousands of deaths in the trenches of the Somme, Verdun, the battlefields of Mesopotamia, Palestine, Italy, and the Eastern Front, the Great War was still hopelessly stalemated. New fronts had been opened, new techniques tried, but they all came to the same end: An entire generation of western youth was being relentlessly slaughtered. It had to be different in 1917.

The war's leaders were characteristically optimistic. The Russians were planning a huge offensive. The Germans were to begin unrestricted submarine warfare. General Erich Ludendorff, head of the German General Staff, had a scheme to take Russia out of the war and was implementing a greatly improved defense system on the Western Front. The French had a new Commander in Chief, the enthusiastic General Robert Nivelle, who claimed his innovative offensive methods could finally bring the war to an end. General Douglas Haig, the British commander on the Western Front, was now gathering enough tanks, trucks, and supporting aircraft to create a different form of combat: mechanized warfare. London was also building a formidable strategic bombing force. Air raids deep into the heart of Germany might be possible. It could be different in 1917.

But to Admiral Reginald H. Bacon, the Royal Navy officer responsible for the defense of the English Channel, New Year's optimism was tempered with a healthy dose of skepticism. If the newly planned Allied efforts on the Western Front were not successful, the war might grind down to a negotiated peace, leaving the Germans still holding a good part of the Belgian coast. That, in turn, raised the Royal Navy's age-old horror: At war's end, Britain could be facing hostile ports on the Channel, and isolation from the Continent would be a distinct possibility.

Bacon worked long and hard to convince both his superiors and Haig of the importance of taking the Belgian coast out of German hands. Haig was committed to a summer attack in Belgium—as part of a general Allied offensive, not an operation aimed primarily at liberating the coast. But as the U-boat toll on Allied shipping mounted alarmingly that spring, the elimination of submarine bases at the Belgian ports of Ostende and Zeebrugge seemed ever more urgent. Haig warmed to Bacon's ideas, and the two officers worked together, developing a novel amphibious plan. Their target was a stretch of beach a few miles north of the Yser River, close to the point where the Western Front ended in the North Sea dunes. Among the confidants, the resulting scheme was referred to as "the Great Landing."

Bacon and Haig's plan had to satisfy a number of demanding tests to be considered "great," or even promising. First, since most offensive military operations (particularly amphibious operations) hinge on surprise, there had to be secrecy during the preparations. Second, the plan had to include neutralizing German beach defenses. This would be difficult because the Germans had fortified the Belgian coast with no less than 100 guns, ranging in caliber from 4 to 11 inches. Third, even if the invaders managed to silence the German guns, they still had to ensure the rapid disembarkation of a ground force. After all, the inability to quickly build up strength ashore had been one of the prime reasons for British grief in the Dardanelles landing two years earlier.

The Dardanelles tragedy also suggested a fourth and vital planning factor: The landing force had to be positioned so that the Germans could not isolate it. There had to be provisions for substantial reinforcement; the Great Landing had to be in close proximity to a general British advance. It was essential that the defenders be hard-pressed and pinned down. Finally, the gains of the plan had to outweigh the inevitable costs.

The two commanders had begun their work in 1916; surprise and secrecy were foremost in their minds. When he described his plans for the summer, Haig was careful to avoid telling his ally, Nivelle, of the intended amphibious assault. The French general was known to talk too much. Haig waited until April before informing the prospective leader of the operation, and swore his subordinate to secrecy. Bacon was equally careful. Ships, boats, and landing craft were sequestered in uninhabited estuaries along the English coast, their crews under a strict quarantine. A special staff of censors read all outgoing mail, and a hospital ship was provided so that sick or injured crewmen did not have to be evacuated from restricted areas. The landing craft were placed in a separate hideaway, apart from the supporting ships, and consolidation for rehearsals was done mostly under cover of darkness.

The landing force—the 13,000-man British 1st Division—was assembled under similar quarantine conditions in late July, but on the French coast near Dunkirk, far away from the invasion craft. The two forces were to be united at night and make their way up the coast so as to begin the run in to the beach just at dawn. A feint was planned farther up the coast, well away from the actual landing site. The British hoped to confuse the Germans further by employing eighty smoke-generating boats that would precede the invasion flotilla almost up to the shoreline.

Secrecy would probably end with the appearance of seven British monitors. These huge, shallow-draft, heavily armored, battleshiplike vessels mounted 12- and 14-inch cannon and were normally used as seagoing gun platforms. They were Bacon's antidote to the German coastal-defense system.

The monitors were also vital to the rapid-debarkation requirement. Six of them worked in pairs, each pair attached on either side to an enormous steel pontoon over 550 feet long. Troops and equipment of the 1st Division were to be distributed on the six monitors and three giant pontoons. In effect the invasion force was creating an artificial port by bringing its own three piers, already loaded with artillery, vehicles, and troops. Trials indicated the entire division would be on dry land twenty minutes after the bows of the pontoons touched Belgian soil.

Bacon went to great lengths to ensure that monitors and pontoons would not ground short of the waterline. His biggest problem was the lack of accurate data for depths along the shoreline. He solved the problem by sending aircraft over the coast to photograph the outgoing tide every twenty minutes or so. Relying, too, on figures supplied by a depth-sounding submarine, Bacon was able to calculate the beach slope accurately.

As early as September 1916, Haig had encouraged Bacon to include tanks in the landing force. But the energetic admiral and his staff ran into a new problem: a formidable seawall only a few yards from the beach. The wall's steepest slope was sixty degrees, and British tanks could negotiate only a thirty-degree incline. Bacon's men built a replica of the wall, then fashioned a triangular ramp of timber and fitted it to the nose of a tank. The contraption could be dropped from inside the tank onto the wall in front of the machine's treads. The test was a success. Bacon could assure Haig that the thirty artillery pieces, twenty-four motorcycles, and six motor ambulances of the landing force would now be led by nine tanks in the initial assault.

Once ashore, the 1st Division might join a battle already in progress. The division would assault German artillery units that were a mile and a half behind the enemy front line. The Germans were going to be suffering a tremendous artillery bombardment during the landing, from both the Royal Navy and Allied artillery units opposite German lines. While the first pair of monitors and their attached pontoon landed troops near German artillery, the other two pairs would be landing troops farther to the German rear, behind the enemy's second line of defense. The three landing sites were to be about a mile apart from each other. With an attack on the German front in progress, the amphibious operation was designed to take the Germans in the flank and rear. The idea was to "unhinge" German forces from the beach. Of the possible options, this scheme was probably the least likely to result in isolated and stranded British amphibious units.

The invasion would actually be part of a combined operation, which seemed to further guarantee its success. Even as the 1st Division was landing, units holding a shallow bridgehead north of the Yser would push forward and join it. In June the British relieved French units along the coast and quickly put a company of Australian miners to work digging a tunnel from the bridgehead trenches toward the German defensive position on the dunes. Tunnels had not been attempted in the sandy coast before, but the Australians developed a technique of shoring their excavations with a rapid timbering process. The unsuspecting German defenders were to be not only attacked from the sea but also bombarded by 636 British guns and literally blown up by explosives planted beneath them.

The trouble was that the Germans were not unsuspecting. "This is supposed to be the lull before the storm which is to break upon us simultaneously from land and sea," a diarist noted on June 24, after a visit to the front line on the beach. Ludendorff considered those beach positions weak and had long planned to reduce the bridgehead held by the Allies forward of the Yser. A successful German assault here would provide a stronger defensive position, a line with the Yser as an obstacle.

ON JULY 10 THE GERMANS LAUNCHED THEIR SURPRISE ATTACK AND GAINED MOST of the bridgehead. On capturing the tunnel, their suspicions were confirmed about the possibility of an amphibious operation. Still, they persisted in their belief that the British would land at Ostende or even in Holland. The German attack made little difference to the British. They simply decided to cross the Yser in boats in conjunction with the planned amphibious operation.

Haig now determined to launch the attack from the sea when his offensive in Flanders reached the Belgian town of Roulers, a little more than ten miles to the east of Ypres. With Roulers in British hands, one rail line the Germans used to supply their coastal units would be cut and another would be in range of British guns. Strategically, the German position in Belgium was shallow. The amphibious operation, coupled with the seizure of Roulers, might be enough to cause Ludendorff to pull back from the coast, which would force him to hold about forty more miles of front. Both sides were short of manpower, but a new front might stretch Berlin to an uncomfortable limit.

THE GREAT LANDING NEVER CAME TO PASS. TROOPS, TANKS, SHIPS' CREWS, AND staffs waited in readiness through July and August. September came and went. Finally, in mid-October, the 1st Division packed up and moved from its secret embarkation point. The decision to cancel the enterprise had nothing to do with weather, tides, or enemy discovery; both Bacon and the 1st Division staff had remained confident of success. The problem was that Roulers had not been taken. Haig's Flanders offensive was bogged down short of its objective. The British attack had proven unable to get beyond a village five miles short of Roulers: Passchendaele.

The Great Landing thus became one of the Great War's many might-have-beens, perhaps for good reason. To later generations, jaded by massive attacks from the sea during World War II, Haig and Bacon's plan seems of minor interest. First of all, it could be criticized for being too cautious—it would have amounted to little more than a tactical envelopment; the landing was not envisioned as a deep attack on the German rear. Second, with the benefit of hindsight—knowing what worked in a later war—it is clear the plan might not have succeeded. The invasion was less than thirty yards wide at the critical point of landing (the combined width of the three ramps of the pontoons). If a few German guns had survived the preparatory bombardment, the assault might well have been added to the list of London's disasters. A little more than a month after the operation was abandoned, direct-fire artillery proved tragically effective against tanks at Cambrai. A good case can be made that the Great Landing was ill conceived—a waste of time, troops, and energy.

On closer examination, however, Haig and Bacon's plan deserves better. Some measure of surprise probably would have been achieved: Bacon noted that the Germans anticipated a landing, but farther up the coast; the target landing area was not reinforced by the Germans until months after the plan was canceled. Haig was probably right in selecting a close-in objective. The Dardanelles had proved amphibious operations to be risky at best in the early part of the twentieth century. His chosen beach might have been a bloody one, but chances of the Germans isolating the 1st Division were small. Then, too, German machine guns probably would have been overcome by the tanks, and any muzzle flashes from German guns would have resulted in point-blank fire from the massive guns of the monitors. Haig recognized enough risk to insist on a precondition, the seizure of Roulers. A year later, in fact, Ludendorff did withdraw from the coast when Haig's troops finally took Roulers. Haig's 1917 judgment therefore cannot be dismissed out of hand.

The most important aspect of the Great Landing, however, centers on the concept, not on what might have happened in 1917. Up to 1915, amphibious landings were little more than ancillary extensions of sea power. Troops were put ashore from ships' boats, lighters—whatever was handy—and landings were often limited to undefended beaches and entailed long marches to objectives. Haig and Bacon's enterprise constituted a significant change in thinking about amphibious operations. Their plan called for specially constructed landing craft, artificial ports, the use of armor in the initial assault, and detailed preparations. These innovations promoted the ability to launch an attack directly into the teeth of a substantial coastal defense, with a landing on the objective. They put us a long step closer to D Day—and in that sense, the Great Landing earned its name.

THE BREAKING OF ARMIES
John Keegan

———

YPRES WAS ALWAYS MORE IMPORTANT AS A LABORATORY of war, whether it was military technology like poison gas or a tactical innovation like defense in depth, than for any strategic advantage it conferred on the opponents. The longer they contended for this shell-fire trap, once a picturesque medieval town but now a smoking ruin, the more it established itself as the Verdun of Flanders. The novelist R. H. Mottram, who served there, remembered the town as "a place in which a whole generation of men had lived, so that it became a part of Britain, to be defended, and something more than that which I cannot put in words." A temporary part of Britain Ypres may have been, but the ordinary soldier loathed its killing fields. Perhaps half a million men, British, French, Belgian, and German, died in the vicinity of this monument to meaninglessness. "The worst has happened," one British diarist lamented early in 1917. "Destination orders have come in and we shall be in action in the Ypres salient."

But nothing that had come before would prepare men for the events of the last half of 1917. Haig's offensive here lasted from July 31 until November 10, a month less than the Somme campaign. The casualties may have been lighter but the collective memories of the battle were far worse. It was officially known as the Third Ypres, but the ordinary Tommy called it simply Passchendaele, after the flattened hamlet on a not-too-distant ridge where the fighting ended, an impossible five miles away from its start. Wyndham Lewis, that disputatious point man of the English avant garde, who was himself present as an artillery officer, played with the name. He found "its suggestion of *splashiness* and of *passion* at once . . . subtly appropriate. The nonsense could not have come to its full flower at any place but at *Passchendaele*. It was pre-ordained."

Haig assumed that his divisions would reach that fish-hook-shaped ridge in the first couple of days of his offensive; it took him more than three months. Bad luck, in the form of the wettest weather in years, bogged him down. But he also created his own misfortune. The millions of shells his artillery poured on the Germans may have killed and maimed thousands of the enemy but they also destroyed the intricate drainage system, rigorously maintained for centuries. Instead of clearing the way for his advance, the bombardment created an impassable morass. At times the forward rate of an attack slowed down to twenty feet per minute—and there was one case in which progress was less than a yard a minute.

As John Keegan writes here, in an excerpt originally taken from his *The First World War,* "the fighting was assuming for those caught up in it a relentlessly baleful character: constant exposure to enemy view in a landscape swept bare of buildings and vegetation, sodden with rain and in wide areas actually under water, on to which well-aimed shellfire fell almost without pause and was concentrated in lethal torrents whenever an assault was attempted against objectives that, nearby in distance, came to seem unattainably remote as failure succeeded failure."

Toward the end of the battle, Haig's chief of staff paid a visit to the fighting front, unbelievably his first. As his automobile bumped through the swamplike edges of the battlefield, he burst into tears and exclaimed, "Good God, did we really send men to fight in that?"

"It's worse further on up," remarked the officer sitting beside him.

Passchendaele, Keegan concludes, "defies explanation." There is evidence that early in October Haig's generals tried to persuade him to call off his offensive: He overruled them, thereby assuring another 100,000 casualties, men who would be missed when Erich Ludendorff's German armies hit back in 1918. Passchendaele finally fell on November 6; the following day the Bolsheviks seized power in Russia. Hostilities ceased on the Eastern Front. "From the end of November onward," Ludendorff wrote in his memoirs, "troop-trains were incessantly passing from East to West." Germany's holdings now stretched from the North Sea to the Black Sea. Ludendorff would strike that next spring and the entire five miles of the Ypres salient that the British had gained in three months would be relinquished in a matter of days.

———

JOHN KEEGAN, who was for many years senior lecturer at the Royal Military Academy, Sandhurst, has taught at Princeton University and Vassar College, and is defense correspondent for *The Daily Telegraph* in London. He is the author of sixteen books, including *The Face of Battle; The Price of Admiralty; The Second World War; A History of Warfare;* and the bestselling *The First World War.*

THE GERMAN RESUMPTION OF UNRESTRICTED SUBMARINE WARFARE ON February 1, 1917, had the effect of driving Britain to undertake what would become its most notorious land campaign of the war, the Third Battle of Ypres, or Passchendaele, so called after the Belgian village destroyed in the course of the offensive, which became its ultimate objective. At the First Battle of Ypres in October and November 1914, the old British Expeditionary Force (BEF) had succeeded in closing the gap between the open wing of the French army and the Flemish coast, thereby completing the Western Front. In the second battle, in April 1915, the BEF had sustained the first gas attack of the war on the Western Front and, though surrendering critical ground in front of the city of Ypres, had held the line.

In 1917, the military situation in the British army's sector was a novel one. The Germans, despite their success against the French and Romanians, and despite the progressive enfeeblement of the Russian army, were no longer in a position, as they had been in 1916 at Verdun, to undertake offensive operations. Their armies were overextended, and Field Marshal Paul von Hindenburg and General Erich Ludendorff awaited a strategic shift of balance—perhaps to be brought by a U-boat victory, perhaps by a final Russian collapse—before they could realign their forces for a new and decisive effort. In the meantime, the British, who had assumed the burden of carrying on the war in the west after French General Robert Nivelle's aborted May 1917 Chemin des Dames offensive, considered their position.

Douglas Haig, the hero of the first battle and defender of Ypres in the second, had long nurtured plans to make the Ypres salient the starting point for a counteroffensive that would break the German line, while an amphibious attack cleared the coast, depriving the Germans of their naval bases at Blankenberghe and Ostend, and thus also dealing, it was hoped, a deadly blow to the U-boats. Haig had first proposed the scheme on January 7, 1916, soon after he succeeded Field Marshal Sir John French in command of the BEF. He reworked the plan for consideration at the Allies' conference at Chantilly in December, only to see it set aside in favor of Nivelle's project for a breakthrough on the Chemin des Dames.

With the failure of Nivelle's offensive, Haig's Flanders plan took on a certain inevitability. It was discussed at an Anglo-French conference in Paris on

May 4–5, 1917, when General Henri-Philippe Pétain, Nivelle's successor, gave assurances that the French would support it with up to four attacks of their own. By June the French could no longer conceal from their British allies that such attacks could not be delivered. On June 7, Haig met Pétain at Cassel, near Ypres, and was told that "two French Divisions had refused to go and relieve two Divisions in the front line." The true figure was more than fifty and Pétain's assurance that "the situation in the French army was serious at the moment but is now more satisfactory" was wholly meretricious. Lloyd George had, at Paris, guessed at the truth when he had challenged Pétain to deny that "for some reason or other you won't fight." Pétain had then merely smiled and said nothing. By June, with the truth of the French mutinies no longer deniable, it was clear that the British would have to fight alone. The matter of the moment was to find a justification for them doing so.

Haig was adamant that the British troops should attack on their own and believed they would win a victory, the best of all reasons for fighting a battle. South of the Ypres salient, local events in June lent credence to his case. There on June 7, the same day he heard from Pétain the first admission of the French army's troubles, General Sir Herbert Plumer's Second Army had mounted a long-prepared assault on Messines Ridge with complete success. Messines continues the line of Flemish heights east of Ypres—elevations held by the Germans since the first battle of October 1914—southward toward the valley of the Lys, which divides the plains of Belgium from those of France. So gradual are the gradients that, to the eye of the casual observer, no commanding ground presents itself to view. More careful observation reveals that the positions occupied by the Germans dominated those of the British all the way to the only true high ground in Flanders, Mount Kemmel and the Mont des Cats, while denying the British observation into the German rear areas between Ypres and Lille, France.

It had long been an ambition of the British commanders at Ypres to take possession of the Messines crest, and during 1917 their tunneling companies had driven forward nineteen galleries, culminating in mine chambers packed with a million pounds of explosives. Just before dawn on June 7, 1917, the mines were detonated with a noise heard all the way to England, and nine divisions, including the 3d Australian, the New Zealand, and—veterans of the first day of the Somme—the 16th Irish and 36th Ulster, moved forward. Nearly three weeks of bombardment, during which three and a half million shells had been fired, had preceded the attack. When the assault waves arrived on the Messines crest, permanently altered by the exploded mines and shelling, they found the surviving defenders unable to offer resistance, and they took possession of what remained of the German trenches with negligible casualties. At a

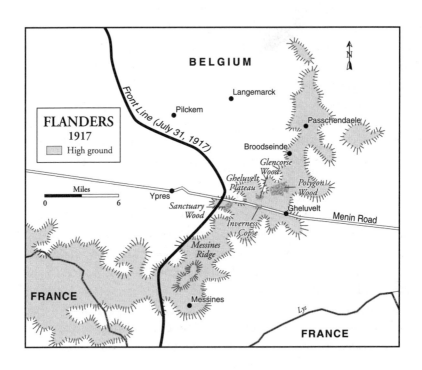

BELGIUM

Front Line (July 31, 1917)

Langemarck

Pilckem

Passchendaele

FLANDERS
1917
High ground

Broodseinde

Glencorse
Wood

Gheluvelt
Plateau

Polygon
Wood

Miles

0   6

Ypres

Sanctuary
Wood

Gheluvelt

Menin Road

Inverness
Copse

Messines
Ridge

FRANCE

Messines

Lys

FRANCE

blow the British had driven the enemy from the southern wing of the Ypres salient. Haig's ambition to drive in the center and thence advance to the Flemish coast was now greatly enhanced.

The obstacle to a second major Western Front offensive, to follow the Somme offensive of the previous year, remained the hesitation of Prime Minister David Lloyd George. He was oppressed by the rising tide of British casualties, already a quarter-million dead, and the paltry military return gained by the sacrifice. The prime minister looked for alternatives—in Italy against the Austrians, even against the Turks in the Middle East—policies that came to be known as "knocking away the props" of Germany's central military position. None commended themselves, and Haig's insistent demand for permission to launch a great Flanders offensive gained strength. Haig's belief in its promise was not shared by Lloyd George's principal military adviser, General Sir William Robertson, a former cavalryman whose innate intelligence and strength of character had carried him to the British army's highest position. Yet he, despite his doubts, preferred Haig's military single-mindedness to the prime minister's political evasions and, when required to throw his weight one way or the other, threw it behind Haig.

In June Lloyd George formed yet another inner committee of the cabinet, in succession to the Dardanelles Committee and the War Council, to assume the higher direction of the war. The Committee on War Policy, which included Lords Curzon and Milner and the South African General Jan Smuts, first met on June 11. Its most important sessions, however, took place on June 19–21, when Haig outlined his plans and asked for their endorsement. Lloyd George was relentless in his interrogation and criticism. He expressed doubts all too accurate about Haig's belief in the importance of Russia's Kerensky offensive, an abortive attempt to drive back the Germans and Austrians; questioned the likelihood of capturing the U-boat ports; and inquired how the offensive was to be made to succeed with a bare superiority, at best, in infantry and nothing more than equality in artillery. Haig was unshaken throughout two days of debate. Despite Lloyd George's fears about casualties, compounded by the difficulties in finding any more men from civilian life to replace those lost, Haig insisted that "it was necessary for us to go on engaging the enemy . . . and he was quite confident, he could reach the first objective," which was the crest of the Ypres ridges.

This was the nub of the difference: Haig wanted to fight, Lloyd George did not. The prime minister could see good reasons for avoiding a battle: It would lose many men for little material gain, it would not win the war (though Haig at times spoke of "great results this year"), and neither the French nor the Russians would help. The Americans were coming and, in consequence, the best strategy was for a succession of small attacks ("Pétain tactics") rather than a repetition of the Somme. Lloyd George weakened his case by urging help for Italy as a means of driving Austria out of the war, but his chief failing, unexpected in a man who so easily dominated his party and parliamentary colleagues, was a lack of will to talk Haig, and his supporter, Robertson, down. At the end, he felt unable, as a civilian prime minister, "to impose my strategical views on my military advisers" and was therefore obliged to accept theirs.

The consequences would be heavy. The "Flanders Position," as the Germans called it, was one of the strongest on the Western Front, both geographically and militarily. From the low heights of Passchendaele, Broodseinde, and Gheluvelt, the enemy front line looked down on an almost level plain from which three years of constant shelling had removed every trace of vegetation. It had also destroyed the field drainage system, elaborated over centuries, so that the onset of rain, frequent in that coastal region, rapidly flooded the battlefield's surface and soon returned it to swamp.

To the quagmire and absence of concealment the Germans had added to the BEF's difficulties by extending the depth of their trench system and its wire entanglements and by building a network of concrete pillboxes and bunkers, often constructed inside ruined buildings, which offered concealment to the construction teams and camouflage to the finished work. The completed Flanders Position was actually several layers thick: In front, a line of listening posts in shell holes covered three lines of breastworks or trenches in which the defending division's frontline battalions were sheltered; next a battle zone consisting of machine-gun posts was supported by a line of pillboxes; finally, in the rearward battle zone, the counterattack units of the division were sheltered in concrete bunkers interspersed between the positions of the supporting artillery batteries.

AS IMPORTANT AS THE PHYSICAL LAYOUT OF THE DEFENSES WAS THE DEPLOYMENT of troops. The German army had, by the fourth summer of the war, recognized that the defense of a position required two separate formations and had reorganized their divisions accordingly. The trench garrison, which was expected to bear the initial assault, had been thinned out to comprise only the companies and battalions of the division in line. Behind it, in the rearward battle zone, were disposed the counterattack divisions, whose mission was to move forward once the enemy assault had been stopped by the fixed defenses and local ripostes of the troops in front.

The defenders of the Flanders Position belonged, in July 1917, to ten divisions, including such solid and well-tried formations as the 3d Guard and the 111th, in which German author Ernst Jünger was serving with the 73d Hanoverian Fusiliers. On the main line of defense, that to be attacked by the British Fifth Army, 1,556 field and heavy guns were deployed along seven miles of front. The British had concentrated 2,299 guns, or one every five yards—ten times the density seen on the Somme fourteen months earlier. The Fifth Army, commanded by the impetuous cavalryman General Sir Hubert Gough, also deployed more than a division to each mile. They included the Guards, the 15th Scottish, and the Highland Divisions, arrayed shoulder to shoulder between Pilckem, where the British Guards faced the German Guards north of Ypres, to the torn stumps of Sanctuary Wood, south of the city, which had given shelter to the original BEF in 1914.

The Fifth Army had also been allotted 180 aircraft, out of a total of 508 in the battle area. Their role was to achieve air superiority above the front to a depth of five miles, where the German observation-balloon line began. Visibility, in good conditions, from the basket of a captive balloon was as much as sixty miles, allowing the observer, via a telephone wire attached to the tethering cable, to correct the artillery's fall of shot with a high degree of accuracy and speed. Improvements in wireless communication were also allowing two-seat observation aircraft to direct artillery fire. The war in the air, which in 1918 would take a dramatic leap forward into the fields of ground attack and long-range strategic bombing, remained during 1917 largely stuck at the level of artillery observation, "balloon busting," and dogfighting to gain or retain air superiority.

The French Air Service, though a branch of the army, was unaffected by the disorders that paralyzed the ground formations during 1917. It operated effectively against the German air raids over the Aisne in April and May and lent important support to the Royal Flying Corps during the Third Battle of Ypres. Its best aircraft, the Spad 12 and 13, were superior to most of those flown by the Germans at the beginning of the year, and it produced a succession of aces, the most celebrated being Captain Georges Guynemer and Captain René Fonck, whose air-fighting skills were deadly. When Guynemer was killed during Third Ypres on September 11, the French Senate ceremonially enshrined the victor of fifty-three aerial combats in the Pantheon. The year was also to see, however, the emergence of the most famous German aces, including Lieutenant Werner Voss and the legendary "Red Baron," Captain Manfred von Richthofen, whose achievements were owed not just to their airmanship and aggressiveness but also to the delivery of several new types of aircraft, particularly the maneuverable Fokker Dr.I triplane, which displayed a significant edge in aerial combat over its British and French counterparts.

Aeronautical technology during the First World War permitted very rapid swings in superiority between one side and the other. "Lead times" in the development of aircraft, now measured in decades, then lasted months, sometimes only weeks. A slightly more powerful engine—when power output ranged between 200 and 300 horsepower at most—or a minor refinement of airframe could confer a startling advantage. During 1917 the Royal Flying Corps received three rapidly developed and advanced aircraft, the single-seat Sopwith Camel and SE-5 and the two-seat Bristol Fighter, which provided the material to make its numbers, inexperienced as many of its pilots were, tell against the German veterans. The Royal Flying Corps also began to produce its own aces to match those of the French and German air forces, the most famous being Major Edward Mannock, Major James McCudden, and Captain Albert Ball. McCudden, an ex-private soldier, and Mannock, a convinced Socialist, were coldhearted technicians of dogfighting from backgrounds wholly at variance with the majority of public-school pilots whom Albert Ball typified. Of whatever class or nation, however, all successful participants in the repetitive and unrelenting stress of aerial fighting came eventually to display the characteristic physiognomy described by Alvin Kernan, a veteran of the Pacific carrier war: "skeletal hands, sharpened noses, tight-drawn cheek bones, the bared teeth of a rictus smile and the fixed, narrowed gaze of men in a state of controlled fear."

THE OUTCOME OF THE THIRD BATTLE OF YPRES WOULD BE DECIDED, HOWEVER, ON the ground, not in the skies above it. As at Verdun and the Somme, the key question at the outset was: Could the weight of artillery preparation crush the enemy's defenses and defenders sufficiently quickly and completely for the attackers to seize positions within his lines from which counterattack would not expel them? There was to be no initial attempt, as Nivelle had desired on the Aisne, for an immediate breakthrough. Instead, the first objectives had been fixed 6,000 yards away from the British start line, within supporting field-gun range. Once those had been taken, the artillery was to be moved forward and the process recommenced, until, bite by bite, the German defenses had been chewed through, the enemy's reserves destroyed, and a way opened to the undefended rear area. The key feature to be taken in the first stage was the Gheluvelt Plateau east of Ypres and two miles distant from the British front line, whose slight elevation above the surrounding lowland conferred important advantages of observation.

The bombardment, which had begun fifteen days earlier and expended more than four million shells—a million had been fired before the Somme—reached its crescendo just before four o'clock on the morning of July 31. At three-fifty, the assaulting troops of the Second and Fifth Armies, with a portion of the French First Army lending support on the left, moved forward, accompanied by 136 tanks. Although the ground was churned and pockmarked by years of shelling, the surface was dry; only two tanks bogged—though many more ditched later—and the infantry also managed to make steady progress. Progress on the left, toward the summit of Pilckem Ridge, was rapid, at Gheluvelt less so. By late morning, moreover, the familiar breakdown of communication between infantry and guns had occurred; cables were everywhere cut, low cloud cover prevented aerial observation, historian Martin Farndale noted, and "some pigeons got through but the only news from the assault was by runners, who sometimes took hours to get back, if indeed they ever did."

Then, at two in the afternoon, the German counterattack was unleashed. An intense bombardment fell on the soldiers of XVIII and XIX Corps as they struggled toward Gheluvelt, so heavy that the leading troops were driven to flight. To the rain of German shells was added a torrential downpour that soon turned the broken battlefield to soupy mud. The rain persisted during the next three days as the British infantry renewed their assaults, and their artillery was dragged forward to new positions to support them. On August 4 a British battery commander, the future Lord Belhaven, wrote of "simply awful [mud], worse I think than winter. The ground is churned up to a depth of ten feet and is the consistency of porridge . . . the middle of the shell craters are so soft that one might sink out of sight . . . there must be hundreds of German dead buried here and now their own shells are re-plowing the area and turning them up."

Rain and lack of progress prompted Sir Douglas Haig to call a halt to the offensive on August 4 until the position could be consolidated. He insisted to the War Cabinet in London, nevertheless, that the attack had been "highly satisfactory and the losses slight." By comparison with the Somme, when 20,000 men had died on the opening day, losses seemed bearable; between July 31 and August 3 the Fifth Army reported 7,800 dead and missing and the Second Army more than 1,000. Wounded included, total casualties—with those of the French First Army—numbered about 35,000, and the Germans had suffered similarly. The Germans, however, remained in command of the vital ground and had committed none of their counterattack divisions. Crown Prince Rupprecht, on the evening of July 31, had recorded in his diary that he was "very satisfied with the results."

Yet, the battle had only just begun. Rupprecht could not reckon with Haig's determination to persist however high the losses mounted or wet the battlefield became. On August 16 he committed the Fifth Army to an attack against Langemarck, scene of the BEF's encounter with the German volunteer divisions in October 1914 where 500 yards of ground were gained. Simultaneously, he committed the Canadian Corps to a diversionary offensive in the coal fields around Lens, that awful wasteland of smashed villages and mine spoil heaps where the BEF had suffered so pointlessly during the winter and spring of 1915. He also continued a series of fruitless assaults on the Gheluvelt Plateau, from which the Germans dominated all action on the lower ground. Little ground was gained and much life lost.

On August 24, after the failure of a third attack on Gheluvelt, Haig decided to transfer responsibility for the main effort at Ypres from Gough's Fifth Army to Plumer's Second. Gough, a young general by the war's gerontocratic standards, had recommended himself to Haig as a fellow cavalryman, noted for his dash and impatience with obstacles. His troops had already learned reasons to feel less confidence in his generalship than his superior held. Plumer, by contrast, was not only older than Gough but looked older than he was and had an elderly caution and concern for those in his charge. He had commanded the Ypres sector for two years, knew all its dangerous corners, and had endeared himself to his soldiers, insofar as any general of World War I could, by his concern for their well-being. He now decided that there must be a pause to allow careful preparation for the next phase, which would take the form of a succession of thrusts into the German line even shallower than Gough had attempted.

BEFORE THE PAUSE, THERE WAS TO BE ONE LAST ACTION ON AUGUST 27 TO attempt the capture of two long-vanished woods, Glencorse Wood and Inverness Copse, just north of the remains of Gheluvelt village. The British army's *Official History* of the war admits that the ground was "so slippery from the rain and so broken by the water-filled shell holes that the pace was slow and the protection of the creeping barrage was soon lost" by soldiers who had been marched up during the night and kept waiting ten hours for the battle to start. When it did, just before two in the afternoon, the advance was soon held up by impassable ground and heavy German fire. Edwin Vaughan, a wartime officer of the 1st Battalion, 8th Warwickshire Regiment, described the effort of his unit to get forward:

> Up the road we staggered, shells bursting around us. A man stopped dead in front of me, and exasperated I cursed him and butted him with my knee. Very gently he said, "I'm blind, Sir," and turned to show me his eyes and nose torn away by a piece of shell. "Oh God! I'm sorry, sonny," I said.

"Keep going on the hard part," and left him staggering back in his darkness. . . . A tank had churned its way slowly behind Springfield and opened fire: a moment later I looked and nothing remained of it but a crumpled heap of iron; it had been hit by a large shell. It was now almost dark and there was no firing from the enemy; plowing across the final stretch of mud, I saw grenades bursting around the pillbox and a party of British rushed in from the other side. As we all closed in, the Boche garrison ran out with their hands up . . . we sent the 16 prisoners back across the open but they had only gone a hundred yards when a German machine gun mowed them down.

Inside the pillbox Vaughan found a wounded German officer. A stretcher-bearer party appeared with a wounded British officer who greeted Vaughan cheerily. " 'Where are you hit?' I asked. 'In the back near the spine. Could you shift my gas helmet from under me?' I cut away the satchel and dragged it out; then he asked for a cigarette. Dunham produced one and he put it between his lips; I struck a match and held it across, but the cigarette had fallen on to his chest and he was dead."

Outside the pillbox Vaughan came across a party of German soldiers eager to surrender.

The prisoners clustered around me, bedraggled and heartbroken, telling me of the terrible time they had been having, *"Nichts essen, Nichts trlnken,"* always, shells, shells, shells. . . . I could not spare a man to take them back, so I put them into shell holes with my men who made a great fuss of them, sharing their scanty rations with them.

From other shell holes from the darkness on all sides came the groans and wails of wounded men; faint, long, sobbing moans of agony, and despairing shrieks. It was too horribly obvious that dozens of men with serious wounds must have crawled for safety into new shell holes, and now the water was rising about them and, powerless to move, they were slowly drowning. Horrible visions came to me with those cries, [of men] lying maimed out there trusting that their pals would find them, and now dying terribly, alone amongst the dead in the inky darkness. And we could do nothing to help them; Dunham was crying quietly beside me, and all the men were affected by the piteous cries.

This was almost the end of Lieutenant Vaughan's experience of August 27. Just before midnight his unit was relieved by another, and he led his survivors back to the lines they had left on August 25:

The cries of the wounded had much diminished now, and as we staggered down the road, the reason was only too apparent, for the water was right over the tops of the shell holes. I hardly recognized [the headquarters pillbox], for it had been hit by shell after shell and its entrance was a long mound of bodies. Crowds [of soldiers] had run there for cover and had been wiped out by shrapnel. I had to climb over them to enter HQ and as I did so a hand stretched out and clung to my equipment. Horrified I dragged a living man from amongst the corpses.

Next morning, when Vaughan awoke to take part in a muster parade, "my worst fears were realized. Standing near the cookers were four small groups of bedraggled, unshaven men from whom the quartermaster sergeants were gathering information concerning any of their pals they had seen killed or wounded. It was a terrible list . . . out of our happy little band of 90 men, only 15 remained."

Vaughan's experience was typical of what the Third Battle of Ypres was becoming. Despite losses lighter than those suffered on the Somme in a comparable period—18,000 killed and missing (the dead drowned in shell holes accounting for many of the missing), and 50,000 wounded since July 31—the fighting was assuming for those caught up in it a relentlessly baleful character: constant exposure to enemy view in a landscape swept bare of buildings and vegetation, sodden with rain, and in wide areas actually underwater, onto which well-aimed shell fire fell almost without pause and was concentrated in lethal torrents whenever an assault was attempted against objectives that, nearby in distance, came to seem unattainably remote as failure succeeded failure.

On September 4, Haig was summoned to London to justify the continuation of the offensive, even in the limited form proposed by the prudent Plumer. The prime minister, reviewing the whole state of the war, argued that, with Russia no longer a combatant and France barely so, strategic wisdom lay in husbanding British resources until the Americans arrived in force in 1918. Haig, supported by Robertson, insisted that, precisely because of the other Allies' weakness, Third Ypres must continue. His case was bad—Ludendorff was actually withdrawing divisions from the Western Front to assist the Austrians—but because Lloyd George advanced worse arguments of his own, in particular that there were decisions to be won against the Turks and on the Italian front, Haig got his way. Henry Wilson, the superseded subchief of the General Staff and a fanatical supporter of maintaining the effort on the Western Front, commented with characteristic cynicism in his diary that Lloyd George's scheme was to give Haig enough rope to hang himself. The assessment that the prime minister wished to relieve his principal military subordinate but dared not until he was compromised by overt failure was probably accurate. There was, however, no obvious successor to Haig, and so, however ill-judged his strategy and harmful its effect on his long-suffering army, it was to be continued for want of a better man or plan.

PLUMER'S "STEP-BY-STEP" STRATEGY, FOR WHICH THE PAUSE IN EARLY SEPTEMBER was the preparation, was conceived in three stages. In each, a long bombardment was to precede a short advance of 1,500 yards, mounted by divisions on a frontage of 1,000 yards, or ten infantrymen for each yard of front. After three weeks of bombardment, the 1st and 2d Australian divisions, with the 23d and 41st British, attacked up the Menin road east of Ypres. The accompanying barrage fell on a defensive belt 1,000 yards deep, and, under that devastating weight of fire, the Germans fell back. The same results were achieved in the Battles of Polygon Wood, September 26, and Broodseinde, October 4. Plumer's "bite and hold" tactics had been successful. The Gheluvelt Plateau had at last been taken, and the immediate area in front of Ypres put out of German observation (troops, nevertheless, continued to march out of the ruined town through its western end and circle back to reach the battlefield, as they had done since the salient had been drawn tight around it in 1915, to escape long-range shelling on the only roads that rose above the waterlogged plain).

The question was whether the next series of bite and hold attacks could be justified. The first three, particularly that on Broodseinde, had hit the enemy hard. Plumer's artillery barrage had caught the German counterattack divisions massed too far forward on October 4 and had caused heavy casualties, particularly in the 4th Guard Division. As a result, the Germans once again decided to refine their system of holding the front. Before Broodseinde they had brought their counterattack divisions close up into the battle zone, to catch the British infantry as they emerged from their protective barrage. As the result had been merely to expose them to the ever heavier weight and deeper thrust of the British artillery, Ludendorff now ordered a reversal: The front was to be thinned out again and the counterattack divisions held farther to the rear, in positions from which they were not to move until a deliberate riposte, supported by a weighty bombardment and barrage, could be organized.

In essence, British and German tactics for the conduct of operations on the awful, blighted, blasted, and half-drowned surface of the Ypres battlefield had now been brought, as if by consultation, to resemble each other exactly. The attackers were to shatter the defenders with a monstrous weight of shell fire and occupy the narrow belt of ground on which it had fallen. The defenders were then to repeat the process in the opposite direction, hoping to regain the ground lost. It was, if decisive victory were the object, a wholly futile exercise, and Haig might, from the evidence with which events almost daily confronted him, have declined to join the enemy in prolonging the agony the struggle inflicted on both sides.

Even the most enthusiastic technical historians of the Great War, ever ready to highlight the overlooked significance of an improvement in the fusing of field-artillery shells or range of trench mortars, concede that Haig should have stopped after Broodseinde. He determined adamantly otherwise. Before Broodseinde he told his army commanders, "the Enemy is faltering and . . . a good decisive blow might lead to decisive results." Immediately after, at a time when Lloyd George was surreptitiously trying to limit the number of reinforcements sent to France to make good losses suffered at Ypres, he wrote to Robertson, the Chief of the Imperial General Staff, "the British Armies alone can be made capable of a great offensive effort [so that] it is beyond argument that everything should be done . . . to make that effort as strong as possible."

The battle of the mud at Ypres—Passchendaele, as it would become known, after the smear of brick that represented all that remained of the village that was its final objective—would therefore continue. Not, however, with British soldiers in the vanguard. Some of the best divisions in the BEF—the Guards, the 8th (one of the old Regular divisions), the 15th Scottish, the 16th Irish, the 38th Welsh, the 56th London—had fought themselves out in August and early September. The only reliable assault divisions Haig had left were in his Australian and New Zealand Army Corps (ANZAC) and Canadian Corps, which had been spared both the first stages of the battle and the worst of the Somme a year earlier.

In what was called the First Battle of Passchendaele, the New Zealand and 3d Australian divisions tried on October 12 to reach the remains of the village on the highest point of ground east of Ypres, 150 feet above sea level, where the Germans' Second Flanders Position of trenches and pillboxes marked the last obstacle between the BEF and the enemy's rear area. "We are practically through the enemy's defenses," Haig told a meeting of war correspondents on October 9. "The enemy has only flesh and blood against us." Flesh and blood, in the circumstances, proved sufficient. Caught in front and flank by machine-gun fire, the ANZACs eventually retreated to the positions from which they had started their advance on that sodden day. So wet was the ground that shells from their supporting artillery buried themselves in the mud without exploding, and the New Zealanders alone suffered nearly 3,000 casualties in attempting to pass through uncut wire.

Having consigned the Second ANZAC Corps to a pointless sacrifice, Haig then turned to the Canadians. General Sir Arthur Currie, commanding the Canadian Corps, had known the Ypres salient since 1915. He did not want to lose any more of his soldiers there, and his precise, schoolmaster's mind forecast that the assault Haig requested would cost 16,000 casualties. Although he had means of recourse to his own government and might have declined, he nevertheless, after protest, complied with Haig's order. The early winter had brought almost continuous rain, and the only way forward toward the top of the ridge was along two narrow causeways surrounded by bogs and streams.

On October 26, the first day of the Second Battle of Passchendaele, the Canadians broke the First Flanders Position and, at a heavy cost in lives, advanced about 500 yards. The 11th Bavarian Division, defending the sector, also lost heavily and was taken out of the line. On October 30 the battle was resumed and a little more ground taken, three soldiers of the 3d and 4th Canadian Divisions earning the Victoria Cross. The 1st and 2d Canadian Divisions took over the front of attack for a fresh assault on November 6, which captured what was left of Passchendaele village, and a final assault was made on November 10, when the line was consolidated. The Second Battle of Passchendaele had cost the four divisions of the Canadian Corps 15,634 killed and wounded, almost exactly the figure Currie had predicted in October.

The point of Passchendaele, as the Third Battle of Ypres has come to be known, defies explanation. It may have relieved pressure on the French in the aftermath of the mutinies, though there is no evidence that Hindenburg and Ludendorff knew enough of Pétain's troubles to plan to profit by them. They had too much trouble of their own, in propping up their Austrian allies and in settling the chaos of the Russian front, to mount another Verdun. Moreover, by the autumn of 1917, Pétain's program of rehabilitation was having its effect on the French army, which staged an attack near the Chemin des Dames on October 23 that recaptured more than seven miles of front, to a depth of three miles, in four days—a result equivalent to that achieved with such effort and suffering at Ypres in ninety-nine. Sir James Edmonds, the official British historian, justified Haig's constant renewal of the Passchendaele battle with the argument that it attracted eighty-eight divisions to the Ypres front, while "the total Allied force engaged was only six French divisions and forty-three British and Dominion [Australian, New Zealand, and Canadian] divisions."

Context puts his judgment in perspective: Eighty-eight divisions represented only a third of the German army, while Haig's forty-three were more than half of his. What is unarguable is that nearly 70,000 of his soldiers had been killed in the muddy wastes of the Ypres battlefield and more than

170,000 wounded. The Germans may have suffered worse—statistical disputes make the argument profitless—but, while the British had given their all, Hindenburg and Ludendorff had another army in Russia with which to begin the war in the west all over again.

Britain had no other army. Like France—though it had adopted conscription later and as an exigency of war, not as a principle of national policy—Britain had by the end of 1917 enlisted every man who could be spared from farm and factory and had begun to compel into the ranks recruits whom the new armies in the heyday of volunteering of 1914–15 would have rejected on sight: the hollow-chested, the round-shouldered, the stunted, the myopic, the overage. Their physical deficiencies were evidence of Britain's desperation for soldiers and Haig's profligacy with men. On the Somme he had sent the flower of British youth to death or mutilation; at Passchendaele he had tipped the survivors into the slough of despond.

MARCH 21, 1918

O'Brien Browne

—

ERICH LUDENDORFF (THE "VON" HE LATER ADDED WAS AN affectation) has to be the central actor of the first half of 1918. This arrogant self-made man came from the bourgeoisie: cold-eyed and hard-faced, he had the look, and the instincts, of an overfed piranha. The Great War had rescued a career that his deliberate tactlessness had threatened to sidetrack. In August 1914 he had rallied demoralized troops to capture the citadel of the Belgian fortress city of Liège. He became an instant national hero. Later that month, with Field Marshal Paul von Hindenburg—a genuine aristocrat—he had presided over the destruction of a Russian army at Tannenberg; the two men became a famous tandem. They were largely responsible for the Eastern Front triumphs of 1915. The following summer Hindenburg would be appointed Chief of the General Staff, with Ludendorff as his deputy. Increasingly, they would act as the de facto rulers of Germany. It has been said that the aged Hindenburg (he turned seventy in 1917) supplied the integrity, Ludendorff, the brains.

Planning for a spring offensive on the Western Front began on November 11, 1917—prophetic date—even as Haig's Passchendaele offensive finally subsided into the mud. O'Brien Browne describes the battle that Ludendorff believed would win the war for Germany. It would be called the *Kaiserschlacht*—"the kaiser's battle"—and was code-named Operation Michael. Since success depended on delivering a knockout blow before the arrival of fresh American millions, Ludendorff scheduled the beginning of his great gamble for victory on the first day of spring, March 21. He believed that would give him time enough. His offensive would strike the sector around the city of St. Quentin, where the British and French forces joined. Three fresh German armies would take on one overstretched British army and part of another. The German General Staff made a careful study of the Allied Western Front offensives and the causes of their failures. The principal reason was readily apparent: an almost total lack of surprise. British defensive preparations played into Ludendorff's hands. They had tried to emulate the German defense-in-depth tactics that had been so successful at Passchendaele; but it was plain that many commanders were uncomfortable with them. Along much of the targeted front, defense lines only existed on the map. Moreover, the British had begun to feel acutely the human wastage of three and a half years of war. Still, Haig was convinced that he could deal with any German attack—and he was certain one was coming. But he expected it to be "a long drawn out" affair, hardly different from the sort of offensives he had initiated. As he confided to his diary in mid-March, he was only afraid that the enemy would *not* attack.

What Haig and his commanders did not count on was Ludendorff's propensity to innovate and his support of fresh tactical ideas. On March 21, at four-forty in the morning, as Browne tells us, the bombardment began: It was intensive and carefully phased—and caught the British by surprise. It did not just kill men but everywhere destroyed communications. Division and brigade headquarters lost touch with the troops they commanded. Confusion reigned. As Tim Travers writes in his landmark study, *How the War Was Won,* the British commanders "had become so welded to a set-piece type of warfare, that, when open warfare occurred, they failed to appreciate the situation, and were unable to function independent of a fixed headquarters." Meanwhile, elite storm troops went forward, aided by a thick fog that has become legendary. Avoiding forward outposts, they headed for the rear, leaving the mopping up to the conventional infantry that followed them. Like Brusilov's attackers two years earlier, the storm troops adhered to the principal of directing the strongest force against the weakest point. In cases, British garrisons did not even realize that they were being bypassed until it was too late.

By the third day of the battle, the Germans opened a fifty-mile-wide gap and were pouring into open country: Ludendorff had broken the long trench stalemate in the west. His original plan called for a pivot to the northwest, which might have succeeded in rolling up the British flank and driving it back to the sea. The British were in total disarray. Haig was panicking. The possibility of that German turning movement remains one of the great "What Ifs" of the March 21 offensive. But Ludendorff chose to take the route of least resistance. "We chop a hole," he said, "the rest follows." The opportunity would pass. By the end of the month his tactical masterpiece would fade into strategic inconsequence.

Meanwhile, the desperate Allies would agree on a step they should have taken long before: putting their armies under a single commander. Their choice was Ferdinand Foch, whose good fortune had been to sit out the disasters of 1917. He, and not Ludendorff, would emerge as the dominant figure of the last year of the war.

———

O'BRIEN BROWNE, who lives in Germany, writes frequently about the Great War.

O N MARCH 21, 1918, WIND AND RAIN RAKED ACROSS THE DESOLATE, crater-scarred fields of northern France. Then, as day edged into night, the storm subsided and a fog began to creep in, covering the land. The early hours of the first day of spring were, as warfare goes, eerily quiet. "There was," recalled British Minister of Munitions Winston Churchill, who was at the front at the time, "a rumble of artillery fire, mostly distant, and the thudding explosions of aeroplane raids. And then," Churchill continued, "exactly as a pianist runs his hands across a keyboard from treble to bass, there rose in less than one minute the most tremendous cannonade I shall ever hear. It swept around us in a wide curve of red flame. . . ."

Churchill was present at the opening fury of the *Kaiserschlacht*—"the kaiser's battle." It was to be Imperial Germany's last, desperate bid to win the Great War and the Allies' greatest crisis since the Battle of the Marne in 1914. Before it was over, the Allied lines had been pushed back up to forty miles, new tactics had revolutionized warfare, command structures had changed, and tens of thousands of men had been killed, wounded, or made prisoner. Its scale was huge, its speed of advance unprecedented, its destructive force immense. It was, said Ernst Jünger, a German soldier who participated, "The final battle . . . [in which] the destiny of the peoples was to be decided. . . ."

But as 1918 opened, Germany's position in Europe had seemed virtually unassailable. To some it appeared that it might even win the war. Kaiser Wilhelm II's armies occupied virtually all of Belgium and a huge part of northern France. No enemy soldier tread on German soil. The Central Powers' armies had knocked Romania and Serbia out of the war. Food was pouring in from the captured fields of Poland and the Ukraine. And the war in the east appeared to be almost over. In addition, Germany's enemies were still recovering from mistakes and failures made in 1917. The British army had nearly bled itself to death in the sucking mud of the disastrous Passchendaele offensive, the French were still reorganizing after mutinies had swept through their ranks in the wake of the futile Nivelle offensive, and the Italian army was reeling in disorder after the bloodletting at Caporetto. Indeed, since the conflict had begun, every Allied attempt at breaking through the German lines had ended in costly failure.

Although the Allied naval blockade was causing some shortages, particularly in raw materials, the German soldier's morale remained high, and he put his faith in good equipment, unassailable positions, and, for the most part, the intelligent leadership of his generals.

For those Germans who could look ahead, however, the future did not appear so full of promise. General Erich Ludendorff was one of those who saw trouble in the future. Arrogant, creative, energetic, and publicity-loving, the fifty-three-year-old Ludendorff had ridden to the top of the German high command through his successful partnership with Field Marshal Paul von Hindenburg. Together, this duo had repeatedly defeated Csar Nicholas II's numerically superior forces and had removed the Russian menace from Germany's rear. Their victories were so important that the two became Germany's de facto rulers. Through contacts with industrial heads and influential conservatives, Ludendorff and Hindenburg had transformed Germany, turning it almost completely into a war machine—socially, politically, and economically. By 1917, they wielded more power than the kaiser himself.

But power did not bring peace of mind. Ludendorff's chief worry was America's entry into the war and the prospect of millions of fresh U.S. troops relieving embattled Allied armies. Indeed, the first American divisions had already landed. Back home in Germany, shortages caused by the Allied blockade and war weariness were beginning to affect the civilian population's willingness to keep sacrificing their sons for a cause that seemed endless. There had even been large-scale antiwar strikes. In addition, Germany was running out of men. So desperate had the kaiser's army become for replacements that now even industrial workers were being called up. Ludendorff needed a grand and dramatic act to secure victory quickly.

The defeat of Russia in late 1917 provided him with the opportunity he had been looking for. With Russia out of the war, Germany could transfer divisions from east to west. Utilizing an excellent rail system and interior lines, Ludendorff was able to increase his forces in the west to 192 divisions. A hard, massive blow with these troops, he reckoned, would shatter his enemies' armies before the Americans arrived in sufficient numbers to alter the situation. With luck, the war would be over by summer and a victorious Germany could dictate the terms of the peace.

In November 1917 at a conference at Mons, Ludendorff put forth his plan for *Kaiserschlacht*. It was given the code name Operation Michael—although many Germans simply called it The Great Battle. Ludendorff chose the area around Saint-Quentin as the most promising site for an attack. Near the joint between the French and British armies, it was a guaranteed weak point, and rupturing the line there would threaten the Allied communications and supply base at Amiens.

The attack that Ludendorff envisioned would be carried out on a fifty-mile front stretching from Arras in the north to Barisis in the south. General Oskar von Hutier's Eighteenth Army was to break through the British lines along a twenty-four-mile front, reach the British troops at the Somme, and then prevent the French from coming north to assist. Farther north, the Seventeenth Army, under General Otto von Below, and the Second Army, under General Georg von der Marwitz, were tasked with striking near Arras, wheeling northward, and pinning the British against the English Channel. Once the British had been neutralized, the Germans could concentrate on driving the French all the way to Paris.

Operation Michael, however, was just one part of a larger plan that encompassed a series of five battles. Stretching from March to July, these blows were intended to keep the Allies off balance, seize the initiative on the Western Front, and punch enough deep holes in the Allied lines to create breakthroughs that would lead to the destruction of the British and French forces.

For such an audacious plan to succeed, Ludendorff realized that the old way of attempting a breakthrough—a long artillery barrage followed by a massed infantry assault—would be insufficient. A new method of attack was required if the Germans were to secure the tactical surprise so necessary to victory.

Ludendorff's plan called for a fluid, flexible offensive, like an onrush of water sweeping irresistibly forward, swirling past large obstacles to gain territory and maintain initiative. His orders emphasized striking with overwhelming force at the enemy's weakest sectors; strong points could be dealt with later. Tactics superseded strategy. "We chop a hole," said Ludendorff, "the rest follows."

To chop this hole, the general brought in Colonel Georg "Durchbruch" ("Breakthrough") Bruchmüller, an innovative artillery tactician. Instead of ranging guns when they were at the front, and thus letting the enemy know that something was happening, Bruchmüller had his artillery preregistered when it was well behind the lines, calibrating each gun's ballistics to meteorological conditions. The attack would open with a short, intense bombardment. Then the Allies' gun emplacements, headquarters, and communications were to be shelled as well as specific pre-located targets. Bruchmüller would also use large quantities of gas in his bombardments, immobilizing and panicking enemy troops. Ingeniously, two types of gas were used. First, lachrymators, such as tear gas, were fired. This would irritate the eyes of the enemy and force them to rip off their gas masks. Deadly phosgene and chlorine gases would then finish off the unprotected men. The artillery would lay down a precisely timed creeping barrage to screen advancing German infantry while at the same time stunning or killing Allied defenders who had escaped the effects of the gas attack. For Operation Michael, 6,473 medium and heavy guns and 3,532 mortars were concentrated behind the German lines near the point of attack.

The *Luftstreitkrafte*, the German Air Service, was also to play an important role. Special squadrons, flying rugged two-seater Hannover CL.IIIs or Halberstadt CL.IIs, were organized into *Schlachtstaffeln*, "battle squadrons," and instructed to provide infantry support. Meanwhile, bomber squadrons would hit Allied supply dumps, airfields, communication centers, and ports while fighters roamed the skies for enemy aircraft. Forty-five percent of the Air Service's fighters were assigned to the offensive, along with almost a third of its artillery spotters and half of its bomber force.

German troops involved in the attack were given a three-week training course in rapid-advance infiltration tactics. The spearhead troops—called *Stosstruppen*, "storm troopers"—were young, battle-hardened, and tough. Their job was to advance behind a creeping artillery barrage, armed with submachine guns, rifles, flamethrowers, light mortars, and bags of hand grenades. Instead of slowly moving across open ground, storm troopers were instructed to use the contours of the terrain and rush forward in small groups. Command decisions were to be made by officers on the spot, not by some general ensconced miles from the action. Hard pockets of resistance were to be left for infantry units following behind the storm troopers. To add surprise to the shock of the attack, troops would be brought to the front lines at midnight, with the second wave a mile behind them and the reserves moving forward as well. All troops were to be on hand to join the fight quickly.

Training was hard, realistic, and thorough. Storm troopers studied aerial photographs of the areas they were to attack and even had maps sewn to their tunics. They practiced rapid, long-distance marches. To further inspire the men, officers told them that Operation Michael was the attack that could win the war, and that Allied soldiers were starved of rations and supplies because of Germany's U-boat campaign. The troops were confident, believing that the end was near.

In order to ensure the vital element of surprise, the artillery was brought into position just a few days before the attack. Storm troop and infantry units were marched or trucked in under cover of darkness. As a final security measure, many of the troops did not know where they would begin their attack. Air force squadrons were transported by train, truck, and even horse-drawn wagons to preselected airfields, where they hurriedly set up canvas hangars and assembled their airplanes. Raids and ruses carried out against the French lines to the south drew increasing numbers of *poilus* away from the British positions. On the eve of the battle, the kaiser himself arrived at Ludendorff's advanced headquarters at Avesnes. The great engine of destruction was now poised to strike.

Across the lines from Ludendorff's storm troopers, the men of the British Fifth Army were huddling in their trenches. Their commander, General Sir Hubert Gough, knew that General von Hutier was opposite him, and despite German deception efforts, believed an attack was in the offing. An arrogant and dashing former cavalry officer, Gough had earned the nickname "Thruster" because of his tenacity in a fight. He had taken over the Fifth Army during the 1917 Somme offensive and built up a reputation as a hard fighter but a poor administrator.

Knowing that the defeat of Russia meant the Germans could now turn their full attention to breaking the stalemate in the west, the British resolved to strengthen their positions based on the German model of a deep, multilayered defense system. No longer a single continually held line, the new British defensive positions consisted of a forward area of fortified dugouts and machine-gun nests, a battle zone where the attacker was to be decimated by artillery fire and the main concentration of infantry, and a secondary battle zone where Germans who had broken through the first defenses could be contained and then eliminated.

Gough's army, however, had not been provided with enough men to complete these sophisticated defenses. Instead, thousands of workmen were toiling miles behind the front, building railway lines and roads to the Channel ports.

Thus, Gough's defenses were unfinished at just the moment that the Germans were about to launch their great attack. Although the forward lines had been completed, the second and third were still insufficient. A further oversight was that no plans had been developed for the conduct of an orderly withdrawal to the Channel ports should that become necessary.

To make matters worse, Gough's forces had taken control of twenty-five miles of the front line from the French. This was the result of an agreement between Field Marshal Sir Douglas Haig, commander of the British Expeditionary Force (BEF), and French Commander in Chief General Henri-Philippe Pétain. By the time of the German attack, Gough's thinly stretched divisions had to face the might of two German armies.

Gough's unenviable position was in part due to decisions made by his commander, Haig. Although a fine military technician, Haig was a stubborn, inarticulate man, insensitive to the sufferings of others. A mediocre and uninspired student at Staff College, he rose to prominence largely through his marriage to a maid of honor to the royal family and through political connections. After disastrous losses of men and matériel in the Somme and Passchendaele battles, Haig's relations with the government in London had deteriorated. By 1918,

Prime Minister David Lloyd George had decided to hold back reserves from the army because he feared that Haig would simply throw away more lives in another senseless battle.

Lloyd George attempted to outmaneuver Haig by creating a body above him, the Supreme War Council, that would control the flow of all Allied reserves and thus limit Haig's freedom of action. A skilled political infighter, Haig countered Lloyd George by refusing to add seven divisions to the pool of reserves. The commander was determined to keep his hands firmly on British reserves. Fearful that the Germans might attack to the north around Arras, Haig concentrated his forces there.

In order to both protect his southern lines and circumvent the council, Haig worked out a plan with Pétain stipulating that the French would support the British with up to six divisions in case of a massive German attack. Pétain, for his part, feared that the blow would come in the Compiègne sector, and his own strategy featured a fighting withdrawal to protect Paris.

Pétain had long and bitter experience fighting the Germans. A cautious but thorough general, his motto was "firepower kills," and he was averse to sending men to face machine guns and shell fire. As commanding general during the final stages of the Battle of Verdun, he had uttered the famous rallying cry *"Ils ne passeront pas!"*—"They shall not pass!"—and brilliantly organized a twenty-four-hour supply train along "the Sacred Way" to keep the French armies around Verdun fighting. When he resisted mounting an offensive across Verdun's strategically useless ground, Pétain was replaced as commander. But he was recalled when elements of the French army mutinied. Pétain's compassion for the plight of the *poilu* earned him the respect and love of his troops. His strength was in defensive operations, and he relied heavily on artillery to keep the enemy at bay. A dogged fighter, Pétain was prone to pessimism, although he would have called it realism.

As spring approached, Allied intelligence obtained quite specific information as to the coming attack. On March 7, the French were aware of German troop movements, and on the twelfth they noticed that the Germans had changed their telegraph codes, as was normally done prior to an assault. German soldiers captured in trench raids even gave the exact date of the attack. Unfortunately, the information came too late, and all Gough could do was to inform his men of the impending assault and order them to brace themselves for the onslaught.

At about four-forty in the morning on March 22, the German bombardment exploded with an intensity hitherto unseen on the Western Front. In five short hours, more than a million shells were fired, smashing trenches, tearing up wire, wrecking artillery pieces, and killing men. Added to the smoke and flying debris was a thick fog that descended onto the battlefield. At nine-forty German storm troopers, looking like monstrous insects in their gas masks, rose up from their trenches and advanced behind a creeping rain of shells. In all, seventy-six German divisions attacked that first day, slamming into a mere twenty-eight British divisions.

With the fog serving as a natural smoke screen, the Germans captured British machine-gun emplacements and strongpoints with relative ease. Storm trooper Ernst Jünger recalled how "without difficulties we zig-zagged through the shredded wire. . . ." The British soldiers, wrote Lieutenant Reinhold Spengler, "carried no weapons and had raised their arms in the air as a sign of surrender. Coming closer, I could see by the expressions on their faces that they had experienced a terrifying time during the last few hours of our bombardment." Sometimes the defenders did not even see their attackers until they were upon them. To add to British difficulties, Gough had violated his own strategy by placing too many men in the front lines. These forward troops became instant victims of the terrific artillery barrage. During the German advance, so many prisoners were taken that they were simply told to march east.

Lieutenant Rudolf Stark, a pilot with Jagdstaffel 34, was flying over the battle during the storm troopers' advance and described the hectic scene: "Below us a battery is firing, infantry are advancing to storm. Columns take cover in trenches and behind rising ground. Everywhere I see flashes—smoking, flaming mouths of the cannon. . . ." In these first days of the attack, German planes outnumbered the Allies' and they were able to provide greater support to advancing ground troops than had previously been the case, a fact quite apparent to the harassed Allied soldiers. Meanwhile, giant Gotha bombers raided French ports and the airfield at Doullens.

The Fifth Army resisted as best it could, but the attack was simply too massive and furious for the British troops to hold out for long, and they were forced to fall back to their secondary defenses. The Germans soon encircled a salient at Flesquières, in front of Bapaume, and Gough ordered a general retreat to keep his left flank from being turned. The Fifth Army pulled back seven miles behind the Crozat Canal. Nearby railway bridges had to be blown. These were under French control and because communications had broken down, Gough could not receive permission to destroy them. They fell into German hands intact.

By the end of the first day of Operation Michael, the Germans had advanced up to four and a half miles and inflicted almost thirty thousand casualties on the British. Hindenburg later laconically commented that "The results of the day appeared to me to be satisfactory."

The next day the attack continued, again assisted by a thick layer of fog.

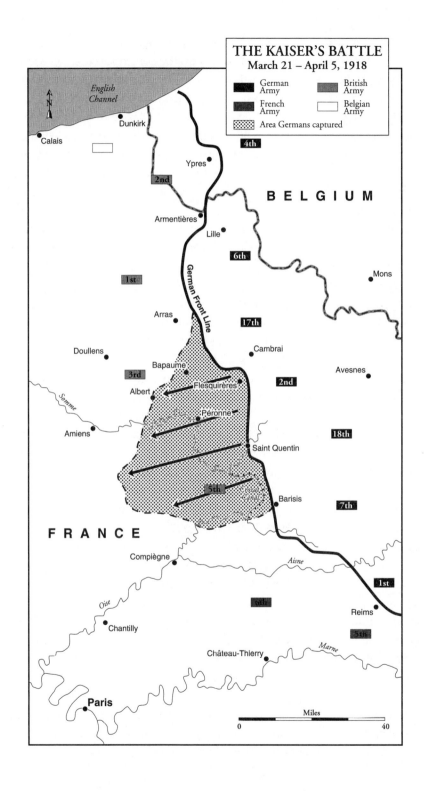

THE KAISER'S BATTLE
March 21 – April 5, 1918

German Army
British Army
French Army
Belgian Army
Area Germans captured

English Channel

Calais

Dunkirk

4th

Ypres

2nd

BELGIUM

Armentières

Lille

6th

Mons

1st

German Front Line

Arras

17th

Doullens

Cambrai

Avesnes

Bapaume

3rd

Albert

Flesquirères

2nd

Péronne

Amiens

18th

Saint Quentin

5th

Crozat Canal

Barisis

7th

FRANCE

Somme

Compiègne

Aisne

1st

Oise

6th

Reims

Chantilly

5th

Château-Thierry

Marne

Paris

Miles

0

40

The Fifth Army was now reeling as the storm troopers pressed forward. Once they had been pushed out of their trenches, the British soldiers, unused to a flexible, dynamic war of movement after years of static trench fighting, fell into disarray. Many were cut down in the open ground. In the confusion it was falsely reported to Gough that the Crozat Canal had been crossed by the Germans. As a result, he ordered another retreat, this time to positions behind the Somme River. In the north, however, the German Seventeenth Army was meeting fierce resistance outside Arras. Still, they had penetrated the Third Army's forward lines, and Marwitz's Second Army was now rushing toward the vital Allied base at Amiens.

Ludendorff could smell victory. To the south, his armies were threatening to split the French from the British and take Amiens; to the north, the attacks on Arras were continuing with the possibility of breaking through and smashing the British armies against the sea. The German juggernaut was now pushing what remained of the British Third Army across the shattered battlefields of the 1916 Somme offensive. At the same time, specially designed Krupp guns had begun lobbing massive shells into Paris, seventy miles away. Now back in Berlin, Kaiser Wilhelm gloated, "the battle won, the English utterly defeated." Meanwhile, a worried Lloyd George telegraphed the British ambassador in Washington to implore President Woodrow Wilson to speed up the transport of American troops to France.

Against the dictates of his own "strongest force against the weakest point" strategy, Ludendorff continued to attempt to take Arras. He sent General Below three more divisions, while directing Marwitz to keep driving toward the town. At the same time, Hutiers' Eighteenth Army had achieved what no other army in four years of fighting on the Western Front had effected—a breakthrough into open country. But, dazzled perhaps or made cautious by the rapidity and scope of his own success, Ludendorff did not exploit this opening.

To the Allies, however, Ludendorff's armies seemed unstoppable; they had now started to cross the Somme. Confronted with this latest disaster, Haig and Pétain met on the evening of March 23, the French commander telling his British counterpart that the promised French reserves were being sent to shore up the crumbling British line. In his diary, Haig described Pétain as coolheaded and reassuring, nevertheless, the situation was grave. After this meeting Haig dashed off a wire to London requesting that the chief of the Imperial General Staff, General Sir Henry Wilson, and the war minister, Viscount Alfred Milner, come immediately to France. Unbeknown to Haig, Milner was already on his way to meet with Georges Clemenceau, France's feisty prime minister, in order to discuss the crisis and the need for a unified Allied command.

Upon seeing the British Commander in Chief, Wilson wrote: "Haig is cowed. He said that unless the whole of the French Army comes up, we were beaten and it would be better to make peace on any terms we could." Seconding this grim assessment, Clemenceau, who had visited the front, reported, "I saw Gough's army spread out like the white of an egg." On the evening of the twenty-fifth, American Expeditionary Force (AEF) commander General John Pershing went to Pétain at Chantilly and offered him the use of the few U.S. divisions he had available to help stem the tide. This was an extraordinary move on Pershing's part, because he had been stubbornly resisting Allied pressure to divide the young American army along different sectors of the front. But the gravity of the hour made such considerations trivial.

On the twenty-sixth, Gough ordered the remnants of his army to hold Amiens. His soldiers were now hunkered down in shallow trenches first dug in 1915. The U.S. 6th Engineers, who had been building roads and bridges behind the lines at the start of the attack, dropped their shovels and picked up rifles to assist the British at Amiens, earning the dubious distinction of becoming the first American unit to engage the Germans on the Western Front.

Meanwhile, the Germans took Albert and forced Byng's Third Army back once again. Amid this crisis, at Doullens, a few miles behind Arras, momentous decisions were being made. Clemenceau had arrived at the *hôtel de ville* in the early morning in order to conduct a high-level meeting with Milner, Wilson, and Haig. French President Raymond Poincaré was also present, as was a pensive Pétain and French General Ferdinand Foch, a buoyantly optimistic man and head of the Supreme War Council.

During the conference it was determined that Amiens should be held at all costs. Then Clemenceau and Milner went into a corner and spoke together for some time. At the end of their discussion, the French prime minister announced that General Foch would be placed in command of all Allied forces in order to coordinate the war effort. Unity of command, long resisted by Haig, had now been forced upon him by the crisis. Before the meeting ended, one last piece of business had to be settled. Gough was relieved of command and two days later was back in Britain. General Sir Henry Rawlinson took over the shattered Fifth Army. Haig, his highly attuned political sense perhaps realizing the need for a scapegoat, did not fight for his general.

Back on the battlefield, Ludendorff continued to violate his own principles by repeatedly throwing his armies against Arras and Amiens. The British, however, now bolstered by French divisions, were beginning to hold their own. The end was now approaching. The German army, after advancing faster and farther than any army since the early days of 1914, was becoming a spent force. With transportation stuck in mud caused by rain and hailstorms and held up on the cratered, debris-strewn earth of the old Somme battlefields, supply lines were breaking down. German soldiers had long been told that the Allies were suffering enormous shortages of food and matériel because of the U-boat campaign. Now they were surprised and disheartened to capture British supply dumps brimming with new equipment and heaps of food. Ernst Jünger's unit overran a dugout formerly occupied by British artillery officers. In one room they came across stores of whiskey and tobacco. "An adjoining room," Jünger wrote, "contained the kitchen where we marveled in awe at the supplies." Jünger and his men filled their pockets with fresh eggs, marmalade, coffee substitute, and onions. In other sectors of the front, German soldiers had stopped advancing to plunder well-provisioned Allied bunkers. Perhaps the Germans believed the war had already been won and it was time to celebrate. Or more likely they had simply reached the point of exhaustion.

Ludendorff, weary from the strain of command, ordered more attacks against Amiens. In the air, the British and French air forces had recovered, fought the Germans to a standstill, and were even achieving the upper hand. On April 5, the offensive was called off. "The enemy's resistance," Ludendorff said, "is beyond our strength."

The killing, however, did not end. Subsequent German attacks struck the Allies from Armentières to Château-Thierry, where the Germans came within forty miles of Paris. These thrusts lasted until July. But by then the French were aggressively counterattacking, more than a million American troops had landed in France, and reinforcements had replenished the BEF's battered armies. Ludendorff's grand gamble to win the war had failed.

The price of *Kaiserschlacht* was enormous. British casualties and prisoners amounted to 177,739, or a daily rate of 11,000 men. The French lost 77,000. In addition, 1,300 Allied guns plus scores of machine guns and tanks had been captured or destroyed. The Germans had hammered a bulge in the Allied lines of up to forty miles and seized 1,200 square miles of bitterly contested territory. To achieve those territorial gains, however, they had suffered almost a quarter of a million casualties.

Ludendorff's vision had emphasized tactics over strategy. Accordingly, he won a tactical, not a strategic, victory. During the battle he seemed at times to be overwhelmed by his own armies' speedy successes, and his radical doctrine of sweeping infiltration followed by mopping up operations became lost as he dashed his men against the enemy's strongest points. Although it had gained impressive amounts of territory, the German army had stretched itself to the limit. The cost was unsupportable both for Ludendorff's forces and for the German economy.

The failure of *Kaiserschlacht* also highlighted the weaknesses of the German government. Essentially dominated by the Hindenburg-Ludendorff "silent dictatorship," government officials had virtually no check on the military, leaving national strategy superseded to the needs of the military. The destiny of Germany depended almost solely upon the success or failure of its generals' war plans. Thus Ludendorff's failure helped to bring about the ultimate defeat of his country.

It also broke his army. For the German soldier, *Kaiserschlacht's* failure bred cynicism, frustration, and disillusionment. The great battle had not won the war for them, and peace and a triumphant return to the homeland were as distant as before. These men no longer believed the propaganda of their own government. They had seen with their own eyes that the Allies had the men and supplies to keep fighting. Although they would continue to fulfill their duty in the long, bloody months ahead, that vital, unquestioning belief in their country's cause had been damaged beyond repair.

In this most ironic of battles, in which the winner was the loser and the loser the ultimate winner, the Allies emerged stronger and more unified than ever. They could now sense victory, although it was still many lives and battles away. The decision at the Doullens conference to make Foch the supreme Allied leader was an important step in achieving that final victory.

Today, *Kaiserschlacht* finds little room in our collective consciousness. Yet it proved to both Germany and the Allies that after four years of bitter struggle the end was near.

DIE PARISKANONE
Robert L. O'Connell

—

LIKE POISON GAS AND THE FLAMETHROWER, THE *Pariskanone,* or "Paris gun," was a terror weapon pure and simple. It was neither accurate nor capable of doing significant damage. But the point of it was to hurl a shell a seemingly impossible distance, one that would strike a French capital that, except for scattered bombing raids, had been mostly immune to destruction. It was the lottery aspect of the weapon that frightened, as well as the mystery of what it was and where it was hidden. On March 24, the day after the first shells hit Paris, killing eight people, *The New York Times* reported that

> officials in Washington do not believe in the existence of a gun capable of firing more than 62 miles. The shots may have been fired by giant airplanes bearing 9.5in howitzers. Others believe that the shots were fired by a British or French gun, manned by mutineers. There may also have been a giant centrifuge, throwing these shells.

Where terror is concerned, timing as much as surprise is of the essence. The first shells—for so they proved to be—landed just when German troops were flooding British rear areas and bursting into the open in the downlands of Picardy. For the Allies this was the moment when Ludendorff's spring offensive assumed truly threatening proportions.

Robert L. O'Connell notes here that "the *Pariskanone* was conceived as a strategic weapon . . . intended to bring Paris to its knees, disrupting both government and war industries. . . . Had the shells carried not high explosives but poison gas, the gun might have been a knife in the heart."

Even so, the 210mm *Pariskanone*, with its 118-foot-long barrel, was the most sophisticated weapon of the Great War. The gun put a man-made object into the stratosphere for the first time in history: In its three-minute flight, a shell would reach a height of twenty-five miles, or some 130,000 feet. By the end of the war, modified versions of the gun could reach a distance of 100 miles, a record not exceeded until the 1960s. But its story is, as Robert L. O'Connell writes, enshrouded in a "body of legend and half-truths." Part of the reason for so much mystery is that almost all information about the gun disappeared after the war. Barrels with their specially developed strengthening alloys were cut up and consigned to the furnace. Plans and calculations were also destroyed. Only a handful of photographs remain. With much effort, the Nazis tried to reproduce the *Pariskanone*. But their copies never attained the range of the original. The German artillery expert Herbert Jäger notes that "they were deployed in 1940 . . . on the French coast of the Channel, firing seventy-two rounds altogether until 1941, most of them innocent of any damage to British property."

———

ROBERT L. O'CONNELL, long a contributing editor to *MHQ: The Quarterly Journal of Military History,* is a former member of the U.S. Delegation to the Conference on Disarmament in Geneva. His books include *Of Arms and Men: A History of War, Weapons, and Aggression; Ride of the Second Horseman: The Birth and Death of War; Soul of the Sword;* and a novel, *Fast Eddie.*

A ROAR, FOLLOWED IMMEDIATELY BY AN EXPLOSION IN THE PLACE DE la République, shattered the early-spring Paris morning. It was seven-twenty on March 23, 1918—the beginning of the third day of the immense German offensive in Picardy that was already threatening to drive a wedge between the French and British armies. Twenty minutes later there was an identical explosion in front of the Gare de l'Est entrance to the Métro. When the smoke and dust cleared, eight lay dead and thirteen others had been seriously injured. What was it? Almost instinctively, worried eyes combed the skies for the German bombers that had taken to staging nightly raids over the city. There was nothing—no aerial silhouettes, not even the drone of aircraft engines. Yet the explosions continued, twenty-five that first day, killing sixteen people and wounding twenty-nine more. By noon the city, already bewildered and terrified by events to the north, had come almost to a standstill.

With an alacrity learned from years of continuous warfare, the Paris Defense Service immediately began gathering metal fragments and subjecting them to careful analysis. In less than three hours, they reached an altogether startling conclusion: Paris was not being bombed, but being shelled by artillery. Yet the nearest point along the German lines was sixty-seven miles away, and adding an extra ten miles for even moderate safety from counterbattery fire, this meant that the offending cannon had to have a range of nearly eighty miles! As improbable as this seemed, further study of the fragments allowed French ordnance experts to hypothesize a projectile approximately eight inches in diameter, with abnormally thick sidewalls and rifling grooves cut into the steel body of the shell—all features corresponding to the enormous chamber pressures necessary to hurl a round this distance. Further, analysts were able to pinpoint a probable location in a stand of woods in German-held territory near the village of Crépy, almost seventy-five miles from the center of Paris.

By evening, orders went out to detach a battery of 305mm rail-mounted cannon within range of the designated spot. The very next day, March 24, the German gunners—*Pariskanoniers,* as they were called—found themselves subjected to a disconcerting, if not lethal, barrage. Amazingly, in almost every detail of the great gun's configuration, performance, and location, the French ballistic experts had been right on the mark. Theirs was an exceptional feat of analysis, diametrically opposed in its realism to the body of legend and half-truths by which the *Pariskanone* is remembered today.

Even its name is a matter of misinformation, being frequently confused with either "Big Bertha," a 420mm siege howitzer named after Gustav Krupp's wife, or "Long Max," a 380mm rail-mounted naval rifle that was the technological jumping-off point for the much more specialized *Pariskanone*. Similarly, more important considerations, such as the extent of its use and the number of casualties inflicted, have been chronically exaggerated.

William Manchester, in his otherwise excellent book about the Krupp family, states that during the 139 days of the big gun's operation it launched a shell every twenty minutes, for a total of about 10,000 shots. Yet on the very same page, he indicates that the barrel, the length of a ten-story building, had to be straightened after every shot and replaced after every sixty-five—making such a high rate of fire very unlikely.

In fact, the gun (or guns, because there were three in all, with seven barrels) was fired at Paris 367 times during four separate phases between March 23 and August 9, 1918. The tubes were subject to drooping and did require periodic straightening, using a sophisticated bore-sighting mechanism and a cable-based bracing system resembling one half of a suspension bridge running along the barrel's top. But this wasn't necessary after every shot. Tube life was actually as short as fifty shots at first. The barrels were then returned to the Kruppwerke, where they were rebored to around nine inches. This greatly increased their durability but also shortened the gun's range, prompting several laborious moves closer to Paris; hence the intermittent periods of activity.

Krupp chroniclers Manchester and Peter Batty both state that over 1,000 Parisians were killed by the *Pariskanone*. The real figure is less than 260. The *Pariskanone*'s reputation as a wanton killer is derived from one horrific incident: On March 29 the gun scored a direct hit on the Church of Saint-Gervais, packed with Good Friday worshipers, of whom eighty-eight were killed and sixty-eight injured. This kind of lethality was never even approximated before or after. During its initial phase of firings, the gun accounted for 122 dead and 247 wounded. Casualties soon declined dramatically as Parisians learned not to congregate in groups during shellings. Thereafter, when they died, it was by twos and threes, like traffic deaths; and most shells did not kill anyone. Nonetheless, the gun's early success and the subsequent reaction of its intended victims say a good deal about its mission and results.

The *Pariskanone* was conceived as a strategic weapon, an integral part of the supreme German effort in the spring of 1918. The gun was intended to bring Paris to its knees, disrupting both government and war industries while

German shock troops first cleaved the British and French forces, then drove the hapless *poilus* out of the trenches and back toward their capital.

Today the *Pariskanone* is most notable for its portentous similarity to the ballistic missiles that hold us hostage, and this may be why it is tinged with an aura of such fear and loathing. But the citizens of Paris, who knew nothing of nuclear warheads and world-girding missiles, found it possible to adjust to fewer than 400 explosions—which were, after all, rather small and frequently hit nothing in particular. When the German retreat in early August 1918 forced the gun out of range and ended five months of shelling, the great cannon had accomplished essentially nothing. As with the Gotha bombers that had struck London the previous year, the creators of the *Pariskanone* had confused the concept of *Schrecklichkeit*, "frightfulness," with its reality. True enough, the winds of change were blowing in this direction. But to work as advertised, terror weapons had to be really terrible. Had the shells carried not high explosives but poison gas, the gun might have been a knife in the heart.

Technologically the *Pariskanone* was much more impressive, but even here its legacy remains mixed. Purely as a piece of artillery, it was a formidable achievement, a statistical *tour de force*. Developed over the space of two years at the Kruppwerke by Dr. Otto von Eberhard and Ordnance Director Fritz Rausenberger, the gun was essentially a 15-inch naval rifle, tubed down to 8.26 inches, vastly reinforced, and almost doubled in length. What emerged was a veritable infernal engine.

Fueled by 432 pounds of smokeless powder, the gun developed nine million horsepower as it accelerated its 264-pound projectile to 5,500 feet per second. The shell reached a height of twelve miles in less than half a minute and a maximum height of twenty-four miles in a minute and a half. For at least fifty miles of its range, the projectile traveled in a near-vacuum—so high and so far that the calculation of its trajectory had to take into account the earth's curvature and rotation. The atmospherics within the gun were just as extreme, with the dynamic pressure on the breech lock and firing chamber reaching nearly 70,000 pounds per square inch, or approximately 4,700 times normal barometric pressure.

It was remarkable that any movable breech could withstand such forces— and as if to drive that point home, tube number three blew up on March 25 after only three shots, killing five of its picked crew from the Kruppwerke. And it was not just a matter of pressure; the heat and corrosive forces of the propellant gases had to be rammed progressively farther up the barrel until the tube lost all consistency of performance. The gun also had such enormous recoil that a 210-ton emplacement was needed to keep it from driving itself into the earth like a giant spike. The weight of the emplacement and the 180-ton dead-weight of the gun and cradle amounted to over three quarters of a million pounds of the finest Krupp steel to shoot a 264-pound projectile.

This is a telling point. For all its fabulous statistics and analogies to today's ballistic missiles, its technological overachieving, the *Pariskanone* was a gun like other guns. The future, it turned out, belonged to rocketry and inertial guidance. Or so it seemed until a Canadian, Dr. Gerald Bull, entered the international arms market in the 1970s.

Something of a prodigy, Bull spent a decade working on guided missiles for the Canadian government before leaving to pursue his real interest: very big guns. He was convinced that a super-cannon could be developed to launch small payloads into low earth orbit at a cost far below that of rockets. In the 1960s he obtained a previously unknown manuscript detailing Fritz Rausenberger's work on the *Pariskanone*. Using that data, Bull did a computer analysis of the gun's performance. He also developed a series of experimental guns, culminating in HARP I (High Altitude Research Project), two 16-inch naval rifles welded together, which in 1967 succeeded in shooting a projectile 112 miles into low space.

The U.S. and Canadian governments soon withdrew support in favor of missiles. Determined to build his supergun, Bull formed his own company. Apparently to finance it, he entered the international arms market with an innovative 155mm gun; in 1980 he was sentenced to six months in a U.S. prison for supplying it to South Africa.

He then moved to Brussels, where he forged close links to Iraq. Later, rumors spread that Iraq was financing a series of guns that would lead to the development of Bull's supergun, 487 feet long with a range of 900 miles. In April 1990 the British government seized what appeared to be sections of a 200-foot gun barrel, labeled as oil piping and scheduled for shipment to Iraq. Other gun parts were seized in Germany and Turkey, but nearly 85 percent of the weapon reportedly did reach Iraq.

By then, however, Bull was dead. On March 22, just outside his Brussels apartment, an unknown assassin shot him twice in the head—ironically, perhaps, at point-blank range.

IRON GENERAL
Thomas Fleming

——

I N HIS PORTRAIT OF GENERAL JOHN J. PERSHING, THE
Commander in Chief of the American Expeditionary Force
(AEF) on the Western Front, Thomas Fleming quotes B. H.
Liddell Hart's assessment: "[T]here was perhaps no other man
who would or could have built the structure of the American
army on the scale he planned. And without that army the war
could hardly have been saved and could not have been won."

Allied commanders like Haig or Foch (as well as many recent military historians) would take a harsher view of the
man, the role he played, and even the ultimate value of the
American contribution. Late in October 1918, Haig told
Pershing to his face that the American Expeditionary Force
(AEF) "cannot be counted on for much." (Pershing made him
back down but the damage was done.) Foch's staff described
Pershing's army as a "comparatively weak asset." After having been caught up for hours in a monumental American traffic jam in the Argonne, an enraged French premier, Georges
Clemenceau, lobbied to have Pershing removed. Almost until
the end, the greatest fear of French commanders was that the
Germans would, in one final effort, rout the Americans and
regain the initiative they had lost in midsummer.

How do you separate reason from rancor? Pershing, as
Fleming writes, was inflexible to a fault—something the Allied
leadership soon learned when it attempted to "amalgamate"
American troops into their divisions under French and British
commanders. Woodrow Wilson backed his insistence on a
separate American army. Though admired by many, as it has

often been said, this frigidly laconic general was loved by few (and many of those were women). The military writer S.L.A. Marshall once commented that Pershing "was the perfect picture of the indomitable commander, tailor-made for monuments." In May 1917, when he was appointed to lead the AEF, perhaps that was what America most needed. And indeed, Pershing became a symbol as much as anything, and the war was over before the public had a chance to question either his accomplishments or the lack of them. Historians would only begin their chipping away at the granite man later on.

That Pershing was able to shepherd 2,080,000 men across the Atlantic in just a year and a half—1.4 million of whom would reach the front—may be, as Liddell Hart said, his greatest accomplishment. It may be sufficient to note that the British needed two years to create from scratch an army also of 1.4 million men: The first action that many of its citizen soldiers would experience was July 1, 1916, hardly a recommendation. Realistically, the Allies could not expect the hastily raised AEF to perform at its best until 1919—and the universal expectation was that the war would last that long. But it didn't, of course, and Pershing would not get the break of history accorded to generals like Haig, Foch, and Franchet d'Esperey, all men who had the good fortune to fail upward into success. Pershing was just beginning to correct his worst mistakes when the war abruptly ended.

Had the fighting continued, his troops certainly would have been better trained. Pershing's army was ill-prepared for the attritional warfare it would face on the Western Front. "The average doughboy at the Meuse Argonne," David M. Kennedy writes in *Over Here: The First World War and American Society*, "had seen perhaps four months of training in camp. Many had seen but a few weeks. Some had been cycled so swiftly from induction center to war zone that they had never handled a rifle, and had to be given a quick ten-day course of instruction upon arrival in France." Their introduction to the modern battlefield was a rude one. The trench stalemate may have ended in 1918 but fighting in the open tends to be even more lethal than position warfare. Open warfare, Pershing maintained, was the only way to beat the Germans. Lives would not be spared.

Ironically, the inflexible man preached a doctrine of mobility, flexibility, and individual initiative, in which the rifle would be the primary weapon. Pershing viewed open warfare as characteristically American, and it was his rationale for fighting as a separate army. He was appalled at what he viewed as the fixation of the British and French with trench warfare and its weapons. But to his critics, it sometimes seemed that he was trying to replay 1914. Liddell Hart wrote that Pershing's offensive doctrine, like that of the French in the early phase of the war, "foundered on the rock of machine guns. . . . It may even be said that he omitted but one factor from his calculations—German machine guns—and was right in all his calculations but one—their effect." Paul F. Braim, who analyzed the Argonne in *The Test of Battle*, wrote: "Were I a draftee in 1918 at the foot of Montfaucon, ordered to attack directly into machine gun fire, I might think less of Pershing." The author's own father had fought in the Argonne, and as a boy young Fleming listened to his stories about the machine gun's killing power. Teddy Fleming had gone on to officers' training school immediately after the Armistice, and in a notebook he recorded the newly recognized way to deal with the weapons: "If enemy infantry or MGs resist, hit the ground. Some men outflank enemy under covering fire of platoon. Then assault with grenades and bayonets. . . . The platoon that advances all at once, plays into the enemy's hands." For too many, that advice came too late.

But then, Pershing learned many things when it was too late. The size of the American cemeteries is evidence of that. Had his insistence on a separate American army been overly rigid? He considered it his foremost achievement. But there are an increasing number of historians, Fleming included, who feel that the AEF would have benefited from being brigaded with French and British combat units. Pershing (who apparently suffered a brief breakdown early in October 1918) at least recognized his limitations as a combat leader and handed over command of the First Army to the remarkable Hunter Liggett. In the meantime, Americans were now arriving in France at the rate of 300,000 a month. Largely thanks to Pershing, it was the arithmetic of victory.

––––––––

THOMAS FLEMING is the author of more than forty books of history and fiction, including, most recently, *Liberty!: The American Revolution; Duel: Alexander Hamilton, Aaron Burr and the Future of America;* and *The New Dealers' War.*

ON FEBRUARY 5, 1917, THE REAR GUARD OF THE 11,000-MAN PUNITIVE Expedition to Mexico recrossed the Rio Grande to American soil. With them was John J. Pershing, the lean, grim-lipped, jut-jawed major general who had managed to pursue Pancho Villa around northern Mexico for nearly eleven months without starting a war. Although he had not captured the guerrilla chieftain, Pershing had scattered Villa's army and killed a number of his lieutenants—and silently swallowed his frustration when President Woodrow Wilson ordered a withdrawal. Within hours of his return to the United States, Pershing called a conference of the newspapermen who had followed him into Mexico. "We have broken diplomatic relations with Germany," he said. "That means we will send an expedition abroad. I'd like to command it. . . . Tell me how I can help you so that you can help me."

It was neither the first nor the last time Pershing would reveal the shrewd self-promotion that lay behind the image of the "Iron General." When he had invaded Mexico, he had obligingly posed on horseback fording the Rio Grande with his staff. Actually, he had traveled across the inhospitable Chihuahuan Desert in a Dodge touring car. In many surprising ways, large and small, Pershing was a very modern major general. In other ways, he was a man of his own time.

Pershing had graduated from West Point in 1886 as first captain of the cadet corps, a coveted title that testified to an aptitude for things military. Scholastically he was in the middle of his seventy-seven-man class. Post–Civil War West Point was intellectually moribund, turning out men who learned by rote what little was taught. If they acquired anything from their four-year indoctrination, it was a ferocious dedication to discipline and military minutiae.

Robert Lee Bullard, who graduated a year ahead of Pershing and would later serve under him, admired his ability to give orders, which seemed to come naturally to him. The Alabama-born Bullard also noted that Pershing inspired admiration and respect, but not affection. There was something impersonal, almost detached, in his style of command. With women, on the other hand, a different man emerged, full of wit and charm. He was a "spoony" cadet, with a pretty girl on his arm for every hop. Later, as a cavalryman on the western frontier and a guerrilla fighter in the Philippines, he gravitated inevitably toward the prettiest woman in sight.

Another large factor in his life soon emerged—what some people called "Pershing luck." Others called it an uncanny ability to ingratiate himself with men in high places. Having watched Pershing in action during the last of the Indian Wars, Nelson Miles selected the young man as his aide after he became commanding general of the army. In 1896, Miles sent Pershing to New York to represent him at a National Guard tournament in Madison Square Garden. Avery Andrews, a classmate who had retired from the army to go into business, invited Pershing to share his box. Another guest was Theodore Roosevelt, on his way to becoming President William McKinley's assistant secretary of the navy. An avid western buff and admirer of soldiers, Roosevelt was fascinated by Pershing's skirmishes with Sioux who were part of the Ghost Dance cult, his knowledge of Indian dialects, and his Missourian enthusiasm for the West's potential. A friendship was born that became a pivot of Pershing's career.

In the West, Pershing had served with the black troopers of the 10th Cavalry. Posted to West Point in 1897, he became the most unpopular tactical officer in recent memory—an accomplishment in itself. In retaliation for his uncompromising discipline, the cadets nicknamed him "Nigger Jack"—a reference to his service with the 10th and a sad commentary on the racism of the era. (It was later softened to "Black Jack"—a name that stuck, largely because most people thought it had something to do with the potentially deadly nature of the instrument of the same name.) When the Spanish-American War broke out in 1898, Pershing rejoined the regiment and went up San Juan Hill with the dismounted black Regulars, proving himself "as cool as a bowl of cracked ice" against Spanish sharpshooters who killed or wounded 50 percent of the regiment's officers.

In 1902, while serving in the Philippines, Captain Pershing pacified much of Mindanao with 700 troops, cajoling Moro *dattus* out of their forts whenever possible, demolishing them in short, savage attacks when necessary. His exploits won headlines in many newspapers. His friend Theodore Roosevelt, now ensconced in the White House, tried to promote Pershing to brigadier general. But not even the president could alter the rigid, seniority-based promotion system.

A military celebrity, back in Washington for service on the General Staff, Pershing in 1905 married a vivacious Wellesley graduate, Helen Frances Warren, the daughter of the wealthy Wyoming senator who headed the Military Affairs Committee. Confronted with subtle threats to their annual budgets, the army's higher ranks became more amenable to Pershing's promotion. In 1906, Roosevelt vaulted him over 862 senior officers to brigadier, making most of these gentlemen instant enemies. They retaliated with a smear campaign about his sex life in the Philippines, claiming he had had a series of native women as mistresses and had sired several children. He denied everything, but the scandal stained his reputation so badly that, six years later, newspapers howled when he was proposed as superintendent of West Point.

Marrying influential daughters was an old army custom. Nelson Miles had married the daughter of Senator John Sherman, who was the brother of General William Tecumseh Sherman and the most powerful senator of his day. In Pershing's case, surviving letters and diaries make it clear the marriage was loving. As his honeymoon ended, Pershing confided to his diary that he was "the happiest man in the world." Four children, three girls and a boy, were born to Jack and "Frankie."

On August 27, 1915, while Pershing was patrolling the restive Mexican border against guerrilla incursions, an excited reporter called headquarters and got the general himself. Without realizing to whom he was talking, the newsman blurted out that Pershing's wife and three daughters had been killed in a midnight fire at their quarters in the Presidio in San Francisco. Only his six-year-old son, Warren, had survived, saved by a courageous orderly. A devastated Pershing wrote a friend: "All the promotion in the world would make no difference now."

Pershing seemed to deal with his sorrow through work, responsibility, and the grinding details of duty. That is one explanation of his pursuit of the command of the American Expeditionary Force (AEF). Another is the very strong probability that he thought he was the best man for the job. One of Pershing's characteristics was his matter-of-fact assumption of his ability.

He courted Woodrow Wilson with a fulsome letter praising the president's speech of April 2 before Congress, calling for a war to make the world safe for democracy. He wrote a similar letter to Secretary of War Newton D. Baker. Senator Warren worked hard on Pershing's behalf, telegraphing him at one point to ask about his knowledge of French. Pershing had barely passed the subject at West Point, but he replied that he could easily acquire "a satisfactory working knowledge" of the language.

There was only one other major general who could compete with Pershing for the job: Frederick Funston. He had won instant fame by capturing rebel leader Emilio Aguinaldo and crippling the Philippine insurrection in 1901. On February 19, 1917, Funston dropped dead in the lobby of a San Antonio hotel—perhaps another instance of Pershing luck.

In early May, Pershing got the job—leaping over five major generals senior to him. What he found in Washington, D.C., would have daunted a less confident man. The U.S. Army had little more than 11,000 combat-ready Regulars. The 122,000-man National Guard was a joke. Fully half its members had never fired a rifle. Hugh Scott, the aging chief of staff, frequently fell asleep at meetings with his officers. The only plan Scott had on his desk was the brain-child of Wilson and Secretary Baker—to send Pershing at the head of a 12,000-man division to France as part of a "flexible" response to the war.

French and British missions swarmed to American shores to deluge the War Department and the president with frantic pleas for men. Instead of Wilson and Baker's symbolic 12,000, they wanted 500,000 men immediately—and they did not particularly want John J. Pershing, or any other American general. The British suggested that the half-million recruits be shipped directly to depots in England, to be trained there and sent to France in British uniforms, under British officers. The French were a bit more polite, but it came down to the same thing: They wanted American soldiers to become part of their army.

From the day he heard the idea, Pershing opposed amalgamation of forces. He had no intention of becoming superfluous in France. For the time being, Wilson, Baker, and General Tasker H. Bliss—the large, slow-moving military politician who soon succeeded Scott as chief of staff—agreed with him. Not without some conflict, Pershing also opposed a proposal by his friend Theodore Roosevelt to raise 50,000 volunteers and lead them himself to Europe to bol-ster the Allies' sagging morale. As an observer in Manchuria during the Russo-Japanese War in 1904, Pershing had seen a modern battlefield, and he did not think there was room on it for amateurs like Roosevelt. He may also have sensed, with his finely honed instinct for command, that there could be only one American leader in Europe.

Pershing saw himself not only as that American leader but as the general who could win the war. He thought he had the answer to breaking the bloody stalemate on the Western Front—"open warfare." This idea was a variation on the doctrine taught at West Point by Dennis Hart Mahan, the man who domi-nated the academy for much of the nineteenth century. Speed, fire, and move-ment were the essence of Mahan's ideas, along with seizing and holding the initiative. Pershing believed the American soldier's natural gifts as a marksman and wielder of the bayonet would shock the German army—and the Allies' armies—out of their trenches.

Three weeks after his appointment, Pershing sailed for Europe with a 191-man staff. In London, people liked what they saw. One American reporter, Hey-wood Broun, opined, "No man ever looked more like the ordained leader of fighting men." Another, Floyd Gibbons, called him "lean, clean, keen." But even as he was charming the newsmen, Pershing was requesting from Washington the power to impose rigid censorship on everything they wrote in France.

In Paris the population went berserk, chanting the "Marseillaise" and pelt-ing Pershing and the staff with flowers as they rode to the Hotel Crillon. On the balcony overlooking the place de la Concorde, when the wind whipped a tricolor toward him, Pershing reverently kissed its folds. The crowd screamed its approval. Inside, he got a very different reception. The American ambassador, William Sharp, said: "I hope you have not arrived too late." The writer Dorothy Canfield Fisher, an old friend, told Pershing the French were beaten: They had had two million casualties, and "there is a limit to what flesh and blood . . . can stand."

Pershing learned even worse news from General Henri-Philippe Pétain, the French Commander in Chief. In April, after a disastrous offensive on the Aisne River that cost 120,000 casualties, the French army had mutinied. Most of it was still in a state of "collective indiscipline," as Pétain put it. Russia, with its immense reservoir of manpower, was even closer to military collapse. The March revolution, which ousted the csar, had failed to add vigor or coherence to their army. More bad news soon arrived from the British front, where Field Marshal Sir Douglas Haig was in the process of squandering 300,000 men on futile attacks in the Ypres salient. An appalled Pershing told his military censor, Major Frederick Palmer, that he feared the worst: "Look at what is expected of us and what we have to start with! No army ready and no ships to bring over an army if we had one."

Pershing soon decided he could not rely on the General Staff in Washington for anything; it took weeks to get a reply from anyone. Tasker Bliss was still writing orders with the stub of a pencil and hiding urgent telegrams under his blotter while he made up his mind what to do with them. Pershing set up his own general staff in France—a far more efficient one than the fumbling team in Washington.

For his chief of staff, Pershing chose Major James Harbord. Neither a West Pointer nor a close friend, but extremely intelligent, Harbord had caught Pershing's eye in the Philippines. He was his commander's opposite in many ways—genial, warm, a man with first-class diplomatic instincts. Harbord kept a voluminous diary, from which we get a good picture of Pershing on the job.

> He thinks very clearly . . . and goes to his conclusions directly when matters call for decision. He can talk straighter to people calling them down than anyone I have ever seen. . . . He loses his temper occasionally, and stupidity and vagueness irritate him more than anything else. . . . He develops great fondness for people whom he likes . . . but . . . is relentless when convinced of inefficiency. . . .
>
> He does not fear responsibility. . . . He decides big things much more quickly than he does trivial ones. Two weeks ago, without any authority from Washington, he placed an order . . . for $50,000,000 worth of airplanes . . . and did not cable the fact until too late for Washington to

countermand it. . . . He did it without winking an eye, as easily as though ordering a postage stamp.

Alfred Thayer Mahan, Dennis Mahan's son, was fond of saying that war is business. As commander of the AEF, Pershing proved it. Until he took charge, each army bureau and department had its own supply officer with its own budget, a system that caused immense confusion and duplication of effort and expense. (For example, the various bureaus had ordered a total of thirty million pairs of shoes when nine million were needed!) Pershing organized the AEF's purchases around a single man, an old friend and future vice president, Charles Dawes. A canny businessman, Dawes had absolute authority to buy anything and everything the army needed from the French and British at the best possible price.

The decisions Pershing and his staff made to prepare the AEF for battle were awesome. Along with French planes for their newly created independent air force, they bought French 75s for their artillery; the English Enfield rifle and steel helmet and the French light machine gun, the Chauchat, for their infantry; and the French light tank, the Renault, for George S. Patton's embryonic tank corps. Pershing also decided to make an AEF division, an entity that did not exist in the prewar American army, of 28,000 men, twice the size of an Allied or German division. He wanted an organization large enough to mount a sustained attack under the command of a single general. Unfortunately, he did not double the size of the new division's artillery, the first symptom of his inability to appreciate the lethal increase in firepower that had transformed warfare on the Western Front.

Pershing also strove to put his own stamp on the spirit of the AEF. In October 1917, he announced: "The standards for the American Army will be those of West Point. The . . . upright bearing, attention to detail, uncomplaining obedience to instruction required of the cadet will be required of every officer and soldier of our armies in France." To have every private behaving like a Pershing was an impossible dream, but the Iron General never wavered in his insistence. To improve the appearance of the officer corps, he ordered them to wear the British Sam Browne belt and authorized the use of canes. The first item was hated by many officers, the second mocked by enlisted men, but they became part of the dress code nonetheless.

Heywood Broun, who followed Pershing around France for a while, was bewildered by the general's appetite for details. He climbed into haylofts where soldiers were quartered and discussed onions with cooks, to make sure men were being billeted in reasonable health and comfort. Broun derided this attention to detail, sneering that Pershing thought he could read a man's soul "through his boots or his buttons." The reporter quoted a junior officer who thought Pershing's favorite biblical figure was Joshua, "because he made the sun and moon stand at attention." Broun's candor got him kicked out of France; Pershing's AEF censors had a low tolerance for such negative remarks. The rest of the press corps remained firmly in Pershing's corner.

One man who never succumbed to the system was Charles Dawes. Pershing made him a brigadier general to give him some weight with his French counterparts, but Dawes remained a civilian. His shoes went unshined, and his uniform was usually a rumpled mess. Pershing would frequently button Dawes's shirt or coat before they would appear together in public. Once, when he walked into a Dawes conference, everyone rose and saluted. But Dawes neglected to take a large cigar out of his mouth. "Charlie," Pershing said, "the next time you salute, put the cigar on the other side of your mouth."

Although he could relax that way with close friends, and make visual gestures for photographers or admiring crowds, the one thing Pershing could not do was inspire soldiers or civilians with a ringing phrase. He was astute enough psychologically to trace this limitation to a boyhood episode, in which he forgot a speech during an elocution performance. A speech his staff wrote for him to make at Lafayette's tomb on July 4, 1917, ended with the oratorical high note, "Lafayette, we are here." Pershing crossed it out and wrote "not in character" beside it. He let one of his staff officers who spoke good French say it instead.

Another flaw, which drove Harbord and the rest of his staff to near distraction, was a complete lack of a sense of time. Pershing constantly arrived late to dinners or receptions, leaving kings, queens, prime ministers, and Allied generals impatiently tapping their VIP feet. The explanation was his appetite for detail. Devouring a report on weapons procurement or shipping schedules, Pershing would lose touch with the external world.

The euphoria of Pershing's arrival soon vanished: The promise of American aid remained unfulfilled. In the fall, the Germans and Austrians wrecked the Italian army at Caporetto. The Bolsheviks, having seized power in Moscow, took Russia out of the war, freeing an estimated seventy-seven German divisions for service on the Western Front. As a handful of American divisions trickled into Saint-Nazaire on their way to training areas in Lorraine, the Allies put more and more pressure on Pershing to give them control of his army.

The French and British generals summoned political reinforcements. Premier Paul Painlevé and Prime Minister David Lloyd George assailed Washington, D.C., with warnings of disaster and grave doubts about Pershing's capacity—simultaneously arranging for Pershing to be made aware of these fires being ignited in his rear. The only reinforcement Pershing got from Wilson was Bliss, an Anglophile who immediately sided with the British on amalgamation. Bliss said they should cable their opposing views to Washington and let the president decide. Pershing responded with some very straight talk. "Bliss," he said, "do you know what would happen if we did that? We would both be relieved from further duty in France and that is exactly what we should deserve." Bliss capitulated for the time being, a tribute not to the inferiority of his ideas but to the force of Pershing's personality.

The amalgamation pressure hardened Pershing's determination to make the AEF the best army in Europe. He was particularly tough on the 1st Division, which arrived in time to march through Paris on July 4—without the precision he expected. He took an instant dislike to the division's commander, Major General William Siebert, an engineering officer with little field experience. In October, inspecting the division, Pershing blasted Siebert in front of his officers. A young staff captain, George C. Marshall, stepped forward and launched a passionate defense of the general and the division, which was hampered by shortages of everything from motor transport to ammunition. The rest of the staff watched, wide-eyed, certain that Marshall and his military career were about to be obliterated. Instead, Pershing studied him for a long thoughtful moment and more or less apologized for his bad temper. It was the beginning of Marshall's rise to a colonel's rank and a dominant role on the AEF staff.

But Marshall did not change Pershing's opinion of Siebert. "Slow of speech and of thought . . . slovenly in dress . . . utterly hopeless as an instructor or tactician" were among his comments. Within a month, Bullard had replaced Siebert as commander of the 1st Division. Pershing was equally unrelenting about most of the other generals who were shipped to Europe to survey the Western Front while their divisions were training in the United States. "Too old," "very fat and inactive," "could not begin to stand the strain" were some of the judgments he made of them. Washington ignored his criticisms and sent almost all of these losers back to France, giving Pershing the unwelcome job of relieving them—a task he performed with grim efficiency.

Ironically, one of the few who escaped Pershing's lash was the fattest general in the army, Hunter Liggett. Pershing kept him because Liggett, former head of the Army War College, had a brain. The Pershing within the Iron General had enough humor to like Liggett's defense of his bulk: There was nothing wrong with fat as long as it was not above the collar.

In the fall of 1917, Pershing moved AEF headquarters to Chaumont, a hilly town of 20,000, some 140 miles east of Paris. There, he and the staff were less exposed to the temptations of the *guerre de luxe*, as more cynical types called service in the City of Light. But Pershing had already succumbed. In September he had begun a liaison with a twenty-three-year-old Romanian artist, Micheline Resco, who had been commissioned by the French government to paint his portrait. He visited her by night in her apartment on the rue Descombes, sitting up front with his chauffeur on his way there and back, the windshield signs with the U.S. flag and his four stars flat on the dashboard, out of sight. Contrary to appearances, it was another love match, and it lasted, without benefit of clergy, for the rest of his life.

The Germans gave him other things to think about. In November they raided the 1st Division just after it entered the lines, killing three Americans, wounding five, and taking twelve prisoners. When Pershing heard the news he wept—not with grief for the dead, but with the humiliation of even a small defeat, which he knew would lead to more French and British condescension and demands for amalgamation. When the 1st Division planned a retaliatory raid of its own, the AEF commander supervised it personally. It was a humiliating flop. The infantry and the engineers failed to meet in no-man's-land and, without the latter's bangalore torpedoes, no one could get through the German barbed wire.

Eventually the division pulled off a successful raid, led by Theodore Roosevelt's oldest son, Ted, but these trivial skirmishes only intensified Allied disillusion with Pershing. The new French premier, Georges Clemenceau, locally known as the Tiger, bared his claws and remarked that Pershing's chief preoccupation seemed to be having dinner in Paris.

As 1918 began, Pershing had only four divisions in France, and three of them were short a total of 20,000 men. None but the 1st had fired a shot at the Germans. Wilson complicated Pershing's life by issuing his own peace terms, the Fourteen Points, infuriating the French and English with the president's blissful ignorance of political realities. The Germans ignored Wilson and continued to shift divisions to the Western Front—with new tactics designed to create their own version of open warfare.

The tactics had been developed by the German General Staff and first used in Italy and on the Eastern Front. They depended heavily on surprise. German artillerists had solved the problem of aiming guns accurately at night without registering fire, which had previously announced offensives on both sides. The key troops were elite *Sturmtruppen* with mission-oriented orders—rather than the detailed timetables that had hobbled earlier offensives. Instead of being assigned a particular objective, the storm troopers were told to penetrate as deeply as possible and disrupt the enemy rear areas. Commanders would commit additional infantry only at breakthroughs, leaving enemy strongpoints isolated and eventually vulnerable to assault from the rear.

On March 21, 1918, the Germans unleashed these innovations on the British Fifth Army, guarding the hinge between the two Allied forces in Picardy. In three days, 90,000 Tommies surrendered, and another 90,000 became casualties. The Fifth Army ceased to exist, and the Germans menaced Amiens, the key rail hub connecting the British and French armies. The frantic Allies convened a conference at Doullens, to which they did not even bother to invite Pershing or any other American. The only general who seemed interested in fighting was Ferdinand Foch, until recently in disgrace for squandering his men in suicidal attacks. The politicians persuaded Haig and Pétain to accept Foch as the Supreme Commander, to coordinate the collapsing battle line.

Instead of sulking over being ignored, Pershing made his only grand gesture of the war. He drove to Foch's headquarters outside Paris and, in reasonably good French, declared: "I have come to tell you that the American people would consider it a great honor for our troops to be engaged in the present battle. I ask you for this in their name and my own." Everyone applauded the performance. It made headlines. But Pershing soon learned he had embraced a rattlesnake.

Instead of taking the four available American divisions and putting them into line as an army corps, which was what Pershing wanted, Foch assigned them to quiet sectors, piecemeal, after the battle for Amiens subsided. Next, behind Pershing's back, Foch dispatched a cable to Wilson telling him that unless 600,000 infantrymen were shipped to Europe in the next three months, unattached, for use as replacements in the French and British armies, the war was lost.

Pershing fought the Frenchman with his only weapon: an immense stubbornness and rocklike faith in his vision of an independent American army. Even when the secretary of war was cajoled into backing Foch by the devious Bliss, who seized the first opportunity to revoke his capitulation to Pershing, the Iron General clung to his determination. In May, soon after a second German offensive had come perilously close to smashing through the northern end of the British line and seizing the Channel ports, the Allies convened another conference at Abbeville. Pershing faced Lloyd George, Clemenceau, and Italian prime minister, Vittorio Emanuele Orlando, plus Haig, Foch, and a half-dozen other generals and cabinet officers. Bliss said not a word in his support. The others raged, screamed, cursed, and pleaded—but Pershing would not change his mind. He absolutely refused to let the Americans fight in units smaller than a division—and he insisted that even this concession would be temporary, pending the formation of an American army.

"Are you willing to risk our being driven back to the Loire?" Foch shouted.

"Gentlemen," Pershing said after another forty minutes of wrangling, "I have thought this program over very deliberately and I will not be coerced."

Pershing was taking one of the greatest gambles in history. On May 27, the Germans struck again, this time at the French along the Chemin des Dames ridge northeast of Soissons. Once more, the German artillery's fiendish combination of high explosives and poison gas tore apart the front lines, and the storm troopers poured through the gaps. The French Sixth Army evaporated. In a week Soissons and Château-Thierry fell, and the Germans were on the Marne, only fifty miles from Paris.

This time, American divisions were not diverted to quiet sectors. The 2d and 3d Divisions went into line around Château-Thierry as *poilus* streamed past them shouting, *"La guerre finie."* Except for some lively skirmishing, the Germans did not attack. Their infantry went on the defensive, while the generals brought up their artillery and tried to decide what to do with the huge salient they had carved in the French lines between Soissons and Reims.

The French commander of the sector, General Jean-Marie-Joseph Degoutte, was, like Foch, an apostle of the school of frontal attack—which had done little thus far but pile up Allied bodies in front of German machine-gun emplacements. Finding himself in possession of fresh American troops, he went on the offensive, ordering an attack on Belleau Wood. He found a willing collaborator in Colonel Preston Brown, the 2d Division's chief of staff. Brown—who dominated the overage and incompetent division commander, Omar Bundy—was burning to demonstrate American prowess. He accepted at face value French reports that the Germans held only the northern corner of the wood. In fact, they occupied it to the last inch with infantry supported by machine guns set up for interlocking fields of fire.

On June 6, without sending out a single patrol to find more information, Brown and Harbord, recently reassigned to the division as commander of the 4th Marine Brigade, ordered their men forward in a frontal assault. The Marines advanced in massed formations unseen on the Western Front since 1914. Incredulous German machine gunners mowed them down in windrows. The slaughter revealed the limitations of Pershing's doctrine of open warfare. As Liggett later mournfully remarked, no one, including Pershing, had thought it out.

The Marines eventually captured Belleau Wood, after the French pulled them back and treated the Germans to a fourteen-hour artillery barrage that smashed the place flat. Pershing rewarded Harbord for his incompetence (there were 50 percent casualties) by making him commander of the 2d Division in place of Bundy, who had stood around during the battle without saying a word while Harbord and Brown made their bloody blunders.

The desperate French trumpeted Belleau Wood as a major victory in their newspapers, and reporters around the world followed suit. Pershing went along because he was even more desperate for proof that his men could stand up to the Germans. The battering he had taken from Foch, Haig, and others had broadened his definition of what constituted a battlefield success. Henceforth, Pershing would countenance the pernicious idea that high casualties were proof of a commander's fighting ability.

Beginning on the night of July 14, seven American divisions (troops were starting to arrive in ever-greater numbers) played crucial roles in smashing the next German offensive, code-named FRIEDENSTURM—the "peace assault." Casualties were relatively light because the Allies, perhaps borrowing a bit of Pershing luck, discovered the exact day and hour of the attack from a captured German officer. Ignoring Foch's senseless order to hold every inch of sacred soil, General Pétain created an elastic defense that inflicted enormous losses on the *Sturmtruppen*. Pershing was only a spectator at this three-day clash, his divisions being temporarily under the orders of French generals.

Foch, an apostle of attack, at last became the right general in the right place at the right time. He threw the American 1st and 2d Divisions and a French colonial division into the soft left flank of the German Marne salient around Soissons. The first day, July 18, was a sensational success, but on the second day the Germans recovered from their surprise. Their machine guns sprouted everywhere, and casualties mounted. Again and again, Americans advanced across open ground without concealment or cover—with predictable results. The 1st and 2d had 12,000 casualties. The 2d, already bled by Belleau Wood, collapsed and was withdrawn after two days. The 1st, equally battered (the 26th Infantry Regiment lost 3,000 out of 3,200 men), was withdrawn the following day. This was hardly the staying power Pershing had envisioned for his double-sized divisions. But he ignored the danger signs and told Harbord that even if the two divisions never fired another shot, they had made their commanders "immortal."

Having seized the initiative, Foch was determined not to relinquish it. For the next six weeks, he ordered attacks all around the Marne salient. In the vanguard were American divisions, fighting under French generals. This little-studied Aisne-Marne offensive proved the courage of the American infantrymen—and the limitations of their open-warfare tactics. Before it ended in early September, over 90,000 Americans were dead or wounded.

Inept tactics were not the only problem. Too often, Americans found their flanks exposed by the failure of a French division to keep pace with their attack. Bullard, who by then was supposed to be supervising American operations as commander of the III Corps, fretted about the murderous casualties but did little else. There is no record of Pershing saying anything.

The climax of this messy operation was on August 27, when an isolated company of the 28th Division was annihilated in Fismette, on the north bank of the Vesle River. Bullard had tried to withdraw the soldiers—they were the only Americans on that side of the river, surrounded by some 200,000 Germans—but Degoutte, now commander of the Sixth Army, had revoked the order. When Bullard reported the episode a few days later, Pershing asked, "Why didn't you disobey the order?"

"I did not answer. It was not necessary to answer," Bullard wrote in his memoirs.

By this time, five other American divisions were training with the British army. On August 8, the British had made a successful attack on the western flank of the salient that the Germans had created when they routed the Fifth Army in Picardy. Pershing had permitted these divisions to go directly into British training areas when they arrived in Europe—an example of the partial surrenders of control extracted from him by Foch and Haig, with the help of the German army. But Pershing stubbornly discounted the possibility that perhaps this was the best way to use the Americans finally flooding into France—brigading them with British or French armies, who already had sophisticated staffs and supply systems in place.

Instead, the Iron General never stopped insisting on a totally independent army. On August 10, he opened First Army headquarters; five days later, he handed Foch a plan for an attack on the Saint-Mihiel salient, another huge bulge into the French lines, south of Verdun. He withdrew three of his five divisions from a choleric Haig, and all that were under French control.

On August 28, as the Americans moved into the lines, Foch descended on Pershing with one last attempt to utilize the AEF in—from the viewpoint of the Supreme Commander—a more rational way. He announced a master plan he had conceived while visiting Haig. The whole German battlefront, he said, was one huge salient that should be attacked from the north, the south, and the center. He therefore wanted Pershing more or less to abort the Saint-Mihiel operation, limiting it to a few divisions, and transfer the rest of his army back to French control for attacks in the Aisne and Argonne theaters.

A vehement argument ensued. At one point, both men were on their feet screaming curses at each other. "Do you wish to take part in the battle?" Foch shrilled, the ultimate insult one general could throw at another. For a moment, Pershing seriously thought of flattening the little Frenchman with a roundhouse right. "As an American army and in no other way!" he replied.

"I must insist on the arrangement!" Foch shouted.

Pershing squared his jaw. "Marshal Foch, you may insist all you please, but I decline absolutely to agree to your plan. While our army will fight wherever you decide, it will fight only as an independent American army."

After another week of wrangling, Pershing accepted a dangerous compromise. He would attack the Saint-Mihiel salient on September 12, as planned, then transfer the bulk of his 500,000-man army west of the Meuse to attack north through the Argonne as part of the overall Allied offensive on September 26. It was an ambitious assignment for a general who had never commanded more than 11,000 men in action and a staff that had yet to fight a single battle. Only a man with Pershing's self-confidence would have tried it. To compound his potential woes, he accepted a battle plan from Foch that gave French generals command east of the Meuse and west of the Argonne Forest, violating a primary military maxim: An attacking army should be responsible for both sides of a natural obstacle such as a forest or a river.

On September 5, Pershing, disturbed by AEF casualties in the Aisne-Marne offensive, made a stab at defining open warfare. In a general order issued to the First Army, he contrasted it to trench warfare, which he claimed was "marked by uniform formations, the regulation of space and time by higher commands down to the smallest details and little initiative." Open warfare had "irregular . . . formations, comparatively little regulation of space and time . . . and the greatest possible use of the infantry's own firepower to enable it to get forward . . . [plus] brief orders and the greatest possible use of individual initiative." It was much too late for such complex ideas to filter down even to division staffs, much less to the captains and lieutenants leading companies. Nor did this inchoate rhetoric offer a clue to how to deal with the primary defensive weapon on the Western Front—the machine gun.

At first, Pershing luck seemed to hold. The Saint-Mihiel offensive was the walkover of the war. The Germans were in the process of withdrawing from the salient when the Americans attacked. Resistance was perfunctory. The bag of prisoners and captured guns was big enough to make headlines, although the take was not nearly as large as originally hoped. Pershing and his staff now tried to imitate the Germans and achieve surprise in the Argonne. He left most of his veteran divisions in Saint-Mihiel and shifted largely green units west. No significant snafus developed on the roads, thanks to the planning genius of George C. Marshall, who was nicknamed the Wizard for managing the sixty-mile transfer in wretched rainy weather.

On September 26, after a German-style, 4,000-gun artillery barrage, Pershing threw 250,000 men in three corps at an estimated 50,000 unprepared German defenders in the twenty-mile-wide Argonne valley. A massive hogback ran down the center, forcing the attackers into defiles on both sides. It was, Liggett said, a natural fortress that made the Virginia wilderness seem like a park. Yet Pershing's plan called for no less than a ten-mile-abreast advance the first day to crack the German defensive line.

Five of Pershing's nine divisions had never been in action before. Even experienced divisions such as the 77th, which had been blooded under the

French, were full of green replacements. The 77th received 2,100 men who had never fired a rifle the day before they attacked. Everything imaginable proceeded to go wrong with Pershing's army. The Germans fell back to well-prepared defenses and began machine-gunning charging Americans. Massive amounts of enemy artillery on the heights east of the Meuse and along the edge of the Argonne Forest which loomed a thousand feet above the valley floor, exacted an even heavier toll.

Rigid orders, issued by Pershing's own staff, held up whole divisions at crucial moments. The 4th Division could have captured the key height of Montfaucon the first day, but it stood still for four hours, waiting for the green 79th Division, assigned the objective, to come abreast of it. By the time Montfaucon fell the following day, the Germans had poured in five first-class divisions, and the American advance had stumbled to a bloody halt.

In the north, where the British and French were attacking, the Germans could give ground for sixty or a hundred miles before yielding anything vital. But only twenty-four miles from the American jumping-off point in the Argonne was the Sedan-Mézières four-track railroad, which supplied almost all the food and ammunition to the Germans' northern armies. They were fighting to protect their jugular in the Argonne. By October 4, they had elements of twenty-three divisions in line or local reserve.

Withdrawing his green divisions, Pershing replaced them with the veteran units he had left in Saint-Mihiel and tried to resume the attack. He was on the road constantly, visiting corps and division headquarters, urging generals and colonels to inject their men with more "drive" and "push." But Pershing was discovering that rhetoric could not silence a machine gun.

His men bled, and also began to starve. Food did not get forward as monumental traffic jams developed on the few roads into the Argonne. Wounded lay unevacuated. Clemenceau, caught in a jam while visiting the front, lost half a day and departed vowing to get rid of Pershing. Stragglers were another problem. Liggett estimated that at the height of the battle, 100,000 fugitives were wandering around the First Army's rear areas. One division reported an effective frontline strength of only 1,600 men. Early in October, Pershing authorized officers to shoot down any man who ran away—proof of his growing desperation.

Worsening Pershing's woes, while the Americans were withdrawing the wreckage of the green divisions, was a visit from Foch's chief of staff, who informed Pershing that the generalissimo thought he had too many men in the Argonne. Foch proposed shifting six divisions to nearby French armies. Recent historians have been inclined to think Foch was probably right. The French on

Pershing's right and left were making little progress and could have used some help. But by now, Pershing hated Foch too much to take his advice about anything. He told the Supreme Commander to go to hell. Foch retaliated with a formal on-the-record letter ordering him to attack continuously "without any [further] interruptions."

Killing fire from the guns east of the Meuse stopped the veteran divisions when they jumped off on October 4. German counterattacks drove them back again and again. Only the 1st Division, under the Cromwellian Charles Summerall, gained some ground, plunging up the left defile for a half-dozen miles—at a cost of 9,387 casualties. On October 8, Pershing sent two divisions east of the Meuse to join the French in an attempt to silence the artillery. The attack faltered and collapsed into a pocket on the banks of the Meuse, deluged by gas and shell fire.

Pershing drove himself as hard as he did his men. He sat up until three or four in the morning reading reports and pondering maps. Rumors drifted into headquarters that Foch and Clemenceau were urging Wilson to replace him with Bliss. One day, in his car with his favorite aide, Major James Collins, a played-out Pershing put his head in his hands and, speaking to his dead wife, moaned: "Frankie . . . Frankie . . . my God, sometimes I don't know how I can go on."

Outwardly, no one else saw anything but the Iron General, still in charge. "Things are going badly," he told Major General Henry Allen, commander of the 90th Division. "But by God, Allen, I was never so much in earnest in my life, and we are going to get through." Marshall thought this was Pershing's finest hour. More critical recent historians, pointing to the substantial gains being made and the huge numbers of prisoners and guns being captured by French and British armies on other fronts, suggest Pershing was hopelessly out of his depth but was refusing to admit it.

There may be some truth to this assertion—except for the last part. On October 12, tacitly admitting he did not have the answer to the Argonne, Pershing gave Liggett command of the First Army and created a Second Army, under Bullard, to operate east of the Meuse. Pershing became the commander of the army group—chairman of the board instead of chief executive officer. The First Army continued to attack for another seven days, finally breaching the Kriemhilde Stellung on October 19. It had taken three weeks and 100,000 casualties to achieve what Pershing and his staff had thought they could do in a single day.

At this point, the First Army was, in the opinion of one staff officer, "a disorganized and wrecked army." Liggett promptly went on the defensive. When

Pershing persisted in hanging around headquarters, talking about launching another attack, Liggett told him to "go away and forget it." Pershing meekly obeyed.

It was just as well, because he soon had a more serious topic on his mind. Early in October, the Germans had announced they were willing to accept peace on the basis of Wilson's Fourteen Points. As Wilson began negotiating with them, Pershing came perilously close to making the president look foolish by issuing a public statement that he favored unconditional surrender.

The Wilson administration was infuriated. Many people assumed Pershing's statement was the opening salvo of a run for the presidency. On the contrary, Pershing was motivated by two things. His political mentor, Theodore Roosevelt, was savaging Wilson back in the United States with a similar call for unconditional surrender. The Iron General was also seething because Haig, the British commander, had recommended an armistice, arguing that the British and French were close to exhaustion and the American army was too inept to bear any substantial share of another offensive. Pershing wanted more war to make Haig eat those words.

Under fierce pressure from Wilson, Pershing accepted the idea of armistice. But he remained convinced it was a mistake. When the First Army resumed the offensive on November 1, he urged it forward with ferocious intensity, hoping it could smash the Germans before negotiators agreed on terms. Rested and reorganized, imbued with new tactics that urged infiltration and flank attacks rather than piling men against enemy strongpoints, the Americans were sensationally successful. They stormed across the Meuse, cutting the Sedan-Mézières railroad and threatening the German armies in the north with imminent starvation and collapse. At Pershing's insistence, they kept attacking until the Armistice went into effect at eleven in the morning on November 11. "If they had given us another ten days," Pershing said, "we would have rounded up the entire German army, captured it, humiliated it." There are strong reasons to doubt this postwar Pershing boast, however. In the final days, replacements had become a major AEF problem. The German army was still a formidable fighting force—and a policy of unconditional surrender might have inspired them to resist with desperate ferocity, as they demonstrated in World War II.

In these same final days, Pershing, still fuming over Foch's condescension and Clemenceau's sneers, attempted to retaliate with a ploy that seriously endangered the fragile alliance. He decided the Americans would capture Sedan, the city where the French had ingloriously surrendered to Bismarck's Germans in 1870. Ignoring a boundary drawn by Foch that placed Sedan in the zone of the French Fourth Army, he ordered the First Army to capture the city and deprive the French of this symbolic honor. The order—which directed the I Corps, spearheaded by the 42d Division, to make the main thrust, "assisted on their right by the V Corps"—was so vague that it encouraged General Summerall, by then the commander of the V Corps, to march the 1st Division across the front of the 42d Division to get there first. In the darkness and confusion, the 1st Division captured Douglas MacArthur, one of the 42d's brigadiers, who looked like a German officer because of his unorthodox headgear. It was a miracle that the two divisions did not shoot each other to pieces. If the German army had been in any kind of fighting shape, a counterattack would have wreaked havoc. The episode suggests Pershing's limitations as a practitioner of coalition warfare. In the end, the French Fourth Army was permitted to capture Sedan. Liggett wanted to court-martial Summerall, but Pershing dismissed the whole affair.

When the bells rang out across France and the people erupted into mad joy, not even Pershing could resist the emotions of victory. In perhaps his most significant summary of the war, he said several times, "The men were willing to pay the price." Perhaps this was as close as the Iron General came to admitting he had made some mistakes.

For the rest of his long life—he did not die until 1948—Pershing spent a good deal of his time fostering the career of the man who would lead America's armies in World War II. Marshall served as his aide when he was Chief of Staff after the war, they became close friends, and Pershing was best man at Marshall's wedding in 1927. When MacArthur, then the army chief of staff, tried to short-circuit Marshall's advancement by appointing him senior instructor to the Illinois National Guard in 1933, Pershing visited him in Chicago, creating headlines for the obscure young colonel. The next chief of staff, a Pershing man, brought Marshall back to Washington as his assistant. In 1939, Pershing persuaded Franklin Delano Roosevelt to make Marshall the Chief of Staff.

In his private life, Pershing was a dutiful father to his only son, Warren. He made no objection when Warren chose a civilian rather than a military career. Pershing remained devoted to Micheline Resco, but he was frequently linked romantically to other women. He once remarked that if he married all the women he was reported to be romancing, he would have to start a harem. Near the end of his life, apparently, Pershing did marry Resco in a secret service.

Trying to sum up Pershing, almost everyone found him full of contradictions. Secretary of War Baker wondered how a man could combine such large views with an obsessive concern for buttons. "If he was not a great man," wrote the newsman Frank Simonds, "there were few stronger." The British military thinker B. H. Liddell Hart said no other man could have built the AEF, and "without that army the war could hardly have been saved and could not have been won." Perhaps his unmilitary friend Charles Dawes came closest to the Iron General's inner secret: "John Pershing, like Lincoln, recognized no superior on the face of the earth." Unquestionably, Pershing left something to be desired as a field commander. But without him, American doughboys might have become cannon fodder for French and British generals—a development that would have caused a huge political backlash on the home front. Meanwhile, he and his men learned the bitter lessons of how to fight on the Western Front. Fortunately for Pershing, the doughboys were willing to pay the price.

BELLEAU WOOD:
ONE MAN'S INITIATION
Allan R. Millett

—

EAGER TO HAVE U.S. MARINES FIGHT IN WORLD WAR I AS part of General John J. Pershing's American Expeditionary Forces, the Marine Corps commandant, Major General George Barnett, successfully persuaded the War Department to accept a Marine brigade as part of the token force sent to France in 1917. Eventually organized as the 4th Brigade of the U.S. 2d Division, it consisted of a brigade headquarters, a machine-gun battalion, and two infantry regiments, the 5th and 6th Marines.

One member of the 1st Battalion, 6th Marines, was a twenty-one-year-old former football player from Bloomington, Illinois, named Gerald C. Thomas. Like most of his comrades, Thomas volunteered for the Marine Corps in the spring of 1917. Like many of the new Marines he also expected to be an officer, since he had completed three years of college at Illinois Wesleyan University, and Commandant Barnett had announced that he wanted college men to be the lieutenants in the expanded corps. Barnett had more officer candidates than openings, however, so Jerry Thomas had to serve first as a corporal and then as a sergeant in the 75th Company until German bullets created sufficient openings in 1918. Before he left the Marine Corps at the end of 1955, General Gerald C. Thomas had fought in three wars and served as assistant commandant and chief of staff of the Marine Corps. His own service reputation, which soared on Guadalcanal and in Korea, began at the Battle of Belleau Wood.

When the German army mounted its last attempt to win the war on the Western Front in March 1918, it found no Americans except scattered soldiers training with the British. By the end of the spring, General Pershing had committed the four divisions he considered more or less combat-ready to the French armies attempting to hold positions north and east of Paris. Late in May, the Germans shattered a mixed Anglo-French force along the Chemin des Dames ridge, and the 2d Division joined the French XXI Corps (under Général de Division Jean Degoutte), which was fighting a confused withdrawal north of the Marne River near the town of Château-Thierry.

Having had a taste of trench warfare in March, Thomas's battalion entered its first major battle with some combat experience, but as its officers and men left their camp near Paris by truck on May 30, none of them could have foreseen the ferocious battle that awaited. At the van of the 4th Brigade (under Brigadier General James G. Harbord, United States Army—no Marine brigadier generals had been immediately available to fill that opening), the 6th Marines moved into an extemporized (and poorly chosen) defensive position anchored on the farming village of Lucy-le-Bocage. From their hastily dug rifle pits, the Marines of the 75th Company, 1st Battalion, 6th Marines, looked across the pasture and wheat field in front of them and saw a thick wood. Sergeant Thomas, by now acting platoon sergeant of the 75th Company's 3d Platoon, certainly had no idea that the wood to his front would prove historic to him and the entire United States Marine Corps.

———

ALLAN R. MILLETT is the General Raymond E. Mason, Jr., Professor of Military History at The Ohio State University. The following article is excerpted from his biography of Gerald C. Thomas, *In Many a Strife: General Gerald C. Thomas and the U.S. Marine Corps, 1917–1956.* Millett is (with Williamson Murray) the author of *A War to Be Won: Fighting the Second World War.*

A DARK FORTRESS OF TALL HARDWOODS, BELLEAU WOOD STRETCHED FOR about a mile along the edge of a low plateau a few miles from the Marne River. It took its name from the farming village of Belleau, beyond the wood's northeast corner. Belleau's only noteworthy feature—a clear, cold spring—gave the town its name ("beautiful water"). Neither the wood nor the town had any importance except that both lay between two major roads that gave the attacking Germans, the IV Reserve Corps, a way to flank the Allied positions along the nearby Paris–Metz highway.

The wood provided an excellent place to assemble an attack force safe from Allied observers. Moreover, German spotters on its western edge could see the Marine brigade's positions around Lucy-le-Bocage. The wood also made an excellent defensive position. Used by a rich Paris businessman as a hunting preserve, Belleau Wood deceived the Americans who watched it from a mile away. Inside the outer edge of trees, it was a tangle of brush and second growth, cut by deep ravines and studded with rock outcroppings and large boulders. Only narrow paths and rocky streams provided access through the wood. Little light penetrated the trees. A haven for game birds and animals, it was meant for hunting by men, not for the killing of men. In June 1918, however, the 4th Marine Brigade and the German 28th and 237th Divisions made Belleau Wood a battlefield.

On the morning of June 3, 1918, General de Infanterie Richard von Conta, commander of the German IV Reserve Corps, ordered a three-division attack on the French forces screening the 2d Division. As the fighting increased, German artillery, assisted by spotters in aircraft and balloons, crashed down upon the Marines' defensive positions. The 1st Battalion, 6th Marines, did not occupy well-built trenches, only quickly dug foxholes. As the shells dropped, shovels and picks rose and fell. Jerry Thomas and the 75th Company soon learned that only a direct hit or a near miss would destroy a foxhole; the 75th pulled the ground around itself and endured. Nevertheless, it suffered casualties: a curious Marine decapitated when he looked outside his hole, two men knocked senseless by a near miss, a carrying party destroyed on its way forward with water. French soldiers began to drift back through Lucy. To the north, small-arms fire swelled as the first German patrols made contact with a battalion of the 5th Marines defending the woods and high ground west of the

Torcy–Lucy road. The 75th Company could hear the noise of troops moving in Belleau Wood.

Soon the French delaying action collapsed, and the only sign of French combativeness was the occasional group of *poilus* who stayed with the Marines. In Jerry Thomas's position, the 3d Platoon gained a Hotchkiss machine-gun crew, a welcome addition since Marine machine-gun teams did not arrive until late in the day. The 6th Marines was spread thin, for its commander, Colonel Albertus W. Catlin, had committed three of his four reserve companies to his endangered left flank, where the 5th Marines had first met the Germans. In the late afternoon the 1st Battalion shifted positions to meet an expected attack to its left, which meant that Thomas's platoon moved from the edge of the village into an open field.

Hardly had the platoon scooped out shallow holes than a German battalion—probably between 400 and 500 men—emerged from Belleau Wood in lines of skirmishers and squad columns and started across the fields toward Lucy. At a range of 400 yards the 1st Battalion opened fire, savaging the German infantry with rapid, accurate rifle fire. The French Hotchkiss crew raked the Germans, and Thomas watched soldiers in baggy *feldgrau* uniforms spin and slump into the wheat and poppies. The attack collapsed, and the survivors scuttled back into Belleau Wood, where the rest of the 461st Infantry Regiment, 237th Division (about 1,200 officers and men), had concentrated for another attack.

Uncertain about the nature of the new resistance his corps had encountered, General von Conta halted the advance on the afternoon of June 3 and instead continued his assault on the 4th Marine Brigade's lines with artillery fire. As the heavier German guns and trench mortars moved into range, the Marines felt the increased weight of the bombardment. They especially disliked the heavy mortar shells, which they could see curling in on top of them and which detonated with both fearsome noise and destructiveness. Much of the artillery fire, in fact, was now falling on positions to the rear where the Germans guessed—incorrectly—the enemy might have its reserve infantry and artillery positions. The next day (June 4) the infantrymen on either side remained in their holes as German and Allied artillery swept the front with a desultory bombardment. On the left flank of the 6th Marines' position, a German patrol found a Marine's corpse and identified its foe for the first time. Von Conta shifted to the defense while he awaited the German 7th Army's decision on whether the IV Reserve Corps should make another extreme effort to reach the Paris–Metz highway from the north.

Meanwhile, the 6th Marines continued to improve its defensive position by building up its artillery and logistical support. Thomas and two companions were dispatched to map the battalion positions in the sector. The battalion commander, Major John A. ("Johnny the Hard") Hughes, liked their work—but not their findings. The entire 1st Battalion position had neither adequate cover nor concealment. In fact, Hughes told Colonel Catlin that the entire regiment was exposed and persuaded the colonel to order a withdrawal that night to a reverse-slope defense two miles to the rear.

However, General Degoutte, headmaster of the school of the unrelenting attack, had other plans for the 2d Division, and a withdrawal was not part of his concept of operations. Degoutte's XXI Corps was, for all practical purposes, the French 167th Division, the U.S. 2d Division, and some French artillery regiments, for his other two French divisions no longer existed as effective fighting organizations. At midafternoon on June 5, Degoutte ordered the 167th and 2d divisions to attack the Germans the next day in order to disrupt the massing of German artillery and infantry reserves in the Clignon River valley north of Torcy. Hill 142, at the left of the line held by the Marines, was their first objective. The 2d Division received a second objective—Belleau Wood—which was to be attacked as soon as possible after the completion of the attack to the north.

The 1st Battalion, 6th Marines, was sent back to a reserve position. Hughes was not unhappy. He did not like the attack plan, a straight-ahead advance like Pickett's Charge. The 1st Battalion marched five miles to the rear into a protected, defiladed wood near Nanteuil, a village on the Marne. Arriving by daybreak, the Marines stripped off their sodden equipment, ate their first hot meal in a week, and collapsed in sleep in the welcome haylofts. In the meantime, the roar of artillery at the front introduced a new phase in the battle for Belleau Wood.

THE 4TH BRIGADE ATTACKS OF JUNE 6, 1918, PRODUCED A FURY OF HEROISM AND sacrifice that remained fixed as a high point of valor in the history of the American Expeditionary Forces and the Marine Corps in World War I. Although Degoutte's and Harbord's conduct of operations on that day showed little skill, no one then or now has faulted the Marines for their efforts to turn bad plans into good victories. The first mistake was Degoutte's in insisting that the attacks begin on June 6 rather than a day later, after the attacking battalions had time to enter the front lines, to conduct some reconnaissance, and to make their own analyses of the situation. Artillery-fire support could certainly have profited by the delay. As it was, the battalions had to conduct a relief of frontline positions and also mount an attack within hours after a night movement, no ingredient for success. Moreover, a 6th Marines nighttime patrol had reported that Belleau Wood was strongly defended. This report reached brigade, but it made no difference. The attacks proceeded on the assumption that the German front was lightly held, reinforced by reports that French aerial observers saw little movement in the area.

The early-morning attack on Hill 142, mounted by only two 5th Marine companies, produced a costly victory that widened with the arrival of four more Marine companies and supporting machine gunners, who beat back a series of German counterattacks. The action ended around nine o'clock in the morning. Afterward, General Harbord ordered the Belleau Wood attack to begin at five o'clock. His order reflected an optimism unjustified by the stiffness of the German resistance that morning, for he expected Catlin to take Belleau Wood and the town of Bouresches with only three battalions—perhaps 2,000 men. (Two of these battalions had additional assignments that prevented them from using all four of their rifle companies.) Presumably, the fire of thirteen Allied artillery battalions would clear the way of Germans. In any event, Catlin mounted the attack as ordered—although Harbord's concept of "infiltration" changed to a converging standard battalion advance of two companies up, two back—and saw the better part of three battalions shot to pieces by German machine-gun positions along the western and southern edges of Belleau Wood.

From the west, Major Benjamin S. Berry's 3d Battalion, 5th Marines, barely entered the wood; so few, shocked, and exhausted were the survivors that they could advance no farther. Most of the battalion remained in a wheat field, dead or wounded. The southern attack by the 3d Battalion, 6th Marines, penetrated the wood at sufficient depth to hold a position, but only at great cost. Casualties in these two battalions approached 60 percent, with losses among officers and noncommissioned officers (NCOs) even higher. The two-company attack on Bouresches, on the other hand, produced success, even though the two companies also took prohibitive losses. The Germans quickly recognized that the loss of Bouresches menaced their lines of communications, so they counterattacked heavily, thus drawing the rest of the 2d Battalion, 6th Marines (under Major Thomas Holcomb), into the battle. Whatever its original tactical value, Belleau Wood had to be taken in order to protect the left flank of the Bouresches salient.

As he analyzed the scattered reports that arrived at his post of command (PC) during the evening of June 6, General Harbord began to understand that the Marine brigade had not taken Belleau Wood and that it had lost more than a thousand officers and men—including Colonel Catlin, who was wounded by a sniper's bullet while observing the attack. More Marines had become casualties in a few hours than the corps had suffered in its entire history. Although

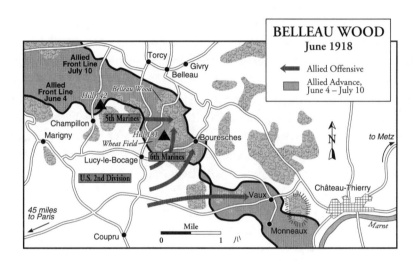

BELLEAU WOOD
June 1918

→ Allied Offensive

■ Allied Advance,
June 4 – July 10

Allied
Front Line
July 10

Allied
Front Line
June 4

Torcy
Givry
Belleau
Belleau Wood
Hill 142
5th Marines
Champillon
Marigny
Hill 181
Wheat Field
6th Marines
Lucy-le-Bocage
U.S. 2nd Division
Bouresches

to Metz

N

Château-Thierry

45 miles
to Paris

Vaux

Marne

Mile
Coupru
0   1

Monneaux

the attacks on Hill 142 and Bouresches had succeeded, the attack on the wood itself had not. Perhaps stung by his own shortcomings as a commander, Harbord lashed out at Catlin's replacement, Lieutenant Colonel Harry Lee, and demanded the attack be resumed. At that point, Belleau Wood basically remained German except for a corner of its southern edge held by the 3d Battalion, 6th Marines.

As the situation cleared during June 7, Harbord assumed that the 6th Marines could hold Bouresches—with help from the U.S. 23d Infantry Regiment to its right—so he ordered Lee to continue the attack within the wood itself. His Marines fought alone in Belleau Wood, without making much progress. Neither side could mount overwhelming artillery support, since the opposing positions were imprecise and too close; the battle pitted German machine-gun and mortar crews, supported by infantry, against Marine infantrymen, who depended primarily on rifles and grenades. Small groups of Marines crawled up to the machine-gun positions, threw grenades, then rushed in with bayonets. Few German prisoners survived. The Marines ran out of grenades, however, which increased their own casualties. By midmorning of June 8, the battalion had little fight left, and it withdrew from the wood. There were no Marines there now.

Harbord let the 2d Division artillery shell Belleau Wood for the rest of that day, while he organized his next attack. Degoutte had decided that he would not press the attack against Torcy, so Harbord could use his only two relatively unscathed battalions—2d Battalion, 5th Marines (under Lieutenant Colonel Frederic M. Wise), and 1st Battalion, 6th Marines—for another attack on Belleau Wood. On the evening of the eighth, Harbord ordered Major Hughes to move his battalion into woods southeast of Lucy-le-Bocage. Although the general had not yet committed himself to a particular plan, Hughes believed that Harbord wanted him in position to move into Belleau Wood the following afternoon.

Hughes again sent Sergeant Jerry Thomas on a reconnoitering expedition, this time to locate the mouth of a sunken road that could lead the battalion to the front along a gulley, which would provide cover and concealment. Thomas found the mouth of the sunken road, then jogged back to the battalion. He reported to Captain George A. Stowell, the senior company commander and a veteran of three Caribbean operations, who would move the battalion while Hughes conferred with Harbord at the PC.

The battalion stepped out around nine o'clock—and, in the dark, entered a nightmare of confusion and wrong turns. It did not reach the sunken road until midnight. There, the column met First Lieutenant Charles A. Etheridge, the new battalion intelligence officer. Thomas thought Etheridge knew the rest of the route, but Etheridge had not reconnoitered the trail because Hughes had not told him to do so. As dawn broke, the 1st Battalion strayed into the open fields west of Lucy-le-Bocage and into the view of German observation-balloon spotters. Stowell quickly ordered the men into a nearby wood, where they would have to stay until night came again. Furious, Hughes rejoined his battalion and relieved Stowell of command. (Stowell later returned to the battalion and had a distinguished career.)

Stowell's 76th Company went to First Lieutenant Macon C. Overton, a thin, handsome, laconic, twenty-six-year-old Georgian who had joined the corps as an enlisted man in 1914. Later in the day (June 9) Harbord ordered Hughes to resume his approach march and to be in position on June 10 to enter Belleau Wood behind a crushing barrage. After dark, the wandering 1st Battalion set off again for the front. This time it did not become lost. On the other hand, it also had nothing between it and the Germans but the outposts of one 2d Battalion company. The attack on Belleau Wood would have to start again from scratch.

Despite the setback of June 6, Harbord did not change his concept of attack for the June 10 operation. The 1st Battalion would attack the southern part of the wood while the 2d Battalion, 5th Marines, would later attack the northern part from the west. The two battalions would join one another at Belleau Wood's narrow, middle neck. It was a maneuver that looked good on a map, but it worked poorly on the battlefield because of the roughness of the terrain. Fortunately, the extra day of shelling had persuaded the German defenders—still battalions from the 237th and 28th Divisions—to concede the wood's southern edge. But the German combat teams still manned a thick belt of defenses that covered the wheat fields to the west and faced the trails inside the southern woods. The Allied artillery bombardment had taken its toll, but had not crushed the defenders. The Germans endured the intense barrage at daybreak on the tenth and then manned their positions to wait for the next two Marine battalions.

Disobeying Major Hughes's orders to remain near the phones at the battalion PC, Sergeant Thomas joined the waves of Marines as they left the woods and started across the lower-lying wheat field for Belleau Wood. The moment had seized him: "The sight of those brave waves moving through the wheat with bayonets fixed and rifles carried at the high post in our first offensive was a little too much to bear." With two companies forward and two back in the standard French attack formation, the battalion marched steadily across the Lucy–Bouresches road. Rifles at the high port, bayonets fixed, unreliable Chauchat automatic rifles pointed to the front, the Marines crossed the swale between the highway and the trees and entered the wood. During the advance,

Thomas ran through the wheat until he caught up with the 3d Platoon of the 75th Company, avoiding the bodies of Marines killed in the June 6 attack. Much to the battalion's surprise, not a shot was fired at it. Instead of entering the wood, Thomas started back to the PC, for he recalled "that I had another job to do." He met Hughes, who was elated by the attack and wanted to report his success by phone. The battalion commander did not censure him for joining the attack, but told him to move the PC across the road to the raised bank at the edge of Belleau Wood. As Thomas helped reestablish the battalion PC, he heard the roar of gunfire within the wood. The 1st Battalion had discovered the Germans.

For the 1st Battalion, 6th Marines, the battle began around six o'clock in the morning on June 10 and did not end until it left the wood seven days later, an exhausted, smaller, but still combative group of veteran Marines. Jerry Thomas fought with his battalion from start to finish. He learned to cope with stress, fear, hunger, thirst, exhaustion, and the death of friends over a protracted period of combat. The fighting on June 10 struck hard at Thomas's 75th Company, which moved through the wood with Lieutenant Overton's 76th Company on the left, in the center of the battalion front. When the company struck a strongpoint of three German machine guns, Thomas lost a dozen comrades from the 3d Platoon. The Marines crawled forward through "a great mass of rocks and boulders," Thomas later recalled, until they could throw grenades at the machine-gun nests.

Through most of the day, Thomas remained with Hughes at the battalion PC to manage scouting missions and analyze the vague company reports. During the afternoon the regimental intelligence officer, First Lieutenant William A. Eddy, came forward and told Hughes that Colonel Lee wanted an accurate report of the German positions. Taking Thomas with him to prepare sketch maps, Eddy crawled around the woods and quickly learned that no one could see much through the brush. Then, against Thomas's advice, he climbed a tree. Eddy immediately tumbled from the branches into Thomas's lap and said, "My God! I was looking square at a German in a machine-gun nest right down in front of us!" Eddy and Thomas returned to Hughes to report that the Germans still held Hill 181, a rocky rise that divided the western and southern wheat fields. Any attack across the western wheat field would still meet flanking fire from Belleau Wood. Having taken thirty-one casualties in the wood on June 10, Hughes agreed with Eddy's assessment that one battalion could not clear out the remaining Germans.

General Harbord then committed the 2d Battalion, 5th Marines, to the battle, establishing its attack for four-thirty the next day. Hughes's left-flank company, Overton's 76th, was supposed to protect the right flank of Wise's battalion. Hughes assigned Thomas the job of ensuring that Overton contacted Wise's battalion as Harbord directed and "conformed to the progress of the attack," as noted in the brigade attack order. As the rolling barrage lifted, Thomas and one of his scouts left the wood and found Wise's battalion moving across the same deadly wheat field that had become the graveyard of Berry's battalion on June 6. Its passage was only slightly less disastrous. As the battalion neared Belleau Wood, German artillery fire crashed down upon it and machine-gun fire raked its front and flanks. Instead of pivoting to the north, the Marines plunged straight ahead into the wood's narrow neck and across the front of the 1st Battalion, 6th Marines, which had joined the attack, too.

Pressured by his own company commanders for help, Wise asked Thomas where the 76th Company was and why it had not appeared on his right flank. Off Thomas went again, back into the wood. He found Overton, whose company was indeed in action and successfully so. Under Overton's inspired and intelligent direction, the 76th Company had destroyed the last German positions around Hill 181 and opened Belleau Wood for Wise's battalion. Overton found Wise's anger mildly amusing and wondered why the 5th Marines could not use the available cover. Certain that Overton had the situation under control, Thomas returned to Hughes's PC and told Johnny the Hard that the 76th Company had fulfilled its mission.

The two-battalion battle for Belleau Wood became a muddled slugfest, with Wise moving east when he should have been moving north. His battalion engaged the strongest German positions, and suffered accordingly. At one point, Wise, Lee, and Harbord all thought that the Marines had seized Belleau Wood. Hughes knew better, but his battalion had its own problems as the Germans responded to the attack with intense artillery fire and reinforcing infantry.

Jerry Thomas continued his duties in Hughes's PC. Each morning and each evening for the next five days, he checked the company positions and discussed the enemy situation with the battalion's four company commanders. "On occasion enemy artillery made my journey a warm one." He helped draft situation reports as well as messages for the regiment, interrogated couriers and occasional prisoners of war (POWs), and carried messages himself to the company commanders. Thomas and Lieutenant Etheridge were all the operational staff Hughes had, since the adjutant and supply officer had their hands full with administrative problems. Thomas and Etheridge watched the battalion's effectiveness wane from lack of sleep, water, and food, and they recognized their own limited capacity. Thirst accelerated fatigue, dulling everyone's judgment and ardor. "Food was not a problem—there just wasn't any during our first week in the wood," he recalled later. The Marines stripped all casualties of water and food, then worried about ammunition. Everyone moved as if in a drunken stupor.

In the early morning of June 13, the Germans mounted heavy counterattacks on the Marines, punishing positions on the 1st Battalion's left flank, still held by the 76th Company. Macon Overton asked battalion headquarters to investigate the fire to the rear, since he thought it might be coming from the disoriented 2d Battalion, 5th Marines. Etheridge and Thomas, who were reconnoitering the lines, decided to check Overton's report. Working their way through the wood, which was now splintered and reeking of cordite smoke and souring corpses, they found an isolated 5th Marines company.

The commander, a young lieutenant named L.Q.C.L. Lyle, told him that he was sure the firing came from bypassed Germans. He had no contact with the company to his left. Etheridge volunteered to scout the gap in the 5th Marines' lines, but before he and Thomas had moved very far, they saw some Germans who had just killed a group of Wise's Marines and occupied their foxholes. Before the German's could react with accurate rifle fire, the two Marines sprinted back to Lyle's position and told him about the Germans. Lyle gave Etheridge a scratch squad armed with grenades, and Thomas and Etheridge led the group back through the wood until they again found the German position. In the short but intense fight that followed, the Marines killed four Germans and captured a sergeant, who showed them another German stay-behind position, which the 6th Marines attacked and wiped out later the same day. Impressed with Thomas's performance in this action, Hughes had him cited in brigade orders for bravery in combat.

The German prisoner also provided Thomas with a temporary reprieve from battle, for brigade headquarters wanted to interrogate the POW immediately. Hughes ordered Thomas to escort the sergeant to the rear. When he arrived at the brigade PC, Thomas reported to Harbord's aide, Lieutenant R. Norris Williams (in civilian life, a nationally known tennis player). Williams asked him when he had last eaten a real meal. Thomas knew exactly: five days. The lieutenant sent him to the brigade mess, where a sergeant who had obviously not been missing his meals fixed Thomas a large plate of bacon, bread, and molasses, accompanied by hot coffee. Food had seldom tasted so good.

Jerry Thomas returned to a 1st Battalion that had reached the limit of its endurance. German shell fire had increased with intensity and accuracy on June 12, continuing through the night and the next day until around 5,000 rounds had fallen on the two Marine battalions in the wood. Two company commanders were killed, and one 1st Battalion company, the 74th, was all but wiped out. By the end of June 13, the 1st Battalion had also lost its commander: Major Hughes, staggering with fatigue, his eyes swollen shut from gas, allowed himself to be evacuated. His own condition, however, did not prevent his telling Harbord that his battalion could defend itself, but could no longer advance: "Have had terrific bombardment and attack. I have every man, except a few odd ones, in line now. . . . Everything is OK now. Men digging in again. Trenches most obliterated by shellfire. . . . The conduct of everyone is magnificent. Can't you get hot coffee and water to me using prisoners?" Before Hughes could receive an answer, he had been replaced by Major Franklin B. Garrett, a forty-one-year-old Louisianan who had spent most of his fourteen years as a Marine officer aboard ship, administering barracks detachments, and in Caribbean assignments that did not include combat operations. At the moment, however, the 1st Battalion, 6th Marines, did not need a heroic leader. It needed rest.

The effects of sleep deprivation, hunger, and thirst were severe, exacerbated now by gas attacks. The Marines fought in their masks, but had to remove them often to clear condensed water and mucus, increasing the chances of inhaling gas. They simply endured burns over the rest of their bodies. The Germans tried no more infantry counterattacks, but they pummeled the battalion with heavy mortars and Austrian 77mm cannon, which fired a flat-trajectory, high-velocity shell dubbed a "whiz bang." In the meantime, Wise's battalion (or rather its remnants) and the 2d Battalion, 6th Marines, had finally reached the northern section of Belleau Wood, but could advance no farther without help. The 1st Battalion, 6th Marines, completed the occupation and defense of the southern woods. On June 15 the battalion learned it would finally be replaced, by a battalion of the U.S. 7th Infantry. Two days later, at less than half their original strength, they shuffled out of Belleau Wood.

FOR ALL THEIR EXHAUSTION, THE 1ST BATTALION, 6TH MARINES, AND SERGEANT Jerry Thomas had proved themselves tough and skillful during their week in Belleau Wood. After the "lost march" of June 8–9, their performance had been exemplary. Largely because of Johnny the Hard's tactical skill and an extra day of artillery preparation and planning, theirs had been the only one of five Marine battalions to enter Belleau Wood without suffering serious casualties. If the 74th Company had not been destroyed by gas and high-explosive shell fire on June 13, the battalion would have fought within the wood with fewer losses than the other Marine battalions. Its men also captured their objectives, and never lost cohesion.

Although casualty statistics are difficult to assess then and now, the 1st Battalion, 6th Marines, appears to have suffered between fifty and sixty casualties a day on June 10, 11, and 12. On the night of June 12, Hughes reported that he had around 700 effectives. The shelling on June 13, however, cost the battalion over 200 casualties, many of them from gas. Casualties on June 13–15 numbered less than fifty. By comparison, the 2d Battalion, 5th Marines, reported that it had only 350 effectives by the night of June 12, after two days of fighting. Total losses for the two Marine infantry regiments (May 31 to July 9, 1918) were ninety-nine officers and 4,407 enlisted men. In the 4th Brigade overall, 112 officers and 4,598 enlisted men were casualties (including 933 killed), more than half the brigade's original strength.

Although no one could determine which of the infantry battalions killed the most Germans in Belleau Wood—from German accounts, Allied artillery probably inflicted the greatest casualties—the 1st Battalion at least shared with Wise's battalion the claim of destroying the German 461st Infantry Regiment, which had fallen from around 1,000 effectives on June 5 to only nine officers and 149 men a week later. In addition, the battle of June 10–12 had cost the German 40th Infantry Regiment of the 28th Division almost 800 men killed, wounded, or missing. A battalion from the 5th Guards Division had also fallen to the Marines. The 1st Battalion and Wise's battalion had captured ten heavy mortars, more than fifty heavy machine guns, and at least 400 prisoners. Within the wood, the 1st Battalion, 6th Marines, and 2d Battalion, 5th Marines, broke the back of the German defense, even though the battle did not actually end for another two weeks.

The tactical effectiveness of the 1st Battalion, 6th Marines—to which Jerry Thomas had made an important contribution—became obscured by the valor of the entire 4th Brigade in the battles for Hill 142, Belleau Wood, and Bouresches. Paired with the performance of the U.S. 1st Division at Cantigny (May 28–31), the 4th Brigade's fight proved to the Germans and Allies alike that the AEF would be a significant force in offensive combat on the Western Front. (The 2d Division's 3d Brigade reinforced this conclusion by seizing Vaux on July 1.) The intelligence section of the German IV Reserve Corps filed a major report praising the valor of the Marines and predicting glumly that their tactical skill might soon match their heroism:

> The Second American Division must be considered a very good one and may even perhaps be considered as a storm troop. The different attacks on Belleau Wood were carried out with bravery and dash. The moral effect of our gunfire cannot seriously impede the advance of the American infantry. The Americans' nerves are not yet worn out.
>
> The qualities of the men individually may be described as remarkable. They are physically well set up, their attitude is good, and they range in age from eighteen to twenty-eight years. They lack at present only

training and experience to make formidable adversaries. The men are in fine spirits and are filled with naive assurance; the words of a prisoner are characteristic—WE KILL OR WE GET KILLED!

French and American headquarters up to and including Pershing's staff and the French Grand Quartier Général (or Army General Staff) praised the 4th Brigade's performance. At the emotional level, however, their reactions varied. Pershing and his staff believed that the Marines had received altogether too much newspaper coverage, especially for the attacks of June 6 and 11. (The AEF censor was at fault, not the Marines.) The French, on the other hand, proved as always capable of the classic *beau geste:* They awarded the 4th Brigade a unit Croix de guerre with Palm and renamed Belleau Wood the Bois de la Brigade de Marine. For Marines of the twentieth century, Belleau Wood became the battle that established the corps' reputation for valor, and Jerry Thomas had been part of it all.

FOR THE 1ST BATTALION, 6TH MARINES, THE BATTLE FOR BELLEAU WOOD REALLY ended when the battalion returned to the rest area at Nanteuil-sur-Marne on June 17, but it did not leave the sector until the entire division departed in early July. On the road to Nanteuil, the battalion found its kitchens and enjoyed hot stew ("slum") and café au lait that tasted like a five-star meal. For three days the battalion did little but sleep and eat. The Marne River became a welcome Marine bathtub. Ten-day beards and dirt came off; thin faces and sunken eyes took longer to return to normal.

The battalion returned to the Belleau Wood sector on June 20–21 in order to give Harbord two fresh battalions in brigade reserve. The battle in the northern wood had grown as the Germans committed a fresh regiment, and Harbord had countered with an attack by the 7th Infantry and the 5th Marines. After the 5th Marines' attacks finally cleared the north woods on June 26—Harbord could report accurately, "Belleau Wood now U.S. Marine Corps entirely"—the battalion marched back into the wood, a doleful walk through the clumps of unburied German and American dead. Except for occasional harassing shell fire, the battalion did not have to deal with live Germans, although the smell of the dead ones was bad enough.

Jerry Thomas spent most of his time in the PC or checking the battalion observation posts. His last special duty in Belleau Wood was to help guide the U.S. 104th Infantry, 26th Division, into the sector. Learning that the relieving "Yankee Division" had already lost men to German artillery fire, he once again proved his intelligence and force by persuading an army lieutenant colonel to move the 104th Infantry into the wood by a longer but more protected route than the one the colonel intended to use. Thomas had no desire to add more Americans to the 800 or so dead who were scattered throughout the 6th Marines' sector.

JUST AS DAWN WAS BREAKING, THE 1ST BATTALION LEFT BELLEAU WOOD FOR THE last time. "Led by our chunky commander, Major Garrett, we traversed the three quarters of a mile to Lucy at a ragged double time." Pushing along on his weary legs, Sergeant Jerry Thomas turned his back on Belleau Wood, at last certain that he would never see it again, at least in wartime. The battle, however, had made him a charter member of a Marine Corps elite, the veterans of the Battle of Belleau Wood. From this group the Marine Corps would eventually draw many of its leaders for the next forty years, including four commandants (Wendell C. Neville, Thomas Holcomb, Clifton B. Cates, and Lemuel C. Shepherd, Jr.). On June 10, 1918, Jerry Thomas had entered Belleau Wood a sergeant whose early performance in France had marked him as a courageous and conscientious noncommissioned officer. He left the wood a proven leader of Marines in combat, a young man clearly capable of assuming greater responsibilities in the most desperate of battles.

THE MYTHICAL MORNING
OF SERGEANT YORK
John Bowers

———

MOST EPISODES OF HEROISM ARE PERFORMED IN A FEW minutes at most, sometimes in only moments. Alvin C. York's, it has been calculated, lasted three hours and fifteen minutes, from the time he moved down a knob called Hill 223 at ten minutes past six on the morning of October 8, 1918, until he arrived at the command port of the 2d Battalion, 328th Regiment of the 82d Division with a bag of 132 prisoners. Along the way, he had also killed twenty-five of the enemy. It was by then twenty-five minutes after nine. He would have to spend the rest of the morning marching his prisoners several miles to the nearest prisoner cages. He would be awarded the Congressional Medal of Honor.

York's feat, which a fellow Tennesseean, John Bowers, recalls here, took place near Châtel-Chéhéry, a single muddy street of crushed farmhouses and barns perched on a hillside at the edge of the Argonne forest. This was a countryside of wooded ridges, sudden drop-offs, and deep ravines, which gave way to fields along the bottomlands of a little river, the Aire. The prospect was not unlike that of York's home in the Valley of the Three Forks of the Wolf River. The resemblance was probably not the sort of thing he had much time to reflect on that crowded morning, but it might have helped in making instinctive choices. When he took on machine gunners with his rifle, he did what he had done at Fentress County turkey shoots. The only difference was that the helmeted heads were bigger.

York, the rifleman of "independent character" (Pershing's phrase), was the sort of democratic nonpareil that open warfare was supposed to depend on as well as create. But as the casualty lists swelled that fall, the ideal was fast losing its luster. The forty-seven-day Meuse-Argonne offensive, which was launched on September 26, would cost Pershing 122,000 casualties, of whom 26,277 died. The average day's human wastage was 2,600. Those were figures worthy of Passchendaele. Maneuver was too often abandoned in favor of wave assaults against heavily fortified positions: The gains were small, the losses great. They were the tactics of the Battle of Malvern Hill and Pickett's Charge. To quote the historian Harvey DeWeerd: "The AEF learned to fight through bitter experience, not through legerdemain with the rifle." The men York killed and the prisoners he took mattered less than the thirty-five machine guns he silenced.

The story of York's division, the 82d, or All-American, points up many of the problems the American Expeditionary Force (AEF) faced. The division claimed to have soldiers from every state. A few were illiterate. Of the 25,500 men in the division, only 266 had college degrees. One out of every five was foreign-born, and some could barely speak English; the division had to institute language courses. "Many were buried as American soldiers before they became American citizens," writes James J. Cooke in his history of the division. Experienced officers and men with technical skills were constantly transferred; others were sent to fill up divisions about to depart for France. The result was that a division like the 82d remained in an uneven state of training. There were no training camps purely for replacements. Secretary of War Newton Baker explained why: "If we had set up camps containing, say, one hundred thousand men for the training of replacement troops as such, the country at the onset would have been shocked to discover how large we thought the losses would be." Talk of a defining essence of the war.

That was not all. The artillery had no guns to train with. There were no trench mortars or modern sniping rifles. The only Chauchat automatic rifles were the few brought to the New World camps by French advisers—who found they had nothing to do as long as recruits were still learning right-face or left-face. Men never had a chance to practice throwing the key weapons of trench warfare, grenades; industry hadn't begun to produce them. The 1st U.S. Gas Regiment sailed for France without gas masks.

In its first major action, the Saint-Mihiel offensive in mid-September, the 82d (and York's regiment in particular) had been badly manhandled. German artillery and machine guns on the flank of the American attack had in a few minutes killed or maimed 275 members of a battalion, not York's, attacking a village called Vandières. The division machine-gun officer, Lieutenant Colonel Emory Pike kept the survivors from bolting and helped them to secure the town. He was wounded but refused to be evacuated until he was certain that his men had found shelter and set up a defensive line; he died the next day. Pike was the 82d's other winner of the Congressional Medal of Honor.

It is tempting to see only the negative about the 82d's performance or that of the AEF in general. It has become something of the historical fashion these days. Just consider the rigors of the landscape. Hunter Liggett, who commanded the I Corps and then the entire First Army, described the Argonne as "a natural fortress beside which the wilderness in which Grant fought Lee was a park." That was not just the self-aggrandizing opinion of a memoir-writing general. There were no worse places to fight in northern France. But Liggett did rely on maneuver. The divisions, including the 82d, that battered the Germans around Châtel-Chéhéry took the Argonne from the flank and succeeded in forcing them out of the forest. For a couple of days the American advance was so rapid that no one took time to bury their dead. Everyone, German and American, was exhausted. Everyone fought in damp, mud-caked uniforms. Everyone suffered from hunger and thirst and diarrhea. "I think the Germans will haft to quit before long," York wrote his fiancée. But the 82d, which had lost upwards of 6,000 men in the Argonne, was at the end of its rope as well.

York didn't stop fighting. As Bowers tells us, he was nearly killed by a shell's near miss. He was promoted to sergeant. He was on leave in Aix-les-Bains when the war ended on November 11. "They sure was a time in that city that day and night," he later remembered. "It was awful noisy. All the French were drunk, whooping and hollering. . . . I never did anything much, just went to church and wrote home and read a little. I did not go out that night. I was all tired. I was glad the Armistice was signed, glad it was all over. . . . [W]e were ready to go home."

———

JOHN BOWERS is the author of a number of books, including *Stonewall Jackson: Portrait of a Soldier* and *Chickamauga and Chattanooga: The Battles That Doomed the Confederacy.* Born and raised in Tennessee, he now lives in New York and teaches writing at Columbia University.

H E HAD ONCE BEEN A CONSCIENTIOUS OBJECTOR WHO HAD HARDLY ANY schooling; he was a die-hard individualist from the isolated mountains of east Tennessee who had trouble taking orders from anyone; and he became the most honored and best-known citizen-soldier in the American army in World War I. He was played by Gary Cooper in the movie version of his life. He was Alvin C. York.

York (1887–1964) grew up on a small spread in the Valley of the Three Forks of the Wolf River near the hamlet of Pall Mall, in Fentress County, Tennessee. Higher up lay Jamestown (dubbed Jimtown by the natives), the county seat. In Jamestown, Mark Twain's parents grew up and married; Twain himself was conceived in Fentress County, though his parents moved to Missouri before he was born. This section of east Tennessee, not far from the Kentucky border, was spared Civil War battles, but it did suffer from marauders and bushwhackers. The region was officially on the Northern side—both York grandfathers served as Union soldiers—but the populace of Fentress County argued both ways. As in other matters, they relished being contrary.

Although the spirit of Mark Twain lingers in Fentress County, York himself seems to have stepped out of the fervid imagination of a New Englander, the late Al Capp, who created the comic-strip hero Li'l Abner. In his youth, York was rangy, broad-shouldered, and seemingly endowed with a mystical ability to walk unscathed through any calamity. He was the prototypical Southern mountaineer—not a *hillbilly*. Mountaineers do not like to be called by that epithet (unless they do it themselves). I know; I am one. I come from upper east Tennessee, and I have known an Alvin York or two. (Actually, I once encountered *the* Alvin York at some gathering at the University of Tennessee in the late 1940s; no longer thin, with a substantial heft and apple cheeks, he bore his fame with a sly chuckle, a little uncomfortable.) Where I come from, males were taught from the cradle on to engage in roughhouse and blood-causing sports, never to back down from a fight, and to bond to the death with those who carried your blood and spoke with your accent. Loyalty and perseverance were two much-loved traits.

It was beautiful beyond belief in the hills of east Tennessee, weather and scenery alike, and you took it for granted that God looked down kindly on you.

Some unfortunate by-products, though, sometimes came in the form of pig-headedness to an extreme, a hesitancy to accept any help, and a tendency to escape life's complexity through either the spirits of the bottle or the spirit of the Lord.

Alvin York never went past the third grade, in a school that used split logs as desks and held classes for only the three months a year after the crops were brought in. York was third in a family of eleven children, born, like Lincoln, a little over a hundred miles north in Kentucky, in a one-room log cabin. Alvin's father, William, eked out a living as a blacksmith and from what a seventy-five-acre farm produced. His mother, Mary, took in neighbors' laundry. Alvin went to work before he was six, hoeing corn and doing household chores. In summer he went barefoot, and in winter he wore brass-toed brogans, made by his father, that in his words "took the hide off my heels." It was a tough life, made even harder when York's father died in November 1911. Alvin, at age twenty-four, the oldest son still at home, became the man of the house, in charge of caring for his mother and younger siblings. He stood six feet tall, large for a man back then. He worked his father's smithy, until a chance fire destroyed it. He then hired out as a day laborer, his best job being on a construction crew that built U.S. Route 127 through Fentress County. His pay: one dollar and sixty cents per backbreaking day.

York sought release in the usual. He reveled in moonshine, card playing, and fights. He was a crack shot from early on, using a homemade muzzle-loader—or hog rifle, as it was called in the mountains. He usually grabbed the prize in shooting matches, which had been around since frontier days, and, with each shooter throwing in a quarter or so to compete, he raked in pots that were known to reach as much as two hundred dollars—what would take him about half a year to make on the road crew. Another version featured a turkey tied behind a log, with only its head exposed. The shooter who took off the bird's bobbing head took home the meat. This lively type of contest was prominently shown in the movie about his life.

York's drinking, carousing, and general hell-raising came to an end when he went through a religious conversion to a fundamentalist Christian faith. The phenomenon of "being saved" is well known in that land. He had always gone to church, loving to blast out hymns in his strong tenor, but attending a revival, led by a fiery visiting evangelist, did the final job. York renounced his wicked ways and joined the Church of Christ in Christian Union. His courtship of a neighbor girl, Gracie Williams, influenced him to change his rowdy ways, too. She came from a large family and had a similar upbringing. He was thirteen years older, and he claimed that he picked her as his future bride the moment he saw her in a cradle a few days after her birth. Their marriage after World War I was, by all accounts, a happy and enduring one.

His conversion, however, did not make his soldiering in the war run smoothly. At first he claimed exemption from the draft because of his religious beliefs, but he was turned down after four appeals. It was unusual that the minister of his church, Pastor Rosier Pile, was head of the local draft board, too. York was drafted into the army reluctantly, to put it mildly, and initially he had grave doubts that, as a devout Christian, he could ever kill another soul. He expressed his concern to his company commander, Captain Edward Danforth, a Harvard-educated Georgian, who immediately took the distraught York to the battalion commander, Major George Edward Buxton, a New Englander who was a devout Christian himself. It was not the ordinary military response to a complaint from the ranks, but Buxton's knowledge of Scripture caused York to rethink his pacifist position. Buxton gave York a ten-day pass to go home and think things over. At the end, Buxton said, if York was still convinced that the words of Jesus forbade his fighting, then Buxton would give him a noncombat assignment. York went home, climbed a mountain, and prayed all night for guidance. He came down the next day convinced that he should fight, and that no harm would come to him; the Lord had told him so. He was so taken with Major Buxton that he later named a son after him.

York's outfit, the 82d Division, landed in Liverpool, England, on May 16, 1918, and was in Le Havre, France, five days later. The soldiers' first order of business was to turn in their Springfields for 1917 British Enfields that had a ten-shot magazine and a caliber of .303 inches. York hated to part with his trusted five-shot Springfield, but he recognized the worth of the Enfield. After some final training, the 82d took its place on the Western Front in late June, along the long-quiet Saint-Mihiel salient, which jutted 200 square miles deep into the Allied line. At the end of the summer, the 82d took part in the five-day push that eliminated the salient. On September 12, York's Company G—in which he was a squad leader—went over the top to help take the village of Norroy, on the left bank of the Moselle River. The assault was successful, but the four days of heavy fighting passed in a blur for York. The Germans struck with mustard gas, causing him to don a hated gas mask for hours on end. He saw fellow soldiers go berserk under pressure, tearing off their masks and gulping in the fatal brew. He saw some Americans lying dead and mutilated, and others whimpering in pain. He experienced the full horror of war, but he believed in his cause, and he kept trusting in the Lord.

He was carrying on as a squad leader without much distinction. "I [was supposed to] lead the squad," he wrote in his 1928 autobiography. "I kinder think they almost led me." Then, on October 8, he became something else, something irrevocable. He became an American hero. It happened in the Argonne, whose terrain, with its steep, wooded hills and deep gullies, resembled the Tennessee hills that York had just come from.

Here is what happened, as best we know it:

Corporal York's 164th Infantry Brigade, 82d Division, had been chosen in early October to assault the high ground along the northeast corner of the Argonne. On October 6, the brigade slogged toward its objective in what had become a given of this war, of so many wars really—mud. In the late afternoon, a cold, steady rain fell. The miserably drenched troops slid and groped their way forward, pulling their equipment, while enemy fire shattered the air and raked the ground around them. When darkness fell, they forded the swollen Aire River, the last obstacle between them and the Argonne. At first light on October 7, as a blanket of fog covered their position, they moved out to attack. The 164th had two goals: to take Hill 223, to the west of the village of Châtel-Chéhéry in the open country along the Aire valley; and to drive about two miles farther and take the Decauville Railroad, a north-south German supply line. By nightfall, Hill 223 had been taken. (A side benefit to this successful advance was that the Germans surrounding the trapped "Lost Battalion" in the Argonne, a few miles to the west, were forced to retreat; the next afternoon, the small number of American survivors stole to safety.)

York had not been in the fight to take Hill 223. He and the rest of the 2d Battalion of the 328th Infantry Regiment had spent October 7 hunkered down west of Châtel-Chéhéry, watching the 1st Battalion do the job. Before first light the next day, however, York's 2d Battalion was creeping up to Hill 223, preparing to move on to the Decauville Railroad. The eternal drizzle fell. More discomforting, German shells burst above and poison gas settled over them. Sniper fire popped unexpectedly, and now and then came the clatter of machine guns, for Hill 223 had not completely become a safe haven. It was free enough, though, for Captain Danforth of Company G to give orders to his men, one of whom was York: two platoons were to attack, with the other two used as support. York led a support squad, on the left, under the command of Sergeant Harry M. Parsons. When the whistle blew, the 2d Battalion started down Hill 223 to cross a valley to where the enemy waited 500 yards away.

The 2d Landwehr ("Territorial") Division, comprising Württembergers from the uplands of southern Germany, had held positions in the Argonne since 1914: When they were not being used as service troops, they manned a sector that, until the American offensive began on September 26, had long been quiet. Most of its youthful members had been transferred to other units in more active parts of the front, leaving behind men in their thirties and early forties. These troops were not about to be inspired to make a last-ditch, to-the-death stand. Though the 2d Landwehr Division's journal complains of the low morale of the men, they were veterans who had been in continuous combat for nearly two weeks, had put up surprisingly stiff resistance in the fight for the Aire valley, and had lost some 5,000 men—more than half the strength of the division. Now they held the high ground that looked down on the Americans moving forward. In an area that until now had not seen fighting, the woods were still thick and the undergrowth tangled. When York's 2d Battalion reached the center of the valley, the heights around them crackled with fire. Mortar shells rained down. Doughboys leaped into the first available shell hole, bobbed up a little later, then raced to one farther along. York observed his company's executive officer get shot, rise, go forward, then fall with a fatal wound.

Sergeant Parsons realized that his forward platoons were trapped. The only remedy was to silence the machine guns that were taking deadly aim from a wooded hill to the left. He told Sergeant Bernard Early to take those machine guns with his three squads. The squads totaled seventeen men, including Early; only a short time before there had been twenty-four. Parsons understood that he was ordering these men to what looked like certain death, but he had no choice.

York was among the patrol that moved out. Protected by a dense forest growth, they eased their way around the German flank. But the forest benefited both sides: the Americans were not too sure where the Germans were. While probing, they suddenly ran across two Germans with Red Cross armbands. One threw up his hands; the other took off to sound an alarm.

What follows shows the chaos of battle: how blunders, ineptitude, chance, daring, and, yes, heroism, influence its outcome. It shows how a hero is both born *and* made. In charge of the German line was First Lieutenant Vollmer of the 1st Battalion, 120th Landwehr Infantry. Like many commanders in a raging battle, he was confused and unhappy. Heavy shelling had forced him to retreat, and he was groping forward again to find the position assigned to his unit. In the wooded terrain, he lost contact with the troops on his left. He was busy setting up nests of machine guns when he heard a commotion to his rear. Rushing back, he found several dozen of his men lounging at breakfast, belts off, weapons down. They were exhausted. He began imploring them to move forward, and then he suddenly saw some Americans who had just broken through underbrush and begun firing. It was York's patrol. Everyone was startled—York thought he had run across a headquarters detachment—but the Germans were more surprised. For all they knew, this could be the van of an entire regiment. All of the Germans surrendered—save one. He made the mistake of firing at York, and missing. York shot him dead.

Before the Americans could deal with their prisoners, a burst of machine-gun bullets raked the open area. The Germans in their midst had conveniently dropped to the ground a second before, on signal from their comrades above, and none of them were hit. But nine Americans fell dead or wounded. Sergeant Early took a bad hit, as did one corporal, and Corporal Murray Savage—York's best friend—was killed. With his fellow soldiers seeking cover or pinned down, York found himself alone to deal with the situation. Calmly, he hit the ground and began firing. He made sure to fall beside some prisoners so that the machine gunners would have to risk striking their own men to get him. The gunners were scarcely thirty yards up a hillside from him—so close, in fact, that they had to depress their gun barrels to come anywhere near hitting him. Here is York's account, as recorded in his autobiography:

> At first I was shooting from a prone position; that is lying down; jes like we often shoot at the targets in the shooting matches in the mountains of Tennessee; and it was jes about the same distance. But the targets here were bigger. I jes couldn't miss a German's head or body at that distance. And I didn't. . . . Every time a head come up I done knocked it down.

York's offhand recounting of the event is in keeping with the actual casualness with which he dispatched the Germans.

> In the middle of the fight a German officer and five men done jumped out of a trench and charged me with fixed bayonets. They had about twenty-five yards to come and they were coming right smart. I only had about half a clip left in my rifle; but I had my pistol ready. I done flipped it out fast and teched them off, too.

Now followed a coup de main York had picked up in Tennessee, something duplicated on the set of the movie, *Sergeant York:*

> I teched off the sixth man first; then the fifth; then the fourth; and so on. That's the way we shoot wild turkeys at home. You see we don't want the front ones to know that we're getting the back ones, and then they keep on coming until we get them all. Of course, I hadn't time to think of that. I guess I jes naturally did it. I knowed, too, that if the front ones wavered, or if I stopped them the rear ones would drop down and pump a volley into me and get me.

York showed no mercy that day, emptying his ten-clip Enfield and then, when the Germans rushed forward after realizing he had used his last shot, pumping away with his .45 Colt automatic. As he later wrote, he got a lieutenant "right through the stomach and he dropped and screamed a lot." In the end, his barrel smoking, ammunition low, he stood, gesturing and shouting for the Germans to lay down their arms.

While York had been firing up the hillside, Lieutenant Vollmer had been busy shooting at him from another direction—but he could not hit him. York had survived a machine-gun assault, a bayonet charge, and Vollmer's fusillade. Vollmer had seen enough. He called out, "English?" He had once worked in Chicago and knew the language well.

"No, American," York replied.

"Good Lord," the German said, and then he surrendered. York put the .45 to Vollmer's head and then collected prisoners. Now what? No more machine guns spat down on him, no bullets whizzed by him, but he was now in charge of a sizable group of Germans and had much enemy terrain to travel before he could get back inside his own lines. Vollmer blew a whistle and Germans came down the hillside and out of the brush with hands raised. One German remained unmollified and had the ill luck to lob a grenade York's way. York shot him immediately.

A strange double column of men then moved out. York led the way, placing Germans on either side of himself as cover. He ordered the Germans to carry the American wounded, and he aligned the few walking Americans to guard the sides and rear. Curiously, York had to ask Vollmer the way to the American lines. Vollmer said one way; York, his mountaineer suspicions raised, went the other. And then he ran into other machine-gun nests. A Lieutenant Thoma, who was technically under Vollmer's command, had guns leveled down on the double column that now came suddenly marching toward him out of nowhere. Before the Germans could fire, however, Vollmer called out, "It is useless, we are surrounded." York took more prisoners. Others fell in along the way. York kept his .45 pointed at Vollmer and captured German after German. One gunner refused, and York shot him dead. In miraculous fashion, York was silencing the guns that had caused such havoc on the Americans crossing the valley from Hill 223. York's single-handed exploit was an essential ingredient in the eventual capture of the Decauville Railroad.

In getting back, York had other problems to face besides German fire. He feared friendly artillery might mistake his prisoners for a German counterattack and shell them. That did not happen. But when he finally reached battalion headquarters, he learned that they could not handle his prisoners. He marched them to regimental headquarters. The results were the same. He kept them going, all the way to division headquarters, where he finally found a home for them.

> We were constantly under heavy shell fire and I had to double-time them to get them through safely. There was nothing to be gained by having any more of them wounded or killed. They done surrendered to me and it was up to me to look after them. And so I done done it. I had orders to report to Brigadier General Lindsay, our brigadier commander, and he said to me, "Well, York, I hear you have captured the whole damned German army." And I told him I only had 132.

York didn't get much of a breather right after the fight. His outfit continued to take heavy losses through the Argonne offensive, and once an exploding shell blew him into the air as he desperately dug a foxhole; however, he was unhurt. But on November 1, ten days before the Armistice, he was rotated to a rest area and given the rank of sergeant.

YORK HAD MARCHED INTO THE ROUGH WOODS OF THE ARGONNE AN OBSCURE corporal. He emerged a mythical hero: Sergeant York. He was given credit for killing twenty-five Germans, capturing 132, and silencing thirty-five machine guns. He did it virtually all on his own, armed with just an Enfield rifle, a .45 pistol, and his own brand of fortitude. He had seen his best friend slaughtered in the first rounds of machine-gun fire on the slope; he had kept going. He had seen things that he tried unsuccessfully to forget until his death in 1964, often dropping to his knees to pray for the souls of the Americans as well as Germans who died that day. Medals began showering down on him; his tunic was unable to hold them all. Marshal Ferdinand Foch pinned the Croix de guerre on him. Even little Montenegro handed out a medal. The United States, of course, did the most. York won an immediate Distinguished Service Cross and, after the usual investigation, was awarded the Medal of Honor. The press discovered him; the pivotal story was written by the veteran war correspondent George Pattullo for the *Saturday Evening Post,* which had a circulation of over two million and greatly shaped public opinion.

York landed in Hoboken, New Jersey, on May 22, 1919, met by streamers and a throng of reporters and well-wishers. He was feted in New York and Washington, then finally allowed to go back to Tennessee for his discharge and a return to the hills from whence he came.

When the dust settled, when all the hoopla ended, some disagreements developed. His exploit did seem like more than one man could do. The scene of the fight had been wild and chaotic, shrouded in fog, dust, smoke, and confusion. When the army first gathered sworn affidavits from the American soldiers who had been there, a short time after the event, they confirmed what has since been handed down as history. York himself had kept a diary, in which he chronicled his day-to-day army experiences, including those of October 8. (Stubborn to the end, he had gone against orders in keeping a diary that might fall into enemy hands if he were captured; he said he hadn't come to France to be captured.) Even before York landed in America, some members of his old patrol had found time to become disgruntled. They wanted some credit, too. They felt that York was hogging it all. It wasn't York, though, who was creating the clamor; it was a public thirsting for an authentic hero in the war, someone to personify the common, ordinary doughboy. York himself was keeping his usual quiet profile, never a man to enjoy a fuss, never anyone to brag, but his buddies' carping did reach his ears. His lone reply: "They raised their right hands and swore to those affidavits."

It would be unthinkable for the Germans not to come forward after the war to disagree with the American version of the event. In 1929, a German living in Sweden ran across York's story in a newspaper. He became outraged at what he considered an insult to the German soldier, and he sent off a hot letter to the German minister of war, suggesting that Germans investigate York's alleged exploit. This was done by the Reichsarchiv, the government records office, which tracked down twenty-two soldiers—including Vollmer—who had been west of Châtel-Chéhéry on October 8, 1918, and got *their* affidavits. They all said York was a fine and brave soldier but it had not happened the way the Americans said. York had not killed all those Germans, he had not put those machine guns out of action, he had not corralled all those prisoners. Throughout the reports, understandably, is the umbrage they took that the German fighting soldier, who was world renowned, was shown in this case to have something lacking. No lone American soldier could have done what York had done. Other troops had helped; the Germans had been surrounded; York had taken credit for prisoners someone else had already captured—and so on and so forth. The Reichsarchiv even got indignant, ten years after the fact, that York had put a pistol to the head of the unfortunate Vollmer and threatened to blow his brains out if he did not cooperate.

Nevertheless, as an American major general, George Duncan, had told reporters in 1919, "The more we investigated [York's] exploit the more remarkable it appeared." In 1935, after investigation after investigation, York's old company commander, Captain Danforth, summed up the official American conclusion: "Credit was given where credit was due." As amazing as it seems, as far as it is humanly possible to know, York did it.

But why Alvin C. York, from Fentress County, Tennessee? Much has been made of his backwoods character, his Southern heritage. It is true that a great deal of American soldiering has fallen on the shoulders of Southerners. Audie Murphy, the most decorated American soldier in World War II, had a background not dissimilar to York's. He had a hardscrabble past and he was from Texas. But for all the Yorks and Murphys in the South, there are countless others who are far meeker and might choose the backward path or cower for cover before the enemy. And some become heroes only after initial failure. For example, Sam Ervin, the famed chairman of the Senate Watergate Committee in 1973, was a Southerner from Morganton, North Carolina, which was a range or two over from the Cumberlands. He was as thorough and honorable a Southerner as York. In France during World War I, as a second lieutenant on the Saint-Mihiel salient—flu-ridden, cold, unable to command the respect of his men—he abandoned his post, in the face of the enemy, for a safe, dry dugout. He got broken to the rank of private and suffered the indignity of having to return to the ranks with men he used to command. Fortified with that bit of humiliation, he went on to battlefield glory. He won the Silver Star, the Distinguished Service Cross, and the French Fourragère for bravery. Under heavy fire, he led a rescue party several times to the front lines to remove the wounded; he was badly wounded himself. He had become fearless in the face of fire. He may have passed the ultimate test of bravery, in swallowing the bitterness of his first failure, returning to the fray, and then persevering no matter what. In so doing, he was following a scenario that was not unknown in American battlefield lore. In Stephen Crane's *The Red Badge of Courage*, Henry Fleming flees from the horrendous sight of battlefield carnage at what is presumed to be Chancellorsville and then, when the shame of it hits him, returns to carry the colors forward, a warrior. Ervin's and Fleming's stories give us comfort because we ordinary souls, removed to the hammock or the easy chair when we read about them, can see ourselves in their tales. We can anticipate being a coward in battle, but we hope we will stand firm. We like to believe there are second chances in life.

What, then, is true heroism? Medals, ticker-tape parades, adoration in the press, fall to those we deem worthy. Surely they should feel they are of a special breed. But no Medal of Honor winner has ever been known to claim publicly that a different kind of blood flows through his veins than in the ordinary man. The standard reply from these heroes, almost to the man, is "You'd have done the same thing given the circumstances." York, Audie Murphy—their responses are the same: They just did what they had to do. In a strange way, those who do not go forward, who may run backward or freeze, repeat the same refrain: You'd have done the same thing, brother, if you'd been there. I know a solid citizen who had once been a shavetail second lieutenant at Omaha beach during the early fighting at Normandy. He said he hugged a tree for an entire day, unable to make his body move an inch. He said, probably correctly, "You'd have done the same, believe me."

A popular hero may be needed by the people at the time, but he tends to be soon forgotten. General John J. Pershing, the commander of the American Expeditionary Force, made only one offhand acknowledgment of York. In his mind there were others just as deserving, or more so. He had wanted First Lieutenant Samuel Woodfill, a Regular Army man who, by himself, silenced three machine-gun nests on October 12, 1918, to be the one and only popularly acclaimed, mud-spattered, indomitable hero. Like York, Woodfill won the Congressional Medal of Honor for heroism.

There were others as well. Major Charles Whittlesey, a New York lawyer before the war, led his surrounded "Lost Battalion" against impossible odds. He took 600 men into battle and, after clinging to a steep bank and a bit of swale for six days, came out with 194. He had kept his cool, dispatching patrols and carrier pigeons and never giving up. He won the Medal of Honor, became a hero, but under continuing strain committed suicide in 1921 by jumping over the side of a vacation liner bound for Cuba. Lieutenant Harold D. Furlong won the same medal by personally taking on four machine guns and twenty enemy soldiers—and prevailing. "There was no choice to do anything different," he said afterward. Gunnery Sergeant Fred Stockham of the U.S. Marines carried wounded and gassed Marines from Belleau Wood. When a shell ripped through the gas mask of a man he was carrying, he pulled off his own and gave it to the man. Choking and coughing, he made several trips without a mask to retrieve more wounded before finally collapsing. He died nine days later. His lieutenant's recommendation for a medal was lost, but years later his comrades pressed his case, and in 1939, through a special act of Congress, he was posthumously awarded the Medal of Honor.

All of these Medal of Honor winners were heroes as much as York. But it was York who captured the public's imagination. York was rangy, freckle-faced, and steadfast as steel, and he had a girl in gingham waiting for him back home. It could be that Whittlesey's Yankee comportment, Woodfill's Regular Army status, and simply the luck of the draw took them and others out of the sweepstakes; in any case, it was York who became the doughboy hero. His story had everything.

The right moment and the right training must come together for a popular hero to emerge. A person must go through several stages before that decisive moment can happen, that moment that elevates him to an exalted stature, even if only for a short time. York had expert training and experience with the rifle; he had been subjected to fire; and he had also become convinced of the rightness of his cause. He had no trouble killing the enemy and believing it was necessary to prevail. York fit right in with the doctrine of the American war machine, from Pershing on down, which was that advances should be achieved by infantry rushes. In World War I, Americans didn't rely on the machine gun offensively; they relied on the rifle. And when Americans engaged the enemy, Pershing believed, the "independent character" of the American soldier would prevail. York was certainly independent, and he had practically been born with a rifle in his hand. When York went into those wooded slopes, the man and the moment came together.

Most men do not like to fire at another human being. In *Men Against Fire,* S.L.A. Marshall states that in World War II only about 15 percent of the men in a company normally fired their weapons at the enemy during an engagement; in exceptional circumstances, the number might rise to 25 or 30 percent. Not all military experts agree with Marshall, but no one contends that in war every soldier fires his weapon at other people as he is expected to. Some soldiers receive all the training there is, listen to all the lectures and propaganda, end up on the front lines, and then fire up in the air when the enemy appears. Others fight, and keep fighting, even when they are held to a foxhole and a line of tanks is rumbling toward them. Research commissioned by the Department of the Army in 1957 of 310 men who had fought in Korea found that the more intelligent a man and the more stable the home life he came from, the better fighter he made. The smart man might find troubling a war that his conscience said was morally wrong; but, once convinced of its right, he makes a far better fighter than the dim, plodding person who accepts everything at face value. He makes a better leader. And anyone who has had a taste of the violence of sports knows something—remotely, it is granted—of war. Stephen Crane, who wrote *The Red Badge of Courage* in ten days in a vacation cottage in Lakeview, New Jersey, had played quarterback in the new game of football only a few years earlier, but he had never fought in the Civil War—or even been in any other war. He said, "I do believe I got my sense of the rage of conflict on the football field."

In the Howard Hawks film *Sergeant York,* which won an Academy Award for best actor, Gary Cooper, as York, returns to a glorious storybook farm that the appreciative citizens of Tennessee have bought for their hero. In truth, York returned to four hundred acres of undeveloped, mortgaged land that he mostly had to pay off himself. After heroic deeds, a hero in America often finds fate far less accommodating. Medals, ticker-tape parades, and newspaper features go only so far. Audie Murphy could sleep only with a pistol beneath his pillow, made good money but worse investments, and died in a plane crash in 1971 at age forty-six, a bankrupt.

In later life, York did nothing that would separate him from the myth that had been created around him. He went to the grave in 1964 a symbol of patriotism, piety, and deadly aim with a firearm. It was not easy. He turned down chances to make a bundle in vaudeville. He was offered money to endorse chewing gum, a brand of rifle, and any number of other products—and he refused. He married his Tennessee sweetheart, Gracie Williams, stayed married, and produced three sons. Like Murphy, though, he did not have much luck with investments. He had to turn into a nearly perpetual fund-raising machine to pay off farm debts, keep the York Agricultural Institute afloat, and head off the Internal Revenue Service at the pass. The institute grew out of a dream he had of bringing the modern age to the mountains, of doing away with illiteracy. York might butcher the King's English, but the love of learning had been passed down to him as a Scots-Irish heritage. Poverty, not an absence of desire, accounts for the meager education in the hills. Stonewall Jackson, the strict Presbyterian from the hills of West Virginia, studied by the light of a burning pine knot. Abraham Lincoln's formal education lasted just one year—but he borrowed books and worked out problems on the back of a wooden shovel, which he then shaved clean so he could use it again. Given the chance, these people of pioneer stock go to great lengths to acquire knowledge and bring the outside to their region.

York was of this stripe, but the school he started had chronic trouble paying for itself, and he proved far less able with administration than with marksmanship. Like the boxing heavyweight Joe Louis and the literary heavyweight Edmund Wilson and many others, York ran afoul of the IRS. According to David D. Lee in *Sergeant York: An American Hero,* in 1959 York was taking care of himself, his wife, and a sister-in-law on $3,483.15 a year, including the ten dollars a month awarded every Medal of Honor winner. He owed the government $172,723.10. It took the divine intervention of the powerful Speaker of the House Sam Rayburn to cut a deal with the tax people and arrange for popular donations to pay the reduced bill.

York did make money and had a certain shrewdness to him, but what came in went out for good works and to support a farm that never paid off. As an example of York's perspicacity, no more needs to be said than that in wrangling over a contract for the movie rights to his life's story, he demanded a percentage of the *gross* receipts, not the *net.* York hadn't traded mules for nothing. But the money he got went to his school and contributed to his downward spiral with the IRS. He hit oil on his property in 1947 and thought his money problems were over, but then he dug several dry holes that wiped out his gain;

he ended up collecting around $300 a year in oil revenue. He could probably have been elected to any office in Tennessee but could never bring himself to suffer the indignity of a campaign. During World II he briefly considered running against a young, unknown congressman, Albert Gore. He decided not to. (Gore went on to become a senator and the father of the former vice president.)

York was mortal. He spent his last years bedridden from strokes and various ailments. The historian Edward M. Coffman, a young man in the late 1950s, was passing through Tennessee. He took a chance and called on York in his big white house. York was gracious and welcoming. It was August, and York was propped up in a little room off the kitchen, in a hospital bed, with a gas heater on nearby. Coffman remembers him as a big man with a high-pitched voice, his hair still red. And though he could not move from bed, he seemed, in Coffman's recollection, to be in full command of the household and to control the movement of the large extended family that filtered in and out of the adjacent kitchen.

York was more sophisticated and worldly than might be supposed. After the war he took as his secretary a devoted man who came from Brooklyn. Arthur Bushing had wandered into the mountains by chance, fallen in love, and married a native girl. The Brooklynite became one of York's closest confidants and advisers. York didn't seem to be bothered by ethnic differences as some of his hill brethren were. As he said about his old outfit:

> There were some mountaineers. Not many of them, though. Jes a few. There were Jews from the East Side of New York; there were English and Irish boys from the mill towns of New England; there were Greeks and Italians from some of the big cities in the East; there were Poles and Slavs from the coal mines of Pennsylvania; there were farmers from the Middle West; there were cow punchers from Oklahoma and Texas; and there were even some German boys.

To the end, the onetime conscientious objector was ready to mix it up and fight. He favored aid to Britain before the United States entered World War II, and he wanted to "bust up all of old man Hitler's ships and submarines." He tried to enlist when war was declared but flunked the physical. When the Korean War broke out in June 1950, he was ready again. He blamed the Soviets, and—sad to report—was ready to drop the atomic bomb from the 38th parallel all the way to Moscow. He was good to have next to you in a foxhole, not so good to determine the fate of the world.

In the end, we are perhaps left more with the myth than the man in trying to capture Alvin York. Gary Cooper, as York, finds religion when lightning strikes him one stormy night in the middle of a road and destroys his rifle. It is a dramatic scene, so effective that even one of York's sons believed it was true. It never happened. York's conversion was triggered by a revival in which lightning played no part. The storybook farm never happened. I recently saw the movie again, and I can report that few of the Tennessee accents are accurate—not Cooper's, not Walter Brennan's, certainly not that of Joan Leslie as Gracie Williams, York's sweetheart and later wife. Only one certified mountain twang comes through—that of Robert Porterfield, who played the cowardly rival for Gracie's hand. Porterfield was a consummate actor. He started the Barter Theater in Abington, Virginia, which was composed of out-of-work actors in the Depression who brought Broadway plays to schoolhouse auditoriums throughout Appalachia. I saw my first play because of Porterfield, and I can only describe the experience as momentous. He was, in his own small way, a hero, too. Alvin C. York, with rifle, family, and love of the land, was many things, hero among them. But one thing we may safely say he was not: He was no Gary Cooper.

PART SEVEN

AFTERMATH

THE MOURNING PARENTS
Robert Cowley

—

LEANING UP THE DEVASTATION OF THE WAR, ESPECIALLY
in the areas of France and Belgium that the trenches
had run through, would last through the 1920s. In his book,
The Human Costs of the War, an American Red Cross official
named Homer Folks estimated in 1919 that "about 6,000
square miles of France or the equivalent, roughly, of a strip
two miles wide stretching from New York to San Francisco,
has become for all practical purposes a wilderness." The
French government counted 410,000 damaged buildings, of
which 240,000 had been totally destroyed. Battlefields like
Verdun were treeless deserts that sprouted only scrub groves
of crosses. The French talked about turning Somme into a national forest—if trees would ever grow there again—and work
gangs closed up tunnel entrances: It was thought that bandits
might take refuge in old dugouts. But refugees returned to
their land, fields were flattened and plowed, and villages were
rebuilt. Before long, former soldiers looking for traces of the
old front line in areas like South Flanders could only tell where
it had once run by connecting the dots of the cemeteries. Even
today, though, formidable (but ever-shrinking) traces of the
Western Front remain: an abundance of concrete bunkers
around Ypres, the tunnels, craters, and trenches (a bit pretti-
fied) at Vimy Ridge, the huge Lochnager Crater on the Somme,
the intricate trench systems concealed in the Argonne, the
battered forts of Verdun, and near Apremont (as of this writing), a few stands of original barbed wire.

If most of the landscape damage disappeared with surprising rapidity, the emotional, physical, and psychological traumas of the Great War would linger to haunt Europe. In the Midlands cities of England in the 1920s, there were entire blocks empty of men. In France, women in black were everywhere. Almost one out of every five Frenchmen who had been mobilized was a skeleton or was heaped in an ossuary bone-pile. Germany lost more than a third of the men between the ages of nineteen and twenty-two at the time the war started. Men without a leg or an arm begged on Berlin street corners. French ex-soldiers with *gueule-cassées*—"broken faces"—hesitated to show themselves in public; the government established special homes for them. But soldiers, this concluding article points out, were not the only victims. "They included the women reduced to poverty by the death of a husband and wage earner; the children left to roam wild while their mothers worked; the families broken apart; the parents deprived not just of the consolation of heirs but of support in their old age. . . . Grief, spread wide enough, and the anger that inevitably follows, can be an unspoken ingredient of social breakdown. . . ." The most visible result was Nazism.

Käthe Kollwitz was both typical—one son was killed in the autumn of 1914—and, as an artist of note, exceptional. For years after Peter Kollwitz's death in a night battle in Belgium, she succumbed to a paralyzing anguish: "I walk in half-darkness," she wrote, "there is seldom a star, the sun has set, long ago and forever." But as she began to recover, she would begin work on a project that would evolve into a memorial like no other. Käthe Kollwitz's eighteen-year struggle to create it gives new meaning to the phrase "home front." As she wrote, "First he fell in battle, and then I did." But then, not all war stories take place on the front lines.

––––––

ROBERT COWLEY, the editor of this volume, is the founding editor and former editor in chief of *MHQ: The Quarterly Journal of Military History*. Most of Käthe Kollwitz's writings quoted here are from *The Diary and Letters of Kaethe Kollwitz*, translated by Richard and Clara Winston.

PEOPLE IN ENGLAND AND FRANCE KEPT TELLING ME ABOUT THE STATUES. They were—to use a Michelin guidebook phrase that skips so easily off European tongues—"worth a visit." I was preparing for a trip along the old Western Front and I was eager not to miss anything important. The statues had been done by the German artist Käthe Kollwitz as a memorial to her son; they presided over a German military cemetery near a village a few miles in from the Belgian coast, Vladslo. I had to ask someone to spell it.

These days Käthe Kollwitz seems consigned to the same obscurity. She is not so much dismissed as ignored. A half century ago, however, many considered her Germany's leading woman artist. She was a folk heroine of the Left, her work suppressed by the Nazis. Later, feminists made canonizing motions, which never took. People like their saints to be influential, but Kollwitz was out of the mainstream of modern art, primarily a graphic artist who worked almost exclusively in black and white at a time when color had ignited a revolution in German painting. Kollwitz produced no paintings to speak of, no works acclaimed as major. I might amend the last when it comes to statues—but that is getting ahead of my story.

For me, that story began as I floundered around the back roads of rural Belgium. I drove in circles searching for the cemetery with the Kollwitz statues. This is some of the most densely populated agricultural land in Europe—in places there are nearly nine hundred people per square mile—though you would never know it from casual observation. The people are well hidden. The farmers here tend to live not in isolated houses but in villages, and those villages crop up around every other bend. Take any of the narrow, tree-arched lanes that lead off from the main traveled roads and you will find not the mingy, land-consuming roadside development of our rural sticks but yet another tidy, prosperous, dark brick settlement. Strip development in the American manner hardly exists.

In these Flanders villages, it's true, you'll find the tentative beginnings of an outward spread, the new brick split-level villas edging into the farmland; the Flemish are fast becoming a population of managers and service workers, with suburban nesting habits similar to ours. But the fields still crowd in on the houses, rather than the other way around, and the rural maze remains as mazy as ever. Is it any wonder that in 1914 whole armies blundered down these same country lanes as blindly as I was doing now?

I found the Vladslo Military Cemetery, eventually, recognizing it by the brownstone gatehouse all but hidden in a long hedge. I had to pass through a gloomy chamber, its walls laden with a claustrophobic throng of names— "these intolerably nameless names," Siegfried Sassoon called them, forever trapped in the elevator of history. Beyond, in the late-afternoon shadows, trees crowded in on a darkening lawn, their leaves an unbearably lush summer green. I felt a little as though I had come on a forest clearing in a tale by the brothers Grimm, a glade where a malign dwarf might once have guarded the waters of life. Military cemeteries, with their deliberately unreal celebration of the cult of the fallen, have that fairy-tale quality, as if enveloped by a sinister unquiet quiet.

But there was also something faintly industrial about this place. The lines of flat, square, basalt gravestones barely rising above the grass looked like sky-lights on a factory roof. Each stone—and there were hundreds of them—listed the names and death dates of as many as twenty men per grave. A total of 25,664 men are buried at Vladslo, including Käthe Kollwitz's son Peter.

I spotted the statues at the far end of the cemetery, backed up against a dark beech hedge—"the height of a man," an official German pamphlet notes. The statues themselves are a bit larger than life-size, kneeling figures of a man and a woman who look down from a pair of rough stone pedestals: *The Mourning Parents.* This is not the usual sort of martial monument, but perhaps the Belgians wouldn't have allowed one. Perhaps, too, the diplomatic skids were greased by the fact that the figures were carved in Belgian granite. A blue-gray stone, it is not a true granite but is durable enough. The statues have been placed side by side—everything is so symmetrical here—as if contemplating the skylights from that defunct workshop of Mars. (In Cologne, another version of the *Parents*, executed posthumously, is angled so that the two figures half-face each other, giving an effect of intimacy that I missed at Vladslo.)

The two figures are recognizably Käthe Kollwitz and her husband, Karl, the artist and the working-class doctor from Berlin, each possessed of a saintly single-mindedness—in stone as in life, curiously connected and curiously re-mote, an enduring mismatch. Here are two people perched on the edge of a chasm of sorrow, trying to pull back before it is too late. Wasn't it Nietzsche who said that if you stare into a chasm long enough, the chasm will begin to stare back at you?

Käthe Kollwitz always chose her models close to home, mostly because she couldn't afford professionals. Karl's face is all detail; Käthe's, less face than ef-face: In grief as in everything else, women had their place in those days. Around his full, downwardly sloping lips, lips that seem on the verge of a tremor, deep lines incise melancholy parentheses. His nose is long and bony;

Death's head shows through those features. His eyes, half-closed, seem focused inward, as if filled to brimming with the second sight of memory. An optical illusion? They are unforgettable. He is a man locked in a prison of grief. Could that explain the lank hair and the loose tunic that might almost belong to a convict?

Beside him, wrapped in a shawl, his wife stares at the ground, her chin sunk into her chest and, in contrast to his severely upright posture, her shoulders slumped. Her hair is pulled back to form a kind of skullcap, emphasizing the familiar wide Kollwitz nose, the heavy-lidded eyes, the broad-boned face— that prematurely old face, its fresh and resilient youthful contours long gone, "that place of suffering" one acquaintance called it. They kneel, their arms folded against their bodies, hugging themselves as if to ward off a palpable chill, one that would not disappear in their lifetime.

Only in my own has it begun to lift.

YOU MIGHT AS WELL SAY IT: PETER KOLLWITZ IS PRETTY MUCH A CIPHER, AN unperson. Only a few photographs survive. He had his mother's full mouth and prominent nose, his father's long face. Intelligence and a likable wryness are written over that countenance; bad luck is not. There is a final snapshot taken just three weeks before he was killed. In his tunic and field cap Peter slouches against a barracks wall; he holds a cigarette with studied nonchalance. Underneath the youthful bravado, though, you sense a certain edgy vulnerability, as if aware of a future suddenly become finite.

Käthe Kollwitz's diaries have survived, but they are chiefly valuable as records of her moods (mostly depressed) and the progress of her work; they tell us little about Peter. It's not easy to re-create a personality out of her reactive vision: Hers was an art of one-sided confrontation; everything was seen from the point of view of the sufferer. Peter now exists mainly as a reflection of his mother's grief. In that sense he is a universal soldier, more universal, perhaps, than *The Mourning Parents*, who were supposed to be just that.

We are left with a smattering of clues to his nature. He was born in Berlin in 1896, while his mother was working on a series of prints about a weavers' uprising; they earned her a gold medal, which the kaiser vetoed, calling them "art from the gutter." We hear Peter's voice only once. In 1903, when he was seven, Kollwitz was beginning an etching called *Woman with Dead Child*. She held Peter across her lap, glancing up at a mirror while she sketched. She groaned from the effort. "Be quiet, Mother," the boy said, "it is going to be very beautiful." Years later she would call the finished etching prophetic.

Like all the Kollwitzes and most young Germans of his time, Peter was a prodigious hiker. He and his older brother, Hans, who became a doctor like his father, staged amateur theatricals. He was a collector—but then, most teenagers are. In his room he kept a cupboard full of stones and a head of Narcissus, which he may have picked up during the months he had once spent with his mother in Italy. He showed talent as an artist, and was obviously the favorite of her two sons. After his death she took to sleeping in his room.

When war was declared, the Kollwitzes were in Königsberg, the Baltic town in East Prussia where she had been born in 1867. "I remember hearing the departing soldiers singing as they marched past our hotel," she wrote later. "Karl ran out to see them. I sat on the bed and cried, and cried, and cried. Even then I knew it all beforehand."

Peter, who was eighteen, rushed to volunteer. His wild outpouring of enthusiasm for the war briefly convinced his mother. Everyone was stuck on the notion of sacrifice and the *death of the hero.* "Heroism" was the enchanted word that united an unstable nation, one in which the distinctions and divisions of class were deep and bitter. Rivers of heroes' blood, one poem proclaimed, would flow homeward and revitalize the nation. "Rushing off to war," as the historian Robert Wheldon Whalen points out, "was an act of love." Peter Kollwitz was no exception. "It always strikes me as strange," his mother later wrote, "when masses of young people profess to be pacifists. I simply don't believe them. All it takes is one spark falling among them, and their pacifism is forgotten."

For the record, Peter Kollwitz served in the 4th Company in the 207th Infantry Reserve Regiment in the 44th Reserve Division in the XXII Reserve Corps in the Fourth German Army. The sense of unit anonymity builds. His mother made one last visit to his army barracks and listened to a sermon blessing the departing volunteers. She gave him a flower before she left, a pink.

His division entrained for the Western Front in mid-October and went into action at Dixmude on the twenty-second, a day when the Battle of the Yser River was approaching a crisis. The first Germans had pushed across the tiny stream and were threatening to pierce the last Allied line of resistance. Peter's division was still on the other side. There had been showers throughout the day and heavy fog. The 44th Reserve Division was ordered to cross that night. Bullets whistled indiscriminately, haystacks caught fire, and Dixmude was in flames. The shellbursts reminded one French Marine officer of thunder in a summer storm just before the rain falls. Wild firing broke out; officers couldn't keep control, and the attackers gave themselves away. Men overran enemy trenches, burst into loud hurrahs, and stopped. Units became mixed with other units; headlong attacks were followed by interludes of milling around. The attackers were in turn taken from the rear. By daylight—"that great friend of humanity," the French officer called it—the Germans were back where they had started. Sometime during those hours, Peter Kollwitz had been killed, the first man of his regiment to die.

When we next hear from Käthe Kollwitz, it is November; the Yser is, for Germany, another lost opportunity; and she is writing to two friends:

> Your pretty shawl will no longer be able to warm our boy. He lies dead under the earth. . . . He did not suffer.
>
> At dawn the regiment buried him; his friends laid him in the grave. Then they went on with their terrible tasks. We thank God that he was so gently taken away before the carnage.
>
> Please do not come to see us yet. . . .

"He did not suffer." This decorous euphemism for home consumption generally meant one of two things: Either a bullet had struck a man in the head or else a shell had blown him apart. Käthe Kollwitz was still swallowing the party line, as it were, on sacrifice. Maybe it was the only way she could cope with Peter's death at first. She was not yet ready to go public with her deeper feelings.

Grief such as she experienced was another, less reported part of the Western Front story, and it was woven like a black band into the fabric of subsequent European history. People were unprepared for so much loss, loss that left few untouched. There was an eerie, offstage quality about all that dying. (The same thing had happened in other wars, of course, but never on such a vast scale.) Men boarded a train or waved good-bye at a barracks gate, and disappeared forever. No wonder survivors could remember the day, the hour, the weather, the last words exchanged, with such clarity.

That unreality was underscored by the way you found out that your husband or son had died—"gone west" was the soldier's phrase. If you were lucky, an official letter or telegram brought you the news. But sometimes you simply glimpsed the name of a loved one on a huge casualty list posted on a city wall, or your last letter to the front came back to you stamped "Dead—Return to Sender." People reacted with bewilderment and, only much later, resentment. They were even denied the purging ritual of a funeral. (In that respect the recent American custom of shipping war dead home, often to be viewed in an open coffin, is healthy. But even American ingenuity would be hard put to return hundreds of thousands of bodies.)

There was nothing remote about the aftereffects of loss. Soldiers, as has been pointed out, were not the only war victims. They included the women reduced to poverty by the death of a husband and wage earner; the children left to roam wild while their mothers worked; the families broken apart; the parents deprived not just of the consolation of heirs but of support in their old age; the intellectual and political movers and shakers stripped of their imaginative energy, their power to persuade. Considered in this light, the phrase "home front" takes on new meaning. "First he fell in battle," she wrote, "and then I did." So much of nineteenth-century optimism had been founded on a belief in the future, and for millions that was gone now. "I walk in half-darkness, there is seldom a star, the sun has set, long ago and forever."

Grief, spread wide enough, and the anger that inevitably follows, can be an unspoken ingredient of social breakdown, a negative force; and the paralysis it brings, a very real affliction. For years after Peter was killed, Käthe Kollwitz produced hardly anything. As she wrote, and she was not talking only about herself: "If all the people who have been hurt in the war were to exclude joy from their lives, it would almost be as if they had died. Men without joy seem like corpses. They seem to obstruct life."

These words come from Kollwitz's diary, which can be read as a fever chart of her grief, and of her growing opposition to war. More important, in those papers she has left us a record of the conception and painful execution of the statues at Vladslo, which would consume her for eighteen years, the span of Peter's own life.

She began bravely. "Conceived the plan for a memorial for Peter tonight," she wrote on December 1, 1914, "but abandoned it again because it seemed to me impossible of execution." At forty-seven, she was new to sculpture and was not yet sure of her skills. But the next morning the idea was back, and now she was thinking of asking the city of Berlin to donate a place for the memorial, to commemorate the deaths of all young volunteers, on heights overlooking the lake called the Havel. "The monument would have Peter's form, lying stretched out, the father at the head, the mother at the feet." Several days later the design seemed to take clearer shape.

> My boy! On your memorial I want your figure on top, above the parents. You will lie outstretched, holding out your hands in answer to the call for sacrifice: "Here I am." Your eyes—perhaps—open wide, so that you see the blue sky above you, and the clouds and birds. Your mouth smiling. And at your breast the pink I gave you.

But there was little indication of progress during the next months: Grief, like the damp, catarrhish chill of a Berlin winter, had settled in. "The idea of eternity and immortality doesn't mean anything to me at present. . . . When one says so simply that someone has 'lost his life'—what a meaning there is in that—to lose one's life." And: "Recently Karl said, 'His death has made us no better.' " Her project seemed to be floundering. On February 21, 1916, the day the Germans attacked at Verdun, she noted, with no great optimism, "Perhaps the work on the memorial will bring me back to simplicity." But she reported on March 31 that she was

> overcome by a terrible depression. . . . When I am . . . in the midst of artists who are all thinking about their own art, I also think of mine. Once I am back home this horrible and difficult life weighs down upon me again with all its might. Then only one thing matters: the war.

Now it was mid-April, a time when Peter's regiment, the 207th Reserve, was being chewed up in the Mort Homme sector of the Verdun front. "Worked. I am making progress on the mother." But another summer came, the summer of the Somme—Peter's regiment suffered cruelly there, too—and still nothing went right: "Stagnation in my work." She told of making a drawing in which a mother lets her dead son slide into her arms. "I might make a hundred such drawings and yet I do not get any closer to him." Peter, she was convinced, was "somewhere" in her work, and yet she could not find him. Was it worth going on? "I have the feeling that I can no longer do it. I am too shattered, weakened, drained by tears."

Two years after Peter's death, Kollwitz was touching bottom, and the next pages are painful to contemplate. "My work seems so hopeless that I have decided to stop for the time being. My inward feeling is one of emptiness. . . . Talking to people means nothing at all. Nothing and no one can help me. I see Peter far, far in the distance."

As Peter's image receded, so did the ideal of sacrifice. A new theme would come to dominate: the futility of this war, of all wars. Suddenly she was writing not of her own paralysis but of the paralysis of "this frightful insanity—the youth of Europe hurling themselves at one another." She recalled that last day at the barracks outside Berlin and the sermon that a minister had delivered before a final blessing of the volunteers:

> He spoke of the Roman youth who leaped into the abyss and so closed it. That was one boy. Each of these boys felt that he must act like that one. But [she could write in October 1916] what came of it was something very different. The abyss has not closed. It has swallowed up millions, and it still gapes wide. And Europe, all Europe, is still like Rome, sacrificing its finest and most precious treasure—but the sacrifice has no effect.

Kollwitz was giving in to stranger feelings, though, the sort that must have been shared, and occasionally acted out in pathetic conjurations, behind closed doors everywhere as the heaven of an old world tried to strike a deal with the oblivion of a new. She contemplated a reunion with Peter's spirit: "I can hope . . . that when I too am dead we may find ourselves in a new form, come back to one another, run together like two streams." She claimed that she could often sense his presence: "He consoles me, he helps me in my work. . . . I am aware of him approving or rejecting, glad or sad."

Kollwitz looked back at other signs, or what seemed like signs. She thought Peter must have exerted some mysterious sway over his brother, Hans, at the moment he died: That was the night when Hans decided to go into the Medical Corps and not into the infantry. And "Wasn't it a sign when on October 13"— the date on which he had left for the front—"I visited the place where your memorial is to stand, and there was the same flower that I gave you when you departed?" Theosophists, she noted, maintained that you could train your faculties so that you could feel your way "toward that other world." Was it then possible to establish such a connection—or was it just "an intellectual jest"?

It is common for people at home to experience similar clairvoyant "signs." Conan Doyle received "messages" from his brother-in-law, killed in the retreat from Mons in 1914; they played a part in his conversion to spiritualism the following year. His eldest son and his brother served on the Western Front, and also died. Doyle's belief in an afterlife seems to have made their losses easier to bear. "You might laugh at me because of this," a German woman wrote, "but my husband and I had promised each other that if one of us died anywhere in the world without being able to tell the other, the one who died would somehow contact the one still living." He left for the front, and one night she dreamed that she saw him. "As he came closer, I awoke with a terrible scream, since what was staring at me was a death's head." Not long after, she received the notification that she expected. Some hours before the dream, her husband had been killed.

BY 1917, THE YEAR OF HER FIFTIETH BIRTHDAY, KOLLWITZ SEEMED TO HAVE PUT the worst behind her. "I work without effort and without tiring," she wrote at the end of July. "It is as if a fog had lifted." She felt there was a chance of finishing the plaster cast of the woman that fall; then work could be started on the final, stone version. (This big work still included a figure of Peter, wrapped in a blanket, only the head left free.)

She learned that Peter's body had been dug up from its solitary grave and reburied in a so-called concentration cemetery at Eessen-Roggevelde, a couple of miles east of Dixmude. (It would not be the last journey for those poor bones.) In addition to the major sculpture group destined for the Berlin hillside, Kollwitz now thought of doing a life-size relief in stone of the grieving parents; it would be placed at the entrance to the cemetery, with some short but suitable inscription engraved on it. She toyed with various possibilities: "Here lies German youth"—or simply, somberly, bitterly: "Here lie the young."

Depression overtook her, as it had so often in the past. The mother was still uncompleted. In October, Kollwitz returned from vacation, but when she went to work again, she "felt no sense of refreshment at all. On the contrary, I'd lost the conception; everything was trite. I let the mother alone for a while, took up the clay figure of the father, and then dropped it too." Now she was resigned to the possibility that it might be years before the sculptures were done.

But then, as the country headed for the "turnip winter" of 1917–18, depression was general. Cracks were beginning to appear in the military facade, too. Ypres was turning into an unimaginable horror. The new division that Peter's regiment now belonged to had been so roughed up at Verdun that it had to be pulled out of the line and reorganized. The French mutinies are well known, and at least one major disturbance erupted behind the British lines. But the Germans also had to deal with soldier insurrections in 1917. The men in at least one replacement unit in Germany refused to leave for the Western Front, and their mutiny was apparently tolerated. Others, though, were arrested when they refused to board troop trains. Some 30,000 deserters wandered the streets of Cologne, and there are indications that other German cities had a similar floating Absent Without Leave (AWOL) population.

From then on, work on the statues went forward in a halfhearted way, if at all. But Kollwitz's drawing, which she had pretty much given up in the last years, was another matter: "Curious how the sluices are opening up again," she noted on December 17, 1917. The need to end the war consumed her thoughts. She was overcome by the feeling that by "letting them go simply to the slaughterhouse," she had betrayed her sons. "Peter would still be living had it not been for this terrible betrayal. Peter and millions, many millions of other boys. All betrayed."

That was her entry for March 19, 1918. Two days later, the German supreme commander, Erich Ludendorff, would take the first of his gambles for victory on the Western Front, the great offensive in Picardy. By the time it ground to a halt, after an unheard-of gain of forty miles and the beginning of the end of trench warfare as it had been known for three and a half years, Peter's regiment would be so weakened that it could hold no more than 160 yards of front. One thing is clear: Even if he had survived the Yser, Peter Kollwitz would have had plenty of other chances to die.

"Germany is near the end," his mother wrote on October 1, 1918. "Wildly contradictory feelings. Germany is losing the war." It seemed madness to continue fighting. Toward the end of that wild month, the poet Richard Dehmel published a manifesto in which he called on all fit men to volunteer for a last stand to save Germany's honor. Kollwitz immediately penned a reply, taking passionate issue with him. Those men, she pointed out, would consist mainly of boys in their teens, the same age group that had died so plentifully in 1914. How could the nation any longer justify the deaths of the very people on which its future depended? "In my opinion such a loss would be worse and more irreparable for Germany than the loss of whole provinces."

It was a view that geneticists might agree with—though considering the history of the next quarter century, you might be tempted to add that too many of the best had gone already. "There has been enough of dying!" Kollwitz wrote. "Let not another man fall!" And she quoted the words of Goethe: " 'Seed for the planting must not be ground.' " A few days later, the Great War would be over, but not before the grinding of more planting seed.

It was as if Kollwitz, like her own country, had weathered a terrible illness: The crisis had passed, but a debilitating weakness remained. For her, as for Germany, that illness, the war, had become an obsession; her very inspiration depended on it. The following summer she took what may have been an inescapable, and certainly purging, decision: She abandoned her big work. "Tomorrow," she wrote on June 25, 1919, "it will all be taken down." She stood by the scaffold regarding Peter's face and then kissed the cold clay of his effigy. "I thought of Germany. For Germany's cause was his cause, and Germany's cause is lost now as my work is lost."

Two years went by. On the seventh anniversary of Peter's death, Käthe Kollwitz sat alone in his room, the room where she now slept alone, and stared at the cupboard still full of his stone collection. She could barely remember how he had looked. "His image is dissolved, even as his body has become wholly earth"—smudged by the clumsy eraser of time. There were compensations: The anguish of bereavement had vanished, too. "I am glad to be alive, intensely glad when I can work. . . ."

The story could have ended here, on a slightly upbeat note, but it didn't, of course.

I ALWAYS IMAGINE KÄTHE KOLLWITZ IN SHADES OF BLACK AND WHITE; NOT EVEN in her little studio room next to her husband's dispensary was there a hint of color. Color did not become her. But her monotones were as bright as any primary, and became brighter as the war receded. The 1920s were a rich period for her art. Her suffering mothers, her child victims, her hollow-eyed fraternity of the proletarian dispossessed proliferated. There was a new and fearful simplicity to her graphics, an eschewing of detail that yet hinted of deeper complexities: a highly politicized art that rose above politics. The abyss does stare back at us, and the result still has the power to unsettle. You can write it off to a maturing command of technique and the old artist's impatience with fussy detail. But had something else been liberated after the long dry spell of grief, like a dark flower blooming in a desert of chalk?

It was a good time for other reasons. Käthe Kollwitz *was* glad to be alive. She grew closer to her husband. Karl had brought her through the crisis of Peter's death, and his quiet strength, more than anything, seems to have cemented their uncertain union. They traveled to Russia. Though she was much acclaimed there, she would never embrace communism, which she found too intrinsically warlike. She delighted in her four grandchildren. (The eldest was named Peter, and he would die on the Eastern Front in the next war, hardly older than the uncle for whom he was named.) Occasionally she would unwrap the figures for the memorial, only to cover them once more. And then one day—her diary indicates that it was in October 1925, just before the mournful anniversary came round for the eleventh time—she went back to them.

Even at this late date, she still had two distinct works in mind: the major memorial complex for Berlin and a more modest monument for the cemetery at Roggevelde. Perhaps that grandiose scheme, so alluring in concept, so difficult in execution, had been one of her troubles all along. Although she had simplified her design for the latter, taking the kneeling figures of the parents out of relief, it sometimes seemed that she was almost willing herself not to finish. There were mishaps that a psychiatrist might not find curious. In a period of only a few days, she twice knocked the figure of the mother off its turntable and had to reconstruct completely what she had destroyed.

June 1926 was another important date for Käthe Kollwitz. That month she and Karl made their first visit to Peter's grave. From this point on, her energies would be devoted to one monument only: *The Mourning Parents.*

Käthe and Karl Kollwitz boarded one of those trolleylike local trains at Dixmude, rode south a few miles, and then set off on foot. Hedges had already grown up along the road, though as yet few trees; they could see fields beyond and an occasional brick farmhouse, already rebuilt. The war was still in evidence. There were dugouts everywhere. A creepy rural silence enveloped them, though she noted that "the larks sing gladly."

This was a scene repeated countless times in those years. The hesitant and perplexed elderly parents or the widows with children grown into their teens searching for the right grove of crosses—too often it was a forest—with its predictably monotonous rows of soldiers' graves. These stragglers rarely came in busloads, like the British to Ypres or the delegations of Gold Star Mothers from America, and they were careful not to give offense in the land of the victors.

They could be hindered, too, by their inability to speak the language. I think of that German guidebook to the Western Front, which gives key phrases and sentences, with their equivalent in French: Driver! Are you free? Can you take me to cemetery X? How much do you charge? In what part of the cemetery can I find grave number . . . ? Do you know the address of a photographer who can take a shot of it? Where can I purchase a wreath? *Was ist der Preis? Quel est le prix?* . . .

THE KOLLWITZES FOUND THEMSELVES LOST IN A FLATLAND LABYRINTH, A wizardless Oz, even as I would decades later at Vladslo. Finally a friendly young peasant led them to an opening in a hedge, bent aside some strands of barbed wire that blocked it, and left them alone. "What an impression: cross upon cross." Roggevelde was actually medium-size as Western Front cemeteries went, with only 855 occupants. The Kollwitzes soon located Peter's cross, low, tin, and marked like all the others with a metal identification plaque—a kind of dogtag of the dead. She described the scene in a letter to Hans:

> All that is left of him lies there in a row-grave. None of the mounds are separated: there are only the same little crosses placed quite close together . . . and almost everywhere is the naked, yellow soil. Here and there relatives have planted flowers, mostly wild roses, which are lovely because they cover and arch over the grave and reach out to the adjoining graves which no one tends, for to the right and left at least half the graves bear the inscription *allemand inconnu.*

They cut three roses from a wild briar and placed them at the foot of Peter's cross.

Käthe Kollwitz immediately set about looking for the best place to put her figures. They would not fit amid the graves; the rows were too close together. She decided that she would like to place them just across from the entrance, where "a kind of garden plot" was now laid out. "Then the kneeling figures would have the whole cemetery before them." The mourning parents left, walking back to Dixmude.

She had one further happening to report to her surviving son. "Tonight," she wrote, "I dreamed there would be another war. . . ."

——

FROM NOW ON, NOTHING MATTERED QUITE AS MUCH AS THE MEMORIAL FOR Roggevelde. "It is beginning," she exulted on October 22, 1926—that day again—after a helper had built up the scaffolding and clay for the figure of the mother. "I feel as if I now stand directly before the last stage of my work."

But completion still eluded her. Another year went by, and then three more. She ran into technical problems—on, of all things, clothing. "The naturalistic folds disgust me and the stylized folds disgust me." (In the end she struck a successful bargain between the two.) Advancing age and diminishing physical capacities haunted her. "Sixty years old—how can I manage to do anything important anymore?" (She underestimated her staying power; she would live another seventeen vigorous years.) She worried that the father figure "had no soul" and she tried crossing his arms over his chest. (That was her eventual, and utterly moving, solution.)

She also experienced moments of undeniable inspiration. An acquaintance was sitting for her, modeling for the head of the mother. Kollwitz suddenly realized that the face was all wrong. She dug out a self-portrait in plaster and unwrapped the head. "It was as if the scale fell from my eyes. I saw that my own head could be used after all." Of course. Could the mother have been anyone else but Käthe Kollwitz?

In April 1930 two friends visited her studio, and Kollwitz did something she had never done in all her years of work on her memorial to Peter: She showed the two figures, nearly completed in clay. "The figures seemed to make the impression I had hoped for." She felt "agitated . . . euphoric"—and then (this is pure Kollwitz) was overcome by "dull indifference." But she had gone too far now not to finish.

Still, it took exactly a year more before she actually exhibited the sculptures of The Mourning Parents, in plaster, at the Prussian Academy of the Arts, Germany's most esteemed cultural institution—where she was now head of the Department of Graphic Arts. (Two years later the Nazis would force her out, and she would never again be allowed to exhibit her work in Germany.) She was pleased with the acclaim the figures received from her fellow artists. All that remained was to have them converted to stone. She was in the final stretch, truly and at last, starting work with two sculptor-masons, one for the mother, the other for the father. "In the fall—Peter—I shall bring it to you."

But for Kollwitz, things were never quite so easy. The year 1931 passed. Now events were catching up with her. These were the months when Japan invaded Manchuria; the Kreditanstalt failed, bringing the banking system of central Europe down with it; Herbert Hoover made his vain, gallant attempt to head off the spread of worldwide depression by seeking a moratorium on German war debts; the unemployed were gathering around Berlin in tent cities organized with military precision; and, like trench raiders bursting out of the shadows, the Nazis were closing in on power. "The Misery," Kollwitz noted in her diary. "People sinking into dark wretchedness, the repulsive political hate-campaigns." The Armistice was proving to be just that—not an end but an intermission in what basically would be a continuous world war. Käthe Kollwitz's nightmare was coming alive.

Eighteen years in the making and finally and irrevocably committed to stone, the figures were exhibited in the entrance hall of the National Gallery at the beginning of June 1932. Kollwitz would have preferred to show them outdoors, but she feared that Nazi vandals might cover her memorial with swastikas and other political graffiti. The day before the figures were to be moved to the museum, she was still fiddling with them, still refining. She had to let them go now—and was predictably overcome by emptiness. Then followed a Saturday packed with press interviews. Workers set up benches around the figures, swept the floor, and gave them a last going-over with a dust cloth. "Finished! Even to the dusting." Admiring crowds circled *The Mourning Parents;* a two-week exhibit was extended to three. There would be no more hitches.

THE STATE OF PRUSSIA HAD, AT THE END, GIVEN KOLLWITZ A GRANT TO HELP PAY for the conversion to stone. It hardly covered her expenses, but the state did arrange to waive toll and freight charges to Belgium, and the German war-graves people supplied the foundations and pedestals. The Roggevelde cemetery had changed since the Kollwitzes visited six years earlier. The small tin crosses had been replaced with low, thick, wooden ones, all alike, and the rows had been straightened out, to run with perfect regularity and cover a rectangle that was now walled in. "Only three graves are planted with roses. On Peter's grave they are in bloom, red ones." (This is one of her few references to color. It also indicates two things: that the numbers of visitors was diminishing—and that someone must have put in a bush for the benefit of the Kollwitzes.) She found the whole effect of the improvements a bit monotonous. But then, she reflected, "a war cemetery ought to be somber."

It took two days to set up the figures and to make sure that they had the proper forward view. As the workers lowered the father onto his pedestal, she experienced a moment of dismay: His line of vision was too low; instead of looking out over the graves, he seemed to be staring downward, brooding, as if too much caught up in his own thoughts, his private grief. No amount of raising and adjusting could change it. Kollwitz left, "sad rather than happy." Had eighteen years of work come down to a misplaced glance?

The next morning, a Friday, she packed. It rained. Memorial rain. All along the old front line—Scott Fitzgerald's words are suddenly apt—"infinitesimal sections of Würtembergers, Prussian Guards, Chasseurs Alpins, Manchester mill hands and old Etonians" pursued "their eternal dissolution in the warm rain." Forever young—though Peter Kollwitz actually would have been thirty-six in July 1932, on the threshold of middle age.

Around four in the afternoon, a war-graves caretaker came round with a car and drove the Kollwitzes out to the cemetery. The skies had cleared. Her depression of the previous day had "lifted." She was, she now reported, "able to see it all in the right light." Of course: That downward, inward look of the father is precisely what gives his face the power to haunt. The war-graves man withdrew discreetly; the old couple approached the statues. Käthe Kollwitz seemed to know that she would never see them again.

"I stood before the woman, looked at her—my own face—and I wept and stroked her cheeks. Karl stood close behind me—I did not even realize it. I heard him whisper, 'yes, yes.' How close we were to one another then!"

POSTSCRIPT: PETER KOLLWITZ'S POSTHUMOUS TRAVELS WERE NOT QUITE OVER. AT the time *The Mourning Parents* were erected, there were 128 German burial grounds in Belgium, ranging from single graves to clusters of thousands. But after the Second World War, the Belgian government demanded that the Germans consolidate them into four cemeteries of several acres each. The pressure of an expanding live population was the reason given. So, in the 1950s, Peter Kollwitz's remains (a curiously cold and remote word, that) were moved to an existing cemetery at Vladslo. The statues came too, along with the bones of almost 22,000 men from all over Belgium. You can find Peter Kollwitz in the back row, slightly to the left of his mother's figure, sharing a stone with thirteen others.

"Since it was impossible to keep bones separate during exhumation," a German war-graves official remarked, "they could not be buried in individual graves." There could be less efficient ways, I suppose, of creating a universal soldier.

Now, the shadows of early evening thickened and spread, enveloping that cheerless Vladslo glade—those same creeping shadows that Käthe Kollwitz always, but imperfectly, managed to keep at arm's length. As I was about to leave, a middle-aged couple approached *The Mourning Parents*. They were speaking in hushed German—there is nothing about this place that encourages a natural tone of voice. The woman was dressed in a yellow, short-sleeved blouse and bright red slacks, a still trim figure in her traveling uniform. Käthe Kollwitz must have been about her age when Peter was killed. She carried a bouquet of crimson roses wrapped in a shroud of stiff cellophane; her husband had a camera around his neck. She peeled off the cellophane and handed it to him. He folded it neatly, tucked it into his trouser pocket, and motioned to his wife to stand between the pedestals. She cradled the roses as if presenting arms. He brought the camera to his eye, she stiffened, and the mirror of his single-lens reflex banged back with a sound that reverberated through that dead space. Then, still for the benefit of the camera, she placed the roses on the flagstones in front of the statues. There hardly seemed enough light for a picture, and yet he continued to snap away. It sometimes seems that we spend our lives denying the night.

"Pain," as Käthe Kollwitz once wrote, "is very dark."

ACKNOWLEDGMENTS

I wish to express my special thanks to Byron Hollinshead and Sabine Russ

at American Historical Publications, and to Katie Hall and Robert D. Loomis

at Random House, for their assistance and encouragement

in all aspects of this book.

PERMISSION ACKNOWLEDGMENTS

All articles were previously published in *MHQ: The Quarterly Journal of Military History*. The following essays were excerpted from books and are reprinted by permission of the publishers:

"Europe 1914" from Sir Michael Howard, *The Coming of the First World War*, Oxford University Press. "A Bad Afternoon at Aubers Ridge" from *Lionel Sotheby's Great War*, edited by Donald C. Richter, Ohio University Press, Athens, Ohio. "Jutland" from John Keegan, *The Price of Admiralty*, Viking Press. "The Fokker Menace" from Michael Spick, *The Ace Factor: Air Combat and the Role of Situational Awareness*, Airlife Publishing (UK). "The Breaking of Armies" from John Keegan, *The First World War*, copyright © 1998 by John Keegan, Alfred A. Knopf, a division of Random House, Inc. "Belleau Wood: One Man's Initiation" from Allan R. Millett, *In Many a Strife: General Gerald C. Thomas and the U.S. Marine Corps, 1917–1956*, Naval Institute Press. All other articles are reprinted by permission of the authors.

Excerpt from "Memorial Rain," *Collected Poems 1917–1982* by Archibald MacLeish. Copyright © 1985 by the Estate of Archibald MacLeish. Reprinted by permission of Houghton Mifflin Company. All rights reserved. Originally published in *Street in the Moon*, 1926.

INDEX

ABOUT THE EDITOR

ROBERT COWLEY is the editor of *What If?* and
*What If? 2; No End Save Victory: Perspectives on
World War II;* and *With My Face to the Enemy:
Perspectives on the Civil War,* and the founding editor
of *MHQ: The Quarterly Journal of Military History,*
which was nominated for a National Magazine
Award for General Excellence.
He lives in Connecticut.

ABOUT THE TYPE

This book was set in Photina, a typeface designed
by José Mendoza in 1971. It is a very elegant
design with high legibility, and its close character
fit has made it a popular choice for use in quality
magazines and art gallery publications.